THE BOOK OF TWEETS

VOLUME 2

THE BOOK OF TWEETS

VOLUME 2

THE TWEETS OF PRESIDENT DONALD J. TRUMP, VOLUME 2: JULY 4, 2018 – JULY 4, 2019

JUDGE HAL MOROZ

NEW YORK   ATLANTA   RICHMOND   WASHINGTON

The Book of Tweets

The Tweets of President Donald J. Trump,
Volume 2: July 4, 2018 – July 4, 2019

Judge Hal Moroz

Access to the vast public records and writings contained in this book
is available through a wide range of sources in the public domain.
The author of this work wishes to thank and acknowledge President Donald J. Trump, The White House, the Library of Congress, the National Archives, the Smithsonian Institution, the U.S. Senate, and the exceptionally outstanding archives of The Ronald Reagan Presidential Foundation located in Simi Valley, California.
The author is a member of the Foundation, and encourages everyone interested in supporting and preserving the legacy of President Ronald Reagan to join the Foundation. Membership can be obtained by writing The Ronald Reagan Presidential Foundation, 40 Presidential Drive, Simi Valley, California 93065, or via the internet at http://www.reaganfoundation.org

Unless otherwise noted, Scripture quotations are from
The King James Version of the Bible.

Printed in the United States of America

Introduction

America's Continuing Re-Birth of Freedom

These are the Tweets of President Donald J. Trump.

This is Volume 2 in a series of historical documented Tweets of America's 45th President, which includes the Tweets of @realDonaldTrump from July 4, 2018 through July 4, 2019.

Volume 1 of *The Book of Tweets*, available for purchase separately, chronicles January 20, 2017 (the day he took office) through July 4, 2018.

We are now fully engaged in a great struggle to determine the future of America, and no one communicates the #MakeAmericaGreatAgain and #KeepAmericaGreat agendas better than our President, Donald J. Trump. That is why this book was created. President Trump's plans for returning power to We the People, re-establishing the Constitution, rebuilding America's economic and military might, defending our borders, and the restoring of our Founding Christian Principles are here to read, share, treasure, and live!

We are now fully engaged in a great struggle to determine the future of America, and no one communicates the #MakeAmericaGreatAgain and #KeepAmericaGreat agendas better than our President, Donald J. Trump. That is why this book was created. President Trump's plans for returning power to We the People, re-establishing the Constitution, rebuilding America's economic and military might, defending our borders, and the restoring of our Founding Christian Principles are here to read, share, treasure, and live!

In this book, President Trump's Tweets are chronicled from the period July 4, 2018 through July 4, 2019. These daily, sometime minute-to-minute, Tweets provide a unique and captivating insight into our 45th POTUS and the social media revolution he championed to usher in America's new birth of freedom.

This volume of *The Book of Tweets* is a key addition to any #MAGA library. It is also a great gift to any American or friend of the republic desiring to cut through the spin and #FakeNews of the mainstream media outlets. It is the unfiltered voice of America's Constitutionally-elected Chief Executive officer. Both volumes of *The Book of Tweets* are a MUST for every real American library!

Enjoy!

At your service,

Hal Moroz

Make America Great Again!

When America is united, America is totally unstoppable!

There should be no fear! We are protected, and we will always be protected! We will be protected by the great men and women of our military and law enforcement and, most importantly, we are protected by God!

Now arrives the hour of action! Do not let anyone tell you it cannot be done! No challenge can match the heart and fight and spirit of America! We will not fail! Our country will thrive and prosper again!

Together, We will make America strong again! We will make wealthy again! We will make America proud again! We will make America safe again! And yes, together, we will make America great again!

Thank you! God bless you! And God bless America!

~ President Donald J. Trump,
January 20, 2017

Freedom is never more than one generation away from extinction. We didn't pass it to our children in the bloodstream. It must be fought for, protected, and handed on for them to do the same, or one day we will spend our sunset years telling our children and our children's children what it was once like in the United States where men were free.

~ President Ronald Reagan

All to the Glory of God

If my people, which are called by my name, shall humble themselves, and pray, and seek my face, and turn from their wicked ways; then will I hear from heaven, and will forgive their sin, and will heal their land.

~ 2 Chronicles 7:14, KJV

The Crusade Continues!

Volume 2 Begins July 4, 2018

[NOTE: These are the original, unedited Tweets of @realDonaldTrump. They include the misspellings and any syntax errors as written. If you see a hyperlink after the text, it means the POTUS included an attachment.]

Donald J. Trump ✓
@realDonaldTrump

(Follow) ⌄

Happy Fourth of July....Our Country is doing GREAT!

7:42 AM · 4 Jul 2018

53 Retweets **114** Likes

💬 44   ↻ 53   ♡ 114

Jul 4, 2018 09:42:38 AM Happy Fourth of July....Our Country is doing GREAT! [Twitter for iPhone]

Jul 4, 2018 09:44:53 AM https://t.co/ue5JEZy85v [Twitter for iPhone]

Jul 4, 2018 03:46:00 PM The OPEC Monopoly must remember that gas prices are up & they are doing little to help. If anything, they are driving prices higher as the United States defends many of their members for very little $'s. This must be a two way street. REDUCE PRICING NOW! [Twitter for iPhone]

Jul 4, 2018 09:47:35 PM Happy Birthday, America! https://t.co/SIi6xXsfof [Twitter for iPhone]

Jul 5, 2018 09:08:57 AM Congress must pass smart, fast and reasonable Immigration Laws now. Law Enforcement at the Border is doing a great job, but the laws they are forced to work with are insane. When people, with or without children, enter our Country, they must be told to leave without our........ [Twitter for iPhone]

Jul 5, 2018 09:16:07 AM .....Country being forced to endure a long and costly trial. Tell the people "OUT," and they must leave, just as they would if they were standing on your front lawn. Hiring thousands of "judges" does not work and is not acceptable - only Country in the World that does this! [Twitter for iPhone]

Jul 5, 2018 09:17:23 AM Congress - FIX OUR INSANE IMMIGRATION LAWS NOW! [Twitter for iPhone]

Jul 5, 2018 02:37:57 PM I have accepted the resignation of Scott Pruitt as the Administrator of the Environmental Protection Agency. Within the Agency Scott has done an outstanding job, and I will always be thankful to him for this. The Senate confirmed Deputy at EPA, Andrew Wheeler, will... [Twitter for iPhone]

Jul 5, 2018 02:37:58 PM ...on Monday assume duties as the acting Administrator of the EPA. I have no doubt that Andy will continue on with our great and lasting EPA agenda. We have made tremendous progress and the future of the EPA is very bright! [Twitter for iPhone]

Jul 5, 2018 07:11:09 PM It was my great honor to join proud, hardworking American Patriots in Montana tonight. I love you - thank you! #MAGA https://t.co/475ct7hW3D [Twitter for iPhone]

Jul 5, 2018 07:44:17 PM A vote for Democrats in November is a vote to let MS-13 run wild in our communities, to let drugs pour into our cities, and to take jobs and benefits away from hardworking Americans. Democrats want anarchy, amnesty and chaos - Republicans want LAW, ORDER and JUSTICE! [Twitter for iPhone]

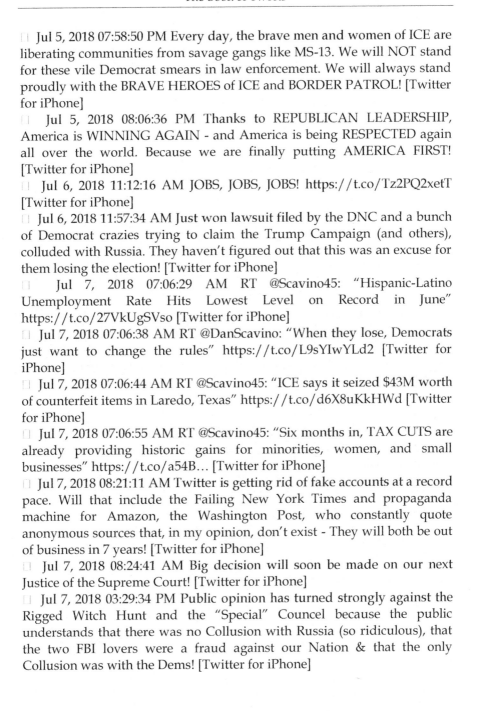

Jul 5, 2018 07:58:50 PM Every day, the brave men and women of ICE are liberating communities from savage gangs like MS-13. We will NOT stand for these vile Democrat smears in law enforcement. We will always stand proudly with the BRAVE HEROES of ICE and BORDER PATROL! [Twitter for iPhone]

Jul 5, 2018 08:06:36 PM Thanks to REPUBLICAN LEADERSHIP, America is WINNING AGAIN - and America is being RESPECTED again all over the world. Because we are finally putting AMERICA FIRST! [Twitter for iPhone]

Jul 6, 2018 11:12:16 AM JOBS, JOBS, JOBS! https://t.co/Tz2PQ2xetT [Twitter for iPhone]

Jul 6, 2018 11:57:34 AM Just won lawsuit filed by the DNC and a bunch of Democrat crazies trying to claim the Trump Campaign (and others), colluded with Russia. They haven't figured out that this was an excuse for them losing the election! [Twitter for iPhone]

Jul 7, 2018 07:06:29 AM RT @Scavino45: "Hispanic-Latino Unemployment Rate Hits Lowest Level on Record in June" https://t.co/27VkUgSVso [Twitter for iPhone]

Jul 7, 2018 07:06:38 AM RT @DanScavino: "When they lose, Democrats just want to change the rules" https://t.co/L9sYIwYLd2 [Twitter for iPhone]

Jul 7, 2018 07:06:44 AM RT @Scavino45: "ICE says it seized $43M worth of counterfeit items in Laredo, Texas" https://t.co/d6X8uKkHWd [Twitter for iPhone]

Jul 7, 2018 07:06:55 AM RT @Scavino45: "Six months in, TAX CUTS are already providing historic gains for minorities, women, and small businesses" https://t.co/a54B... [Twitter for iPhone]

Jul 7, 2018 08:21:11 AM Twitter is getting rid of fake accounts at a record pace. Will that include the Failing New York Times and propaganda machine for Amazon, the Washington Post, who constantly quote anonymous sources that, in my opinion, don't exist - They will both be out of business in 7 years! [Twitter for iPhone]

Jul 7, 2018 08:24:41 AM Big decision will soon be made on our next Justice of the Supreme Court! [Twitter for iPhone]

Jul 7, 2018 03:29:34 PM Public opinion has turned strongly against the Rigged Witch Hunt and the "Special" Councel because the public understands that there was no Collusion with Russia (so ridiculous), that the two FBI lovers were a fraud against our Nation & that the only Collusion was with the Dems! [Twitter for iPhone]

Jul 7, 2018 03:42:48 PM Public opinion has turned strongly against the Rigged Witch Hunt and the "Special" Counsel because the public understands that there was no Collusion with Russia (so ridiculous), that the two FBI lovers were a fraud against our Nation & that the only Collusion was with the Dems! [Twitter for iPhone]

Jul 7, 2018 05:24:02 PM The Rigged Witch Hunt, originally headed by FBI lover boy Peter S (for one year) & now, 13 Angry Democrats, should look into the missing DNC Server, Crooked Hillary's illegally deleted Emails, the Pakistani Fraudster, Uranium One, Podesta & so much more. It's a Democrat Con Job! [Twitter for iPhone]

Jul 8, 2018 08:14:13 AM The U.S. is working very closely with the Government of Thailand to help get all of the children out of the cave and to safety. Very brave and talented people! [Twitter for iPhone]

Jul 8, 2018 09:55:55 AM RT @CortesSteve: Today's report: Hispanic jobs hit another record, unemployment at an all-time low. Of 9 months in history under 5% jobless... [Twitter for iPhone]

Jul 8, 2018 03:29:27 PM Iranian Harassment of U.S. Warships: 2015: 22 2016: 36 2017: 14 2018: 0 Source: @USNavy [Twitter for iPhone]

Jul 8, 2018 04:27:17 PM Looking forward to announcing my final decision on the United States Supreme Court Justice at 9:00pmE tomorrow night at the @WhiteHouse. An exceptional person will be chosen! [Twitter for iPhone]

Jul 8, 2018 04:58:52 PM They just didn't get it, but they do now! https://t.co/9T50NupkDy [Media Studio]

Jul 9, 2018 06:55:01 AM The United States is spending far more on NATO than any other Country. This is not fair, nor is it acceptable. While these countries have been increasing their contributions since I took office, they must do much more. Germany is at 1%, the U.S. is at 4%, and NATO benefits....... [Twitter for iPhone]

Jul 9, 2018 07:04:02 AM ...Europe far more than it does the U.S. By some accounts, the U.S. is paying for 90% of NATO, with many countries nowhere close to their 2% commitment. On top of this the European Union has a Trade Surplus of $151 Million with the U.S., with big Trade Barriers on U.S. goods. NO! [Twitter for iPhone]

Jul 9, 2018 07:14:43 AM I have long heard that the most important decision a U.S. President can make is the selection of a Supreme Court Justice - Will be announced tonight at 9:00 P.M. [Twitter for iPhone]

Jul 9, 2018 09:25:06 AM I have confidence that Kim Jong Un will honor the contract we signed &, even more importantly, our handshake. We agreed to the denuclearization of North Korea. China, on the other hand, may be exerting negative pressure on a deal because of our posture on Chinese Trade-Hope Not! [Twitter for iPhone]

Jul 9, 2018 12:04:04 PM The failing NY Times Fake News story today about breast feeding must be called out. The U.S. strongly supports breast feeding but we don't believe women should be denied access to formula. Many women need this option because of malnutrition and poverty. [Twitter for iPhone]

Jul 9, 2018 12:08:29 PM Pfizer & others should be ashamed that they have raised drug prices for no reason. They are merely taking advantage of the poor & others unable to defend themselves, while at the same time giving bargain basement prices to other countries in Europe & elsewhere. We will respond! [Twitter for iPhone]

Jul 9, 2018 05:22:40 PM HAPPY 100TH BIRTHDAY to our amazing current and former Army Warrant Officers. Thank you for your century of service, as the indispensable guardians of our great @USArmy's technology! #CenturyOfService https://t.co/hD42XseaTG [Twitter for iPhone]

Jul 9, 2018 08:01:17 PM RT @WhiteHouse: President Trump Announces the Nominee for Associate Justice of the Supreme Court https://t.co/rVMTOMpurr [Twitter for iPhone]

Jul 9, 2018 09:54:10 PM Tonight, it was my honor and privilege to nominate Judge Brett Kavanaugh to the United States Supreme Court. #SCOTUS https://t.co/97clc9zifm [Twitter for iPhone]

Jul 10, 2018 04:00:10 AM RT @Scavino45: Judge Brett Kavanaugh watches with his family as President Donald J. Trump signs the document Monday evening, July 9, 2018,... [Twitter for iPhone]

Jul 10, 2018 04:00:47 AM RT @Scavino45: "The Rule of Law is our Nation's proud heritage. It is the cornerstone of our Freedom. It is what guarantees equal justice -... [Twitter for iPhone]

Jul 10, 2018 04:03:04 AM RT @realDonaldTrump: Iranian Harassment of U.S. Warships: 2015: 22 2016: 36 2017: 14 2018: 0 Source: @USNavy [Twitter for iPhone]

Jul 10, 2018 04:07:47 AM RT @KatrinaPierson: The stupidity of the left was on full display in Oakland. The #AbolishICE protest was actually the execution of a warra... [Twitter for iPhone]

Jul 10, 2018 04:35:05 AM Getting ready to leave for Europe. First meeting - NATO. The U.S. is spending many times more than any other country in order to protect them. Not fair to the U.S. taxpayer. On top of that we lose $151 Billion on Trade with the European Union. Charge us big Tariffs (& Barriers)! [Twitter for iPhone]

Jul 10, 2018 05:42:43 AM NATO countries must pay MORE, the United States must pay LESS. Very Unfair! [Twitter for iPhone]

Jul 10, 2018 05:44:29 AM RT @ShennaFoxxx: @realDonaldTrump #TrumpUKVisitGB To the 45th @POTUS Donald J Trump @FLOTUS @MELANIATRUMP The British people are looking f... [Twitter for iPhone]

Jul 10, 2018 05:59:30 AM Thank you to all of my great supporters, really big progress being made. Other countries wanting to fix crazy trade deals. Economy is ROARING. Supreme Court pick getting GREAT REVIEWS. New Poll says Trump, at over 90%, is the most popular Republican in history of the Party. Wow! [Twitter for iPhone]

Jul 10, 2018 06:38:10 AM RT @realDonaldTrump: They just didn't get it, but they do now! https://t.co/9T50NupkDy [Twitter for iPhone]

Jul 10, 2018 07:39:18 AM On behalf of the United States, congratulations to the Thai Navy SEALs and all on the successful rescue of the 12 boys and their coach from the treacherous cave in Thailand. Such a beautiful moment - all freed, great job! [Twitter for iPhone]

Jul 10, 2018 09:40:12 AM I am on Air Force One flying to NATO and hear reports that the FBI lovers, Peter Strzok and Lisa Page are getting cold feet on testifying about the Rigged Witch Hunt headed by 13 Angry Democrats and people that worked for Obama for 8 years. Total disgrace! [Twitter for iPhone]

Jul 10, 2018 09:49:17 AM Informing the Republican Senators of my nomination of Judge Brett Kavanaugh. #SCOTUS https://t.co/O5cAaVAtQt [Twitter for iPhone]

Jul 10, 2018 12:01:30 PM Many countries in NATO, which we are expected to defend, are not only short of their current commitment of 2% (which is low), but are also delinquent for many years in payments that have not been made. Will they reimburse the U.S.? [Twitter for iPhone]

Jul 10, 2018 01:42:21 PM A recent Emerson College ePoll said that most Americans, especially Hispanics, feel that they are better off under President Trump than they were under President Obama. [Twitter for iPhone]

Jul 10, 2018 01:52:21 PM The European Union makes it impossible for our farmers and workers and companies to do business in Europe (U.S. has a $151 Billion trade deficit), and then they want us to happily defend them through NATO, and nicely pay for it. Just doesn't work! [Twitter for iPhone]

Jul 10, 2018 05:37:28 PM Just talked with Pfizer CEO and @SecAzar on our drug pricing blueprint. Pfizer is rolling back price hikes, so American patients don't pay more. We applaud Pfizer for this decision and hope other companies do the same. Great news for the American people! [Twitter for iPhone]

Jul 11, 2018 03:04:45 AM Bilateral Breakfast with NATO Secretary General in Brussels, Belgium... https://t.co/l0EP3lzhCM [Twitter for iPhone]

Jul 11, 2018 05:37:42 AM RT @realDonaldTrump: Bilateral Breakfast with NATO Secretary General in Brussels, Belgium... https://t.co/l0EP3lzhCM [Twitter for iPhone]

Jul 11, 2018 07:40:31 AM I am in Brussels, but always thinking about our farmers. Soy beans fell 50% from 2012 to my election. Farmers have done poorly for 15 years. Other countries' trade barriers and tariffs have been destroying their businesses. I will open... [Twitter for iPhone]

Jul 11, 2018 07:40:32 AM ...things up, better than ever before, but it can't go too quickly. I am fighting for a level playing field for our farmers, and will win! [Twitter for iPhone]

Jul 11, 2018 11:41:12 AM Democrats in Congress must no longer Obstruct - vote to fix our terrible Immigration Laws now. I am watching what is going on from Europe - it would be soooo simple to fix. Judges run the system and illegals and traffickers know how it works. They are just using children! [Twitter for iPhone]

Jul 11, 2018 11:50:49 AM What good is NATO if Germany is paying Russia billions of dollars for gas and energy? Why are their only 5 out of 29 countries that have met their commitment? The U.S. is paying for Europe's protection, then loses billions on Trade. Must pay 2% of GDP IMMEDIATELY, not by 2025. [Twitter for iPhone]

Jul 11, 2018 12:07:27 PM What good is NATO if Germany is paying Russia billions of dollars for gas and energy? Why are there only 5 out of 29 countries that have met their commitment? The U.S. is paying for Europe's protection, then loses billions on Trade. Must pay 2% of GDP IMMEDIATELY, not by 2025. [Twitter for iPhone]

Jul 11, 2018 04:09:01 PM If the Democrats want to win Supreme Court and other Court picks, don't Obstruct and Resist, but rather do it the good ol' fashioned way, WIN ELECTIONS! [Twitter for iPhone]

Jul 11, 2018 04:10:11 PM RT @Scavino45: President Donald J. Trump and First Lady Melania Trump participate in the Tri-Mission Embassy Meet and Greet Wednesday, July... [Twitter for iPhone]

Jul 11, 2018 04:10:24 PM RT @realDonaldTrump: Democrats in Congress must no longer Obstruct - vote to fix our terrible Immigration Laws now. I am watching what is g... [Twitter for iPhone]

Jul 11, 2018 04:10:31 PM RT @realDonaldTrump: I am in Brussels, but always thinking about our farmers. Soy beans fell 50% from 2012 to my election. Farmers have don... [Twitter for iPhone]

Jul 11, 2018 04:10:46 PM RT @realDonaldTrump: ...things up, better than ever before, but it can't go too quickly. I am fighting for a level playing field for our fa... [Twitter for iPhone]

Jul 11, 2018 04:11:20 PM RT @Scavino45: President @realDonaldTrump meets with Chancellor Angela Merkel of Germany, along with their respective delegations at #NATOS... [Twitter for iPhone]

Jul 11, 2018 04:11:36 PM RT @Scavino45: President @realDonaldTrump and President @EmmanuelMacron of France meeting earlier today at #NATOSummit2018 in Brussels, Bel... [Twitter for iPhone]

Jul 11, 2018 04:11:54 PM RT @realDonaldTrump: What good is NATO if Germany is paying Russia billions of dollars for gas and energy? Why are there only 5 out of 29 c... [Twitter for iPhone]

Jul 11, 2018 04:53:26 PM Ex-FBI LAYER Lisa Page today defied a House of Representatives issued Subpoena to testify before Congress! Wow, but is anybody really surprised! Together with her lover, FBI Agent Peter Strzok, she worked on the Rigged Witch Hunt, perhaps the most tainted and corrupt case EVER! [Twitter for iPhone]

Jul 11, 2018 05:47:16 PM How can the Rigged Witch Hunt proceed when it was started, influenced and worked on, for an extended period of time, by former FBI Agent/Lover Peter Strzok? Read his hate filled and totally biased Emails and the answer is clear! [Twitter for iPhone]

Jul 11, 2018 06:33:33 PM Billions of additional dollars are being spent by NATO countries since my visit last year, at my request, but it isn't nearly enough. U.S. spends too much. Europe's borders are BAD! Pipeline dollars to Russia are not acceptable! [Twitter for iPhone]

Jul 12, 2018 12:55:24 AM As I head out to a very important NATO meeting, I see that FBI Lover/Agent Lisa Page is dodging a Subpoena & is refusing to show up and testify. What can she possibly say about her statements and lies. So much corruption on the other side. Where is the Attorney General? @FoxNews [Twitter for iPhone]

Jul 12, 2018 01:03:29 AM Presidents have been trying unsuccessfully for years to get Germany and other rich NATO Nations to pay more toward their protection from Russia. They pay only a fraction of their cost. The U.S. pays tens of Billions of Dollars too much to subsidize Europe, and loses Big on Trade! [Twitter for iPhone]

Jul 12, 2018 01:12:05 AM ....On top of it all, Germany just started paying Russia, the country they want protection from, Billions of Dollars for their Energy needs coming out of a new pipeline from Russia. Not acceptable! All NATO Nations must meet their 2% commitment, and that must ultimately go to 4%! [Twitter for iPhone]

Jul 12, 2018 05:57:06 AM #NATOSummit2018 Press Conference in Brussels, Belgium: https://t.co/iEOeGV6YBI [Twitter for iPhone]

Jul 12, 2018 09:12:41 AM Thank you #NATO2018! https://t.co/nk85QBv1u7 [Twitter for iPhone]

Jul 12, 2018 10:00:43 AM RT @dougmillsnyt: .@realDonaldTrump's shadow is reflected on the wall as he makes a statement and answers questions as he departs the NATO... [Twitter for iPhone]

Jul 12, 2018 10:00:54 AM RT @dougmillsnyt: .@realDonaldTrump & @FLOTUS walk off Air Force One as they arrive at London Stansted Airport in Stansted, England. https:... [Twitter for iPhone]

Jul 12, 2018 10:10:51 AM "Trump has been the most consequential president in history when it comes to minority employment. In June, for instance, the unemployment rate for Hispanics and Latinos 16 years and older fell to 4.6%, its lowest level ever, from 4.9% in May." https://t.co/ex9jizOyAV [Twitter for iPhone]

Jul 12, 2018 11:32:21 AM A very nice note from Chairman Kim of North Korea. Great progress being made! https://t.co/6NI6AqL0xt [Twitter for iPhone]

Jul 12, 2018 12:52:33 PM Great success today at NATO! Billions of additional dollars paid by members since my election. Great spirit! [Twitter for iPhone]

Jul 13, 2018 01:02:42 AM Congressman Matt Gaetz of Florida is one of the finest and most talented people in Congress. Strong on Crime, the Border, Illegal Immigration, the 2nd Amendment, our great Military & Vets, Matt worked tirelessly on helping to get our Massive Tax Cuts. He has my Full Endorsement! [Twitter for iPhone]

Jul 13, 2018 01:12:25 AM RT @MagaGoldHat: @RonDeSantisFL event July 18 th in Orlando with @DonaldJTrumpJr https://t.co/C5B5UwQZXa [Twitter for iPhone]

Jul 13, 2018 09:07:29 AM Joint Press Conference with Prime Minister Theresa May... https://t.co/XQLkayYKlM [Twitter for iPhone]

Jul 13, 2018 01:04:59 PM USGB https://t.co/CwnBfe3smd [Twitter for iPhone]

Jul 14, 2018 04:16:26 AM RT @realDonaldTrump: "Trump has been the most consequential president in history when it comes to minority employment. In June, for instanc... [Twitter for iPhone]

Jul 14, 2018 04:17:24 AM RT @realDonaldTrump: ....On top of it all, Germany just started paying Russia, the country they want protection from, Billions of Dollars f... [Twitter for iPhone]

Jul 14, 2018 04:18:40 AM This is now changing - for the first time! https://t.co/bRgrMbdDPp [Twitter for iPhone]

Jul 14, 2018 04:43:04 AM I have arrived in Scotland and will be at Trump Turnberry for two days of meetings, calls and hopefully, some golf - my primary form of exercise! The weather is beautiful, and this place is incredible! Tomorrow I go to Helsinki for a Monday meeting with Vladimir Putin. [Twitter for iPhone]

Jul 14, 2018 04:46:55 AM The Stock Market hit 25,000 yesterday. Jobs are at an all time record - and that is before we fix some of the worst trade deals and conditions ever seen by any government. It is all happening! [Twitter for iPhone]

Jul 14, 2018 04:53:13 AM The stories you heard about the 12 Russians yesterday took place during the Obama Administration, not the Trump Administrations. Why didn't they do something about it, especially when it was reported that President Obama was informed by the FBI in September, before the Election? [Twitter for iPhone]

Jul 14, 2018 04:57:53 AM ....Where is the DNC Server, and why didn't the FBI take possession of it? Deep State? [Twitter for iPhone]

Jul 14, 2018 05:08:23 AM The stories you heard about the 12 Russians yesterday took place during the Obama Administration, not the Trump Administration. Why didn't they do something about it, especially when it was reported that President Obama was informed by the FBI in September, before the Election? [Twitter for iPhone]

Jul 14, 2018 06:24:13 AM So funny! I just checked out Fake News CNN, for the first time in a long time (they are dying in the ratings), to see if they covered my takedown yesterday of Jim Acosta (actually a nice guy). They didn't! But they did say I already lost in my meeting with Putin. Fake News...... [Twitter for iPhone]

Jul 14, 2018 06:34:32 AM ....Remember, it was Little Jeff Z and his people, who are told exactly what to say, who said I could not win the election in that "there was no way to 270" (over & over again) in the Electoral College. I got 306! They were sooooo wrong in their election coverage. Still hurting! [Twitter for iPhone]

Jul 14, 2018 07:44:05 AM Our prayers are with those affected by the flooding in Japan. We commend the rescue efforts and offer condolences to all who were injured or lost loved ones. https://t.co/AIgJMyT7qS [Twitter for iPhone]

Jul 14, 2018 01:17:37 PM These Russian individuals did their work during the Obama years. Why didn't Obama do something about it? Because he thought Crooked Hillary Clinton would win, that's why. Had nothing to do with the Trump Administration, but Fake News doesn't want to report the truth, as usual! [Twitter for iPhone]

Jul 15, 2018 08:33:14 AM RT @Scavino45: "Texas grand jury indicts MS-13 gang members after machete attacks" https://t.co/GGTCEDOcVh [Twitter for iPhone]

Jul 15, 2018 08:33:15 AM RT @Scavino45: "Asylum-Seeking Central American Discovered to Be MS-13 Gang Member" https://t.co/76ZizQSNKI [Twitter for iPhone]

Jul 15, 2018 08:33:15 AM RT @Scavino45: "MS-13 Gang Member Arrested Again After 4 Deportations" https://t.co/wuNqERJmPN [Twitter for iPhone]

Jul 15, 2018 08:33:15 AM RT @Scavino45: "About 1-in-5 illegal alien adults crossing the United States-Mexico border with toddlers under the age of five are either c… [Twitter for iPhone]

Jul 15, 2018 08:33:15 AM RT @Scavino45: "Mike Pence op-ed: Trump White House phenomenally successful" https://t.co/L2WaPpxxgg [Twitter for iPhone]

Jul 15, 2018 08:33:15 AM RT @realDonaldTrump: These Russian individuals did their work during the Obama years. Why didn't Obama do something about it? Because he t… [Twitter for iPhone]

Jul 15, 2018 08:40:23 AM RT @Scavino45: "Criminal Illegal Alien Deported 11 Times Attacked Woman with Chainsaw, @ICEgov Says" https://t.co/wU7rk1OOzj [Twitter for iPhone]

Jul 15, 2018 08:40:55 AM RT @realDonaldTrump: The stories you heard about the 12 Russians yesterday took place during the Obama Administration, not the Trump Admini… [Twitter for iPhone]

Jul 15, 2018 11:11:13 AM There hasn't been a missile or rocket fired in 9 months in North Korea, there have been no nuclear tests and we got back our hostages. Who knows how it will all turn out in the end, but why isn't the Fake News talking about these wonderful facts? Because it is FAKE NEWS! [Twitter for iPhone]

Jul 15, 2018 11:18:10 AM Heading to Helsinki, Finland – looking forward to meeting with President Putin tomorrow. Unfortunately, no matter how well I do at the Summit, if I was given the great city of Moscow as retribution for all of the sins and evils committed by Russia... [Twitter for iPhone]

Jul 15, 2018 11:18:11 AM ...over the years, I would return to criticism that it wasn't good enough – that I should have gotten Saint Petersburg in addition! Much of our news media is indeed the enemy of the people and all the Dems... [Twitter for iPhone]

Jul 15, 2018 11:18:12 AM ...know how to do is resist and obstruct! This is why there is such hatred and dissension in our country – but at some point, it will heal! [Twitter for iPhone]

Jul 15, 2018 12:03:03 PM Congratulations to France, who played extraordinary soccer, on winning the 2018 World Cup. Additionally, congratulations to President Putin and Russia for putting on a truly great World Cup Tournament -- one of the best ever! [Twitter for iPhone]

Jul 15, 2018 11:28:10 PM RT @Scavino45: President @realDonaldTrump and @FLOTUS Melania are wheels down in Helsinki, Finland...photo via motorcade en route to hotel.… [Twitter for iPhone]

⟨⟩ Jul 15, 2018 11:28:24 PM RT @SecPompeo: Landed in #Finland for #helsinki2018 where @POTUS & Prez Putin are set to discuss US/Russian relations. POTUS meeting is in… [Twitter for iPhone]

⟨⟩ Jul 16, 2018 12:23:50 AM Received many calls from leaders of NATO countries thanking me for helping to bring them together and to get them focused on financial obligations, both present & future. We had a truly great Summit that was inaccurately covered by much of the media. NATO is now strong & rich! [Twitter for iPhone]

⟨⟩ Jul 16, 2018 12:37:05 AM President Obama thought that Crooked Hillary was going to win the election, so when he was informed by the FBI about Russian Meddling, he said it couldn't happen, was no big deal, & did NOTHING about it. When I won it became a big deal and the Rigged Witch Hunt headed by Strzok! [Twitter for iPhone]

⟨⟩ Jul 16, 2018 01:05:29 AM Our relationship with Russia has NEVER been worse thanks to many years of U.S. foolishness and stupidity and now, the Rigged Witch Hunt! [Twitter for iPhone]

⟨⟩ Jul 16, 2018 03:56:58 AM It was an honor to join you this morning. Thank you! https://t.co/NOUTroe8MV [Twitter for iPad]

⟨⟩ Jul 16, 2018 11:11:26 AM Joint Press Conference from Helsinki, Finland: https://t.co/fadLMDuGiY [Twitter for iPhone]

⟨⟩ Jul 16, 2018 11:51:20 AM Thank you Helsinki, Finland! https://t.co/rh4NUjPSwU [Twitter for iPhone]

⟨⟩ Jul 16, 2018 02:40:23 PM As I said today and many times before, "I have GREAT confidence in MY intelligence people." However, I also recognize that in order to build a brighter future, we cannot exclusively focus on the past -- as the world's two largest nuclear powers, we must get along! #HELSINKI2018 [Twitter for iPhone]

⟨⟩ Jul 16, 2018 03:29:54 PM I would rather take a political risk in pursuit of peace, than to risk peace in pursuit of politics. #HELSINKI2018 https://t.co/XdlrJWLPIh [Twitter for iPhone]

⟨⟩ Jul 16, 2018 03:34:07 PM A productive dialogue is not only good for the United States and good for Russia, but it is good for the world. #HELSINKI2018 https://t.co/Q2Y1PhM9au [Twitter for iPhone]

⟨⟩ Jul 16, 2018 05:53:47 PM Will be interviewed on @seanhannity tonight at 9pmE and @TuckerCarlson tomorrow night at 8pmE. Enjoy! [Twitter for iPhone]

⟨⟩ Jul 17, 2018 07:59:36 AM Thank you @RandPaul, you really get it! "The President has gone through a year and a half of totally partisan investigations - what's he supposed think?" [Twitter for iPhone]

Jul 17, 2018 08:53:39 AM I had a great meeting with NATO. They have paid $33 Billion more and will pay hundreds of Billions of Dollars more in the future, only because of me. NATO was weak, but now it is strong again (bad for Russia). The media only says I was rude to leaders, never mentions the money! [Twitter for iPhone]

Jul 17, 2018 09:22:28 AM While I had a great meeting with NATO, raising vast amounts of money, I had an even better meeting with Vladimir Putin of Russia. Sadly, it is not being reported that way - the Fake News is going Crazy! [Twitter for iPhone]

Jul 17, 2018 09:33:47 AM Thank you @RandPaul. "The President has gone through a year and a half of totally partisan investigations - what's he supposed to think?" [Twitter for iPhone]

Jul 17, 2018 09:39:08 AM The economy of the United States is stronger than ever before! [Twitter for iPhone]

Jul 17, 2018 07:21:54 PM The meeting between President Putin and myself was a great success, except in the Fake News Media! [Twitter for iPhone]

Jul 17, 2018 07:27:37 PM The Democrats want to abolish ICE, which will mean more crime in our country. I want to give ICE a big cheer! Vote Republican in November. [Twitter for iPhone]

Jul 17, 2018 11:10:19 PM "Prosperity is returning. Donald Trump is doing exactly what he said he would do as a candidate, now as the most effective president, the most successful president, in modern American history." Thank you to the great Lou Dobbs! [Twitter for iPhone]

Jul 18, 2018 04:53:41 AM So many people at the higher ends of intelligence loved my press conference performance in Helsinki. Putin and I discussed many important subjects at our earlier meeting. We got along well which truly bothered many haters who wanted to see a boxing match. Big results will come! [Twitter for iPhone]

Jul 18, 2018 05:08:36 AM While the NATO meeting in Brussels was an acknowledged triumph, with billions of dollars more being put up by member countries at a faster pace, the meeting with Russia may prove to be, in the long run, an even greater success. Many positive things will come out of that meeting.. [Twitter for iPhone]

Jul 18, 2018 05:16:50 AM ....Russia has agreed to help with North Korea, where relationships with us are very good and the process is moving along. There is no rush, the sanctions remain! Big benefits and exciting future for North Korea at end of process! [Twitter for iPhone]

Jul 18, 2018 05:44:18 AM Congratulations to Martha Roby of The Great State of Alabama on her big GOP Primary win for Congress. My endorsement came appropriately late, but when it came the "flood gates" opened and you had the kind of landslide victory that you deserve. Enjoy! [Twitter for iPhone]

⊔ Jul 18, 2018 06:03:05 AM "A lot of Democrats wished they voted for the Tax Cuts because the economy is booming - we could have 4% growth now and the Fed said yesterday that unemployment could drop again." @foxandfriends @kilmeade [Twitter for iPhone]

⊔ Jul 18, 2018 06:27:59 AM Some people HATE the fact that I got along well with President Putin of Russia. They would rather go to war than see this. It's called Trump Derangement Syndrome! [Twitter for iPhone]

⊔ Jul 18, 2018 06:33:34 AM 3.4 million jobs created since our great Election Victory - far greater than ever anticipated, and only getting better as new and greatly improved Trade Deals start coming to fruition! [Twitter for iPhone]

⊔ Jul 18, 2018 12:12:53 PM RT @SecretService: In Remembrance: Special Agent Nole E. Remagen. This week the U.S. Secret Service lost one of America's finest. We ask fo… [Twitter for iPhone]

⊔ Jul 18, 2018 02:25:30 PM Brian Kemp is running for Governor of the great state of Georgia. The Primary is on Tuesday. Brian is tough on crime, strong on the border and illegal immigration. He loves our Military and our Vets and protects our Second Amendment. I give him my full and total endorsement. [Twitter for iPhone]

⊔ Jul 18, 2018 04:29:06 PM Thank you to Congressman Kevin Yoder! He secured $5 BILLION for Border Security. Now we need Congress to support. Kevin has been strong on Crime, the Border, the 2nd Amendment, and he loves our Military and Vets. @RepKevinYoder has my full and total endorsement! [Twitter for iPhone]

⊔ Jul 18, 2018 04:30:19 PM The two biggest opponents of ICE in America today are the Democratic Party and MS-13! [Twitter for iPhone]

⊔ Jul 18, 2018 04:34:12 PM RT @SecAzar: .@POTUS has made clear that it's time for drug companies to put American Patients First -- Novartis halting its prescription dr… [Twitter for iPhone]

⊔ Jul 18, 2018 08:35:33 PM A total disgrace that Turkey will not release a respected U.S. Pastor, Andrew Brunson, from prison. He has been held hostage far too long. @RT_Erdogan should do something to free this wonderful Christian husband & father. He has done nothing wrong, and his family needs him! [Twitter for iPhone]

⊔ Jul 19, 2018 05:23:14 AM Thank you to Novartis for not increasing your prices on prescription drugs. Likewise to Pfizer. We are making a big push to actually reduce the prices, maybe substantially, on prescription drugs. [Twitter for iPhone]

⊔ Jul 19, 2018 05:29:15 AM The Democrats have a death wish, in more ways than one - they actually want to abolish ICE. This should cost them heavily in the Midterms. Yesterday, the Republicans overwhelmingly passed a bill supporting ICE! [Twitter for iPhone]

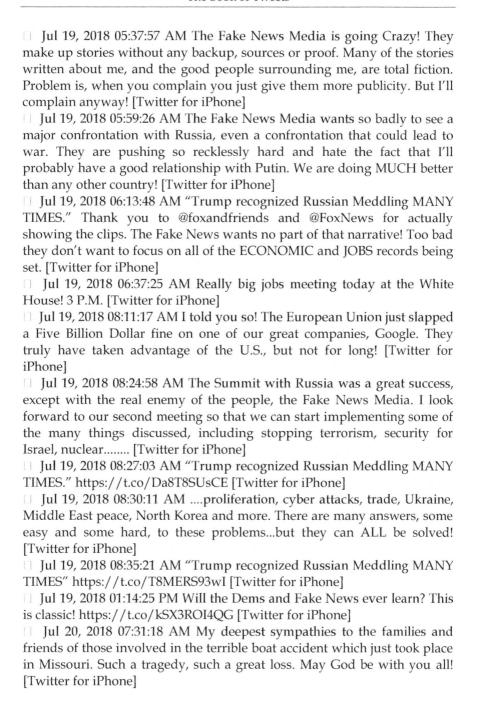

Jul 19, 2018 05:37:57 AM The Fake News Media is going Crazy! They make up stories without any backup, sources or proof. Many of the stories written about me, and the good people surrounding me, are total fiction. Problem is, when you complain you just give them more publicity. But I'll complain anyway! [Twitter for iPhone]

Jul 19, 2018 05:59:26 AM The Fake News Media wants so badly to see a major confrontation with Russia, even a confrontation that could lead to war. They are pushing so recklessly hard and hate the fact that I'll probably have a good relationship with Putin. We are doing MUCH better than any other country! [Twitter for iPhone]

Jul 19, 2018 06:13:48 AM "Trump recognized Russian Meddling MANY TIMES." Thank you to @foxandfriends and @FoxNews for actually showing the clips. The Fake News wants no part of that narrative! Too bad they don't want to focus on all of the ECONOMIC and JOBS records being set. [Twitter for iPhone]

Jul 19, 2018 06:37:25 AM Really big jobs meeting today at the White House! 3 P.M. [Twitter for iPhone]

Jul 19, 2018 08:11:17 AM I told you so! The European Union just slapped a Five Billion Dollar fine on one of our great companies, Google. They truly have taken advantage of the U.S., but not for long! [Twitter for iPhone]

Jul 19, 2018 08:24:58 AM The Summit with Russia was a great success, except with the real enemy of the people, the Fake News Media. I look forward to our second meeting so that we can start implementing some of the many things discussed, including stopping terrorism, security for Israel, nuclear........ [Twitter for iPhone]

Jul 19, 2018 08:27:03 AM "Trump recognized Russian Meddling MANY TIMES." https://t.co/Da8T8SUsCE [Twitter for iPhone]

Jul 19, 2018 08:30:11 AM ....proliferation, cyber attacks, trade, Ukraine, Middle East peace, North Korea and more. There are many answers, some easy and some hard, to these problems...but they can ALL be solved! [Twitter for iPhone]

Jul 19, 2018 08:35:21 AM "Trump recognized Russian Meddling MANY TIMES" https://t.co/T8MERS93wI [Twitter for iPhone]

Jul 19, 2018 01:14:25 PM Will the Dems and Fake News ever learn? This is classic! https://t.co/kSX3ROI4QG [Twitter for iPhone]

Jul 20, 2018 07:31:18 AM My deepest sympathies to the families and friends of those involved in the terrible boat accident which just took place in Missouri. Such a tragedy, such a great loss. May God be with you all! [Twitter for iPhone]

Jul 20, 2018 07:43:05 AM China, the European Union and others have been manipulating their currencies and interest rates lower, while the U.S. is raising rates while the dollars gets stronger and stronger with each passing day - taking away our big competitive edge. As usual, not a level playing field... [Twitter for iPhone]

Jul 20, 2018 07:51:45 AM ....The United States should not be penalized because we are doing so well. Tightening now hurts all that we have done. The U.S. should be allowed to recapture what was lost due to illegal currency manipulation and BAD Trade Deals. Debt coming due & we are raising rates - Really? [Twitter for iPhone]

Jul 20, 2018 08:04:44 AM Farmers have been on a downward trend for 15 years. The price of soybeans has fallen 50% since 5 years before the Election. A big reason is bad (terrible) Trade Deals with other countries. They put on massive Tariffs and Barriers. Canada charges 275% on Dairy. Farmers will WIN! [Twitter for iPhone]

Jul 20, 2018 09:33:57 AM RT @Scavino45: "Senate GOP breaks record on confirming Trump picks for key court" https://t.co/CB5Zsl5iSG [Twitter for iPhone]

Jul 20, 2018 09:34:11 AM RT @Scavino45: "Former Harvard law students praise Kavanaugh in letter" https://t.co/1ihzCwPToF [Twitter for iPhone]

Jul 20, 2018 09:34:44 AM RT @Scavino45: "More Winning: American Jobless Claims Drop to Lowest Level Since 1969" https://t.co/eBGUs7GlSU [Twitter for iPhone]

Jul 20, 2018 09:35:49 AM So important. Should have been done years ago! https://t.co/TFIqsaZWBt [Twitter for iPhone]

Jul 20, 2018 09:35:59 AM RT @realDonaldTrump: Will the Dems and Fake News ever learn? This is classic! https://t.co/kSX3ROI4QG [Twitter for iPhone]

Jul 20, 2018 09:39:02 AM RT @realDonaldTrump: The Summit with Russia was a great success, except with the real enemy of the people, the Fake News Media. I look forw… [Twitter for iPhone]

Jul 20, 2018 09:39:21 AM RT @realDonaldTrump: I told you so! The European Union just slapped a Five Billion Dollar fine on one of our great companies, Google. They… [Twitter for iPhone]

Jul 20, 2018 04:50:30 PM I got severely criticized by the Fake News Media for being too nice to President Putin. In the Old Days they would call it Diplomacy. If I was loud & vicious, I would have been criticized for being too tough. Remember when they said I was too tough with Chairman Kim? Hypocrites! [Twitter for iPhone]

Jul 20, 2018 04:51:11 PM RT @IvankaTrump: .@WhiteHouse National Council for the American Worker together w/ the private sector is working to equip students + worker… [Twitter for iPhone]

Jul 20, 2018 05:17:21 PM The NFL National Anthem Debate is alive and well again - can't believe it! Isn't it in contract that players must stand at attention, hand on heart? The $40,000,000 Commissioner must now make a stand. First time kneeling, out for game. Second time kneeling, out for season/no pay! [Twitter for iPhone]

Jul 21, 2018 07:10:58 AM Inconceivable that the government would break into a lawyer's office (early in the morning) - almost unheard of. Even more inconceivable that a lawyer would tape a client - totally unheard of & perhaps illegal. The good news is that your favorite President did nothing wrong! [Twitter for iPhone]

Jul 21, 2018 05:40:06 PM The Rigged Witch Hunt, headed by the 13 Angry Democrats (and now 4 more have been added, one who worked directly for Obama W.H.), seems intent on damaging the Republican Party's chances in the November Election. This Democrat excuse for losing the '16 Election never ends! [Twitter for iPhone]

Jul 21, 2018 05:50:38 PM No Collusion, No Obstruction - but that doesn't matter because the 13 Angry Democrats, who are only after Republicans and totally protecting Democrats, want this Witch Hunt to drag out to the November Election. Republicans better get smart fast and expose what they are doing! [Twitter for iPhone]

Jul 21, 2018 06:00:42 PM Brian Kemp, who is running for Governor of Georgia and has my full endorsement, is campaigning tonight with @MikePenceVP. Brian is very strong on Crime and Borders, LOVES our Military, Vets and the 2nd Amendment. He will be a GREAT Governor! [Twitter for iPhone]

Jul 21, 2018 06:10:57 PM Brian Kemp, who is running for Governor of Georgia and has my full endorsement, is campaigning tonight with VP @mike_pence. Brian is very strong on Crime and Borders, LOVES our Military, Vets and the 2nd Amendment. He will be a GREAT Governor! [Twitter for iPhone]

Jul 21, 2018 06:23:34 PM Troy Balderson of Ohio is running for Congress against a Nancy Pelosi Liberal who is WEAK on Crime & Borders. Troy is the total opposite, and loves our Military, Vets & 2nd Amendment. EARLY VOTING just started with Election Day on August 7th. Troy has my Full & Total Endorsement! [Twitter for iPhone]

Jul 21, 2018 07:21:01 PM Watching Los Angeles possible hostage situation very closely. Active barricaded suspect. L.A.P.D. working with Federal Law Enforcement. [Twitter for iPhone]

Jul 22, 2018 05:28:40 AM Congratulations to @JudicialWatch and @TomFitton on being successful in getting the Carter Page FISA documents. As usual they are ridiculously heavily redacted but confirm with little doubt that the Department of "Justice" and FBI misled the courts. Witch Hunt Rigged, a Scam! [Twitter for iPhone]

Jul 22, 2018 05:49:25 AM Looking more & more like the Trump Campaign for President was illegally being spied upon (surveillance) for the political gain of Crooked Hillary Clinton and the DNC. Ask her how that worked out - she did better with Crazy Bernie. Republicans must get tough now. An illegal Scam! [Twitter for iPhone]

Jul 22, 2018 07:22:49 AM Andrew McCarthy - "I said this could never happen. This is so bad that they should be looking at the judges who signed off on this stuff, not just the people who gave it. It is so bad it screams out at you." On the whole FISA scam which led to the rigged Mueller Witch Hunt! [Twitter for iPhone]

Jul 22, 2018 07:56:15 AM .@PeteHegseth on @FoxNews "Source #1 was the (Fake) Dossier. Yes, the Dirty Dossier, paid for by Democrats as a hit piece against Trump, and looking for information that could discredit Candidate #1 Trump. Carter Page was just the foot to surveil the Trump campaign..." ILLEGAL! [Twitter for iPhone]

Jul 22, 2018 08:15:18 AM I had a GREAT meeting with Putin and the Fake News used every bit of their energy to try and disparage it. So bad for our country! [Twitter for iPhone]

Jul 22, 2018 03:58:44 PM Happy Birthday @SenatorDole! https://t.co/MiVoB7qC6A [Twitter for iPhone]

Jul 22, 2018 05:23:52 PM So President Obama knew about Russia before the Election. Why didn't he do something about it? Why didn't he tell our campaign? Because it is all a big hoax, that's why, and he thought Crooked Hillary was going to win!!! [Twitter for iPhone]

Jul 22, 2018 10:24:19 PM To Iranian President Rouhani: NEVER, EVER THREATEN THE UNITED STATES AGAIN OR YOU WILL SUFFER CONSEQUENCES THE LIKES OF WHICH FEW THROUGHOUT HISTORY HAVE EVER SUFFERED BEFORE. WE ARE NO LONGER A COUNTRY THAT WILL STAND FOR YOUR DEMENTED WORDS OF VIOLENCE & DEATH. BE CAUTIOUS! [Twitter for iPhone]

Jul 23, 2018 05:13:52 AM Tom Fitton on @foxandfriends at 6:15 A.M. NOW! Judicial Watch. [Twitter for iPhone]

Jul 23, 2018 05:30:11 AM So we now find out that it was indeed the unverified and Fake Dirty Dossier, that was paid for by Crooked Hillary Clinton and the DNC, that was knowingly & falsely submitted to FISA and which was responsible for starting the totally conflicted and discredited Mueller Witch Hunt! [Twitter for iPhone]

Jul 23, 2018 05:52:10 AM "It was classified to cover up misconduct by the FBI and the Justice Department in misleading the Court by using this Dossier in a dishonest way to gain a warrant to target the Trump Team. This is a Clinton Campaign document. It was a fraud and a hoax designed to target Trump.... [Twitter for iPhone]

Jul 23, 2018 06:01:15 AM ....and the DOJ, FBI and Obama Gang need to be held to account. Source #1 was the major source. Avoided talking about it being the Clinton campaign behind it. Misled the Court to provide a pretext to SPY on the Trump Team. Not about Carter Page..was all about getting Trump..... [Twitter for iPhone]

Jul 23, 2018 06:09:39 AM ....."Carter Page wasn't a spy, wasn't an agent of the Russians - he would have cooperated with the FBI. It was a fraud and a hoax designed to target Trump." Tom Fitton @JudicialWatch A disgrace to America. They should drop the discredited Mueller Witch Hunt now! [Twitter for iPhone]

Jul 23, 2018 07:25:02 AM When you hear the Fake News talking negatively about my meeting with President Putin, and all that I gave up, remember, I gave up NOTHING, we merely talked about future benefits for both countries. Also, we got along very well, which is a good thing, except for the Corrupt Media! [Twitter for iPhone]

Jul 23, 2018 08:06:18 AM A Rocket has not been launched by North Korea in 9 months. Likewise, no Nuclear Tests. Japan is happy, all of Asia is happy. But the Fake News is saying, without ever asking me (always anonymous sources), that I am angry because it is not going fast enough. Wrong, very happy! [Twitter for iPhone]

Jul 23, 2018 08:21:15 AM The Amazon Washington Post has gone crazy against me ever since they lost the Internet Tax Case in the U.S. Supreme Court two months ago. Next up is the U.S. Post Office which they use, at a fraction of real cost, as their "delivery boy" for a BIG percentage of their packages.... [Twitter for iPhone]

Jul 23, 2018 08:35:20 AM ....In my opinion the Washington Post is nothing more than an expensive (the paper loses a fortune) lobbyist for Amazon. Is it used as protection against antitrust claims which many feel should be brought? [Twitter for iPhone]

Jul 23, 2018 08:35:37 PM Robert will do a great job for our Vets. We also recently won Choice! https://t.co/hE0GDuCBET [Twitter for iPhone]

Jul 23, 2018 08:44:06 PM Lou Barletta was one of my first supporters. He is tough on Crime and Borders. Will be a great Senator from Pennsylvania. His opponent is WEAK on Crime, ICE and Borders. We need Lou! https://t.co/dcMSi4CPfb [Twitter for iPhone]

Jul 23, 2018 09:07:39 PM #MadeInAmerica Showcase! https://t.co/rT0WIE99yP [Twitter for iPhone]

Jul 24, 2018 06:01:13 AM RT @DanScavino: "Lockheed Martin will add 400 workers to boost production of the F-35 fighter jet, the most expensive in U.S. history, afte… [Twitter for iPhone]

Jul 24, 2018 06:01:27 AM RT @DanScavino: "Coast Guard seizes $729M worth of cocaine from boats moving drugs from Central America to the US" https://t.co/R7fFD5BJTb [Twitter for iPhone]

Jul 24, 2018 06:09:12 AM Countries that have treated us unfairly on trade for years are all coming to Washington to negotiate. This should have taken place many years ago but, as the saying goes, better late than never! [Twitter for iPhone]

Jul 24, 2018 06:29:50 AM Tariffs are the greatest! Either a country which has treated the United States unfairly on Trade negotiates a fair deal, or it gets hit with Tariffs. It's as simple as that - and everybody's talking! Remember, we are the "piggy bank" that's being robbed. All will be Great! [Twitter for iPhone]

Jul 24, 2018 08:39:49 AM Today is the day to vote for Brian Kemp. Will be great for Georgia, full Endorsement! https://t.co/yPND2bJ219 [Twitter for iPhone]

Jul 24, 2018 08:46:22 AM Our Country is doing GREAT. Best financial numbers on the Planet. Great to have USA WINNING AGAIN! [Twitter for iPhone]

Jul 24, 2018 08:52:56 AM Heading to Missouri to be with many of my great friends. VFW here we come! [Twitter for iPhone]

Jul 24, 2018 08:54:19 AM MAKE AMERICA GREAT AGAIN! [Twitter for iPhone]

Jul 24, 2018 10:50:37 AM I'm very concerned that Russia will be fighting very hard to have an impact on the upcoming Election. Based on the fact that no President has been tougher on Russia than me, they will be pushing very hard for the Democrats. They definitely don't want Trump! [Twitter for iPhone]

Jul 24, 2018 12:51:28 PM #VFWConvention @VFWHQ https://t.co/dBQx526axz [Twitter for iPhone]

Jul 24, 2018 02:15:36 PM I want to thank the @VFWHQ for your devotion to our fallen heroes, unknown soldiers, Prisoners of War, those Missing in Action, and their families. #VFWConvention https://t.co/15ygFhCudR [Twitter for iPhone]

Jul 24, 2018 05:25:07 PM On the heels of the VERY successful launch of the @WhiteHouse National Council for the American Worker, Congress should reauthorize #PerkinsCTE and ensure the American workforce remains stronger than EVER! #Jobs #Workforce [Twitter for iPhone]

Jul 24, 2018 05:33:30 PM Today, it was my great honor to be in Kansas City, Missouri to pay tribute to the men and women who make FREEDOM possible! Thank you @VFWHQ! #VFWConvention https://t.co/E6TYsNmWO8 [Twitter for iPhone]

Jul 24, 2018 07:08:01 PM The European Union is coming to Washington tomorrow to negotiate a deal on Trade. I have an idea for them. Both the U.S. and the E.U. drop all Tariffs, Barriers and Subsidies! That would finally be called Free Market and Fair Trade! Hope they do it, we are ready - but they won't! [Twitter for iPhone]

Jul 24, 2018 07:39:16 PM So sad and unfair that the FCC wouldn't approve the Sinclair Broadcast merger with Tribune. This would have been a great and much needed Conservative voice for and of the People. Liberal Fake News NBC and Comcast gets approved, much bigger, but not Sinclair. Disgraceful! [Twitter for iPhone]

Jul 24, 2018 08:05:05 PM "The Russia Hoax, The Illicit Scheme To Clear Hillary Clinton & Frame Donald Trump" is a Hot Seller, already Number One! More importantly, it is a great book that everyone is talking about. It covers the Rigged Witch Hunt brilliantly. Congratulations to Gregg Jarrett! [Twitter for iPhone]

Jul 25, 2018 06:01:05 AM Every time I see a weak politician asking to stop Trade talks or the use of Tariffs to counter unfair Tariffs, I wonder, what can they be thinking? Are we just going to continue and let our farmers and country get ripped off? Lost $817 Billion on Trade last year. No weakness! [Twitter for iPhone]

Jul 25, 2018 06:08:39 AM When you have people snipping at your heels during a negotiation, it will only take longer to make a deal, and the deal will never be as good as it could have been with unity. Negotiations are going really well, be cool. The end result will be worth it! [Twitter for iPhone]

Jul 25, 2018 06:20:28 AM China is targeting our farmers, who they know I love & respect, as a way of getting me to continue allowing them to take advantage of the U.S. They are being vicious in what will be their failed attempt. We were being nice - until now! China made $517 Billion on us last year. [Twitter for iPhone]

Jul 25, 2018 07:34:58 AM What kind of a lawyer would tape a client? So sad! Is this a first, never heard of it before? Why was the tape so abruptly terminated (cut) while I was presumably saying positive things? I hear there are other clients and many reporters that are taped - can this be so? Too bad! [Twitter for iPhone]

Jul 25, 2018 07:41:14 AM Congratulations to Brian Kemp on your very big win in Georgia last night. Wow, 69-30, those are big numbers. Now go win against the open border, crime loving opponent that the Democrats have given you. She is weak on Vets, the Military and the 2nd Amendment. Win! [Twitter for iPhone]

Jul 25, 2018 03:57:24 PM The United States and the European Union have a $1 TRILLION bilateral trade relationship – the largest economic relationship in the world. We want to further strengthen this trade relationship to the benefit of all American and European citizens... https://t.co/4zlmEEtCpG [Media Studio]

Jul 25, 2018 05:33:01 PM This week, my Administration is hosting the first-ever #IRFMinisterial. The U.S. will continue to promote #ReligiousFreedom around the world. Nations that support religious freedom are far more free, prosperous & peaceful. Great job, @VP, @SecPompeo, @IRF_Ambassador & @StateDept! [Twitter for iPhone]

Jul 25, 2018 05:45:49 PM Sergio Marchionne, who passed away today, was one of the most brilliant & successful car executives since the days of the legendary Henry Ford. It was a great honor for me to get to know Sergio as POTUS, he loved the car industry, and fought hard for it. He will be truly missed! [Twitter for iPhone]

Jul 25, 2018 05:59:35 PM Thank you very much, working hard! https://t.co/cSzbFfq2NW [Twitter for iPhone]

Jul 25, 2018 06:42:23 PM Great meeting on Trade today with @JunckerEU and representatives of the European Union. We have come to a very strong understanding and are all believers in no tariffs, no barriers and no subsidies. Work on documents has already started and the process is moving... [Twitter for iPhone]

Jul 25, 2018 06:42:24 PM ...along quickly. European Union Nations will be open to the United States and at the same time benefiting by everything we are doing for them. There was great warmth and feeling in the room - a breakthrough has been quickly made that nobody thought possible! [Twitter for iPhone]

Jul 25, 2018 06:49:34 PM Obviously the European Union, as represented by @JunckerEU and the United States, as represented by yours truly, love each other! https://t.co/42ImacgCN0 [Twitter for iPhone]

Jul 25, 2018 07:16:32 PM Thank you Georgia! They say that my endorsement last week of Brian Kemp, in the Republican Primary for Governor against a very worthy opponent, lifted him from 5 points down to a 70% to 30% victory! Two very good and talented men in a great race, but congratulations to Brian! [Twitter for iPhone]

Jul 25, 2018 07:57:19 PM RT @Scavino45: "We met today...to launch a new phase in the relationship between the U.S. & the EU – a phase of close friendship, of strong… [Twitter for iPhone]

Jul 25, 2018 08:01:08 PM Great to be back on track with the European Union. This was a big day for free and fair trade! [Twitter for iPhone]

Jul 25, 2018 08:07:28 PM European Union representatives told me that they would start buying soybeans from our great farmers immediately. Also, they will be buying vast amounts of LNG! [Twitter for iPhone]

Jul 26, 2018 06:46:09 AM Twitter "SHADOW BANNING" prominent Republicans. Not good. We will look into this discriminatory and illegal practice at once! Many complaints. [Twitter for iPhone]

⬜ Jul 26, 2018 09:11:30 AM Heading to Dubuque, Iowa and then Granite City, Illinois. Looking forward to being with many great friends! [Twitter for iPhone]

⬜ Jul 26, 2018 09:52:18 AM This is great - on my way, see you soon @IAGovernor Kim Reynolds! https://t.co/SXfkk12Uig [Twitter for iPhone]

⬜ Jul 26, 2018 10:22:39 AM The United States will impose large sanctions on Turkey for their long time detainment of Pastor Andrew Brunson, a great Christian, family man and wonderful human being. He is suffering greatly. This innocent man of faith should be released immediately! [Twitter for iPhone]

⬜ Jul 26, 2018 04:12:45 PM Thank you @U_S_Steel and Granite City, Illinois! https://t.co/6RsUvGF6rg [Twitter for iPhone]

⬜ Jul 26, 2018 04:43:13 PM PROMISES KEPT! https://t.co/vR2R5WXPVD [Twitter for iPhone]

⬜ Jul 26, 2018 05:48:38 PM .@AlanDersh, a brilliant lawyer, who although a Liberal Democrat who probably didn't vote for me, has discussed the Witch Hunt with great clarity and in a very positive way. He has written a new and very important book... [Twitter for iPhone]

⬜ Jul 26, 2018 05:48:40 PM ...called "The Case Against Impeaching Trump," which I would encourage all people with Trump Derangement Syndrome to read! [Twitter for iPhone]

⬜ Jul 26, 2018 09:37:00 PM America is OPEN FOR BUSINESS and U.S. Steel is back! https://t.co/lJTcr6JHBW [Twitter for iPhone]

⬜ Jul 26, 2018 10:50:54 PM The Remains of American Servicemen will soon be leaving North Korea and heading to the United States! After so many years, this will be a great moment for so many families. Thank you to Kim Jong Un. [Twitter for iPhone]

⬜ Jul 27, 2018 05:56:17 AM Way to go Jerry. This is what the league should do! https://t.co/yEP1jK57xi [Twitter for iPhone]

⬜ Jul 27, 2018 06:26:20 AM Arrived back in Washington last night from a very emotional reopening of a major U.S. Steel plant in Granite City, Illinois, only to be greeted with the ridiculous news that the highly conflicted Robert Mueller and his gang of 13 Angry Democrats obviously cannot find Collusion... [Twitter for iPhone]

⬜ Jul 27, 2018 06:38:32 AM ....,the only Collusion with Russia was with the Democrats, so now they are looking at my Tweets (along with 53 million other people) - the rigged Witch Hunt continues! How stupid and unfair to our Country....And so the Fake News doesn't waste my time with dumb questions, NO,.... [Twitter for iPhone]

Jul 27, 2018 06:56:15 AM .....I did NOT know of the meeting with my son, Don jr. Sounds to me like someone is trying to make up stories in order to get himself out of an unrelated jam (Taxi cabs maybe?). He even retained Bill and Crooked Hillary's lawyer. Gee, I wonder if they helped him make the choice! [Twitter for iPhone]

Jul 27, 2018 08:17:09 AM GREAT GDP numbers just released. Will be having a news conference soon! [Twitter for iPhone]

Jul 27, 2018 10:53:20 AM ...John is strong on crime and borders, loves our Military, our Vets and our Second Amendment. He will be a star. He has my full and total Endorsement! [Twitter for iPhone]

Jul 27, 2018 10:53:20 AM .@JohnJamesMI, who is running in the Republican Primary in the great state of Michigan, is SPECTACULAR! Vote on August 7th. Rarely have I seen a candidate with such great potential. West Point graduate, successful businessman and a African American leader... [Twitter for iPhone]

Jul 27, 2018 10:58:45 AM .@Troy_Balderson of Ohio is running for Congress - so important to the Republican Party. Cast you early vote or vote on August 7th. Troy is strong on crime and borders, loves our Military, our Vets and our Second Amendment. He has my full and total Endorsement! [Twitter for iPhone]

Jul 27, 2018 11:12:14 AM I am thrilled to announce that in the second quarter of this year, the U.S. Economy grew at the amazing rate of 4.1%! https://t.co/xeAPwAAOXN [Twitter for iPhone]

Jul 27, 2018 11:20:37 AM We have accomplished an economic turnaround of HISTORIC proportions! https://t.co/vnmMtPv0kk [Twitter for iPhone]

Jul 27, 2018 01:16:46 PM The @USNavy's first female Admiral, Alene Duerk once said: "It was a nice distinction to have, and to be recognized as the first, but I wanted to make certain that I used that notoriety to do as much positive as I could." Alene did just that, and America is forever grateful! https://t.co/tOqkzqGVG7 [Twitter for iPhone]

Jul 27, 2018 02:23:07 PM Private business investment has surged from 1.8 percent the year BEFORE I came into office to 9.4 percent this year -- that means JOBS, JOBS, JOBS! https://t.co/evO63CpqPP [Twitter for iPhone]

Jul 27, 2018 03:08:06 PM Congressman David Kustoff has been a champion for the Trump Agenda - I greatly appreciate his support. David is strong on crime and borders, loves our Military, Vets and Second Amendment. Get out and vote for David on Thursday, August 2nd. He has my full and total Endorsement! [Twitter for iPhone]

Jul 27, 2018 05:45:56 PM Democrats, who want Open Borders and care little about Crime, are incompetent, but they have the Fake News Media almost totally on their side! [Twitter for iPhone]

Jul 27, 2018 07:47:58 PM The only things the Democrats do well is "Resist," which is their campaign slogan, and "Obstruct." Cryin' Chuck Schumer has almost 400 great American people that are waiting "forever" to serve our Country! A total disgrace. Mitch M should not let them go home until all approved! [Twitter for iPhone]

Jul 27, 2018 08:53:48 PM Join me in Tampa, Florida next Tuesday, July 31st at 7:00pmE for a #MAGA Rally! Tickets: https://t.co/Q2PMyTACl8 https://t.co/URjvN8Owoe [Twitter for iPhone]

Jul 28, 2018 11:37:29 AM https://t.co/E3xvdUGZqa [Media Studio]

Jul 29, 2018 06:31:52 AM Tom Homan, fmr ICE Director: "There is nobody that has done more for border security & public safety than President Trump. I've worked for six presidents, and I respect them all, but nobody has done more than this Administration & President Trump, that's just a stone cold fact!" [Twitter for iPhone]

Jul 29, 2018 06:44:00 AM Wow, highest Poll Numbers in the history of the Republican Party. That includes Honest Abe Lincoln and Ronald Reagan. There must be something wrong, please recheck that poll! [Twitter for iPhone]

Jul 29, 2018 06:52:49 AM Do you think the Fake News Media will ever report on this tweet from Michael? https://t.co/kXLCKZO5Fr [Twitter for iPhone]

Jul 29, 2018 06:58:09 AM Please understand, there are consequences when people cross our Border illegally, whether they have children or not - and many are just using children for their own sinister purposes. Congress must act on fixing the DUMBEST & WORST immigration laws anywhere in the world! Vote "R" [Twitter for iPhone]

Jul 29, 2018 06:59:26 AM RT @realDonaldTrump: Democrats, who want Open Borders and care little about Crime, are incompetent, but they have the Fake News Media almos… [Twitter for iPhone]

Jul 29, 2018 06:59:30 AM RT @realDonaldTrump: The only things the Democrats do well is "Resist," which is their campaign slogan, and "Obstruct." Cryin' Chuck Schume… [Twitter for iPhone]

Jul 29, 2018 07:00:13 AM RT @realDonaldTrump: Congressman David Kustoff has been a champion for the Trump Agenda - I greatly appreciate his support. David is strong… [Twitter for iPhone]

Jul 29, 2018 07:30:04 AM Had a very good and interesting meeting at the White House with A.G. Sulzberger, Publisher of the New York Times. Spent much time talking about the vast amounts of Fake News being put out by the media & how that Fake News has morphed into phrase, "Enemy of the People." Sad! [Twitter for iPhone]

Jul 29, 2018 07:42:52 AM The biggest and best results coming out of the good GDP report was that the quarterly Trade Deficit has been reduced by $52 Billion and, of course, the historically low unemployment numbers, especially for African Americans, Hispanics, Asians and Women. [Twitter for iPhone]

Jul 29, 2018 08:13:59 AM I would be willing to "shut down" government if the Democrats do not give us the votes for Border Security, which includes the Wall! Must get rid of Lottery, Catch & Release etc. and finally go to system of Immigration based on MERIT! We need great people coming into our Country! [Twitter for iPhone]

Jul 29, 2018 02:09:17 PM When the media - driven insane by their Trump Derangement Syndrome - reveals internal deliberations of our government, it truly puts the lives of many, not just journalists, at risk! Very unpatriotic! Freedom of the press also comes with a responsibility to report the news... [Twitter for iPhone]

Jul 29, 2018 02:09:18 PM ...dying newspaper industry. No matter how much they try to distract and cover it up, our country is making great progress under my leadership and I will never stop fighting for the American people! As an example, the failing New York Times... [Twitter for iPhone]

Jul 29, 2018 02:09:18 PM ...accurately. 90% of media coverage of my Administration is negative, despite the tremendously positive results we are achieving, it's no surprise that confidence in the media is at an all time low! I will not allow our great country to be sold out by anti-Trump haters in the... [Twitter for iPhone]

Jul 29, 2018 02:09:19 PM ...and the Amazon Washington Post do nothing but write bad stories even on very positive achievements - and they will never change! [Twitter for iPhone]

Jul 29, 2018 02:35:14 PM There is No Collusion! The Robert Mueller Rigged Witch Hunt, headed now by 17 (increased from 13, including an Obama White House lawyer) Angry Democrats, was started by a fraudulent Dossier, paid for by Crooked Hillary and the DNC. Therefore, the Witch Hunt is an illegal Scam! [Twitter for iPhone]

Jul 29, 2018 03:12:15 PM Is Robert Mueller ever going to release his conflicts of interest with respect to President Trump, including the fact that we had a very nasty & contentious business relationship, I turned him down to head the FBI (one day before appointment as S.C.) & Comey is his close friend.. [Twitter for iPhone]

Jul 29, 2018 03:20:39 PM ....Also, why is Mueller only appointing Angry Dems, some of whom have worked for Crooked Hillary, others, including himself, have worked for Obama....And why isn't Mueller looking at all of the criminal activity & real Russian Collusion on the Democrats side-Podesta, Dossier? [Twitter for iPhone]

Jul 29, 2018 06:04:20 PM RT @Scavino45: "@realDonaldTrump tells @ICEgov agents: 'We always will stand with you'" https://t.co/o1P17H7IVq [Twitter for iPhone]

Jul 30, 2018 06:57:34 AM We must have Border Security, get rid of Chain, Lottery, Catch & Release Sanctuary Cities - go to Merit based Immigration. Protect ICE and Law Enforcement and, of course, keep building, but much faster, THE WALL! [Twitter for iPhone]

Jul 30, 2018 07:06:39 AM RT @GOPChairwoman: "David Burritt, U.S. Steel's president and CEO, said the company was experiencing a 'renaissance' and credited @realDona... [Twitter for iPhone]

Jul 30, 2018 12:22:27 PM It is my great honor to welcome Prime Minister @GiuseppeConteIT of Italy to the @WhiteHouse! Join us at 2:00pmE for our joint press conference: https://t.co/XAchZ3zUSe https://t.co/5t4QVsKKqH [Twitter for iPhone]

Jul 30, 2018 02:31:31 PM USIT https://t.co/1SSUCRtMEE [Twitter for iPhone]

Jul 30, 2018 04:20:37 PM Congratulations to General John Kelly. Today we celebrate his first full year as @WhiteHouse Chief of Staff! https://t.co/JWCaJ3GhHV [Twitter for iPhone]

Jul 30, 2018 05:28:20 PM .@Troy_Balderson of Ohio is running for Congress - so important to the Republican Party. Troy is strong on crime and Borders, loves our Military, our Vets and our Second Amendment. Troy will strongly protect... [Twitter for iPhone]

Jul 30, 2018 05:28:21 PM ...your Social Security and Medicare! Cast your early vote, or vote on August 7th, Election Day. He has my full and total Endorsement! [Twitter for iPhone]

Jul 30, 2018 05:29:05 PM RT @realDonaldTrump: .@JohnJamesMI, who is running in the Republican Primary in the great state of Michigan, is SPECTACULAR! Vote on August... [Twitter for iPhone]

Jul 30, 2018 05:29:06 PM RT @realDonaldTrump: ...John is strong on crime and borders, loves our Military, our Vets and our Second Amendment. He will be a star. He h... [Twitter for iPhone]

Jul 30, 2018 05:31:20 PM Congratulations to Judge Jeanine on the tremendous success of her new #1 best-selling book, "Liars, Leakers, and Liberals – The Case Against the Anti-Trump Conspiracy!" [Twitter for iPhone]

Jul 30, 2018 05:34:21 PM Illegal immigration is a top National Security problem. After decades of playing games, with the whole World laughing at the stupidity of our immigration laws, and with Democrats thinking... [Twitter for iPhone]

⊔ Jul 30, 2018 05:34:22 PM ...that Open Borders, large scale Crime, and abolishing ICE is good for them, we must get smart and finally do what must be done for the Safety and Security of our Country! [Twitter for iPhone]

⊔ Jul 30, 2018 05:36:02 PM Thank you to @RandPaul for your YES on a future great Justice of the Supreme Court, Brett Kavanaugh. Your vote means a lot to me, and to everyone who loves our Country! [Twitter for iPhone]

⊔ Jul 30, 2018 05:44:12 PM Congratulations to our new @DeptVetAffairs Secretary, Robert Wilkie! https://t.co/6erqWJzuiK [Twitter for iPhone]

⊔ Jul 30, 2018 07:56:16 PM A highly respected Federal judge today stated that the "Trump Administration gets great credit" for reuniting illegal families. Thank you, and please look at the previous administrations record - not good! [Twitter for iPhone]

⊔ Jul 30, 2018 09:01:02 PM MAKING AMERICA GREAT AGAIN! https://t.co/OnMGXvldVT [Media Studio]

⊔ Jul 31, 2018 05:14:18 AM The globalist Koch Brothers, who have become a total joke in real Republican circles, are against Strong Borders and Powerful Trade. I never sought their support because I don't need their money or bad ideas. They love my Tax & Regulation Cuts, Judicial picks & more. I made..... [Twitter for iPhone]

⊔ Jul 31, 2018 05:23:41 AM ....them richer. Their network is highly overrated, I have beaten them at every turn. They want to protect their companies outside the U.S. from being taxed, I'm for America First & the American Worker - a puppet for no one. Two nice guys with bad ideas. Make America Great Again! [Twitter for iPhone]

⊔ Jul 31, 2018 05:29:59 AM RT @dougmillsnyt: .@realDonaldTrump pumps his fist after his new Secretary of Veterans Affairs Robert Wilkie is sworn-in by @VP Mike Pence… [Twitter for iPhone]

⊔ Jul 31, 2018 05:30:23 AM RT @dougmillsnyt: .@realDonaldTrump walks with Giuseppe Conte, Prime Minister of the Italy following a joint news conference in the East Ro… [Twitter for iPhone]

⊔ Jul 31, 2018 05:50:28 AM Rush Limbaugh is a great guy who truly gets it! [Twitter for iPhone]

⊔ Jul 31, 2018 06:00:41 AM One of the reasons we need Great Border Security is that Mexico's murder rate in 2017 increased by 27% to 31,174 people killed, a record! The Democrats want Open Borders. I want Maximum Border Security and respect for ICE and our great Law Enforcement Professionals! @FoxNews [Twitter for iPhone]

⊔ Jul 31, 2018 06:58:58 AM Collusion is not a crime, but that doesn't matter because there was No Collusion (except by Crooked Hillary and the Democrats)! [Twitter for iPhone]

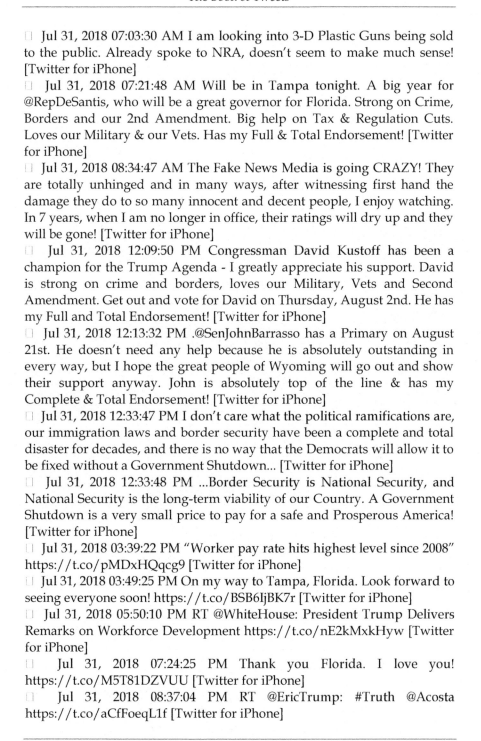

Jul 31, 2018 07:03:30 AM I am looking into 3-D Plastic Guns being sold to the public. Already spoke to NRA, doesn't seem to make much sense! [Twitter for iPhone]

Jul 31, 2018 07:21:48 AM Will be in Tampa tonight. A big year for @RepDeSantis, who will be a great governor for Florida. Strong on Crime, Borders and our 2nd Amendment. Big help on Tax & Regulation Cuts. Loves our Military & our Vets. Has my Full & Total Endorsement! [Twitter for iPhone]

Jul 31, 2018 08:34:47 AM The Fake News Media is going CRAZY! They are totally unhinged and in many ways, after witnessing first hand the damage they do to so many innocent and decent people, I enjoy watching. In 7 years, when I am no longer in office, their ratings will dry up and they will be gone! [Twitter for iPhone]

Jul 31, 2018 12:09:50 PM Congressman David Kustoff has been a champion for the Trump Agenda - I greatly appreciate his support. David is strong on crime and borders, loves our Military, Vets and Second Amendment. Get out and vote for David on Thursday, August 2nd. He has my Full and Total Endorsement! [Twitter for iPhone]

Jul 31, 2018 12:13:32 PM .@SenJohnBarrasso has a Primary on August 21st. He doesn't need any help because he is absolutely outstanding in every way, but I hope the great people of Wyoming will go out and show their support anyway. John is absolutely top of the line & has my Complete & Total Endorsement! [Twitter for iPhone]

Jul 31, 2018 12:33:47 PM I don't care what the political ramifications are, our immigration laws and border security have been a complete and total disaster for decades, and there is no way that the Democrats will allow it to be fixed without a Government Shutdown... [Twitter for iPhone]

Jul 31, 2018 12:33:48 PM ...Border Security is National Security, and National Security is the long-term viability of our Country. A Government Shutdown is a very small price to pay for a safe and Prosperous America! [Twitter for iPhone]

Jul 31, 2018 03:39:22 PM "Worker pay rate hits highest level since 2008" https://t.co/pMDxHQqcg9 [Twitter for iPhone]

Jul 31, 2018 03:49:25 PM On my way to Tampa, Florida. Look forward to seeing everyone soon! https://t.co/BSB6IjBK7r [Twitter for iPhone]

Jul 31, 2018 05:50:10 PM RT @WhiteHouse: President Trump Delivers Remarks on Workforce Development https://t.co/nE2kMxkHyw [Twitter for iPhone]

Jul 31, 2018 07:24:25 PM Thank you Florida. I love you! https://t.co/M5T81DZVUU [Twitter for iPhone]

Jul 31, 2018 08:37:04 PM RT @EricTrump: #Truth @Acosta https://t.co/aCfFoeqL1f [Twitter for iPhone]

⌐⌐ Aug 1, 2018 08:03:08 AM "FBI Agent Peter Strzok (on the Mueller team) should have recused himself on day one. He was out to STOP THE ELECTION OF DONALD TRUMP. He needed an insurance policy. Those are illegal, improper goals, trying to influence the Election. He should never, ever been allowed to........ [Twitter for iPhone]

⌐⌐ Aug 1, 2018 08:15:24 AM .....remain in the FBI while he himself was being investigated. This is a real issue. It won't go into a Mueller Report because Mueller is going to protect these guys. Mueller has an interest in creating the illusion of objectivity around his investigation." ALAN DERSHOWITZ.... [Twitter for iPhone]

⌐⌐ Aug 1, 2018 08:24:03 AM ..This is a terrible situation and Attorney General Jeff Sessions should stop this Rigged Witch Hunt right now, before it continues to stain our country any further. Bob Mueller is totally conflicted, and his 17 Angry Democrats that are doing his dirty work are a disgrace to USA! [Twitter for iPhone]

⌐⌐ Aug 1, 2018 08:34:03 AM Paul Manafort worked for Ronald Reagan, Bob Dole and many other highly prominent and respected political leaders. He worked for me for a very short time. Why didn't government tell me that he was under investigation. These old charges have nothing to do with Collusion - a Hoax! [Twitter for iPhone]

⌐⌐ Aug 1, 2018 09:01:53 AM Russian Collusion with the Trump Campaign, one of the most successful in history, is a TOTAL HOAX. The Democrats paid for the phony and discredited Dossier which was, along with Comey, McCabe, Strzok and his lover, the lovely Lisa Page, used to begin the Witch Hunt. Disgraceful! [Twitter for iPhone]

⌐⌐ Aug 1, 2018 10:23:13 AM "We already have a smocking gun about a campaign getting dirt on their opponent, it was Hillary Clinton. How is it OK for Hillary Clinton to proactively seek dirt from the Russians but the Trump campaign met at the Russians request and that is bad?" Marc Thiessen, Washington Post [Twitter for iPhone]

⌐⌐ Aug 1, 2018 10:35:47 AM Looking back on history, who was treated worse, Alfonse Capone, legendary mob boss, killer and "Public Enemy Number One," or Paul Manafort, political operative & Reagan/Dole darling, now serving solitary confinement - although convicted of nothing? Where is the Russian Collusion? [Twitter for iPhone]

⌐⌐ Aug 1, 2018 10:56:31 AM "We already have a smoking gun about a campaign getting dirt on their opponent, it was Hillary Clinton. How is it OK for Hillary Clinton to proactively seek dirt from the Russians but the Trump campaign met at the Russians request and that is bad?" Marc Thiessen, Washington Post [Twitter for iPhone]

⌐⌐ Aug 1, 2018 01:55:56 PM It was my great honor to be joined by leading pastors and faith leaders from across our Nation today at the @WhiteHouse! https://t.co/6sS1zGA1p7 [Twitter for iPhone]

Aug 1, 2018 02:22:01 PM #PledgeToAmericasWorkers https://t.co/qIJQfQ3bos [Twitter for iPhone]

Aug 1, 2018 04:04:18 PM Join me tomorrow night at 7pmE in Wilkes-Barre Township, Pennsylvania for a MAKE AMERICA GREAT AGAIN RALLY! Tickets: https://t.co/dR6EzS3Q8L https://t.co/c52kIxvdF7 [Twitter for iPhone]

Aug 1, 2018 04:16:11 PM "Private payrolls boom in July, increasing by 219,000 vs 185,000 estimate: ADP" https://t.co/SeU9kGpima [Twitter for iPhone]

Aug 1, 2018 10:32:14 PM Incredibly beautiful ceremony as U.S. Korean War remains are returned to American soil. Thank you to Honolulu and all of our great Military participants on a job well done. A special thanks to Vice President Mike Pence on delivering a truly magnificent tribute! [Twitter for iPhone]

Aug 1, 2018 10:40:24 PM RT @realDonaldTrump: "Worker pay rate hits highest level since 2008" https://t.co/pMDxHQqcg9 [Twitter for iPhone]

Aug 1, 2018 11:38:15 PM Congratulations to @GreggJarrett on The TREMENDOUS success of his just out book, "The Russia Hoax, The Illicit Scheme To Clear Hillary Clinton & Frame Donald Trump." Already number one on Amazon. Hard work from a brilliant guy. It's the Real Story of the Rigged Witch Hunt! [Twitter for iPhone]

Aug 1, 2018 11:47:25 PM Thank you to Chairman Kim Jong Un for keeping your word & starting the process of sending home the remains of our great and beloved missing fallen! I am not at all surprised that you took this kind action. Also, thank you for your nice letter - l look forward to seeing you soon! [Twitter for iPhone]

Aug 2, 2018 05:38:15 AM Charles Koch of Koch Brothers, who claims to be giving away millions of dollars to politicians even though I know very few who have seen this (?), now makes the ridiculous statement that what President Trump is doing is unfair to "foreign workers." He is correct, AMERICA FIRST! [Twitter for iPhone]

Aug 2, 2018 06:04:04 AM Wow, @foxandfriends is blowing away the competition in the morning ratings. Morning Joe is a dead show with very few people watching and sadly, Fake News CNN is also doing poorly. Too much hate and inaccurately reported stories - too predictable! [Twitter for iPhone]

Aug 2, 2018 12:23:50 PM Working hard, thank you! https://t.co/pNXbFNcf8z [Twitter for iPhone]

Aug 2, 2018 01:45:49 PM Congressman Steve Stivers of Ohio has done a fantastic job as Chairman of the @NRCC. He is a great Congressman who is tough on crime & borders & an inspiration to our Military & Vets. Big on 2nd Amendment. Get out and vote for Steve on Aug 7th. He has my full & total endorsement! [Twitter for iPhone]

Aug 2, 2018 01:53:58 PM Looking forward to being in the Great State of Pennsylvania where we had a tremendous victory in the Election. Will be campaigning hard for an original supporter, Lou Barletta, to replace a weak an ineffective Senator, Bob Casey. Lou is tough and smart, loves PA and our Country! [Twitter for iPhone]

Aug 2, 2018 01:55:23 PM Pennsylvania has to love Trump because unlike all of the others before me, I am bringing STEEL BACK in a VERY BIG way. Plants opening up in Pennsylvania, and all over the Country, and Congressman Lou Barletta, who is running for the Senate in Pennsylvania, is really helping! [Twitter for iPhone]

Aug 2, 2018 01:57:44 PM When the House and Senate meet on the very important Farm Bill – we love our farmers - hopefully they will be able to leave the WORK REQUIREMENTS FOR FOOD STAMPS PROVISION that the House approved. Senate should go to 51 votes! [Twitter for iPhone]

Aug 2, 2018 02:08:37 PM Looking forward to being in the Great State of Ohio on Saturday night where I will be campaigning hard for a truly talented future Congressman, @Troy_Balderson. See you all then! Tickets: https://t.co/8UOykaI8uf https://t.co/jHdtAy5fgj [Twitter for iPhone]

Aug 2, 2018 03:24:33 PM They asked my daughter Ivanka whether or not the media is the enemy of the people. She correctly said no. It is the FAKE NEWS, which is a large percentage of the media, that is the enemy of the people! [Twitter for iPhone]

Aug 2, 2018 07:30:28 PM Thank you Pennsylvania. I love you! https://t.co/qoswnBZb3f [Twitter for iPhone]

Aug 3, 2018 09:21:48 AM Congratulations to Bill Lee of Tennessee on his big primary win for Governor last night. He ran a great campaign and now will finish off the job in November. Bill has my total and enthusiastic Endorsement! [Twitter for iPhone]

Aug 3, 2018 12:39:06 PM Congratulations Marsha! https://t.co/JSMiOWfbxa [Twitter for iPhone]

Aug 3, 2018 01:50:03 PM RT @Rasmussen_Poll: Today's @realDonaldTrump approval ratings among black voters: 29% This time last year: 15% https://t.co/mazBCWoIMy @… [Twitter for iPhone]

Aug 3, 2018 03:31:52 PM "Pastor praises Trump as 'pro-black' at prison reform event" https://t.co/xFKf1arebx [Twitter for iPhone]

Aug 3, 2018 05:00:39 PM Marsha Blackburn had a BIG win last night in the Tennessee primary for U.S. Senate. She is an outstanding person & great supporter of mine. Congratulations Marsha, we need you very badly in the Senate to vote for our agenda. Your next opponent will vote against all we are doing! [Twitter for iPhone]

Aug 3, 2018 05:10:35 PM July is just the ninth month since 1970 that unemployment has fallen below 4%. Our economy has added 3.7 million jobs since I won the Election. 4.1 GDP. More than 4 million people have received a pay raise due to tax reform. $400 Billion brought back from "overseas." @FoxNews [Twitter for iPhone]

Aug 3, 2018 05:43:03 PM NASA, which is making a BIG comeback under the Trump Administration, has just named 9 astronauts for Boeing and Spacex space flights. We have the greatest facilities in the world and we are now letting the private sector pay to use them. Exciting things happening. Space Force! [Twitter for iPhone]

Aug 3, 2018 05:55:38 PM "The media are good news fire extinguishers!" @greggutfeld @TheFive [Twitter for iPhone]

Aug 3, 2018 05:59:47 PM Almost 500,000 Manufacturing Jobs created since I won the Election. Remember when my opponents were saying that we couldn't create this type of job anymore. Wrong, in fact these are among our best and most important jobs! [Twitter for iPhone]

Aug 3, 2018 08:06:28 PM Great photo from Ocean City, Maryland. Thank you. MAKE AMERICA GREAT AGAIN! https://t.co/kILZz31yDJ [Twitter for iPhone]

Aug 3, 2018 10:01:46 PM Congratulations to Gregg Jarrett on his book, "THE RUSSIA HOAX, THE ILLICIT SCHEME TO CLEAR HILLARY CLINTON AND FRAME DONALD TRUMP," going to #1 on @nytimes and Amazon. It is indeed a HOAX and WITCH HUNT, illegally started by people who have already been disgraced. Great book! [Twitter for iPhone]

Aug 3, 2018 10:05:00 PM RT @Scavino45: "Pro-Trump pastor: Trump is 'the most pro-black' president I've ever seen" https://t.co/5GoQOoeCP3 [Twitter for iPhone]

Aug 3, 2018 10:05:04 PM RT @Scavino45: .@POTUS @realDonaldTrump and @UFC's @DanaWhite in the Oval Office earlier today at the @WhiteHouse.... https://t.co/JC9jPsn4... [Twitter for iPhone]

Aug 3, 2018 10:05:20 PM RT @Scavino45: ✓"US workers see biggest pay, benefit increase in 10 years" https://t.co/eD9vxbBMBb [Twitter for iPhone]

Aug 3, 2018 10:05:55 PM RT @realDonaldTrump: "Private payrolls boom in July, increasing by 219,000 vs 185,000 estimate: ADP" https://t.co/SeU9kGpima [Twitter for iPhone]

Aug 3, 2018 10:08:55 PM RT @DRUDGE_REPORT: Hispanic unemployment record low... https://t.co/ky1W0I6pQ2 [Twitter for iPhone]

Aug 3, 2018 10:09:16 PM RT @DRUDGE_REPORT: RECORD 155,965,000 EMPLOYED https://t.co/SPazgBPyz2 [Twitter for iPhone]

Aug 3, 2018 10:10:55 PM RT @DRUDGE_REPORT: Manufacturing +37,000... https://t.co/XparcYpi3G [Twitter for iPhone]

Aug 3, 2018 10:15:23 PM RT @WhiteHouse: Under President Trump, the economy is roaring, jobs are soaring, and the American worker is seeing more money in their payc... [Twitter for iPhone]

Aug 3, 2018 10:17:51 PM RT @DRUDGE_REPORT: NYT editorial board member: 'Kill More Men,' 'F*ck The Police'... https://t.co/f7Vu1dycyi [Twitter for iPhone]

Aug 3, 2018 10:24:48 PM RT @WhiteHouse: "This is probably the most pro-active administration regarding urban America and the faith-based community in my lifetime.... [Twitter for iPhone]

Aug 3, 2018 10:28:06 PM ...Dianne is the person leading our Nation on "Collusion" with Russia (only done by Dems). Will she now investigate herself? https://t.co/OG6l04bBwg [Twitter for iPhone]

Aug 3, 2018 10:29:41 PM RT @VinceMcMahon: Grateful for our special #MakeAWish guest at @WWE HQ. Thanks for visiting us, Tyler ... and for making yourself comfortable... [Twitter for iPhone]

Aug 3, 2018 10:30:30 PM RT @seanhannity: https://t.co/RAVcGZwsiS [Twitter for iPhone]

Aug 3, 2018 10:37:36 PM Lebron James was just interviewed by the dumbest man on television, Don Lemon. He made Lebron look smart, which isn't easy to do. I like Mike! [Twitter for iPhone]

Aug 4, 2018 07:49:49 AM Will be going to Ohio tonight to campaign for Troy Balderson for the big Congressional Special Election on Tuesday. Early voting is on. Troy is strong on Crime, the Border & loves our Military, Vets & 2nd Amendment. His opponent is a puppet of Nancy Pelosi/high taxes. [Twitter for iPhone]

Aug 4, 2018 08:02:36 AM Troy Balderson, running for Congress from Ohio, is in a big Election fight with a candidate who just got caught lying about his relationship with Nancy Pelosi, who is weak on Crime, Borders & your 2nd Amendment-and wants to raise your Taxes (by a lot). Vote for Troy on Tuesday! [Twitter for iPhone]

Aug 4, 2018 10:18:53 AM HAPPY BIRTHDAY @USCG! https://t.co/cQo41jcoKn [Twitter for iPhone]

Aug 4, 2018 02:47:40 PM Tariffs are working far better than anyone ever anticipated. China market has dropped 27% in last 4months, and they are talking to us. Our market is stronger than ever, and will go up dramatically when these horrible Trade Deals are successfully renegotiated. America First....... [Twitter for iPhone]

Aug 4, 2018 02:53:22 PM ....Tariffs have had a tremendous positive impact on our Steel Industry. Plants are opening all over the U.S., Steelworkers are working again, and big dollars are flowing into our Treasury. Other countries use Tariffs against, but when we use them, foolish people scream! [Twitter for iPhone]

Aug 4, 2018 02:58:06 PM ....Tariffs will make our country much richer than it is today. Only fools would disagree. We are using them to negotiate fair trade deals and, if countries are still unwilling to negotiate, they will pay us vast sums of money in the form of Tariffs. We win either way...... [Twitter for iPhone]

Aug 4, 2018 03:03:39 PM ....China, which is for the first time doing poorly against us, is spending a fortune on ads and P.R. trying to convince and scare our politicians to fight me on Tariffs- because they are really hurting their economy. Likewise other countries. We are Winning, but must be strong! [Twitter for iPhone]

Aug 4, 2018 03:28:09 PM Heading to Ohio! [Twitter for iPhone]

Aug 4, 2018 03:53:39 PM Iran, and it's economy, is going very bad, and fast! I will meet, or not meet, it doesn't matter - it is up to them! [Twitter for iPhone]

Aug 4, 2018 03:54:49 PM RT @realDonaldTrump: Troy Balderson, running for Congress from Ohio, is in a big Election fight with a candidate who just got caught lying... [Twitter for iPhone]

Aug 4, 2018 07:28:25 PM Thank you Ohio. I love you! https://t.co/HYSaQOB6GW [Twitter for iPhone]

Aug 4, 2018 08:43:00 PM A great night in Ohio's 12th Congressional District with Troy Balderson! Troy loves Ohio, and he loves the people of Ohio. He will be fighting for you all the way... [Twitter for iPhone]

Aug 4, 2018 08:43:01 PM ...Danny O'Connor is a total puppet for Nancy Pelosi and Maxine Waters – Danny wants to raise your taxes, open your borders, and take away your 2nd Amendment. Vote for Troy on Tuesday! [Twitter for iPhone]

Aug 5, 2018 06:38:12 AM The Fake News hates me saying that they are the Enemy of the People only because they know it's TRUE. I am providing a great service by explaining this to the American People. They purposely cause great division & distrust. They can also cause War! They are very dangerous & sick! [Twitter for iPhone]

Aug 5, 2018 06:59:29 AM Tariffs are working big time. Every country on earth wants to take wealth out of the U.S., always to our detriment. I say, as they come,Tax them. If they don't want to be taxed, let them make or build the product in the U.S. In either event, it means jobs and great wealth..... [Twitter for iPhone]

Aug 5, 2018 07:06:25 AM ..Because of Tariffs we will be able to start paying down large amounts of the $21 Trillion in debt that has been accumulated, much by the Obama Administration, while at the same time reducing taxes for our people. At minimum, we will make much better Trade Deals for our country! [Twitter for iPhone]

Aug 5, 2018 07:35:43 AM Fake News reporting, a complete fabrication, that I am concerned about the meeting my wonderful son, Donald, had in Trump Tower. This was a meeting to get information on an opponent, totally legal and done all the time in politics - and it went nowhere. I did not know about it! [Twitter for iPhone]

Aug 5, 2018 07:45:56 AM ...Why aren't Mueller and the 17 Angry Democrats looking at the meetings concerning the Fake Dossier and all of the lying that went on in the FBI and DOJ? This is the most one sided Witch Hunt in the history of our country. Fortunately, the facts are all coming out, and fast! [Twitter for iPhone]

Aug 5, 2018 07:49:21 AM Too bad a large portion of the Media refuses to report the lies and corruption having to do with the Rigged Witch Hunt - but that is why we call them FAKE NEWS! [Twitter for iPhone]

Aug 5, 2018 03:01:17 PM Presidential Approval numbers are very good - strong economy, military and just about everything else. Better numbers than Obama at this point, by far. We are winning on just about every front and for that reason there will not be a Blue Wave, but there might be a Red Wave! [Twitter for iPhone]

Aug 5, 2018 04:52:57 PM RT @realDonaldTrump: A great night in Ohio's 12th Congressional District with Troy Balderson! Troy loves Ohio, and he loves the people of O… [Twitter for iPhone]

Aug 5, 2018 04:53:11 PM RT @realDonaldTrump: ...Danny O'Connor is a total puppet for Nancy Pelosi and Maxine Waters – Danny wants to raise your taxes, open your bo… [Twitter for iPhone]

Aug 5, 2018 05:06:42 PM California wildfires are being magnified & made so much worse by the bad environmental laws which aren't allowing massive amount of readily available water to be properly utilized. It is being diverted into the Pacific Ocean. Must also tree clear to stop fire spreading! [Twitter for iPhone]

Aug 6, 2018 09:13:10 AM "Collusion with Russia was very real. Hillary Clinton and her team 100% colluded with the Russians, and so did Adam Schiff who is on tape trying to collude with what he thought was Russians to obtain compromising material on DJT. We also know that Hillary Clinton paid through.... [Twitter for iPhone]

Aug 6, 2018 09:25:56 AM ....a law firm, eventually Kremlin connected sources, to gather info on Donald Trump. Collusion is very real with Russia, but only with Hillary and the Democrats, and we should demand a full investigation." Dan Bongino on @foxandfriends Looking forward to the new IG Report! [Twitter for iPhone]

Aug 6, 2018 09:52:46 AM Great financial numbers being announced on an almost daily basis. Economy has never been better, jobs at best point in history. Fixing our terrible Trade Deals is a priority-and going very well. Immigration on Merit Based System to take care of the companies coming back to U.S.A. [Twitter for iPhone]

Aug 6, 2018 10:48:40 AM Kris Kobach, a strong and early supporter of mine, is running for Governor of the Great State of Kansas. He is a fantastic guy who loves his State and our Country - he will be a GREAT Governor and has my full & total Endorsement! Strong on Crime, Border & Military. VOTE TUESDAY! [Twitter for iPhone]

Aug 6, 2018 12:43:57 PM Governor Jerry Brown must allow the Free Flow of the vast amounts of water coming from the North and foolishly being diverted into the Pacific Ocean. Can be used for fires, farming and everything else. Think of California with plenty of Water - Nice! Fast Federal govt. approvals. [Twitter for iPhone]

Aug 6, 2018 02:13:42 PM John James is a potential Republican Star who has a Senate primary election tomorrow in Michigan. If he becomes the Republican candidate, he will beat the Open Borders, weak on Crime, Democrat, Debbie Stabenow. Vote for John James and Make America Great Again! [Twitter for iPhone]

Aug 6, 2018 04:41:20 PM Democrats want Open Borders and they want to abolish ICE, the brave men and women that our protecting our Country from some of the most vicious and dangerous people on earth! Sorry, we can't let that happen!Also, change the rules in the Senate and approve STRONG Border Security! [Twitter for iPhone]

Aug 6, 2018 04:44:00 PM RT @realDonaldTrump: Presidential Approval numbers are very good - strong economy, military and just about everything else. Better numbers… [Twitter for iPhone]

Aug 6, 2018 04:46:47 PM Democrats want Open Borders and they want to abolish ICE, the brave men and women that are protecting our Country from some of the most vicious and dangerous people on earth! Sorry, we can't let that happen! Also, change the rules in the Senate and approve STRONG Border Security! [Twitter for iPhone]

Aug 6, 2018 04:53:42 PM California wildfires are being magnified & made so much worse by the bad environmental laws which aren't allowing massive amounts of readily available water to be properly utilized. It is being diverted into the Pacific Ocean. Must also tree clear to stop fire from spreading! [Twitter for iPhone]

Aug 7, 2018 04:31:46 AM The Iran sanctions have officially been cast. These are the most biting sanctions ever imposed, and in November they ratchet up to yet another level. Anyone doing business with Iran will NOT be doing business with the United States. I am asking for WORLD PEACE, nothing less! [Twitter for iPhone]

Aug 7, 2018 05:46:45 AM Ohio, vote today for Troy Balderson for Congress. His opponent, controlled by Nancy Pelosi, is weak on Crime, the Border, Military, Vets, your 2nd Amendment - and will end your Tax Cuts. Troy will be a great Congressman. #MAGA [Twitter for iPhone]

Aug 7, 2018 09:03:05 AM RT @EricTrump: Ohio make sure to get out and vote today! We need Troy Balderson in Congress. Visit https://t.co/ypMnbPQzqk to find your pol… [Twitter for iPhone]

Aug 7, 2018 01:25:13 PM Today, on the 236th anniversary of the Purple Heart, we honor the members of our Armed Forces for serving as the vanguard of American democracy and freedom around the world. #PurpleHeartDay https://t.co/NghmQ4BOKh [Twitter for iPhone]

Aug 7, 2018 09:59:39 PM When I decided to go to Ohio for Troy Balderson, he was down in early voting 64 to 36. That was not good. After my speech on Saturday night, there was a big turn for the better. Now Troy wins a great victory during a very tough time of the year for voting. He will win BIG in Nov. [Twitter for iPhone]

Aug 7, 2018 10:18:36 PM .....Congratulations to Troy Balderson on a great win in Ohio. A very special and important race! [Twitter for iPhone]

Aug 7, 2018 10:23:54 PM Congratulations to a future STAR of the Republican Party, future Senator John James. A big and bold victory tonight in the Great State of Michigan - the first of many. November can't come fast enough! [Twitter for iPhone]

Aug 7, 2018 10:52:43 PM Congratulations to Bill Schuette. You will have a Big win in November and be a tremendous Governor for the Great State of Michigan. Lots of car and other companies moving back! [Twitter for iPhone]

Aug 7, 2018 11:28:09 PM Congratulations to Josh Hawley on your big Senate Primary win in Missouri. I look forward to working with you toward a big win in November. We need you in Washington! [Twitter for iPhone]

Aug 8, 2018 09:31:14 AM 5 for 5! [Twitter for iPhone]

Aug 8, 2018 10:14:26 AM The Republicans have now won 8 out of 9 House Seats, yet if you listen to the Fake News Media you would think we are being clobbered. Why can't they play it straight, so unfair to the Republican Party and in particular, your favorite President! [Twitter for iPhone]

Aug 8, 2018 10:25:55 AM As long as I campaign and/or support Senate and House candidates (within reason), they will win! I LOVE the people, & they certainly seem to like the job I'm doing. If I find the time, in between China, Iran, the Economy and much more, which I must, we will have a giant Red Wave! [Twitter for iPhone]

Aug 8, 2018 01:07:43 PM Congratulations to @LenaEpstein of Michigan on a job well done. Also, thanks for your great support! [Twitter for iPhone]

Aug 8, 2018 01:51:39 PM RED WAVE! [Twitter for iPhone]

Aug 9, 2018 08:22:39 AM "There has been no evidence whatsoever that Donald Trump or the campaign was involved in any kind of collusion to fix the 2016 election. In fact the evidence is the opposite, that Hillary Clinton & the Democrats colluded with the Russians to fix the 2016 election." @GrahamLedger [Twitter for iPhone]

Aug 9, 2018 11:02:33 AM This is an illegally brought Rigged Witch Hunt run by people who are totally corrupt and/or conflicted. It was started and paid for by Crooked Hillary and the Democrats. Phony Dossier, FISA disgrace and so many lying and dishonest people already fired. 17 Angry Dems? Stay tuned! [Twitter for iPhone]

Aug 9, 2018 11:03:30 AM Space Force all the way! [Twitter for iPhone]

Aug 9, 2018 12:00:42 PM Congressman Ted Yoho of Florida is doing a fantastic job and has my complete and total Endorsement! Tough on Crime and Borders, Ted was really helpful on Tax Cuts. Vote all the way for Ted in the upcoming Primary - he will never let you down! [Twitter for iPhone]

Aug 9, 2018 02:43:25 PM @LindseyGrahamSC "Why didn't the FBI tell President Trump that they had concerns about Carter Page? Is there a double standard here?" They told Senator Diane Feinstein that she had a spy - but not Trump. Is that entrapment or did they just want to use Page as an excuse to SPY? [Twitter for iPhone]

Aug 9, 2018 05:50:31 PM Jenna Ellis "FBI thought they wouldn't get caught because they thought that Hillary was going to win. There is overt bias and that depends on whether you are Democrat or Republican - a double standard that needs to stop." [Twitter for iPhone]

Aug 10, 2018 06:49:48 AM .@MariaBartiromo "No evidence to launch even an investigation into potential collusion between Donald Trump and the Russians - and here we are, a year and a half later." [Twitter for iPhone]

Aug 10, 2018 07:18:55 AM The NFL players are at it again - taking a knee when they should be standing proudly for the National Anthem. Numerous players, from different teams, wanted to show their "outrage" at something that most of them are unable to define. They make a fortune doing what they love...... [Twitter for iPhone]

Aug 10, 2018 07:32:40 AM .....Be happy, be cool! A football game, that fans are paying soooo much money to watch and enjoy, is no place to protest. Most of that money goes to the players anyway. Find another way to protest. Stand proudly for your National Anthem or be Suspended Without Pay! [Twitter for iPhone]

Aug 10, 2018 07:47:42 AM I have just authorized a doubling of Tariffs on Steel and Aluminum with respect to Turkey as their currency, the Turkish Lira, slides rapidly downward against our very strong Dollar! Aluminum will now be 20% and Steel 50%. Our relations with Turkey are not good at this time! [Twitter for iPhone]

Aug 10, 2018 04:30:43 PM Democrats, please do not distance yourselves from Nancy Pelosi. She is a wonderful person whose ideas & policies may be bad, but who should definitely be given a 4th chance. She is trying very hard & has every right to take down the Democrat Party if she has veered too far left! [Twitter for iPhone]

Aug 10, 2018 05:47:45 PM Had a very good phone call with @EmmanuelMacron, President of France. Discussed various subjects, in particular Security and Trade. Many other calls and conversations today. Looking forward to dinner tonight with Tim Cook of Apple. He is investing big dollars in U.S.A. [Twitter for iPhone]

Aug 10, 2018 05:58:05 PM Thank you to Kanye West and the fact that he is willing to tell the TRUTH. One new and great FACT - African American unemployment is the lowest ever recorded in the history of our Country. So honored by this. Thank you Kanye for your support. It is making a big difference! [Twitter for iPhone]

Aug 10, 2018 06:12:58 PM Deal with Mexico is coming along nicely. Autoworkers and farmers must be taken care of or there will be no deal. New President of Mexico has been an absolute gentleman. Canada must wait. Their Tariffs and Trade Barriers are far too high. Will tax cars if we can't make a deal! [Twitter for iPhone]

Aug 11, 2018 07:35:31 AM Why isn't the FBI giving Andrew McCabe text massages to Judicial Watch or appropriate governmental authorities. FBI said they won't give up even one (I may have to get involved, DO NOT DESTROY). What are they hiding? McCabe wife took big campaign dollars from Hillary people...... [Twitter for iPhone]

Aug 11, 2018 07:49:02 AM .....Will the FBI ever recover it's once stellar reputation, so badly damaged by Comey, McCabe, Peter S and his lover, the lovely Lisa Page, and other top officials now dismissed or fired? So many of the great men and women of the FBI have been hurt by these clowns and losers! [Twitter for iPhone]

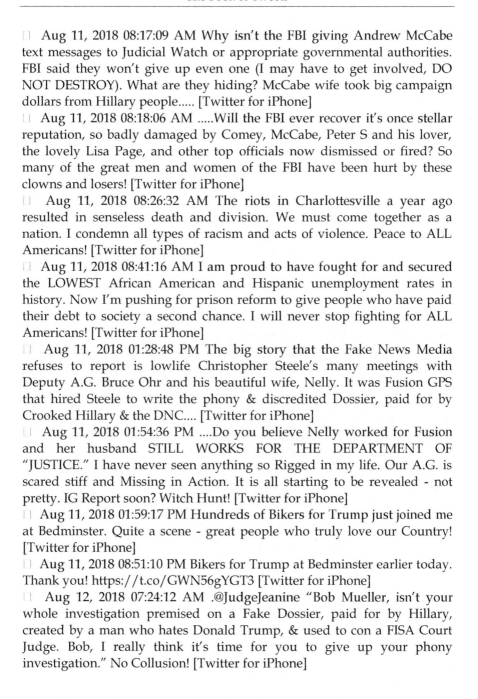

Aug 11, 2018 08:17:09 AM Why isn't the FBI giving Andrew McCabe text messages to Judicial Watch or appropriate governmental authorities. FBI said they won't give up even one (I may have to get involved, DO NOT DESTROY). What are they hiding? McCabe wife took big campaign dollars from Hillary people..... [Twitter for iPhone]

Aug 11, 2018 08:18:06 AM .....Will the FBI ever recover it's once stellar reputation, so badly damaged by Comey, McCabe, Peter S and his lover, the lovely Lisa Page, and other top officials now dismissed or fired? So many of the great men and women of the FBI have been hurt by these clowns and losers! [Twitter for iPhone]

Aug 11, 2018 08:26:32 AM The riots in Charlottesville a year ago resulted in senseless death and division. We must come together as a nation. I condemn all types of racism and acts of violence. Peace to ALL Americans! [Twitter for iPhone]

Aug 11, 2018 08:41:16 AM I am proud to have fought for and secured the LOWEST African American and Hispanic unemployment rates in history. Now I'm pushing for prison reform to give people who have paid their debt to society a second chance. I will never stop fighting for ALL Americans! [Twitter for iPhone]

Aug 11, 2018 01:28:48 PM The big story that the Fake News Media refuses to report is lowlife Christopher Steele's many meetings with Deputy A.G. Bruce Ohr and his beautiful wife, Nelly. It was Fusion GPS that hired Steele to write the phony & discredited Dossier, paid for by Crooked Hillary & the DNC.... [Twitter for iPhone]

Aug 11, 2018 01:54:36 PM ....Do you believe Nelly worked for Fusion and her husband STILL WORKS FOR THE DEPARTMENT OF "JUSTICE." I have never seen anything so Rigged in my life. Our A.G. is scared stiff and Missing in Action. It is all starting to be revealed - not pretty. IG Report soon? Witch Hunt! [Twitter for iPhone]

Aug 11, 2018 01:59:17 PM Hundreds of Bikers for Trump just joined me at Bedminster. Quite a scene - great people who truly love our Country! [Twitter for iPhone]

Aug 11, 2018 08:51:10 PM Bikers for Trump at Bedminster earlier today. Thank you! https://t.co/GWN56gYGT3 [Twitter for iPhone]

Aug 12, 2018 07:24:12 AM .@JudgeJeanine "Bob Mueller, isn't your whole investigation premised on a Fake Dossier, paid for by Hillary, created by a man who hates Donald Trump, & used to con a FISA Court Judge. Bob, I really think it's time for you to give up your phony investigation." No Collusion! [Twitter for iPhone]

⊔ Aug 12, 2018 07:34:06 AM .@GovMikeHuckabee "Your paycheck is bigger, your pension is stronger." @foxandfriends Unemployment numbers are better than they have been in 50 years, & perhaps ever. Our country is booming like never before - and it will get even better! Many companies moving back to the U.S.A. [Twitter for iPhone]

⊔ Aug 12, 2018 07:57:39 AM Many @harleydavidson owners plan to boycott the company if manufacturing moves overseas. Great! Most other companies are coming in our direction, including Harley competitors. A really bad move! U.S. will soon have a level playing field, or better. [Twitter for iPhone]

⊔ Aug 12, 2018 08:25:55 AM "Seems like the Department of Justice (and FBI) had a program to keep Donald Trump from becoming President". @DarrellIssa @foxandfriends If this had happened to the other side, everybody involved would be in jail. This is a Media coverup of the biggest story of our time. [Twitter for iPhone]

⊔ Aug 13, 2018 08:27:08 AM Wacky Omarosa, who got fired 3 times on the Apprentice, now got fired for the last time. She never made it, never will. She begged me for a job, tears in her eyes, I said Ok. People in the White House hated her. She was vicious, but not smart. I would rarely see her but heard.... [Twitter for iPhone]

⊔ Aug 13, 2018 08:50:27 AM ...really bad things. Nasty to people & would constantly miss meetings & work. When Gen. Kelly came on board he told me she was a loser & nothing but problems. I told him to try working it out, if possible, because she only said GREAT things about me - until she got fired! [Twitter for iPhone]

⊔ Aug 13, 2018 09:21:46 AM While I know it's "not presidential" to take on a lowlife like Omarosa, and while I would rather not be doing so, this is a modern day form of communication and I know the Fake News Media will be working overtime to make even Wacky Omarosa look legitimate as possible. Sorry! [Twitter for iPhone]

⊔ Aug 13, 2018 10:12:31 AM The very unpopular Governor of Ohio (and failed presidential candidate) @JohnKasich hurt Troy Balderson's recent win by tamping down enthusiasm for an otherwise great candidate. Even Kasich's Lt. Governor lost Gov. race because of his unpopularity. Credit to Troy on the BIG WIN! [Twitter for iPhone]

⊔ Aug 13, 2018 11:04:51 AM Agent Peter Strzok was just fired from the FBI - finally. The list of bad players in the FBI & DOJ gets longer & longer. Based on the fact that Strzok was in charge of the Witch Hunt, will it be dropped? It is a total Hoax. No Collusion, No Obstruction - I just fight back! [Twitter for iPhone]

Aug 13, 2018 11:09:41 AM Just fired Agent Strzok, formerly of the FBI, was in charge of the Crooked Hillary Clinton sham investigation. It was a total fraud on the American public and should be properly redone! [Twitter for iPhone]

Aug 13, 2018 11:13:11 AM Wacky Omarosa already has a fully signed Non-Disclosure Agreement! [Twitter for iPhone]

Aug 13, 2018 12:11:21 PM Brooks Koepka just won his third Golf Major, and he did it not only with his powerful game, but with his powerful mind. He has been a man of steel on the Tour and will have many Victories, including Majors, ahead of him. Congrats to Brooks and his great team on a job well done! [Twitter for iPad]

Aug 13, 2018 12:14:21 PM RT @MichaelCohen212: LTo the many dozens of #journalists who called me, questioning @OMAROSA claim in her new book that @POTUS @realDonaldT… [Twitter for iPad]

Aug 13, 2018 12:14:40 PM RT @FrankLuntz: I'm in @Omarosa's book on page 149. She claims to have heard from someone who heard from me that I heard Trump use the N-wo… [Twitter for iPad]

Aug 13, 2018 01:19:29 PM Just landed at Fort Drum, New York. Looking forward to making a speech about our GREAT HEROES! [Twitter for iPhone]

Aug 13, 2018 02:37:25 PM Great to be in Fort Drum, New York with our HEROES! https://t.co/Ke54QGZbU7 [Twitter for iPhone]

Aug 13, 2018 03:42:37 PM Pete Stauber is running for Congress in Minnesota. He will make for a great Congressman. Pete is strong on crime and borders, loves our Military, Vets and Second Amendment. Vote for Pete tomorrow. He has my full and total Endorsement! [Twitter for iPhone]

Aug 13, 2018 05:36:15 PM It was my great honor to sign our new Defense Bill into law and to pay tribute to the greatest soldiers in the history of the world: THE U.S. ARMY. The National Defense Authorization Act is the most significant investment in our Military and our warfighters in modern history! https://t.co/M6VI1c0Sgx [Twitter for iPhone]

Aug 13, 2018 07:11:32 PM "Trump's foreign policy is actually boosting America's standing" https://t.co/oC7Xs38uRo [Twitter for iPhone]

Aug 13, 2018 08:37:19 PM Scott Walker of Wisconsin is a tremendous Governor who has done incredible things for that Great State. He has my complete & total Endorsement! He brought the amazing Foxconn to Wisconsin with its 15,000 Jobs-and so much more. Vote for Scott on Tuesday in the Republican Primary! [Twitter for iPhone]

Aug 13, 2018 08:37:40 PM https://t.co/Gm9KE8cHpS [Twitter for iPhone]

Aug 13, 2018 08:50:05 PM .@MarkBurnettTV called to say that there are NO TAPES of the Apprentice where I used such a terrible and disgusting word as attributed by Wacky and Deranged Omarosa. I don't have that word in my vocabulary, and never have. She made it up. Look at her MANY recent quotes saying.... [Twitter for iPhone]

Aug 13, 2018 08:57:55 PM ....such wonderful and powerful things about me - a true Champion of Civil Rights - until she got fired. Omarosa had Zero credibility with the Media (they didn't want interviews) when she worked in the White House. Now that she says bad about me, they will talk to her. Fake News! [Twitter for iPhone]

Aug 14, 2018 05:59:33 AM Tom Fitton of Judicial Watch: "The Strzok firing is as much about the Mueller operation as anything else. There would be no Mueller Special Councel to investigate so called collusion but for the machinations of Strzok & his colleagues at the top levels of the FBI. We know this... [Twitter for iPhone]

Aug 14, 2018 06:07:00 AM ....guy was corrupt and had anti-Trump animus. Strzok and others at the FBI should be criminally investigated for the way the conducted this investigation. Instead, Mueller is pretending nothing went wrong. He used Strzok, he used the Clinton DNC Dossier...the whole thing.... [Twitter for iPhone]

Aug 14, 2018 06:13:26 AM ....should be shut down. The Strzok firing shows that the fundamental underpinnings of the investigation were corrupt. It should be shut down by the courts or by honest prosecutors." Thank you Judicial Watch, I couldn't have said it better myself! [Twitter for iPhone]

Aug 14, 2018 06:21:48 AM Lou Dobbs: "This cannot go forward...this Special Councel with all of his conflicts, with his 17 Angry Democrats, without any evidence of collusion by the Trump Campaign and Russia. The Dems are the ones who should be investigated." Thank you Lou, so true! [Twitter for iPhone]

Aug 14, 2018 06:31:11 AM When you give a crazed, crying lowlife a break, and give her a job at the White House, I guess it just didn't work out. Good work by General Kelly for quickly firing that dog! [Twitter for iPhone]

Aug 14, 2018 06:42:11 AM Another terrorist attack in London...These animals are crazy and must be dealt with through toughness and strength! [Twitter for iPhone]

Aug 14, 2018 06:55:01 AM Bruce Ohr of the "Justice" Department (can you believe he is still there) is accused of helping disgraced Christopher Steele "find dirt on Trump." Ohr's wife, Nelly, was in on the act big time - worked for Fusion GPS on Fake Dossier. @foxandfriends [Twitter for iPhone]

Aug 14, 2018 07:06:55 AM "They were all in on it, clear Hillary Clinton and FRAME Donald Trump for things he didn't do." Gregg Jarrett on @foxandfriends If we had a real Attorney General, this Witch Hunt would never have been started! Looking at the wrong people. [Twitter for iPhone]

Aug 14, 2018 08:01:50 AM Fired FBI Agent Peter Strzok is a fraud, as is the rigged investigation he started. There was no Collusion or Obstruction with Russia, and everybody, including the Democrats, know it. The only Collusion and Obstruction was by Crooked Hillary, the Democrats and the DNC! [Twitter for iPhone]

Aug 14, 2018 08:10:30 AM Strzok started the illegal Rigged Witch Hunt - why isn't this so-called "probe" ended immediately? Why aren't these angry and conflicted Democrats instead looking at Crooked Hillary? [Twitter for iPhone]

Aug 14, 2018 08:15:58 AM Lou Dobbs: "This cannot go forward...this Special Counsel with all of his conflicts, with his 17 Angry Democrats, without any evidence of collusion by the Trump Campaign and Russia. The Dems are the ones who should be investigated." Thank you Lou, so true! [Twitter for iPhone]

Aug 14, 2018 01:21:51 PM "Hope and Change in an Alabama Coal Mine" https://t.co/IwLEO9ff9X [Twitter for iPhone]

Aug 15, 2018 07:30:38 AM Great Republican election results last night. So far we have the team we want. 8 for 9 in Special Elections. Red Wave! [Twitter for iPhone]

Aug 15, 2018 07:44:12 AM "People who enter the United States without our permission are illegal aliens and illegal aliens should not be treated the same as people who enters the U.S. legally." Chuck Schumer in 2009, before he went left and haywire! @foxandfriends [Twitter for iPhone]

Aug 15, 2018 07:54:11 AM Congratulations to Leah Vukmir of Wisconsin on your great win last night. You beat a very tough and good competitor and will make a fantastic Senator after winning in November against someone who has done very little. You have my complete and total Endorsement! [Twitter for iPhone]

Aug 15, 2018 08:02:23 AM Congratulations to Bryan Steil on a wonderful win last night. Your will be replacing a great guy in Paul Ryan, and your win in November will make the entire State of Wisconsin very proud. You have my complete and total Endorsement! [Twitter for iPhone]

Aug 15, 2018 08:07:05 AM Scott Walker is very special and will have another great win in November. He has done a fantastic job as Governor of Wisconsin and will always have my full support and Endorsement! [Twitter for iPhone]

Aug 15, 2018 08:12:48 AM Jeff Johnson of Minnesota had a big night in winning the Republican nomination for Governor against a very strong and well known opponent! Thanks for all of the support you showed me. You have my complete and total Endorsement. You will win in November! [Twitter for iPhone]

Aug 15, 2018 08:14:19 AM Congratulations to Bryan Steil on a wonderful win last night. You will be replacing a great guy in Paul Ryan, and your win in November will make the entire State of Wisconsin very proud. You have my complete and total Endorsement! [Twitter for iPhone]

Aug 15, 2018 08:18:43 AM "People who enter the United States without our permission are illegal aliens and illegal aliens should not be treated the same as people who entered the U.S. legally." Chuck Schumer in 2009, before he went left and haywire! @foxandfriends [Twitter for iPhone]

Aug 15, 2018 08:31:30 AM .@PeteStauber won big last night in Minnesota. A big star in Hockey, he will be an even bigger star in politics. It all begins with a win in November. Pete has my complete and total Endorsement! [Twitter for iPhone]

Aug 15, 2018 08:39:35 AM It is about time that Connecticut had a real and talented Governor. Bob Stefanowski is the person needed to do the job. Tough on crime, Bob is also a big cutter of Taxes. He will win in November and make a Great Governor, a major difference maker. Bob has my total Endorsement! [Twitter for iPhone]

Aug 15, 2018 08:51:12 AM My friend and very early supporter Kris Kobach won the Republican Nomination for Governor of Kansas last night in a tough race against a very fine opponent. Kris will win in November and be a great Governor. He has my complete and total Endorsement! [Twitter for iPhone]

Aug 15, 2018 09:08:18 AM The Rigged Russian Witch Hunt goes on and on as the "originators and founders" of this scam continue to be fired and demoted for their corrupt and illegal activity. All credibility is gone from this terrible Hoax, and much more will be lost as it proceeds. No Collusion! [Twitter for iPhone]

Aug 15, 2018 09:15:07 AM "The action (the Strzok firing) was a decisive step in the right direction in correcting the wrongs committed by what has been described as Comey's skinny inner circle." Chris Swecker, former FBI Assistant Director. [Twitter for iPhone]

Aug 15, 2018 09:57:20 AM Happy Birthday to the leader of the Democrat Party, Maxine Waters! [Twitter for iPhone]

Aug 15, 2018 10:04:16 AM Our Country was built on Tariffs, and Tariffs are now leading us to great new Trade Deals - as opposed to the horrible and unfair Trade Deals that I inherited as your President. Other Countries should not be allowed to come in and steal the wealth of our great U.S.A. No longer! [Twitter for iPhone]

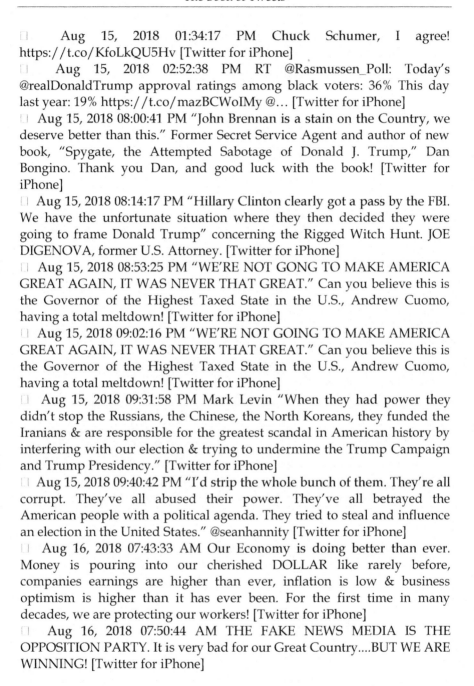

⬜ Aug 15, 2018 01:34:17 PM Chuck Schumer, I agree! https://t.co/KfoLkQU5Hv [Twitter for iPhone]

⬜ Aug 15, 2018 02:52:38 PM RT @Rasmussen_Poll: Today's @realDonaldTrump approval ratings among black voters: 36% This day last year: 19% https://t.co/mazBCWoIMy @... [Twitter for iPhone]

⬜ Aug 15, 2018 08:00:41 PM "John Brennan is a stain on the Country, we deserve better than this." Former Secret Service Agent and author of new book, "Spygate, the Attempted Sabotage of Donald J. Trump," Dan Bongino. Thank you Dan, and good luck with the book! [Twitter for iPhone]

⬜ Aug 15, 2018 08:14:17 PM "Hillary Clinton clearly got a pass by the FBI. We have the unfortunate situation where they then decided they were going to frame Donald Trump" concerning the Rigged Witch Hunt. JOE DIGENOVA, former U.S. Attorney. [Twitter for iPhone]

⬜ Aug 15, 2018 08:53:25 PM "WE'RE NOT GONG TO MAKE AMERICA GREAT AGAIN, IT WAS NEVER THAT GREAT." Can you believe this is the Governor of the Highest Taxed State in the U.S., Andrew Cuomo, having a total meltdown! [Twitter for iPhone]

⬜ Aug 15, 2018 09:02:16 PM "WE'RE NOT GOING TO MAKE AMERICA GREAT AGAIN, IT WAS NEVER THAT GREAT." Can you believe this is the Governor of the Highest Taxed State in the U.S., Andrew Cuomo, having a total meltdown! [Twitter for iPhone]

⬜ Aug 15, 2018 09:31:58 PM Mark Levin "When they had power they didn't stop the Russians, the Chinese, the North Koreans, they funded the Iranians & are responsible for the greatest scandal in American history by interfering with our election & trying to undermine the Trump Campaign and Trump Presidency." [Twitter for iPhone]

⬜ Aug 15, 2018 09:40:42 PM "I'd strip the whole bunch of them. They're all corrupt. They've all abused their power. They've all betrayed the American people with a political agenda. They tried to steal and influence an election in the United States." @seanhannity [Twitter for iPhone]

⬜ Aug 16, 2018 07:43:33 AM Our Economy is doing better than ever. Money is pouring into our cherished DOLLAR like rarely before, companies earnings are higher than ever, inflation is low & business optimism is higher than it has ever been. For the first time in many decades, we are protecting our workers! [Twitter for iPhone]

⬜ Aug 16, 2018 07:50:44 AM THE FAKE NEWS MEDIA IS THE OPPOSITION PARTY. It is very bad for our Great Country....BUT WE ARE WINNING! [Twitter for iPhone]

Aug 16, 2018 09:00:00 AM The Boston Globe, which was sold to the the Failing New York Times for 1.3 BILLION DOLLARS (plus 800 million dollars in losses & investment), or 2.1 BILLION DOLLARS, was then sold by the Times for 1 DOLLAR. Now the Globe is in COLLUSION with other papers on free press. PROVE IT! [Twitter for iPhone]

Aug 16, 2018 09:10:17 AM There is nothing that I would want more for our Country than true FREEDOM OF THE PRESS. The fact is that the Press is FREE to write and say anything it wants, but much of what it says is FAKE NEWS, pushing a political agenda or just plain trying to hurt people. HONESTY WINS! [Twitter for iPhone]

Aug 16, 2018 10:36:26 AM The Queen of Soul, Aretha Franklin, is dead. She was a great woman, with a wonderful gift from God, her voice. She will be missed! [Twitter for iPhone]

Aug 16, 2018 01:43:22 PM Great @Cabinet meeting today at the @WhiteHouse! https://t.co/RwOhQF9SEv [Twitter for iPhone]

Aug 16, 2018 01:55:35 PM Thank you for the kind words Omarosa! https://t.co/PMmNG6iIsi [Twitter for iPhone]

Aug 16, 2018 06:30:26 PM Turkey has taken advantage of the United States for many years. They are now holding our wonderful Christian Pastor, who I must now ask to represent our Country as a great patriot hostage. We will pay nothing for the release of an innocent man, but we are cutting back on Turkey! [Twitter for iPhone]

Aug 16, 2018 06:37:15 PM "The FBI received documents from Bruce Ohr (of the Justice Department & whose wife Nelly worked for Fusion GPS)." Disgraced and fired FBI Agent Peter Strzok. This is too crazy to be believed! The Rigged Witch Hunt has zero credibility. [Twitter for iPhone]

Aug 16, 2018 06:45:01 PM "While Steele shopped the document to multiple media outlets, he also asked for help with a RUSSIAN Oligarch." Catherine Herridge of @FoxNews @LouDobbs In other words, they were colluding with Russia! [Twitter for iPhone]

Aug 16, 2018 06:53:55 PM "Very concerned about Comey's firing, afraid they will be exposed," said Bruce Ohr. DOJ's Emails & Notes show Bruce Ohr's connection to (phony & discredited) Trump Dossier. A creep thinking he would get caught in a dishonest act. Rigged Witch Hunt! [Twitter for iPhone]

Aug 16, 2018 07:45:22 PM .@TuckerCarlson speaking of John Brennan: "How did somebody so obviously limited intellectually get to be CIA Director in the first place?" Now that is a really good question! Then followed by "Richard Blumenthal of Connecticut is a FAKE War Hero..." So true, a total Fake! [Twitter for iPhone]

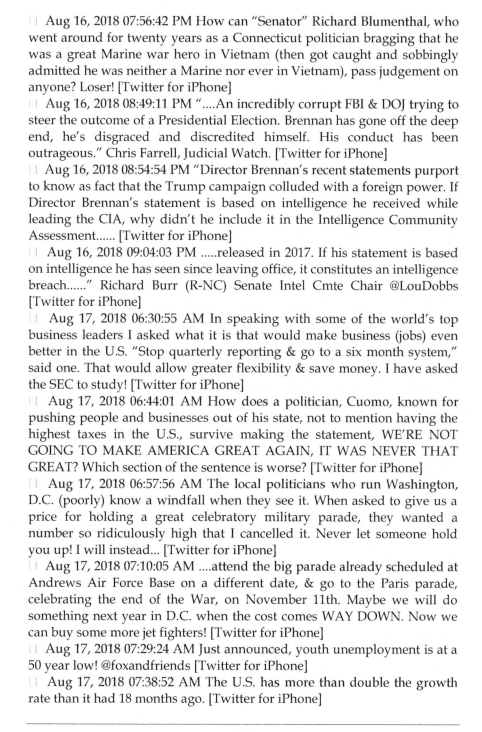

Aug 16, 2018 07:56:42 PM How can "Senator" Richard Blumenthal, who went around for twenty years as a Connecticut politician bragging that he was a great Marine war hero in Vietnam (then got caught and sobbingly admitted he was neither a Marine nor ever in Vietnam), pass judgement on anyone? Loser! [Twitter for iPhone]

Aug 16, 2018 08:49:11 PM "....An incredibly corrupt FBI & DOJ trying to steer the outcome of a Presidential Election. Brennan has gone off the deep end, he's disgraced and discredited himself. His conduct has been outrageous." Chris Farrell, Judicial Watch. [Twitter for iPhone]

Aug 16, 2018 08:54:54 PM "Director Brennan's recent statements purport to know as fact that the Trump campaign colluded with a foreign power. If Director Brennan's statement is based on intelligence he received while leading the CIA, why didn't he include it in the Intelligence Community Assessment...... [Twitter for iPhone]

Aug 16, 2018 09:04:03 PM .....released in 2017. If his statement is based on intelligence he has seen since leaving office, it constitutes an intelligence breach......" Richard Burr (R-NC) Senate Intel Cmte Chair @LouDobbs [Twitter for iPhone]

Aug 17, 2018 06:30:55 AM In speaking with some of the world's top business leaders I asked what it is that would make business (jobs) even better in the U.S. "Stop quarterly reporting & go to a six month system," said one. That would allow greater flexibility & save money. I have asked the SEC to study! [Twitter for iPhone]

Aug 17, 2018 06:44:01 AM How does a politician, Cuomo, known for pushing people and businesses out of his state, not to mention having the highest taxes in the U.S., survive making the statement, WE'RE NOT GOING TO MAKE AMERICA GREAT AGAIN, IT WAS NEVER THAT GREAT? Which section of the sentence is worse? [Twitter for iPhone]

Aug 17, 2018 06:57:56 AM The local politicians who run Washington, D.C. (poorly) know a windfall when they see it. When asked to give us a price for holding a great celebratory military parade, they wanted a number so ridiculously high that I cancelled it. Never let someone hold you up! I will instead... [Twitter for iPhone]

Aug 17, 2018 07:10:05 AM ....attend the big parade already scheduled at Andrews Air Force Base on a different date, & go to the Paris parade, celebrating the end of the War, on November 11th. Maybe we will do something next year in D.C. when the cost comes WAY DOWN. Now we can buy some more jet fighters! [Twitter for iPhone]

Aug 17, 2018 07:29:24 AM Just announced, youth unemployment is at a 50 year low! @foxandfriends [Twitter for iPhone]

Aug 17, 2018 07:38:52 AM The U.S. has more than double the growth rate than it had 18 months ago. [Twitter for iPhone]

Aug 17, 2018 09:06:13 AM Wow! Big pushback on Governor Andrew Cuomo of New York for his really dumb statement about America's lack of greatness. I have already MADE America Great Again, just look at the markets, jobs, military- setting records, and we will do even better. Andrew "chocked" badly, mistake! [Twitter for iPhone]

Aug 17, 2018 09:10:25 AM Wow! Big pushback on Governor Andrew Cuomo of New York for his really dumb statement about America's lack of greatness. I have already MADE America Great Again, just look at the markets, jobs, military- setting records, and we will do even better. Andrew "choked" badly, mistake! [Twitter for iPhone]

Aug 17, 2018 09:17:03 AM When a politician admits that "We're not going to make America great again," there doesn't seem to be much reason to ever vote for him. This could be a career threatening statement by Andrew Cuomo, with many wanting him to resign-he will get higher ratings than his brother Chris! [Twitter for iPhone]

Aug 17, 2018 02:25:52 PM Which is worse, Hightax Andrew Cuomo's statement, "WE'RE NOT GOING TO MAKE AMERICA GREAT AGAIN, IT WAS NEVER THAT GREAT" or Hillary Clinton's "DEPLORABLES" statement... [Twitter for iPhone]

Aug 17, 2018 02:25:53 PM ...I say Andrew's was a bigger and more incompetent blunder. He should easily win his race against a Super Liberal Actress, but his political career is over! [Twitter for iPhone]

Aug 17, 2018 04:25:20 PM https://t.co/TmICRUV9uo [Twitter for iPhone]

Aug 17, 2018 05:29:15 PM "Fox News has learned that Bruce Ohr wrote Christopher Steele following the firing of James Comey saying that he was afraid the anti-Trump Russia probe will be exposed." Charles Payne @FoxBusiness How much more does Mueller have to see? They have blinders on - RIGGED! [Twitter for iPhone]

Aug 17, 2018 08:37:58 PM "Bruce Ohr of DOJ is in legal jeopardy, it's astonishingthat he's still employed. Bruce & Nelly Ohr's bank account is getting fatter & fatter because of the Dossier that they are both peddling. He doesn't disclose it under Fed Regs. Using your Federal office for personal....... [Twitter for iPhone]

Aug 17, 2018 08:46:26 PM "Bruce Ohr of DOJ is in legal jeopardy, it's astonishing that he's still employed. Bruce & Nelly Ohr's bank account is getting fatter & fatter because of the Dossier that they are both peddling. He doesn't disclose it under Fed Regs. Using your Federal office for personal....... [Twitter for iPhone]

Aug 17, 2018 08:47:44 PM ....financial gain is a Federal Gratuity Statute Violation, Bribery Statute Violation, Honest Services Violation....all Major Crimes....because the DOJ is run by BLANK Jeff Sessions......" Gregg Jarrett. So when does Mueller do what must be done? Probably never! @FoxNews [Twitter for iPhone]

Aug 18, 2018 06:23:00 AM Social Media is totally discriminating against Republican/Conservative voices. Speaking loudly and clearly for the Trump Administration, we won't let that happen. They are closing down the opinions of many people on the RIGHT, while at the same time doing nothing to others....... [Twitter for iPhone]

Aug 18, 2018 06:32:17 AM .....Censorship is a very dangerous thing & absolutely impossible to police. If you are weeding out Fake News, there is nothing so Fake as CNN & MSNBC, & yet I do not ask that their sick behavior be removed. I get used to it and watch with a grain of salt, or don't watch at all.. [Twitter for iPhone]

Aug 18, 2018 06:40:11 AM ....Too many voices are being destroyed, some good & some bad, and that cannot be allowed to happen. Who is making the choices, because I can already tell you that too many mistakes are being made. Let everybody participate, good & bad, and we will all just have to figure it out! [Twitter for iPhone]

Aug 18, 2018 06:46:14 AM All of the fools that are so focused on looking only at Russia should start also looking in another direction, China. But in the end, if we are smart, tough and well prepared, we will get along with everyone! [Twitter for iPhone]

Aug 18, 2018 08:06:30 AM https://t.co/5kIR5EggBp [Twitter for iPhone]

Aug 18, 2018 08:12:43 AM Has anyone looked at the mistakes that John Brennan made while serving as CIA Director? He will go down as easily the WORST in history & since getting out, he has become nothing less than a loudmouth, partisan, political hack who cannot be trusted with the secrets to our country! [Twitter for iPhone]

Aug 18, 2018 08:34:49 AM Great Job Rachel Campos-Duffy on @foxandfriends. [Twitter for iPhone]

Aug 18, 2018 08:39:28 AM The Economy is stronger and better than ever before. Importantly, there remains tremendous potential - it will only get better with time! [Twitter for iPhone]

Aug 18, 2018 02:39:35 PM https://t.co/TfRmZA8RWQ [Twitter for iPhone]

Aug 18, 2018 04:51:11 PM The United States has ended the ridiculous 230 Million Dollar yearly development payment to Syria. Saudi Arabia and other rich countries in the Middle East will start making payments instead of the U.S. I want to develop the U.S., our military and countries that help us! [Twitter for iPhone]

⊔   Aug 18, 2018 05:04:48 PM I allowed White House Counsel Don McGahn, and all other requested members of the White House Staff, to fully cooperate with the Special Councel. In addition we readily gave over one million pages of documents. Most transparent in history. No Collusion, No Obstruction. Witch Hunt! [Twitter for iPhone]

⊔   Aug 18, 2018 05:12:30 PM I allowed White House Counsel Don McGahn, and all other requested members of the White House Staff, to fully cooperate with the Special Counsel. In addition we readily gave over one million pages of documents. Most transparent in history. No Collusion, No Obstruction. Witch Hunt! [Twitter for iPhone]

⊔   Aug 19, 2018 06:01:47 AM The failing @nytimes wrote a Fake piece today implying that because White House Councel Don McGahn was giving hours of testimony to the Special Councel, he must be a John Dean type "RAT." But I allowed him and all others to testify - I didn't have to. I have nothing to hide...... [Twitter for iPhone]

⊔   Aug 19, 2018 06:15:12 AM ....and have demanded transparency so that this Rigged and Disgusting Witch Hunt can come to a close. So many lives have been ruined over nothing - McCarthyism at its WORST! Yet Mueller & his gang of Dems refuse to look at the real crimes on the other side - Media is even worse! [Twitter for iPhone]

⊔   Aug 19, 2018 06:30:41 AM No Collusion and No Obstruction, except by Crooked Hillary and the Democrats. All of the resignations and corruption, yet heavily conflicted Bob Mueller refuses to even look in that direction. What about the Brennan, Comey, McCabe, Strzok lies to Congress, or Crooked's Emails! [Twitter for iPhone]

⊔   Aug 19, 2018 07:06:43 AM The Failing New York Times wrote a story that made it seem like the White House Councel had TURNED on the President, when in fact it is just the opposite - & the two Fake reporters knew this. This is why the Fake News Media has become the Enemy of the People. So bad for America! [Twitter for iPhone]

⊔   Aug 19, 2018 07:14:44 AM Some members of the media are very Angry at the Fake Story in the New York Times. They actually called to complain and apologize - a big step forward. From the day I announced, the Times has been Fake News, and with their disgusting new Board Member, it will only get worse! [Twitter for iPhone]

⊔   Aug 19, 2018 07:24:38 AM Study the late Joseph McCarthy, because we are now in period with Mueller and his gang that make Joseph McCarthy look like a baby! Rigged Witch Hunt! [Twitter for iPhone]

⊔   Aug 20, 2018 06:28:45 AM Disgraced and discredited Bob Mueller and his whole group of Angry Democrat Thugs spent over 30 hours with the White House Councel, only with my approval, for purposes of transparency. Anybody needing that much time when they know there is no Russian Collusion is just someone.... [Twitter for iPhone]

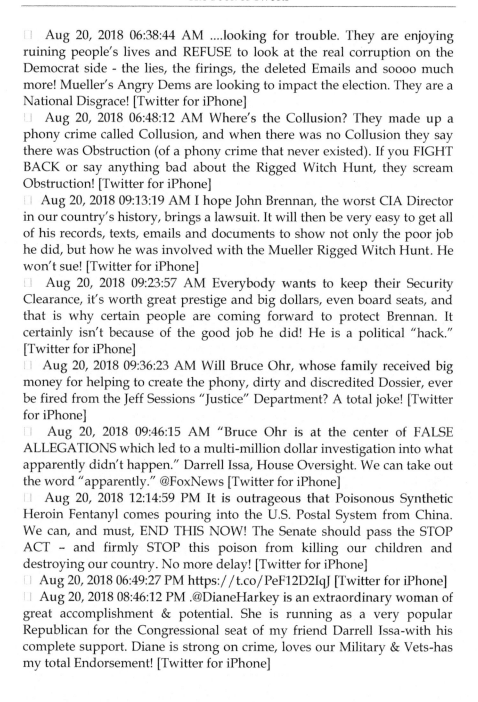

Aug 20, 2018 06:38:44 AM ....looking for trouble. They are enjoying ruining people's lives and REFUSE to look at the real corruption on the Democrat side - the lies, the firings, the deleted Emails and soooo much more! Mueller's Angry Dems are looking to impact the election. They are a National Disgrace! [Twitter for iPhone]

Aug 20, 2018 06:48:12 AM Where's the Collusion? They made up a phony crime called Collusion, and when there was no Collusion they say there was Obstruction (of a phony crime that never existed). If you FIGHT BACK or say anything bad about the Rigged Witch Hunt, they scream Obstruction! [Twitter for iPhone]

Aug 20, 2018 09:13:19 AM I hope John Brennan, the worst CIA Director in our country's history, brings a lawsuit. It will then be very easy to get all of his records, texts, emails and documents to show not only the poor job he did, but how he was involved with the Mueller Rigged Witch Hunt. He won't sue! [Twitter for iPhone]

Aug 20, 2018 09:23:57 AM Everybody wants to keep their Security Clearance, it's worth great prestige and big dollars, even board seats, and that is why certain people are coming forward to protect Brennan. It certainly isn't because of the good job he did! He is a political "hack." [Twitter for iPhone]

Aug 20, 2018 09:36:23 AM Will Bruce Ohr, whose family received big money for helping to create the phony, dirty and discredited Dossier, ever be fired from the Jeff Sessions "Justice" Department? A total joke! [Twitter for iPhone]

Aug 20, 2018 09:46:15 AM "Bruce Ohr is at the center of FALSE ALLEGATIONS which led to a multi-million dollar investigation into what apparently didn't happen." Darrell Issa, House Oversight. We can take out the word "apparently." @FoxNews [Twitter for iPhone]

Aug 20, 2018 12:14:59 PM It is outrageous that Poisonous Synthetic Heroin Fentanyl comes pouring into the U.S. Postal System from China. We can, and must, END THIS NOW! The Senate should pass the STOP ACT – and firmly STOP this poison from killing our children and destroying our country. No more delay! [Twitter for iPhone]

Aug 20, 2018 06:49:27 PM https://t.co/PeF12D2IqJ [Twitter for iPhone]

Aug 20, 2018 08:46:12 PM .@DianeHarkey is an extraordinary woman of great accomplishment & potential. She is running as a very popular Republican for the Congressional seat of my friend Darrell Issa-with his complete support. Diane is strong on crime, loves our Military & Vets-has my total Endorsement! [Twitter for iPhone]

Aug 20, 2018 09:06:08 PM Just watched former Intelligence Official Phillip Mudd become totally unglued and weird while debating wonderful @PARISDENNARD over Brennan's Security Clearance. Dennard destroyed him but Mudd is in no mental condition to have such a Clearance. Should be REVOKED? @seanhannity [Twitter for iPhone]

Aug 20, 2018 10:40:49 PM Will be going to the Great State of West Virginia on Tuesday Night to campaign & do a Rally Speech for a hard working and spectacular person, A.G. Patrick Morrisey, who is running for the U.S. Senate. Patrick has great Energy & Stamina-I need his VOTE to MAGA. Total Endorsement! [Twitter for iPhone]

Aug 20, 2018 10:53:49 PM I am hearing so many great things about the Republican Party's California Gubernatorial Candidate, John Cox. He is a very successful businessman who is tired of high Taxes & Crime. He will Make California Great Again & make you proud of your Great State again. Total Endorsement! [Twitter for iPhone]

Aug 21, 2018 05:38:19 AM A Blue Wave means Crime and Open Borders. A Red Wave means Safety and Strength! [Twitter for iPhone]

Aug 21, 2018 05:55:03 AM Even James Clapper has admonished John Brennan for having gone totally off the rails. Maybe Clapper is being nice to me so he doesn't lose his Security Clearance for lying to Congress! [Twitter for iPhone]

Aug 21, 2018 06:10:49 AM Fake News, of which there is soooo much (this time the very tired New Yorker) falsely reported that I was going to take the extraordinary step of denying Intelligence Briefings to President Obama. Never discussed or thought of! [Twitter for iPhone]

Aug 21, 2018 06:41:46 AM I am sorry to have to reiterate that there are serious and unpleasant consequences to crossing the Border into the United States ILLEGALLY! If there were no serious consequences, our country would be overrun with people trying to get in, and our system could not handle it! [Twitter for iPhone]

Aug 21, 2018 06:57:19 AM Big Rally tonight in West Virginia. Patrick Morrisey is running a GREAT race for U.S. Senate. I have done so much for West Virginia, against all odds, and having Patrick, a real fighter, by my side, would make things so much easier. See you later. CLEAN COAL!!!! [Twitter for iPhone]

Aug 21, 2018 09:15:18 AM Bill DeBlasio, the high taxing Mayor of NYC, just stole my campaign slogan: PROMISES MADE PROMISES KEPT! That's not at all nice. No imagination! @foxandfriends [Twitter for iPhone]

Aug 21, 2018 09:56:31 AM To the incredible people of the Great State of Wyoming: Go VOTE TODAY for Foster Friess - He will be a fantastic Governor! Strong on Crime, Borders & 2nd Amendment. Loves our Military & our Vets. He has my complete and total Endorsement! [Twitter for iPhone]

Aug 21, 2018 10:22:04 AM Join me tonight at the Charleston Civic Center in West Virginia at 7:00pmE! Tickets: https://t.co/OX8gGhdmg9 [Twitter for iPhone]

Aug 21, 2018 04:32:31 PM Just landed in West Virginia. Big crowd, looking forward to seeing everyone soon! #MAGA [Twitter for iPhone]

Aug 21, 2018 07:38:32 PM MAKING AMERICA GREAT AGAIN! https://t.co/gZqP81bclE [Twitter for iPhone]

Aug 21, 2018 07:45:19 PM Thank you West Virginia. I love you! https://t.co/K1OQ98wOh4 [Twitter for iPhone]

Aug 22, 2018 07:44:08 AM If anyone is looking for a good lawyer, I would strongly suggest that you don't retain the services of Michael Cohen! [Twitter for iPhone]

Aug 22, 2018 08:21:29 AM I feel very badly for Paul Manafort and his wonderful family. "Justice" took a 12 year old tax case, among other things, applied tremendous pressure on him and, unlike Michael Cohen, he refused to "break" - make up stories in order to get a "deal." Such respect for a brave man! [Twitter for iPhone]

Aug 22, 2018 08:34:16 AM A large number of counts, ten, could not even be decided in the Paul Manafort case. Witch Hunt! [Twitter for iPhone]

Aug 22, 2018 08:37:34 AM Michael Cohen plead guilty to two counts of campaign finance violations that are not a crime. President Obama had a big campaign finance violation and it was easily settled! [Twitter for iPhone]

Aug 22, 2018 08:52:33 AM Thank you to Democrat Assemblyman Dov Hikind of New York for your very gracious remarks on @foxandfriends for our deporting a longtime resident Nazi back to Germany! Others worked on this for decades. [Twitter for iPhone]

Aug 22, 2018 10:05:30 AM Everyone in the path of #HurricaneLane please prepare yourselves, heed the advice of State and local officials, and follow @NWSHonolulu for updates. Be safe! https://t.co/kCwtL8UxNI [Twitter for iPhone]

Aug 22, 2018 11:13:34 AM https://t.co/OGqKufBeHn [Media Studio]

Aug 22, 2018 03:05:05 PM https://t.co/mJtO0AFLus [Twitter for iPhone]

Aug 22, 2018 03:07:29 PM Longest bull run in the history of the stock market, congratulations America! [Twitter for iPhone]

Aug 22, 2018 05:24:57 PM https://t.co/wYCNmkkaNR [Twitter for iPhone]

Aug 22, 2018 06:01:24 PM https://t.co/15ibBbf34U [Twitter for iPhone]

Aug 22, 2018 07:46:53 PM RT @Scavino45: Today, President Trump welcomed the family of @usairforce Tech. Sgt. John A. Chapman, Medal of Honor recipient, to the Oval... [Twitter for iPhone]

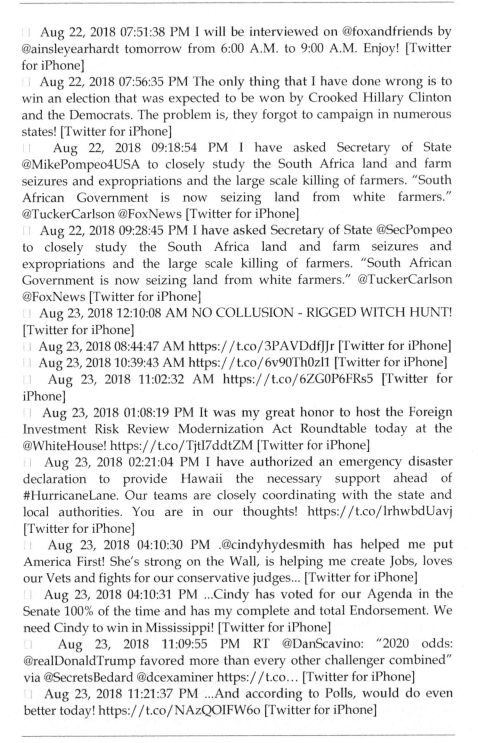

⊔ Aug 22, 2018 07:51:38 PM I will be interviewed on @foxandfriends by @ainsleyearhardt tomorrow from 6:00 A.M. to 9:00 A.M. Enjoy! [Twitter for iPhone]

⊔ Aug 22, 2018 07:56:35 PM The only thing that I have done wrong is to win an election that was expected to be won by Crooked Hillary Clinton and the Democrats. The problem is, they forgot to campaign in numerous states! [Twitter for iPhone]

⊔ Aug 22, 2018 09:18:54 PM I have asked Secretary of State @MikePompeo4USA to closely study the South Africa land and farm seizures and expropriations and the large scale killing of farmers. "South African Government is now seizing land from white farmers." @TuckerCarlson @FoxNews [Twitter for iPhone]

⊔ Aug 22, 2018 09:28:45 PM I have asked Secretary of State @SecPompeo to closely study the South Africa land and farm seizures and expropriations and the large scale killing of farmers. "South African Government is now seizing land from white farmers." @TuckerCarlson @FoxNews [Twitter for iPhone]

⊔ Aug 23, 2018 12:10:08 AM NO COLLUSION - RIGGED WITCH HUNT! [Twitter for iPhone]

⊔ Aug 23, 2018 08:44:47 AM https://t.co/3PAVDdfJJr [Twitter for iPhone]

⊔ Aug 23, 2018 10:39:43 AM https://t.co/6v90Th0zl1 [Twitter for iPhone]

⊔ Aug 23, 2018 11:02:32 AM https://t.co/6ZG0P6FRs5 [Twitter for iPhone]

⊔ Aug 23, 2018 01:08:19 PM It was my great honor to host the Foreign Investment Risk Review Modernization Act Roundtable today at the @WhiteHouse! https://t.co/Tjtl7ddtZM [Twitter for iPhone]

⊔ Aug 23, 2018 02:21:04 PM I have authorized an emergency disaster declaration to provide Hawaii the necessary support ahead of #HurricaneLane. Our teams are closely coordinating with the state and local authorities. You are in our thoughts! https://t.co/lrhwbdUavj [Twitter for iPhone]

⊔ Aug 23, 2018 04:10:30 PM .@cindyhydesmith has helped me put America First! She's strong on the Wall, is helping me create Jobs, loves our Vets and fights for our conservative judges... [Twitter for iPhone]

⊔ Aug 23, 2018 04:10:31 PM ...Cindy has voted for our Agenda in the Senate 100% of the time and has my complete and total Endorsement. We need Cindy to win in Mississippi! [Twitter for iPhone]

⊔ Aug 23, 2018 11:09:55 PM RT @DanScavino: "2020 odds: @realDonaldTrump favored more than every other challenger combined" via @SecretsBedard @dcexaminer https://t.co… [Twitter for iPhone]

⊔ Aug 23, 2018 11:21:37 PM ...And according to Polls, would do even better today! https://t.co/NAzQOIFW6o [Twitter for iPhone]

Aug 24, 2018 04:57:15 AM Target CEO raves about the Economy. "This is the best consumer environment I've seen in my career." A big statement from a top executive. But virtually everybody is saying this, & when our Trade Deals are made, & cost cutting done, you haven't seen anything yet! @DRUDGE_REPORT [Twitter for iPhone]

Aug 24, 2018 05:04:45 AM Our Economy is setting records on virtually every front - Probably the best our country has ever done. Tremendous value created since the Election. The World is respecting us again! Companies are moving back to the U.S.A. [Twitter for iPhone]

Aug 24, 2018 05:17:34 AM "Department of Justice will not be improperly influenced by political considerations." Jeff, this is GREAT, what everyone wants, so look into all of the corruption on the "other side" including deleted Emails, Comey lies & leaks, Mueller conflicts, McCabe, Strzok, Page, Ohr...... [Twitter for iPhone]

Aug 24, 2018 05:28:37 AM ....FISA abuse, Christopher Steele & his phony and corrupt Dossier, the Clinton Foundation, illegal surveillance of Trump Campaign, Russian collusion by Dems - and so much more. Open up the papers & documents without redaction? Come on Jeff, you can do it, the country is waiting! [Twitter for iPhone]

Aug 24, 2018 06:10:13 AM Ex-NSA contractor to spend 63 months in jail over "classified" information. Gee, this is "small potatoes" compared to what Hillary Clinton did! So unfair Jeff, Double Standard. [Twitter for iPhone]

Aug 24, 2018 06:34:13 AM Social Media Giants are silencing millions of people. Can't do this even if it means we must continue to hear Fake News like CNN, whose ratings have suffered gravely. People have to figure out what is real, and what is not, without censorship! [Twitter for iPhone]

Aug 24, 2018 11:10:25 AM https://t.co/0a25gApyJ6 [Twitter for iPhone]

Aug 24, 2018 12:36:00 PM I have asked Secretary of State Mike Pompeo not to go to North Korea, at this time, because I feel we are not making sufficient progress with respect to the denuclearization of the Korean Peninsula... [Twitter for iPhone]

Aug 24, 2018 12:36:01 PM ...Additionally, because of our much tougher Trading stance with China, I do not believe they are helping with the process of denuclearization as they once were (despite the UN Sanctions which are in place)... [Twitter for iPhone]

Aug 24, 2018 12:36:02 PM ...Secretary Pompeo looks forward to going to North Korea in the near future, most likely after our Trading relationship with China is resolved. In the meantime I would like to send my warmest regards and respect to Chairman Kim. I look forward to seeing him soon! [Twitter for iPhone]

Aug 24, 2018 06:26:02 PM Thank you. I love you Ohio! https://t.co/RQ9Gj0SETz [Twitter for iPhone]

⬜ Aug 24, 2018 07:20:53 PM I spoke with Governor David Ige of Hawaii today to express our full support for the people of Hawaii as the State is impacted by #HurricaneLane. The Federal Government is fully committed to helping the people of Hawaii. https://t.co/P35yAAovIk [Twitter for iPhone]

⬜ Aug 24, 2018 07:27:13 PM Congratulations to new Australian Prime Minister Scott Morrison. There are no greater friends than the United States and Australia! [Twitter for iPhone]

⬜ Aug 24, 2018 07:40:21 PM Great to see the Senate working on solutions to end the secrecy around ridiculously high drug prices, something I called for in my drug pricing Blueprint. Will now work with the House to help American patients! #AmericanPatientsFirst [Twitter for iPhone]

⬜ Aug 24, 2018 09:13:13 PM Great #StateDinner2018 in Ohio tonight! Together, we are MAKING AMERICA GREAT AGAIN! https://t.co/ALU1PHEsvh [Twitter for iPhone]

⬜ Aug 24, 2018 10:35:21 PM Happy birthday Vince, you are truly one of the greats! https://t.co/b8zV5MfojY [Twitter for iPhone]

⬜ Aug 25, 2018 07:16:53 AM Michaels Cohen's attorney clarified the record, saying his client does not know if President Trump knew about the Trump Tower meeting (out of which came nothing!). The answer is that I did NOT know about the meeting. Just another phony story by the Fake News Media! [Twitter for iPhone]

⬜ Aug 25, 2018 07:36:33 AM Jeff Sessions said he wouldn't allow politics to influence him only because he doesn't understand what is happening underneath his command position. Highly conflicted Bob Mueller and his gang of 17 Angry Dems are having a field day as real corruption goes untouched. No Collusion! [Twitter for iPhone]

⬜ Aug 25, 2018 07:46:18 AM .@LindseyGrahamSC "Every President deserves an Attorney General they have confidence in. I believe every President has a right to their Cabinet, these are not lifetime appointments. You serve at the pleasure of the President." [Twitter for iPhone]

⬜ Aug 25, 2018 08:05:42 AM Big story out that the FBI ignored tens of thousands of Crooked Hillary Emails, many of which are REALLY BAD. Also gave false election info. I feel sure that we will soon be getting to the bottom of all of this corruption. At some point I may have to get involved! [Twitter for iPhone]

⬜ Aug 25, 2018 08:11:28 AM "The FBI only looked at 3000 of 675,000 Crooked Hillary Clinton Emails." They purposely didn't look at the disasters. This news is just out. @FoxNews [Twitter for iPhone]

⬜ Aug 25, 2018 08:14:15 AM "The FBI looked at less than 1%" of Crooked's Emails! [Twitter for iPhone]

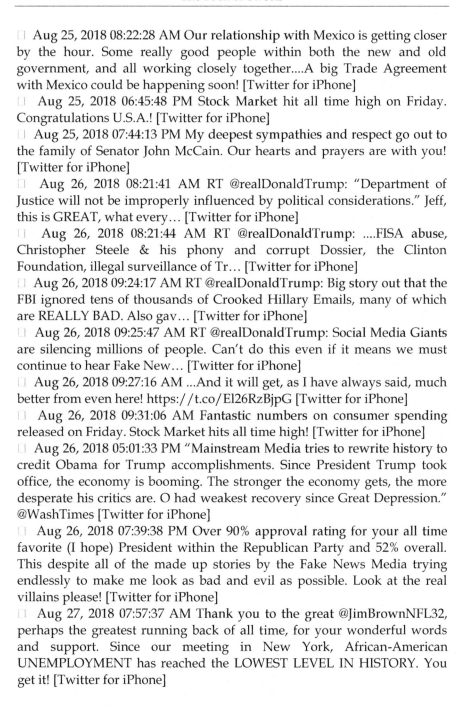

Aug 25, 2018 08:22:28 AM Our relationship with Mexico is getting closer by the hour. Some really good people within both the new and old government, and all working closely together....A big Trade Agreement with Mexico could be happening soon! [Twitter for iPhone]

Aug 25, 2018 06:45:48 PM Stock Market hit all time high on Friday. Congratulations U.S.A.! [Twitter for iPhone]

Aug 25, 2018 07:44:13 PM My deepest sympathies and respect go out to the family of Senator John McCain. Our hearts and prayers are with you! [Twitter for iPhone]

Aug 26, 2018 08:21:41 AM RT @realDonaldTrump: "Department of Justice will not be improperly influenced by political considerations." Jeff, this is GREAT, what every... [Twitter for iPhone]

Aug 26, 2018 08:21:44 AM RT @realDonaldTrump: ....FISA abuse, Christopher Steele & his phony and corrupt Dossier, the Clinton Foundation, illegal surveillance of Tr... [Twitter for iPhone]

Aug 26, 2018 09:24:17 AM RT @realDonaldTrump: Big story out that the FBI ignored tens of thousands of Crooked Hillary Emails, many of which are REALLY BAD. Also gav... [Twitter for iPhone]

Aug 26, 2018 09:25:47 AM RT @realDonaldTrump: Social Media Giants are silencing millions of people. Can't do this even if it means we must continue to hear Fake New... [Twitter for iPhone]

Aug 26, 2018 09:27:16 AM ...And it will get, as I have always said, much better from even here! https://t.co/El26RzBjpG [Twitter for iPhone]

Aug 26, 2018 09:31:06 AM Fantastic numbers on consumer spending released on Friday. Stock Market hits all time high! [Twitter for iPhone]

Aug 26, 2018 05:01:33 PM "Mainstream Media tries to rewrite history to credit Obama for Trump accomplishments. Since President Trump took office, the economy is booming. The stronger the economy gets, the more desperate his critics are. O had weakest recovery since Great Depression." @WashTimes [Twitter for iPhone]

Aug 26, 2018 07:39:38 PM Over 90% approval rating for your all time favorite (I hope) President within the Republican Party and 52% overall. This despite all of the made up stories by the Fake News Media trying endlessly to make me look as bad and evil as possible. Look at the real villains please! [Twitter for iPhone]

Aug 27, 2018 07:57:37 AM Thank you to the great @JimBrownNFL32, perhaps the greatest running back of all time, for your wonderful words and support. Since our meeting in New York, African-American UNEMPLOYMENT has reached the LOWEST LEVEL IN HISTORY. You get it! [Twitter for iPhone]

⑴ Aug 27, 2018 08:37:39 AM The Fake News Media worked hard to get Tiger Woods to say something that he didn't want to say. Tiger wouldn't play the game - he is very smart. More importantly, he is playing great golf again! [Twitter for iPhone]

⑴ Aug 27, 2018 08:39:02 AM A big deal looking good with Mexico! [Twitter for iPhone]

⑴ Aug 27, 2018 12:19:20 PM Rick Scott of Florida is doing a fantastic job as Governor. Jobs are pouring into the State and its economic health is better than ever before. He is strong on Crime, Borders, and loves our Military and Vets. Vote for Rick on Tuesday! [Twitter for iPhone]

⑴ Aug 27, 2018 12:20:15 PM Congressman Ron DeSantis is a special person who has done an incredible job. He is running in Tuesdays Primary for Governor of Florida….Strong on Crime, Borders and wants Low Taxes. He will be a great Governor and has my full and total Endorsement! [Twitter for iPhone]

⑴ Aug 27, 2018 12:22:07 PM Governor Doug Ducey of Arizona is doing a great job. It would be really nice to show your support tomorrow by voting for him in Tuesdays Primary. Doug is strong on Crime, the Border, and our Second Amendment. Loves our Military & our Vets. He has my full and complete Endorsement. [Twitter for iPhone]

⑴ Aug 27, 2018 01:11:20 PM United States-Mexico Trade Agreement: https://t.co/E1AzveYPli https://t.co/ZYbHt1pD8a [Twitter for iPhone]

⑴ Aug 27, 2018 05:07:45 PM RT @FLOTUS: It was a pleasure having @FirstLadyKenya at the @WhiteHouse today. I enjoyed learning about @BeyondZeroKenya & discussing our… [Twitter for iPhone]

⑴ Aug 27, 2018 05:07:50 PM .@FLOTUS Melania and I were honored to welcome the President of the Republic of Kenya, @UKenyatta and Mrs. Margaret Kenyatta to the @WhiteHouse today! https://t.co/ZU5MovNKt8 [Twitter for iPhone]

⑴ Aug 27, 2018 08:18:38 PM VOTE FOR RON! https://t.co/80NShvQ73u [Twitter for iPhone]

⑴ Aug 28, 2018 04:24:35 AM Google search results for "Trump News" shows only the viewing/reporting of Fake New Media. In other words, they have it RIGGED, for me & others, so that almost all stories & news is BAD. Fake CNN is prominent. Republican/Conservative & Fair Media is shut out. Illegal? 96% of... [Twitter for iPhone]

⑴ Aug 28, 2018 04:34:44 AM ….results on "Trump News" are from National Left-Wing Media, very dangerous. Google & others are suppressing voices of Conservatives and hiding information and news that is good. They are controlling what we can & cannot see. This is a very serious situation-will be addressed! [Twitter for iPhone]

Aug 28, 2018 04:54:32 AM "President Trump has done more for minority groups in this country than any president in decades." @LouDobbs [Twitter for iPhone]

Aug 28, 2018 04:57:51 AM NASDAQ has just gone above 8000 for the first time in history! [Twitter for iPhone]

Aug 28, 2018 09:21:08 AM I smile at Senators and others talking about how good free trade is for the U.S. What they don't say is that we lose Jobs and over 800 Billion Dollars a year on really dumb Trade Deals....and these same countries Tariff us to death. These lawmakers are just fine with this! [Twitter for iPhone]

Aug 28, 2018 10:02:49 AM Google search results for "Trump News" shows only the viewing/reporting of Fake News Media. In other words, they have it RIGGED, for me & others, so that almost all stories & news is BAD. Fake CNN is prominent. Republican/Conservative & Fair Media is shut out. Illegal? 96% of.... [Twitter for iPhone]

Aug 28, 2018 10:02:51 AM ....results on "Trump News" are from National Left-Wing Media, very dangerous. Google & others are suppressing voices of Conservatives and hiding information and news that is good. They are controlling what we can & cannot see. This is a very serious situation-will be addressed! [Twitter for iPhone]

Aug 28, 2018 12:28:28 PM "Consumer confidence pops in August to highest level since October 2000" https://t.co/1Gg5IOtbNa [Twitter for iPhone]

Aug 28, 2018 03:50:34 PM https://t.co/H2FiSVxyOF [Twitter for iPhone]

Aug 28, 2018 07:32:05 PM Such a fantastic win for Ron DeSantis and the people of the Great State of Florida. Ron will be a fantastic Governor. On to November! [Twitter for iPhone]

Aug 28, 2018 07:48:11 PM Congratulations to Governor Rick Scott of Florida on his conclusive Republican Primary Win. He will be a great Senator! [Twitter for iPhone]

Aug 28, 2018 08:16:58 PM Report just out: "China hacked Hillary Clinton's private Email Server." Are they sure it wasn't Russia (just kidding!)? What are the odds that the FBI and DOJ are right on top of this? Actually, a very big story. Much classified information! [Twitter for iPhone]

Aug 28, 2018 08:21:59 PM Add the 2026 World Cup to our long list of accomplishments! [Twitter for iPhone]

Aug 28, 2018 09:19:58 PM Our new Trade Deal with Mexico focuses on FARMERS, GROWTH for our country, tearing down TRADE BARRIERS, JOBS and having companies continue to POUR BACK INTO OUR COUNTRY. It will be a big hit! [Twitter for iPhone]

Aug 28, 2018 09:26:35 PM New Poll - A majority of Americans think that John Brennan and James Comey should have their Security Clearances Revoked. Not surprised! @FoxNews [Twitter for iPhone]

Aug 28, 2018 11:11:45 PM Hillary Clinton's Emails, many of which are Classified Information, got hacked by China. Next move better be by the FBI & DOJ or, after all of their other missteps (Comey, McCabe, Strzok, Page, Ohr, FISA, Dirty Dossier etc.), their credibility will be forever gone! [Twitter for iPhone]

Aug 28, 2018 11:44:54 PM Martha McSally, running in the Arizona Primary for U.S. Senate, was endorsed by rejected Senator Jeff Flake....and turned it down - a first! Now Martha, a great U.S. Military fighter jet pilot and highly respected member of Congress, WINS BIG. Congratulations, and on to November! [Twitter for iPhone]

Aug 29, 2018 07:00:37 AM Not only did Congressman Ron DeSantis easily win the Republican Primary, but his opponent in November is his biggest dream....a failed Socialist Mayor named Andrew Gillum who has allowed crime & many other problems to flourish in his city. This is not what Florida wants or needs! [Twitter for iPhone]

Aug 29, 2018 07:12:38 AM "The Obama people did something that's never been done...They spied on a rival presidential campaign. Would it be OK if Trump did it next? I am losing faith that our system is on the level. I'm beginning to think it is rotten & corrupt. Scary stuff Obama did." @TuckerCarlson DOJ [Twitter for iPhone]

Aug 29, 2018 07:18:10 AM "Hillary Clinton and the DNC paid for information from the Russian government to use against her government - there's no doubt about that!" @TuckerCarlson [Twitter for iPhone]

Aug 29, 2018 07:23:18 AM Big Election Wins last night! The Republican Party will MAKE AMERICA GREAT AGAIN! Actually, it is happening faster than anybody thought possible! It is morphing into KEEP AMERICA GREAT! [Twitter for iPhone]

Aug 29, 2018 07:40:05 AM "Anonymous Sources are really starting to BURN the media." @FoxNews The fact is that many anonymous sources don't even exist. They are fiction made up by the Fake News reporters. Look at the lie that Fake CNN is now in. They got caught red handed! Enemy of the People! [Twitter for iPhone]

Aug 29, 2018 07:41:38 AM When you see "anonymous source," stop reading the story, it is fiction! [Twitter for iPhone]

Aug 29, 2018 07:52:05 AM Martha McSally is an extraordinary woman. She was a very talented fighter jet pilot and is now a highly respected member of Congress. She is Strong on Crime, the Border and our under siege 2nd Amendment. Loves our Military and our Vets. Has my total and complete Endorsement! [Twitter for iPhone]

Aug 29, 2018 09:30:35 AM White House Counsel Don McGahn will be leaving his position in the fall, shortly after the confirmation (hopefully) of Judge Brett Kavanaugh to the United States Supreme Court. I have worked with Don for a long time and truly appreciate his service! [Twitter for iPhone]

Aug 29, 2018 09:56:38 AM Consumer Confidence Index, just out, is the HIGHEST IN 18 YEARS! Also, GDP revised upward to 4.2 from 4.1. Our country is doing great! [Twitter for iPhone]

Aug 29, 2018 10:12:23 AM How the hell is Bruce Ohr still employed at the Justice Department? Disgraceful! Witch Hunt! [Twitter for iPhone]

Aug 29, 2018 03:55:45 PM #StopTheBias https://t.co/xqz599iQZw [Twitter for iPhone]

Aug 29, 2018 04:23:08 PM STATEMENT FROM THE WHITE HOUSE President Donald J. Trump feels strongly that North Korea is under tremendous pressure from China because of our major trade disputes with the Chinese Government. At the same time, we also know that China is providing North Korea with... [Twitter for iPhone]

Aug 29, 2018 04:23:09 PM ...considerable aid, including money, fuel, fertilizer and various other commodities. This is not helpful! Nonetheless, the President believes that his relationship with Kim Jong Un is a very good and warm one, and there is no reason at this time to be spending large amounts... [Twitter for iPhone]

Aug 29, 2018 04:23:10 PM ...differences, they will be resolved in time by President Trump and China's great President Xi Jinping. Their relationship and bond remain very strong. [Twitter for iPhone]

Aug 29, 2018 04:23:10 PM ...of money on joint U.S.-South Korea war games. Besides, the President can instantly start the joint exercises again with South Korea, and Japan, if he so chooses. If he does, they will be far bigger than ever before. As for the U.S.-China trade disputes, and other... [Twitter for iPhone]

Aug 29, 2018 05:43:49 PM CNN is being torn apart from within based on their being caught in a major lie and refusing to admit the mistake. Sloppy @carlbernstein, a man who lives in the past and thinks like a degenerate fool, making up story after story, is being laughed at all over the country! Fake News [Twitter for iPhone]

Aug 29, 2018 07:44:26 PM "Lanny Davis admits being anonymous source in CNN Report." @BretBaier Oh well, so much for CNN saying it wasn't Lanny. No wonder their ratings are so low, it's FAKE NEWS! [Twitter for iPhone]

Aug 29, 2018 08:43:30 PM "Ohr told the FBI it (the Fake Dossier) wasn't true, it was a lie and the FBI was determined to use it anyway to damage Trump and to perpetrate a fraud on the court to spy on the Trump campaign. This is a fraud on the court. The Chief Justice of the U.S. Supreme Court is in...... [Twitter for iPhone]

Aug 29, 2018 08:51:50 PM ...charge of the FISA court. He should direct the Presiding Judge, Rosemary Collier, to hold a hearing, haul all of these people from the DOJ & FBI in there, & if she finds there were crimes committed, and there were, there should be a criminal referral by her...." @GreggJarrett [Twitter for iPhone]

Aug 29, 2018 09:27:24 PM Watch: Kanye West Says Trump Wants to Be the 'Greatest President' for Black Americans https://t.co/ECxTzVNZeG via @BreitbartNews [Twitter for iPhone]

Aug 30, 2018 05:50:20 AM The hatred and extreme bias of me by @CNN has clouded their thinking and made them unable to function. But actually, as I have always said, this has been going on for a long time. Little Jeff Z has done a terrible job, his ratings suck, & AT&T should fire him to save credibility! [Twitter for iPhone]

Aug 30, 2018 06:02:16 AM What's going on at @CNN is happening, to different degrees, at other networks - with @NBCNews being the worst. The good news is that Andy Lack(y) is about to be fired(?) for incompetence, and much worse. When Lester Holt got caught fudging my tape on Russia, they were hurt badly! [Twitter for iPhone]

Aug 30, 2018 06:11:58 AM I just cannot state strongly enough how totally dishonest much of the Media is. Truth doesn't matter to them, they only have their hatred & agenda. This includes fake books, which come out about me all the time, always anonymous sources, and are pure fiction. Enemy of the People! [Twitter for iPhone]

Aug 30, 2018 06:20:48 AM The news from the Financial Markets is even better than anticipated. For all of you that have made a fortune in the markets, or seen your 401k's rise beyond your wildest expectations, more good news is coming! [Twitter for iPhone]

Aug 30, 2018 06:44:28 AM Ivanka Trump & Jared Kushner had NOTHING to do with the so called "pushing out" of Don McGahn.The Fake News Media has it, purposely,so wrong! They love to portray chaos in the White House when they know that chaos doesn't exist-just a "smooth running machine" with changing parts! [Twitter for iPhone]

Aug 30, 2018 06:56:28 AM The only thing James Comey ever got right was when he said that President Trump was not under investigation! [Twitter for iPhone]

Aug 30, 2018 07:12:22 AM I am very excited about the person who will be taking the place of Don McGahn as White House Councel! I liked Don, but he was NOT responsible for me not firing Bob Mueller or Jeff Sessions. So much Fake Reporting and Fake News! [Twitter for iPhone]

Aug 30, 2018 07:54:13 AM Wow, Nellie Ohr, Bruce Ohr's wife, is a Russia expert who is fluent in Russian. She worked for Fusion GPS where she was paid a lot. Collusion! Bruce was a boss at the Department of Justice and is, unbelievably, still there! [Twitter for iPhone]

Aug 30, 2018 08:17:48 AM The Rigged Russia Witch Hunt did not come into play, even a little bit, with respect to my decision on Don McGahn! [Twitter for iPhone]

Aug 30, 2018 08:39:00 AM I am very excited about the person who will be taking the place of Don McGahn as White House Counsel! I liked Don, but he was NOT responsible for me not firing Bob Mueller or Jeff Sessions. So much Fake Reporting and Fake News! [Twitter for iPhone]

Aug 30, 2018 08:49:51 AM Will be going to Evansville, Indiana, tonight for a big crowd rally with Mike Braun, a very successful businessman who is campaigning to be Indiana's next U.S. Senator. He is strong on Crime & Borders, the 2nd Amendment, and loves our Military & Vets. Will be a big night! [Twitter for iPhone]

Aug 30, 2018 11:54:09 AM CNN is working frantically to find their "source." Look hard because it doesn't exist. Whatever was left of CNN's credibility is now gone! [Twitter for iPhone]

Aug 30, 2018 01:30:04 PM Kevin Stitt ran a great winning campaign against a very tough opponent in Oklahoma. Kevin is a very successful businessman who will be a fantastic Governor. He is strong on Crime & Borders, the 2nd Amendment, & loves our Military & Vets. He has my complete and total Endorsement! [Twitter Web Client]

Aug 30, 2018 02:59:32 PM Throwback Thursday! #MAGA https://t.co/8slzITa1l6 [Media Studio]

Aug 30, 2018 08:50:40 PM Thank you Indiana, I love you! https://t.co/To6s9ViMj1 [Twitter for iPhone]

Aug 31, 2018 12:09:01 PM I will be doing a major rally for Senator Ted Cruz in October. I'm picking the biggest stadium in Texas we can find. As you know, Ted has my complete and total Endorsement. His opponent is a disaster for Texas - weak on Second Amendment, Crime, Borders, Military, and Vets! [Twitter for iPhone]

Aug 31, 2018 01:37:04 PM Wow, I made OFF THE RECORD COMMENTS to Bloomberg concerning Canada, and this powerful understanding was BLATANTLY VIOLATED. Oh well, just more dishonest reporting. I am used to it. At least Canada knows where I stand! [Twitter for iPhone]

⊔ Aug 31, 2018 05:07:25 PM "President Donald J. Trump is Strengthening Retirement Security for American Workers" https://t.co/cKeATuKXDe [Twitter for iPhone]

⊔ Aug 31, 2018 07:01:21 PM https://t.co/c79zLeREOA [Twitter for iPhone]

⊔ Aug 31, 2018 09:25:38 PM .@Rasmussen_Poll just came out at 48% approval rate despite the constant and intense Fake News. Higher than Election Day and higher than President Obama. Rasmussen was one of the most accurate Election Day polls! [Twitter for iPhone]

⊔ Aug 31, 2018 09:35:28 PM The ABC/Washington Post Poll was by far the least accurate one 2 weeks out from the 2016 Election. I call it a suppression poll - but by Election Day they brought us, out of shame, to about even. They will never learn! [Twitter for iPhone]

⊔ Aug 31, 2018 09:36:57 PM Great day in North Carolina where Republicans will do very well! [Twitter for iPhone]

⊔ Aug 31, 2018 09:40:23 PM Still can't believe that Bloomberg violated a firm OFF THE RECORD statement. Will they put out an apology? [Twitter for iPhone]

⊔ Sep 1, 2018 06:19:04 AM "I think today what has happened is that news reporting has become part of the adversary system." Alan Dershowitz It has become tainted and corrupt! DJT [Twitter for iPhone]

⊔ Sep 1, 2018 06:21:41 AM I love Canada, but they've taken advantage of our Country for many years! [Twitter for iPhone]

⊔ Sep 1, 2018 07:26:58 AM Report: There were no FISA hearings held over Spy documents."It is astonishing that the FISA courts couldn't hold hearings on Spy Warrants targeting Donald Trump. It isn't about Carter Page, it's about the Trump Campaign. You've got corruption at the DOJ & FBI. The leadership.... [Twitter for iPhone]

⊔ Sep 1, 2018 07:32:59 AM ....of the DOJ & FBI are completely out to lunch in terms of exposing and holding those accountable who are responsible for that corruption." @TomFitton @JudicialWatch [Twitter for iPhone]

⊔ Sep 1, 2018 08:19:20 AM "You have a Fake Dossier, gathered by Steele, paid by the Clinton team to get information on Trump. The Dossier is Fake, nothing in it has been verified. It then filters into our American court system in order to spy on Barrack Obama and Hillary Clinton's political opponent...... [Twitter for iPhone]

⊔ Sep 1, 2018 08:27:05 AM ....Donald Trump, and now we find out that there wasn't even a hearing - that Donald Trump's 4th Amendment right to privacy was signed away...and someone in there is swearing that this stuff is true, when it wasn't? This is the scandal here - a police state." Dan Bongino [Twitter for iPhone]

Sep 1, 2018 10:00:35 AM There is no political necessity to keep Canada in the new NAFTA deal. If we don't make a fair deal for the U.S. after decade of abuse, Canada will be out. Congress should not interfere with these negotiations or I will simply terminate NAFTA entirely & we will be far better off.. [Twitter for iPhone]

Sep 1, 2018 10:03:28 AM There is no political necessity to keep Canada in the new NAFTA deal. If we don't make a fair deal for the U.S. after decades of abuse, Canada will be out. Congress should not interfere w/ these negotiations or I will simply terminate NAFTA entirely & we will be far better off... [Twitter for iPhone]

Sep 1, 2018 10:12:25 AM ....Remember, NAFTA was one of the WORST Trade Deals ever made. The U.S. lost thousands of businesses and millions of jobs. We were far better off before NAFTA - should never have been signed. Even the Vat Tax was not accounted for. We make new deal or go back to pre-NAFTA! [Twitter for iPhone]

Sep 1, 2018 05:51:29 PM No Deal! Trade Talks with Canada Conclude for the Week with No Agreement | Breitbart https://t.co/87vi7OqopY via @BreitbartNews [Twitter for iPhone]

Sep 1, 2018 05:53:07 PM MAKE AMERICA GREAT AGAIN! [Twitter for iPhone]

Sep 1, 2018 05:55:29 PM We shouldn't have to buy our friends with bad Trade Deals and Free Military Protection! [Twitter for iPhone]

Sep 1, 2018 07:46:41 PM "There's no fairness here, if you're a Democrat or a friend of Hillary you get immunity or off scott free. If you're connected to Donald Trump, you get people like Robert Mueller & Andrew Weissman, and his team of partisans, coming after you with a vengeance and abusing their.... [Twitter for iPhone]

Sep 1, 2018 07:53:44 PM ....positions of power. That's part of the story of the Russia Hoax. Christopher Steele is on the payroll of Hillary Clinton & the FBI, & when they fired him for lying, they continued to use him. Violation of FBI regulations. Kept trying to verify the unverifiable." @GreggJarrett [Twitter for iPhone]

Sep 1, 2018 08:01:22 PM "No information was ever given by the Trump Team to Russia, yet the Hillary Clinton campaign paid for information from Kremlin sources and just washed it through an intermediary, Christopher Steele." Jesse Waters [Twitter for iPhone]

Sep 1, 2018 08:21:41 PM "There is no possible way the Trump Tower meeting between Don Trump jr and a couple of Russians, who have very deep connections to both the Clintons & Fusion GPS, & where no information on the Clintons was exchanged, is a crime. Dems are blinded by their hatred of Trump." Bongino [Twitter for iPhone]

Sep 1, 2018 08:23:02 PM RT @realDonaldTrump: We shouldn't have to buy our friends with bad Trade Deals and Free Military Protection! [Twitter for iPhone]

Sep 1, 2018 08:23:10 PM RT @realDonaldTrump: MAKE AMERICA GREAT AGAIN! [Twitter for iPhone]

Sep 1, 2018 08:43:29 PM RT @CoreyStewartVA: Federal workers endured 8 years of hell under Obama, with several rounds of pay freezes and benefit cuts. @realDonald... [Twitter for iPhone]

Sep 2, 2018 08:28:20 AM Tiger Woods showed great class in the way he answered the question about the Office of the Presidency and me. Now they say the so-called "left" is angry at him. So sad, but the "center & right" loves Tiger, Kanye, George Foreman, Jim Brown & so many other greats, even more....... [Twitter for iPhone]

Sep 2, 2018 08:37:51 AM ....The fact is that African/American unemployment is now the lowest in the history of our country. Same with Asian, Hispanic and almost every other group. The Democrats have been all talk and no action. My Administration has already produced like no other, and everyone sees it! [Twitter for iPhone]

Sep 2, 2018 09:10:17 AM RT @realDonaldTrump: .@Rasmussen_Poll just came out at 48% approval rate despite the constant and intense Fake News. Higher than Election D... [Twitter for iPhone]

Sep 3, 2018 06:01:44 AM RT @SecPompeo: On behalf of the American people, special thank you to @Commander_RS GEN Nicholson for his 2+ years of service leading @NATO... [Twitter for iPhone]

Sep 3, 2018 06:05:37 AM RT @CoreyStewartVA: About 200,000 #Virginia residents are federal workers; as I travel the state this #LaborDay weekend, Virginians are say... [Twitter for iPhone]

Sep 3, 2018 06:05:53 AM RT @CoreyStewartVA: In the U.S. Senate I'll be working WITH @realDonaldTrump on his #MAGA agenda -- and that includes having the backs of A... [Twitter for iPhone]

Sep 3, 2018 06:15:44 AM Richard Trumka, the head of the AFL-CIO, represented his union poorly on television this weekend. Some of the things he said were so againt the working men and women of our country, and the success of the U.S. itself, that it is easy to see why unions are doing so poorly. A Dem! [Twitter for iPhone]

Sep 3, 2018 06:28:14 AM Happy Labor Day! Our country is doing better than ever before with unemployment setting record lows. The U.S. has tremendous upside potential as we go about fixing some of the worst Trade Deals ever made by any country in the world. Big progress being made! [Twitter for iPhone]

Sep 3, 2018 07:23:33 AM The Worker in America is doing better than ever before. Celebrate Labor Day! [Twitter for iPhone]

Sep 3, 2018 10:28:33 AM Richard Trumka, the head of the AFL-CIO, represented his union poorly on television this weekend. Some of the things he said were so against the working men and women of our country, and the success of the U.S. itself, that it is easy to see why unions are doing so poorly. A Dem! [Twitter for iPhone]

Sep 3, 2018 12:50:01 PM The U.S. is respected again! https://t.co/NtQ4vsoqnk [Twitter for iPhone]

Sep 3, 2018 12:50:59 PM RT @WhiteHouse: In July, President Trump announced the Pledge to America's Workers. In little more than a month since, MILLIONS of new oppo... [Twitter for iPhone]

Sep 3, 2018 12:57:10 PM RT @IvankaTrump: Today, on #LaborDay, let's also recognize the amazing stay-at-home parents across America, who seldom receive the credit t... [Twitter for iPhone]

Sep 3, 2018 01:25:25 PM Two long running, Obama era, investigations of two very popular Republican Congressmen were brought to a well publicized charge, just ahead of the Mid-Terms, by the Jeff Sessions Justice Department. Two easy wins now in doubt because there is not enough time. Good job Jeff...... [Twitter for iPhone]

Sep 3, 2018 01:39:19 PM ....The Democrats, none of whom voted for Jeff Sessions, must love him now. Same thing with Lyin' James Comey. The Dems all hated him, wanted him out, thought he was disgusting - UNTIL I FIRED HIM! Immediately he became a wonderful man, a saint like figure in fact. Really sick! [Twitter for iPhone]

Sep 3, 2018 01:55:35 PM I see that John Kerry, the father of the now terminated Iran deal, is thinking of running for President. I should only be so lucky - although the field that is currently assembling looks really good - FOR ME! [Twitter for iPhone]

Sep 3, 2018 02:21:26 PM According to the Failing New York Times, the FBI started a major effort to flip Putin loyalists in 2014-2016. "It wasn't about Trump, he wasn't even close to a candidate yet." Rigged Witch Hunt! [Twitter for iPhone]

Sep 3, 2018 05:20:17 PM President Bashar al-Assad of Syria must not recklessly attack Idlib Province. The Russians and Iranians would be making a grave humanitarian mistake to take part in this potential human tragedy. Hundreds of thousands of people could be killed. Don't let that happen! [Twitter for iPhone]

Sep 4, 2018 09:58:21 AM NBC FAKE NEWS, which is under intense scrutiny over their killing the Harvey Weinstein story, is now fumbling around making excuses for their probably highly unethical conduct. I have long criticized NBC and their journalistic standards-worse than even CNN. Look at their license? [Twitter for iPhone]

☐ Sep 4, 2018 01:24:52 PM Everyone in the path of #Gordon please heed the advice of State and local officials and follow @NHC_Atlantic for updates. The Federal Government stands ready to assist. Be safe! https://t.co/sJiL4wnQID [Twitter for iPhone]

☐ Sep 4, 2018 03:40:28 PM Jon Kyl will be an extraordinary Senator representing an extraordinary state, Arizona. I look forward to working with him! [Twitter for iPhone]

☐ Sep 4, 2018 03:41:37 PM The Brett Kavanaugh hearings for the future Justice of the Supreme Court are truly a display of how mean, angry, and despicable the other side is. They will say anything, and are only.... [Twitter for iPhone]

☐ Sep 4, 2018 03:41:38 PM ....looking to inflict pain and embarrassment to one of the most highly renowned jurists to ever appear before Congress. So sad to see! [Twitter for iPhone]

☐ Sep 4, 2018 03:44:49 PM "Pledge to America's Workers" https://t.co/wbGZU6oi9G [Twitter for iPhone]

☐ Sep 4, 2018 03:55:41 PM Paul Cook is a decorated Marine Corps Veteran who loves and supports our Military and Vets. He is Strong on Crime, the Border, and supported Tax Cuts for the people of California. Paul has my total and complete Endorsement! [Twitter for iPhone]

☐ Sep 4, 2018 04:03:50 PM "Judge Brett Kavanaugh is an Exceptionally Qualified and Deserving Nominee for the Supreme Court" https://t.co/nD5XZo9yIm [Twitter for iPhone]

☐ Sep 4, 2018 05:37:09 PM Statement from Secretary of Defense, James Mattis: https://t.co/OneaxKCneV [Twitter for iPhone]

☐ Sep 4, 2018 05:38:06 PM Statement from White House Chief of Staff, General John Kelly: https://t.co/LUN8cDr3N5 [Twitter for iPhone]

☐ Sep 4, 2018 05:49:35 PM Statement from White House @PressSec, Sarah Sanders: https://t.co/mE73HSi6Rl [Twitter for iPhone]

☐ Sep 4, 2018 06:18:08 PM The Woodward book has already been refuted and discredited by General (Secretary of Defense) James Mattis and General (Chief of Staff) John Kelly. Their quotes were made up frauds, a con on the public. Likewise other stories and quotes. Woodward is a Dem operative? Notice timing? [Twitter for iPhone]

☐ Sep 4, 2018 09:50:19 PM Sleepy Eyes Chuck Todd of Fake NBC News said it's time for the Press to stop complaining and to start fighting back. Actually Chuck, they've been doing that from the day I announced for President. They've gone all out, and I WON, and now they're going CRAZY! [Twitter for iPhone]

Sep 4, 2018 10:01:43 PM The already discredited Woodward book, so many lies and phony sources, has me calling Jeff Sessions "mentally retarded" and "a dumb southerner." I said NEITHER, never used those terms on anyone, including Jeff, and being a southerner is a GREAT thing. He made this up to divide! [Twitter for iPhone]

Sep 4, 2018 10:32:16 PM Jim Mattis Calls Woodward Book 'Fiction': 'Product of Someone's Rich Imagination' https://t.co/HGMDiH98nx via @BreitbartNews [Twitter for iPhone]

Sep 4, 2018 10:35:30 PM "Secretary Mattis Nukes Woodward Allegations" https://t.co/H5bPjsVXNb [Twitter for iPhone]

Sep 5, 2018 06:33:18 AM Isn't it a shame that someone can write an article or book, totally make up stories and form a picture of a person that is literally the exact opposite of the fact, and get away with it without retribution or cost. Don't know why Washington politicians don't change libel laws? [Twitter for iPhone]

Sep 5, 2018 08:20:22 AM Almost everyone agrees that my Administration has done more in less than two years than any other Administration in the history of our Country. I'm tough as hell on people & if I weren't, nothing would get done. Also, I question everybody & everything-which is why I got elected! [Twitter for iPhone]

Sep 5, 2018 08:21:07 AM The Trump Economy is booming with help of House and Senate GOP. #FarmBill with SNAP work requirements will bolster farmers and get America back to work. Pass the Farm Bill with SNAP work requirements! [Twitter for iPhone]

Sep 5, 2018 08:39:54 AM Just like the NFL, whose ratings have gone WAY DOWN, Nike is getting absolutely killed with anger and boycotts. I wonder if they had any idea that it would be this way? As far as the NFL is concerned, I just find it hard to watch, and always will, until they stand for the FLAG! [Twitter for iPhone]

Sep 5, 2018 08:51:29 AM Thank you General Kelly, book is total fiction! https://t.co/J5iUONhRin [Twitter for iPhone]

Sep 5, 2018 08:54:35 AM Thank you General Mattis, book is boring & untrue! https://t.co/Bq79ZjF3Dk [Twitter for iPhone]

Sep 5, 2018 02:09:51 PM Join me tomorrow night at 7:00pm MDT in Billings, Montana for a MAKE AMERICA GREAT AGAIN RALLY! Get your tickets here: https://t.co/fyHduA2Peo [Twitter for iPhone]

Sep 5, 2018 04:10:01 PM Today, it was my honor to welcome the Amir of Kuwait to the @WhiteHouse! https://t.co/b5iqsajpOj https://t.co/8wtucJrtEl [Twitter for iPhone]

Sep 5, 2018 04:45:54 PM The Failing New York Times! https://t.co/SHsXvYKpBf [Twitter for iPhone]

Sep 5, 2018 05:15:09 PM TREASON? [Twitter for iPhone]

Sep 5, 2018 06:40:32 PM Does the so-called "Senior Administration Official" really exist, or is it just the Failing New York Times with another phony source? If the GUTLESS anonymous person does indeed exist, the Times must, for National Security purposes, turn him/her over to government at once! [Twitter for iPhone]

Sep 5, 2018 10:22:34 PM I'm draining the Swamp, and the Swamp is trying to fight back. Don't worry, we will win! [Twitter for iPhone]

Sep 6, 2018 05:58:41 AM Kim Jong Un of North Korea proclaims "unwavering faith in President Trump." Thank you to Chairman Kim. We will get it done together! [Twitter for iPhone]

Sep 6, 2018 06:19:30 AM The Deep State and the Left, and their vehicle, the Fake News Media, are going Crazy - & they don't know what to do. The Economy is booming like never before, Jobs are at Historic Highs, soon TWO Supreme Court Justices & maybe Declassification to find Additional Corruption. Wow! [Twitter for iPhone]

Sep 6, 2018 06:31:19 AM Cosumer confidence highest in 18 years, Atlanta Fed forecasts 4.7 GDP, manufacturing jobs highest in many years. "It's the story of the Trump Administration, the Economic Success, that's unnerving his detractors." @MariaBartiromo [Twitter for iPhone]

Sep 6, 2018 09:09:32 AM "The record is quite remarkable. The President has faithfully followed the agenda he campaigned on in 2016. People should focus on the results, and they're extraordinary!" James Freeman - Wall Street Journal [Twitter for iPhone]

Sep 6, 2018 12:16:12 PM Look forward to seeing everyone in Montana tonight! #MAGA https://t.co/fyHduA2Peo [Twitter for iPhone]

Sep 6, 2018 06:12:02 PM Are the investigative "journalists" of the New York Times going to investigate themselves - who is the anonymous letter writer? [Twitter for iPhone]

Sep 6, 2018 06:15:20 PM Landing in Montana now to support Matt Rosendale for U.S. Senate! #MAGA https://t.co/0MIEyWxMbW [Twitter for iPhone]

Sep 6, 2018 08:06:56 PM Getting ready to go on stage for Matt Rosendale, who will be a great Senator. Jon Tester has let the people of Montana down & does not deserve another six years. Matt is strong on Crime, the Borders, & will save your Second Amendment from the onslaught. Loves our Military & Vets! [Twitter for iPhone]

Sep 6, 2018 09:38:26 PM MAKE AMERICA GREAT AGAIN! https://t.co/RPOYiqsHHH [Twitter for iPhone]

Sep 6, 2018 09:48:03 PM Thank you Montana, I love you! https://t.co/9J4Xv2PoNw [Twitter for iPhone]

Sep 7, 2018 05:56:38 AM What was Nike thinking? [Twitter for iPhone]

Sep 7, 2018 06:11:49 AM Matt Rosendale will be a Great Senator from a Great State, Montana! He is a fighter who will be tough on Crime and the Border, fight hard for our 2nd Amendment and loves our Military and our Vets. He has my full and complete Endorsement! [Twitter for iPhone]

Sep 7, 2018 06:32:32 AM The Woodward book is a scam. I don't talk the way I am quoted. If I did I would not have been elected President. These quotes were made up. The author uses every trick in the book to demean and belittle. I wish the people could see the real facts - and our country is doing GREAT! [Twitter for iPhone]

Sep 7, 2018 11:35:57 AM Under our horrible immigration laws, the Government is frequently blocked from deporting criminal aliens with violent felony convictions. House GOP just passed a bill to increase our ability to deport violent felons (Crazy Dems opposed). Need to get this bill to my desk fast! [Twitter for iPhone]

Sep 7, 2018 03:16:18 PM "Unprecedented Jobs Growth Streak Continues as Wages Rise" https://t.co/Mk0WSyjdOe [Twitter for iPhone]

Sep 7, 2018 04:39:37 PM 14 days for $28 MILLION - $2 MILLION a day, No Collusion. A great day for America! [Twitter for iPhone]

Sep 7, 2018 08:03:45 PM RT @Scavino45: .@larry_kudlow: "Job gains, wage growth show Trump's economic boom continues" https://t.co/raDjFB3zrW [Twitter for iPhone]

Sep 7, 2018 08:17:26 PM RT @CalebJHull: "I complained plenty about Fox News, but I never threatened to shut them down." It's probably a good time to remind you th... [Twitter for iPhone]

Sep 7, 2018 08:17:59 PM RT @RichardGrenell: fact check: @realDonaldTrump kicked the Nazi out of NYC after 14 years and multiple Presidents allowed him to stay. htt... [Twitter for iPhone]

Sep 7, 2018 08:22:56 PM RT @ericbolling: Watching @BarackObama take credit for @realDonaldTrump successes is disgraceful. Score So Far- TRUMP: -Unemployment Rate... [Twitter for iPhone]

Sep 8, 2018 09:44:29 AM Dave Hughes is running for Congress in the Great State of Minnesota. He will help us accomplish our America First policies, is strong on Crime, the Border, our 2nd Amendmen, Trade, Military and Vets. Running against Pelosi Liberal Puppet Petterson. Dave has my Total Endorsement! [Twitter for iPhone]

Sep 8, 2018 09:47:08 AM "To this point, President Trump's achievements are unprecedented." @LouDobbs [Twitter for iPhone]

Sep 8, 2018 09:51:29 AM We are breaking all Jobs and Economic Records but, importantly, our Country has TREMENDOUS FUTURE POTENTIAL. We have just begun! [Twitter for iPhone]

Sep 8, 2018 10:45:28 AM Apple prices may increase because of the massive Tariffs we may be imposing on China - but there is an easy solution where there would be ZERO tax, and indeed a tax incentive. Make your products in the United States instead of China. Start building new plants now. Exciting! #MAGA [Twitter for iPhone]

Sep 8, 2018 04:08:41 PM So true! "Mr. Trump remains the single most popular figure in the Republican Party, whose fealty has helped buoy candidates in competitive Republican primaries and remains a hot commodity among general election candidates." Nicholas Fandos, @nytimes [Twitter for iPhone]

Sep 8, 2018 07:07:31 PM Our Social Media (and beyond) Stars, @DiamondandSilk, are terrific people who are doing really well. We are all very proud of them, and their great success! [Twitter for iPhone]

Sep 8, 2018 08:38:38 PM Republicans are doing really well with the Senate Midterms. Races that we were not even thinking about winning are now very close, or even leading. Election night will be very interesting indeed! [Twitter for iPhone]

Sep 8, 2018 08:47:25 PM The Dems have tried every trick in the playbook-call me everything under the sun. But if I'm all of those terrible things, how come I beat them so badly, 306-223? Maybe they're just not very good! The fact is they are going CRAZY only because they know they can't beat me in 2020! [Twitter for iPhone]

Sep 8, 2018 08:51:01 PM So nice, thank you both! https://t.co/IAskDJIILo [Twitter for iPhone]

Sep 8, 2018 08:54:14 PM RT @thejtlewis: @realDonaldTrump President Trump will win in 2020 in an even BIGGER landslide than 2016! You are the greatest President EVE... [Twitter for iPhone]

Sep 9, 2018 08:01:12 AM Happy Anniversary! #ProudDeplorable https://t.co/iHyeu5a8DD [Twitter for iPhone]

Sep 9, 2018 08:10:27 AM "Barrack Obama talked a lot about hope, but Donald Trump delivered the American Dream. All the economic indicators, what's happening overseas, Donald Trump has proven to be far more successful than Barrack Obama. President Trump is delivering the American Dream." Jason Chaffetz [Twitter for iPhone]

Sep 9, 2018 08:12:28 AM RT @realDonaldTrump: Happy Anniversary! #ProudDeplorable https://t.co/iHyeu5a8DD [Twitter for iPhone]

Sep 9, 2018 08:13:54 AM RT @DanScavino: https://t.co/VznqrCTR0C [Twitter for iPhone]

Sep 9, 2018 08:15:12 AM RT @realDonaldTrump: So true! "Mr. Trump remains the single most popular figure in the Republican Party, whose fealty has helped buoy candi... [Twitter for iPhone]

Sep 9, 2018 08:32:04 AM "Barack Obama talked a lot about hope, but Donald Trump delivered the American Dream. All the economic indicators, what's happening overseas, Donald Trump has proven to be far more successful than Barack Obama. President Trump is delivering the American Dream." Jason Chaffetz [Twitter for iPhone]

Sep 9, 2018 08:49:20 AM "Ford has abruptly killed a plan to sell a Chinese-made small vehicle in the U.S. because of the prospect of higher U.S. Tariffs." CNBC. This is just the beginning. This car can now be BUILT IN THE U.S.A. and Ford will pay no tariffs! [Twitter for iPhone]

Sep 9, 2018 09:01:06 AM If the U.S. sells a car into China, there is a tax of 25%. If China sells a car into the U.S., there is a tax of 2%. Does anybody think that is FAIR? The days of the U.S. being ripped-off by other nations is OVER! [Twitter for iPhone]

Sep 9, 2018 09:12:18 AM "Trump has set Economic Growth on fire. During his time in office, the economy has achieved feats most experts thought impossible. GDP is growing at a 3 percent-plus rate. The unemployment rate is near a 50 year low." CNBC...Also, the Stock Market is up almost 50% since Election! [Twitter for iPhone]

Sep 9, 2018 09:42:41 AM Wow, NFL first game ratings are way down over an already really bad last year comparison. Viewership declined 13%, the lowest in over a decade. If the players stood proudly for our Flag and Anthem, and it is all shown on broadcast, maybe ratings could come back? Otherwise worse! [Twitter for iPhone]

Sep 9, 2018 10:21:22 AM North Korea has just staged their parade, celebrating 70th anniversary of founding, without the customary display of nuclear missiles. Theme was peace and economic development. "Experts believe that North Korea cut out the nuclear missiles to show President Trump...... [Twitter for iPhone]

Sep 9, 2018 10:31:58 AM ...its commitment to denuclearize." @FoxNews This is a big and very positive statement from North Korea. Thank you To Chairman Kim. We will both prove everyone wrong! There is nothing like good dialogue from two people that like each other! Much better than before I took office. [Twitter for iPhone]

Sep 9, 2018 12:28:17 PM Melania and I wish all Jewish people Shana Tova and send our warmest greetings to those celebrating Rosh Hashanah and the start of the High Holy Days... https://t.co/uMrHHX5il0 [Twitter for iPhone]

Sep 10, 2018 06:03:40 AM The GDP Rate (4.2%) is higher than the Unemployment Rate (3.9%) for the first time in over 100 years! [Twitter for iPhone]

Sep 10, 2018 06:10:27 AM If the Democrats had won the Election in 2016, GDP, which was about 1% and going down, would have been minus 4% instead of up 4.2%. I opened up our beautiful economic engine with Regulation and Tax Cuts. Our system was choking and would have been made worse. Still plenty to do! [Twitter for iPhone]

Sep 10, 2018 06:22:29 AM The Woodward book is a Joke - just another assault against me, in a barrage of assaults, using now disproven unnamed and anonymous sources. Many have already come forward to say the quotes by them, like the book, are fiction. Dems can't stand losing. I'll write the real book! [Twitter for iPhone]

Sep 10, 2018 06:30:49 AM The White House is running beautifully. We are making some of the greatest and most important deals in our countries history - with many more to come. Big progress! [Twitter for iPhone]

Sep 10, 2018 06:35:54 AM The White House is a "smooth running machine." We are making some of the biggest and most important deals in our country's history - with many more to come! The Dems are going crazy! [Twitter for iPhone]

Sep 10, 2018 06:46:35 AM "I'm taking this book with a grain of salt & everyone should do the same. Multiple sources, but almost every one of them has come out and discredited the claims made by Woodward. You cannot take this book too seriously." Katelyn Caralle, Washington Examiner [Twitter for iPhone]

Sep 10, 2018 07:05:57 AM RT @trueamerica1st: https://t.co/po1LaCbWg1 [Twitter for iPhone]

Sep 10, 2018 07:06:02 AM RT @trueamerica1st: Welcome to 2018 NFL https://t.co/K6YJEc1IXi [Twitter for iPhone]

Sep 10, 2018 07:06:11 AM RT @trueamerica1st: Thank god for Trump! https://t.co/bnPaMHW3tB [Twitter for iPhone]

Sep 10, 2018 07:08:07 AM RT @trueamerica1st: Thank you @realDonaldTrump https://t.co/fpFwNqw5id [Twitter for iPhone]

Sep 10, 2018 07:08:26 AM RT @The_Trump_Train: @realDonaldTrump STAND FOR THE NATIONAL ANTHEM! https://t.co/oHk86YNi0v [Twitter for iPhone]

Sep 10, 2018 07:10:41 AM RT @realDonaldTrump: "Trump has set Economic Growth on fire. During his time in office, the economy has achieved feats most experts thought... [Twitter for iPhone]

Sep 10, 2018 07:11:37 AM RT @realDonaldTrump: The Woodward book is a scam. I don't talk the way I am quoted. If I did I would not have been elected President. These... [Twitter for iPhone]

Sep 10, 2018 07:36:53 AM "It is mostly anonymous sources in here, why should anyone trust you? General Mattis, General Kelly said it's not true." @SavannahGuthrie @TODAYshow Bob Woodward is a liar who is like a Dem operative prior to the Midterms. He was caught cold, even by NBC. [Twitter for iPhone]

Sep 10, 2018 08:57:18 AM The Economy is soooo good, perhaps the best in our country's history (remember, it's the economy stupid!), that the Democrats are flailing & lying like CRAZY! Phony books, articles and T.V. "hits" like no other pol has had to endure-and they are losing big. Very dishonest people! [Twitter for iPhone]

Sep 10, 2018 09:42:34 AM "President Trump would need a magic wand to get to 4% GDP," stated President Obama. I guess I have a magic wand, 4.2%, and we will do MUCH better than this! We have just begun. [Twitter for iPhone]

Sep 10, 2018 02:35:06 PM The Storms in the Atlantic are very dangerous. We encourage anyone in the path of these storms to prepare themselves and to heed the warnings of State and Local officials. The Federal Government is closely monitoring and ready to assist. We are with you! [Twitter for iPhone]

Sep 10, 2018 02:41:17 PM To the incredible citizens of North Carolina, South Carolina and the entire East Coast - the storm looks very bad! Please take all necessary precautions. We have already began mobilizing our assets to respond accordingly, and we are here for you! https://t.co/g74cyD6b6K [Twitter for iPhone]

Sep 10, 2018 04:18:22 PM Chuck Schumer is holding up 320 appointments (Ambassadors, Executives, etc.) of great people who have left jobs and given up so much in order to come into Government. Schumer and the Democrats continue to OBSTRUCT! [Twitter for iPhone]

Sep 10, 2018 04:52:11 PM Was just briefed via phone by @DHSgov @SecNielsen and @FEMA @FEMA_Brock, along with @VP Mike Pence and Chief of Staff, John Kelly on incoming storm which is very dangerous. Heed the directions of your State and Local Officials - and know that WE are here for you. Be SAFE! https://t.co/sN8D5NvrBa [Twitter for iPhone]

Sep 10, 2018 06:17:24 PM My people just informed me that this is one of the worst storms to hit the East Coast in many years. Also, looking like a direct hit on North Carolina, South Carolina and Virginia. Please be prepared, be careful and be SAFE! [Twitter for iPhone]

Sep 10, 2018 06:21:41 PM Just had calls with South Carolina Governor Henry McMaster, North Carolina Governor Roy Cooper, and Virginia Governor Ralph Northam regarding the incoming storm. Federal Government stands by, ready to assist 24/7. [Twitter for iPhone]

Sep 10, 2018 06:35:54 PM https://t.co/Vh47XjGzpt [Twitter for iPhone]

[] Sep 11, 2018 06:08:35 AM "We have found nothing to show collusion between President Trump & Russia, absolutely zero, but every day we get more documentation showing collusion between the FBI & DOJ, the Hillary campaign, foreign spies & Russians, incredible." @SaraCarterDC @LouDobbs [Twitter for iPhone]

[] Sep 11, 2018 06:12:31 AM #NeverForget #September11th https://t.co/ExGrrVtrEf [Twitter for iPhone]

[] Sep 11, 2018 06:19:19 AM New Strzok-Page texts reveal "Media Leak Strategy." @FoxNews So terrible, and NOTHING is being done at DOJ or FBI - but the world is watching, and they get it completely. [Twitter for iPhone]

[] Sep 11, 2018 06:41:33 AM "ERIC Holder could be running the Justice Department right now and it would be behaving no differently than it is." @LouDobbs [Twitter for iPhone]

[] Sep 11, 2018 06:59:08 AM Rudy Giuliani did a GREAT job as Mayor of NYC during the period of September 11th. His leadership, bravery and skill must never be forgotten. Rudy is a TRUE WARRIOR! [Twitter for iPhone]

[] Sep 11, 2018 07:24:52 AM Departing Washington, D.C. to attend a Flight 93 September 11th Memorial Service in Shanksville, Pennsylvania with Melania. #NeverForget https://t.co/O2sFUeRqeb [Twitter for iPhone]

[] Sep 11, 2018 07:58:10 AM 17 years since September 11th! [Twitter for iPhone]

[] Sep 11, 2018 10:32:28 AM #NeverForget #September11th https://t.co/l8WZer3UOL [Twitter for iPhone]

[] Sep 11, 2018 11:48:49 AM Small Business Optimism Soars to Highest Level Ever | Breitbart https://t.co/T6rFhfPz6n via @BreitbartNews [Twitter for iPhone]

[] Sep 11, 2018 03:16:49 PM The safety of American people is my absolute highest priority. Heed the directions of your State and Local Officials. Please be prepared, be careful and be SAFE! https://t.co/YP7ssITwW9 https://t.co/LZIUCgdPTH [Twitter for iPhone]

[] Sep 11, 2018 05:51:35 PM RT @WhiteHouse: .@realDonaldTrump and @FLOTUS visited the Flight 93 National Memorial in Pennsylvania this morning to honor the memories of… [Twitter for iPhone]

[] Sep 11, 2018 07:19:43 PM #NeverForget #September11th https://t.co/POd8D1WfBa [Twitter for iPhone]

[] Sep 11, 2018 08:16:06 PM "You know who's at fault for this more than anyone else, Comey, because he leaked information and laundered it through a professor at Columbia Law School. Shame on that professor, and shame on Comey. He snuck the information to a law professor who collaborated with him in........ [Twitter for iPhone]

Sep 11, 2018 08:28:29 PM ....giving the information, and causing the appointment of a Special C without having the courage of his own convictions....." Alan Dershowitz @TuckerCarlson In other words, the whole thing was illegally and very unfairly set up? [Twitter for iPhone]

Sep 11, 2018 08:55:10 PM Crazy Maxine Waters: "After we impeach Trump, we'll go after Mike Pence. We'll get him." @FoxNews Where are the Democrats coming from? The best Economy in the history of our country would totally collapse if they ever took control! [Twitter for iPhone]

Sep 12, 2018 05:30:15 AM "The President has absolutely demonstrated no wrongdoing whatsoever & that the Special Counsel has no evidence of any wrongdoing. In other words, it's time to end this Witch Hunt." @LouDobbs Russian "collusion" was just an excuse by the Democrats for having lost the Election! [Twitter for iPhone]

Sep 12, 2018 05:51:59 AM We got A Pluses for our recent hurricane work in Texas and Florida (and did an unappreciated great job in Puerto Rico, even though an inaccessible island with very poor electricity and a totally incompetent Mayor of San Juan). We are ready for the big one that is coming! [Twitter for iPhone]

Sep 12, 2018 05:58:43 AM Hurricane Florence is looking even bigger than anticipated. It will be arriving soon. FEMA, First Responders and Law Enforcement are supplied and ready. Be safe! [Twitter for iPhone]

Sep 12, 2018 06:03:39 AM https://t.co/54YVC4DDfe [Twitter for iPhone]

Sep 12, 2018 08:58:01 AM Hurricane Florence may now be dipping a bit south and hitting a portion of the Great State of Georgia. Be ready, be prepared! [Twitter for iPhone]

Sep 12, 2018 09:06:15 AM "I can say, as it relates to the Senate Intelligence Committee Investigation, that we have NO hard evidence of Collusion." Richard Burr (R-NC) Senate Intelligence Committee, Chairman [Twitter for iPhone]

Sep 12, 2018 11:37:33 AM It is imperative that everyone follow local evacuation orders. This storm is extremely dangerous. Be SAFE! #HurricaneFlorence https://t.co/94Ue4e26PD https://t.co/KvF54CwomW [Twitter for iPhone]

Sep 12, 2018 06:16:36 PM #HurricaneFlorence https://t.co/mP7icn0Yzl https://t.co/jOdKT02rbH [Twitter for iPhone]

Sep 12, 2018 06:21:38 PM Tonight, it was my great honor to host a Congressional Medal of Honor Society Reception at the @WhiteHouse! https://t.co/75JQiVtnUT [Twitter for iPhone]

Sep 13, 2018 06:22:00 AM The problem with banker Jamie Dimon running for President is that he doesn't have the aptitude or "smarts" & is a poor public speaker & nervous mess - otherwise he is wonderful. I've made a lot of bankers, and others, look much smarter than they are with my great economic policy! [Twitter for iPhone]

Sep 13, 2018 06:39:42 AM We are completely ready for hurricane Florence, as the storm gets even larger and more powerful. Be careful! [Twitter for iPhone]

Sep 13, 2018 07:06:15 AM More text messages between former FBI employees Peter Strzok and Lisa Page are a disaster and embarrassment to the FBI & DOJ. This should never have happened but we are learning more and more by the hour. "Others were leaking like mad" in order to get the President! .... [Twitter for iPhone]

Sep 13, 2018 07:10:19 AM ....."It is a cesspool of corruption, and the people who did this need to be brought to justice." @GreggJarrett [Twitter for iPhone]

Sep 13, 2018 07:16:11 AM RT @realDonaldTrump: "We have found nothing to show collusion between President Trump & Russia, absolutely zero, but every day we get more... [Twitter for iPhone]

Sep 13, 2018 07:16:19 AM RT @realDonaldTrump: https://t.co/Vh47XjGzpt [Twitter for iPhone]

Sep 13, 2018 07:17:24 AM RT @realDonaldTrump: "President Trump would need a magic wand to get to 4% GDP," stated President Obama. I guess I have a magic wand, 4.2%,... [Twitter for iPhone]

Sep 13, 2018 07:18:35 AM RT @realDonaldTrump: "I can say, as it relates to the Senate Intelligence Committee Investigation, that we have NO hard evidence of Collusi... [Twitter for iPhone]

Sep 13, 2018 07:25:25 AM "Middle-Class Income Hits All-Time High!" @foxandfriends And will continue to rise (unless the Dems get in and destroy what we have built). [Twitter for iPhone]

Sep 13, 2018 07:37:27 AM 3000 people did not die in the two hurricanes that hit Puerto Rico. When I left the Island, AFTER the storm had hit, they had anywhere from 6 to 18 deaths. As time went by it did not go up by much. Then, a long time later, they started to report really large numbers, like 3000... [Twitter for iPhone]

Sep 13, 2018 07:49:12 AM .....This was done by the Democrats in order to make me look as bad as possible when I was successfully raising Billions of Dollars to help rebuild Puerto Rico. If a person died for any reason, like old age, just add them onto the list. Bad politics. I love Puerto Rico! [Twitter for iPhone]

Sep 13, 2018 08:41:44 AM RT @fema: Storm surge is deadly. Anyone in an evacuation zone in the Carolinas and Virginia must leave NOW if they haven't yet. #Florence h... [Twitter for iPhone]

Sep 13, 2018 09:15:55 AM The Wall Street Journal has it wrong, we are under no pressure to make a deal with China, they are under pressure to make a deal with us. Our markets are surging, theirs are collapsing. We will soon be taking in Billions in Tariffs & making products at home. If we meet, we meet? [Twitter for iPhone]

Sep 13, 2018 10:14:54 AM Thank you @USCG! https://t.co/PqddsoZg2I [Twitter for iPhone]

Sep 13, 2018 12:26:22 PM I was just briefed on Hurricane Florence. FEMA, First Responders and Law Enforcement are supplied and ready. We are with you! https://t.co/mP7icn0Yzl https://t.co/a8KQ0lcoSD [Twitter for iPhone]

Sep 13, 2018 12:41:40 PM Thank you @USNationalGuard! #HurricaneFlorence https://t.co/4xWFr1jz9I [Twitter for iPhone]

Sep 13, 2018 12:56:41 PM Senator Debbie Stabenow and the Democrats are totally against approving the Farm Bill. They are fighting tooth and nail to not allow our Great Farmers to get what they so richly deserve. Work requirements are imperative and the Dems are a NO. Not good! [Twitter for iPhone]

Sep 13, 2018 07:11:31 PM RT @DanScavino: Jamie Dimon loves President Trump. If he were to run in 2020, he'd have a ZERO percent chance. ¯_(ツ)_/¯ https://t.co/R5d63… [Twitter for iPhone]

Sep 13, 2018 07:11:52 PM RT @NWS: Important note as #Florence continues to close in on the Carolina coastline, storm surge is not just an "ocean" problem tonight. S… [Twitter for iPhone]

Sep 13, 2018 07:28:12 PM RT @LouDobbs: #FakeNews- The Hurricane Maria death tolls have been inflated & President @realDonaldTrump was right to call out organization… [Twitter for iPhone]

Sep 13, 2018 08:10:33 PM John Kerry had illegal meetings with the very hostile Iranian Regime, which can only serve to undercut our great work to the detriment of the American people. He told them to wait out the Trump Administration! Was he registered under the Foreign Agents Registration Act? BAD! [Twitter for iPhone]

Sep 13, 2018 09:37:22 PM Gina is Great! https://t.co/TyLQ2W42y5 [Twitter for iPhone]

Sep 14, 2018 06:28:05 AM RT @fema: Stay safe and shelter away from windows on the lowest floor that's not subject to flooding. If you get trapped in a flooded build… [Twitter for iPhone]

Sep 14, 2018 06:28:33 AM RT @NCDOT: We cannot share this enough: In case of flooding, MOVE TO HIGHER GROUND. And DO NOT DRIVE into standing or flooded water. If you… [Twitter for iPhone]

Sep 14, 2018 06:28:53 AM RT @VDEM: For travel information call 5-1-1 or follow local VDOT social media accounts. To find out how Hurricane Florence impacts your are… [Twitter for iPhone]

⬜ Sep 14, 2018 06:29:18 AM RT @SCEMD: As #HurricaneFlorence begins to affect #SC, residents who were unable to evacuate should stay indoors during the #hurricane & aw... [Twitter for iPhone]

⬜ Sep 14, 2018 06:31:06 AM RT @SCEMD: 6 inches of moving water can knock an adult off their feet. STAY AWAY from moving water! #FloodSafety #Florence #HurricaneFloren... [Twitter for iPhone]

⬜ Sep 14, 2018 06:31:46 AM RT @DHSgov: North Carolina iTunes: https://t.co/ikyhB27ZO8 Google Play: https://t.co/qfFgjM7C03 Virginia iTunes: https://t.co/Eu4YVGqFsh G... [Twitter for iPhone]

⬜ Sep 14, 2018 06:32:18 AM RT @DHSgov: For those in the path of Hurricane #Florence, make sure you have downloaded your states (SC, NC, VA) official emergency app + t... [Twitter for iPhone]

⬜ Sep 14, 2018 06:32:35 AM RT @RedCross: More than 1,500 Red Cross disaster workers are helping #HurricaneFlorence relief efforts. Some 80 emergency response vehicles... [Twitter for iPhone]

⬜ Sep 14, 2018 06:33:11 AM RT @NHC_Atlantic: Do not focus on the wind speed category of #Hurricane #Florence! Life-threatening storm surge flooding, catastrophic fla... [Twitter for iPhone]

⬜ Sep 14, 2018 06:33:31 AM RT @fema: If you're in a mandatory evacuation zone for #Florence, your window of time to leave is closing rapidly. Here are the zones for S... [Twitter for iPhone]

⬜ Sep 14, 2018 06:33:46 AM RT @HHSGov: If you're ordered to evacuate ahead of #HurricaneFlorence: ➡️⬜ Take only essential items ➡️⬜ Turn off the gas, electricity, an... [Twitter for iPhone]

⬜ Sep 14, 2018 06:34:26 AM RT @RedCross: We are on the ground helping prepare for #HurricaneFlorence. More than 1,600 people spent last night in 36 Red Cross and comm... [Twitter for iPhone]

⬜ Sep 14, 2018 06:35:02 AM RT @FEMAespanol: Hoy es el último día para desalojar. Si está en la ruta de #Florence, escuche a las autoridades locales para órdenes de de... [Twitter for iPhone]

⬜ Sep 14, 2018 06:35:40 AM RT @fema: We have created a rumor control page for Hurricane #Florence that will be updated regularly. During disasters, it's critical to a... [Twitter for iPhone]

⬜ Sep 14, 2018 06:37:48 AM RT @USNationalGuard: Today, nearly 3,000 National Guard members from Guam, Hawaii, Maryland, North Carolina, South Carolina and Virginia ar... [Twitter for iPhone]

⬜ Sep 14, 2018 07:19:59 AM Incredible job being done by FEMA, First Responders, Law Enforcement and all. Thank you! [Twitter for iPhone]

⬜ Sep 14, 2018 08:29:32 AM RT @NHC_Atlantic: NEW: #Hurricane #Florence has made landfall near Wrightsville Beach, North Carolina at 7:15 AM EDT (1115 UTC) with estima... [Twitter for iPhone]

⬜ Sep 14, 2018 08:29:42 AM RT @NCEmergency: #FlorenceNC safety tips: - STAY INDOORS. Do not venture out during the storm. - Do NOT drive or walk through stagnant or m… [Twitter for iPhone]

⬜ Sep 14, 2018 11:44:56 AM RT @NCEmergency: Use these resources to get help or more info. For emergencies, call 911. To receive info on shelters, evacuations & storm… [Twitter for iPhone]

⬜ Sep 14, 2018 12:04:12 PM RT @DeptofDefense: More than 7,000 #ServiceMembers, @USNationalGuard and #ActiveDuty, are standing by to assist as #HurricaneFlorence hits… [Twitter for iPhone]

⬜ Sep 14, 2018 04:34:15 PM RT @NOAASatellites: #GOESEast captured these two dramatic views of #HurricaneFlorence shortly after the storm made landfall near Wrightsvil… [Twitter for iPhone]

⬜ Sep 14, 2018 04:40:28 PM We love the #CajunNavy - THANK YOU! #FlorenceHurricane2018 https://t.co/RuP55jWX8e [Twitter for iPhone]

⬜ Sep 14, 2018 04:42:32 PM RT @fema: Over 1,150 @FEMA Urban Search and Rescue personnel are integrated with state & local teams in NC, SC, & VA to help with rescues a… [Twitter for iPhone]

⬜ Sep 14, 2018 04:43:43 PM Keep up the great work - THANK YOU! https://t.co/qCKts6CfN4 [Twitter for iPhone]

⬜ Sep 14, 2018 05:35:00 PM "They say all these people died in the storm in Puerto Rico, yet 70% of the power was out before the storm. So when did people start dying? At what point do you recognize that what they are doing is a political agenda couched in the nice language of journalism?" @GeraldoRivera [Twitter for iPhone]

⬜ Sep 14, 2018 07:31:40 PM "The story of Puerto Rico is the rebuilding that has occurred. The President has done an extraordinary job of cleanup, rebuilding electrical stuff and everything else." @EdRollins "The people of Puerto Rico have one of the most corrupt governments in our country." @LouDobbs [Twitter for iPhone]

⬜ Sep 14, 2018 07:43:59 PM My thoughts and prayers are with Evelyn Rodriguez this evening, along with her family and friends. #RIPEvelyn https://t.co/wMwxRdjBHM [Twitter for iPhone]

⬜ Sep 14, 2018 08:54:17 PM Great job FEMA, First Responders and Law Enforcement - not easy, very dangerous, tremendous talent. America is proud of you. Keep it all going - finish strong! [Twitter for iPhone]

⬜ Sep 14, 2018 09:05:02 PM "When Trump visited the island territory last October, OFFICIALS told him in a briefing 16 PEOPLE had died from Maria." The Washington Post. This was long AFTER the hurricane took place. Over many months it went to 64 PEOPLE. Then, like magic, "3000 PEOPLE KILLED." They hired…. [Twitter for iPhone]

Sep 14, 2018 09:23:26 PM ....GWU Research to tell them how many people had died in Puerto Rico (how would they not know this?). This method was never done with previous hurricanes because other jurisdictions know how many people were killed. FIFTY TIMES LAST ORIGINAL NUMBER - NO WAY! [Twitter for iPhone]

Sep 14, 2018 10:08:11 PM When President Obama said that he has been to "57 States," very little mention in Fake News Media. Can you imagine if I said that...story of the year! @IngrahamAngle [Twitter for iPhone]

Sep 15, 2018 03:26:44 PM Thank you @nycemergencymgt! https://t.co/8jR4DLm99t [Twitter for iPhone]

Sep 15, 2018 03:30:46 PM RT @NCEmergency: New Evacuation Orders are in place. Go to https://t.co/Yx3twhyOqj to see if you are in an area with a mandatory or volunte... [Twitter for iPhone]

Sep 15, 2018 03:41:45 PM Thank you Brock – it is my honor! "We (@FEMA) have never had the support that we have had from this President." Administrator @FEMA_Brock [Twitter for iPhone]

Sep 15, 2018 03:43:58 PM Congressman Pete Sessions of Texas is doing a great job. He is a fighter who will be tough on Crime and the Border, fight hard for our Second Amendment and loves our Military and our Vets. He has my full and complete Endorsement! [Twitter for iPhone]

Sep 15, 2018 03:54:31 PM Congressman Keith Rothfus continues to do a great job for the people of Pennsylvania. Keith is strong on Crime, the Border, and our Second Amendment. Loves our Military and our Vets. He has my total Endorsement! [Twitter for iPhone]

Sep 15, 2018 03:57:48 PM .@DannyTarkanian of Nevada is a great friend who supports the Trump Agenda. He is Strong on Crime, the Border and our under siege 2nd Amendment. Danny Loves our Military and our Vets. He has my total and complete Endorsement! [Twitter for iPhone]

Sep 15, 2018 05:08:30 PM While my (our) poll numbers are good, with the Economy being the best ever, if it weren't for the Rigged Russian Witch Hunt, they would be 25 points higher! Highly conflicted Bob Mueller & the 17 Angry Democrats are using this Phony issue to hurt us in the Midterms. No Collusion! [Twitter for iPhone]

Sep 15, 2018 05:38:35 PM When will Republican leadership learn that they are being played like a fiddle by the Democrats on Border Security and Building the Wall? Without Borders, we don't have a country. With Open Borders, which the Democrats want, we have nothing but crime! Finish the Wall! [Twitter for iPhone]

Sep 15, 2018 05:42:10 PM Five deaths have been recorded thus far with regard to hurricane Florence! Deepest sympathies and warmth go out to the families and friends of the victims. May God be with them! [Twitter for iPhone]

Sep 15, 2018 07:50:51 PM RT @fema: ⚡ "Hurricane Florence Response" Disaster response requires teamwork and coordination at all levels. Check out the incredible t… [Twitter for iPhone]

Sep 15, 2018 09:27:07 PM Exclusive -- Donald Trump Jr. to Obama: My Dad Fixed the Economy You Could Not https://t.co/HXuSBGFmf2 via @BreitbartNews [Twitter for iPhone]

Sep 16, 2018 09:20:07 AM The illegal Mueller Witch Hunt continues in search of a crime. There was never Collusion with Russia, except by the Clinton campaign, so the 17 Angry Democrats are looking at anything they can find. Very unfair and BAD for the country. ALSO, not allowed under the LAW! [Twitter for iPhone]

Sep 16, 2018 11:09:08 AM FEMA, First Responders and Law Enforcement are working really hard on hurricane Florence. As the storm begins to finally recede, they will kick into an even higher gear. Very Professional! [Twitter for iPhone]

Sep 16, 2018 11:25:19 AM Just watched Sunday Morning Futures with @MariaBartiromo on @FoxNews. This show is MANDATORY watching if you want to understand the massive governmental corruption and the Russian Hoax. It will be rebroadcast this evening at 6:00 P.M. on @FoxBusiness. A must see! [Twitter for iPhone]

Sep 16, 2018 12:39:05 PM RT @FoxNews: .@DevinNunes: "I think full transparency is in order here." #SundayFutures @MariaBartiromo https://t.co/RmjFNRysWN [Twitter for iPhone]

Sep 16, 2018 04:28:46 PM Congratulations to all of our Mexican friends on National Independence Day. We will be doing great things together! [Twitter for iPhone]

Sep 16, 2018 04:40:19 PM Watch @MariaBartiromo at 6:00 P.M. on @FoxBusiness. Russian Hoax the big topic! Mainstream Media, often referred to as the Fake News Media, hates to discuss the real facts! [Twitter for iPhone]

Sep 16, 2018 05:18:10 PM Best economic numbers in decades. If the Democrats take control, kiss your newfound wealth goodbye! [Twitter for iPhone]

Sep 16, 2018 08:06:27 PM Consumer Sentiment hit its highest level in 17 years this year. Sentiment fell 11% in 2015, an Obama year, and rose 16% since the Election, #TrumpTime! [Twitter for iPhone]

Sep 17, 2018 04:39:15 AM RT @FEMAespanol: Por favor comparta este mensaje de seguridad y exhorte a todos estar pendientes a las predicciones del clima. #Florence co… [Twitter for iPhone]

Sep 17, 2018 04:40:16 AM RT @FEMAespanol: #Florence sigue causando inundaciones repentinas y tornados. Manténgase seguro y asegúrese de recibir actualizaciones por… [Twitter for iPhone]

Sep 17, 2018 04:41:57 AM RT @SCNationalGuard: #SCGuard Soldiers w/4-118 Combined Arms Battalion conducted high water rescue & evacuation in Chesterfield County S.C... [Twitter for iPhone]

Sep 17, 2018 04:42:54 AM RT @Norad_Northcom: "I would like to highlight the incredible work that is being done by the state & local first responders. We are posture... [Twitter for iPhone]

Sep 17, 2018 04:43:10 AM RT @DeptofDefense: #Pets are family, too. 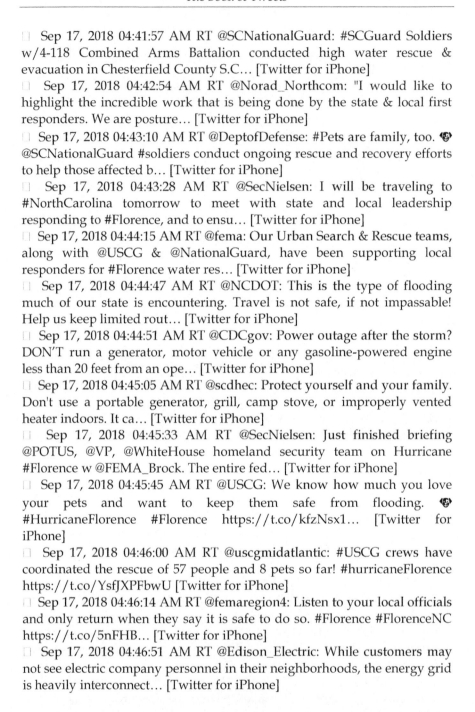 @SCNationalGuard #soldiers conduct ongoing rescue and recovery efforts to help those affected b... [Twitter for iPhone]

Sep 17, 2018 04:43:28 AM RT @SecNielsen: I will be traveling to #NorthCarolina tomorrow to meet with state and local leadership responding to #Florence, and to ensu... [Twitter for iPhone]

Sep 17, 2018 04:44:15 AM RT @fema: Our Urban Search & Rescue teams, along with @USCG & @NationalGuard, have been supporting local responders for #Florence water res... [Twitter for iPhone]

Sep 17, 2018 04:44:47 AM RT @NCDOT: This is the type of flooding much of our state is encountering. Travel is not safe, if not impassable! Help us keep limited rout... [Twitter for iPhone]

Sep 17, 2018 04:44:51 AM RT @CDCgov: Power outage after the storm? DON'T run a generator, motor vehicle or any gasoline-powered engine less than 20 feet from an ope... [Twitter for iPhone]

Sep 17, 2018 04:45:05 AM RT @scdhec: Protect yourself and your family. Don't use a portable generator, grill, camp stove, or improperly vented heater indoors. It ca... [Twitter for iPhone]

Sep 17, 2018 04:45:33 AM RT @SecNielsen: Just finished briefing @POTUS, @VP, @WhiteHouse homeland security team on Hurricane #Florence w @FEMA_Brock. The entire fed... [Twitter for iPhone]

Sep 17, 2018 04:45:45 AM RT @USCG: We know how much you love your pets and want to keep them safe from flooding. 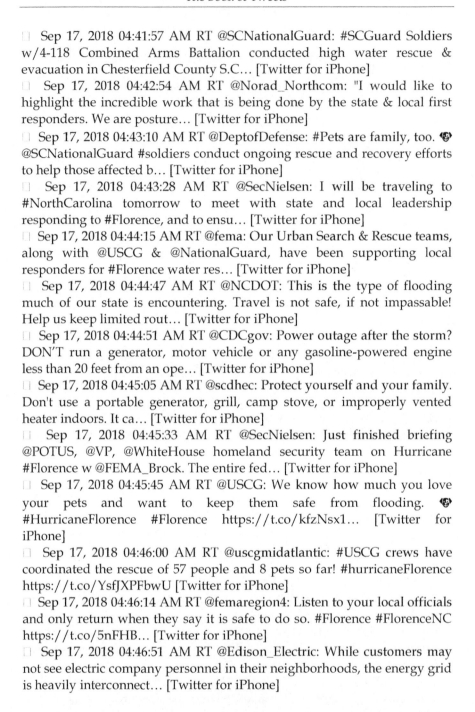 #HurricaneFlorence #Florence https://t.co/kfzNsx1... [Twitter for iPhone]

Sep 17, 2018 04:46:00 AM RT @uscgmidatlantic: #USCG crews have coordinated the rescue of 57 people and 8 pets so far! #hurricaneFlorence https://t.co/YsfJXPFbwU [Twitter for iPhone]

Sep 17, 2018 04:46:14 AM RT @femaregion4: Listen to your local officials and only return when they say it is safe to do so. #Florence #FlorenceNC https://t.co/5nFHB... [Twitter for iPhone]

Sep 17, 2018 04:46:51 AM RT @Edison_Electric: While customers may not see electric company personnel in their neighborhoods, the energy grid is heavily interconnect... [Twitter for iPhone]

Sep 17, 2018 04:47:07 AM RT @CBPFlorida: us@CBP personnel and assets are in place responding with @fema. Aircrews and teams□ from across the country are staging at… [Twitter for iPhone]

Sep 17, 2018 04:47:32 AM RT @DHSgov: If you see something, tell local authorities who or what you saw; when you saw it; where it occurred; and why it's suspicious.… [Twitter for iPhone]

Sep 17, 2018 04:48:08 AM RT @fema: Rain from #Florence these next few days will cause flooding in many parts of the Carolinas. Expect flash flooding at any time and… [Twitter for iPhone]

Sep 17, 2018 05:01:30 AM "A lot of small & medium size enterprises are registering very good profit, sometimes record profits-there stocks are doing very well, low income workers are getting big raises. There are an awful lot of good things going on that weren't during Pres. Obama's Watch." Peter Morici [Twitter for iPhone]

Sep 17, 2018 05:11:31 AM Tariffs have put the U.S. in a very strong bargaining position, with Billions of Dollars, and Jobs, flowing into our Country - and yet cost increases have thus far been almost unnoticeable. If countries will not make fair deals with us, they will be "Tariffed!" [Twitter for iPhone]

Sep 17, 2018 05:15:52 AM Our Steel Industry is the talk of the World. It has been given new life, and is thriving. Billions of Dollars is being spent on new plants all around the country! [Twitter for iPhone]

Sep 17, 2018 09:23:27 AM "Lisa Page Testimony- NO EVIDENCE OF COLLUSION BEFORE MUELLER APPOINTMENT." @FoxNews by Catherine Herridge. Therefore, the case should never have been allowed to be brought. It is a totally illegal Witch Hunt! [Twitter for iPhone]

Sep 17, 2018 09:36:06 AM Immediately after Comey's firing Peter Strzok texted to his lover, Lisa Page "We need to Open the case we've been waiting on now while Andy (McCabe, also fired) is acting. Page answered, "We need to lock in (redacted). In a formal chargeable way. Soon." Wow, a conspiracy caught? [Twitter for iPhone]

Sep 17, 2018 01:10:09 PM Americans deserve to know the lowest drug price at their pharmacy, but "gag clauses" prevent your pharmacist from telling you! I support legislation that will remove gag clauses and urge the Senate to act. #AmericanPatientsFirst [Twitter for iPhone]

Sep 17, 2018 01:22:01 PM Join me in Las Vegas, Nevada at 7:00pm for a MAKE AMERICA GREAT AGAIN RALLY! Tickets: https://t.co/keENWZEd0F https://t.co/xJzQ9foOTL [Twitter for iPhone]

Sep 17, 2018 02:27:38 PM Happy Constitution Day! https://t.co/9KiLowP3Hh [Twitter for iPhone]

Sep 17, 2018 03:53:51 PM https://t.co/Vu2b2hhwHu [Twitter for iPhone]

Sep 17, 2018 04:53:11 PM It was my great honor to host today's Inaugural Meeting of the "President's National Council for the American Worker" in the Roosevelt Room! Read more: https://t.co/mi7MVljnBa https://t.co/vyvlw2YP91 [Twitter for iPhone]

Sep 17, 2018 05:07:35 PM Just met John James of Michigan. He has every single quality to be your next Great Senator from Michigan. When the people of Michigan get to know John, they will say he is a true star. Also, distinguished Military and a Combat Vet! https://t.co/thRBoBkuFL [Twitter for iPhone]

Sep 17, 2018 07:21:09 PM Today, as we celebrate Hispanic Heritage Month, we share our gratitude for all the ways Hispanic-Americans make our country flourish and prosper. Today, and every day, we honor, cherish, and celebrate Hispanic-American Workers, Families, Students, Businesses, and Leaders... https://t.co/2AxlbluB2S [Twitter for iPhone]

Sep 18, 2018 07:42:02 AM "What will be disclosed is that there was no basis for these FISA Warrants, that the important information was kept from the court, there's going to be a disproportionate influence of the (Fake) Dossier. Basically you have a counter terrorism tool used to spy on a presidential... [Twitter for iPhone]

Sep 18, 2018 07:45:09 AM ....campaign, which is unprecedented in our history." Congressman Peter King Really bad things were happening, but they are now being exposed. Big stuff! [Twitter for iPhone]

Sep 18, 2018 07:50:29 AM China has openly stated that they are actively trying to impact and change our election by attacking our farmers, ranchers and industrial workers because of their loyalty to me. What China does not understand is that these people are great patriots and fully understand that..... [Twitter for iPhone]

Sep 18, 2018 07:55:04 AM .....China has been taking advantage of the United States on Trade for many years. They also know that I am the one that knows how to stop it. There will be great and fast economic retaliation against China if our farmers, ranchers and/or industrial workers are targeted! [Twitter for iPhone]

Sep 18, 2018 08:26:09 AM Happy 71st Birthday to our GREAT United States Air Force! https://t.co/r9Sa7DJQ76 [Twitter for iPhone]

Sep 18, 2018 10:50:55 AM Right now, everybody is saying what a great job we are doing with Hurricane Florence – and they are 100% correct. But don't be fooled, at some point in the near future the Democrats will start ranting... [Twitter for iPhone]

Sep 18, 2018 10:50:57 AM ...that FEMA, our Military, and our First Responders, who are all unbelievable, are a disaster and not doing a good job. This will be a total lie, but that's what they do, and everybody knows it! [Twitter for iPhone]

⬜ Sep 18, 2018 10:59:58 AM Thank you to our great Coast Guard for doing such a tremendous job - thousands of lives being saved! https://t.co/Ud8AT1orf8 https://t.co/YEFnGMmwoV [Twitter for iPhone]

⬜ Sep 18, 2018 01:21:47 PM Today, I took action to strengthen our Nation's defenses against biological threats. For the first time in history, the Federal Government has a National Biodefense Strategy to address the FULL RANGE of biological threats! https://t.co/kW7Ug1DA6q [Twitter for iPhone]

⬜ Sep 18, 2018 04:20:46 PM Today, it was my great honor to welcome @prezydentpl Andrzej Duda of Poland to the @WhiteHouse! https://t.co/VdsTYdq9MN [Twitter for iPhone]

⬜ Sep 18, 2018 06:42:22 PM https://t.co/G0BjCXEnaX [Twitter for iPhone]

⬜ Sep 18, 2018 10:45:38 PM The Supreme Court is one of the main reasons I got elected President. I hope Republican Voters, and others, are watching, and studying, the Democrats Playbook. [Twitter for iPhone]

⬜ Sep 18, 2018 11:04:32 PM Kim Jong Un has agreed to allow Nuclear inspections, subject to final negotiations, and to permanently dismantle a test site and launch pad in the presence of international experts. In the meantime there will be no Rocket or Nuclear testing. Hero remains to continue being........ [Twitter for iPhone]

⬜ Sep 18, 2018 11:11:39 PM ....returned home to the United States. Also, North and South Korea will file a joint bid to host the 2032 Olympics. Very exciting! [Twitter for iPhone]

⬜ Sep 19, 2018 06:34:29 AM "The recovery got started on Election Day 2016. It took Trump's Tax Cuts and Regulation Cuts to get the economy booming. Before that it was the worst and slowest economic recovery since the Great Depression. It took just 6 months for Trump to get to 3%, even though they said..... [Twitter for iPhone]

⬜ Sep 19, 2018 06:40:37 AM ....it was impossible - and then already it's over 4%, and I expect it's going to grow faster and faster. We're just getting started here." Peter Ferrara, former advisor to President Reagan. @foxandfriends [Twitter for iPhone]

⬜ Sep 19, 2018 06:43:44 AM "North Korea recommits to denuclearization - we've come a long way." @FoxNews [Twitter for iPhone]

⬜ Sep 19, 2018 12:49:19 PM "President Donald J. Trump's Administration is Providing Support to Those Impacted by Hurricane Florence" https://t.co/3neafSgQ1h [Twitter for iPhone]

⬜ Sep 19, 2018 06:37:25 PM Just returned to the White House from the Great States of North Carolina and South Carolina where incredible work is being done on the ongoing fight against hurricane Florence. Tremendous talent and spirit! [Twitter for iPhone]

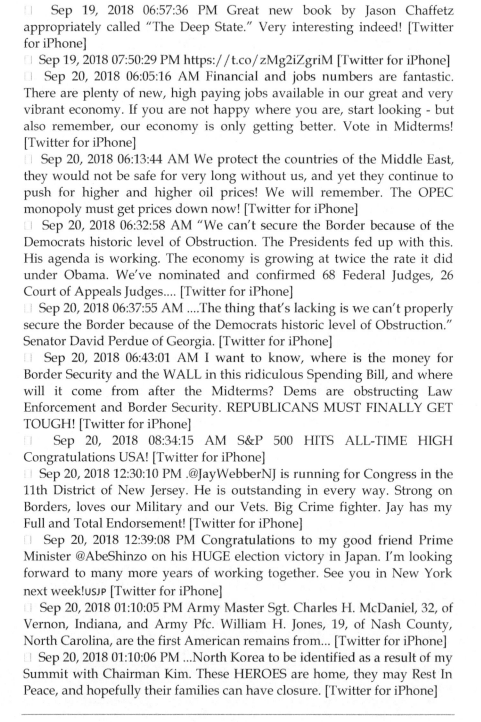

Sep 19, 2018 06:57:36 PM Great new book by Jason Chaffetz appropriately called "The Deep State." Very interesting indeed! [Twitter for iPhone]

Sep 19, 2018 07:50:29 PM https://t.co/zMg2iZgriM [Twitter for iPhone]

Sep 20, 2018 06:05:16 AM Financial and jobs numbers are fantastic. There are plenty of new, high paying jobs available in our great and very vibrant economy. If you are not happy where you are, start looking - but also remember, our economy is only getting better. Vote in Midterms! [Twitter for iPhone]

Sep 20, 2018 06:13:44 AM We protect the countries of the Middle East, they would not be safe for very long without us, and yet they continue to push for higher and higher oil prices! We will remember. The OPEC monopoly must get prices down now! [Twitter for iPhone]

Sep 20, 2018 06:32:58 AM "We can't secure the Border because of the Democrats historic level of Obstruction. The Presidents fed up with this. His agenda is working. The economy is growing at twice the rate it did under Obama. We've nominated and confirmed 68 Federal Judges, 26 Court of Appeals Judges.... [Twitter for iPhone]

Sep 20, 2018 06:37:55 AM ....The thing that's lacking is we can't properly secure the Border because of the Democrats historic level of Obstruction." Senator David Perdue of Georgia. [Twitter for iPhone]

Sep 20, 2018 06:43:01 AM I want to know, where is the money for Border Security and the WALL in this ridiculous Spending Bill, and where will it come from after the Midterms? Dems are obstructing Law Enforcement and Border Security. REPUBLICANS MUST FINALLY GET TOUGH! [Twitter for iPhone]

Sep 20, 2018 08:34:15 AM S&P 500 HITS ALL-TIME HIGH Congratulations USA! [Twitter for iPhone]

Sep 20, 2018 12:30:10 PM .@JayWebberNJ is running for Congress in the 11th District of New Jersey. He is outstanding in every way. Strong on Borders, loves our Military and our Vets. Big Crime fighter. Jay has my Full and Total Endorsement! [Twitter for iPhone]

Sep 20, 2018 12:39:08 PM Congratulations to my good friend Prime Minister @AbeShinzo on his HUGE election victory in Japan. I'm looking forward to many more years of working together. See you in New York next week!USJP [Twitter for iPhone]

Sep 20, 2018 01:10:05 PM Army Master Sgt. Charles H. McDaniel, 32, of Vernon, Indiana, and Army Pfc. William H. Jones, 19, of Nash County, North Carolina, are the first American remains from... [Twitter for iPhone]

Sep 20, 2018 01:10:06 PM ...North Korea to be identified as a result of my Summit with Chairman Kim. These HEROES are home, they may Rest In Peace, and hopefully their families can have closure. [Twitter for iPhone]

Sep 20, 2018 01:34:14 PM https://t.co/RzqoiQ4SmD [Twitter for iPhone]

Sep 20, 2018 04:54:39 PM On my way to Las Vegas, Nevada. Look forward to seeing everyone tonight! #MAGA https://t.co/wTeerIUJvd [Twitter for iPhone]

Sep 20, 2018 06:57:13 PM https://t.co/LdXQb42Imc [Twitter for iPhone]

Sep 20, 2018 08:27:45 PM Landing in Las Vegas now for a Make America Great Again Rally supporting @DeanHeller and @DannyTarkanian. Also doing interview there with @seanhannity live on @FoxNews. Big crowd, long lines. Will be great! #MAGA [Twitter for iPhone]

Sep 20, 2018 10:29:03 PM MAKE AMERICA GREAT AGAIN! https://t.co/OYJUkiEUid [Twitter for iPhone]

Sep 20, 2018 10:33:30 PM Thank you Las Vegas, Nevada - I love you! #MAGAus https://t.co/GBZO84PyQ1 [Twitter for iPhone]

Sep 20, 2018 11:05:52 PM AMERICA IS WINNING AGAIN! https://t.co/6HcBjLAAQB [Twitter for iPhone]

Sep 21, 2018 07:56:46 AM Judge Brett Kavanaugh is a fine man, with an impeccable reputation, who is under assault by radical left wing politicians who don't want to know the answers, they just want to destroy and delay. Facts don't matter. I go through this with them every single day in D.C. [Twitter for iPhone]

Sep 21, 2018 08:14:33 AM I have no doubt that, if the attack on Dr. Ford was as bad as she says, charges would have been immediately filed with local Law Enforcement Authorities by either her or her loving parents. I ask that she bring those filings forward so that we can learn date, time, and place! [Twitter for iPhone]

Sep 21, 2018 08:23:32 AM I will Chair the United Nations Security Council meeting on Iran next week! [Twitter for iPhone]

Sep 21, 2018 08:29:47 AM The radical left lawyers want the FBI to get involved NOW. Why didn't someone call the FBI 36 years ago? [Twitter for iPhone]

Sep 21, 2018 08:33:16 AM RT @trueamerica1st: https://t.co/02E9bG17Mf [Twitter for iPhone]

Sep 21, 2018 08:34:19 AM RT @trueamerica1st: @realDonaldTrump https://t.co/w7EBsA5aTT [Twitter for iPhone]

Sep 21, 2018 09:35:11 AM I met with the DOJ concerning the declassification of various UNREDACTED documents. They agreed to release them but stated that so doing may have a perceived negative impact on the Russia probe. Also, key Allies' called to ask not to release. Therefore, the Inspector General..... [Twitter for iPhone]

Sep 21, 2018 09:41:18 AM ....has been asked to review these documents on an expedited basis. I believe he will move quickly on this (and hopefully other things which he is looking at). In the end I can always declassify if it proves necessary. Speed is very important to me - and everyone! [Twitter for iPhone]

Sep 21, 2018 10:25:58 AM Senator Feinstein and the Democrats held the letter for months, only to release it with a bang after the hearings were OVER - done very purposefully to Obstruct & Resist & Delay. Let her testify, or not, and TAKE THE VOTE! [Twitter for iPhone]

Sep 21, 2018 10:29:34 AM Senator Feinstein and the Democrats held the letter for months, only to release it with a bang after the hearings were OVER - done very purposefully to Obstruct & Resist & Delay. Let her testify, or not, and TAKE THE VOTE! [Twitter for iPhone]

Sep 21, 2018 12:22:35 PM Throughout American history, the men and women of our Armed Forces have selflessly served our Country, making tremendous sacrifices to defend our liberty. On National POW/MIA Recognition Day, we honor all American Prisoners of War: https://t.co/ZGiqdYbats https://t.co/OEetrLzgcJ [Twitter for iPhone]

Sep 21, 2018 03:11:48 PM Promises Kept for our GREAT Veterans! https://t.co/C0h8cW4FuH [Twitter for iPhone]

Sep 21, 2018 03:21:27 PM RT @LindseyGrahamSC: Great job tonight by President @realDonaldTrump in Las Vegas laying out how strong America has become economically and... [Twitter for iPhone]

Sep 21, 2018 03:22:11 PM RT @GOP: "We're fighting every day for our factories, our ranchers, our great miners, our farmers, and we are now the largest producer of e... [Twitter for iPhone]

Sep 21, 2018 03:23:11 PM RT @NVGOP: Energy and excitement for President @realDonaldTrump and his #AmericaFirst agenda is through the roof! #MAGA https://t.co/KNywCE... [Twitter for iPhone]

Sep 21, 2018 03:24:14 PM RT @MikeTokes: We are outside the Trump rally in Las Vegas. There are THOUSANDS of conservatives here and the line extends all the way arou... [Twitter for iPhone]

Sep 21, 2018 03:24:20 PM RT @MikeTokes: What an amazing Trump rally in Las Vegas, Nevada. There must have been over 10,000 people here and trust me when I say it, w... [Twitter for iPhone]

Sep 21, 2018 03:25:20 PM RT @RamonaGiwargis: The crowd roars as @realDonaldTrump takes the stage. Says he's thrilled to be back in Ne-vah-da. "You have to say that... [Twitter for iPhone]

Sep 21, 2018 03:26:58 PM RT @W7VOA: View of the line outside Las Vegas Convention Center of those waiting to get into the @realDonaldTrump #MAGA rally. (Photos sent... [Twitter for iPhone]

Sep 21, 2018 03:51:44 PM https://t.co/hIw1AQdRpY [Twitter for iPhone]

Sep 21, 2018 04:44:11 PM Remarks by President Trump at the Signing of H.R. 5895: https://t.co/tfKJJGMevo https://t.co/7hcD22Txvy [Twitter for iPhone]

Sep 21, 2018 08:05:00 PM Thank you Missouri - I love you! https://t.co/rx3mtd7yOy [Twitter for iPhone]

Sep 21, 2018 08:31:42 PM Thank you Missouri - Together, we are MAKING AMERICA GREAT AGAIN! https://t.co/onl1HmM2Gz [Twitter for iPhone]

Sep 21, 2018 10:09:25 PM RT @FoxBusiness: .@POTUS: "The stock market is up 55%... Your 401(k)s are up 50, 60, 70% in some cases." https://t.co/g38SD65pMW [Twitter for iPhone]

Sep 21, 2018 10:09:52 PM RT @juliehdavis: For 2nd night in row at Trump rally (tonite in Springfield, last nite in Las Vegas), crowd spontaneously breaks into cheer... [Twitter for iPhone]

Sep 21, 2018 10:11:53 PM RT @dcexaminer: "We are standing up for your values," Trump said closing his rally in Springfield, Missouri. "We are standing up for our na... [Twitter for iPhone]

Sep 21, 2018 10:13:26 PM RT @RSBNetwork: President @realDonaldTrump absolutely packs the house at JQH Arena in Springfield, MO. #TrumpRally #RedWave https://t.co/1c... [Twitter for iPhone]

Sep 21, 2018 10:20:49 PM GOD BLESS THE U.S.A.! https://t.co/n9OkDlqz11 [Twitter for iPhone]

Sep 22, 2018 09:01:05 AM New Economic Records being set on a daily basis - and it is not by accident! [Twitter for iPhone]

Sep 22, 2018 09:56:35 AM https://t.co/MgkotGmkJ0 [Twitter for iPhone]

Sep 22, 2018 02:39:15 PM https://t.co/qZSEifBNaP [Twitter for iPhone]

Sep 23, 2018 03:43:52 PM Tiger is playing great. Looks like a big win could happen. Very exciting! @TigerWoods [Twitter for iPhone]

Sep 23, 2018 03:52:37 PM Going to New York. Will be with Prime Minister Abe of Japan tonight, talking Military and Trade. We have done much to help Japan, would like to see more of a reciprocal relationship. It will all work out! [Twitter for iPhone]

Sep 23, 2018 05:48:33 PM Prime Minster @AbeShinzo is coming up to Trump Tower for dinner but, most importantly, he just had a great landslide victory in Japan. I will congratulate him on behalf of the American people! [Twitter for iPhone]

Sep 24, 2018 09:13:22 AM RT @SCEMD: Now is the time to put safety first above everything else. Evacuate to a shelter if you need to, take your pets with you. Your l... [Twitter for iPhone]

Sep 24, 2018 09:17:26 AM "Remarks by President Trump at 'Global Call to Action on the World Drug Problem' Event" #UNGA → https://t.co/kvUZegWdlH https://t.co/BGdrQeZuId [Twitter for iPhone]

Sep 24, 2018 11:55:18 AM Today, we commit to fighting the drug epidemic together! #UNGA https://t.co/XgaYTOBrSK [Twitter for iPhone]

Sep 24, 2018 03:42:22 PM It was my great honor to welcome and meet with President @moonriver365 Jae-in of South Korea today, in New York City! https://t.co/7f3eOYGxDn #UNGA https://t.co/B6rVeeBTCc [Twitter for iPhone]

Sep 24, 2018 03:44:24 PM US-Korea Free Trade Agreement Signing Ceremony! https://t.co/yLFkAZgagG [Twitter for iPhone]

Sep 24, 2018 04:33:33 PM Brett Kavanaugh and his wife, Ashley, will be interviewed tonight at 7pmE on @marthamaccallum @FoxNews. This is an outstanding family who must be treated fairly! [Twitter for iPhone]

Sep 24, 2018 04:46:22 PM Joint Statement on the United States-Korea Free Trade Agreement: https://t.co/m0jW8nqdQW https://t.co/lcrhsJtv00 [Twitter for iPhone]

Sep 24, 2018 05:33:39 PM It was my great honor to welcome President @AlsisiOfficial of Egypt to the United States this afternoon, in New York City. Great meetings! #UNGA https://t.co/dsMZWodpWr [Twitter for iPad]

Sep 24, 2018 05:53:04 PM RT @realDonaldTrump: Brett Kavanaugh and his wife, Ashley, will be interviewed tonight at 7pmE on @marthamaccallum @FoxNews. This is an out... [Twitter for iPhone]

Sep 24, 2018 06:41:37 PM It was my great honor to welcome President @EmmanuelMacron of France to the United States, here in New York City, this evening! #UNGA https://t.co/Gd7pCBFUCg [Twitter for iPhone]

Sep 24, 2018 07:22:46 PM https://t.co/FXqSWusSTV [Twitter for iPhone]

Sep 24, 2018 09:37:58 PM The Democrats are working hard to destroy a wonderful man, and a man who has the potential to be one of our greatest Supreme Court Justices ever, with an array of False Acquisitions the likes of which have never been seen before! [Twitter for iPhone]

Sep 24, 2018 09:38:39 PM REMEMBER THE MIDTERMS! [Twitter for iPhone]

Sep 24, 2018 09:50:09 PM The Democrats are working hard to destroy a wonderful man, and a man who has the potential to be one of our greatest Supreme Court Justices ever, with an array of False Accusations the likes of which have never been seen before! [Twitter for iPhone]

Sep 25, 2018 05:41:20 AM Republican Party Favorability is the highest it has been in 7 years - 3 points higher than Democrats! Gallup [Twitter for iPhone]

Sep 25, 2018 05:53:41 AM Despite requests, I have no plans to meet Iranian President Hassan Rouhani. Maybe someday in the future. I am sure he is an absolutely lovely man! [Twitter for iPhone]

Sep 25, 2018 08:14:04 AM Will be speaking at the United Nations this morning. Our country is much stronger and much richer than it was when I took office less than two years ago. We are also MUCH safer! [Twitter for iPhone]

Sep 25, 2018 10:27:35 AM https://t.co/h43dehf0WV [Twitter for iPhone]

Sep 25, 2018 11:36:02 AM Thank you Mark! https://t.co/NVGs6WbQe2 [Twitter for iPhone]

Sep 25, 2018 11:37:43 AM Thank you Dr. Jeffress! https://t.co/cm7NjQh0ti [Twitter for iPhone]

Sep 25, 2018 11:45:36 AM Rush Limbaugh to Republicans: "You can kiss the MIDTERMS goodbye if you don't get highly qualified Kavanaugh approved." [Twitter for iPhone]

Sep 25, 2018 12:19:44 PM "Remarks by President Trump to the 73rd Session of the United Nations General Assembly" → https://t.co/Oshhko61zY https://t.co/Fm8LSse417 [Twitter for iPhone]

Sep 25, 2018 02:28:26 PM "Remarks by President Trump at a Luncheon Hosted by the Secretary-General of the United Nations" https://t.co/ShHaLmoSDL https://t.co/k62KGgD8j6 [Twitter for iPhone]

Sep 25, 2018 03:27:25 PM "Consumer confidence rose in September, notching its highest level in about 18 years. The Consumer Board's index rose to 138.4 this month from 134.7 in August..." https://t.co/ZbxjnrRvAX [Twitter for iPhone]

Sep 25, 2018 05:06:33 PM 73rd Session of the United Nations General Assembly #UNGA https://t.co/xJyx7RrH5F [Twitter for iPhone]

Sep 25, 2018 09:38:54 PM "These law enforcement people took the law into their own hands when it came to President Trump." @LindseyGrahamSC [Twitter for iPhone]

Sep 25, 2018 09:55:20 PM The Democrats are playing a high level CON GAME in their vicious effort to destroy a fine person. It is called the politics of destruction. Behind the scene the Dems are laughing. Pray for Brett Kavanaugh and his family! [Twitter for iPhone]

Sep 26, 2018 05:54:59 AM Consumer confidence hits an 18 year high, close to breaking the all-time record. A big jump from last 8 years. People are excited about the USA again! We are getting Bigger and Richer and Stronger. WAY MORE TO GO! [Twitter for iPhone]

Sep 26, 2018 05:57:30 AM Jobless Claims fell to their lowest level in 49 years! [Twitter for iPhone]

Sep 26, 2018 11:47:06 AM Avenatti is a third rate lawyer who is good at making false accusations, like he did on me and like he is now doing on Judge Brett Kavanaugh. He is just looking for attention and doesn't want people to look at his past record and relationships - a total low-life! [Twitter for iPhone]

Sep 26, 2018 12:26:54 PM China is actually placing propaganda ads in the Des Moines Register and other papers, made to look like news. That's because we are beating them on Trade, opening markets, and the farmers will make a fortune when this is over! https://t.co/ppdvTX7oz1 [Twitter for iPhone]

Sep 26, 2018 12:28:54 PM RT @newtgingrich: President Trump's United Nations speech today is a remarkable outline of the power of patriotism, the importance of natio… [Twitter for iPhone]

Sep 26, 2018 12:31:40 PM RT @PeteHegseth: This @realDonaldTrump speech to the #UNGA should be required viewing in American high schools. A beautiful articulation of… [Twitter for iPhone]

Sep 26, 2018 12:34:34 PM Congressman Lee Zeldin is doing a fantastic job in D.C. Tough and smart, he loves our Country and will always be there to do the right thing. He has my Complete and Total Endorsement! [Twitter for iPhone]

Sep 26, 2018 02:23:03 PM RT @WhiteHouse: Earlier today, President Trump participated in a bilateral meeting with Prime Minister @netanyahu of Israel. USI☐ https://t… [Twitter for iPhone]

Sep 26, 2018 02:23:07 PM RT @WhiteHouse: This afternoon, President Trump participated in a bilateral meeting with Prime Minister Abe. USJP https://t.co/PvSINQY7yq [Twitter for iPhone]

Sep 26, 2018 03:47:16 PM RT @WhiteHouse: President Trump and Prime Minister Theresa May met for a bilateral meeting in New York US GB https://t.co/VdJztUmD9T [Twitter for iPhone]

Sep 26, 2018 03:48:12 PM Join me this Saturday in Wheeling, West Virginia at 7pmE! Tickets: https://t.co/JyRaBps0eR https://t.co/hiruLIxa7w [Twitter for iPhone]

Sep 26, 2018 06:52:51 PM https://t.co/9o5gZlJiTd [Twitter for iPhone]

Sep 27, 2018 05:46:17 PM Judge Kavanaugh showed America exactly why I nominated him. His testimony was powerful, honest, and riveting. Democrats' search and destroy strategy is disgraceful and this process has been a total sham and effort to delay, obstruct, and resist. The Senate must vote! [Twitter for iPhone]

Sep 28, 2018 07:27:17 PM Just started, tonight, our 7th FBI investigation of Judge Brett Kavanaugh. He will someday be recognized as a truly great Justice of The United States Supreme Court! [Twitter for iPhone]

Sep 29, 2018 03:33:51 PM Senator Richard Blumenthal must talk about his fraudulent service in Vietnam, where for 12 years he told the people of Connecticut, as their Attorney General, that he was a great Marine War Hero. Talked about his many battles of near death, but was never in Vietnam. Total Phony! [Twitter for iPhone]

Sep 29, 2018 03:36:43 PM Heading to West Virginia now. Big Rally. Will be live on @FoxNews tonight. Long lines, but will be great! [Twitter for iPhone]

Sep 29, 2018 07:51:22 PM https://t.co/BxlF4grr9k [Twitter for iPhone]

Sep 29, 2018 07:52:25 PM Thank you West Virginia - I love you! https://t.co/Ou2umCfKp9 [Twitter for iPhone]

Sep 29, 2018 09:49:55 PM NBC News incorrectly reported (as usual) that I was limiting the FBI investigation of Judge Kavanaugh, and witnesses, only to certain people. Actually, I want them to interview whoever they deem appropriate, at their discretion. Please correct your reporting! [Twitter for iPhone]

Sep 30, 2018 11:57:45 AM Like many, I don't watch Saturday Night Live (even though I past hosted it) - no longer funny, no talent or charm. It is just a political ad for the Dems. Word is that Kanye West, who put on a MAGA hat after the show (despite being told "no"), was great. He's leading the charge! [Twitter for iPhone]

Sep 30, 2018 12:47:03 PM So if African-American unemployment is now at the lowest number in history, median income the highest, and you then add all of the other things I have done, how do Democrats, who have done NOTHING for African-Americans but TALK, win the Black Vote? And it will only get better! [Twitter for iPhone]

Sep 30, 2018 01:56:27 PM Wow! Just starting to hear the Democrats, who are only thinking Obstruct and Delay, are starting to put out the word that the "time" and "scope" of FBI looking into Judge Kavanaugh and witnesses is not enough. Hello! For them, it will never be enough - stay tuned and watch! [Twitter for iPhone]

Oct 1, 2018 05:30:08 AM Late last night, our deadline, we reached a wonderful new Trade Deal with Canada, to be added into the deal already reached with Mexico. The new name will be The United States Mexico Canada Agreement, or USMCA. It is a great deal for all three countries, solves the many...... [Twitter for iPhone]

Oct 1, 2018 05:40:24 AM .....deficiencies and mistakes in NAFTA, greatly opens markets to our Farmers and Manufacturers, reduce Trade Barriers to the U.S. and will bring all three Great Nations closer together in competition with the rest of the world. The USMCA is a historic transaction! [Twitter for iPhone]

Oct 1, 2018 05:53:28 AM ....deficiencies and mistakes in NAFTA, greatly opens markets to our Farmers and Manufacturers, reduces Trade Barriers to the U.S. and will bring all three Great Nations together in competition with the rest of the world. The USMCA is a historic transaction! [Twitter for iPhone]

Oct 1, 2018 05:56:22 AM Congratulations to Mexico and Canada! [Twitter for iPhone]

Oct 1, 2018 07:08:26 AM News conference on the USMCA this morning at 11:00 - Rose Garden of White House. [Twitter for iPhone]

Oct 1, 2018 07:25:44 PM https://t.co/5UmYGFLyLK [Twitter for iPhone]

Oct 1, 2018 07:37:49 PM Thank you Tennessee - I love you! https://t.co/1swpoY7F5x [Twitter for iPhone]

Oct 1, 2018 07:50:23 PM WOW - THANK YOU TENNESSEE! https://t.co/38UUDqfIz5 [Twitter for iPhone]

Oct 2, 2018 09:52:52 AM Happy 7th birthday to Tristan, a very special member of the Trump family! [Twitter for iPhone]

Oct 2, 2018 10:02:03 AM Great reviews on the new USMCA. Thank you! Mexico and Canada will be wonderful partners in Trade (and more) long into the future. [Twitter for iPhone]

Oct 2, 2018 11:08:25 AM THE ONLY REASON TO VOTE FOR A DEMOCRAT IS IF YOU'RE TIRED OF WINNING! [Twitter for iPhone]

Oct 2, 2018 11:18:58 AM Yesterday, it was my great honor to present the Medal of Honor to Ronald J. Shurer II, for his actions on April 6, 2008, when he braved enemy fire to treat multiple injured Soldiers. Read more: https://t.co/Nrrcp2JJUL https://t.co/A0KLHmIPZs [Twitter for iPhone]

Oct 2, 2018 12:22:36 PM Proud of our great First Lady - and she loves doing this! https://t.co/VD7wlqeJoR [Twitter for iPhone]

Oct 2, 2018 01:18:35 PM "USMCA Wins Praise as a Victory for American Industries and Workers" → https://t.co/UWhPhNXiiL https://t.co/eBVv0nXXRT [Twitter for iPhone]

Oct 2, 2018 04:17:08 PM RT @WhiteHouse: "America will always be a nation of great builders, because in America, we honor work, we honor grit, we honor craftsmanshi... [Twitter for iPhone]

Oct 2, 2018 04:20:05 PM This is really an incredible time for our Nation - WE are RESPECTED AGAIN! https://t.co/94KusYcDAj [Twitter for iPhone]

Oct 2, 2018 08:18:08 PM Thank you Mississippi - I love you! https://t.co/eH6x1NBNQG [Twitter for iPhone]

Oct 2, 2018 08:25:33 PM GOD BLESS THE U.S.A.! #MAGAus https://t.co/pquqyy5S3G [Twitter for iPhone]

Oct 2, 2018 09:15:03 PM "National wage growth is at the highest it's been in nearly 17 months -- and, according to a new study released by Glassdoor, it's not expected to slow down anytime soon...." https://t.co/G0Ts6yVqF9 [Twitter for iPhone]

Oct 2, 2018 09:18:03 PM Today, my Administration provided HISTORIC levels of funding to improve school safety through STOP School Violence grants – a top priority for @sandyhook. I am committed to keeping our children SAFE in their schools! [Twitter for iPhone]

Oct 2, 2018 09:58:22 PM Thank you Mississippi - Together, we are MAKING AMERICA GREAT AGAIN! https://t.co/npnRirjcFG [Twitter for iPhone]

Oct 2, 2018 10:56:24 PM RT @DHSgov: REMINDER: Tomorrow, 10/3 at 2:18 PM EDT, there will be a nationwide test of the Wireless Emergency Alert system, in coordinatio... [Twitter for iPhone]

Oct 3, 2018 07:35:52 AM Congressman @PeteSessions of Texas is a true fighter and patriot. Highly respected in D.C. by all, he always gets what his district, and our country, wants and needs. Strong on Crime, Border, Military, Vets and 2nd Amendment. Pete has my Full and Total Endorsement. A great guy! [Twitter for iPhone]

Oct 3, 2018 07:53:35 AM The Failing New York Times did something I have never seen done before. They used the concept of "time value of money" in doing a very old, boring and often told hit piece on me. Added up, this means that 97% of their stories on me are bad. Never recovered from bad election call! [Twitter for iPhone]

Oct 3, 2018 08:04:02 AM The Stock Market just reached an All-Time High during my Administration for the 102nd Time, a presidential record, by far, for less than two years. So much potential as Trade and Military Deals are completed. [Twitter for iPhone]

Oct 3, 2018 08:16:08 AM https://t.co/w04sqlMIYm [Twitter for iPhone]

Oct 3, 2018 08:23:34 AM Thank you Governor Phil Bryant - it was my great honor to be there! #MAGA https://t.co/UbY7Qu2fMt [Twitter for iPhone]

Oct 3, 2018 09:02:10 AM Thank you to Congressman Tom Reed of New York for your wonderful comments on our great new Trade Deal with Mexico and Canada, the USMCA. I have long ago given you my Full Endorsement, and for good reason. Keep up the Great Work! @Varneyco [Twitter for iPhone]

Oct 3, 2018 09:05:28 AM Blowout numbers on New Jobs and, separately, Services. Market up! [Twitter for iPhone]

Oct 3, 2018 09:13:42 AM Mexico, Canada and the United States are a great partnership and will be a very formidable trading force. We will now, because of the USMCA, work very well together. Great Spirit! [Twitter for iPhone]

Oct 3, 2018 09:29:25 AM I see it each time I go out to Rallies in order to help some of our great Republican candidates. VOTERS ARE REALLY ANGRY AT THE VICIOUS AND DESPICABLE WAY DEMOCRATS ARE TREATING BRETT KAVANAUGH! He and his wonderful family deserve much better. [Twitter for iPhone]

Oct 3, 2018 09:35:48 AM Just spoke to President-Elect Andres Manuel Lopez Obrador of Mexico. Great call, we will work well together! [Twitter for iPhone]

Oct 3, 2018 07:01:09 PM My thoughts and prayers are with the Florence County Sheriff's Office and the Florence Police Department tonight, in South Carolina. We are forever grateful for what our Law Enforcement Officers do 24/7/365. https://t.co/ZwDmDthItD [Twitter for iPhone]

Oct 3, 2018 09:23:11 PM Wow, such enthusiasm and energy for Judge Brett Kavanaugh. Look at the Energy, look at the Polls. Something very big is happening. He is a fine man and great intellect. The country is with him all the way! [Twitter for iPhone]

Oct 4, 2018 07:16:41 AM The harsh and unfair treatment of Judge Brett Kavanaugh is having an incredible upward impact on voters. The PEOPLE get it far better than the politicians. Most importantly, this great life cannot be ruined by mean & despicable Democrats and totally uncorroborated allegations! [Twitter for iPhone]

Oct 4, 2018 08:34:16 AM Our country's great First Lady, Melania, is doing really well in Africa. The people love her, and she loves them! It is a beautiful thing to see. [Twitter for iPhone]

Oct 4, 2018 08:54:58 AM This is a very important time in our country. Due Process, Fairness and Common Sense are now on trial! [Twitter for iPhone]

Oct 4, 2018 09:01:13 AM RT @ChatByCC: While armed with the power of our Vote, we proudly & peacefully revolted Never doubt this was an American revolution #MAGA... [Twitter for iPhone]

Oct 4, 2018 09:17:01 AM This is now the 7th. time the FBI has investigated Judge Kavanaugh. If we made it 100, it would still not be good enough for the Obstructionist Democrats. [Twitter for iPhone]

Oct 4, 2018 12:38:08 PM Working hard, thank you! https://t.co/6HQVaEXH0I [Twitter for iPhone]

Oct 4, 2018 02:17:28 PM Statement on National Strategy for Counterterrorism: https://t.co/ajFBg9Elsj https://t.co/Qr56ycjMAV [Twitter for iPhone]

Oct 4, 2018 02:29:27 PM "U.S. Stocks Widen Global Lead" https://t.co/Snhv08ulcO [Twitter for iPhone]

Oct 4, 2018 05:17:48 PM Congressman Bishop is doing a GREAT job! He helped pass tax reform which lowered taxes for EVERYONE! Nancy Pelosi is spending hundreds of thousands of dollars on his opponent because they both support a liberal agenda of higher taxes and wasteful spending! [Twitter for iPhone]

Oct 4, 2018 05:58:21 PM Just made my second stop in Minnesota for a MAKE AMERICA GREAT AGAIN rally. We need to elect @KarinHousley to the U.S. Senate, and we need the strong leadership of @TomEmmer, @Jason2CD, @JimHagedornMN and @PeteStauber in the U.S. House! [Twitter for iPhone]

Oct 4, 2018 07:52:20 PM Thank you Minnesota - I love you! https://t.co/eQC2NqdIil [Twitter for iPhone]

Oct 4, 2018 08:03:25 PM Beautiful evening in Rochester, Minnesota. VOTE, VOTE, VOTE! https://t.co/SyxrxvTpZE [Twitter for iPhone]

Oct 5, 2018 06:25:42 AM RT @Scavino45: 🎥 Happening Now | 2:08amE; Our great @FLOTUS, Melania Trump...visiting a Kenyan elephant orphanage...https://t.co/rW2cWXaswf [Twitter for iPhone]

Oct 5, 2018 06:28:02 AM RT @newsobserver: Presidential adviser and daughter @IvankaTrump will make 3 stops in NC to see hurricane relief efforts, thank first respo… [Twitter for iPhone]

Oct 5, 2018 06:29:15 AM RT @RealJamesWoodss: Whether you love or hate him, Trump's ascendancy to the presidency was a once-in-a-century miracle. He was literally t… [Twitter for iPhone]

Oct 5, 2018 08:03:06 AM The very rude elevator screamers are paid professionals only looking to make Senators look bad. Don't fall for it! Also, look at all of the professionally made identical signs. Paid for by Soros and others. These are not signs made in the basement from love! #Troublemakers [Twitter for iPhone]

Oct 5, 2018 08:06:08 AM Just out: 3.7% Unemployment is the lowest number since 1969! [Twitter for iPhone]

Oct 5, 2018 09:59:41 AM Very proud of the U.S. Senate for voting "YES" to advance the nomination of Judge Brett Kavanaugh! [Twitter for iPhone]

Oct 5, 2018 04:29:49 PM RT @FLOTUS: Thank you Ghana! US G□ https://t.co/d34cqFyRdN [Twitter for iPhone]

Oct 5, 2018 04:29:54 PM RT @FLOTUS: Thank you Malawi! US □□ https://t.co/rE03LMNzOZ [Twitter for iPhone]

Oct 5, 2018 10:46:07 PM RT @realDonaldTrump: Thank you Minnesota - I love you! https://t.co/eQC2NqdIil [Twitter for iPhone]

Oct 6, 2018 09:40:53 AM Women for Kavanaugh, and many others who support this very good man, are gathering all over Capital Hill in preparation for a 3-5 P.M. VOTE. It is a beautiful thing to see - and they are not paid professional protesters who are handed expensive signs. Big day for America! [Twitter for iPhone]

Oct 6, 2018 11:08:57 AM Women for Kavanaugh, and many others who support this very good man, are gathering all over Capitol Hill in preparation for a 3-5 P.M. VOTE. It is a beautiful thing to see - and they are not paid professional protesters who are handed expensive signs. Big day for America! [Twitter for iPhone]

Oct 6, 2018 03:06:01 PM I have asked Steve Daines, our great Republican Senator from Montana, to attend his daughter Annie's wedding rather than coming to today's vote. Steve was ready to do whatever he had to, but we had the necessary number. To the Daines Family, congratulations- have a wonderful day! [Twitter for iPhone]

Oct 6, 2018 03:15:30 PM I applaud and congratulate the U.S. Senate for confirming our GREAT NOMINEE, Judge Brett Kavanaugh, to the United States Supreme Court. Later today, I will sign his Commission of Appointment, and he will be officially sworn in. Very exciting! [Twitter for iPhone]

Oct 6, 2018 04:57:09 PM The crowd in front of the U.S. Supreme Court is tiny, looks like about 200 people (& most are onlookers) - that wouldn't even fill the first couple of rows of our Kansas Rally, or any of our Rallies for that matter! The Fake News Media tries to make it look sooo big, & it's not! [Twitter for iPhone]

Oct 6, 2018 07:49:56 PM Thank you Kansas - I love you! https://t.co/ymCFNr9WQY [Twitter for iPhone]

Oct 6, 2018 08:15:00 PM Beautiful evening in Topeka, Kansas. VOTE, VOTE, VOTE! #MAGA https://t.co/bomRqsaYfm [Twitter for iPhone]

Oct 6, 2018 08:21:22 PM You don't hand matches to an arsonist, and you don't give power to an angry left-wing mob. Democrats have become too EXTREME and TOO DANGEROUS to govern. Republicans believe in the rule of law - not the rule of the mob. VOTE REPUBLICAN! [Twitter for iPhone]

Oct 7, 2018 09:42:25 AM .@SecPompeo had a good meeting with Chairman Kim today in Pyongyang. Progress made on Singapore Summit Agreements! I look forward to seeing Chairman Kim again, in the near future. https://t.co/bUa2pkq80s [Twitter for iPhone]

Oct 7, 2018 01:15:22 PM RT @FLOTUS: Thank you Kenya KE US https://t.co/JrHncob8Qp [Twitter for iPhone]

Oct 8, 2018 08:36:11 AM Christopher Columbus's spirit of determination & adventure has provided inspiration to generations of Americans. On #ColumbusDay, we honor his remarkable accomplishments as a navigator, & celebrate his voyage into the unknown expanse of the Atlantic Ocean. https://t.co/Mg3dxRfPuN [Twitter for iPhone]

Oct 8, 2018 10:31:51 AM Departing Washington, D.C. for the International Association of Chiefs of Police Annual Convention in Orlando, Florida. Look forward to seeing everyone soon! #IACP2018 https://t.co/EwSd7IU9t1 [Twitter for iPhone]

Oct 8, 2018 01:32:51 PM It was my great honor to address the International Association of Chiefs of Police Annual Convention in Orlando, Florida. Thank you! #IACP2018 #LESM https://t.co/Z0nY5bSNr6 [Twitter for iPhone]

Oct 8, 2018 01:57:07 PM America's police officers have earned the everlasting gratitude of our Nation. In moments of danger & despair you are the reason we never lose hope – because there are men & women in uniform who face down evil & stand for all that is GOOD and JUST and DECENT and RIGHT! #IACP2018 https://t.co/N0Dq50DkbP [Twitter for iPhone]

Oct 8, 2018 02:27:41 PM We thank you. We salute you. We honor you. And we promise you: we will ALWAYS have your BACK – now and FOREVER! #IACP2018 https://t.co/nvUUIuvouj [Twitter for iPhone]

Oct 8, 2018 02:37:36 PM Every day, our police officers race into darkened allies, deserted streets, & onto the doorsteps of the most hardened criminals. They see the worst of humanity & they respond with the best of the American Spirit. America's LEOs have earned the everlasting gratitude of our Nation! https://t.co/RquS91Vz7o [Twitter for iPhone]

Oct 8, 2018 02:44:49 PM Great to see @AGPamBondi launch a cutting-edge statewide school safety APP in Florida today - named by Parkland Survivors. BIG PRIORITY and Florida is getting it done! #FortifyFL [Twitter for iPhone]

Oct 8, 2018 06:43:34 PM https://t.co/k2bOxapRtR [Twitter for iPhone]

Oct 8, 2018 08:34:56 PM https://t.co/4ySIkmfllE [Twitter for iPhone]

Oct 9, 2018 07:18:39 AM RT @fema: ⚠ If you're told to evacuate for Hurricane #Michael, don't delay. Leave as soon as possible. Listen to @FLSERT and local offici... [Twitter for iPhone]

Oct 9, 2018 07:19:53 AM RT @NWSTallahassee: 8am Intermediate Advisory from @NHC_Atlantic upgrades #HurricaneMichael into a category 2 hurricane. Keep in mind, wind... [Twitter for iPhone]

Oct 9, 2018 07:32:46 AM The paid D.C. protesters are now ready to REALLY protest because they haven't gotten their checks - in other words, they weren't paid! Screamers in Congress, and outside, were far too obvious - less professional than anticipated by those paying (or not paying) the bills! [Twitter for iPhone]

Oct 9, 2018 07:37:55 AM Great evening last night at the White House honoring Justice Kavanaugh and family. Our country is very proud of them! [Twitter for iPhone]

Oct 9, 2018 08:10:01 AM Will be going to Iowa tonight for Rally, and more! The Farmers (and all) are very happy with USMCA! [Twitter for iPhone]

Oct 9, 2018 08:23:21 AM RT @realDonaldTrump: https://t.co/4ySIkmfllE [Twitter for iPhone]

Oct 9, 2018 09:18:47 AM Big announcement with my friend Ambassador Nikki Haley in the Oval Office at 10:30am. [Twitter for iPhone]

Oct 9, 2018 11:00:04 AM Hurricane on its way to the Florida Pan Handle with major elements arriving tomorrow. Could also hit, in later stage, parts of Georgia, and unfortunately North Carolina, and South Carolina, again... [Twitter for iPhone]

Oct 9, 2018 11:00:05 AM ...Looks to be a Cat. 3 which is even more intense than Florence. Good news is, the folks in the Pan Handle can take care of anything. @FEMA and First Responders are ready - be prepared! #HurricaneMichael [Twitter for iPhone]

Oct 9, 2018 11:07:03 AM FLORIDA - It is imperative that you heed the directions of your State and Local Officials. Please be prepared, be careful and be SAFE! #HurricaneMichael https://t.co/VP6PBXfzm9 https://t.co/aKmaDNgZve [Twitter for iPhone]

Oct 9, 2018 11:36:48 AM REGISTER TO VOTE! https://t.co/0pWiwCHGbh https://t.co/3vYfDmpqiH [Twitter for iPhone]

Oct 9, 2018 02:08:57 PM "President Donald J. Trump Approves Florida Emergency Declaration" https://t.co/TnTDCvs41W [Twitter for iPhone]

Oct 9, 2018 04:34:50 PM RT @Scavino45: Congratulations to our 114th Supreme Court Justice, Brett M. Kavanaugh! #SCOTUS us [10] https://t.co/c3YdNNcU7c https://t.co/A... [Twitter for iPhone]

Oct 9, 2018 04:39:22 PM .@FLGovScott has been relentless in securing the funding to fix the algae problem from Lake Okeechobee - we will solve this! Congress must follow through on the Government's plan on the Everglades Reservoir. Bill Nelson has been no help! [Twitter for iPhone]

Oct 9, 2018 04:59:51 PM RT @FLOTUS: Thank you Kenya KE US https://t.co/5FXP7Ki3Zw [Twitter for iPhone]

Oct 9, 2018 04:59:52 PM RT @FLOTUS: Thank you Egypt EG US https://t.co/7i0POn29XN [Twitter for iPhone]

Oct 9, 2018 05:18:13 PM RT @fema: Flooding from Hurricane #Michael will affect several states. Finish preparations ASAP and get ready to shelter in a safe location… [Twitter for iPhone]

Oct 9, 2018 08:09:41 PM Beautiful evening in Iowa. GOD BLESS THE U.S.A.! #MAGAus https://t.co/Zi0rwyajrz [Twitter for iPhone]

Oct 9, 2018 08:18:12 PM https://t.co/CPf3oxgdRX [Twitter for iPhone]

Oct 9, 2018 08:23:49 PM THANK YOU IOWA & NEBRASKA! VOTE, VOTE, VOTE! https://t.co/0pWiwCHGbh https://t.co/tzkiQ4IlEd [Twitter for iPhone]

Oct 9, 2018 09:28:10 PM RT @FLGovScott: If you're in an evacuation zone, I am urging you to leave RIGHT NOW. Do not risk your life or the lives of your loved ones-… [Twitter for iPhone]

Oct 10, 2018 07:47:01 AM Walker Stapleton is running as the highly respected Republican Candidate for Governor of the Great State of Colorado. His credentials and talents are impeccable. He has my complete and total Endorsement! [Twitter for iPhone]

Oct 10, 2018 07:47:57 AM RT @fema: As Hurricane #Michael nears land, take shelter & stay safe. ▯Follow weather updates on your phone or radio. ◈ In a tornado WARN… [Twitter for iPhone]

Oct 10, 2018 07:48:11 AM RT @NHC_Atlantic: NHC Director Ken Graham will provide a Facebook Live broadcast regarding Category 4 Hurricane #Michael at 8:45 a.m. EDT (… [Twitter for iPhone]

Oct 10, 2018 07:48:26 AM RT @NHC_Atlantic: A Storm Surge Warning remains in effect for much of the Florida Panhandle and Big Bend region, where life-threatening sto… [Twitter for iPhone]

Oct 10, 2018 07:48:41 AM RT @NHC_Atlantic: Hurricane force winds are expected to extend well inland over portions of the Florida Panhandle and portions of southeast… [Twitter for iPhone]

Oct 10, 2018 07:48:59 AM RT @NHC_Atlantic: Hurricane #Michael. In addition to the life-threatening storm surge and wind impacts, heavy rainfall is expected across… [Twitter for iPhone]

Oct 10, 2018 07:49:08 AM RT @FLSERT: Hurricane shelter locations are accessible from: https://t.co/Hop887IoiC #HurricaneMichael https://t.co/Ljk8boFaSw [Twitter for iPhone]

Oct 10, 2018 07:50:06 AM RT @FAANews: Due to #HurricaneMichael, flights in your area could be delayed and possibly cancelled. Please continue to check the status of... [Twitter for iPhone]

Oct 10, 2018 07:50:56 AM RT @NHC_Surge: A destructive and life-threatening storm surge event will occur along portions of the Florida Panhandle, Big Bend, and Natur... [Twitter for iPhone]

Oct 10, 2018 08:01:05 AM Despite so many positive events and victories, Media Reseach Center reports that 92% of stories on Donald Trump are negative on ABC, CBS and ABC. It is FAKE NEWS! Don't worry, the Failing New York Times didn't even put the Brett Kavanaugh victory on the Front Page yesterday-A17! [Twitter for iPhone]

Oct 10, 2018 11:05:55 AM We are with you Florida! https://t.co/qzrVLeFbyF https://t.co/HVVhSmBg7S https://t.co/rcB6OCwLeH [Twitter for iPhone]

Oct 10, 2018 11:43:12 AM RT @EricTrump: All my friends in Missouri, today is your LAST CHANCE to register to vote this November! It is very easy to do - simply go t... [Twitter for iPhone]

Oct 10, 2018 11:52:17 AM RT @FLGuard: #HurricaneMichael is here, but so are we. Stay safe, Florida. #FloridaFirst #FLNGAlwaysThere https://t.co/e2rVNXFERp [Twitter for iPhone]

Oct 10, 2018 12:39:59 PM RT @USATODAY: .@usatodayopinion: Democrats want to outlaw private health care plans, taking away freedom to choose plans while letting anyo... [Twitter for iPhone]

Oct 10, 2018 02:52:23 PM Departing the @WhiteHouse for Erie, Pennsylvania. I cannot disappoint the thousands of people that are there - and the thousands that are going. I look forward to seeing everyone this evening. [Twitter for iPhone]

Oct 10, 2018 04:01:55 PM Couldn't let these great people down. They have been lined up since last night - see you soon Pennsylvania! https://t.co/jSrsmncw85 [Twitter for iPhone]

Oct 10, 2018 04:05:08 PM RT @WhiteHouse: Earlier today: President @realDonaldTrump, joined by Homeland Security @SecNielsen, listens as @FEMA_Brock briefs reporters... [Twitter for iPhone]

Oct 10, 2018 05:33:37 PM RT @USNationalGuard: LIVE UPDATE: @AlabamaNG, @GeorgiaGuard, @FLGuard and @NCNationalGuard vehicles and personnel are staged and ready to p... [Twitter for iPhone]

Oct 10, 2018 05:33:48 PM RT @fema: It's extremely important to keep sheltering in a safe place and to stay aware as #Michael continues to move inland! https://t.co/... [Twitter for iPhone]

Oct 10, 2018 07:52:29 PM Thank you Erie, Pennsylvania! Remember to get out and VOTE! #MAGAus https://t.co/X8IEW8h9qP [Twitter for iPhone]

⬜ Oct 10, 2018 08:00:18 PM Massive overflow crowd tonight in Erie, Pennsylvania. THANK YOU to everyone who came out and joined us. Together, we are MAKING AMERICA GREAT AGAIN! https://t.co/FkPNNVpccX [Twitter for iPhone]

⬜ Oct 10, 2018 08:33:21 PM Thank you Jacksonville Sheriff's Office! #HurricaneMichael https://t.co/fuy7stLMJI [Twitter for iPhone]

⬜ Oct 10, 2018 08:35:15 PM Thank you to @FEMA and all First Responders! #HurricaneMichael https://t.co/vwN8BbrkkJ [Twitter for iPhone]

⬜ Oct 10, 2018 10:44:00 PM Florida Highway Patrol Troopers are all en route to the Panhandle, from all across the state of Florida - to help those affected by #HurricaneMichael. If you see them, be sure to shake their hands and say THANK YOU! #LESM https://t.co/rB7uNBudY5 [Twitter for iPhone]

⬜ Oct 11, 2018 09:41:01 AM https://t.co/h47S6T9u8V [Media Studio]

⬜ Oct 11, 2018 09:43:33 AM https://t.co/rsxEwbFZht [Media Studio]

⬜ Oct 11, 2018 11:21:53 AM https://t.co/xJ9QYGMJXa [Media Studio]

⬜ Oct 11, 2018 12:23:27 PM RT @WhiteHouse: Moments ago, President Trump signed the Music Modernization Act, which will close loopholes in our digital royalty laws to... [Twitter for iPhone]

⬜ Oct 11, 2018 05:14:23 PM RT @WhiteHouse: President Trump provides an update on the response to Hurricane Michael: https://t.co/zmnHXKakYw [Twitter for iPhone]

⬜ Oct 11, 2018 05:49:26 PM RT @FLGuard: There are serious communication issues in the Panhandle after #HurricaneMichael. If you are worried about someone, visit https... [Twitter for iPhone]

⬜ Oct 12, 2018 08:42:04 AM Working very hard on Pastor Brunson! [Twitter for iPhone]

⬜ Oct 12, 2018 08:54:46 AM So nice, everyone wants Ivanka Trump to be the new United Nations Ambassador. She would be incredible, but I can already hear the chants of Nepotism! We have great people that want the job. [Twitter for iPhone]

⬜ Oct 12, 2018 08:59:06 AM My thoughts and prayers are with Pastor Brunson, and we hope to have him safely back home soon! [Twitter for iPhone]

⬜ Oct 12, 2018 09:26:00 AM PASTOR BRUNSON JUST RELEASED. WILL BE HOME SOON! [Twitter for iPhone]

⬜ Oct 12, 2018 10:57:52 AM REGISTER TO VOTE! https://t.co/0pWiwCHGbh https://t.co/EOCLoJJ24B [Twitter for iPhone]

⬜ Oct 12, 2018 11:43:13 AM PROMISES MADE, PROMISES KEPT! https://t.co/2lk8Fjspe4 [Twitter for iPhone]

Oct 12, 2018 01:09:17 PM People have no idea how hard Hurricane Michael has hit the great state of Georgia. I will be visiting both Florida and Georgia early next week. We are working very hard on every area and every state that was hit - we are with you! [Twitter for iPhone]

Oct 12, 2018 02:10:51 PM Don't miss our GREAT @FLOTUS, Melania, on @ABC @ABC2020 tonight at 10pmE. Enjoy! [Twitter for iPhone]

Oct 12, 2018 02:37:27 PM Happy #NationalFarmersDay! With the recent #USMCA our GREAT FARMERS will do better than ever before!! https://t.co/PMS4z2EScY [Twitter for iPhone]

Oct 12, 2018 04:30:27 PM RT @WhiteHouse: https://t.co/IqLBKtgNEf [Twitter for iPhone]

Oct 12, 2018 05:02:19 PM https://t.co/HHTwwbuKa2 [Twitter for iPhone]

Oct 12, 2018 05:14:44 PM The GREAT football (and lacrosse) player, Jim Brown outside the West Wing of the @WhiteHouse. He is also a tremendous man and mentor to many young people! https://t.co/yo7MxoGL6C [Twitter for iPhone]

Oct 12, 2018 07:30:16 PM Beautiful MAKE AMERICA GREAT AGAIN rally in Lebanon, Ohio. Thank you! #ICYMI, watch here: https://t.co/UGQAmARPKR https://t.co/6nsoV8yTx3 [Twitter for iPhone]

Oct 12, 2018 08:17:01 PM RT @realDonaldTrump: Don't miss our GREAT @FLOTUS, Melania, on @ABC @ABC2020 tonight at 10pmE. Enjoy! [Twitter for iPhone]

Oct 13, 2018 08:31:27 AM Happy 243rd Birthday to our GREAT @USNavy! #243NavyBday https://t.co/m1YtoKSHFw [Twitter for iPhone]

Oct 13, 2018 09:06:26 AM Pastor Andrew Brunson, released by Turkey, will be with me in the Oval Office at 2:30 P.M. (this afternoon). It will be wonderful to see and meet him. He is a great Christian who has been through such a tough experience. I would like to thank President @RT_Erdogan for his help! [Twitter for iPhone]

Oct 13, 2018 09:17:57 AM There was NO DEAL made with Turkey for the release and return of Pastor Andrew Brunson. I don't make deals for hostages. There was, however, great appreciation on behalf of the United States, which will lead to good, perhaps great, relations between the United States & Turkey! [Twitter for iPhone]

Oct 13, 2018 12:03:06 PM "From a Turkish prison to the White House in 24 hours." Kristin Fisher of @FoxNews Very cool! [Twitter for iPhone]

Oct 13, 2018 12:43:02 PM Highly respected Congressman Keith Rothfus (R) of Pennsylvania is in the fight of his life because the Dems changed the District Map. He must win. Strong on crime, borders, big tax & reg cuts, Military & Vets. Opponent Lamb a Pelosi puppet-weak on crime. BIG ENDORSEMENT FOR KEITH [Twitter for iPhone]

Oct 13, 2018 12:52:26 PM Heading to the Great State of Kentucky - Big Rally for Congressman Andy Barr - Fantastic guy, need his vote for MAGA! Strong on Crime, Tax Cuts, Military, Vets & 2nd A. His opponent will NEVER vote for us, only for Pelosi. Andy has my Strongest Endorsement!!! See you in Kentucky. [Twitter for iPhone]

Oct 13, 2018 03:42:22 PM https://t.co/uIaENHQoPK [Twitter for iPhone]

Oct 13, 2018 03:48:09 PM WELCOME HOME PASTOR ANDREW BRUNSON! https://t.co/HijeAGU1gy [Twitter for iPhone]

Oct 13, 2018 04:06:19 PM On my way to Richmond, Kentucky for a MAKE AMERICA GREAT AGAIN rally at 7:00pmE. The crowds are once again, massive. See everyone in a couple of hours! #MAGA https://t.co/D1FYNgW0nL https://t.co/d0VBFeePLk [Twitter for iPhone]

Oct 13, 2018 08:16:43 PM Thank you Kentucky! #MAGAus https://t.co/iCUqrQ91gF https://t.co/xwsa1S2dIU [Twitter for iPhone]

Oct 13, 2018 10:42:43 PM Big day! Pastor Andrew Brunson, who could have spent 35 years in a Turkish prison, was returned safely home to his family today. Met in Oval Office, great people! Then off to Kentucky for a Rally for Congressman Andy Barr. Tremendous crowd & spirit! Just returned to White House. [Twitter for iPhone]

Oct 13, 2018 10:53:09 PM Congratulations to Tucker Carlson on the great success of his book, "Ship of Fools." It just went to NUMBER ONE! [Twitter for iPhone]

Oct 14, 2018 08:56:12 AM NBC News has totally and purposely changed the point and meaning of my story about General Robert E Lee and General Ulysses Grant. Was actually a shoutout to warrior Grant and the great state in which he was born. As usual, dishonest reporting. Even mainstream media embarrassed! [Twitter for iPhone]

Oct 14, 2018 09:02:07 AM Princess Eugenie of York was a truly beautiful bride yesterday. She has been through so much, and has come out a total winner! [Twitter for iPhone]

Oct 14, 2018 01:06:16 PM Will be interviewed tonight by @LesleyRStahl on @60Minutes @CBSNews at 7:30 P.M. Eastern. Enjoy! https://t.co/eUTAP0u0Uh [Twitter for iPhone]

Oct 14, 2018 02:39:16 PM I will be interviewed on "60 Minutes" tonight at 7:00 P.M., after NFL game. Enjoy! [Twitter for iPhone]

⎕ Oct 14, 2018 02:44:20 PM RT @IVT2020: @realDonaldTrump https://t.co/cvYbnieQ4H [Twitter for iPhone]

⎕ Oct 14, 2018 02:45:05 PM Thank you! https://t.co/CrExOML9Mi [Twitter for iPhone]

⎕ Oct 14, 2018 02:54:20 PM Thank you to NBC for the correction! https://t.co/L2mX3vREOl [Twitter for iPhone]

⎕ Oct 14, 2018 05:44:59 PM RT @realDonaldTrump: I will be interviewed on "60 Minutes" tonight at 7:00 P.M., after NFL game. Enjoy! [Twitter for iPhone]

⎕ Oct 15, 2018 06:46:39 AM "The only way to shut down the Democrats new Mob Rule strategy is to stop them cold at the Ballot Box. The fight for America's future is never over!" Ben Shapiro [Twitter for iPhone]

⎕ Oct 15, 2018 07:11:29 AM The crowds at my Rallies are far bigger than they have ever been before, including the 2016 election. Never an empty seat in these large venues, many thousands of people watching screens outside. Enthusiasm & Spirit is through the roof. SOMETHING BIG IS HAPPENING - WATCH! [Twitter for iPhone]

⎕ Oct 15, 2018 07:25:13 AM Will be leaving for Florida and Georgia with the First Lady to tour the hurricane damage and visit with FEMA, First Responders and Law Enforcement. Maximum effort is taking place, everyone is working very hard. Worst hit in 50 years! [Twitter for iPhone]

⎕ Oct 15, 2018 07:37:05 AM Just spoke to the King of Saudi Arabia who denies any knowledge of whatever may have happened "to our Saudi Arabian citizen." He said that they are working closely with Turkey to find answer. I am immediately sending our Secretary of State to meet with King! [Twitter for iPhone]

⎕ Oct 15, 2018 08:48:13 AM On our way to Florida and Georgia! [Twitter for iPhone]

⎕ Oct 15, 2018 10:45:43 AM Just arrived in Florida. Also thinking about our GREAT Alabama farmers and our many friends in North and South Carolina today. We are with you! [Twitter for iPhone]

⎕ Oct 15, 2018 05:03:23 PM RT @WhiteHouse: "First responders, @fema, the job they've done is incredible," President @realDonaldTrump said as he toured damage from #Hu… [Twitter for iPhone]

⎕ Oct 15, 2018 05:27:00 PM RT @WhiteHouse: Thank you to the law enforcement, first responders, and state, local, and Federal officials who are helping in recovery eff… [Twitter for iPhone]

⎕ Oct 15, 2018 06:51:59 PM Open enrollment starts today on lower-priced Medicare Advantage plans so loved by our great seniors. Crazy Bernie and his band of Congressional Dems will outlaw these plans. Disaster! [Twitter for iPhone]

⎕ Oct 15, 2018 07:26:23 PM TOGETHER, WE WILL PREVAIL! https://t.co/C1TLMVkDmt [Twitter for iPhone]

Oct 16, 2018 07:06:31 AM Pocahontas (the bad version), sometimes referred to as Elizabeth Warren, is getting slammed. She took a bogus DNA test and it showed that she may be 1/1024, far less than the average American. Now Cherokee Nation denies her, "DNA test is useless." Even they don't want her. Phony! [Twitter for iPhone]

Oct 16, 2018 07:16:35 AM Now that her claims of being of Indian heritage have turned out to be a scam and a lie, Elizabeth Warren should apologize for perpetrating this fraud against the American Public. Harvard called her "a person of color" (amazing con), and would not have taken her otherwise! [Twitter for iPhone]

Oct 16, 2018 07:24:51 AM Thank you to the Cherokee Nation for revealing that Elizabeth Warren, sometimes referred to as Pocahontas, is a complete and total Fraud! [Twitter for iPhone]

Oct 16, 2018 07:55:38 AM "Op-Ed praises Trump Administrations efforts at the Border." @FoxNews The Washington Examiner States, "Finally, the government has taken steps to stop releasing unaccompanied minors to criminals and traffickers." This was done by the Obama Administration! [Twitter for iPhone]

Oct 16, 2018 08:05:04 AM The United States has strongly informed the President of Honduras that if the large Caravan of people heading to the U.S. is not stopped and brought back to Honduras, no more money or aid will be given to Honduras, effective immediately! [Twitter for iPhone]

Oct 16, 2018 08:08:24 AM "8X more new manufacturing jobs now than with Obama." @FoxNews @cvpayne [Twitter for iPhone]

Oct 16, 2018 08:15:18 AM For the record, I have no financial interests in Saudi Arabia (or Russia, for that matter). Any suggestion that I have is just more FAKE NEWS (of which there is plenty)! [Twitter for iPhone]

Oct 16, 2018 09:12:06 AM Incredible number just out, 7,036,000 job openings. Astonishing - it's all working! Stock Market up big on tremendous potential of USA. Also, Strong Profits. We are Number One in World, by far! [Twitter for iPhone]

Oct 16, 2018 10:04:32 AM "Federal Judge throws out Stormy Danials lawsuit versus Trump. Trump is entitled to full legal fees." @FoxNews Great, now I can go after Horseface and her 3rd rate lawyer in the Great State of Texas. She will confirm the letter she signed! She knows nothing about me, a total con! [Twitter for iPhone]

Oct 16, 2018 10:18:51 AM "Conflict between Glen Simpson's testimony to another House Panel about his contact with Justice Department official Bruce Ohr. Ohr was used by Simpson and Steele as a Back Channel to get (FAKE) Dossier to FBI. Simpson pleading Fifth." Catherine Herridge. Where is Jeff Sessions? [Twitter for iPhone]

⬜ Oct 16, 2018 10:26:33 AM Is it really possible that Bruce Ohr, whose wife Nellie was paid by Simpson and GPS Fusion for work done on the Fake Dossier, and who was used as a Pawn in this whole SCAM (WITCH HUNT), is still working for the Department of Justice????? Can this really be so????? [Twitter for iPhone]

⬜ Oct 16, 2018 11:18:08 AM RT @WhiteHouse: https://t.co/RNqLpOtS3O [Twitter for iPhone]

⬜ Oct 16, 2018 11:22:11 AM REGISTER TO https://t.co/0pWiwCHGbh! #MAGAus https://t.co/ACTMe53TZU [Twitter for iPhone]

⬜ Oct 16, 2018 01:40:18 PM Just spoke with the Crown Prince of Saudi Arabia who totally denied any knowledge of what took place in their Turkish Consulate. He was with Secretary of State Mike Pompeo... [Twitter for iPhone]

⬜ Oct 16, 2018 01:40:19 PM ...during the call, and told me that he has already started, and will rapidly expand, a full and complete investigation into this matter. Answers will be forthcoming shortly. [Twitter for iPhone]

⬜ Oct 16, 2018 01:50:54 PM WOW, John James is making headway in Michigan. We are bringing jobs back to the State, and the People of Michigan appreciate it. Debbie Stabenow has been no help, if anything, a major hindrance. John James is a star, I hope the voters see it. Polls are tightening! [Twitter for iPhone]

⬜ Oct 16, 2018 06:28:44 PM RT @FoxBusiness: TONIGHT: @POTUS talks 2020 election in an exclusive interview with @trish_regan. Don't miss the full interview on 'Trish R... [Twitter for iPhone]

⬜ Oct 16, 2018 06:43:42 PM I will be interviewed tonight by Trish Regan on @FoxBusiness at 8:00 P.M., right after the great Lou Dobbs! [Twitter for iPhone]

⬜ Oct 16, 2018 08:19:20 PM We have today informed the countries of Honduras, Guatemala and El Salvador that if they allow their citizens, or others, to journey through their borders and up to the United States, with the intention of entering our country illegally, all payments made to them will STOP (END)! [Twitter for iPhone]

⬜ Oct 16, 2018 08:24:30 PM Anybody entering the United States illegally will be arrested and detained, prior to being sent back to their country! [Twitter for iPhone]

⬜ Oct 16, 2018 09:36:30 PM Elizabeth Warren is being hammered, even by the Left. Her false claim of Indian heritage is only selling to VERY LOW I.Q. individuals! [Twitter for iPhone]

⬜ Oct 16, 2018 09:39:24 PM Stock Market up 548 points today. Also, GREAT jobs numbers! [Twitter for iPhone]

Oct 17, 2018 06:30:21 AM "Trump could be the most honest president in modern history. When you look at the real barometer of presidential truthfulness, which is promise keeping, he is probably the most honest president in American history. He's done exactly what he said he would do." Marc Thiessen, WPost [Twitter for iPhone]

Oct 17, 2018 06:52:19 AM Watched the debate last night & Beto O'Rourke, who wants higher taxes and far more regulations, is not in the same league with Ted Cruz & what the great people of Texas stand for & want. Ted is strong on Crime, Border & 2nd A, loves our Military, Vets, Low Taxes. Beto is a Flake! [Twitter for iPhone]

Oct 17, 2018 07:00:11 AM Ted Cruz has done so much for Texas, including massive cuts in taxes and regulations - which has brought Texas to the best jobs numbers in the history of the state. He watches carefully over your 2nd Amendment. O'Rourke would blow it all! Ted has long had my Strong Endorsement! [Twitter for iPhone]

Oct 17, 2018 07:09:52 AM AP headline was very different from my quote and meaning in the story. They just can't help themselves. FAKE NEWS! [Twitter for iPhone]

Oct 17, 2018 07:31:18 AM August job openings hit a record 7.14 million. Congratulations USA! [Twitter for iPhone]

Oct 17, 2018 07:40:15 AM "Network News gave Zero coverage to the Big Day the Stock Market had yesterday." @foxandfriends [Twitter for iPhone]

Oct 17, 2018 08:45:33 AM Hard to believe that with thousands of people from South of the Border, walking unimpeded toward our country in the form of large Caravans, that the Democrats won't approve legislation that will allow laws for the protection of our country. Great Midterm issue for Republicans! [Twitter for iPhone]

Oct 17, 2018 08:48:25 AM Republicans must make the horrendous, weak and outdated immigration laws, and the Border, a part of the Midterms! [Twitter for iPhone]

Oct 17, 2018 12:11:45 PM RT @GOP: TODAY is the LAST day to register to vote in Massachusetts and Wisconsin! Register today →☐ https://t.co/CZsNCAAomd https://t.co/3... [Twitter for iPhone]

Oct 17, 2018 12:11:48 PM RT @GOP: You can cast your ballot before Election Day in: →☐KS →☐NC →☐TN Get out and vote →☐ https://t.co/YIO9A13Uio https://t.co/bxkCMApisn [Twitter for iPhone]

Oct 17, 2018 12:18:53 PM "President Donald J. Trump is Following Through on His Promise to Cut Burdensome Red Tape and Unleash the American Economy" Read more: https://t.co/SrBaQzpq4E https://t.co/zF8fEsw3in [Twitter for iPhone]

Oct 17, 2018 12:29:30 PM https://t.co/afqHydsMB5 [Twitter Media Studio]

Oct 17, 2018 12:38:17 PM https://t.co/CMxxW2fEDq [Twitter Media Studio]

Oct 17, 2018 12:41:26 PM https://t.co/MadlgNheSe [Twitter Media Studio]

Oct 17, 2018 12:52:36 PM https://t.co/mNkDYgu5sr [Twitter Media Studio]

Oct 17, 2018 02:24:44 PM College educated women want safety, security and healthcare protections – very much along with financial and economic health for themselves and our Country. I supply all of this far better than any Democrat (for decades, actually). That's why they will be voting for me! [Twitter for iPhone]

Oct 17, 2018 02:36:08 PM Congressman Neal Dunn (@DunnCampaign) of Florida has done an outstanding job at everything having to do with #MAGA. Now working hard on hurricane relief and rebuild. Strong on Crime, strong on Borders, loves our Military and our Vets. Neal has my highest Endorsement! [Twitter for iPhone]

Oct 17, 2018 03:11:53 PM RT @USMC: LIVE from the White House: Sgt. Maj. John Canley becomes the 300th Marine to receive the Medal of Honor. https://t.co/sD93rrqaoZ [Twitter for iPhone]

Oct 17, 2018 05:03:52 PM This afternoon, it was my great honor to present @USMC Sergeant Major John Canley the Medal of Honor in the East Room of the @WhiteHouse! https://t.co/EI1DD4AkC9 https://t.co/6JJm1SRcQ9 [Twitter for iPhone]

Oct 17, 2018 09:03:35 PM Ever since his vicious and totally false statements about Admiral Ron Jackson, the highly respected White House Doctor for Obama, Bush & me, Senator John Tester looks to be in big trouble in the Great State of Montana! He behaved worse than the Democrat Mob did with Justice K! [Twitter for iPhone]

Oct 18, 2018 06:25:54 AM I am watching the Democrat Party led (because they want Open Borders and existing weak laws) assault on our country by Guatemala, Honduras and El Salvador, whose leaders are doing little to stop this large flow of people, INCLUDING MANY CRIMINALS, from entering Mexico to U.S..... [Twitter for iPhone]

Oct 18, 2018 06:35:06 AM ....In addition to stopping all payments to these countries, which seem to have almost no control over their population, I must, in the strongest of terms, ask Mexico to stop this onslaught - and if unable to do so I will call up the U.S. Military and CLOSE OUR SOUTHERN BORDER!.. [Twitter for iPhone]

Oct 18, 2018 06:45:43 AM ....The assault on our country at our Southern Border, including the Criminal elements and DRUGS pouring in, is far more important to me, as President, than Trade or the USMCA. Hopefully Mexico will stop this onslaught at their Northern Border. All Democrats fault for weak laws! [Twitter for iPhone]

Oct 18, 2018 08:28:45 AM Congressman @DaveBratVA7th is one of the hardest working, and smartest, people in Washington. He is strong on the Border, Crime, the Military, our Vets and the 2nd Amendment. He is a powerful vote for MAGA and loves the Great State of Virginia. Dave has my Total Endorsement! [Twitter for iPhone]

Oct 18, 2018 10:40:23 AM ...the Crown Prince. He is waiting for the results of the investigations being done by the Saudis and Turkey, and just gave a news conference to that effect. [Twitter for iPhone]

Oct 18, 2018 10:40:23 AM Secretary of State Mike Pompeo returned last night from Saudi Arabia and Turkey. I met with him this morning wherein the Saudi situation was discussed in great detail, including his meeting with... [Twitter for iPhone]

Oct 18, 2018 10:53:10 AM .@StateDept @SecPompeo outside of the West Wing after our meeting this morning in the Oval Office... https://t.co/4GrmMdOhS1 [Twitter for iPhone]

Oct 18, 2018 11:46:09 AM See you tonight Missoula, Montana! #MAGARallyushttps://t.co/2HZ66y4BS7 [Twitter for iPhone]

Oct 18, 2018 02:43:32 PM All Republicans support people with pre-existing conditions, and if they don't, they will after I speak to them. I am in total support. Also, Democrats will destroy your Medicare, and I will keep it healthy and well! [Twitter for iPhone]

Oct 18, 2018 03:04:03 PM Can you believe this, and what Democrats are allowing to be done to our Country? https://t.co/4aDpASkjIU [Twitter for iPhone]

Oct 18, 2018 04:22:53 PM Look forward to being there. Something's happening! #MAGA https://t.co/Cev7giQexE [Twitter for iPhone]

Oct 18, 2018 05:51:42 PM Thank you Mexico, we look forward to working with you! https://t.co/wf7sE0DHFT [Twitter for iPhone]

Oct 18, 2018 06:49:45 PM Prime Minister @AbeShinzo of Japan has been working with me to help balance out the one-sided Trade with Japan. These are some of the investments they are making in our Country - just the beginning! https://t.co/ib2yB3Akkt [Twitter for iPhone]

Oct 18, 2018 07:04:52 PM Will be landing soon. Looking forward to seeing our next Senator from Montana, Matt Rosendale. He will represent our Country well, far better than Jon Tester who will vote with Cryin' Chuck Schumer and Nancy Pelosi - never with us! [Twitter for iPhone]

Oct 18, 2018 07:11:14 PM The only thing keeping Tester alive is he has millions and millions of dollars from outside liberals and leftists, who couldn't care less about our Country! [Twitter for iPhone]

Oct 18, 2018 08:54:52 PM Thank you Missoula, Montana. Get out and VOTE for @MattForMontana and @GregForMontana!! #MAGAus https://t.co/6XgaceUu1e https://t.co/nEndInSOhw [Twitter for iPhone]

⎵⎵ Oct 18, 2018 10:11:46 PM Jon Tester says one thing to voters and does the EXACT OPPOSITE in Washington. Tester takes his orders form Pelosi & Schumer. Tester wants to raise your taxes, take away your 2A, open your borders, and deliver MOB RULE. Retire Tester & Elect America-First Patriot Matt Rosendale! [Twitter for iPhone]

⎵⎵ Oct 18, 2018 10:23:02 PM #JobsNotMobs! [Twitter for iPhone]

⎵⎵ Oct 19, 2018 09:02:49 AM Congressman Andy Biggs is doing a great job for Arizona and our Country! https://t.co/V561vXRpzx [Twitter for iPhone]

⎵⎵ Oct 19, 2018 09:04:45 AM When referring to the USA, I will always capitalize the word Country! [Twitter for iPhone]

⎵⎵ Oct 19, 2018 12:26:19 PM Secretary of State Mike Pompeo was never given or shown a Transcript or Video of the Saudi Consulate event. FAKE NEWS! [Twitter for iPhone]

⎵⎵ Oct 19, 2018 12:34:07 PM Beto O'Rourke is a total lightweight compared to Ted Cruz, and he comes nowhere near representing the values and desires of the people of the Great State of Texas. He will never be allowed to turn Texas into Venezuela! [Twitter for iPhone]

⎵⎵ Oct 19, 2018 01:41:29 PM #JobsNotMobs! https://t.co/U1suRW5j6G [Twitter for iPhone]

⎵⎵ Oct 19, 2018 06:47:06 PM This is what it is all about for the Republican Party! #JobsNotMobs https://t.co/8OabccPec5 [Twitter for iPhone]

⎵⎵ Oct 19, 2018 07:51:02 PM WOW - Mesa, Arizona! Look forward to joining everyone soon. Something's happening!! #MAGAus https://t.co/z6LNGYoICO [Twitter for iPhone]

⎵⎵ Oct 19, 2018 08:23:25 PM On my way - see you all shortly! https://t.co/0pWiwCq4MH https://t.co/ahDmLiwPZi [Twitter for iPhone]

⎵⎵ Oct 19, 2018 10:13:08 PM This was outside of the massive totally full hangar tonight in Mesa, Arizona! https://t.co/0pWiwCq4MH #MAGAus https://t.co/7mx98y515I [Twitter for iPhone]

⎵⎵ Oct 19, 2018 10:17:36 PM Beautiful evening in Mesa, Arizona with GREAT PATRIOTS - thank you! https://t.co/0pWiwCq4MH #MAGARallyusreplay: https://t.co/6vHEaB37VH https://t.co/pHmU6pMKh7 [Twitter for iPhone]

⎵⎵ Oct 20, 2018 09:35:39 AM If the Democrats would stop being obstructionists and come together, we could write up and agree to new immigration laws in less than one hour. Look at the needless pain and suffering that they are causing. Look at the horrors taking place on the Border. Chuck & Nancy, call me! [Twitter for iPhone]

Oct 20, 2018 09:43:02 AM Georgia Secretary of State Brian Kemp will be a great governor. He has been successful at whatever he has done, and has prepared for this very difficult and complex job for many years. He has my Strong Endorsement. His opponent is totally unqualified. Would destroy a great state! [Twitter for iPhone]

Oct 20, 2018 09:46:00 AM Get out and Early Vote for Brian Kemp. He will be a GREAT GOVERNOR for the State of Georgia! [Twitter for iPhone]

Oct 20, 2018 09:56:32 AM Ron @RonDeSantisFL DeSantis is working hard. A great Congressman and top student at Harvard & Yale, Ron will be a record setting governor for Florida. Rick Scott gave him tremendous foundations to further build on. His opponent runs one of the worst & most corrupt cities in USA! [Twitter for iPhone]

Oct 20, 2018 10:03:27 AM Rick Scott is known as easily one of the best Governors in the USA. Florida is setting records in almost every category of success. Amazing achievement-the envy of the World. Ron DeSantis will build on this success. His incompetent opponent will destroy Florida - next Venezuela! [Twitter for iPhone]

Oct 20, 2018 11:19:05 AM Leaving Arizona after a fantastic Rally last night, in Mesa, honoring, and for, Martha @RepMcSally McSally. She is an inspiration & will be a GREAT SENATOR for the people of Arizona. Her opponent is a Nancy Pelosi puppet, really bad for State. Early Voting NOW! Will be back soon. [Twitter for iPhone]

Oct 20, 2018 11:30:00 AM Heading to Nevada to help a man who has become a good friend, Senator Dean Heller. He is all about #MAGA and I need his Help and Talent in Washington. Also, Adam Laxalt will be a GREAT GOVERNOR, and has my complete and total Endorsement. Winners Both! [Twitter for iPhone]

Oct 20, 2018 03:12:52 PM Beautiful afternoon in Elko, Nevada. Thank you! Get out and VOTE TODAY!! #MAGAus#JobsNotMobs https://t.co/0pWiwCq4MH https://t.co/AKfGzjrqCM [Twitter for iPhone]

Oct 20, 2018 07:36:13 PM All levels of government and Law Enforcement are watching carefully for VOTER FRAUD, including during EARLY VOTING. Cheat at your own peril. Violators will be subject to maximum penalties, both civil and criminal! [Twitter for iPhone]

Oct 20, 2018 09:45:20 PM Watched North Dakota's Rep. Kevin Cramer easily win debate with Senator Heidi Heitkamp. Great job Kevin, you will be a great Senator! [Twitter for iPhone]

Oct 21, 2018 02:11:52 PM Full efforts are being made to stop the onslaught of illegal aliens from crossing our Souther Border. People have to apply for asylum in Mexico first, and if they fail to do that, the U.S. will turn them away. The courts are asking the U.S. to do things that are not doable! [Twitter for iPhone]

Oct 21, 2018 02:14:24 PM The Caravans are a disgrace to the Democrat Party. Change the immigration laws NOW! [Twitter for iPhone]

Oct 21, 2018 02:26:12 PM Best Jobs Numbers in the history of our great Country! Many other things likewise. So why wouldn't we win the Midterms? Dems can never do even nearly as well! Think of what will happen to your now beautiful 401-k's! [Twitter for iPhone]

Oct 21, 2018 05:48:55 PM Facebook has just stated that they are setting up a system to "purge" themselves of Fake News. Does that mean CNN will finally be put out of business? [Twitter for iPhone]

Oct 21, 2018 08:49:29 PM Ron @RonDeSantisFL DeSantis had a great debate victory tonight against Andrew Gillum, a mayor who presides over one of the worst run, and most corrupt, cities in Florida. Ron will build on the great job done by Governor Rick Scott. Gillum will make Florida the next Venezuela! [Twitter for iPhone]

Oct 22, 2018 07:26:10 AM Congressman Tom Reed of New York's 23rd District has done a great job. He has my complete and total Endorsement! [Twitter for iPhone]

Oct 22, 2018 07:37:40 AM Sadly, it looks like Mexico's Police and Military are unable to stop the Caravan heading to the Southern Border of the United States. Criminals and unknown Middle Easterners are mixed in. I have alerted Border Patrol and Military that this is a National Emergy. Must change laws! [Twitter for iPhone]

Oct 22, 2018 07:49:31 AM Every time you see a Caravan, or people illegally coming, or attempting to come, into our Country illegally, think of and blame the Democrats for not giving us the votes to change our pathetic Immigration Laws! Remember the Midterms! So unfair to those who come in legally. [Twitter for iPhone]

Oct 22, 2018 07:57:48 AM Guatemala, Honduras and El Salvador were not able to do the job of stopping people from leaving their country and coming illegally to the U.S. We will now begin cutting off, or substantially reducing, the massive foreign aid routinely given to them. [Twitter for iPhone]

Oct 22, 2018 07:58:39 AM Big Night In Texas!!!! [Twitter for iPhone]

Oct 22, 2018 12:52:46 PM "Shock report: US paying more for illegal immigrant births than Trump's wall" https://t.co/FX3ljN7kPS [Twitter for iPhone]

Oct 22, 2018 01:00:32 PM "America: the Cleanest Air in the World - BY FAR!" https://t.co/rMtxHSnof4 [Twitter for iPhone]

Oct 22, 2018 02:18:31 PM ....I say of course they're low - because for the first time in 50 years I am making them pay a big price for doing business with America. Why should they like me? — But I still like them! [Twitter for iPhone]

Oct 22, 2018 02:18:31 PM The Fake News Media has been talking about recent approval ratings of me by countries around the world, including the European Union, as being very low.... [Twitter for iPhone]

Oct 22, 2018 02:27:20 PM WOW - thank you Houston, Texas! I am departing @Andrews_JBA now. See you in a few hours!! #MAGAus https://t.co/UxZCo19cxT [Twitter for iPhone]

Oct 22, 2018 02:54:04 PM Last day to register to VOTE in Alabama, California, South Dakota and Wyoming! #JobsNotMobs https://t.co/0pWiwCq4MH https://t.co/hmQgqgmbyE [Twitter for iPhone]

Oct 22, 2018 02:55:58 PM Let's go FLORIDA! https://t.co/0pWiwCq4MH https://t.co/6kaVM1TaiB [Twitter for iPhone]

Oct 22, 2018 04:35:03 PM Massive crowds inside and outside of the @ToyotaCenter in Houston, Texas. Landing shortly - see everyone soon! #MAGAushttps://t.co/0pWiwCq4MH https://t.co/tj5S6Z2GY7 [Twitter for iPhone]

Oct 22, 2018 08:23:33 PM https://t.co/flKQuv9MnX [Twitter for iPhone]

Oct 22, 2018 08:30:28 PM THANK YOU HOUSTON, TEXAS. Get out and https://t.co/0pWiwCHGbh! #JobsNotMobs https://t.co/JXiFjDFH6R https://t.co/Ebc1JfgUys [Twitter for iPhone]

Oct 22, 2018 09:06:24 PM We send our deepest condolences to Lou and the entire Barletta family - he has been working so hard despite this terrible situation for the people of Pennsylvania. Our thoughts and prayers are with you Lou! [Twitter for iPhone]

Oct 22, 2018 09:13:36 PM At stake in this Election is whether we continue the extraordinary prosperity we have achieved - or whether we let the Radical Democrat Mob take a giant wrecking ball to our Country and our Economy! #JobsNotMobs https://t.co/POhRivl1BZ [Twitter for iPhone]

Oct 22, 2018 09:30:03 PM Today's Democrat Party would rather protect criminal aliens than AMERICAN CITIZENS - which is why the Democrats must be voted OUT of OFFICE! #JobsNotMobs https://t.co/0pWiwCq4MH https://t.co/axUEOzBAsZ [Twitter for iPhone]

⊔ Oct 22, 2018 09:44:52 PM We send our deepest condolences to @RepLouBarletta and the entire Barletta family, on the passing of his brother. Lou has been working so hard despite this terrible situation for the people of Pennsylvania. Our thoughts and prayers are with Lou and the entire Barletta family! [Twitter for iPhone]

⊔ Oct 22, 2018 11:22:03 PM Congressman Erik Paulsen of the Great State of Minnesota has done a fantastic job in cutting Taxes and Job Killing Regulations. Hard working and very smart. Keep Erik in Congress. He has my Strong Endorsement! [Twitter for iPhone]

⊔ Oct 23, 2018 08:53:31 AM Jay Webber of New Jersey, running for Congress, is doing a great job against a person who is looking to raise Taxes substantially. Jay wants big Tax Cuts and Changes. A Harvard graduate and father of seven, Jay will be great for New Jersey and get the job done-and I will help! [Twitter for iPhone]

⊔ Oct 23, 2018 10:24:18 AM The people of Puerto Rico are wonderful but the inept politicians are trying to use the massive and ridiculously high amounts of hurricane/disaster funding to pay off other obligations. The U.S. will NOT bail out long outstanding & unpaid obligations with hurricane relief money! [Twitter for iPhone]

⊔ Oct 23, 2018 10:41:03 AM Congressman John Faso of New York has worked hard and smart. Strong on Crime, Borders and our 2nd Amendment, John is respected by all. Vote for John. He has my complete and total Endorsement! [Twitter for iPhone]

⊔ Oct 23, 2018 11:23:30 AM https://t.co/6R85sd4LLD [Twitter for iPhone]

⊔ Oct 23, 2018 11:29:19 AM #JobsNotMobs https://t.co/0pWiwCHGbh https://t.co/DsJ82fArcq [Twitter for iPhone]

⊔ Oct 23, 2018 11:43:46 AM Billions of dollars are, and will be, coming into United States coffers because of Tariffs. Great also for negotiations - if a country won't give us a fair Trade Deal, we will institute Tariffs on them. Used or not, jobs and businesses will be created. U.S. respected again! [Twitter for iPhone]

⊔ Oct 23, 2018 04:51:51 PM RT @DeptofDefense: Never forgotten! On Oct. 23, 1983, the #Beirut Marine Barracks bombing took the lives of 241 #Marines, #sailors and #sol… [Twitter for iPhone]

⊔ Oct 23, 2018 06:18:23 PM I agree with President Obama 100%! https://t.co/PI3aW1Zh5Q [Twitter for iPhone]

⊔ Oct 24, 2018 06:52:29 AM For those who want and advocate for illegal immigration, just take a good look at what has happened to Europe over the last 5 years. A total mess! They only wish they had that decision to make over again. [Twitter for iPhone]

⊔ Oct 24, 2018 06:56:41 AM We are a great Sovereign Nation. We have Strong Borders and will never accept people coming into our Country illegally! [Twitter for iPhone]

Oct 24, 2018 07:35:15 AM Brian Kemp will be a GREAT Governor of Georgia. Stacey Abrams will destroy the State. Sooooo important, get out and VOTE for Brian! [Twitter for iPhone]

Oct 24, 2018 07:45:10 AM Republicans will totally protect people with Pre-Existing Conditions, Democrats will not! Vote Republican. [Twitter for iPhone]

Oct 24, 2018 11:04:27 AM I agree wholeheartedly! https://t.co/ndzu0A30vU [Twitter for iPhone]

Oct 24, 2018 01:55:42 PM The safety of the American People is my highest priority. I have just concluded a briefing with the FBI, Department of Justice, Department of Homeland Security, and the U.S. Secret Service... https://t.co/nEUBcq4NOh [Twitter for iPhone]

Oct 24, 2018 06:54:32 PM Just arrived in Wisconsin to help two great people, @ScottWalker and @LeahVukmir! https://t.co/Pu1Yyl5K0G [Twitter for iPhone]

Oct 24, 2018 08:43:41 PM Just leaving Wisconsin. @ScottWalker and @LeahVukmir are fantastic people, badly needed for our Country! #MAGA https://t.co/6dLOBO6UQy [Twitter for iPhone]

Oct 25, 2018 05:54:42 AM The so-called experts on Trump over at the New York Times wrote a long and boring article on my cellphone usage that is so incorrect I do not have time here to correct it. I only use Government Phones, and have only one seldom used government cell phone. Story is soooo wrong! [Twitter for iPhone]

Oct 25, 2018 06:05:12 AM Brandon Judd of the National Border Patrol Council is right when he says on @foxandfriends that the Democrat inspired laws make it tough for us to stop people at the Border. MUST BE CHANDED, but I am bringing out the military for this National Emergency. They will be stopped! [Twitter for iPhone]

Oct 25, 2018 06:18:18 AM A very big part of the Anger we see today in our society is caused by the purposely false and inaccurate reporting of the Mainstream Media that I refer to as Fake News. It has gotten so bad and hateful that it is beyond description. Mainstream Media must clean up its act, FAST! [Twitter for iPhone]

Oct 25, 2018 08:57:27 AM The New York Times has a new Fake Story that now the Russians and Chinese (glad they finally added China) are listening to all of my calls on cellphones. Except that I rarely use a cellphone, & when I do it's government authorized. I like Hard Lines. Just more made up Fake News! [Twitter for iPhone]

Oct 25, 2018 11:21:46 AM "Remarks by President Trump on a Year of Historic Progress and Action to Combat the Opioid Crisis" https://t.co/YBTzMSOozW https://t.co/njGYwHff4t [Twitter for iPhone]

Oct 25, 2018 01:31:07 PM To those in the Caravan, turnaround, we are not letting people into the United States illegally. Go back to your Country and if you want, apply for citizenship like millions of others are doing! [Twitter for iPhone]

Oct 25, 2018 01:42:05 PM Spoke with French President @EmmanuelMacron this morning. Discussed many topics including the very exciting upcoming visit to Paris where @FLOTUS Melania and I will attend the Armistice Day Centennial Commemoration! [Twitter for iPhone]

Oct 25, 2018 01:47:10 PM Just spoke with Prime Minister @GiuseppeConteIT of Italy concerning many subjects, including the fact that Italy is now taking a very hard line on illegal immigration... [Twitter for iPhone]

Oct 25, 2018 01:47:11 PM ...I agree with their stance 100%, and the United States is likewise taking a very hard line on illegal immigration. The Prime Minister is working very hard on the economy of Italy - he will be successful! [Twitter for iPhone]

Oct 25, 2018 02:55:37 PM .@JohnChrin of Pennsylvania is fantastic. He is strong on the Border, Crime, the Military, our Vets and the 2nd Amendment. He is a powerful vote for #MAGA and loves the Great State of Pennsylvania. Please get out and vote for John, he has my Total and very Strong Endorsement! [Twitter for iPhone]

Oct 25, 2018 02:56:00 PM .@Troy_Balderson of Ohio is doing a great job as your Congressman, already very respected in Washington. Get out and VOTE for Troy - we need him – great guy – has my Total Endorsement! [Twitter for iPhone]

Oct 25, 2018 03:22:52 PM .@LloydSmuckerPA is doing a great job for the people of Pennsylvania. He is strong on the Border, Crime, the Military, our Vets and the 2nd Amendment. Lloyd has my Total Endorsement! [Twitter for iPhone]

Oct 25, 2018 03:24:40 PM .@MikeDunleavyGov will make a fantastic Governor of Alaska. Mike is for Energy and Jobs, is tough on Crime, loves our Vets and our Great Second Amendment. Mike has my Complete and Total Endorsement! [Twitter for iPhone]

Oct 25, 2018 03:39:16 PM .@BrucePoliquin from Maine is a great Congressman. He is in a tough fight against a very liberal Nancy Pelosi Democrat. Bruce has helped bring JOBS back to his State and totally protects your Great Second Amendment. We need to keep Bruce in Washington. He has my Full Endorsement! [Twitter for iPhone]

Oct 25, 2018 06:13:53 PM We are gathered together on this solemn occasion to fulfill our most reverent and sacred duty. 35 years ago, 241 American service members were murdered in the terrorist attack on our Marine Barracks in Beirut, Lebanon. Today, we honor our fallen heroes... https://t.co/zPgjSFj9BM [Twitter for iPhone]

Oct 25, 2018 06:19:40 PM In 1983, roughly 1,800 Marines were in Beirut to keep the peace in a Nation torn apart by Civil War. Terrorists had bombed the U.S. Embassy earlier that year, killing 63 people, including 17 Americans... https://t.co/Mp73AYv7J0 [Twitter for iPhone]

Oct 25, 2018 06:21:30 PM The Service Members who died that day included brave young Marines just out of high school, accomplished officers in the middle of their military careers, and enlisted men who had served in theaters all over the world... https://t.co/82Wkru7JAb [Twitter for iPhone]

Oct 26, 2018 02:14:39 AM Funny how lowly rated CNN, and others, can criticize me at will, even blaming me for the current spate of Bombs and ridiculously comparing this to September 11th and the Oklahoma City bombing, yet when I criticize them they go wild and scream, "it's just not Presidential!" [Twitter for iPhone]

Oct 26, 2018 08:55:48 AM The United States has been spending Billions of Dollars a year on Illegal Immigration. This will not continue. Democrats must give us the votes to pass strong (but fair) laws. If not, we will be forced to play a much tougher hand. [Twitter for iPhone]

Oct 26, 2018 09:05:49 AM Twitter has removed many people from my account and, more importantly, they have seemingly done something that makes it much harder to join - they have stifled growth to a point where it is obvious to all. A few weeks ago it was a Rocket Ship, now it is a Blimp! Total Bias? [Twitter for iPhone]

Oct 26, 2018 09:19:39 AM Republicans are doing so well in early voting, and at the polls, and now this "Bomb" stuff happens and the momentum greatly slows - news not talking politics. Very unfortunate, what is going on. Republicans, go out and vote! [Twitter for iPhone]

Oct 26, 2018 10:41:19 AM I will be speaking at the Young Black Leadership Summit in 15 minutes where I will address the investigation into the bomb packages. [Twitter for iPhone]

Oct 26, 2018 12:23:31 PM I would like to begin today's remarks by providing an update on the packages and devices that have been mailed to high-profile figures throughout our Country, and a media org. I am pleased to inform you that law enforcement has apprehended the suspect and taken him into custody. https://t.co/UFjwjjUkLd [Twitter Media Studio]

⬜ Oct 26, 2018 12:59:12 PM I want to applaud the FBI, Secret Service, Department of Justice, the U.S. Attorneys' Office for the Southern District of New York, the NYPD, and all Law Enforcement partners across the Country for their incredible work, skill and determination! [Twitter for iPhone]

⬜ Oct 26, 2018 01:22:12 PM It is my great honor to be with so many brilliant, courageous, patriotic, and PROUD AMERICANS. Seeing all of you here today fills me with extraordinary confidence in America's future. Each of you is taking part in the Young Black Leadership Summit because you are true leaders... https://t.co/lIlZBxKjuG [Twitter for iPhone]

⬜ Oct 26, 2018 01:48:29 PM Whether you are African-American, Hispanic-American or ANY AMERICAN at all – you have the right to live in a Country that puts YOUR NEEDS FIRST! https://t.co/hwDICbpOT7 [Twitter for iPhone]

⬜ Oct 26, 2018 04:22:40 PM It was my great honor, thank you! https://t.co/U2Nt1hpaVv [Twitter for iPhone]

⬜ Oct 26, 2018 04:47:16 PM If you meet every day with optimism – if you confront every obstacle with determination – if you refuse to give up, if you never quit, if you face every challenge with confidence and pride – then there is no goal you cannot achieve, and no dream beyond your reach! #YBLS2018 https://t.co/Uqmw5fLmxW [Twitter for iPhone]

⬜ Oct 26, 2018 07:58:44 PM Fantastic evening in Charlotte, North Carolina with great PATRIOTS. Get out and VOTE for @buddforcongress and @MarkHarrisNC9! https://t.co/0pWiwCHGbh #MAGARally replay: https://t.co/bKVTylqDvE https://t.co/O1QiZSw4cU [Twitter for iPhone]

⬜ Oct 27, 2018 08:28:56 AM Trump Thunders at Media for Smearing His Supporters after Bomb Scares https://t.co/Ggdhs9reY3 via @BreitbartNews [Twitter for iPhone]

⬜ Oct 27, 2018 08:38:46 AM A big change is coming - don't want the Dems anymore! https://t.co/O6wp2gjPUY [Twitter for iPhone]

⬜ Oct 27, 2018 08:41:22 AM Good luck Mary! https://t.co/qEBpqS0vli [Twitter for iPhone]

⬜ Oct 27, 2018 08:45:53 AM Thank you Charlie! https://t.co/U2Nt1h7A3X [Twitter for iPhone]

⬜ Oct 27, 2018 08:46:33 AM RT @GOPChairwoman: .@realDonaldTrump is delivering results for all Americans, and it's inspiring our future leaders to get involved in the... [Twitter for iPhone]

⬜ Oct 27, 2018 08:51:41 AM Martha McSally is a great warrior, her opponent a Nancy Pelosi Wacko! https://t.co/QEUdPWDDud [Twitter for iPhone]

⬜ Oct 27, 2018 08:54:15 AM Budd and Mark, two great patriots for Congress! https://t.co/xx0cqUf7wj [Twitter for iPhone]

Oct 27, 2018 08:55:12 AM RT @DiamondandSilk: LIVE: President @realdonaldtrump #MAGA rally in Charlotte, NC https://t.co/mi9Nh8TecI [Twitter for iPhone]

Oct 27, 2018 09:02:36 AM #Walkaway Walkaway from the Democrat Party movement marches today in D.C. Congratulations to Brandon Straka for starting something very special. @foxandfriends [Twitter for iPhone]

Oct 27, 2018 10:08:28 AM Watching the events unfolding in Pittsburgh, Pennsylvania. Law enforcement on the scene. People in Squirrel Hill area should remain sheltered. Looks like multiple fatalities. Beware of active shooter. God Bless All! [Twitter for iPhone]

Oct 27, 2018 11:26:23 AM Events in Pittsburgh are far more devastating than originally thought. Spoke with Mayor and Governor to inform them that the Federal Government has been, and will be, with them all the way. I will speak to the media shortly and make further statement at Future Farmers of America. [Twitter for iPhone]

Oct 27, 2018 02:43:45 PM As you know, earlier today there was a horrific shooting targeting and killing Jewish Americans at the Tree of Life Synagogue in Pittsburgh, Pennsylvania. The shooter is in custody, and federal authorities have been dispatched to support state and local police... https://t.co/WqO7GfPyMT [Twitter for iPhone]

Oct 27, 2018 03:07:24 PM RT @WhiteHouse: Just now: President Trump invited Rabbi Benjamin Sendrow to offer a prayer for the victims of the attack in Pittsburgh. htt… [Twitter for iPhone]

Oct 27, 2018 04:41:35 PM ...This evil Anti-Semitic attack is an assault on humanity. It will take all of us working together to extract the poison of Anti-Semitism from our world. We must unite to conquer hate. [Twitter for iPhone]

Oct 27, 2018 04:41:35 PM All of America is in mourning over the mass murder of Jewish Americans at the Tree of Life Synagogue in Pittsburgh. We pray for those who perished and their loved ones, and our hearts go out to the brave police officers who sustained serious injuries... [Twitter for iPhone]

Oct 27, 2018 10:46:45 PM Watching the Dodgers/Red Sox final innings. It is amazing how a manager takes out a pitcher who is loose & dominating through almost 7 innings, Rich Hill of Dodgers, and brings in nervous reliever(s) who get shellacked. 4 run lead gone. Managers do it all the time, big mistake! [Twitter for iPhone]

Oct 27, 2018 10:57:41 PM Very interesting! https://t.co/ZmSA4v5fKi [Twitter for iPhone]

Oct 28, 2018 11:53:15 AM Thank you to Steve Rogers, FBI Joint Terror Task Force (Ret), for his very kind and generous remarks about me and my relationship to Law Enforcement. @JudgeJeanine [Twitter for iPhone]

⊔ Oct 28, 2018 12:03:47 PM Just watched Wacky Tom Steyer, who I have not seen in action before, be interviewed by @jaketapper. He comes off as a crazed & stumbling lunatic who should be running out of money pretty soon. As bad as their field is, if he is running for President, the Dems will eat him alive! [Twitter for iPhone]

⊔ Oct 28, 2018 07:12:57 PM The Fake News is doing everything in their power to blame Republicans, Conservatives and me for the division and hatred that has been going on for so long in our Country. Actually, it is their Fake & Dishonest reporting which is causing problems far greater than they understand! [Twitter for iPhone]

⊔ Oct 29, 2018 07:03:13 AM There is great anger in our Country caused in part by inaccurate, and even fraudulent, reporting of the news. The Fake News Media, the true Enemy of the People, must stop the open & obvious hostility & report the news accurately & fairly. That will do much to put out the flame... [Twitter for iPhone]

⊔ Oct 29, 2018 07:07:51 AM ....of Anger and Outrage and we will then be able to bring all sides together in Peace and Harmony. Fake News Must End! [Twitter for iPhone]

⊔ Oct 29, 2018 07:28:08 AM Had a very good conversation with the newly elected President of Brazil, Jair Bolsonaro, who won his race by a substantial margin. We agreed that Brazil and the United States will work closely together on Trade, Military and everything else! Excellent call, wished him congrats! [Twitter for iPhone]

⊔ Oct 29, 2018 09:41:56 AM Many Gang Members and some very bad people are mixed into the Caravan heading to our Southern Border. Please go back, you will not be admitted into the United States unless you go through the legal process. This is an invasion of our Country and our Military is waiting for you! [Twitter for iPhone]

⊔ Oct 29, 2018 09:54:25 AM In Florida there is a choice between a Harvard/Yale educated man named @RonDeSantisFL who has been a great Congressman and will be a great Governor - and a Dem who is a thief and who is Mayor of poorly run Tallahassee, said to be one of the most corrupt cities in the Country! [Twitter for iPhone]

⊔ Oct 29, 2018 09:57:42 AM Great job being done by Congressman Keith Rothfus of Pennsylvania. Thank you Keith! [Twitter for iPhone]

⊔ Oct 29, 2018 07:00:23 PM CNN and others in the Fake News Business keep purposely and inaccurately reporting that I said the "Media is the Enemy of the People." Wrong! I said that the "Fake News (Media) is the Enemy of the People," a very big difference. When you give out false information - not good! [Twitter for iPhone]

Oct 29, 2018 07:14:17 PM Check out tweets from last two days. I refer to Fake News Media when mentioning Enemy of the People - but dishonest reporters use only the word "Media." The people of our Great Country are angry and disillusioned at receiving so much Fake News. They get it, and fully understand! [Twitter for iPhone]

Oct 29, 2018 07:31:36 PM I will be interviewed by Laura Ingraham tonight at 10:00 P.M. on @FoxNews [Twitter for iPhone]

Oct 29, 2018 07:39:17 PM So Revealing! https://t.co/wR0Z4694ei [Twitter for iPhone]

Oct 29, 2018 08:53:05 PM RT @realDonaldTrump: I will be interviewed by Laura Ingraham tonight at 10:00 P.M. on @FoxNews [Twitter for iPhone]

Oct 29, 2018 08:56:19 PM .@troybalderson is doing a great job as Congressman from Ohio. We need him in D.C. Vote for Troy - He has my total Endorsement! [Twitter for iPhone]

Oct 29, 2018 09:01:38 PM RT @realDonaldTrump: I will be interviewed by Laura Ingraham tonight at 10:00 P.M. on @FoxNews [Twitter for iPhone]

Oct 29, 2018 09:11:37 PM .@Troy_Balderson is doing a great job as Congressman from Ohio. We need him in D.C. Vote for Troy - He has my total Endorsement! [Twitter for iPhone]

Oct 29, 2018 09:50:31 PM Congressman @DenverRiggleman of the 5th District in Virginia is a popular guy who really knows how to get the job done! Really big help with Tax Cuts, the Military and our great Vets. He has my Total Endorsement! [Twitter for iPhone]

Oct 29, 2018 10:01:40 PM .@ErikPaulson, @JasonLewis, @JimHagedornMN and @PeteStauber love our Country and the Great State of Minnesota. They are winners and always get the job done We need them all in Congress for #MAGA. Border, Military, Vets, 2nd A. Go Vote Minnesota. They have my Strong Endorsement! [Twitter for iPhone]

Oct 29, 2018 10:05:14 PM .@Denver4VA of the 5th District in Virginia is a popular guy who really knows how to get the job done! Really big help with Tax Cuts, the Military and our great Vets. He has my Total Endorsement! [Twitter for iPhone]

Oct 29, 2018 10:07:15 PM Congressman @RodBlum of Iowa got a desperately needed Flood Wall for Cedar Rapids that was almost impossible to get. He makes a BIG difference for Iowa! Border, Military, Vets etc. We need Rod in D.C. He has my Strong Endorsement! [Twitter for iPhone]

Oct 29, 2018 10:13:13 PM Congresswoman @cathymcmorris of Washington State is an incredible leader who is respected by everyone in Congress. We need her badly in D.C. to keep building on #MAGA. She has my Strong Endorsement! [Twitter for iPhone]

Oct 29, 2018 10:18:12 PM .@Erik_Paulsen, @Jason2CD, @JimHagedornMN and @PeteStauber love our Country and the Great State of Minnesota. They are winners and always get the job done We need them all in Congress for #MAGA. Border, Military, Vets, 2nd A. Go Vote Minnesota. They have my Strong Endorsement! [Twitter for iPhone]

Oct 29, 2018 10:19:42 PM Congressman @DaveBratVA7th is a fighter who is doing a great job for Virginia and for our Country. Border, Military, Vets, 2nd Amendment and all else. We need Dave in D.C. He has my Strong Endorsement! [Twitter for iPhone]

Oct 29, 2018 10:21:36 PM .@Erik_Paulsen, @Jason2CD, @JimHagedornMN and @PeteStauber love our Country and the Great State of Minnesota. They are winners and always get the job done. We need them all in Congress for #MAGA. Border, Military, Vets, 2nd A. Go Vote Minnesota. They have my Strong Endorsement! [Twitter for iPhone]

Oct 30, 2018 07:12:25 AM Congressman Andy Barr of Kentucky, who just had a great debate with his Nancy Pelosi run opponent, has been a winner for his State. Strong on Crime, the Border, Tax Cuts, Military, Vets and 2nd Amendment, we need Andy in D.C. He has my Strong Endorsement! [Twitter for iPhone]

Oct 30, 2018 07:25:07 AM Congressman Kevin Brady of Texas is so popular in his District, and far beyond, that he doesn't need any help - but I am giving it to him anyway. He is a great guy and the absolute "King" of Cutting Taxes. Highly respected by all, he loves his State & Country. Strong Endorsement! [Twitter for iPhone]

Oct 30, 2018 07:33:39 AM The Stock Market is up massively since the Election, but is now taking a little pause - people want to see what happens with the Midterms. If you want your Stocks to go down, I strongly suggest voting Democrat. They like the Venezuela financial model, High Taxes & Open Borders! [Twitter for iPhone]

Oct 30, 2018 07:53:03 AM "If the Fed backs off and starts talking a little more Dovish, I think we're going to be right back to our 2,800 to 2,900 target range that we've had for the S&P 500." Scott Wren, Wells Fargo. [Twitter for iPhone]

Oct 30, 2018 10:10:39 AM Just out: Consumer Confidence hits highest level since 2000. [Twitter for iPhone]

Oct 30, 2018 12:37:49 PM ....Richard Cordray will let you down, just like he did when he destroyed the government agency that he ran. Clone of Pocahontas, that's not for Ohio. Mike has my Total Endorsement! [Twitter for iPhone]

Oct 30, 2018 12:37:49 PM .@MikeDeWine will be a great Governor for the People of Ohio. He is an outstanding man who loves his State – and always produces big.... [Twitter for iPhone]

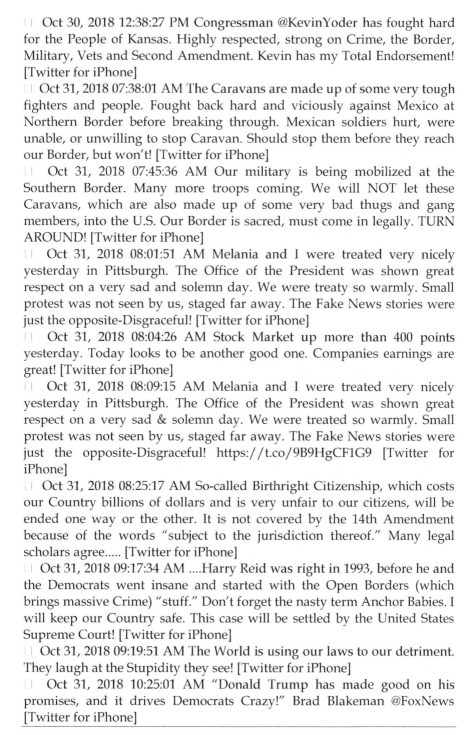

Oct 30, 2018 12:38:27 PM Congressman @KevinYoder has fought hard for the People of Kansas. Highly respected, strong on Crime, the Border, Military, Vets and Second Amendment. Kevin has my Total Endorsement! [Twitter for iPhone]

Oct 31, 2018 07:38:01 AM The Caravans are made up of some very tough fighters and people. Fought back hard and viciously against Mexico at Northern Border before breaking through. Mexican soldiers hurt, were unable, or unwilling to stop Caravan. Should stop them before they reach our Border, but won't! [Twitter for iPhone]

Oct 31, 2018 07:45:36 AM Our military is being mobilized at the Southern Border. Many more troops coming. We will NOT let these Caravans, which are also made up of some very bad thugs and gang members, into the U.S. Our Border is sacred, must come in legally. TURN AROUND! [Twitter for iPhone]

Oct 31, 2018 08:01:51 AM Melania and I were treated very nicely yesterday in Pittsburgh. The Office of the President was shown great respect on a very sad and solemn day. We were treaty so warmly. Small protest was not seen by us, staged far away. The Fake News stories were just the opposite-Disgraceful! [Twitter for iPhone]

Oct 31, 2018 08:04:26 AM Stock Market up more than 400 points yesterday. Today looks to be another good one. Companies earnings are great! [Twitter for iPhone]

Oct 31, 2018 08:09:15 AM Melania and I were treated very nicely yesterday in Pittsburgh. The Office of the President was shown great respect on a very sad & solemn day. We were treated so warmly. Small protest was not seen by us, staged far away. The Fake News stories were just the opposite-Disgraceful! https://t.co/9B9HgCF1G9 [Twitter for iPhone]

Oct 31, 2018 08:25:17 AM So-called Birthright Citizenship, which costs our Country billions of dollars and is very unfair to our citizens, will be ended one way or the other. It is not covered by the 14th Amendment because of the words "subject to the jurisdiction thereof." Many legal scholars agree..... [Twitter for iPhone]

Oct 31, 2018 09:17:34 AM ....Harry Reid was right in 1993, before he and the Democrats went insane and started with the Open Borders (which brings massive Crime) "stuff." Don't forget the nasty term Anchor Babies. I will keep our Country safe. This case will be settled by the United States Supreme Court! [Twitter for iPhone]

Oct 31, 2018 09:19:51 AM The World is using our laws to our detriment. They laugh at the Stupidity they see! [Twitter for iPhone]

Oct 31, 2018 10:25:01 AM "Donald Trump has made good on his promises, and it drives Democrats Crazy!" Brad Blakeman @FoxNews [Twitter for iPhone]

Oct 31, 2018 10:28:57 AM Republicans will protect people with pre-existing conditions far better than the Dems! [Twitter for iPhone]

Oct 31, 2018 11:43:19 AM Paul Ryan should be focusing on holding the Majority rather than giving his opinions on Birthright Citizenship, something he knows nothing about! Our new Republican Majority will work on this, Closing the Immigration Loopholes and Securing our Border! [Twitter for iPhone]

Oct 31, 2018 12:19:27 PM Harry Reid, when he was sane, agreed with us on Birthright Citizenship! https://t.co/ypiE1QWKag [Twitter for iPhone]

Oct 31, 2018 02:24:22 PM Yesterday in Pittsburgh I was really impressed with Congressman Keith Rothfus (far more so than any other local political figure). His sincere level of compassion, grief and sorrow for the events that took place was, in its own way, very inspiring. Vote for Keith! [Twitter for iPhone]

Oct 31, 2018 02:25:29 PM #JOBSNOTMOBS! VOTE REPUBLICAN NOW!! https://t.co/wso9ZHIvyF [Twitter for iPhone]

Oct 31, 2018 03:18:07 PM It is outrageous what the Democrats are doing to our Country. Vote Republican now! https://t.co/0pWiwCHGbh https://t.co/2crea9HF7G [Twitter for iPhone]

Oct 31, 2018 07:53:19 PM THANK YOU FLORIDA! Get out and VOTE Republican! #MAGAus https://t.co/v3hpKOPBik [Twitter for iPhone]

Oct 31, 2018 08:43:15 PM Fantastic evening in Florida with great PATRIOTS at a beautiful #MAGARally. Get out and https://t.co/0pWiwCq4MH so we can continue MAKING AMERICA SAFE & GREAT AGAIN! https://t.co/c3fqrEdzFU https://t.co/VrmaMHPhl3 [Twitter for iPhone]

Oct 31, 2018 10:33:01 PM That's because they treat me fairly! "@FoxNews tops @CNN and @MSNBC combined in October cable news ratings" https://t.co/QX56Pwlmj4 [Twitter for iPhone]

Oct 31, 2018 10:34:07 PM RT @realDonaldTrump: Harry Reid, when he was sane, agreed with us on Birthright Citizenship! https://t.co/ypiE1QWKag [Twitter for iPhone]

Oct 31, 2018 10:34:15 PM RT @realDonaldTrump: #JOBSNOTMOBS! VOTE REPUBLICAN NOW!! https://t.co/wso9ZHIvyF [Twitter for iPhone]

Nov 1, 2018 09:09:10 AM Just had a long and very good conversation with President Xi Jinping of China. We talked about many subjects, with a heavy emphasis on Trade. Those discussions are moving along nicely with meetings being scheduled at the G-20 in Argentina. Also had good discussion on North Korea! [Twitter for iPhone]

Nov 1, 2018 01:33:41 PM Thank you to Rick Breckenridge and congratulations to Matt Rosendale (@MattForMontana). This is very big - see you in Montana on Saturday! Tickets: https://t.co/zX9sj0qUzN https://t.co/UWuHHs6Y0u [Twitter for iPhone]

Nov 1, 2018 01:37:15 PM .@WalkerStapleton will be an extraordinary Governor for the State of Colorado. He is strong, smart, and has been successful at everything he has ever done.... [Twitter for iPhone]

Nov 1, 2018 01:37:17 PM ....His opponent, Jared Polis, is weak on crime and weak on borders – could never do the job. Get out and VOTE – Walker has my Complete and Total Endorsement! [Twitter for iPhone]

Nov 1, 2018 03:54:49 PM Illegal immigration affects the lives of all Americans. Illegal Immigration hurts American workers, burdens American taxpayers, undermines public safety, and places enormous strain on local schools, hospitals and communities... https://t.co/eN1IqPNBJY [Twitter for iPhone]

Nov 1, 2018 05:11:42 PM On my way to Columbia, Missouri for a #MAGARally. Look forward to seeing everyone soon! https://t.co/0pWiwCHGbh https://t.co/oD6v3E13bk [Twitter for iPhone]

Nov 1, 2018 05:46:35 PM Together, we are Making America Safe and Great Again! https://t.co/0pWiwCHGbh https://t.co/rWl5aSpY3O [Twitter for iPhone]

Nov 1, 2018 09:23:20 PM Beautiful evening at a #MAGARally with great American Patriots. Loyal citizens like you helped build this Country and together, we are taking back this Country – returning power to YOU, the AMERICAN PEOPLE. Get out and https://t.co/0pWiwCHGbh! https://t.co/9nCTLdFVW4 https://t.co/wBOUVedVtT [Twitter for iPhone]

Nov 1, 2018 09:43:46 PM I love you Missouri! Under Republican leadership, America is BOOMING, America is THRIVING, and America is WINNING - because we are finally putting AMERICA FIRST. Get out and VOTE Josh @HawleyMO for the United States Senate! #MAGAus https://t.co/opp35qPPy3 [Twitter for iPhone]

Nov 2, 2018 08:46:49 AM Wow! The U.S. added 250,000 Jobs in October - and this was despite the hurricanes. Unemployment at 3.7%. Wages UP! These are incredible numbers. Keep it going, Vote Republican! [Twitter for iPhone]

Nov 2, 2018 08:54:58 AM Will be going to West Virginia and Indiana today, TWO RALLIES! Don't tell anyone (big secret), but I will be bringing Coach Bobby Knight to Indiana. He's been a supporter right from the beginning of the Greatest Political Movement in American History! [Twitter for iPhone]

Nov 2, 2018 11:01:44 AM https://t.co/nk2vKvHuaL [Twitter for iPhone]

Nov 2, 2018 04:54:06 PM Fantastic #MAGARallyusin West Virginia, thank you. Everyone get out and VOTE for Patrick @MorriseyWV and @CarolMillerWV! https://t.co/N8CQeLmSad [Twitter for iPhone]

Nov 2, 2018 05:14:29 PM JOBS, JOBS, JOBS! #MAGA https://t.co/ZqPjsPUX0t [Twitter for iPhone]

Nov 2, 2018 05:45:52 PM THANK YOU WEST VIRGINIA! https://t.co/0pWiwCHGbh https://t.co/KmrMAt4Cea [Twitter for iPhone]

Nov 2, 2018 05:51:57 PM Just landed - will see everyone in Southport, Indiana shortly! #MAGARallyus https://t.co/zmapQS70CG [Twitter for iPhone]

Nov 2, 2018 06:18:24 PM I need the people of West Virginia to send a message to Chuck Schumer, Maxine Waters, Nancy Pelosi and the Radical Democrats by voting for Carol Miller and Patrick Morrisey! [Twitter for iPhone]

Nov 2, 2018 07:40:33 PM In just 4 days, the people of Indiana are going to send Mike @braun4indiana to the United States Senate, so we can keep MAKING AMERICA GREAT AGAIN! Get out and VOTE!! https://t.co/dO3Nr8nuJi [Twitter for iPhone]

Nov 2, 2018 07:49:30 PM Republicans believe our Country should be a Sanctuary for law-abiding Americans – not criminal aliens. And Republicans will ALWAYS stand with the HEROES of @ICEgov, @CBP, and Law Enforcement! https://t.co/jmnmO26Yb3 [Twitter for iPhone]

Nov 2, 2018 08:27:44 PM Massive #MAGARallyustonight in Indiana, thank you. Everyone get out and https://t.co/0pWiwCHGbh! https://t.co/5jVFO6SIsz [Twitter for iPhone]

Nov 2, 2018 09:56:11 PM Scott Perry of Pennsylvania is fantastic. He is strong on the Border, Crime, the Military, our Vets and the Second Amendment. Scott has my Total Endorsement! [Twitter for iPhone]

Nov 3, 2018 05:54:55 AM Congresswoman Maxine Waters was called the most Corrupt Member of Congress! @FoxNews If Dems win, she would be put in charge of our Country's finances. The beginning of the end! [Twitter for iPhone]

Nov 3, 2018 06:49:45 AM Indiana Rally, and Coach Bobby Knight, were incredible last night. Packed House in Honor of Mike Braun for Senate. Mike will be a GREAT Senator. Don't forget to VOTE! [Twitter for iPhone]

Nov 3, 2018 07:04:35 AM Heading to Montana and Florida today! Everyone is excited about the Jobs Numbers - 250,000 new jobs in October. Also, wages rising. Wow! [Twitter for iPhone]

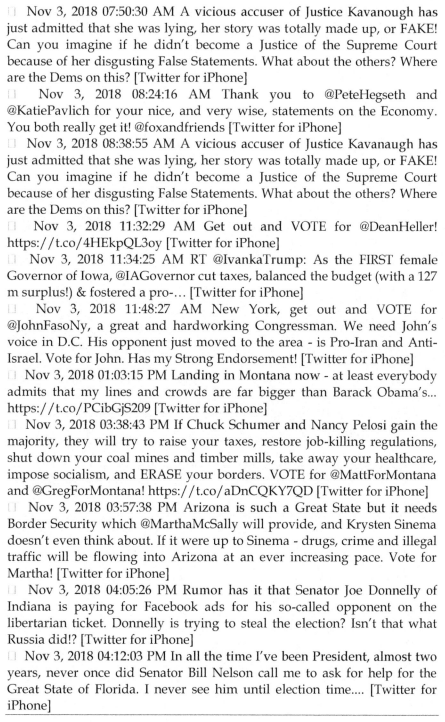

Nov 3, 2018 07:50:30 AM A vicious accuser of Justice Kavanough has just admitted that she was lying, her story was totally made up, or FAKE! Can you imagine if he didn't become a Justice of the Supreme Court because of her disgusting False Statements. What about the others? Where are the Dems on this? [Twitter for iPhone]

Nov 3, 2018 08:24:16 AM Thank you to @PeteHegseth and @KatiePavlich for your nice, and very wise, statements on the Economy. You both really get it! @foxandfriends [Twitter for iPhone]

Nov 3, 2018 08:38:55 AM A vicious accuser of Justice Kavanaugh has just admitted that she was lying, her story was totally made up, or FAKE! Can you imagine if he didn't become a Justice of the Supreme Court because of her disgusting False Statements. What about the others? Where are the Dems on this? [Twitter for iPhone]

Nov 3, 2018 11:32:29 AM Get out and VOTE for @DeanHeller! https://t.co/4HEkpQL3oy [Twitter for iPhone]

Nov 3, 2018 11:34:25 AM RT @IvankaTrump: As the FIRST female Governor of Iowa, @IAGovernor cut taxes, balanced the budget (with a 127 m surplus!) & fostered a pro-... [Twitter for iPhone]

Nov 3, 2018 11:48:27 AM New York, get out and VOTE for @JohnFasoNy, a great and hardworking Congressman. We need John's voice in D.C. His opponent just moved to the area - is Pro-Iran and Anti-Israel. Vote for John. Has my Strong Endorsement! [Twitter for iPhone]

Nov 3, 2018 01:03:15 PM Landing in Montana now - at least everybody admits that my lines and crowds are far bigger than Barack Obama's... https://t.co/PCibGjS209 [Twitter for iPhone]

Nov 3, 2018 03:38:43 PM If Chuck Schumer and Nancy Pelosi gain the majority, they will try to raise your taxes, restore job-killing regulations, shut down your coal mines and timber mills, take away your healthcare, impose socialism, and ERASE your borders. VOTE for @MattForMontana and @GregForMontana! https://t.co/aDnCQKY7QD [Twitter for iPhone]

Nov 3, 2018 03:57:38 PM Arizona is such a Great State but it needs Border Security which @MarthaMcSally will provide, and Krysten Sinema doesn't even think about. If it were up to Sinema - drugs, crime and illegal traffic will be flowing into Arizona at an ever increasing pace. Vote for Martha! [Twitter for iPhone]

Nov 3, 2018 04:05:26 PM Rumor has it that Senator Joe Donnelly of Indiana is paying for Facebook ads for his so-called opponent on the libertarian ticket. Donnelly is trying to steal the election? Isn't that what Russia did!? [Twitter for iPhone]

Nov 3, 2018 04:12:03 PM In all the time I've been President, almost two years, never once did Senator Bill Nelson call me to ask for help for the Great State of Florida. I never see him until election time.... [Twitter for iPhone]

Nov 3, 2018 04:12:07 PM ....Lake Okeechobee and all of the hurricane money were a passion for Rick Scott, who called endlessly on behalf of the People of Florida. Vote @ScottforFlorida! [Twitter for iPhone]

Nov 3, 2018 06:00:22 PM Governor @DougDucey of Arizona is doing a great job. Doug is strong on Crime, the Border, and our Second Amendment. Loves our Military & our Vets. Vote for Doug, he has my full and Complete Endorsement! [Twitter for iPhone]

Nov 3, 2018 06:05:05 PM Heading to Pensacola, Florida - will be there soon. Amazing lines of people wanting to get in - what a crowd! Is this a sign of Republican Strength on Tuesday? https://t.co/te7RHdAeKA [Twitter for iPhone]

Nov 3, 2018 08:29:26 PM Another fantastic #MAGARally tonight in the Great State of Florida. In just 3 days, the People of Florida are going to elect @ScottforFlorida and @RonDeSantisFL to protect your jobs, defend your BORDERS, and CONTINUE MAKING AMERICA GREAT AGAIN! https://t.co/0pWiwCHGbhus https://t.co/sS78uyafOG [Twitter for iPhone]

Nov 3, 2018 08:39:58 PM .@DannyTarkanian is a great guy and a team player. He will represent his District, State and Country at the highest level. Danny is strong on Military, our Vets, Second Amendment and all of the things that we so strongly stand for. Vote for Danny - he has my Strong Endorsement! [Twitter for iPhone]

Nov 3, 2018 08:46:00 PM If you want to protect criminal aliens – VOTE DEMOCRAT. If you want to protect Law-Abiding Americans – VOTE REPUBLICAN! https://t.co/0pWiwCHGbh https://t.co/2YoXSWT0Px [Twitter for iPhone]

Nov 3, 2018 09:47:33 PM Unbelievable crowd in Florida tonight. Get out and VOTE! #MAGAus https://t.co/zPLkAko8If [Twitter for iPhone]

Nov 4, 2018 10:15:42 AM New Fox Poll shows a "40% Approval Rating by African Americans for President Trump, a record for Republicans." Thank you, a great honor! [Twitter for iPhone]

Nov 4, 2018 10:24:58 AM RT @realDonaldTrump: Scott Perry of Pennsylvania is fantastic. He is strong on the Border, Crime, the Military, our Vets and the Second Ame... [Twitter for iPhone]

Nov 4, 2018 10:25:59 AM RT @realDonaldTrump: I need the people of West Virginia to send a message to Chuck Schumer, Maxine Waters, Nancy Pelosi and the Radical Dem... [Twitter for iPhone]

Nov 4, 2018 10:27:21 AM RT @realDonaldTrump: Wow! The U.S. added 250,000 Jobs in October - and this was despite the hurricanes. Unemployment at 3.7%. Wages UP! The... [Twitter for iPhone]

⊔ Nov 4, 2018 10:27:47 AM RT @realDonaldTrump: I love you Missouri! Under Republican leadership, America is BOOMING, America is THRIVING, and America is WINNING - be... [Twitter for iPhone]

⊔ Nov 4, 2018 10:28:22 AM RT @realDonaldTrump: Together, we are Making America Safe and Great Again! https://t.co/0pWiwCHGbh https://t.co/rWl5aSpY3O [Twitter for iPhone]

⊔ Nov 4, 2018 10:28:42 AM RT @realDonaldTrump: Illegal immigration affects the lives of all Americans. Illegal Immigration hurts American workers, burdens American t... [Twitter for iPhone]

⊔ Nov 4, 2018 10:29:17 AM RT @realDonaldTrump: .@WalkerStapleton will be an extraordinary Governor for the State of Colorado. He is strong, smart, and has been succe... [Twitter for iPhone]

⊔ Nov 4, 2018 10:30:14 AM RT @realDonaldTrump: That's because they treat me fairly! "@FoxNews tops @CNN and @MSNBC combined in October cable news ratings" https://t.... [Twitter for iPhone]

⊔ Nov 4, 2018 10:32:05 AM RT @realDonaldTrump: It is outrageous what the Democrats are doing to our Country. Vote Republican now! https://t.co/0pWiwCHGbh https://t.c... [Twitter for iPhone]

⊔ Nov 4, 2018 10:32:18 AM RT @realDonaldTrump: Yesterday in Pittsburgh I was really impressed with Congressman Keith Rothfus (far more so than any other local politi... [Twitter for iPhone]

⊔ Nov 4, 2018 10:39:11 AM RT @realDonaldTrump: Congressman @KevinYoder has fought hard for the People of Kansas. Highly respected, strong on Crime, the Border, Milit... [Twitter for iPhone]

⊔ Nov 4, 2018 10:39:28 AM RT @realDonaldTrump: ....Richard Cordray will let you down, just like he did when he destroyed the government agency that he ran. Clone of... [Twitter for iPhone]

⊔ Nov 4, 2018 10:39:37 AM RT @realDonaldTrump: .@MikeDeWine will be a great Governor for the People of Ohio. He is an outstanding man who loves his State – and alway... [Twitter for iPhone]

⊔ Nov 4, 2018 10:39:46 AM RT @realDonaldTrump: Just out: Consumer Confidence hits highest level since 2000. [Twitter for iPhone]

⊔ Nov 4, 2018 10:40:24 AM RT @realDonaldTrump: .@Erik_Paulsen, @Jason2CD, @JimHagedornMN and @PeteStauber love our Country and the Great State of Minnesota. They ar... [Twitter for iPhone]

⊔ Nov 4, 2018 10:40:35 AM RT @realDonaldTrump: Congressman @DaveBratVA7th is a fighter who is doing a great job for Virginia and for our Country. Border, Military, V... [Twitter for iPhone]

⊔ Nov 4, 2018 10:40:49 AM RT @realDonaldTrump: Congressman @RodBlum of Iowa got a desperately needed Flood Wall for Cedar Rapids that was almost impossible to get. H... [Twitter for iPhone]

Nov 4, 2018 10:41:03 AM RT @realDonaldTrump: .@Troy_Balderson is doing a great job as Congressman from Ohio. We need him in D.C. Vote for Troy - He has my total En... [Twitter for iPhone]

Nov 4, 2018 10:41:45 AM RT @realDonaldTrump: So Revealing! https://t.co/wR0Z4694ei [Twitter for iPhone]

Nov 4, 2018 10:42:32 AM RT @realDonaldTrump: In Florida there is a choice between a Harvard/Yale educated man named @RonDeSantisFL who has been a great Congressman... [Twitter for iPhone]

Nov 4, 2018 10:44:36 AM RT @realDonaldTrump: Martha McSally is a great warrior, her opponent a Nancy Pelosi Wacko! https://t.co/QEUdPWDDud [Twitter for iPhone]

Nov 4, 2018 11:07:14 AM RT @realDonaldTrump: .@DannyTarkanian is a great guy and a team player. He will represent his District, State and Country at the highest le... [Twitter for iPhone]

Nov 4, 2018 01:35:54 PM WOW - Departing the White House shortly. See you soon Georgia! #MAGA https://t.co/Lk0SoU8pie https://t.co/Sn9D9o4fNZ [Twitter for iPhone]

Nov 4, 2018 03:02:53 PM On my way to Macon, Georgia where the crowds are massive, for a 4pmE #MAGARally. Will be in Chattanooga, Tennessee tonight, seen below, for a 7pmE rally. Something's happening! Everyone needs to get out and VOTE! https://t.co/xBXepwpug9 [Twitter for iPhone]

Nov 4, 2018 06:05:44 PM Thank you Macon, Georgia! Get out on Tuesday, November 6th and VOTE for @BrianKempGA as your next Governor to protect your jobs, defend your borders, fight for your values, and continue MAKING AMERICA GREAT AGAIN! https://t.co/Hzbqw35oNM [Twitter for iPhone]

Nov 4, 2018 06:47:01 PM Great to be back in Tennessee. On our way to the McKenzie Arena in Chattanooga for a huge #MAGARally - see everyone soon! https://t.co/RwZt5yGuE5 [Twitter for iPhone]

Nov 4, 2018 08:36:10 PM Thank you for joining us tonight in Tennessee, @TheLeeGreenwood. GOD BLESS THE U.S.A.! https://t.co/hfxi4Ct6Pv [Twitter for iPhone]

Nov 4, 2018 09:00:06 PM In just 2 days, the people of Tennessee are going to elect @VoteMarsha Blackburn to the United States Senate to protect your jobs, defend your borders, and CONTINUE MAKING AMERICA GREAT AGAIN! Get out on Tuesday and VOTE for Marsha! https://t.co/BJhmItntMo [Twitter for iPhone]

Nov 5, 2018 12:04:53 AM John James, running as a Republican for the Senate from Michigan, is a spectacular young star of the future. We should make him a star of the present. A distinguished West Point Grad and Vet, people should Vote Out Schumer Puppet Debbie Stabenow, who does nothing for Michigan! [Twitter for iPhone]

Nov 5, 2018 12:32:10 AM Dana Rohrabacher has been a great Congressman for his District and for the people of Cal. He works hard and is respected by all - he produces! Dems are desperate to replace Dana by spending vast sums to elect a super liberal who is weak on Crime and bad for our Military & Vets! [Twitter for iPhone]

Nov 5, 2018 08:13:20 AM .@DebbieStabenow voted against Tax Cuts, great Healthcare, Supreme Court Justices and all of the many things the people of Michigan wanted and need. She is an automatic far left vote, controlled by her bosses. John James can be a truly great Senator! [Twitter for iPhone]

Nov 5, 2018 08:21:07 AM If @AndrewGillum did the same job with Florida that he has done in Tallahassee as Mayor, the State will be a crime ridden, overtaxed mess. @RonDeSantisFL will be a great Governor. VOTE!!!!!! [Twitter for iPhone]

Nov 5, 2018 08:36:57 AM No matter what she says, Senator Claire McCaskill will always vote against us and the Great State of Missouri! Vote for Josh Hawley - he will be a great Senator! [Twitter for iPhone]

Nov 5, 2018 10:01:43 AM I need @claudiatenney of #NY22 to be re-elected in order to get our big plans moving. Her opponent would be a disaster. Nobody works harder than Claudia, and she is a producer. I look forward to working together with her - she has my Strongest Endorsement! Vote Claudia! [Twitter for iPhone]

Nov 5, 2018 10:18:06 AM So funny to see the CNN Fake Suppression Polls and false rhetoric. Watch for real results Tuesday. We are lucky CNN's ratings are so low. Don't fall for the Suppression Game. Go out & VOTE. Remember, we now have perhaps the greatest Economy (JOBS) in the history of our Country! [Twitter for iPhone]

Nov 5, 2018 10:35:06 AM REMEMBER FLORIDA: I have been President of the United States for almost two years. During that time Senator Bill Nelson didn't call me once. Rick Scott called constantly requesting dollars plus for Florida. Did a GREAT job on hurricanes. VOTE SCOTT! [Twitter for iPhone]

Nov 5, 2018 10:41:48 AM Law Enforcement has been strongly notified to watch closely for any ILLEGAL VOTING which may take place in Tuesday's Election (or Early Voting). Anyone caught will be subject to the Maximum Criminal Penalties allowed by law. Thank you! [Twitter for iPhone]

Nov 5, 2018 12:10:18 PM RT @EricTrump: Friends, We are on the one yard line and need everyone to VOTE Republican tomorrow! America is back! America is winning aga... [Twitter for iPhone]

Nov 5, 2018 12:59:12 PM "Bill Nelson is kind of an empty figure in Washington. You never hear his name, he's never in debates on key issues - he is just under the radar." Chris Wallace on @FoxNews In other words, Nelson is a "stiff." [Twitter for iPhone]

Nov 5, 2018 03:59:42 PM Something's happening America! Get out tomorrow and https://t.co/0pWiwCHGbh so together, we can KEEP MAKING AMERICA GREAT AGAIN!! https://t.co/zajBieMWpl [Twitter for iPhone]

Nov 5, 2018 04:26:24 PM Thank you Ohio! When you enter the voting booth tomorrow you will be making a simple choice. A vote for Republicans is a vote to continue our extraordinary prosperity. A vote for Dems is a vote to bring this Economic Boom crashing to a sudden, screeching halt. Vote @MikeDeWine! https://t.co/iai8bSEgBh [Twitter for iPhone]

Nov 5, 2018 04:40:04 PM Republicans have created the best economy in the HISTORY of our Country – and the hottest jobs market on planet earth. The Democrat Agenda is a Socialist Nightmare. The Republican Agenda is the AMERICAN DREAM! https://t.co/0pWiwCHGbh https://t.co/JfdM1p5xxY [Twitter for iPhone]

Nov 5, 2018 05:28:09 PM Just landed in Fort Wayne, Indiana for a #MAGARally at the Allen County War Memorial Coliseum. See everyone soon! https://t.co/0pWiwCHGbh [Twitter for iPhone]

Nov 5, 2018 08:02:32 PM Thank you Indiana! A vote for Mike @Braun4Indiana is a vote to keep your jobs going up, your wages going up, and your healthcare costs coming down. It's a vote to keep your families safe & to keep criminals, traffickers & drug dealers OUT of our Country! Get out and for for Mike! https://t.co/3AE7WcHZej [Twitter for iPhone]

Nov 5, 2018 08:05:37 PM There is only one way to stop this Democrat-Led assault on our sovereignty – you have to VOTE Republican TOMORROW! Polling locations: https://t.co/0pWiwCHGbh https://t.co/ggs0zcXaQu [Twitter for iPhone]

Nov 5, 2018 08:26:42 PM Massive crowd inside and outside the Allen County War Memorial Coliseum in Fort Wayne, Indiana! Thank you for joining us tonight - and make sure you get out and https://t.co/0pWiwCHGbh tomorrow! https://t.co/8APMivyM0x [Twitter for iPhone]

Nov 5, 2018 08:47:25 PM On my way, see you soon Cape Girardeau, Missouri! #MAGARally https://t.co/0pWiwCHGbh https://t.co/XZdgktuTmL [Twitter for iPhone]

Nov 5, 2018 09:14:58 PM You have been loyal and faithful to your Country, and now you have a President that is loyal and faithful to you. Get out tomorrow, and https://t.co/HfihPERFgZ! https://t.co/Fr6HlmA7y6 [Twitter for iPhone]

Nov 5, 2018 11:58:38 PM RT @DanScavino: .@TheLeeGreenwood singing GOD BLESS THE USA in Cape Girardeau, Missouri at @realDonaldTrump's #MAGARally... https://t.co/Gl... [Twitter for iPhone]

Nov 6, 2018 12:02:31 AM RT @IvankaTrump: Ohio✈️ Indiana✈️ Missouri ususus https://t.co/Xn51CudZUt [Twitter for iPhone]

Nov 6, 2018 12:05:09 AM A fantastic evening in Girardeau, Missouri. Josh @HawleyMO will be a tireless champion for YOU. He is great on jobs, great on tax cuts, and tough on crime. He shares your values, and he will always support our Military, Vets and Police! Get out tomorrow and VOTE for Josh!! https://t.co/8zgyv5x2A6 [Twitter for iPhone]

Nov 6, 2018 12:12:46 AM A vote for Claire McCaskill is a vote for Schumer, Pelosi, Waters, and their socialist agenda. Claire voted IN FAVOR of deadly Sanctuary Cities - she would rather protect criminal aliens than American citizens, which is why she needs to be voted out of office. Vote @HawleyMO! https://t.co/tn2zsEWQJ5 [Twitter for iPhone]

Nov 6, 2018 01:36:22 AM A fantastic evening in Cape Girardeau, Missouri. Josh @HawleyMO will be a tireless champion for YOU. He is great on jobs, great on tax cuts, and tough on crime. He shares your values, and he will always support our Military, Vets and Police! Get out tomorrow and VOTE for Josh!! https://t.co/YPB8nqX2d6 [Twitter for iPhone]

Nov 6, 2018 10:20:08 AM There is a rumor, put out by the Democrats, that Josh Hawley of Missouri left the Arena last night early. It is Fake News. He met me at the plane when I arrived, spoke at the great Rally, & stayed to the very end. In fact, I said goodbye to him and left before he did. Deception! [Twitter for iPhone]

Nov 6, 2018 10:44:46 AM Congressman Peter King of New York is a hardworking gem. Loves his Country and his State. Get out and VOTE for Peter! [Twitter for iPhone]

Nov 6, 2018 11:18:49 AM RT @realDonaldTrump: "Bill Nelson is kind of an empty figure in Washington. You never hear his name, he's never in debates on key issues -... [Twitter for iPhone]

Nov 6, 2018 11:19:12 AM RT @realDonaldTrump: Law Enforcement has been strongly notified to watch closely for any ILLEGAL VOTING which may take place in Tuesday's E... [Twitter for iPhone]

Nov 6, 2018 11:19:24 AM RT @realDonaldTrump: REMEMBER FLORIDA: I have been President of the United States for almost two years. During that time Senator Bill Nelso... [Twitter for iPhone]

Nov 6, 2018 11:19:39 AM RT @realDonaldTrump: I need @claudiatenney of #NY22 to be re-elected in order to get our big plans moving. Her opponent would be a disaster... [Twitter for iPhone]

Nov 6, 2018 11:20:03 AM RT @realDonaldTrump: No matter what she says, Senator Claire McCaskill will always vote against us and the Great State of Missouri! Vote fo... [Twitter for iPhone]

Nov 6, 2018 11:20:17 AM RT @realDonaldTrump: If @AndrewGillum did the same job with Florida that he has done in Tallahassee as Mayor, the State will be a crime rid... [Twitter for iPhone]

Nov 6, 2018 11:21:12 AM RT @realDonaldTrump: Thank you Macon, Georgia! Get out on Tuesday, November 6th and VOTE for @BrianKempGA as your next Governor to protect... [Twitter for iPhone]

Nov 6, 2018 11:23:23 AM RT @realDonaldTrump: Another fantastic #MAGARally tonight in the Great State of Florida. In just 3 days, the People of Florida are going to... [Twitter for iPhone]

Nov 6, 2018 11:23:52 AM RT @realDonaldTrump: In all the time I've been President, almost two years, never once did Senator Bill Nelson call me to ask for help for... [Twitter for iPhone]

Nov 6, 2018 11:24:13 AM RT @realDonaldTrump: ....Lake Okeechobee and all of the hurricane money were a passion for Rick Scott, who called endlessly on behalf of th... [Twitter for iPhone]

Nov 6, 2018 11:24:43 AM RT @realDonaldTrump: Rumor has it that Senator Joe Donnelly of Indiana is paying for Facebook ads for his so-called opponent on the liberta... [Twitter for iPhone]

Nov 6, 2018 11:24:54 AM RT @realDonaldTrump: Arizona is such a Great State but it needs Border Security which @MarthaMcSally will provide, and Krysten Sinema doesn... [Twitter for iPhone]

Nov 6, 2018 11:25:09 AM RT @realDonaldTrump: If Chuck Schumer and Nancy Pelosi gain the majority, they will try to raise your taxes, restore job-killing regulation... [Twitter for iPhone]

Nov 6, 2018 11:25:44 AM RT @realDonaldTrump: New York, get out and VOTE for @JohnFasoNy, a great and hardworking Congressman. We need John's voice in D.C. His oppo... [Twitter for iPhone]

Nov 6, 2018 11:26:15 AM RT @realDonaldTrump: Get out and VOTE for @DeanHeller! https://t.co/4HEkpQL3oy [Twitter for iPhone]

Nov 6, 2018 11:26:37 AM RT @realDonaldTrump: Indiana Rally, and Coach Bobby Knight, were incredible last night. Packed House in Honor of Mike Braun for Senate. Mik... [Twitter for iPhone]

Nov 6, 2018 11:27:29 AM RT @realDonaldTrump: Fantastic #MAGARallyusin West Virginia, thank you. Everyone get out and VOTE for Patrick @MorriseyWV and @CarolMillerW... [Twitter for iPhone]

Nov 6, 2018 12:58:13 PM POLLING LOCATIONS: https://t.co/0pWiwCHGbh [Twitter for iPhone]

Nov 6, 2018 01:08:29 PM Bob Hugin, successful all of his life, would be a Great Senator from New Jersey. He has my complete and total Endorsement! Get out and Vote for Bob. [Twitter for iPhone]

Nov 6, 2018 01:11:30 PM RT @FLOTUS: Vote Red us MAGA us https://t.co/i95OiBimxA https://t.co/ncvDcAP8LZ [Twitter for iPhone]

Nov 6, 2018 01:48:55 PM Epstein all the way in Michigan House 11. She is a wonderful person and, at the same time, a real fighter. Has my Strong Endorsement! [Twitter for iPhone]

Nov 6, 2018 02:52:48 PM Florida, very important - get out and vote for Florida Congressional Candidate Michael Waltz (R). He has my Strong Endorsement! [Twitter for iPhone]

Nov 6, 2018 02:56:34 PM Congressman Randy Hultgren (R) of Illinois is doing a great job. Get out and Vote for Randy - Total Endorsement! [Twitter for iPhone]

Nov 6, 2018 11:14:39 PM Tremendous success tonight. Thank you to all! [Twitter for iPhone]

Nov 7, 2018 01:27:01 AM "There's only been 5 times in the last 105 years that an incumbent President has won seats in the Senate in the off year election. Mr. Trump has magic about him. This guy has magic coming out of his ears. He is an astonishing vote getter & campaigner. The Republicans are......... [Twitter for iPhone]

Nov 7, 2018 01:37:48 AM ....unbelievably lucky to have him and I'm just awed at how well they've done. It's all the Trump magic - Trump is the magic man. Incredible, he's got the entire media against him, attacking him every day, and he pulls out these enormous wins." Ben Stein, "The Capitalist Code" [Twitter for iPhone]

Nov 7, 2018 01:49:40 AM .@DavidAsmanfox "How do the Democrats respond to this? Think of how his position with Republicans improves-all the candidates who won tonight. They realize how important he is because of what he did in campaigning for them. They owe him their political career." Thanks, I agree! [Twitter for iPhone]

Nov 7, 2018 06:21:51 AM Received so many Congratulations from so many on our Big Victory last night, including from foreign nations (friends) that were waiting me out, and hoping, on Trade Deals. Now we can all get back to work and get things done! [Twitter for iPhone]

Nov 7, 2018 06:55:35 AM Ron DeSantis showed great courage in his hard fought campaign to become the Governor of Florida. Congratulations to Ron and family! [Twitter for iPhone]

Nov 7, 2018 07:07:51 AM Those that worked with me in this incredible Midterm Election, embracing certain policies and principles, did very well. Those that did not, say goodbye! Yesterday was such a very Big Win, and all under the pressure of a Nasty and Hostile Media! [Twitter for iPhone]

Nov 7, 2018 07:36:28 AM I will be doing a news conference at The White House - 11:30 A.M. Will be discussing our success in the Midterms! [Twitter for iPhone]

Nov 7, 2018 07:52:39 AM To any of the pundits or talking heads that do not give us proper credit for this great Midterm Election, just remember two words - FAKE NEWS! [Twitter for iPhone]

Nov 7, 2018 08:04:02 AM If the Democrats think they are going to waste Taxpayer Money investigating us at the House level, then we will likewise be forced to consider investigating them for all of the leaks of Classified Information, and much else, at the Senate level. Two can play that game! [Twitter for iPhone]

Nov 7, 2018 08:31:24 AM In all fairness, Nancy Pelosi deserves to be chosen Speaker of the House by the Democrats. If they give her a hard time, perhaps we will add some Republican votes. She has earned this great honor! [Twitter for iPhone]

Nov 7, 2018 10:39:11 AM According to NBC News, Voters Nationwide Disapprove of the so-called Mueller Investigation (46%) more than they Approve (41%). You mean they are finally beginning to understand what a disgusting Witch Hunt, led by 17 Angry Democrats, is all about! [Twitter for iPhone]

Nov 7, 2018 02:44:11 PM We are pleased to announce that Matthew G. Whitaker, Chief of Staff to Attorney General Jeff Sessions at the Department of Justice, will become our new Acting Attorney General of the United States. He will serve our Country well.... [Twitter for iPhone]

Nov 7, 2018 02:44:12 PM ....We thank Attorney General Jeff Sessions for his service, and wish him well! A permanent replacement will be nominated at a later date. [Twitter for iPhone]

Nov 8, 2018 07:38:41 AM I have been fully briefed on the terrible shooting in California. Law Enforcement and First Responders, together with the FBI, are on scene. 13 people, at this time, have been reported dead. Likewise, the shooter is dead, along with the first police officer to enter the bar.... [Twitter for iPhone]

Nov 8, 2018 07:51:21 AM ....Great bravery shown by police. California Highway Patrol was on scene within 3 minutes, with first officer to enter shot numerous times. That Sheriff's Sergeant died in the hospital. God bless all of the victims and families of the victims. Thank you to Law Enforcement. [Twitter for iPhone]

Nov 8, 2018 09:38:22 PM Law Enforcement is looking into another big corruption scandal having to do with Election Fraud in #Broward and Palm Beach. Florida voted for Rick Scott! [Twitter for iPhone]

Nov 9, 2018 09:54:15 AM "Presidential Proclamation Addressing Mass Migration Through the Southern Border of the United States" https://t.co/9blzn1XGyS [Twitter for iPhone]

Nov 9, 2018 10:55:25 AM .@BrianKempGA ran a great race in Georgia – he won. It is time to move on! [Twitter for iPhone]

Nov 9, 2018 10:58:56 AM You mean they are just now finding votes in Florida and Georgia – but the Election was on Tuesday? Let's blame the Russians and demand an immediate apology from President Putin! [Twitter for iPhone]

Nov 9, 2018 11:52:19 AM As soon as Democrats sent their best Election stealing lawyer, Marc Elias, to Broward County they miraculously started finding Democrat votes. Don't worry, Florida - I am sending much better lawyers to expose the FRAUD! [Twitter for iPhone]

Nov 9, 2018 12:10:02 PM Jeff Flake(y) doesn't want to protect the Non-Senate confirmed Special Counsel, he wants to protect his future after being unelectable in Arizona for the "crime" of doing a terrible job! A weak and ineffective guy! [Twitter for iPhone]

Nov 9, 2018 12:36:38 PM Rick Scott was up by 50,000+ votes on Election Day, now they "found" many votes and he is only up 15,000 votes. "The Broward Effect." How come they never find Republican votes? [Twitter for iPhone]

Nov 9, 2018 01:14:03 PM Mayor Gillum conceded on Election Day and now Broward County has put him "back into play." Bill Nelson conceded Election - now he's back in play!? This is an embarrassment to our Country and to Democracy! [Twitter for iPhone]

Nov 9, 2018 01:20:28 PM In the 2016 Election I was winning by so much in Florida that Broward County, which was very late with vote tabulation and probably getting ready to do a "number," couldn't do it because not enough people live in Broward for them to falsify a victory! [Twitter for iPhone]

Nov 9, 2018 01:39:00 PM Thank you @marcorubio for helping to expose the potential corruption going on with respect to Election Theft in Broward and Palm Beach Counties. The WORLD is now watching closely! [Twitter for iPhone]

Nov 9, 2018 03:33:37 PM Just out — in Arizona, SIGNATURES DON'T MATCH. Electoral corruption - Call for a new Election? We must protect our Democracy! [Twitter for iPhone]

Nov 9, 2018 04:10:46 PM President Macron of France has just suggested that Europe build its own military in order to protect itself from the U.S., China and Russia. Very insulting, but perhaps Europe should first pay its fair share of NATO, which the U.S. subsidizes greatly! [Twitter for iPhone]

Nov 9, 2018 10:52:16 PM Matthew G. Whitaker is a highly respected former U.S. Attorney from Iowa. He was chosen by Jeff Sessions to be his Chief of Staff. I did not know Mr. Whitaker. Likewise, as Chief, I did not know Mr. Whitaker except primarily as he traveled with A.G. Sessions. No social contact... [Twitter for iPhone]

Nov 9, 2018 11:04:53 PM ....Mr. Whitaker is very highly thought of by @SenJoniErnst, Senator @ChuckGrassley, Ambassador @TerryBranstad, Leonard Leo of Federalist Society, and many more. I feel certain he will make an outstanding Acting Attorney General! [Twitter for iPhone]

Nov 10, 2018 03:08:52 AM There is no reason for these massive, deadly and costly forest fires in California except that forest management is so poor. Billions of dollars are given each year, with so many lives lost, all because of gross mismanagement of the forests. Remedy now, or no more Fed payments! [Twitter for iPhone]

Nov 10, 2018 03:17:44 AM I am in Paris getting ready to celebrate the end of World War One. Is there anything better to celebrate than the end of a war, in particular that one, which was one of the bloodiest and worst of all time? [Twitter for iPhone]

Nov 10, 2018 09:09:42 AM Happy 243rd Birthday to our GREAT U.S. Marine Corpsus https://t.co/1cPtoMfmxP [Twitter for iPhone]

Nov 10, 2018 02:06:50 PM Had very productive meetings and calls for our Country today. Meeting tonight with World Leaders! [Twitter for iPhone]

Nov 10, 2018 02:09:29 PM Trying to STEAL two big elections in Florida! We are watching closely! [Twitter for iPhone]

Nov 10, 2018 05:19:35 PM More than 4,000 are fighting the Camp and Woolsey Fires in California that have burned over 170,000 acres. Our hearts are with those fighting the fires, the 52,000 who have evacuated, and the families of the 11 who have died. The destruction is catastrophic. God Bless them all. [Twitter for iPhone]

Nov 10, 2018 05:20:40 PM These California fires are expanding very, very quickly (in some cases 80-100 acres a minute). If people don't evacuate quickly, they risk being overtaken by the fire. Please listen to evacuation orders from State and local officials! [Twitter for iPhone]

Nov 11, 2018 04:40:50 AM With proper Forest Management, we can stop the devastation constantly going on in California. Get Smart! [Twitter for iPhone]

Nov 11, 2018 09:16:42 AM On this Veterans Day — the 100th Anniversary of the end of WWI, we honor the brave HEROES who fought for America in the Great War, and every Veteran who has worn the uniform and kept our Nation Safe, Strong and FREE! https://t.co/zBvvYRR7XE https://t.co/YO06ztfvNm [Twitter for iPhone]

Nov 11, 2018 09:52:56 AM Beautiful ceremony today in Paris commemorating the end of World War One. Many World leaders in attendance. Thank you to @EmmanuelMacron, President of France! Now off to Suresnes American Cemetery to make speech in honor of our great heroes! Then back to the U.S.A. [Twitter for iPhone]

Nov 11, 2018 10:43:49 AM RT @WhiteHouse: President Trump Attends the American Commemoration Ceremony at Suresnes American Cemetery https://t.co/P6PgE1zXuE [Twitter for iPhone]

Nov 11, 2018 11:03:35 AM Poland, a great country - Congratulations on the 100th Anniversary of your Independence. I will never forget my time there! https://t.co/gEme6McF1x [Twitter for iPhone]

Nov 11, 2018 03:55:38 PM RT @FLOTUS: Today we remember the brave actions of our troops and those of our allies during WWI. Honored to be spending this day honoring... [Twitter for iPhone]

Nov 11, 2018 11:38:00 PM Exactly 100 years ago today, on November 11th, 1918, World War I came to an end. We are gathered together, at this hallowed resting place, to pay tribute to the brave Americans who gave their last breath in that mighty struggle.... https://t.co/JPUkOr4rW1 [Twitter for iPhone]

Nov 12, 2018 07:03:25 AM Just returned from France where much was accomplished in my meetings with World Leaders. Never easy bringing up the fact that the U.S. must be treated fairly, which it hasn't, on both Military and Trade. We pay for LARGE portions of other countries military protection,........ [Twitter for iPhone]

Nov 12, 2018 07:10:16 AM .....hundreds of billions of dollars, for the great privilege of losing hundreds of billions of dollars with these same countries on trade. I told them that this situation cannot continue - It is, and always has been, ridiculously unfair to the United States. Massive amounts..... [Twitter for iPhone]

Nov 12, 2018 07:21:11 AM .....of money spent on protecting other countries, and we get nothing but Trade Deficits and Losses. It is time that these very rich countries either pay the United States for its great military protection, or protect themselves...and Trade must be made FREE and FAIR! [Twitter for iPhone]

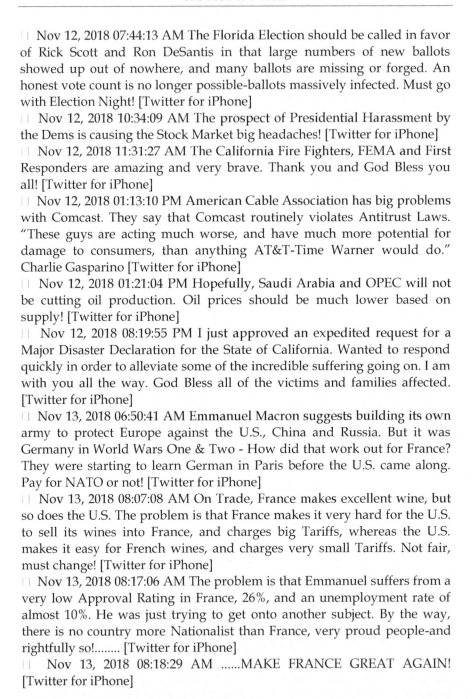

Nov 12, 2018 07:44:13 AM The Florida Election should be called in favor of Rick Scott and Ron DeSantis in that large numbers of new ballots showed up out of nowhere, and many ballots are missing or forged. An honest vote count is no longer possible-ballots massively infected. Must go with Election Night! [Twitter for iPhone]

Nov 12, 2018 10:34:09 AM The prospect of Presidential Harassment by the Dems is causing the Stock Market big headaches! [Twitter for iPhone]

Nov 12, 2018 11:31:27 AM The California Fire Fighters, FEMA and First Responders are amazing and very brave. Thank you and God Bless you all! [Twitter for iPhone]

Nov 12, 2018 01:13:10 PM American Cable Association has big problems with Comcast. They say that Comcast routinely violates Antitrust Laws. "These guys are acting much worse, and have much more potential for damage to consumers, than anything AT&T-Time Warner would do." Charlie Gasparino [Twitter for iPhone]

Nov 12, 2018 01:21:04 PM Hopefully, Saudi Arabia and OPEC will not be cutting oil production. Oil prices should be much lower based on supply! [Twitter for iPhone]

Nov 12, 2018 08:19:55 PM I just approved an expedited request for a Major Disaster Declaration for the State of California. Wanted to respond quickly in order to alleviate some of the incredible suffering going on. I am with you all the way. God Bless all of the victims and families affected. [Twitter for iPhone]

Nov 13, 2018 06:50:41 AM Emmanuel Macron suggests building its own army to protect Europe against the U.S., China and Russia. But it was Germany in World Wars One & Two - How did that work out for France? They were starting to learn German in Paris before the U.S. came along. Pay for NATO or not! [Twitter for iPhone]

Nov 13, 2018 08:07:08 AM On Trade, France makes excellent wine, but so does the U.S. The problem is that France makes it very hard for the U.S. to sell its wines into France, and charges big Tariffs, whereas the U.S. makes it easy for French wines, and charges very small Tariffs. Not fair, must change! [Twitter for iPhone]

Nov 13, 2018 08:17:06 AM The problem is that Emmanuel suffers from a very low Approval Rating in France, 26%, and an unemployment rate of almost 10%. He was just trying to get onto another subject. By the way, there is no country more Nationalist than France, very proud people-and rightfully so!........ [Twitter for iPhone]

Nov 13, 2018 08:18:29 AM ......MAKE FRANCE GREAT AGAIN! [Twitter for iPhone]

Nov 13, 2018 08:30:03 AM By the way, when the helicopter couldn't fly to the first cemetery in France because of almost zero visibility, I suggested driving. Secret Service said NO, too far from airport & big Paris shutdown. Speech next day at American Cemetary in pouring rain! Little reported-Fake News! [Twitter for iPhone]

Nov 13, 2018 10:49:20 AM By the way, when the helicopter couldn't fly to the first cemetery in France because of almost zero visibility, I suggested driving. Secret Service said NO, too far from airport & big Paris shutdown. Speech next day at American Cemetery in pouring rain! Little reported-Fake News! [Twitter for iPhone]

Nov 13, 2018 11:32:09 AM When will Bill Nelson concede in Florida? The characters running Broward and Palm Beach voting will not be able to "find" enough votes, too much spotlight on them now! [Twitter for iPhone]

Nov 13, 2018 12:07:45 PM The story in the New York Times concerning North Korea developing missile bases is inaccurate. We fully know about the sites being discussed, nothing new - and nothing happening out of the normal. Just more Fake News. I will be the first to let you know if things go bad! [Twitter for iPhone]

Nov 13, 2018 02:38:45 PM We mourn for the lives lost and we pray for the victims of the California Wildfires. I want to thank the Firefighters and First Responders for their incredible courage in the face of grave danger.... https://t.co/3YQYZR8OzS [Twitter Media Studio]

Nov 13, 2018 03:33:18 PM Today, we gathered for Diwali, a holiday observed by Buddhists, Sikhs, and Jains throughout the United States & around the world. Hundreds of millions of people have gathered with family & friends to light the Diya and to mark the beginning of a New Year. https://t.co/a1QRfaPm37 https://t.co/LKRTr0nCQl [Twitter for iPhone]

Nov 13, 2018 04:03:38 PM Today, we gathered for Diwali, a holiday observed by Buddhists, Sikhs, and Jains throughout the United States & around the world. Hundreds of millions of people have gathered with family & friends to light the Diya and to mark the beginning of a New Year. https://t.co/epHogpTY1A https://t.co/9LUwnhngWJ [Twitter for iPhone]

Nov 13, 2018 04:20:48 PM It was my great honor to host a celebration of Diwali, the Hindu Festival of Lights, in the Roosevelt Room at the @WhiteHouse this afternoon. Very, very special people! https://t.co/kQk7IvpSFo https://t.co/tYlBABg4JF [Twitter for iPhone]

Nov 13, 2018 04:35:42 PM "Boom: Record high business optimism, need for employees at 45-year high" https://t.co/jBFjEwAcfd [Twitter for iPhone]

Nov 14, 2018 02:28:24 PM Not seen in many years, America's steelworkers get a hard-earned raise because of my Administration's policies to help bring back the U.S. steel industry, which is critical to our National Security. I will always protect America and its workers! [Twitter for iPhone]

Nov 14, 2018 02:35:22 PM Was just briefed by @FEMA_Brock and @SecretaryZinke, who are in California. Thank you to the great Firefighters, First Responders and @FEMA for the incredible job they are doing w/ the California Wildfires. Our Nation appreciates your heroism, courage & genius. God Bless you all! [Twitter for iPhone]

Nov 14, 2018 02:58:17 PM Just spoke to Governor Jerry Brown to let him know that we are with him, and the people of California, all the way! [Twitter for iPhone]

Nov 14, 2018 05:10:27 PM I am grateful to be here today w/ Members of the House & Senate who have poured their time, heart and energy into the crucial issue of Prison Reform. Working together w/ my Admin over the last two years, these members have reached a bipartisan agreement...https://t.co/wflidv2cZr [Twitter for iPhone]

Nov 14, 2018 06:26:38 PM Our pledge to hire American includes those leaving prison and looking for a very fresh start — new job, and new life. The legislation I am supporting today contains many significant reforms. Read more here: https://t.co/BwQ3qd9Fyk https://t.co/6DUY9KNTpR [Twitter for iPhone]

Nov 15, 2018 06:59:19 AM The White House is running very smoothly and the results for our Nation are obviously very good. We are the envy of the world. But anytime I even think about making changes, the FAKE NEWS MEDIA goes crazy, always seeking to make us look as bad as possible! Very dishonest! [Twitter for iPhone]

Nov 15, 2018 07:14:37 AM The inner workings of the Mueller investigation are a total mess. They have found no collusion and have gone absolutely nuts. They are screaming and shouting at people, horribly threatening them to come up with the answers they want. They are a disgrace to our Nation and don't... [Twitter for iPhone]

Nov 15, 2018 07:32:03 AM ....care how many lives the ruin. These are Angry People, including the highly conflicted Bob Mueller, who worked for Obama for 8 years. They won't even look at all of the bad acts and crimes on the other side. A TOTAL WITCH HUNT LIKE NO OTHER IN AMERICAN HISTORY! [Twitter for iPhone]

Nov 15, 2018 09:49:28 AM Universities will someday study what highly conflicted (and NOT Senate approved) Bob Mueller and his gang of Democrat thugs have done to destroy people. Why is he protecting Crooked Hillary, Comey, McCabe, Lisa Page & her lover, Peter S, and all of his friends on the other side? [Twitter for iPhone]

Nov 15, 2018 09:59:28 AM The only "Collusion" is that of the Democrats with Russia and many others. Why didn't the FBI take the Server from the DNC? They still don't have it. Check out how biased Facebook, Google and Twitter are in favor of the Democrats. That's the real Collusion! [Twitter for iPhone]

Nov 15, 2018 03:08:32 PM .@FLOTUS Melania and I were honored to visit with our GREAT U.S. MARINES at the Marine Barracks here in Washington, D.C. We love you @USMC @MBWDC! https://t.co/ASWmDZrDRK https://t.co/xYrPw9zzVv [Twitter Media Studio]

Nov 15, 2018 03:34:20 PM It was my great honor to host a @WhiteHouse Conference on Supporting Veterans & Military Families... To everyone here today who has served our Country in uniform, & to every Veteran & Military family across our land, I want to express the eternal gratitude of our entire Nation! https://t.co/MK8jUaTGFK [Twitter for iPhone]

Nov 15, 2018 03:39:51 PM Last year, I signed the landmark VA Accountability Act to ensure those who mistreat our Veterans can be held fully accountable. Since my inauguration, we have removed more than 3,600 government employees who were not giving our Vets the care they deserve.... https://t.co/KqWXXt7D4U [Twitter for iPhone]

Nov 15, 2018 03:43:42 PM It is our sacred duty to support America's Service Members every single day they wear the uniform – and every day after when they return home as Veterans. Together we will HONOR those who defend us, we will CHERISH those who protect us, and we will celebrate the amazing heroes... https://t.co/kovcIj4fwU [Twitter for iPhone]

Nov 16, 2018 02:35:28 PM People are not being told that the Republican Party is on track to pick up two seats in the U.S. Senate, and epic victory: 53 to 47. The Fake News Media only wants to speak of the House, were the Midterm results were better than other sitting Presidents. [Twitter for iPhone]

Nov 16, 2018 02:35:59 PM Today in the East Room of the @WhiteHouse, it was my true privilege to award seven extraordinary Americans with the Presidential Medal of Freedom...https://t.co/TuEy635mav [Twitter for iPhone]

Nov 16, 2018 02:41:57 PM People are not being told that the Republican Party is on track to pick up two seats in the U.S. Senate, and epic victory: 53 to 47. The Fake News Media only wants to speak of the House, where the Midterm results were better than other sitting Presidents. [Twitter for iPhone]

Nov 16, 2018 04:47:55 PM PRESIDENTIAL MEDAL OF FREEDOM https://t.co/Mgeg4wijTk [Twitter for iPhone]

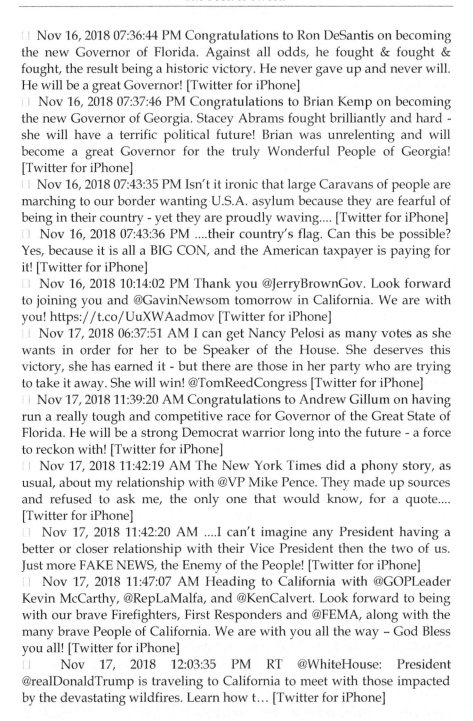

Nov 16, 2018 07:36:44 PM Congratulations to Ron DeSantis on becoming the new Governor of Florida. Against all odds, he fought & fought & fought, the result being a historic victory. He never gave up and never will. He will be a great Governor! [Twitter for iPhone]

Nov 16, 2018 07:37:46 PM Congratulations to Brian Kemp on becoming the new Governor of Georgia. Stacey Abrams fought brilliantly and hard - she will have a terrific political future! Brian was unrelenting and will become a great Governor for the truly Wonderful People of Georgia! [Twitter for iPhone]

Nov 16, 2018 07:43:35 PM Isn't it ironic that large Caravans of people are marching to our border wanting U.S.A. asylum because they are fearful of being in their country - yet they are proudly waving.... [Twitter for iPhone]

Nov 16, 2018 07:43:36 PM ....their country's flag. Can this be possible? Yes, because it is all a BIG CON, and the American taxpayer is paying for it! [Twitter for iPhone]

Nov 16, 2018 10:14:02 PM Thank you @JerryBrownGov. Look forward to joining you and @GavinNewsom tomorrow in California. We are with you! https://t.co/UuXWAadmov [Twitter for iPhone]

Nov 17, 2018 06:37:51 AM I can get Nancy Pelosi as many votes as she wants in order for her to be Speaker of the House. She deserves this victory, she has earned it - but there are those in her party who are trying to take it away. She will win! @TomReedCongress [Twitter for iPhone]

Nov 17, 2018 11:39:20 AM Congratulations to Andrew Gillum on having run a really tough and competitive race for Governor of the Great State of Florida. He will be a strong Democrat warrior long into the future - a force to reckon with! [Twitter for iPhone]

Nov 17, 2018 11:42:19 AM The New York Times did a phony story, as usual, about my relationship with @VP Mike Pence. They made up sources and refused to ask me, the only one that would know, for a quote.... [Twitter for iPhone]

Nov 17, 2018 11:42:20 AM ....I can't imagine any President having a better or closer relationship with their Vice President then the two of us. Just more FAKE NEWS, the Enemy of the People! [Twitter for iPhone]

Nov 17, 2018 11:47:07 AM Heading to California with @GOPLeader Kevin McCarthy, @RepLaMalfa, and @KenCalvert. Look forward to being with our brave Firefighters, First Responders and @FEMA, along with the many brave People of California. We are with you all the way – God Bless you all! [Twitter for iPhone]

Nov 17, 2018 12:03:35 PM RT @WhiteHouse: President @realDonaldTrump is traveling to California to meet with those impacted by the devastating wildfires. Learn how t... [Twitter for iPhone]

Nov 17, 2018 09:48:00 PM Incredible to be with our GREAT HEROES today in California. We will always be with you! https://t.co/B1MCTF83Zf [Twitter for iPhone]

Nov 18, 2018 09:47:28 AM RT @FoxNewsSunday: Chris Wallace during his interview at the White House with President Trump. Check your local listings to watch this Sund... [Twitter for iPhone]

Nov 18, 2018 12:30:30 PM I will be interviewed by Chris Wallace on @FoxNews at 2:00 P.M. and 7:00 P.M. Enjoy! [Twitter for iPhone]

Nov 18, 2018 01:01:09 PM So funny to see little Adam Schitt (D-CA) talking about the fact that Acting Attorney General Matt Whitaker was not approved by the Senate, but not mentioning the fact that Bob Mueller (who is highly conflicted) was not approved by the Senate! [Twitter for iPhone]

Nov 18, 2018 01:42:59 PM The Mayor of Tijuana, Mexico, just stated that "the City is ill-prepared to handle this many migrants, the backlog could last 6 months." Likewise, the U.S. is ill-prepared for this invasion, and will not stand for it. They are causing crime and big problems in Mexico. Go home! [Twitter for iPhone]

Nov 18, 2018 01:44:14 PM RT @realDonaldTrump: I will be interviewed by Chris Wallace on @FoxNews at 2:00 P.M. and 7:00 P.M. Enjoy! [Twitter for iPhone]

Nov 18, 2018 02:55:24 PM Catch and Release is an obsolete term. It is now Catch and Detain. Illegal Immigrants trying to come into the U.S.A., often proudly flying the flag of their nation as they ask for U.S. Asylum, will be detained or turned away. Dems must approve Border Security & Wall NOW! [Twitter for iPhone]

Nov 18, 2018 02:59:41 PM From day one Rick Scott never wavered. He was a great Governor and will be even a greater Senator in representing the People of Florida. Congratulations to Rick on having waged such a courageous and successful campaign! [Twitter for iPhone]

Nov 18, 2018 07:22:44 PM RT @realDonaldTrump: I will be interviewed by Chris Wallace on @FoxNews at 2:00 P.M. and 7:00 P.M. Enjoy! [Twitter for iPhone]

Nov 19, 2018 09:30:37 AM .@cindyhydesmith loves Mississippi and our Great U.S.A. https://t.co/hQPC4CrhDi [Twitter for iPhone]

Nov 19, 2018 10:02:03 AM RT @realDonaldTrump: "Boom: Record high business optimism, need for employees at 45-year high" https://t.co/jBFjEwAcfd [Twitter for iPhone]

Nov 19, 2018 10:26:39 AM Of course we should have captured Osama Bin Laden long before we did. I pointed him out in my book just BEFORE the attack on the World Trade Center. President Clinton famously missed his shot. We paid Pakistan Billions of Dollars & they never told us he was living there. Fools!.. [Twitter for iPhone]

Nov 19, 2018 10:41:19 AM ....We no longer pay Pakistan the $Billions because they would take our money and do nothing for us, Bin Laden being a prime example, Afghanistan being another. They were just one of many countries that take from the United States without giving anything in return. That's ENDING! [Twitter for iPhone]

Nov 19, 2018 02:10:09 PM The Fake News is showing old footage of people climbing over our Ocean Area Fence. This is what it really looks like - no climbers anymore under our Administration! https://t.co/CD4ltRePML [Twitter for iPhone]

Nov 19, 2018 03:56:08 PM RT @WhiteHouse: President Trump and the First Lady Participate in the White House Christmas Tree Delivery https://t.co/O6Nr8k1mnu [Twitter for iPhone]

Nov 19, 2018 09:15:22 PM RT @FLOTUS: The @WhiteHouse is getting ready for the Christmas season! Thank you to the Smith Family & the National Christmas Tree Associat… [Twitter for iPhone]

Nov 19, 2018 11:19:18 PM I hope the discovery and eventual recovery of the Argentine submarine San Juan brings needed closure to the wonderful families of those brave missing sailors. I look forward to hearing more from my friend President @MauricioMacri in Argentina later this month. [Twitter for iPhone]

Nov 20, 2018 03:01:03 PM RT @WhiteHouse: President @realDonaldTrump, joined by @FLOTUS, has officially pardoned this year's National Thanksgiving Turkey, Peas—and h… [Twitter for iPhone]

Nov 20, 2018 10:43:41 PM So-called comedian Michelle Wolf bombed so badly last year at the White House Correspondents' Dinner that this year, for the first time in decades, they will have an author instead of a comedian. Good first step in comeback of a dying evening and tradition! Maybe I will go? [Twitter for iPhone]

Nov 20, 2018 11:40:03 PM AMERICA FIRST! [Twitter for iPhone]

Nov 21, 2018 07:49:51 AM Oil prices getting lower. Great! Like a big Tax Cut for America and the World. Enjoy! $54, was just $82. Thank you to Saudi Arabia, but let's go lower! [Twitter for iPhone]

Nov 21, 2018 07:50:29 AM MAKE AMERICA GREAT AGAIN! [Twitter for iPhone]

Nov 21, 2018 09:16:26 AM "'Trump Imitation Syndrome' is afflicting the president's liberal enemies" Thank you @MGoodwin_NYPost! https://t.co/KpmsrKCaBZ [Twitter for iPhone]

Nov 21, 2018 10:13:33 AM Great new book out, "Mad Politics: Keeping Your Sanity in a World Gone Crazy" by @RealDrGina Loudon. Go out and get your copy today — a great read! [Twitter for iPhone]

Nov 21, 2018 03:51:11 PM Sorry Chief Justice John Roberts, but you do indeed have "Obama judges," and they have a much different point of view than the people who are charged with the safety of our country. It would be great if the 9th Circuit was indeed an "independent judiciary," but if it is why...... [Twitter for iPhone]

Nov 21, 2018 04:09:20 PM .....are so many opposing view (on Border and Safety) cases filed there, and why are a vast number of those cases overturned. Please study the numbers, they are shocking. We need protection and security - these rulings are making our country unsafe! Very dangerous and unwise! [Twitter for iPhone]

Nov 21, 2018 04:31:24 PM "Thank you to President Trump on the Border. No American President has ever done this before." Hector Garza, National Border Patrol Council [Twitter for iPhone]

Nov 21, 2018 04:42:30 PM There are a lot of CRIMINALS in the Caravan. We will stop them. Catch and Detain! Judicial Activism, by people who know nothing about security and the safety of our citizens, is putting our country in great danger. Not good! [Twitter for iPhone]

Nov 21, 2018 05:17:33 PM "79% of these decisions have been overturned in the 9th Circuit." @FoxNews A terrible, costly and dangerous disgrace. It has become a dumping ground for certain lawyers looking for easy wins and delays. Much talk over dividing up the 9th Circuit into 2 or 3 Circuits. Too big! [Twitter for iPhone]

Nov 21, 2018 05:18:24 PM RT @realDonaldTrump: AMERICA FIRST! [Twitter for iPhone]

Nov 21, 2018 05:18:28 PM RT @realDonaldTrump: MAKE AMERICA GREAT AGAIN! [Twitter for iPhone]

Nov 21, 2018 07:23:09 PM Brutal and Extended Cold Blast could shatter ALL RECORDS - Whatever happened to Global Warming? [Twitter for iPhone]

Nov 21, 2018 07:36:06 PM You just can't win with the Fake News Media. A big story today is that because I have pushed so hard and gotten Gasoline Prices so low, more people are driving and I have caused traffic jams throughout our Great Nation. Sorry everyone! [Twitter for iPhone]

Nov 22, 2018 06:58:24 AM "It's a mean & nasty world out there, the Middle East in particular. This is a long and historic commitment, & one that is absolutely vital to America's national security." @SecPompeo I agree 100%. In addition, many Billions of Dollars of purchases made in U.S., big Jobs & Oil! [Twitter for iPhone]

Nov 22, 2018 07:01:51 AM HAPPY THANKSGIVING TO ALL! [Twitter for iPhone]

⬜ Nov 22, 2018 07:21:51 AM Justice Roberts can say what he wants, but the 9th Circuit is a complete & total disaster. It is out of control, has a horrible reputation, is overturned more than any Circuit in the Country, 79%, & is used to get an almost guaranteed result. Judges must not Legislate Security... [Twitter for iPhone]

⬜ Nov 22, 2018 07:30:27 AM ....and Safety at the Border, or anywhere else. They know nothing about it and are making our Country unsafe. Our great Law Enforcement professionals MUST BE ALLOWED TO DO THEIR JOB! If not there will be only bedlam, chaos, injury and death. We want the Constitution as written! [Twitter for iPhone]

⬜ Nov 22, 2018 08:42:29 AM Will be speaking with our great military in different parts of the world, through teleconference, at 9:00 A.M. Eastern. Then it will be off to see our Coast Guard patriots & to thank them for the great job they have been doing, especially with the hurricanes. Happy Thanksgiving! [Twitter for iPhone]

⬜ Nov 22, 2018 10:12:12 AM https://t.co/y4chCfEDke [Twitter for iPhone]

⬜ Nov 22, 2018 04:26:12 PM This is the coldest weather in the history of the Thanksgiving Day Parade in NYC, and one of the coldest Thanksgivings on record! [Twitter for iPhone]

⬜ Nov 22, 2018 06:07:44 PM Our highly trained security professionals are not allowed to do their job on the Border because of the Judicial Activism and Interference by the 9th Circuit. Nevertheless, they are working hard to make America a safer place, though hard to do when anybody filing a lawsuit wins! [Twitter for iPhone]

⬜ Nov 23, 2018 07:41:50 AM Republicans and Democrats MUST come together, finally, with a major Border Security package, which will include funding for the Wall. After 40 years of talk, it is finally time for action. Fix the Border, for once and for all, NOW! [Twitter for iPhone]

⬜ Nov 23, 2018 07:57:18 AM Really good Criminal Justice Reform has a true shot at major bipartisan support. @senatemajldr Mitch McConnell and @senchuckschumer have a real chance to do something so badly needed in our country. Already past, with big vote, in House. Would be a major victory for ALL! [Twitter for iPhone]

⬜ Nov 23, 2018 12:14:19 PM Really good Criminal Justice Reform has a true shot at major bipartisan support. @senatemajldr Mitch McConnell and @SenSchumer have a real chance to do something so badly needed in our country. Already passed, with big vote, in House. Would be a major victory for ALL! [Twitter for iPhone]

Nov 23, 2018 06:48:19 PM I am extremely happy and proud of the job being done by @USTreasury Secretary @StevenMnuchin1. The FAKE NEWS likes to write stories to the contrary, quoting phony sources or jealous people, but they aren't true. They never like to ask me for a quote b/c it would kill their story. [Twitter for iPhone]

Nov 23, 2018 06:49:04 PM RT @realDonaldTrump: The Fake News is showing old footage of people climbing over our Ocean Area Fence. This is what it really looks like -… [Twitter for iPhone]

Nov 24, 2018 01:44:35 PM RT @WhiteHouse: Small Business Saturday has become a staple of the post-Thanksgiving shopping weekend. "This year, Small Business Saturday… [Twitter for iPhone]

Nov 24, 2018 06:49:25 PM Migrants at the Southern Border will not be allowed into the United States until their claims are individually approved in court. We only will allow those who come into our Country legally. Other than that our very strong policy is Catch and Detain. No "Releasing" into the U.S... [Twitter for iPhone]

Nov 24, 2018 06:56:27 PM ....All will stay in Mexico. If for any reason it becomes necessary, we will CLOSE our Southern Border. There is no way that the United States will, after decades of abuse, put up with this costly and dangerous situation anymore! [Twitter for iPhone]

Nov 25, 2018 07:12:34 AM Victor Davis Hanson was a very good and interesting guest of Mark Levin on @FoxNews. He wrote a highly touted book called "The Second World Wars" and a new book will soon be coming out called "The Case For Trump." Recommend both. @marklevinshow [Twitter for iPhone]

Nov 25, 2018 07:30:51 AM I will be in Gulfport and Tupelo, Mississippi, on Monday night doing two Rallies for Senator Hyde-Smith, who has a very important Election on Tuesday. She is an outstanding person who is strong on the Border, Crime, Military, our great Vets, Healthcare & the 2nd A. Needed in D.C. [Twitter for iPhone]

Nov 25, 2018 08:16:56 AM The large and violent French protests don't take into account how badly the United States has been treated on Trade by the European Union or on fair and reasonable payments for our GREAT military protection. Both of these topics must be remedied soon. [Twitter for iPhone]

Nov 25, 2018 08:28:30 AM Would be very SMART if Mexico would stop the Caravans long before they get to our Southern Border, or if originating countries would not let them form (it is a way they get certain people out of their country and dump in U.S. No longer). Dems created this problem. No crossings! [Twitter for iPhone]

Apr 18, 2019 03:37:57 PM Today, I was thrilled to host the @WWP Soldier Ride once again at the @WhiteHouse. We were all deeply honored to be in the presence of TRUE AMERICAN HEROES....https://t.co/q6D5875xCw [Twitter for iPhone]

Apr 18, 2019 04:31:51 PM "Donald Trump was being framed, he fought back. That is not Obstruction." @JesseBWatters I had the right to end the whole Witch Hunt if I wanted. I could have fired everyone, including Mueller, if I wanted. I chose not to. I had the RIGHT to use Executive Privilege. I didn't! [Twitter for iPhone]

Apr 18, 2019 05:29:09 PM It was a really great day for America! A special evening tonight on @TuckerCarlson, @seanhannity & @IngrahamAngle Will be very interesting! [Twitter for iPhone]

Apr 18, 2019 06:28:23 PM Anything the Russians did concerning the 2016 Election was done while Obama was President. He was told about it and did nothing! Most importantly, the vote was not affected. [Twitter for iPhone]

Apr 18, 2019 06:46:58 PM When there is not an underlying crime with regard to Collusion (in fact, the whole thing was a made up fraud), it is difficult to say that someone is obstructing something. There was no underlying crime." @marthamaccallum @FoxNews [Twitter for iPhone]

Apr 18, 2019 06:47:26 PM RT @realDonaldTrump: It was a really great day for America! A special evening tonight on @TuckerCarlson, @seanhannity & @IngrahamAngle Wil... [Twitter for iPhone]

Apr 18, 2019 07:27:34 PM "If dozens of Federal prosecutors spent two years trying to charge you with a crime, and found they couldn't, it would mean there wasn't any evidence you did it - and that's what happened here - that's what we just learned from the Mueller Report." @TuckerCarlson [Twitter for iPhone]

Apr 18, 2019 07:38:16 PM "The Mueller Report is perhaps the single most humiliating thing that has ever happened to the White House Press in the history of this Country. They know they lied...Many reporters lied about Russia Collusion and so much more. Clapper & Brennan, all lies" @TuckerCarlson [Twitter for iPhone]

Apr 18, 2019 09:34:48 PM Kimberley Strassel should get the Pulitzer. She is a treasure (and I don't know her) who correctly called the Russia Hoax right from the start! Others who were soooo wrong will get the Prize. Fake News! https://t.co/TJJPY5MM6X [Twitter for iPhone]

Apr 19, 2019 06:53:09 AM Statements are made about me by certain people in the Crazy Mueller Report, in itself written by 18 Angry Democrat Trump Haters, which are fabricated & totally untrue. Watch out for people that take so-called "notes," when the notes never existed until needed. Because I never.... [Twitter for iPhone]

Apr 19, 2019 07:08:56 AM ...agreed to testify, it was not necessary for me to respond to statements made in the "Report" about me, some of which are total bullshit & only given to make the other person look good (or me to look bad). This was an Illegally Started Hoax that never should have happened, a... [Twitter for iPhone]

Apr 19, 2019 03:47:34 PM ....big, fat, waste of time, energy and money - $30,000,000 to be exact. It is now finally time to turn the tables and bring justice to some very sick and dangerous people who have committed very serious crimes, perhaps even Spying or Treason. This should never happen again Nov 25, 2018 08:46:54 AM So great that oil prices are falling (thank you President T). Add that, which is like a big Tax Cut, to our other good Economic news. Inflation down (are you listening Fed)! [Twitter for iPhone]

Nov 25, 2018 03:13:00 PM Mississippi, Vote for @cindyhydesmith on Tuesday. Respected by all. We need her in Washington!. Thanks! [Twitter for iPhone]

Nov 25, 2018 03:20:36 PM General Anthony Tata: "President Trump is a man of his word & he said he was going to be tough on the Border, and he is tough on the Border. He has rightfully strengthened the Border in the face of an unprecedented threat. It's the right move by President Trump." Thanks General! [Twitter for iPhone]

Nov 25, 2018 03:27:34 PM Europe has to pay their fair share for Military Protection. The European Union, for many years, has taken advantage of us on Trade, and then they don't live up to their Military commitment through NATO. Things must change fast! [Twitter for iPhone]

Nov 25, 2018 03:39:26 PM Clinton Foundation donations drop 42% - which shows that they illegally played the power game. They monetized their political influence through the Foundation. "During her tenure the State Department was put in the service of the Clinton Foundation." Andrew McCarthy [Twitter for iPhone]

Nov 25, 2018 08:59:13 PM .@60Minutes did a phony story about child separation when they know we had the exact same policy as the Obama Administration. In fact a picture of children in jails was used by other Fake Media to show how bad (cruel) we are, but it was in 2014 during O years. Obama separated.... [Twitter for iPhone]

Nov 25, 2018 09:07:27 PM ....children from parents, as did Bush etc., because that is the policy and law. I tried to keep them together but the problem is, when you do that, vast numbers of additional people storm the Border. So with Obama seperation is fine, but with Trump it's not. Fake 60 Minutes! [Twitter for iPhone]

Nov 26, 2018 06:19:41 AM Mexico should move the flag waving Migrants, many of whom are stone cold criminals, back to their countries. Do it by plane, do it by bus, do it anyway you want, but they are NOT coming into the U.S.A. We will close the Border permanently if need be. Congress, fund the WALL! [Twitter for iPhone]

Nov 26, 2018 09:33:12 AM When Mueller does his final report, will he be covering all of his conflicts of interest in a preamble, will he be recommending action on all of the crimes of many kinds from those "on the other side"(whatever happened to Podesta?), and will he be putting in statements from..... [Twitter for iPhone]

Nov 26, 2018 09:44:33 AM ....hundreds of people closely involved with my campaign who never met, saw or spoke to a Russian during this period? So many campaign workers, people inside from the beginning, ask me why they have not been called (they want to be). There was NO Collusion & Mueller knows it! [Twitter for iPhone]

Nov 26, 2018 02:45:16 PM On the ten-year anniversary of the Mumbai terror attack, the U.S. stands with the people of India in their quest for justice. The attack killed 166 innocents, including six Americans. We will never let terrorists win, or even come close to winning! [Twitter for iPhone]

Nov 26, 2018 02:47:29 PM ....and false way. Something has to be done, including the possibility of the United States starting our own Worldwide Network to show the World the way we really are, GREAT! [Twitter for iPhone]

Nov 26, 2018 02:47:29 PM While CNN doesn't do great in the United States based on ratings, outside of the U.S. they have very little competition. Throughout the world, CNN has a powerful voice portraying the United States in an unfair.... [Twitter for iPhone]

Nov 26, 2018 03:20:58 PM Brad Raffensperger will be a fantastic Secretary of State for Georgia - will work closely with @BrianKempGA. It is really important that you get out and vote for Brad - early voting.... [Twitter for iPhone]

Nov 26, 2018 03:20:59 PM ....starts today, election is on December 4th. @VoteBradRaff is tough on Crime and Borders, Loves our Military and Vets. He will be great for jobs! [Twitter for iPhone]

Nov 26, 2018 11:40:22 PM RT @GOP: "I need the great people of Mississippi to send a message to... the radical Democrats by electing @cindyhydesmith." -@realDonaldTrum... [Twitter for iPhone]

Nov 26, 2018 11:40:30 PM RT @GOP: "Only with a strong Senate GOP majority can we defend your tax cuts, defend your Second Amendment, protect your Medicare and Socia... [Twitter for iPhone]

Nov 26, 2018 11:54:58 PM RT @GOP: "Tomorrow, the voters of this state will cast their ballots in one of the most important Senate elections of your lives — of all of… [Twitter for iPhone]

Nov 27, 2018 07:30:37 AM The Phony Witch Hunt continues, but Mueller and his gang of Angry Dems are only looking at one side, not the other. Wait until it comes out how horribly & viciously they are treating people, ruining lives for them refusing to lie. Mueller is a conflicted prosecutor gone rogue…. [Twitter for iPhone]

Nov 27, 2018 07:42:58 AM ….The Fake News Media builds Bob Mueller up as a Saint, when in actuality he is the exact opposite. He is doing TREMENDOUS damage to our Criminal Justice System, where he is only looking at one side and not the other. Heroes will come of this, and it won't be Mueller and his… [Twitter for iPhone]

Nov 27, 2018 08:07:23 AM ….terrible Gang of Angry Democrats. Look at their past, and look where they come from. The now $30,000,000 Witch Hunt continues and they've got nothing but ruined lives. Where is the Server? Let these terrible people go back to the Clinton Foundation and "Justice" Department! [Twitter for iPhone]

Nov 27, 2018 08:32:57 AM Polls are open in Mississippi. We need Cindy Hyde-Smith in Washington. GO OUT AND VOTE. Thanks! [Twitter for iPhone]

Nov 27, 2018 02:05:39 PM ….for electric cars. General Motors made a big China bet years ago when they built plants there (and in Mexico) - don't think that bet is going to pay off. I am here to protect America's Workers! [Twitter for iPhone]

Nov 27, 2018 02:05:39 PM Very disappointed with General Motors and their CEO, Mary Barra, for closing plants in Ohio, Michigan and Maryland. Nothing being closed in Mexico & China. The U.S. saved General Motors, and this is the THANKS we get! We are now looking at cutting all @GM subsidies, including…. [Twitter for iPhone]

Nov 27, 2018 07:31:37 PM The Mueller Witch Hunt is a total disgrace. They are looking at supposedly stolen Crooked Hillary Clinton Emails (even though they don't want to look at the DNC Server), but have no interest in the Emails that Hillary DELETED & acid washed AFTER getting a Congressional Subpoena! [Twitter for iPhone]

Nov 27, 2018 10:38:48 PM Brenda Snipes, in charge of voting in Broward County, Florida, was just spotted wearing a beautiful dress with 300 I VOTED signs on it. Just kidding, she is a fine, very honorable and highly respected voting tactician! [Twitter for iPhone]

Nov 27, 2018 10:42:08 PM Congratulations to Senator Cindy Hyde-Smith on your big WIN in the Great State of Mississippi. We are all very proud of you! [Twitter for iPhone]

Nov 28, 2018 08:39:38 AM While the disgusting Fake News is doing everything within their power not to report it that way, at least 3 major players are intimating that the Angry Mueller Gang of Dems is viciously telling witnesses to lie about facts & they will get relief. This is our Joseph McCarthy Era! [Twitter for iPhone]

Nov 28, 2018 08:40:18 AM RT @The_Trump_Train: https://t.co/FWJRNzBUB3 [Twitter for iPhone]

Nov 28, 2018 08:40:48 AM RT @The_Trump_Train: If GM doesn't want to keep their jobs in the United States, they should pay back the $11.2 billion bailout that was fu... [Twitter for iPhone]

Nov 28, 2018 08:41:14 AM RT @The_Trump_Train: Illegals can get up to $3,874 a month under Federal Assistance program. Our social security checks are on average $120... [Twitter for iPhone]

Nov 28, 2018 08:41:29 AM RT @The_Trump_Train: Will CNN ever ask Border Patrol agents how they felt having large rocks chucked at them by criminal illegals? [Twitter for iPhone]

Nov 28, 2018 09:29:30 AM RT @MikePenceVP: I'm thankful for every day Hillary Clinton is not President! [Twitter for iPhone]

Nov 28, 2018 09:31:18 AM RT @dbongino: What the hell is this? 🤷‍♂️ https://t.co/3haUa6XMRe [Twitter for iPhone]

Nov 28, 2018 09:32:20 AM RT @charliekirk11: WOW - if a conservative said this they would be boycotted and not allowed back in the public arena -- Hillary said "all b... [Twitter for iPhone]

Nov 28, 2018 09:43:31 AM The reason that the small truck business in the U.S. is such a go to favorite is that, for many years, Tariffs of 25% have been put on small trucks coming into our country. It is called the "chicken tax." If we did that with cars coming in, many more cars would be built here..... [Twitter for iPhone]

Nov 28, 2018 09:49:31 AM .....and G.M. would not be closing their plants in Ohio, Michigan & Maryland. Get smart Congress. Also, the countries that send us cars have taken advantage of the U.S. for decades. The President has great power on this issue - Because of the G.M. event, it is being studied now! [Twitter for iPhone]

Nov 28, 2018 11:09:47 AM Steel Dynamics announced that it will build a brand new 3 million ton steel mill in the Southwest that will create 600 good-paying U.S. JOBS. Steel JOBS are coming back to America, just like I predicted. Congratulations to Steel Dynamics! [Twitter for iPhone]

Nov 28, 2018 06:32:11 PM On behalf of @FLOTUS Melania and the entire Trump family, I want to wish you all a very MERRY CHRISTMAS! May this Christmas Season bring peace to your hearts, warmth to your homes, cheer to your spirits and JOY TO THE WORLD! #NCTL2018🎄 https://t.co/XNMJQ5JDSU [Twitter for iPhone]

Nov 28, 2018 11:36:07 PM Sebastian Gorka, a very talented man who I got to know well while he was working at the White House, has just written an excellent book, "Why We Fight." Much will be learned from this very good read! [Twitter for iPhone]

Nov 28, 2018 11:39:03 PM So much happening with the now discredited Witch Hunt. This total Hoax will be studied for years! [Twitter for iPhone]

Nov 29, 2018 06:37:14 AM General Motors is very counter to what other auto, and other, companies are doing. Big Steel is opening and renovating plants all over the country. Auto companies are pouring into the U.S., including BMW, which just announced a major new plant. The U.S.A. is booming! [Twitter for iPhone]

Nov 29, 2018 06:54:16 AM Did you ever see an investigation more in search of a crime? At the same time Mueller and the Angry Democrats aren't even looking at the atrocious, and perhaps subversive, crimes that were committed by Crooked Hillary Clinton and the Democrats. A total disgrace! [Twitter for iPhone]

Nov 29, 2018 07:16:12 AM When will this illegal Joseph McCarthy style Witch Hunt, one that has shattered so many innocent lives, ever end-or will it just go on forever? After wasting more than $40,000,000 (is that possible?), it has proven only one thing-there was NO Collusion with Russia. So Ridiculous! [Twitter for iPhone]

Nov 29, 2018 07:32:13 AM Billions of Dollars are pouring into the coffers of the U.S.A. because of the Tariffs being charged to China, and there is a long way to go. If companies don't want to pay Tariffs, build in the U.S.A. Otherwise, lets just make our Country richer than ever before! [Twitter for iPhone]

Nov 29, 2018 11:34:18 AM Based on the fact that the ships and sailors have not been returned to Ukraine from Russia, I have decided it would be best for all parties concerned to cancel my previously scheduled meeting.... [Twitter for iPhone]

Nov 29, 2018 11:34:19 AM ....in Argentina with President Vladimir Putin. I look forward to a meaningful Summit again as soon as this situation is resolved! [Twitter for iPhone]

Nov 29, 2018 05:03:52 PM .@SteveScalise has written an absolutely fascinating book (BACK IN THE GAME) on the world of D.C. politics, and more. He has experienced so much, in a short period of time. Few people have had his bravery or courage, and he has come all the way back. A big power and great person! [Twitter for iPhone]

Nov 29, 2018 05:14:21 PM .@StephenMoore and Arthur Laffer, two very talented men, have just completed an incredible book on my Economic Policies or, as they call it, #TRUMPONOMICS.... [Twitter for iPhone]

Nov 29, 2018 05:14:22 PM ....They have really done a great job in capturing my long-held views and ideas. This book is on sale now - a terrific read of a really interesting subject! [Twitter for iPhone]

Nov 29, 2018 05:34:18 PM .@DBongino's new book, "Spygate: The Attempted Sabotage of Donald J. Trump," is terrific. He's tough, he's smart, and he really gets it. His book is on sale now, I highly recommend! [Twitter for iPhone]

Nov 29, 2018 05:43:12 PM With all of the new books coming out you can't forget two of the great originals written by @GreggJarrett and @JudgeJeanine Pirro. Their books both went to #1. Go get them now, the phony Witch Hunt is well explained! [Twitter for iPhone]

Nov 29, 2018 05:47:59 PM We have been working hard on this - and it's only going to get better! https://t.co/MtGjmhMO8B [Twitter for iPhone]

Nov 29, 2018 07:04:23 PM As RNC Chair Ronna McDaniel oversaw history defying gains in the Senate and unprecedented fundraising strength. I have asked her to serve another term for my 2020 re-elect, because there is no one better for the job! [Twitter for iPhone]

Nov 29, 2018 08:41:50 PM Just landed in Argentina with @FLOTUS Melania! #G20Summit https://t.co/Zg15gmPazF [Twitter for iPhone]

Nov 29, 2018 09:50:59 PM "This demonstrates the Robert Mueller and his partisans have no evidence, not a whiff of collusion, between Trump and the Russians. Russian project legal. Trump Tower meeting (son Don), perfectly legal. He wasn't involved with hacking." Gregg Jarrett. A total Witch Hunt! [Twitter for iPhone]

Nov 29, 2018 10:04:34 PM Alan Dershowitz: "These are not crimes. He (Mueller) has no authority to be a roving Commissioner. I don't see any evidence of crimes." This is an illegal Hoax that should be ended immediately. Mueller refuses to look at the real crimes on the other side. Where is the IG REPORT? [Twitter for iPhone]

Nov 29, 2018 10:31:14 PM Arrived in Argentina with a very busy two days planned. Important meetings scheduled throughout. Our great Country is extremely well represented. Will be very productive! [Twitter for iPhone]

Nov 30, 2018 04:52:04 AM Oh, I get it! I am a very good developer, happily living my life, when I see our Country going in the wrong direction (to put it mildly). Against all odds, I decide to run for President & continue to run my business-very legal & very cool, talked about it on the campaign trail... [Twitter for iPhone]

Nov 30, 2018 04:59:03 AM ....Lightly looked at doing a building somewhere in Russia. Put up zero money, zero guarantees and didn't do the project. Witch Hunt! [Twitter for iPhone]

Nov 30, 2018 08:08:27 AM #USMCAus□□c□ https://t.co/7CYsYBYbd1 [Twitter for iPhone]

Nov 30, 2018 09:45:18 AM Just signed one of the most important, and largest, Trade Deals in U.S. and World History. The United States, Mexico and Canada worked so well together in crafting this great document. The terrible NAFTA will soon be gone. The USMCA will be fantastic for all! [Twitter for iPhone]

Nov 30, 2018 03:19:12 PM To the Great people of Alaska. You have been hit hard by a "big one." Please follow the directions of the highly trained professionals who are there to help you. Your Federal Government will spare no expense. God Bless you ALL! [Twitter for iPhone]

Nov 30, 2018 03:23:09 PM Great reviews on the USMCA - sooo much better than NAFTA! [Twitter for iPhone]

Nov 30, 2018 07:23:30 PM Great day at the #G20Summit in Buenos Aires, Argentina. Thank you! https://t.co/4IHvUdOygc [Twitter for iPhone]

Nov 30, 2018 09:03:36 PM Watch @seanhannity on @FoxNews NOW. Enjoy! [Twitter for iPhone]

Nov 30, 2018 10:13:24 PM RT @TheBlueHouseENG: President Moon (@moonriver365) and President Trump (@realDonaldTrump) reaffirmed their commitment to closely coordinat... [Twitter for iPhone]

Nov 30, 2018 10:14:18 PM RT @AbeShinzo: アルゼンチンでＧ２０サミットが開幕しました。この機会を活かし、トランプ大統領、モディ首相と、初めてとなる日米印三か国による首脳会談を行いました。「自由で開かれたインド太平洋」という共通の目標に向かって、緊密に連携していくことで一致しました。 htt... [Twitter for iPhone]

Nov 30, 2018 10:16:54 PM RT @EPN: En mi último día como Presidente, me siento muy honrado de haber participado en la firma del nuevo Tratado Comercial entre México,... [Twitter for iPhone]

Dec 1, 2018 12:49:46 AM Statement from President Donald J. Trump and First Lady Melania Trump on the Passing of Former President George H.W. Bush https://t.co/qxPsp4Ggs7 [Twitter for iPhone]

Dec 1, 2018 12:50:09 AM RT @realDonaldTrump: Statement from President Donald J. Trump and First Lady Melania Trump on the Passing of Former President George H.W. B... [Twitter for iPhone]

Dec 1, 2018 06:16:08 AM President George H.W. Bush led a long, successful and beautiful life. Whenever I was with him I saw his absolute joy for life and true pride in his family. His accomplishments were great from beginning to end. He was a truly wonderful man and will be missed by all! [Twitter for iPhone]

Dec 1, 2018 10:21:57 AM I was very much looking forward to having a press conference just prior to leaving Argentina because we have had such great success in our dealing with various countries and their leaders at the G20.... [Twitter for iPhone]

Dec 1, 2018 10:21:58 AM ....However, out of respect for the Bush Family and former President George H.W. Bush we will wait until after the funeral to have a press conference. [Twitter for iPhone]

Dec 2, 2018 03:15:38 PM This week, Jews around the world will celebrate the miracles of Hanukkah. @FLOTUS Melania and I send our very best wishes for a blessed and Happy Hanukkah! https://t.co/LrnGcc86w4 https://t.co/Kdjeyvkzmb [Twitter for iPhone]

Dec 2, 2018 11:00:25 PM China has agreed to reduce and remove tariffs on cars coming into China from the U.S. Currently the tariff is 40%. [Twitter for iPhone]

Dec 3, 2018 07:54:30 AM My meeting in Argentina with President Xi of China was an extraordinary one. Relations with China have taken a BIG leap forward! Very good things will happen. We are dealing from great strength, but China likewise has much to gain if and when a deal is completed. Level the field! [Twitter for iPhone]

Dec 3, 2018 08:01:08 AM Farmers will be a a very BIG and FAST beneficiary of our deal with China. They intend to start purchasing agricultural product immediately. We make the finest and cleanest product in the World, and that is what China wants. Farmers, I LOVE YOU! [Twitter for iPhone]

Dec 3, 2018 08:18:01 AM President Xi and I have a very strong and personal relationship. He and I are the only two people that can bring about massive and very positive change, on trade and far beyond, between our two great Nations. A solution for North Korea is a great thing for China and ALL! [Twitter for iPhone]

Dec 3, 2018 08:30:46 AM I am certain that, at some time in the future, President Xi and I, together with President Putin of Russia, will start talking about a meaningful halt to what has become a major and uncontrollable Arms Race. The U.S. spent 716 Billion Dollars this year. Crazy! [Twitter for iPhone]

Dec 3, 2018 08:45:22 AM We would save Billions of Dollars if the Democrats would give us the votes to build the Wall. Either way, people will NOT be allowed into our Country illegally! We will close the entire Southern Border if necessary. Also, STOP THE DRUGS! [Twitter for iPhone]

Dec 3, 2018 10:24:37 AM "Michael Cohen asks judge for no Prison Time." You mean he can do all of the TERRIBLE, unrelated to Trump, things having to do with fraud, big loans, Taxis, etc., and not serve a long prison term? He makes up stories to get a GREAT & ALREADY reduced deal for himself, and get..... [Twitter for iPhone]

Dec 3, 2018 10:29:31 AM ....his wife and father-in-law (who has the money?) off Scott Free. He lied for this outcome and should, in my opinion, serve a full and complete sentence. [Twitter for iPhone]

Dec 3, 2018 10:48:12 AM "I will never testify against Trump." This statement was recently made by Roger Stone, essentially stating that he will not be forced by a rogue and out of control prosecutor to make up lies and stories about "President Trump." Nice to know that some people still have "guts!" [Twitter for iPhone]

Dec 3, 2018 10:56:06 AM Bob Mueller (who is a much different man than people think) and his out of control band of Angry Democrats, don't want the truth, they only want lies. The truth is very bad for their mission! [Twitter for iPhone]

Dec 3, 2018 11:37:38 AM Looking forward to being with the Bush Family to pay my respects to President George H.W. Bush. [Twitter for iPhone]

Dec 3, 2018 02:42:31 PM Congratulations to newly inaugurated Mexican President @lopezobrador_. He had a tremendous political victory with the great support of the Mexican People. We will work well together for many years to come! [Twitter for iPhone]

Dec 3, 2018 09:21:18 PM #Remembering41 https://t.co/9xbFYlZzNs [Twitter for iPhone]

Dec 4, 2018 09:22:01 AM Looking forward to being with the wonderful Bush family at Blair House today. The former First Lady will be coming over to the White House this morning to be given a tour of the Christmas decorations by Melania. The elegance & precision of the last two days have been remarkable! [Twitter for iPhone]

Dec 4, 2018 09:30:16 AM The negotiations with China have already started. Unless extended, they will end 90 days from the date of our wonderful and very warm dinner with President Xi in Argentina. Bob Lighthizer will be working closely with Steve Mnuchin, Larry Kudlow, Wilbur Ross and Peter Navarro..... [Twitter for iPhone]

Dec 4, 2018 09:55:35 AM ......on seeing whether or not a REAL deal with China is actually possible. If it is, we will get it done. China is supposed to start buying Agricultural product and more immediately. President Xi and I want this deal to happen, and it probably will. But if not remember,...... [Twitter for iPhone]

Dec 4, 2018 10:03:41 AM ....I am a Tariff Man. When people or countries come in to raid the great wealth of our Nation, I want them to pay for the privilege of doing so. It will always be the best way to max out our economic power. We are right now taking in $billions in Tariffs. MAKE AMERICA RICH AGAIN [Twitter for iPhone]

Dec 4, 2018 10:10:00 AM .....But if a fair deal is able to be made with China, one that does all of the many things we know must be finally done, I will happily sign. Let the negotiations begin. MAKE AMERICA GREAT AGAIN! [Twitter for iPhone]

Dec 4, 2018 11:22:24 AM Could somebody please explain to the Democrats (we need their votes) that our Country losses 250 Billion Dollars a year on illegal immigration, not including the terrible drug flow. Top Border Security, including a Wall, is $25 Billion. Pays for itself in two months. Get it done! [Twitter for iPhone]

Dec 4, 2018 11:24:07 AM RT @charliekirk11: There are riots in socialist France because of radical leftist fuel taxes Media barely mentioning this America is boom... [Twitter for iPhone]

Dec 4, 2018 05:56:00 PM I am glad that my friend @EmmanuelMacron and the protestors in Paris have agreed with the conclusion I reached two years ago. The Paris Agreement is fatally flawed because it raises the price of energy for responsible countries while whitewashing some of the worst polluters.... [Twitter for iPhone]

Dec 4, 2018 05:56:01 PM ....in the world. I want clean air and clean water and have been making great strides in improving America's environment. But American taxpayers – and American workers – shouldn't pay to clean up others countries' pollution. [Twitter for iPhone]

Dec 4, 2018 07:20:27 PM We are either going to have a REAL DEAL with China, or no deal at all - at which point we will be charging major Tariffs against Chinese product being shipped into the United States. Ultimately, I believe, we will be making a deal - either now or into the future.... [Twitter for iPhone]

Dec 4, 2018 07:21:41 PM .....China does not want Tariffs! [Twitter for iPhone]

Dec 5, 2018 07:46:28 AM "China officially echoed President Donald Trump's optimism over bilateral trade talks. Chinese officials have begun preparing to restart imports of U.S. Soybeans & Liquified Natural Gas, the first sign confirming the claims of President Donald Trump and the White House that...... [Twitter for iPhone]

Dec 5, 2018 07:49:48 AM .....China had agreed to start "immediately" buying U.S. products." @business [Twitter for iPhone]

Dec 5, 2018 08:19:46 AM Very strong signals being sent by China once they returned home from their long trip, including stops, from Argentina. Not to sound naive or anything, but I believe President Xi meant every word of what he said at our long and hopefully historic meeting. ALL subjects discussed! [Twitter for iPhone]

Dec 5, 2018 08:44:10 AM One of the very exciting things to come out of my meeting with President Xi of China is his promise to me to criminalize the sale of deadly Fentanyl coming into the United States. It will now be considered a "controlled substance." This could be a game changer on what is....... [Twitter for iPhone]

Dec 5, 2018 08:51:07 AM .....considered to be the worst and most dangerous, addictive and deadly substance of them all. Last year over 77,000 people died from Fentanyl. If China cracks down on this "horror drug," using the Death Penalty for distributors and pushers, the results will be incredible! [Twitter for iPhone]

Dec 5, 2018 08:56:31 AM Looking forward to being with the Bush family. This is not a funeral, this is a day of celebration for a great man who has led a long and distinguished life. He will be missed! [Twitter for iPhone]

Dec 5, 2018 09:44:48 AM Hopefully OPEC will be keeping oil flows as is, not restricted. The World does not want to see, or need, higher oil prices! [Twitter for iPhone]

Dec 5, 2018 09:24:40 PM Doug Wead, a truly great presidential historian, had a wonderful take on a very beautiful moment in history, the funeral service today of President Bush. Doug was able to brilliantly cover some very important and interesting periods of time! @LouDobbs [Twitter for iPhone]

Dec 5, 2018 10:32:22 PM Working hard, thank you! https://t.co/3SoWTkZjP6 [Twitter for iPhone]

Dec 6, 2018 10:17:47 AM Without the phony Russia Witch Hunt, and with all that we have accomplished in the last almost two years (Tax & Regulation Cuts, Judge's, Military, Vets, etc.) my approval rating would be at 75% rather than the 50% just reported by Rasmussen. It's called Presidential Harassment! [Twitter for iPhone]

Dec 6, 2018 12:07:29 PM My thoughts and prayers are with the @USMC crew members who were involved in a mid-air collision off the coast of Japan. Thank you to @USForcesJapan for their immediate response and rescue efforts. Whatever you need, we are here for you. @IIIMEF [Twitter for iPhone]

Dec 6, 2018 07:27:11 PM Does the Fake News Media ever mention the fact that Republicans, with the very important help of my campaign Rallies, WON THE UNITED STATES SENATE, 53 to 47? All I hear is that the Open Border Dems won the House. Senate alone approves judges & others. Big Republican Win! [Twitter for iPhone]

Dec 6, 2018 07:56:18 PM Statement from China: "The teams of both sides are now having smooth communications and good cooperation with each other. We are full of confidence that an agreement can be reached within the next 90 days." I agree! [Twitter for iPhone]

Dec 6, 2018 09:58:43 PM Jerome Corsi: "This is not justice, this is not America. This is a political prosecution. The Special Prosecutor (Counsel), to get this plea deal, demanded I lie and violate the law. They're the criminals." He is not alone. 17 Angry Dems. People forced to lie. Sad! @Trish_Regan [Twitter for iPhone]

Dec 6, 2018 10:07:18 PM Trish_Regan: "Did the FBI follow protocol to obtain the FISA warrant? I don't think so. The Dossier was opposition research funded by opponents. Don't use Government resources to take down political foes. Weaponizing Government for gain." Is this really America? Witch Hunt! [Twitter for iPhone]

Dec 6, 2018 10:08:26 PM FAKE NEWS - THE ENEMY OF THE PEOPLE! [Twitter for iPhone]

Dec 6, 2018 10:15:12 PM Arizona, together with our Military and Border Patrol, is bracing for a massive surge at a NON-WALLED area. WE WILL NOT LET THEM THROUGH. Big danger. Nancy and Chuck must approve Boarder Security and the Wall! [Twitter for iPhone]

Dec 7, 2018 06:18:59 AM Robert Mueller and Leakin' Lyin' James Comey are Best Friends, just one of many Mueller Conflicts of Interest. And bye the way, wasn't the woman in charge of prosecuting Jerome Corsi (who I do not know) in charge of "legal" at the corrupt Clinton Foundation? A total Witch Hunt... [Twitter for iPhone]

Dec 7, 2018 06:28:50 AM ....Will Robert Mueller's big time conflicts of interest be listed at the top of his Republicans only Report. Will Andrew Weissman's horrible and vicious prosecutorial past be listed in the Report. He wrongly destroyed people's lives, took down great companies, only to be........ [Twitter for iPhone]

Dec 7, 2018 06:40:53 AM .....overturned, 9-0, in the United States Supreme Court. Doing same thing to people now. Will all of the substantial & many contributions made by the 17 Angry Democrats to the Campaign of Crooked Hillary be listed in top of Report. Will the people that worked for the Clinton.... [Twitter for iPhone]

Dec 7, 2018 06:53:34 AM ....Foundation be listed at the top of the Report? Will the scathing document written about Lyin' James Comey, by the man in charge of the case, Rod Rosenstein (who also signed the FISA Warrant), be a big part of the Report? Isn't Rod therefore totally conflicted? Will all of.... [Twitter for iPhone]

Dec 7, 2018 07:15:58 AM ...the lying and leaking by the people doing the Report, & also Bruce Ohr (and his lovely wife Molly), Comey, Brennan, Clapper, & all of the many fired people of the FBI, be listed in the Report? Will the corruption within the DNC & Clinton Campaign be exposed?..And so much more! [Twitter for iPhone]

Dec 7, 2018 08:13:48 AM China talks are going very well! [Twitter for iPhone]

Dec 7, 2018 08:39:36 AM It has been incorrectly reported that Rudy Giuliani and others will not be doing a counter to the Mueller Report. That is Fake News. Already 87 pages done, but obviously cannot complete until we see the final Witch Hunt Report. [Twitter for iPhone]

Dec 7, 2018 09:46:32 AM Today, we honor those who perished 77 years ago at Pearl Harbor, and we salute every veteran who served in World War II over the 4 years that followed that horrific attack. God Bless America! https://t.co/zbu4NLVr4G https://t.co/5hbLDrqg40 [Twitter for iPhone]

Dec 7, 2018 09:56:46 AM We will be doing a major Counter Report to the Mueller Report. This should never again be allowed to happen to a future President of the United States! [Twitter for iPhone]

Dec 7, 2018 11:16:51 AM I am pleased to announce that Heather Nauert, Spokeswoman for the United States Department of State, will be nominated to serve as United Nations Ambassador. I want to congratulate Heather, and thank Ambassador Nikki Haley for her great service to our Country! [Twitter for iPhone]

Dec 7, 2018 11:18:36 AM I am pleased to announce that I will be nominating The Honorable William P. Barr for the position of Attorney General of the United States. As the former AG for George H.W. Bush.... [Twitter for iPhone]

Dec 7, 2018 11:18:37 AM ....and one of the most highly respected lawyers and legal minds in the Country, he will be a great addition to our team. I look forward to having him join our very successful Administration! [Twitter for iPhone]

Dec 7, 2018 01:48:43 PM RT @WhiteHouse: President Trump Delivers Remarks at the 2018 Project Safe Neighborhoods National Conference https://t.co/5oV86XUX1o [Twitter for iPhone]

Dec 7, 2018 03:02:34 PM Mike Pompeo is doing a great job, I am very proud of him. His predecessor, Rex Tillerson, didn't have the mental capacity needed. He was dumb as a rock and I couldn't get rid of him fast enough. He was lazy as hell. Now it is a whole new ballgame, great spirit at State! [Twitter for iPhone]

Dec 7, 2018 03:56:17 PM Hopefully Mitch McConnell will ask for a VOTE on Criminal Justice Reform. It is extremely popular and has strong bipartisan support. It will also help a lot of people, save taxpayer dollars, and keep our communities safe. Go for it Mitch! [Twitter for iPhone]

Dec 7, 2018 04:49:01 PM It is being reported that Leakin' James Comey was told by Department of Justice attorneys not to answer the most important questions. Total bias and corruption at the highest levels of previous Administration. Force him to answer the questions under oath! [Twitter for iPhone]

Dec 7, 2018 06:00:21 PM Totally clears the President. Thank you! [Twitter for iPhone]

Dec 7, 2018 10:58:04 PM RT @WhiteHouse: This afternoon, President Trump delivered remarks at the 2018 Project Safe Neighborhoods National Conference where he reinf… [Twitter for iPhone]

Dec 8, 2018 07:34:04 AM The Paris Agreement isn't working out so well for Paris. Protests and riots all over France. People do not want to pay large sums of money, much to third world countries (that are questionably run), in order to maybe protect the environment. Chanting "We Want Trump!" Love France. [Twitter for iPhone]

Dec 8, 2018 07:52:39 AM The idea of a European Military didn't work out too well in W.W. I or 2. But the U.S. was there for you, and always will be. All we ask is that you pay your fair share of NATO. Germany is paying 1% while the U.S. pays 4.3% of a much larger GDP - to protect Europe. Fairness! [Twitter for iPhone]

Dec 8, 2018 08:01:56 AM AFTER TWO YEARS AND MILLIONS OF PAGES OF DOCUMENTS (and a cost of over $30,000,000), NO COLLUSION! [Twitter for iPhone]

Dec 8, 2018 09:19:31 AM ….I am thankful to both of these incredible men for their service to our Country! Date of transition to be determined. [Twitter for iPhone]

Dec 8, 2018 09:19:31 AM I am pleased to announce my nomination of four-star General Mark Milley, Chief of Staff of the United States Army -- as the Chairman of the Joint Chiefs of Staff, replacing General Joe Dunford, who will be retiring.... [Twitter for iPhone]

Dec 8, 2018 11:01:39 AM "This is collusion illusion, there is no smoking gun here. At this late date, after all that we have gone through, after millions have been spent, we have no Russian Collusion. There is nothing impeachable here." @GeraldoRivera Time for the Witch Hunt to END! [Twitter for iPhone]

Dec 8, 2018 12:22:32 PM Very sad day & night in Paris. Maybe it's time to end the ridiculous and extremely expensive Paris Agreement and return money back to the people in the form of lower taxes? The U.S. was way ahead of the curve on that and the only major country where emissions went down last year! [Twitter for iPhone]

Dec 8, 2018 01:58:13 PM Watched Da Nang Dick Blumenthal on television spewing facts almost as accurate as his bravery in Vietnam (which he never saw). As the bullets whizzed by Da Nang Dicks head, as he was saving soldiers.... [Twitter for iPhone]

Dec 8, 2018 01:58:14 PM ....left and right, he then woke up from his dream screaming that HE LIED. Next time I go to Vietnam I will ask "the Dick" to travel with me! [Twitter for iPhone]

Dec 8, 2018 02:07:07 PM Great honor to be headed to the Army-Navy game today. Will be there shortly, landing now! https://t.co/ByAfESq8aS [Twitter for iPhone]

Dec 8, 2018 06:22:52 PM #ArmyNavyGameus https://t.co/Yjhq6r6F9h [Twitter for iPhone]

Dec 8, 2018 06:31:15 PM It was my honor to attend today's #ArmyNavyGame in Philadelphia. A GREAT game played all around by our HEROES. Congratulations @ArmyWP_Football on the win! https://t.co/WDLkM6VE2T [Twitter for iPhone]

Dec 9, 2018 08:38:22 AM On 245 occasions, former FBI Director James Comey told House investigators he didn't know, didn't recall, or couldn't remember things when asked. Opened investigations on 4 Americans (not 2) - didn't know who signed off and didn't know Christopher Steele. All lies! [Twitter for iPhone]

Dec 9, 2018 08:53:30 AM Leakin' James Comey must have set a record for who lied the most to Congress in one day. His Friday testimony was so untruthful! This whole deal is a Rigged Fraud headed up by dishonest people who would do anything so that I could not become President. They are now exposed! [Twitter for iPhone]

Dec 9, 2018 05:43:13 PM The Trump Administration has accomplished more than any other U.S. Administration in its first two (not even) years of existence, & we are having a great time doing it! All of this despite the Fake News Media, which has gone totally out of its mind-truly the Enemy of the People! [Twitter for iPhone]

Dec 9, 2018 08:27:23 PM I am in the process of interviewing some really great people for the position of White House Chief of Staff. Fake News has been saying with certainty it was Nick Ayers, a spectacular person who will always be with our #MAGA agenda. I will be making a decision soon! [Twitter for iPhone]

Dec 10, 2018 06:46:11 AM "Democrats can't find a Smocking Gun tying the Trump campaign to Russia after James Comey's testimony. No Smocking Gun...No Collusion." @FoxNews That's because there was NO COLLUSION. So now the Dems go to a simple private transaction, wrongly call it a campaign contribution,... [Twitter for iPhone]

Dec 10, 2018 07:00:00 AM ....which it was not (but even if it was, it is only a CIVIL CASE, like Obama's - but it was done correctly by a lawyer and there would not even be a fine. Lawyer's liability if he made a mistake, not me). Cohen just trying to get his sentence reduced. WITCH HUNT! [Twitter for iPhone]

Dec 10, 2018 09:11:21 PM James Comey's behind closed doors testimony reveals that "there was not evidence of Campaign Collusion" with Russia when he left the FBI. In other words, the Witch Hunt is illegal and should never have been started! [Twitter for iPhone]

Dec 10, 2018 09:28:25 PM "Former FBI Director James Comey under fire for his testimony acknowledging he knew that the Democrats paid for that phony Trump Dossier." @LouDobbs Details on Tuesday night. [Twitter for iPhone]

Dec 11, 2018 06:52:28 AM Despite the large Caravans that WERE forming and heading to our Country, people have not been able to get through our newly built Walls, makeshift Walls & Fences, or Border Patrol Officers & Military. They are now staying in Mexico or going back to their original countries....... [Twitter for iPhone]

Dec 11, 2018 07:04:50 AM .....Ice, Border Patrol and our Military have done a FANTASTIC job of securing our Southern Border. A Great Wall would be, however, a far easier & less expensive solution. We have already built large new sections & fully renovated others, making them like new. The Democrats,..... [Twitter for iPhone]

Dec 11, 2018 07:12:23 AM ....however, for strictly political reasons and because they have been pulled so far left, do NOT want Border Security. They want Open Borders for anyone to come in. This brings large scale crime and disease. Our Southern Border is now Secure and will remain that way....... [Twitter for iPhone]

Dec 11, 2018 07:30:57 AM .....I look forward to my meeting with Chuck Schumer & Nancy Pelosi. In 2006, Democrats voted for a Wall, and they were right to do so. Today, they no longer want Border Security. They will fight it at all cost, and Nancy must get votes for Speaker. But the Wall will get built... [Twitter for iPhone]

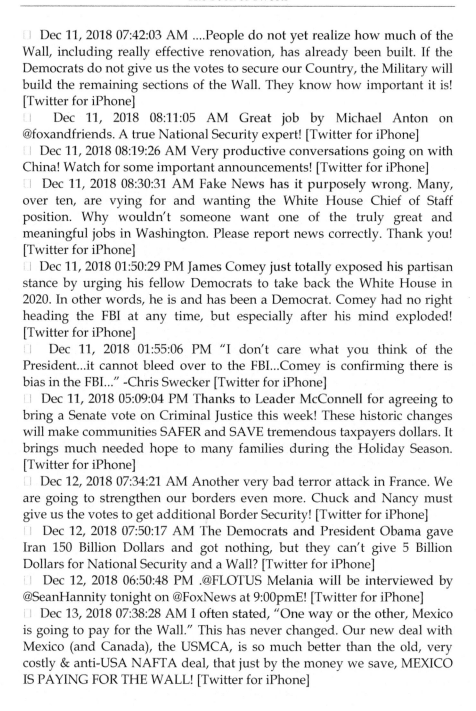

Dec 11, 2018 07:42:03 AM ....People do not yet realize how much of the Wall, including really effective renovation, has already been built. If the Democrats do not give us the votes to secure our Country, the Military will build the remaining sections of the Wall. They know how important it is! [Twitter for iPhone]

Dec 11, 2018 08:11:05 AM Great job by Michael Anton on @foxandfriends. A true National Security expert! [Twitter for iPhone]

Dec 11, 2018 08:19:26 AM Very productive conversations going on with China! Watch for some important announcements! [Twitter for iPhone]

Dec 11, 2018 08:30:31 AM Fake News has it purposely wrong. Many, over ten, are vying for and wanting the White House Chief of Staff position. Why wouldn't someone want one of the truly great and meaningful jobs in Washington. Please report news correctly. Thank you! [Twitter for iPhone]

Dec 11, 2018 01:50:29 PM James Comey just totally exposed his partisan stance by urging his fellow Democrats to take back the White House in 2020. In other words, he is and has been a Democrat. Comey had no right heading the FBI at any time, but especially after his mind exploded! [Twitter for iPhone]

Dec 11, 2018 01:55:06 PM "I don't care what you think of the President...it cannot bleed over to the FBI...Comey is confirming there is bias in the FBI..." -Chris Swecker [Twitter for iPhone]

Dec 11, 2018 05:09:04 PM Thanks to Leader McConnell for agreeing to bring a Senate vote on Criminal Justice this week! These historic changes will make communities SAFER and SAVE tremendous taxpayers dollars. It brings much needed hope to many families during the Holiday Season. [Twitter for iPhone]

Dec 12, 2018 07:34:21 AM Another very bad terror attack in France. We are going to strengthen our borders even more. Chuck and Nancy must give us the votes to get additional Border Security! [Twitter for iPhone]

Dec 12, 2018 07:50:17 AM The Democrats and President Obama gave Iran 150 Billion Dollars and got nothing, but they can't give 5 Billion Dollars for National Security and a Wall? [Twitter for iPhone]

Dec 12, 2018 06:50:48 PM .@FLOTUS Melania will be interviewed by @SeanHannity tonight on @FoxNews at 9:00pmE! [Twitter for iPhone]

Dec 13, 2018 07:38:28 AM I often stated, "One way or the other, Mexico is going to pay for the Wall." This has never changed. Our new deal with Mexico (and Canada), the USMCA, is so much better than the old, very costly & anti-USA NAFTA deal, that just by the money we save, MEXICO IS PAYING FOR THE WALL! [Twitter for iPhone]

Dec 13, 2018 08:17:08 AM I never directed Michael Cohen to break the law. He was a lawyer and he is supposed to know the law. It is called "advice of counsel," and a lawyer has great liability if a mistake is made. That is why they get paid. Despite that many campaign finance lawyers have strongly...... [Twitter for iPhone]

Dec 13, 2018 08:25:27 AM ....stated that I did nothing wrong with respect to campaign finance laws, if they even apply, because this was not campaign finance. Cohen was guilty on many charges unrelated to me, but he plead to two campaign charges which were not criminal and of which he probably was not... [Twitter for iPhone]

Dec 13, 2018 08:34:14 AM ....guilty even on a civil bases. Those charges were just agreed to by him in order to embarrass the president and get a much reduced prison sentence, which he did-including the fact that his family was temporarily let off the hook. As a lawyer, Michael has great liability to me! [Twitter for iPhone]

Dec 13, 2018 08:39:34 AM ....guilty even on a civil basis. Those charges were just agreed to by him in order to embarrass the president and get a much reduced prison sentence, which he did-including the fact that his family was temporarily let off the hook. As a lawyer, Michael has great liability to me! [Twitter for iPhone]

Dec 13, 2018 11:07:50 AM They gave General Flynn a great deal because they were embarrassed by the way he was treated - the FBI said he didn't lie and they overrode the FBI. They want to scare everybody into making up stories that are not true by catching them in the smallest of misstatements. Sad!...... [Twitter for iPhone]

Dec 13, 2018 11:08:16 AM WITCH HUNT! [Twitter for iPhone]

Dec 13, 2018 12:34:14 PM If it was a Conservative that said what "crazed" Mika Brzezinski stated on her show yesterday, using a certain horrible term, that person would be banned permanently from television.... [Twitter for iPhone]

Dec 13, 2018 12:34:15 PM ....She will probably be given a pass, despite their terrible ratings. Congratulations to @RichardGrenell, our great Ambassador to Germany, for having the courage to take this horrible issue on! [Twitter for iPhone]

Dec 13, 2018 01:00:44 PM Just did an interview with @HARRISFAULKNER on @FoxNews, airing now (1pmE.) Enjoy! [Twitter for iPhone]

Dec 13, 2018 01:13:39 PM Happy 382nd Birthday @USNationalGuard. Our entire Nation is forever grateful for all you do 24/7/365. We love you! #Guard382 https://t.co/XLoCxOFvMA [Twitter Media Studio]

Dec 13, 2018 03:24:36 PM Today, it was my honor to welcome our Nation's newly elected Governors to the @WhiteHouse! https://t.co/LCpFIoRglp [Twitter for iPhone]

Dec 13, 2018 04:21:33 PM Let's not do a shutdown, Democrats - do what's right for the American People! https://t.co/bZg07ZKQqo [Twitter Media Studio]

Dec 14, 2018 11:25:59 AM China just announce the there economy is growing much slower than anticipated because of our Trade War with them. They have just suspended U.S. Tariff Hikes. U.S. is doing very well. China wants to make a big and very comprehensive deal. It could happen, and rather soon! [Twitter for iPhone]

Dec 14, 2018 11:35:43 AM China just announced that their economy is growing much slower than anticipated because of our Trade War with them. They have just suspended U.S. Tariff Hikes. U.S. is doing very well. China wants to make a big and very comprehensive deal. It could happen, and rather soon! [Twitter for iPhone]

Dec 14, 2018 01:17:32 PM ....Kim Jong Un sees it better than anyone and will fully take advantage of it for his people. We are doing just fine! [Twitter for iPhone]

Dec 14, 2018 01:17:32 PM Many people have asked how we are doing in our negotiations with North Korea - I always reply by saying we are in no hurry, there is wonderful potential for great economic success for that country.... [Twitter for iPhone]

Dec 14, 2018 01:19:36 PM Thank you to @tim_cook for agreeing to expand operations in the U.S. and thereby creating thousands of jobs! https://t.co/2zOVxp9nTF [Twitter for iPhone]

Dec 14, 2018 05:18:15 PM I am pleased to announce that Mick Mulvaney, Director of the Office of Management & Budget, will be named Acting White House Chief of Staff, replacing General John Kelly, who has served our Country with distinction. Mick has done an outstanding job while in the Administration.... [Twitter for iPhone]

Dec 14, 2018 05:18:16 PM ....I look forward to working with him in this new capacity as we continue to MAKE AMERICA GREAT AGAIN! John will be staying until the end of the year. He is a GREAT PATRIOT and I want to personally thank him for his service! [Twitter for iPhone]

Dec 14, 2018 07:31:44 PM For the record, there were MANY people who wanted to be the White House Chief of Staff. Mick M will do a GREAT job! [Twitter for iPhone]

Dec 14, 2018 09:07:45 PM As I predicted all along, Obamacare has been struck down as an UNCONSTITUTIONAL disaster! Now Congress must pass a STRONG law that provides GREAT healthcare and protects pre-existing conditions. Mitch and Nancy, get it done! [Twitter for iPhone]

Dec 14, 2018 09:16:29 PM Wow, but not surprisingly, ObamaCare was just ruled UNCONSTITUTIONAL by a highly respected judge in Texas. Great news for America! [Twitter for iPhone]

Dec 15, 2018 09:14:54 AM Secretary of the Interior @RyanZinke will be leaving the Administration at the end of the year after having served for a period of almost two years. Ryan has accomplished much during his tenure and I want to thank him for his service to our Nation....... [Twitter for iPhone]

Dec 15, 2018 09:18:29 AM ....The Trump Administration will be announcing the new Secretary of the Interior next week. [Twitter for iPhone]

Dec 15, 2018 10:37:40 AM Never in the history of our Country has the "press" been more dishonest than it is today. Stories that should be good, are bad. Stories that should be bad, are horrible. Many stories, like with the REAL story on Russia, Clinton & the DNC, seldom get reported. Too bad! [Twitter for iPhone]

Dec 15, 2018 11:15:38 AM The pathetic and dishonest Weekly Standard, run by failed prognosticator Bill Kristol (who, like many others, never had a clue), is flat broke and out of business. Too bad. May it rest in peace! [Twitter for iPhone]

Dec 15, 2018 11:45:12 AM Wow, 19,000 Texts between Lisa Page and her lover, Peter S of the FBI, in charge of the Russia Hoax, were just reported as being wiped clean and gone. Such a big story that will never be covered by the Fake News. Witch Hunt! [Twitter for iPhone]

Dec 16, 2018 08:58:54 AM A REAL scandal is the one sided coverage, hour by hour, of networks like NBC & Democrat spin machines like Saturday Night Live. It is all nothing less than unfair news coverage and Dem commercials. Should be tested in courts, can't be legal? Only defame & belittle! Collusion? [Twitter for iPhone]

Dec 16, 2018 09:11:52 AM So where are all the missing Text messages between fired FBI agents Peter S and the lovely Lisa Page, his lover. Just reported that they have been erased and wiped clean. What an outrage as the totally compromised and conflicted Witch Hunt moves ever so slowly forward. Want them! [Twitter for iPhone]

Dec 16, 2018 09:39:50 AM Remember, Michael Cohen only became a "Rat" after the FBI did something which was absolutely unthinkable & unheard of until the Witch Hunt was illegally started. They BROKE INTO AN ATTORNEY'S OFFICE! Why didn't they break into the DNC to get the Server, or Crooked's office? [Twitter for iPhone]

Dec 16, 2018 10:03:22 AM At the request of many, I will be reviewing the case of a "U.S. Military hero," Major Matt Golsteyn, who is charged with murder. He could face the death penalty from our own government after he admitted to killing a Terrorist bomb maker while overseas. @PeteHegseth @FoxNews [Twitter for iPhone]

Dec 16, 2018 10:20:43 AM Judge Ken Starr, former Solicitor Generel & Independent Counsel, just stated that, after two years, "there is no evidence or proof of collusion" & further that "there is no evidence that there was a campaign financing violation involving the President." Thank you Judge. @FoxNews [Twitter for iPhone]

Dec 16, 2018 11:25:51 AM The Democrats policy of Child Seperation on the Border during the Obama Administration was far worse than the way we handle it now. Remember the 2014 picture of children in cages - the Obama years. However, if you don't separate, FAR more people will come. Smugglers use the kids! [Twitter for iPhone]

Dec 16, 2018 03:21:05 PM Required television watching is last weeks @marthamaccallum interview with the wonderful wife of @RodBlagojevich and the @trishregan interview with a Jerome Corsi. If that doesn't tell you something about what has been going on in our Country, nothing will. Very sad! [Twitter for iPhone]

Dec 16, 2018 03:29:48 PM Required television watching is last weeks @marthamaccallum interview with the wonderful wife of Rod Blagojevich and the @trish_regan interview with a Jerome Corsi. If that doesn't tell you something about what has been going on in our Country, nothing will. Very sad! [Twitter for iPhone]

Dec 16, 2018 03:29:52 PM "It looks here as though General Flynn's defenses are incidental to something larger which is for the prosecution to figure out if it can find a path to Donald Trump without quite knowing what that crime might be. It stops looking like prosecution and more looking like...... [Twitter for iPhone]

Dec 16, 2018 03:37:17 PM ....a persecution of the President." Daniel Henninger, The Wall Street Journal. Thank you, people are starting to see and understand what this Witch Hunt is all about. Jeff Sessions should be ashamed of himself for allowing this total HOAX to get started in the first place! [Twitter for iPhone]

Dec 16, 2018 03:56:33 PM ....The Russian Witch Hunt Hoax, started as the "insurance policy" long before I even got elected, is very bad for our Country. They are Entrapping people for misstatements, lies or unrelated things that took place many years ago. Nothing to do with Collusion. A Democrat Scam! [Twitter for iPhone]

Dec 17, 2018 08:02:13 AM The DEDUCTIBLE which comes with ObamaCare is so high that it is practically not even useable! Hurts families badly. We have a chance, working with the Democrats, to deliver great HealthCare! A confirming Supreme Court Decision will lead to GREAT HealthCare results for Americans! [Twitter for iPhone]

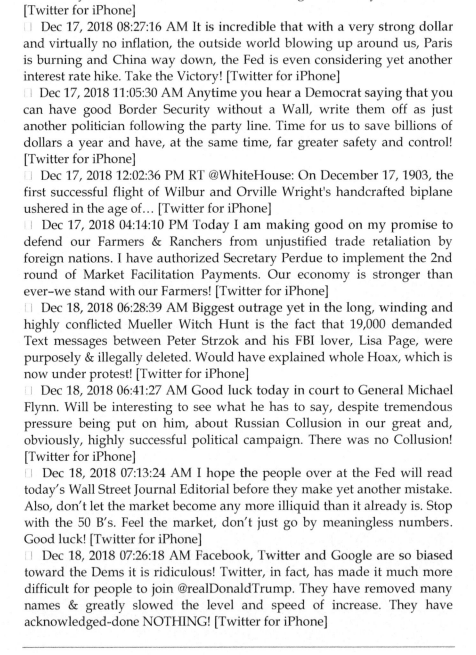

Dec 17, 2018 08:08:38 AM Anytime you hear a Democrat saying that you can have good Boarder Security without a Wall, write them off as just another politician following the party line. Time for us to save billions of dollars a year and have, at the same time, far greater safety and control! [Twitter for iPhone]

Dec 17, 2018 08:27:16 AM It is incredible that with a very strong dollar and virtually no inflation, the outside world blowing up around us, Paris is burning and China way down, the Fed is even considering yet another interest rate hike. Take the Victory! [Twitter for iPhone]

Dec 17, 2018 11:05:30 AM Anytime you hear a Democrat saying that you can have good Border Security without a Wall, write them off as just another politician following the party line. Time for us to save billions of dollars a year and have, at the same time, far greater safety and control! [Twitter for iPhone]

Dec 17, 2018 12:02:36 PM RT @WhiteHouse: On December 17, 1903, the first successful flight of Wilbur and Orville Wright's handcrafted biplane ushered in the age of… [Twitter for iPhone]

Dec 17, 2018 04:14:10 PM Today I am making good on my promise to defend our Farmers & Ranchers from unjustified trade retaliation by foreign nations. I have authorized Secretary Perdue to implement the 2nd round of Market Facilitation Payments. Our economy is stronger than ever–we stand with our Farmers! [Twitter for iPhone]

Dec 18, 2018 06:28:39 AM Biggest outrage yet in the long, winding and highly conflicted Mueller Witch Hunt is the fact that 19,000 demanded Text messages between Peter Strzok and his FBI lover, Lisa Page, were purposely & illegally deleted. Would have explained whole Hoax, which is now under protest! [Twitter for iPhone]

Dec 18, 2018 06:41:27 AM Good luck today in court to General Michael Flynn. Will be interesting to see what he has to say, despite tremendous pressure being put on him, about Russian Collusion in our great and, obviously, highly successful political campaign. There was no Collusion! [Twitter for iPhone]

Dec 18, 2018 07:13:24 AM I hope the people over at the Fed will read today's Wall Street Journal Editorial before they make yet another mistake. Also, don't let the market become any more illiquid than it already is. Stop with the 50 B's. Feel the market, don't just go by meaningless numbers. Good luck! [Twitter for iPhone]

Dec 18, 2018 07:26:18 AM Facebook, Twitter and Google are so biased toward the Dems it is ridiculous! Twitter, in fact, has made it much more difficult for people to join @realDonaldTrump. They have removed many names & greatly slowed the level and speed of increase. They have acknowledged-done NOTHING! [Twitter for iPhone]

Dec 18, 2018 07:55:48 AM Illegal immigration costs the United States more than 200 Billion Dollars a year. How was this allowed to happen? [Twitter for iPhone]

Dec 18, 2018 08:14:40 AM Russia Dossier reporter now doubts dopey Christopher Steele's claims! "When you get into the details of the Steele Dossier, the specific allegations, we have not seen the evidence to support them. There's good grounds to think that some of the more sensational allegations..... [Twitter for iPhone]

Dec 18, 2018 08:22:29 AM ....WILL NEVER BE PROVEN AND ARE LIKELY FALSE." Thank you to Michael Isikoff, Yahoo, for honesty. What this means is that the FISA WARRANTS and the whole Russian Witch Hunt is a Fraud and a Hoax which should be ended immediately. Also, it was paid for by Crooked Hillary & DNC! [Twitter for iPhone]

Dec 18, 2018 08:32:34 AM Michael Isikoff was the first to report Dossier allegations and now seriously doubts the Dossier claims. The whole Russian Collusion thing was a HOAX, but who is going to restore the good name of so many people whose reputations have been destroyed? [Twitter for iPhone]

Dec 18, 2018 11:36:34 AM RT @FLOTUS: Merry Christmas from President Donald J. Trump and First Lady Melania Trump. @POTUS & @FLOTUS are seen Saturday, December 15, i... [Twitter for iPhone]

Dec 18, 2018 11:53:27 AM RT @VP: Today, @POTUS Trump will direct the @DeptofDefense to establish a Combatant Command that will oversee all of our military activitie... [Twitter for iPhone]

Dec 18, 2018 05:42:37 PM "President Donald J. Trump's Commission on School Safety examined ways to make our schools safe for all students and teachers." Read more: https://t.co/Sj3T2B3cKW https://t.co/M0iiESm2fJ [Twitter for iPhone]

Dec 18, 2018 07:59:08 PM Congratulations to @MarthaMcSally on her appointment by Governor @DougDucey as the Great new Senator from Arizona - I have no doubt she will do a fantastic job! [Twitter for iPhone]

Dec 18, 2018 08:13:30 PM ....It will be beautiful and, at the same time, give our Country the security that our citizens deserve. It will go up fast and save us BILLIONS of dollars a month once completed! [Twitter for iPhone]

Dec 18, 2018 08:13:30 PM The Democrats, are saying loud and clear that they do not want to build a Concrete Wall - but we are not building a Concrete Wall, we are building artistically designed steel slats, so that you can easily see through it.... [Twitter for iPhone]

Dec 18, 2018 09:07:01 PM America is the greatest Country in the world and my job is to fight for ALL citizens, even those who have made mistakes. Congratulations to the Senate on the bi-partisan passing of a historic Criminal Justice Reform Bill.... [Twitter for iPhone]

Dec 18, 2018 09:07:02 PM ....This will keep our communities safer, and provide hope and a second chance, to those who earn it. In addition to everything else, billions of dollars will be saved. I look forward to signing this into law! [Twitter for iPhone]

Dec 19, 2018 07:28:47 AM In our Country, so much money has been poured down the drain, for so many years, but the Democrats fight us like cats and dogs when it comes to spending on Boarder Security (including a Wall) and the Military. We won on the Military, it is being completely rebuilt. We will win... [Twitter for iPhone]

Dec 19, 2018 07:35:04 AM In our Country, so much money has been poured down the drain, for so many years, but when it comes to Border Security and the Military, the Democrats fight to the death. We won on the Military, which is being completely rebuilt. One way or the other, we will win on the Wall! [Twitter for iPhone]

Dec 19, 2018 08:43:10 AM Mexico is paying (indirectly) for the Wall through the new USMCA, the replacement for NAFTA! Far more money coming to the U.S. Because of the tremendous dangers at the Border, including large scale criminal and drug inflow, the United States Military will build the Wall! [Twitter for iPhone]

Dec 19, 2018 09:29:49 AM We have defeated ISIS in Syria, my only reason for being there during the Trump Presidency. [Twitter for iPhone]

Dec 19, 2018 09:44:42 AM The Trump Foundation has done great work and given away lots of money, both mine and others, to great charities over the years - with me taking NO fees, rent, salaries etc. Now, as usual, I am getting slammed by Cuomo and the Dems in a long running civil lawsuit started by..... [Twitter for iPhone]

Dec 19, 2018 09:56:11 AM ...sleazebag AG Eric Schneiderman, who has since resigned over horrific women abuse, when I wanted to close the Foundation so as not to be in conflict with politics. Shady Eric was head of New Yorkers for Clinton, and refused to even look at the corrupt Clinton Foundation...... [Twitter for iPhone]

Dec 19, 2018 10:05:29 AM ....In any event, it goes on and on & the new AG, who is now being replaced by yet another AG (who openly campaigned on a GET TRUMP agenda), does little else but rant, rave & politic against me. Will never be treated fairly by these people - a total double standard of "justice." [Twitter for iPhone]

Dec 19, 2018 06:10:35 PM After historic victories against ISIS, it's time to bring our great young people home! https://t.co/xoNjFzQFTp [Twitter Media Studio]

Dec 19, 2018 10:30:00 PM RT @GovMikeHuckabee: It took a British court to reveal it, but more shocking evidence of the REAL "Russian collusion" and it wasn't about @... [Twitter for iPhone]

Dec 20, 2018 12:04:05 AM Col. Jim Carafano on @IngrahamAngle "Trump has made the Middle East a better place. When Trump came into office, ISIS was running amuck in the Middle East. Over a million refugees poured into Western Europe - none of that is happening today. That's all due to Trump." [Twitter for iPhone]

Dec 20, 2018 12:17:12 AM "Trump gets no credit for what he's done in the Middle East." @IngrahamAngle So true, thank you Laura! [Twitter for iPhone]

Dec 20, 2018 06:25:51 AM "I'm proud of the President today to hear that he is declaring victory in Syria." Senator Rand Paul. "I couldn't agree more with the presidents decision. By definition, this is the opposite of an Obama decision. Senator Mike Lee [Twitter for iPhone]

Dec 20, 2018 06:42:57 AM Getting out of Syria was no surprise. I've been campaigning on it for years, and six months ago, when I very publicly wanted to do it, I agreed to stay longer. Russia, Iran, Syria & others are the local enemy of ISIS. We were doing there work. Time to come home & rebuild. #MAGA [Twitter for iPhone]

Dec 20, 2018 06:56:54 AM Does the USA want to be the Policeman of the Middle East, getting NOTHING but spending precious lives and trillions of dollars protecting others who, in almost all cases, do not appreciate what we are doing? Do we want to be there forever? Time for others to finally fight..... [Twitter for iPhone]

Dec 20, 2018 07:16:38 AM ....Russia, Iran, Syria & many others are not happy about the U.S. leaving, despite what the Fake News says, because now they will have to fight ISIS and others, who they hate, without us. I am building by far the most powerful military in the world. ISIS hits us they are doomed! [Twitter for iPhone]

Dec 20, 2018 07:28:34 AM The Democrats, who know Steel Slats (Wall) are necessary for Border Security, are putting politics over Country. What they are just beginning to realize is that I will not sign any of their legislation, including infrastructure, unless it has perfect Border Security. U.S.A. WINS! [Twitter for iPhone]

Dec 20, 2018 07:39:19 AM With so much talk about the Wall, people are losing sight of the great job being done on our Southern Border by Border Patrol, ICE and our great Military. Remember the Caravans? Well, they didn't get through and none are forming or on their way. Border is tight. Fake News silent! [Twitter for iPhone]

Dec 20, 2018 07:41:08 AM RT @realDonaldTrump: After historic victories against ISIS, it's time to bring our great young people home! https://t.co/xoNjFzQFTp [Twitter for iPhone]

⬜ Dec 20, 2018 10:28:54 AM When I begrudgingly signed the Omnibus Bill, I was promised the Wall and Border Security by leadership. Would be done by end of year (NOW). It didn't happen! We foolishly fight for Border Security for other countries - but not for our beloved U.S.A. Not good! [Twitter for iPhone]

⬜ Dec 20, 2018 02:16:07 PM Congress just passed the Criminal Justice Reform Bill known as the #FirstStepAct. Congratulations! This is a great bi-partisan achievement for everybody. When both parties work together we can keep our Country safer. A wonderful thing for the U.S.A.!! [Twitter for iPhone]

⬜ Dec 20, 2018 02:22:19 PM So hard to believe that Lindsey Graham would be against saving soldier lives & billions of $$$. Why are we fighting for our enemy, Syria, by staying & killing ISIS for them, Russia, Iran & other locals? Time to focus on our Country & bring our youth back home where they belong! [Twitter for iPhone]

⬜ Dec 20, 2018 03:14:35 PM Farm Bill signing in 15 minutes! #Emmys #TBT https://t.co/KtSS17xvIn [Twitter for iPhone]

⬜ Dec 20, 2018 04:48:15 PM Democrats, it is time to come together and put the SAFETY of the AMERICAN PEOPLE before POLITICS. Border security must become a #1 priority! https://t.co/Wck6UpQGil [Twitter Media Studio]

⬜ Dec 20, 2018 05:21:07 PM ....equipment. General Mattis was a great help to me in getting allies and other countries to pay their share of military obligations. A new Secretary of Defense will be named shortly. I greatly thank Jim for his service! [Twitter for iPhone]

⬜ Dec 20, 2018 05:21:07 PM General Jim Mattis will be retiring, with distinction, at the end of February, after having served my Administration as Secretary of Defense for the past two years. During Jim's tenure, tremendous progress has been made, especially with respect to the purchase of new fighting.... [Twitter for iPhone]

⬜ Dec 20, 2018 10:13:54 PM Thank you to our GREAT Republican Members of Congress for your VOTE to fund Border Security and the Wall. The final numbers were 217-185 and many have said that the enthusiasm was greater than they have ever seen before. So proud of you all. Now on to the Senate! [Twitter for iPhone]

⬜ Dec 20, 2018 10:20:29 PM Soon to be Speaker Nancy Pelosi said, last week live from the Oval Office, that the Republicans didn't have the votes for Border Security. Today the House Republicans voted and won, 217-185. Nancy does not have to apologize. All I want is GREAT BORDER SECURITY! [Twitter for iPhone]

Dec 21, 2018 06:50:53 AM Senator Mitch McConnell should fight for the Wall and Border Security as hard as he fought for anything. He will need Democrat votes, but as shown in the House, good things happen. If enough Dems don't vote, it will be a Democrat Shutdown! House Republicans were great yesterday! [Twitter for iPhone]

Dec 21, 2018 06:58:29 AM The Democrats are trying to belittle the concept of a Wall, calling it old fashioned. The fact is there is nothing else's that will work, and that has been true for thousands of years. It's like the wheel, there is nothing better. I know tech better than anyone, & technology..... [Twitter for iPhone]

Dec 21, 2018 07:10:36 AM .....on a Border is only effective in conjunction with a Wall. Properly designed and built Walls work, and the Democrats are lying when they say they don't. In Israel the Wall is 99.9% successful. Will not be any different on our Southern Border! Hundreds of $Billions saved! [Twitter for iPhone]

Dec 21, 2018 07:19:46 AM No matter what happens today in the Senate, Republican House Members should be very proud of themselves. They flew back to Washington from all parts of the World in order to vote for Border Security and the Wall. Not one Democrat voted yes, and we won big. I am very proud of you! [Twitter for iPhone]

Dec 21, 2018 07:24:18 AM The Democrats, whose votes we need in the Senate, will probably vote against Border Security and the Wall even though they know it is DESPERATELY NEEDED. If the Dems vote no, there will be a shutdown that will last for a very long time. People don't want Open Borders and Crime! [Twitter for iPhone]

Dec 21, 2018 07:27:47 AM House Republican Vote, 217-185. [Twitter for iPhone]

Dec 21, 2018 07:31:35 AM Shutdown today if Democrats do not vote for Border Security! [Twitter for iPhone]

Dec 21, 2018 07:38:15 AM Even President Ronald Reagan tried for 8 years to build a Border Wall, or Fence, and was unable to do so. Others also have tried. We will get it done, one way or the other! [Twitter for iPhone]

Dec 21, 2018 08:02:35 AM Mitch, use the Nuclear Option and get it done! Our Country is counting on you! [Twitter for iPhone]

Dec 21, 2018 08:08:06 AM Thank you @SteveDaines for being willing to go with the so-called nuclear option in order to win on DESPERATELY NEEDED Border Security! Have my total support. [Twitter for iPhone]

Dec 21, 2018 09:41:59 AM There has never been a president who has been tougher (but fair) on China or Russia - Never, just look at the facts. The Fake News tries so hard to paint the opposite picture. [Twitter for iPhone]

☐ Dec 21, 2018 09:50:29 AM General Anthony Tata, author, "Dark Winter." I think the President is making the exact right move in Syria. All the geniuses who are protesting the withdrawal of troops from Syria are the same geniuses who cooked the books on ISIS intelligence and gave rise to ISIS." [Twitter for iPhone]

☐ Dec 21, 2018 10:07:23 AM The Democrats now own the shutdown! [Twitter for iPhone]

☐ Dec 21, 2018 10:31:41 AM I've done more damage to ISIS than all recent presidents....not even close! [Twitter for iPhone]

☐ Dec 21, 2018 02:28:13 PM Today, it was my great honor to sign the #FirstStepAct - a monumental bi-partisan win for the American people! https://t.co/isy6Bt38iK [Twitter for iPhone]

☐ Dec 21, 2018 02:56:05 PM Today, it was my honor to sign into law H.R. 7213, the "Countering Weapons of Mass Destruction Act of 2018." The Act redesignates the @DHSgov Domestic Nuclear Detection Office as the Countering Weapons of Mass Destruction Office. Read more: https://t.co/XCkyc8pGZF https://t.co/TTvGxBww5n [Twitter for iPhone]

☐ Dec 21, 2018 05:14:14 PM A design of our Steel Slat Barrier which is totally effective while at the same time beautiful! https://t.co/sGltXh0cu9 [Twitter for iPhone]

☐ Dec 21, 2018 06:23:27 PM Some of the many Bills that I am signing in the Oval Office right now. Cancelled my trip on Air Force One to Florida while we wait to see if the Democrats will help us to protect America's Southern Border! https://t.co/ws6LYhKcKl [Twitter for iPhone]

☐ Dec 21, 2018 07:16:55 PM Wishing Supreme Court Justice Ruth Bader Ginsburg a full and speedy recovery! [Twitter for iPhone]

☐ Dec 21, 2018 09:49:05 PM OUR GREAT COUNTRY MUST HAVE BORDER SECURITY! https://t.co/ZGcYygMf3a [Twitter for iPhone]

☐ Dec 22, 2018 12:09:15 AM RT @realDonaldTrump: OUR GREAT COUNTRY MUST HAVE BORDER SECURITY! https://t.co/ZGcYygMf3a [Twitter for iPhone]

☐ Dec 22, 2018 11:18:11 AM I am in the White House, working hard. News reports concerning the Shutdown and Syria are mostly FAKE. We are negotiating with the Democrats on desperately needed Border Security (Gangs, Drugs, Human Trafficking & more) but it could be a long stay. On Syria, we were originally... [Twitter for iPhone]

☐ Dec 22, 2018 11:30:35 AM ....going to be there for three months, and that was seven years ago - we never left. When I became President, ISIS was going wild. Now ISIS is largely defeated and other local countries, including Turkey, should be able to easily take care of whatever remains. We're coming home! [Twitter for iPhone]

Dec 22, 2018 12:02:37 PM Will be having lunch in White House residence with large group concerning Border Security. [Twitter for iPhone]

Dec 22, 2018 03:03:58 PM The crisis of illegal activity at our Southern Border is real and will not stop until we build a great Steel Barrier or Wall. Let work begin! [Twitter for iPhone]

Dec 22, 2018 03:28:21 PM I won an election, said to be one of the greatest of all time, based on getting out of endless & costly foreign wars & also based on Strong Borders which will keep our Country safe. We fight for the borders of other countries, but we won't fight for the borders of our own! [Twitter for iPhone]

Dec 22, 2018 04:12:02 PM Senate adjourns until December 27th. [Twitter for iPhone]

Dec 22, 2018 06:58:43 PM I will not be going to Florida because of the Shutdown - Staying in the White House! #MAGA [Twitter for iPhone]

Dec 22, 2018 08:48:23 PM Brett McGurk, who I do not know, was appointed by President Obama in 2015. Was supposed to leave in February but he just resigned prior to leaving. Grandstander? The Fake News is making such a big deal about this nothing event! [Twitter for iPhone]

Dec 22, 2018 08:59:29 PM If anybody but your favorite President, Donald J. Trump, announced that, after decimating ISIS in Syria, we were going to bring our troops back home (happy & healthy), that person would be the most popular hero in America. With me, hit hard instead by the Fake News Media. Crazy! [Twitter for iPhone]

Dec 22, 2018 09:20:32 PM When President Obama ingloriously fired Jim Mattis, I gave him a second chance. Some thought I shouldn't, I thought I should. Interesting relationship-but I also gave all of the resources that he never really had. Allies are very important-but not when they take advantage of U.S. [Twitter for iPhone]

Dec 23, 2018 09:17:54 AM The only way to stop drugs, gangs, human trafficking, criminal elements and much else from coming into our Country is with a Wall or Barrier. Drones and all of the rest are wonderful and lots of fun, but it is only a good old fashioned Wall that works! [Twitter for iPhone]

Dec 23, 2018 11:46:47 AM I am pleased to announce that our very talented Deputy Secretary of Defense, Patrick Shanahan, will assume the title of Acting Secretary of Defense starting January 1, 2019. Patrick has a long list of accomplishments while serving as Deputy, & previously Boeing. He will be great! [Twitter for iPhone]

Dec 23, 2018 11:59:22 AM I just had a long and productive call with President @RT_Erdogan of Turkey. We discussed ISIS, our mutual involvement in Syria, & the slow & highly coordinated pullout of U.S. troops from the area. After many years they are coming home. We also discussed heavily expanded Trade. [Twitter for iPhone]

Dec 23, 2018 12:13:27 PM Unthinkable devastation from the tsunami disaster in Indonesia. More than two hundred dead and nearly a thousand injured or unaccounted for. We are praying for recovery and healing. America is with you! [Twitter for iPhone]

Dec 23, 2018 02:45:22 PM We signed two pieces of major legislation this week, Criminal Justice Reform and the Farm Bill. These are two Big Deals, but all the Fake News Media wants to talk about is "the mistake" of bringing our young people back home from the Never Ending Wars. It all began 19 years ago! [Twitter for iPhone]

Dec 23, 2018 02:56:37 PM Senator Bob Corker just stated that, "I'm so priveledged to serve in the Senate for twelve years, and that's what I told the people of our state that's what I'd do, serve for two terms." But that is Not True - wanted to run but poll numbers TANKED when I wouldn't endorse him..... [Twitter for iPhone]

Dec 23, 2018 03:20:22 PM .....Bob Corker was responsible for giving us the horrible Iran Nuclear Deal, which I ended, yet he badmouths me for wanting to bring our young people safely back home. Bob wanted to run and asked for my endorsement. I said NO and the game was over. #MAGA I LOVE TENNESSEE! [Twitter for iPhone]

Dec 23, 2018 04:18:49 PM Thanks @RandPaul "I am very proud of the President. This is exactly what he promised, and I think the people agree with him. We've been at war too long and in too many places...spent several trillion dollars on these wars everywhere. He's different...that's why he got elected." [Twitter for iPhone]

Dec 23, 2018 07:42:22 PM RT @RSScott_BP252: USBP Agents will continue to diligently do their sworn duites through the holidays and the furlough -JUST LIKE EVERY OTH… [Twitter for iPhone]

Dec 23, 2018 10:32:49 PM "It should not be the job of America to replace regimes around the world. This is what President Trump recognized in Iraq, that it was the biggest foreign policy disaster of the last several decades, and he's right...The generals still don't get the mistake." @RandPaul [Twitter for iPhone]

Dec 23, 2018 10:47:21 PM Mitch McConnell just told a group of people, and me, that he has been in the U.S. Senate for 32 years and the last two have been by far the best & most productive of his career. Tax & Regulation Cuts, VA Choice, Farm Bill, Criminal Justice Reform, Judgeships & much more. Great! [Twitter for iPhone]

Dec 23, 2018 11:05:26 PM The most important way to stop gangs, drugs, human trafficking and massive crime is at our Southern Border. We need Border Security, and as EVERYONE knows, you can't have Border Security without a Wall. The Drones & Technology are just bells and whistles. Safety for America! [Twitter for iPhone]

Dec 23, 2018 11:26:22 PM "The President has been remarkable. I do not doubt that he will thrive in this new environment, and he will be a constant reminder of what populism is." Thank you to Tammy Bruce and Steve Hilton. Presidential Harassment has been with me from the beginning! [Twitter for iPhone]

Dec 23, 2018 11:54:00 PM President @RT_Erdogan of Turkey has very strongly informed me that he will eradicate whatever is left of ISIS in Syria....and he is a man who can do it plus, Turkey is right "next door." Our troops are coming home! [Twitter for iPhone]

Dec 24, 2018 09:31:50 AM Virtually every Democrat we are dealing with today strongly supported a Border Wall or Fence. It was only when I made it an important part of my campaign, because people and drugs were pouring into our Country unchecked, that they turned against it. Desperately needed! [Twitter for iPhone]

Dec 24, 2018 09:41:02 AM To those few Senators who think I don't like or appreciate being allied with other countries, they are wrong, I DO. What I don't like, however, is when many of these same countries take advantage of their friendship with the United States, both in Military Protection and Trade... [Twitter for iPhone]

Dec 24, 2018 09:59:23 AM ....We are substantially subsidizing the Militaries of many VERY rich countries all over the world, while at the same time these countries take total advantage of the U.S., and our TAXPAYERS, on Trade. General Mattis did not see this as a problem. I DO, and it is being fixed! [Twitter for iPhone]

Dec 24, 2018 10:23:22 AM For all of the sympathizers out there of Brett McGurk remember, he was the Obama appointee who was responsible for loading up airplanes with 1.8 Billion Dollars in CASH & sending it to Iran as part of the horrific Iran Nuclear Deal (now terminated) approved by Little Bob Corker. [Twitter for iPhone]

Dec 24, 2018 10:33:41 AM AMERICA IS RESPECTED AGAIN! [Twitter for iPhone]

Dec 24, 2018 10:55:22 AM The only problem our economy has is the Fed. They don't have a feel for the Market, they don't understand necessary Trade Wars or Strong Dollars or even Democrat Shutdowns over Borders. The Fed is like a powerful golfer who can't score because he has no touch - he can't putt! [Twitter for iPhone]

Dec 24, 2018 11:55:32 AM I never "lashed out" at the Acting Attorney General of the U.S., a man for whom I have great respect. This is a made up story, one of many, by the Fake News Media! [Twitter for iPhone]

Dec 24, 2018 12:10:22 PM The Wall is different than the 25 Billion Dollars in Border Security. The complete Wall will be built with the Shutdown money plus funds already in hand. The reporting has been inaccurate on the point. The problem is, without the Wall, much of the rest of Dollars are wasted! [Twitter for iPhone]

Dec 24, 2018 12:23:22 PM Saudi Arabia has now agreed to spend the necessary money needed to help rebuild Syria, instead of the United States. See? Isn't it nice when immensely wealthy countries help rebuild their neighbors rather than a Great Country, the U.S., that is 5000 miles away. Thanks to Saudi A! [Twitter for iPhone]

Dec 24, 2018 12:32:44 PM I am all alone (poor me) in the White House waiting for the Democrats to come back and make a deal on desperately needed Border Security. At some point the Democrats not wanting to make a deal will cost our Country more money than the Border Wall we are all talking about. Crazy! [Twitter for iPhone]

Dec 24, 2018 04:14:12 PM Christmas Eve briefing with my team working on North Korea – Progress being made. Looking forward to my next summit with Chairman Kim! https://t.co/zPTtDbrP0o [Twitter for iPhone]

Dec 24, 2018 05:24:13 PM I am in the Oval Office & just gave out a 115 mile long contract for another large section of the Wall in Texas. We are already building and renovating many miles of Wall, some complete. Democrats must end Shutdown and finish funding. Billions of Dollars, & lives, will be saved! [Twitter for iPhone]

Dec 24, 2018 09:28:40 PM RT @FLOTUS: Helping children across the country track #Santa is becoming one of my favorite traditions! @Potus and I enjoyed working with... [Twitter for iPhone]

Dec 25, 2018 07:59:08 AM Merry Christmas! [Twitter for iPhone]

Dec 25, 2018 06:18:44 PM I hope everyone, even the Fake News Media, is having a great Christmas! Our Country is doing very well. We are securing our Borders, making great new Trade Deals, and bringing our Troops Back Home. We are finally putting America First. MERRY CHRISTMAS! #MAGA [Twitter for iPhone]

Dec 26, 2018 03:35:25 PM .@FLOTUS Melania and I were honored to visit our incredible troops at Al Asad Air Base in Iraq. GOD BLESS THE U.S.A.! https://t.co/rDlhITDvm1 [Twitter for iPhone]

Dec 27, 2018 06:59:04 AM Just returned from visiting our troops in Iraq and Germany. One thing is certain, we have incredible people representing our Country - people that know how to win! [Twitter for iPhone]

Dec 27, 2018 07:06:25 AM Have the Democrats finally realized that we desperately need Border Security and a Wall on the Southern Border. Need to stop Drugs, Human Trafficking,Gang Members & Criminals from coming into our Country. Do the Dems realize that most of the people not getting paid are Democrats? [Twitter for iPhone]

Dec 27, 2018 02:35:46 PM The reason the DACA for Wall deal didn't get done was that a ridiculous court decision from the 9th Circuit allowed DACA to remain, thereby setting up a Supteme Court case. After ruling, Dems dropped deal - and that's where we are today, Democrat obstruction of the needed Wall. [Twitter for iPhone]

Dec 27, 2018 02:41:45 PM The Democrats OBSTRUCTION of the desperately needed Wall, where they almost all recently agreed it should be built, is exceeded only by their OBSTRUCTION of 350 great people wanting & expecting to come into Government after being delayed for more than two years, a U.S. record! [Twitter for iPhone]

Dec 27, 2018 02:44:49 PM The reason the DACA for Wall deal didn't get done was that a ridiculous court decision from the 9th Circuit allowed DACA to remain, thereby setting up a Supreme Court case. After ruling, Dems dropped deal - and that's where we are today, Democrat obstruction of the needed Wall. [Twitter for iPhone]

Dec 27, 2018 03:39:59 PM "Border Patrol Agents want the Wall." Democrat's say they don't want the Wall (even though they know it is really needed), and they don't want ICE. They don't have much to campaign on, do they? An Open Southern Border and the large scale crime that comes with such stupidity! [Twitter for iPhone]

Dec 27, 2018 04:04:06 PM There is right now a full scale manhunt going on in California for an illegal immigrant accused of shooting and killing a police officer during a traffic stop. Time to get tough on Border Security. Build the Wall! [Twitter for iPhone]

Dec 27, 2018 04:04:24 PM I totally agree! https://t.co/KO8E3bfWfn [Twitter for iPhone]

Dec 27, 2018 04:13:15 PM Brad Blakeman: "The American people understand that we have been played by foreign actors who would rather have us fight their battles for them. The Pesident says look, this is your neighborhood, you've got to stand up to protect yourselves. Don't always look to America." [Twitter for iPhone]

Dec 27, 2018 04:26:10 PM Brad Blakeman: "The American people understand that we have been played by foreign actors who would rather have us fight their battles for them. The President says look, this is your neighborhood, you've got to stand up to protect yourselves. Don't always look to America." [Twitter for iPhone]

Dec 27, 2018 05:10:07 PM This isn't about the Wall, everybody knows that a Wall will work perfectly (In Israel the Wall works 99.9%). This is only about the Dems not letting Donald Trump & the Republicans have a win. They may have the 10 Senate votes, but we have the issue, Border Security. 2020! [Twitter for iPhone]

Dec 27, 2018 06:23:36 PM CNN & others within the Fake News Universe were going wild about my signing MAGA hats for our military in Iraq and Germany. If these brave young people ask me to sign their hat, I will sign. Can you imagine my saying NO? We brought or gave NO hats as the Fake News first reported! [Twitter for iPhone]

Dec 28, 2018 07:16:40 AM We will be forced to close the Southern Border entirely if the Obstructionist Democrats do not give us the money to finish the Wall & also change the ridiculous immigration laws that our Country is saddled with. Hard to believe there was a Congress & President who would approve! [Twitter for iPhone]

Dec 28, 2018 07:42:12 AM ....The United States looses soooo much money on Trade with Mexico under NAFTA, over 75 Billion Dollars a year (not including Drug Money which would be many times that amount), that I would consider closing the Southern Border a "profit making operation." We build a Wall or..... [Twitter for iPhone]

Dec 28, 2018 07:49:26 AM .....close the Southern Border. Bring our car industry back into the United States where it belongs. Go back to pre-NAFTA, before so many of our companies and jobs were so foolishly sent to Mexico. Either we build (finish) the Wall or we close the Border...... [Twitter for iPhone]

Dec 28, 2018 08:06:13 AM .....Honduras, Guatemala and El Salvador are doing nothing for the United States but taking our money. Word is that a new Caravan is forming in Honduras and they are doing nothing about it. We will be cutting off all aid to these 3 countries - taking advantage of U.S. for years! [Twitter for iPhone]

Dec 28, 2018 09:51:07 AM Thank you to Sean Parnell for the nice comments on @foxandfriends about the troops wonderful reaction to Melania and I in Iraq and Germany. Great things are happening! [Twitter for iPhone]

Dec 29, 2018 10:42:50 AM The Mueller Angry Democrats recently deleted approximately 19,000 Text messages between FBI Agent Lisa Page and her lover, Agent Peter S. These Texts were asked for and INVALUABLE to the truth of the Witch Hunt Hoax. This is a total Obstruction of Justice. All Texts Demanded! [Twitter for iPhone]

Dec 29, 2018 10:52:24 AM I am in the White House waiting for the Democrats to come on over and make a deal on Border Security. From what I hear, they are spending so much time on Presidential Harassment that they have little time left for things like stopping crime and our military! [Twitter for iPhone]

Dec 29, 2018 11:03:02 AM Just had a long and very good call with President Xi of China. Deal is moving along very well. If made, it will be very comprehensive, covering all subjects, areas and points of dispute. Big progress being made! [Twitter for iPhone]

Dec 29, 2018 01:30:16 PM Any deaths of children or others at the Border are strictly the fault of the Democrats and their pathetic immigration policies that allow people to make the long trek thinking they can enter our country illegally. They can't. If we had a Wall, they wouldn't even try! The two..... [Twitter for iPhone]

Dec 29, 2018 01:36:17 PM ...children in question were very sick before they were given over to Border Patrol. The father of the young girl said it was not their fault, he hadn't given her water in days. Border Patrol needs the Wall and it will all end. They are working so hard & getting so little credit! [Twitter for iPhone]

Dec 29, 2018 02:25:47 PM For those that naively ask why didn't the Republicans get approval to build the Wall over the last year, it is because IN THE SENATE WE NEED 10 DEMOCRAT VOTES, and they will gives us "NONE" for Border Security! Now we have to do it the hard way, with a Shutdown. Too bad! @FoxNews [Twitter for iPhone]

Dec 29, 2018 04:06:08 PM 2018 is being called "THE YEAR OF THE WORKER" by Steve Moore, co-author of "Trumponomics." It was indeed a great year for the American Worker with the "best job market in 50 years, and the lowest unemployment rate ever for blacks and Hispanics and all workers. Big wage gains." [Twitter for iPhone]

Dec 29, 2018 10:01:28 PM "Absolutely nothing" (on Russian Collusion). Kimberley Strassel, The Wall Street Journal. The Russian Collusion fabrication is the greatest Hoax in the history of American politics. The only Russian Collusion was with Hillary and the Democrats! [Twitter for iPhone]

Dec 29, 2018 10:15:36 PM "It turns out to be true now, that the Department of Justice and the FBI, under President Obama, rigged the investigation for Hillary and really turned the screws on Trump, and now it looks like in a corrupt & illegal way. The facts are out now. Whole Hoax exposed. @JesseBWatters [Twitter for iPhone]

Dec 30, 2018 10:28:35 AM Veterans on President Trump's handling of Border Security - 62% Approval Rating. On being a strong leader - 59%. AP Poll. Thank you! [Twitter for iPhone]

Dec 30, 2018 11:56:09 AM Great work by my Administration over the holidays to save Coast Guard pay during this #SchumerShutdown. No thanks to the Democrats who left town and are not concerned about the safety and security of Americans! [Twitter for iPhone]

Dec 30, 2018 04:59:44 PM President and Mrs. Obama built/has a ten foot Wall around their D.C. mansion/compound. I agree, totally necessary for their safety and security. The U.S. needs the same thing, slightly larger version! [Twitter for iPhone]

Dec 31, 2018 07:51:22 AM An all concrete Wall was NEVER ABANDONED, as has been reported by the media. Some areas will be all concrete but the experts at Border Patrol prefer a Wall that is see through (thereby making it possible to see what is happening on both sides). Makes sense to me! [Twitter for iPhone]

Dec 31, 2018 08:03:05 AM If anybody but Donald Trump did what I did in Syria, which was an ISIS loaded mess when I became President, they would be a national hero. ISIS is mostly gone, we're slowly sending our troops back home to be with their families, while at the same time fighting ISIS remnants...... [Twitter for iPhone]

Dec 31, 2018 08:12:40 AM ...I campaigned on getting out of Syria and other places. Now when I start getting out the Fake News Media, or some failed Generals who were unable to do the job before I arrived, like to complain about me & my tactics, which are working. Just doing what I said I was going to do! [Twitter for iPhone]

Dec 31, 2018 08:19:13 AM .....Except the results are FAR BETTER than I ever said they were going to be! I campaigned against the NEVER ENDING WARS, remember! [Twitter for iPhone]

Dec 31, 2018 08:29:32 AM I campaigned on Border Security, which you cannot have without a strong and powerful Wall. Our Southern Border has long been an "Open Wound," where drugs, criminals (including human traffickers) and illegals would pour into our Country. Dems should get back here an fix now! [Twitter for iPhone]

Dec 31, 2018 09:38:52 AM I am the only person in America who could say that, "I'm bringing our great troops back home, with victory," and get BAD press. It is Fake News and Pundits who have FAILED for years that are doing the complaining. If I stayed in Endless Wars forever, they would still be unhappy! [Twitter for iPhone]

Dec 31, 2018 10:33:15 AM I'm in the Oval Office. Democrats, come back from vacation now and give us the votes necessary for Border Security, including the Wall. You voted yes in 2006 and 3013. One more yes, but with me in office, I'll get it built, and Fast! [Twitter for iPhone]

Dec 31, 2018 10:37:14 AM I'm in the Oval Office. Democrats, come back from vacation now and give us the votes necessary for Border Security, including the Wall. You voted yes in 2006 and 2013. One more yes, but with me in office, I'll get it built, and Fast! [Twitter for iPhone]

Dec 31, 2018 10:39:15 AM It's incredible how Democrats can all use their ridiculous sound bite and say that a Wall doesn't work. It does, and properly built, almost 100%! They say it's old technology - but so is the wheel. They now say it is immoral- but it is far more immoral for people to be dying! [Twitter for iPhone]

Dec 31, 2018 03:02:52 PM ....Senator Schumer, more than a year longer than any other Administration in history. These are people who have been approved by committees and all others, yet Schumer continues to hold them back from serving their Country! Very Unfair! [Twitter for iPhone]

Dec 31, 2018 03:02:52 PM Heads of countries are calling wanting to know why Senator Schumer is not approving their otherwise approved Ambassadors!? Likewise in Government lawyers and others are being delayed at a record pace! 360 great and hardworking people are waiting for approval from.... [Twitter for iPhone]

Dec 31, 2018 06:53:06 PM HAPPY NEW YEAR! https://t.co/bHoPDPQ7G6 [Twitter for iPhone]

Dec 31, 2018 07:40:26 PM MEXICO IS PAYING FOR THE WALL through the many billions of dollars a year that the U.S.A. is saving through the new Trade Deal, the USMCA, that will replace the horrendous NAFTA Trade Deal, which has so badly hurt our Country. Mexico & Canada will also thrive - good for all! [Twitter for iPhone]

Dec 31, 2018 07:51:43 PM The Democrats will probably submit a Bill, being cute as always, which gives everything away but gives NOTHING to Border Security, namely the Wall. You see, without the Wall there can be no Border Security - the Tech "stuff" is just, by comparison, meaningless bells & whistles... [Twitter for iPhone]

Dec 31, 2018 08:05:39 PM ...Remember this. Throughout the ages some things NEVER get better and NEVER change. You have Walls and you have Wheels. It was ALWAYS that way and it will ALWAYS be that way! Please explain to the Democrats that there can NEVER be a replacement for a good old fashioned WALL! [Twitter for iPhone]

Dec 31, 2018 09:01:26 PM RT @WhiteHouse: 2018 has been a year of historic accomplishments! https://t.co/6Iq5CFVdwY [Twitter for iPhone]

Jan 1, 2019 07:51:34 AM Dr. Sebastian Gorka, a very good and talented guy, has a great new book just out, "Why We Fight." Lots of insight - Enjoy! [Twitter for iPhone]

Jan 1, 2019 08:08:29 AM HAPPY NEW YEAR TO EVERYONE, INCLUDING THE HATERS AND THE FAKE NEWS MEDIA! 2019 WILL BE A FANTASTIC YEAR FOR THOSE NOT SUFFERING FROM TRUMP DERANGEMENT SYNDROME. JUST CALM DOWN AND ENJOY THE RIDE, GREAT THINGS ARE HAPPENING FOR OUR COUNTRY! [Twitter for iPhone]

Jan 1, 2019 09:25:32 AM Happy New Year! [Twitter for iPhone]

Jan 1, 2019 09:32:01 AM The Democrats, much as I suspected, have allocated no money for a new Wall. So imaginative! The problem is, without a Wall there can be no real Border Security - and our Country must finally have a Strong and Secure Southern Border! [Twitter for iPhone]

Jan 1, 2019 09:50:39 AM RT @GOPChairwoman: Jobless claims fell last week to a 49-year low. Yet another sign that @realDonaldTrump's economic policies are working a… [Twitter for iPhone]

Jan 1, 2019 09:52:33 AM RT @GOPChairwoman: .@realDonaldTrump made sure the men and women of the Coast Guard continue to get paid during the #SchumerShutdown. Mea… [Twitter for iPhone]

Jan 1, 2019 09:54:32 AM RT @realDonaldTrump: Heads of countries are calling wanting to know why Senator Schumer is not approving their otherwise approved Ambassado… [Twitter for iPhone]

Jan 1, 2019 09:55:01 AM RT @realDonaldTrump: ....Senator Schumer, more than a year longer than any other Administration in history. These are people who have been… [Twitter for iPhone]

Jan 1, 2019 10:32:30 AM "General" McChrystal got fired like a dog by Obama. Last assignment a total bust. Known for big, dumb mouth. Hillary lover! https://t.co/RzOkeHl3KV [Twitter for iPhone]

Jan 1, 2019 10:51:09 AM One thing has now been proven. The Democrats do not care about Open Borders and all of the crime and drugs that Open Borders bring! [Twitter for iPhone]

Jan 1, 2019 01:12:08 PM Congratulations to President @JairBolsonaro who just made a great inauguration speech - the U.S.A. is with you! [Twitter for iPhone]

Jan 1, 2019 02:02:36 PM Border Security and the Wall "thing" and Shutdown is not where Nancy Pelosi wanted to start her tenure as Speaker! Let's make a deal? [Twitter for iPhone]

Jan 1, 2019 05:44:03 PM Gas prices are low and expected to go down this year. This would be good! [Twitter for iPhone]

Jan 1, 2019 05:51:12 PM Washington Examiner - "MAGA list: 205 'historic results' help Trump make case for 2020 re-election." True! [Twitter for iPhone]

Jan 1, 2019 06:11:12 PM "Kim Jong Un says North Korea will not make or test nuclear weapons, or give them to others - & he is ready to meet President Trump anytime." PBS News Hour. I also look forward to meeting with Chairman Kim who realizes so well that North Korea possesses great economic potential! [Twitter for iPhone]

Jan 1, 2019 06:39:32 PM Do you think it's just luck that gas prices are so low, and falling? Low gas prices are like another Tax Cut! [Twitter for iPhone]

Jan 1, 2019 07:43:50 PM For FAR TOO LONG Senate Democrats have been Obstructing more than 350 Nominations. These great Americans left their jobs to serve our Country, but can't because Dems are blocking them, some for two years-historic record. Passed committees, but Schumer putting them on hold. Bad! [Twitter for iPhone]

Jan 2, 2019 07:53:55 AM Here we go with Mitt Romney, but so fast! Question will be, is he a Flake? I hope not. Would much prefer that Mitt focus on Border Security and so many other things where he can be helpful. I won big, and he didn't. He should be happy for all Republicans. Be a TEAM player & WIN! [Twitter for iPhone]

Jan 2, 2019 08:35:30 AM Mexico is paying for the Wall through the new USMCA Trade Deal. Much of the Wall has already been fully renovated or built. We have done a lot of work. $5.6 Billion Dollars that House has approved is very little in comparison to the benefits of National Security. Quick payback! [Twitter for iPhone]

Jan 2, 2019 07:07:37 PM Important meeting today on Border Security with Republican and Democrat Leaders in Congress. Both parties must work together to pass a Funding Bill that protects this Nation and its people – this is the first and most important duty of government... [Twitter for iPhone]

Jan 2, 2019 07:07:38 PM ...I remain ready and willing to work with Democrats to pass a bill that secures our borders, supports the agents and officers on the ground, and keeps America Safe. Let's get it done! [Twitter for iPhone]

Jan 2, 2019 11:09:52 PM Sadly, there can be no REAL Border Security without the Wall! [Twitter for iPhone]

Jan 3, 2019 09:36:57 AM "MAGA list: 205 'historic results' help Trump make case for 2020 re-election" https://t.co/vtqnUwdhjB [Twitter for iPhone]

Jan 3, 2019 09:44:19 AM The Shutdown is only because of the 2020 Presidential Election. The Democrats know they can't win based on all of the achievements of "Trump," so they are going all out on the desperately needed Wall and Border Security - and Presidential Harassment. For them, strictly politics! [Twitter for iPhone]

☐ Jan 3, 2019 09:52:13 AM The United States Treasury has taken in MANY billions of dollars from the Tariffs we are charging China and other countries that have not treated us fairly. In the meantime we are doing well in various Trade Negotiations currently going on. At some point this had to be done! [Twitter for iPhone]

☐ Jan 3, 2019 11:10:31 AM https://t.co/JzfXMAPwKP [Twitter for iPhone]

☐ Jan 3, 2019 12:40:49 PM The RNC has a great Chairwoman in Ronna McDaniel and the @GOP has never been stronger. We achieved historic wins with her help last year! #MAGAus [Twitter for iPhone]

☐ Jan 3, 2019 03:25:18 PM https://t.co/jsOrDtwdEa [Twitter Media Studio]

☐ Jan 3, 2019 08:19:17 PM Michael Pillsbury interviewed by @cvpayne: "They have the motive of making the President look bad – instead of President Trump being portrayed as a HERO. The first President to take China on, it's 20 years overdue.... [Twitter for iPhone]

☐ Jan 3, 2019 08:19:18 PM ....President Trump deserves a lot of credit, but again, you have the anti-Trump people who are not going to give him a lot of credit." [Twitter for iPhone]

☐ Jan 4, 2019 08:06:40 AM As I have stated many times, if the Democrats take over the House or Senate, there will be disruption to the Financial Markets. We won the Senate, they won the House. Things will settle down. They only want to impeach me because they know they can't win in 2020, too much success! [Twitter for iPhone]

☐ Jan 4, 2019 08:16:20 AM How do you impeach a president who has won perhaps the greatest election of all time, done nothing wrong (no Collusion with Russia, it was the Dems that Colluded), had the most successful first two years of any president, and is the most popular Republican in party history 93%? [Twitter for iPhone]

☐ Jan 4, 2019 09:39:07 AM GREAT JOBS NUMBERS JUST ANNOUNCED! [Twitter for iPhone]

☐ Jan 4, 2019 03:36:38 PM "Job growth surges by 312,000 in December" https://t.co/FCSwxFZjUF [Twitter for iPhone]

☐ Jan 4, 2019 04:45:27 PM The story in the New York Times regarding Jim Webb being considered as the next Secretary of Defense is FAKE NEWS. I'm sure he is a fine man, but I don't know Jim, and never met him. Patrick Shanahan, who is Acting Secretary of Defense, is doing a great job! [Twitter for iPhone]

☐ Jan 4, 2019 08:10:43 PM Great new book by Dr. Robert Jeffress, "Choosing the Extraordinary Life." Get it and enjoy! @LouDobbs [Twitter for iPhone]

Jan 5, 2019 07:17:35 AM Thank you to Kanye West for your nice words. Criminal Justice Reform is now law - passed in a very bipartisan way! [Twitter for iPhone]

Jan 5, 2019 07:31:03 AM Great support coming from all sides for Border Security (including Wall) on our very dangerous Southern Border. Teams negotiating this weekend! Washington Post and NBC reporting of events, including Fake sources, has been very inaccurate (to put it mildly)! [Twitter for iPhone]

Jan 5, 2019 07:57:17 AM The Democrats could solve the Shutdown problem in a very short period of time. All they have to do is approve REAL Border Security (including a Wall), something which everyone, other than drug dealers, human traffickers and criminals, want very badly! This would be so easy to do! [Twitter for iPhone]

Jan 5, 2019 08:55:41 AM Many people currently a part of my opposition, including President Obama & the Dems, have had campaign violations, in some cases for very large sums of money. These are civil cases. They paid a fine & settled. While no big deal, I did not commit a campaign violation! [Twitter for iPhone]

Jan 5, 2019 09:48:55 AM I don't care that most of the workers not getting paid are Democrats, I want to stop the Shutdown as soon as we are in agreement on Strong Border Security! I am in the White House ready to go, where are the Dems? [Twitter for iPhone]

Jan 5, 2019 10:16:14 AM We are working hard at the Border, but we need a WALL! In 2018, 1.7 million pounds of narcotics seized, 17,000 adults arrested with criminal records, and 6000 gang members, including MS-13, apprehended. A big Human Trafficking problem. [Twitter for iPhone]

Jan 5, 2019 10:54:42 AM The Democrats want Billions of Dollars for Foreign Aid, but they don't want to spend a small fraction of that number on properly securing our Border. Figure that one out! [Twitter for iPhone]

Jan 5, 2019 11:13:07 AM Great Tweet today by Tyler Q. Houlton @SpoxDHS on the #FakeNews being put out by @CNN, a proud member of the Opposition Party. @TSA is doing a great job! [Twitter for iPhone]

Jan 5, 2019 12:27:18 PM "Former @NYTimes editor Jill Abramson rips paper's 'unmistakably anti-Trump' bias." Ms. Abramson is 100% correct. Horrible and totally dishonest reporting on almost everything they write. Hence the term Fake News, Enemy of the People, and Opposition Party! [Twitter for iPhone]

Jan 5, 2019 03:49:27 PM Drug makers and companies are not living up to their commitments on pricing. Not being fair to the consumer, or to our Country! [Twitter for iPhone]

Jan 5, 2019 04:05:59 PM V.P. Mike Pence and team just left the White House. Briefed me on their meeting with the Schumer/Pelosi representatives. Not much headway made today. Second meeting set for tomorrow. After so many decades, must finally and permanently fix the problems on the Southern Border! [Twitter for iPhone]

Jan 5, 2019 08:00:30 PM "Jobs up big, plus 312,000. Record number working. Manufacturing best in 20 years (Previous administration said this could not happen). Hispanic unemployment lowest ever. Dow plus 747 (for day)." @DRUDGE_REPORT [Twitter for iPhone]

Jan 5, 2019 08:35:32 PM "The number of employed Americans has now set a 14th record under President Trump. Over the year, average hourly earnings have increased by 84 cents, or 3.2%. Participation Rate hits Trump-Era High." CNS NEWS. And we will do even better with new trade deals and all else! [Twitter for iPhone]

Jan 5, 2019 08:47:56 PM AP-NORC POLL: "Immigration among the top concerns in 2019." People want to stop drugs and criminals at the Border. Want Border Security! Tell the Dems to do the inevitable now, rather than later. The wait is costly and dangerous! [Twitter for iPhone]

Jan 5, 2019 09:06:29 PM Will be going to Camp David tomorrow morning for meetings on Border Security and many other topics with @WhiteHouse senior staff. [Twitter for iPhone]

Jan 5, 2019 09:15:10 PM https://t.co/iSFAokoIP7 [Twitter for iPhone]

Jan 6, 2019 07:01:42 AM "We simply cannot allow people to pour into the United States undetected, undocumented, unchecked..." Barrack Obama, 2005. I voted, when I was a Senator, to build a barrier to try to prevent illegal immigrants from coming in..." Hillary Clinton, 2015. [Twitter for iPhone]

Jan 6, 2019 07:33:39 AM ....The only reason they do not want to build a Wall is that Walls Work! 99% of our illegal Border crossings will end, crime in our Country will go way down and we will save billions of dollars a year! A properly planned and constructed Wall will pay for itself many times a year! [Twitter for iPhone]

Jan 6, 2019 07:41:04 AM RT @realDonaldTrump: As I have stated many times, if the Democrats take over the House or Senate, there will be disruption to the Financial... [Twitter for iPhone]

Jan 6, 2019 07:41:23 AM RT @realDonaldTrump: How do you impeach a president who has won perhaps the greatest election of all time, done nothing wrong (no Collusion... [Twitter for iPhone]

Jan 6, 2019 09:59:33 AM Excited to see our friends in Egypt opening the biggest Cathedral in the Middle East. President El-Sisi is moving his country to a more inclusive future! [Twitter for iPhone]

Jan 6, 2019 10:27:49 AM Our GREAT MILITARY has delivered justice for the heroes lost and wounded in the cowardly attack on the USS Cole. We have just killed the leader of that attack, Jamal al-Badawi. Our work against al Qaeda continues. We will never stop in our fight against Radical Islamic Terrorism! [Twitter for iPhone]

Jan 6, 2019 04:53:57 PM V.P. Mike Pence and group had a productive meeting with the Schumer/Pelosi representatives today. Many details of Border Security were discussed. We are now planning a Steel Barrier rather than concrete. It is both stronger & less obtrusive. Good solution, and made in the U.S.A. [Twitter for iPhone]

Jan 7, 2019 07:56:19 AM With all of the success that our Country is having, including the just released jobs numbers which are off the charts, the Fake News & totally dishonest Media concerning me and my presidency has never been worse. Many have become crazed lunatics who have given up on the TRUTH!... [Twitter for iPhone]

Jan 7, 2019 08:09:03 AM ...The Fake News will knowingly lie and demean in order make the tremendous success of the Trump Administration, and me, look as bad as possible. They use non-existent sources & write stories that are total fiction. Our Country is doing so well, yet this is a sad day in America! [Twitter for iPhone]

Jan 7, 2019 08:31:00 AM ....The Fake News Media in our Country is the real Opposition Party. It is truly the Enemy of the People! We must bring honesty back to journalism and reporting! [Twitter for iPhone]

Jan 7, 2019 08:38:34 AM Congressman Adam Smith, the new Chairman of the House Armed Services Committee, just stated, "Yes, there is a provision in law that says a president can declare an emergency. It's been done a number of times." No doubt, but let's get our deal done in Congress! [Twitter for iPhone]

Jan 7, 2019 09:55:05 AM The Failing New York Times has knowingly written a very inaccurate story on my intentions on Syria. No different from my original statements, we will be leaving at a proper pace while at the same time continuing to fight ISIS and doing all else that is prudent and necessary!..... [Twitter for iPhone]

Jan 7, 2019 01:44:41 PM I am pleased to inform you that I will Address the Nation on the Humanitarian and National Security crisis on our Southern Border. Tuesday night at 9:00 P.M. Eastern. [Twitter for iPhone]

Jan 7, 2019 10:50:29 PM Endless Wars, especially those which are fought out of judgement mistakes that were made many years ago, & those where we are getting little financial or military help from the rich countries that so greatly benefit from what we are doing, will eventually come to a glorious end! [Twitter for iPhone]

Jan 8, 2019 08:01:15 AM Economic numbers looking REALLY good. Can you imagine if I had long term ZERO interest rates to play with like the past administration, rather than the rapidly raised normalized rates we have today. That would have been SO EASY! Still, markets up BIG since 2016 Election! [Twitter for iPhone]

Jan 8, 2019 08:13:06 AM "The President is the biggest and best supporter of the Steel Industry in many years. We are now doing really well. The Tariffs let us compete. Was unfair that the Steel Industry lost its jobs to unfair trade laws. Very positive outcome." Mark Glyptis, United Steelworkers [Twitter for iPhone]

Jan 8, 2019 08:16:09 AM Talks with China are going very well! [Twitter for iPhone]

Jan 8, 2019 09:42:39 AM Congratulations to a truly great football team, the Clemson Tigers, on an incredible win last night against a powerful Alabama team. A big win also for the Great State of South Carolina. Look forward to seeing the team, and their brilliant coach, for the second time at the W.H. [Twitter for iPhone]

Jan 8, 2019 09:16:29 PM https://t.co/Ft6FqQmYfl [Twitter for iPhone]

Jan 8, 2019 11:33:59 PM Thank you for soooo many nice comments regarding my Oval Office speech. A very interesting experience! [Twitter for iPhone]

Jan 9, 2019 09:06:09 AM Our Country is doing so well in so many ways. Great jobs numbers, with a record setting December. We are rebuilding our military. Vets finally have Choice & Accountability. Economy & GDP are strong. Tax & Reg cuts historic. Trade deals great. But we MUST fix our Southern Border! [Twitter for iPhone]

Jan 9, 2019 09:36:05 AM Billions of dollars are sent to the State of California for Forrest fires that, with proper Forrest Management, would never happen. Unless they get their act together, which is unlikely, I have ordered FEMA to send no more money. It is a disgraceful situation in lives & money! [Twitter for iPhone]

Jan 9, 2019 10:25:43 AM Billions of dollars are sent to the State of California for Forest fires that, with proper Forest Management, would never happen. Unless they get their act together, which is unlikely, I have ordered FEMA to send no more money. It is a disgraceful situation in lives & money! [Twitter for iPhone]

Jan 9, 2019 02:31:29 PM Thank you to all of America's brave police, deputies, sheriffs, and federal law enforcement on National Law Enforcement Appreciation Day! We love you and will always support you. https://t.co/kGL6kPmpDY [Twitter for iPhone]

Jan 9, 2019 03:34:46 PM Just left a meeting with Chuck and Nancy, a total waste of time. I asked what is going to happen in 30 days if I quickly open things up, are you going to approve Border Security which includes a Wall or Steel Barrier? Nancy said, NO. I said bye-bye, nothing else works! [Twitter for iPad]

Jan 9, 2019 10:43:13 PM The Mainstream Media has NEVER been more dishonest than it is now. NBC and MSNBC are going Crazy. They report stories, purposely, the exact opposite of the facts. They are truly the Opposition Party working with the Dems. May even be worse than Fake News CNN, if that is possible! [Twitter for iPhone]

Jan 9, 2019 10:53:03 PM Gave an OFF THE RECORD luncheon, somewhat of a White House tradition or custom, to network anchors yesterday - and they quickly leaked the contents of the meeting. Who would believe how bad it has gotten with the mainstream media, which has gone totally bonkers! [Twitter for iPhone]

Jan 9, 2019 10:55:30 PM RT @charliekirk11: This is why we need a wall Illegal immigration is a serious threat to our country 90% of all heroin comes across the b... [Twitter for iPhone]

Jan 9, 2019 10:55:59 PM RT @charliekirk11: President Trump is winning this shutdown fight Democrats have no message, and are refusing to open government because t... [Twitter for iPhone]

Jan 9, 2019 10:56:26 PM RT @charliekirk11: Did you know: At our Southern Border, in 2018: 1.7 MILLION pounds of narcotics were seized 17,000 criminals were arre... [Twitter for iPhone]

Jan 9, 2019 10:59:15 PM RT @charliekirk11: Governor Ron DeSantis suspends the horrible Sheriff Scott Israel who is largely responsible for the errors leading up to... [Twitter for iPhone]

Jan 9, 2019 10:59:42 PM RT @parscale: Just received my newest voter score tracking from my team. @realDonaldTrump has reached his highest national approval rating... [Twitter for iPhone]

Jan 9, 2019 11:11:41 PM RT @dbongino: New Poll: Vast Majority of Voters Believe There is "Crisis" or "Problem" at U.S. Border https://t.co/bzFimBid26 [Twitter for iPhone]

Jan 10, 2019 08:24:30 AM Cryin Chuck told his favorite lie when he used his standard sound bite that I "slammed the table & walked out of the room. He had a temper tantrum." Because I knew he would say that, and after Nancy said no to proper Border Security, I politely said bye-bye and left, no slamming! [Twitter for iPhone]

Jan 10, 2019 08:34:10 AM There is GREAT unity with the Republicans in the House and Senate, despite the Fake News Media working in overdrive to make the story look otherwise. The Opposition Party & the Dems know we must have Strong Border Security, but don't want to give "Trump" another one of many wins! [Twitter for iPhone]

Jan 10, 2019 08:41:25 AM "Great support for Border Security and the Wall." @foxandfriends Even greater than anyone would know! "Presidents supporters do not want him to cave." @SteveDoocy I won't! [Twitter for iPhone]

Jan 10, 2019 08:43:15 AM Getting ready to leave for the Great State of Texas! #MAGA [Twitter for iPhone]

Jan 10, 2019 08:43:54 AM MAKE AMERICA GREAT AGAIN! [Twitter for iPhone]

Jan 10, 2019 11:47:11 AM President Obama, thank you for your great support – I have been saying this all along! https://t.co/L506g9Aq4z [Twitter for iPhone]

Jan 10, 2019 01:14:31 PM Because of the Democrats intransigence on Border Security and the great importance of Safety for our Nation, I am respectfully cancelling my very important trip to Davos, Switzerland for the World Economic Forum. My warmest regards and apologies to the @WEF! [Twitter for iPhone]

Jan 10, 2019 01:17:01 PM RT @SenateGOP: Why do we need border security? This is why. These are the facts. #SecureOurBorder https://t.co/dMpYb3p4Wy [Twitter for iPhone]

Jan 10, 2019 05:41:01 PM From the Southern Border.... https://t.co/Vgsf5nEZUH [Twitter for iPhone]

Jan 10, 2019 08:10:49 PM Dear Diary... https://t.co/NAuMaQW6fl [Twitter for iPhone]

Jan 10, 2019 08:45:54 PM Will be interviewed at the Border by @seanhannity on @FoxNews tonight at 9:00. Enjoy! [Twitter for iPhone]

Jan 10, 2019 09:42:46 PM We lose 300 Americans a week, 90% of which comes through the Southern Border. These numbers will be DRASTICALLY REDUCED if we have a Wall! [Twitter for iPhone]

Jan 10, 2019 09:43:00 PM When I took the Oath of Office.... https://t.co/GDhIqteKpv [Twitter for iPhone]

Jan 11, 2019 07:05:00 AM I often said during rallies, with little variation, that "Mexico will pay for the Wall." We have just signed a great new Trade Deal with Mexico. It is Billions of Dollars a year better than the very bad NAFTA deal which it replaces. The difference pays for Wall many times over! [Twitter for iPhone]

Jan 11, 2019 07:40:30 AM H1-B holders in the United States can rest assured that changes are soon coming which will bring both simplicity and certainty to your stay, including a potential path to citizenship. We want to encourage talented and highly skilled people to pursue career options in the U.S. [Twitter for iPhone]

Jan 11, 2019 11:04:25 AM Humanitarian Crisis at our Southern Border. I just got back and it is a far worse situation than almost anyone would understand, an invasion! I have been there numerous times - The Democrats, Cryin' Chuck and Nancy don't know how bad and dangerous it is for our ENTIRE COUNTRY.... [Twitter for iPhone]

Jan 11, 2019 11:16:14 AM ...The Steel Barrier, or Wall, should have been built by previous administrations long ago. They never got it done - I will. Without it, our Country cannot be safe. Criminals, Gangs, Human Traffickers, Drugs & so much other big trouble can easily pour in. It can be stopped cold! [Twitter for iPhone]

Jan 11, 2019 12:50:04 PM The Fake News Media keeps saying we haven't built any NEW WALL. Below is a section just completed on the Border. Anti-climbing feature included. Very high, strong and beautiful! Also, many miles already renovated and in service! https://t.co/UAAGXl5Byr [Twitter for iPhone]

Jan 11, 2019 05:11:30 PM RT @WhiteHouse: This afternoon, President Trump hosted a roundtable discussion with State, local, and community leaders, who spoke on how t... [Twitter for iPhone]

Jan 11, 2019 05:11:34 PM RT @WhiteHouse: This is common sense. Congress must pass a bill that ends the crisis at our border. https://t.co/wD0PPKfpNM [Twitter for iPhone]

Jan 11, 2019 06:00:23 PM I look forward to hosting, right out of the great State of South Carolina, the 2019 NCAA Football Champion Clemson Tigers at the White House on Monday, January 14th. What a game, what a coach, what a team! [Twitter for iPhone]

Jan 11, 2019 06:21:41 PM Drug prices declined in 2018, the first time in nearly half a century. During the first 19 months of my Administration, Americans saved $26 Billion on prescription drugs. Our policies to get cheaper generic drugs to market are working! [Twitter for iPhone]

Jan 11, 2019 06:29:48 PM .@CNN called a San Diego news station (@KUSINews) for negative reports on the Wall. When the station said that Walls work, CNN no longer had interest. #FakeNews https://t.co/IDyXqmDsPq [Twitter for iPhone]

Jan 12, 2019 07:05:36 AM Wow, just learned in the Failing New York Times that the corrupt former leaders of the FBI, almost all fired or forced to leave the agency for some very bad reasons, opened up an investigation on me, for no reason & with no proof, after I fired Lyin' James Comey, a total sleaze! [Twitter for iPhone]

Jan 12, 2019 07:18:35 AM ...Funny thing about James Comey. Everybody wanted him fired, Republican and Democrat alike. After the rigged & botched Crooked Hillary investigation, where she was interviewed on July 4th Weekend, not recorded or sworn in, and where she said she didn't know anything (a lie),.... [Twitter for iPhone]

☐ Jan 12, 2019 07:33:30 AM ....the FBI was in complete turmoil (see N.Y. Post) because of Comey's poor leadership and the way he handled the Clinton mess (not to mention his usurpation of powers from the Justice Department). My firing of James Comey was a great day for America. He was a Crooked Cop...... [Twitter for iPhone]

☐ Jan 12, 2019 07:53:25 AM .....who is being totally protected by his best friend, Bob Mueller, & the 13 Angry Democrats - leaking machines who have NO interest in going after the Real Collusion (and much more) by Crooked Hillary Clinton, her Campaign, and the Democratic National Committee. Just Watch! [Twitter for iPhone]

☐ Jan 12, 2019 08:09:23 AM I have been FAR tougher on Russia than Obama, Bush or Clinton. Maybe tougher than any other President. At the same time, & as I have often said, getting along with Russia is a good thing, not a bad thing. I fully expect that someday we will have good relations with Russia again! [Twitter for iPhone]

☐ Jan 12, 2019 09:20:33 AM Lyin' James Comey, Andrew McCabe, Peter S and his lover, agent Lisa Page, & more, all disgraced and/or fired and caught in the act. These are just some of the losers that tried to do a number on your President. Part of the Witch Hunt. Remember the "insurance policy?" This is it! [Twitter for iPhone]

☐ Jan 12, 2019 09:28:14 AM Democrats should come back to Washington and work to end the Shutdown, while at the same time ending the horrible humanitarian crisis at our Southern Border. I am in the White House waiting for you! [Twitter for iPhone]

☐ Jan 12, 2019 09:42:21 AM 23% of Federal inmates are illegal immigrants. Border arrests are up 240%. In the Great State of Texas, between 2011 & 2018, there were a total of 292,000 crimes by illegal aliens, 539 murders, 32,000 assaults, 3,426 sexual assaults and 3000 weapons charges. Democrats come back! [Twitter for iPhone]

☐ Jan 12, 2019 09:47:04 AM Democrats could solve the Shutdown in 15 minutes! Call your Dem Senator or Congresswoman/man. Tell them to get it done! Humanitarian Crisis. [Twitter for iPhone]

☐ Jan 12, 2019 10:57:23 AM I just watched a Fake reporter from the Amazon Washington Post say the White House is "chaotic, there does not seem to be a strategy for this Shutdown. There is no plan." The Fakes always like talking Chaos, there is NONE. In fact, there's almost nobody in the W.H. but me, and... [Twitter for iPhone]

☐ Jan 12, 2019 11:07:22 AM ....I do have a plan on the Shutdown. But to understand that plan you would have to understand the fact that I won the election, and I promised safety and security for the American people. Part of that promise was a Wall at the Southern Border. Elections have consequences! [Twitter for iPhone]

Jan 12, 2019 11:14:55 AM We have a massive Humanitarian Crisis at our Southern Border. We will be out for a long time unless the Democrats come back from their "vacations" and get back to work. I am in the White House ready to sign! [Twitter for iPhone]

Jan 12, 2019 01:20:13 PM https://t.co/3IH1yW2eTg [Twitter for iPhone]

Jan 12, 2019 08:37:11 PM I will be interviewed by Jeanine Pirro at 9:00 P.M. on @FoxNews. Watch @JesseBWatters before and @greggutfeld after. All terrific people. I am in the White House waiting for Cryin' Chuck and Nancy to call so we can start helping our Country both at the Border and from within! [Twitter for iPhone]

Jan 13, 2019 09:58:26 AM Democrats are saying that DACA is not worth it and don't want to include in talks. Many Hispanics will be coming over to the Republican side, watch! [Twitter for iPhone]

Jan 13, 2019 10:00:53 AM The building of the Wall on the Southern Border will bring down the crime rate throughout the entire Country! [Twitter for iPhone]

Jan 13, 2019 10:05:37 AM I'm in the White House, waiting. The Democrats are everywhere but Washington as people await their pay. They are having fun and not even talking! [Twitter for iPhone]

Jan 13, 2019 10:36:04 AM The damage done to our Country from a badly broken Border - Drugs, Crime and so much that is bad - is far greater than a Shutdown, which the Dems can easily fix as soon as they come back to Washington! [Twitter for iPhone]

Jan 13, 2019 10:45:45 AM Thousands of illegal aliens who have committed sexual crimes against children are right now in Texas prisons. Most came through our Southern Border. We can end this easily - We need a Steel Barrier or Wall. Walls Work! John Jones, Texas Department of Public Safety. @FoxNews [Twitter for iPhone]

Jan 13, 2019 05:01:21 PM Wish I could share with everyone the beauty and majesty of being in the White House and looking outside at the snow filled lawns and Rose Garden. Really is something - SPECIAL COUNTRY, SPECIAL PLACE! [Twitter for iPhone]

Jan 13, 2019 05:53:32 PM Starting the long overdue pullout from Syria while hitting the little remaining ISIS territorial caliphate hard, and from many directions. Will attack again from existing nearby base if it reforms. Will devastate Turkey economically if they hit Kurds. Create 20 mile safe zone.... [Twitter for iPhone]

Jan 13, 2019 06:02:56 PM ....Likewise, do not want the Kurds to provoke Turkey. Russia, Iran and Syria have been the biggest beneficiaries of the long term U.S. policy of destroying ISIS in Syria - natural enemies. We also benefit but it is now time to bring our troops back home. Stop the ENDLESS WARS! [Twitter for iPhone]

Jan 13, 2019 08:45:10 PM So sorry to hear the news about Jeff Bozo being taken down by a competitor whose reporting, I understand, is far more accurate than the reporting in his lobbyist newspaper, the Amazon Washington Post. Hopefully the paper will soon be placed in better & more responsible hands! [Twitter for iPhone]

Jan 13, 2019 09:08:08 PM If Elizabeth Warren, often referred to by me as Pocahontas did this commercial from Bighorn or Wounded Knee instead of her kitchen, with her husband dressed in full Indian garb, it would have been a smash! https://t.co/paf1CvesBa [Twitter for iPhone]

Jan 13, 2019 09:52:59 PM If Elizabeth Warren, often referred to by me as Pocahontas, did this commercial from Bighorn or Wounded Knee instead of her kitchen, with her husband dressed in full Indian garb, it would have been a smash! https://t.co/D5KWr8EPan [Twitter for iPhone]

Jan 13, 2019 10:03:03 PM Best line in the Elizabeth Warren beer catastrophe is, to her husband, "Thank you for being here. I'm glad you're here" It's their house, he's supposed to be there! [Twitter for iPhone]

Jan 13, 2019 10:12:34 PM The Trump portrait of an unsustainable Border Crisis is dead on. "In the last two years, ICE officers made 266,000 arrests of aliens with Criminal Records, including those charged or convicted of 100,000 assaults, 30,000 sex crimes & 4000 violent killings." America's Southern.... [Twitter for iPhone]

Jan 13, 2019 10:18:31 PM ....Border is eventually going to be militarized and defended or the United States, as we have known it, is going to cease to exist...And Americans will not go gentle into that good night. Patrick Buchanan. The great people of our Country demand proper Border Security NOW! [Twitter for iPhone]

Jan 14, 2019 07:14:25 AM "Gas prices drop across the United States because President Trump has deregulated Energy and we are now producing a great deal more oil than ever before." @foxandfriends But this is bad news for Russia, why would President Trump do such a thing? Thought he worked for Kremlin? [Twitter for iPhone]

Jan 14, 2019 07:17:09 AM RT @GOPChairwoman: It didn't get the attention it deserved, but @realDonaldTrump recently signed a bill into law that will empower women al... [Twitter for iPhone]

Jan 14, 2019 07:17:40 AM RT @GOPChairwoman: Chuck Schumer and Nancy Pelosi are not negotiating in good faith with @realDonaldTrump. Instead, Congressional Democra... [Twitter for iPhone]

Jan 14, 2019 07:18:27 AM RT @GeraldoRivera: Based on the record, the allegation/suggestion that the #FBI came close to investigating @realDonaldTrump as a Russian s... [Twitter for iPhone]

Jan 14, 2019 07:18:52 AM RT @GOPChairwoman: Economic policies that @realDonaldTrump and @IvankaTrump have championed are producing some fantastic results for Americ... [Twitter for iPhone]

Jan 14, 2019 07:19:49 AM RT @GOPChairwoman: Smugglers are flooding our communities with drugs. *300 Americans die each week from heroin, 90% of it comes from south... [Twitter for iPhone]

Jan 14, 2019 07:23:11 AM I've been waiting all weekend. Democrats must get to work now. Border must be secured! [Twitter for iPhone]

Jan 14, 2019 07:26:18 AM Nancy and Cryin' Chuck can end the Shutdown in 15 minutes. At this point it has become their, and the Democrats, fault! [Twitter for iPhone]

Jan 14, 2019 07:32:38 AM Getting ready to address the Farm Convention today in Nashville, Tennessee. Love our farmers, love Tennessee - a great combination! See you in a little while. [Twitter for iPhone]

Jan 14, 2019 07:35:13 AM "Dems in Puerto Rico as Shutdown hits day 24." @foxandfriends [Twitter for iPhone]

Jan 14, 2019 08:44:59 AM The Fake News gets crasier and more dishonest every single day. Amazing to watch as certain people covering me, and the tremendous success of this administration, have truly gone MAD! Their Fake reporting creates anger and disunity. Take two weeks off and come back rested. Chill! [Twitter for iPhone]

Jan 14, 2019 10:49:31 AM https://t.co/w5X8jqvtiS [Twitter for iPhone]

Jan 14, 2019 01:44:35 PM Getting ready to go on stage at the #AFBF100 in New Orleans - packed house! I will try and match the great game played yesterday by the New Orleans Saints and their incredible QB, Drew Brees. People here are very excited by the team. Going on stage now! https://t.co/ytZv0HLYun [Twitter for iPhone]

Jan 14, 2019 02:48:31 PM RT @WhiteHouse: President Trump Delivers Remarks at the American Farm Bureau Federation's 100th Annual Convention https://t.co/tMWj5zj3K0 [Twitter for iPhone]

Jan 14, 2019 03:37:44 PM RT @DonaldJTrumpJr: Silence of the Moms: Media Refuse to Discuss Angel Families https://t.co/AoVIquJge2 via @BreitbartNews [Twitter for iPhone]

Jan 14, 2019 03:38:19 PM RT @DonaldJTrumpJr: 'Angel mom' demands Trump's wall, 'we've become collateral damage' https://t.co/FoUPO11tmM [Twitter for iPhone]

Jan 14, 2019 05:12:49 PM Spoke w/ President Erdogan of Turkey to advise where we stand on all matters including our last two weeks of success in fighting the remnants of ISIS, and 20 mile safe zone. Also spoke about economic development between the U.S. & Turkey - great potential to substantially expand! [Twitter for iPhone]

Jan 14, 2019 05:19:49 PM For decades, politicians promised to secure the border, fix our trade deals, bring back our factories, get tough on China, move the Embassy to Jerusalem, make NATO pay their fair share, and so much else - only to do NOTHING (or worse).... [Twitter for iPhone]

⬜ Jan 14, 2019 05:19:50 PM ....I am doing exactly what I pledged to do, and what I was elected to do by the citizens of our great Country. Just as I promised, I am fighting for YOU! [Twitter for iPhone]

⬜ Jan 15, 2019 06:58:52 AM The rank and file of the FBI are great people who are disgusted with what they are learning about Lyin' James Comey and the so-called "leaders" of the FBI. Twelve have been fired or forced to leave. They got caught spying on my campaign and then called it an investigation. Bad! [Twitter for iPhone]

⬜ Jan 15, 2019 07:16:00 AM Just announced that Veterans unemployment has reached an 18 year low, really good news for our Vets and their families. Will soon be an all time low! Do you think the media will report on this and all of the other great economic news? [Twitter for iPhone]

⬜ Jan 15, 2019 07:25:45 AM Volkswagen will be spending 800 million dollars in Chattanooga, Tennessee. They will be making Electric Cars. Congratulations to Chattanooga and Tennessee on a job well done. A big win! [Twitter for iPhone]

⬜ Jan 15, 2019 07:37:55 AM A big new Caravan is heading up to our Southern Border from Honduras. Tell Nancy and Chuck that a drone flying around will not stop them. Only a Wall will work. Only a Wall, or Steel Barrier, will keep our Country safe! Stop playing political games and end the Shutdown! [Twitter for iPhone]

⬜ Jan 15, 2019 07:49:21 AM Polls are now showing that people are beginning to understand the Humanitarian Crisis and Crime at the Border. Numbers are going up fast, over 50%. Democrats will soon be known as the Party of Crime. Ridiculous that they don't want Border Security! [Twitter for iPhone]

⬜ Jan 15, 2019 07:58:29 AM Great being with the National Champion Clemson Tigers last night at the White House. Because of the Shutdown I served them massive amounts of Fast Food (I paid), over 1000 hamberders etc. Within one hour, it was all gone. Great guys and big eaters! [Twitter for iPhone]

⬜ Jan 15, 2019 08:01:36 AM RT @PARISDENNARD: I trust a rancher on the Southern border more than a liberal politician from Northern California https://t.co/mo4oWe1SnI [Twitter for iPhone]

⬜ Jan 15, 2019 08:02:10 AM RT @DonaldJTrumpJr: Worth the read. I'm A Senior Trump Official, And I Hope A Long Shutdown Smokes Out The Resistance https://t.co/6ahfOl… [Twitter for iPhone]

⬜ Jan 15, 2019 08:02:21 AM RT @DonaldJTrumpJr: Since January 1, neither CNN nor MSNBC has booked a single Angel Mom — mothers of children brutally murdered by illegal… [Twitter for iPhone]

⬜ Jan 15, 2019 08:02:49 AM RT @MZHemingway: NYT Reveals FBI Retaliated Against Trump For Lawfully Firing Comey https://t.co/LwJ7w1ctom [Twitter for iPhone]

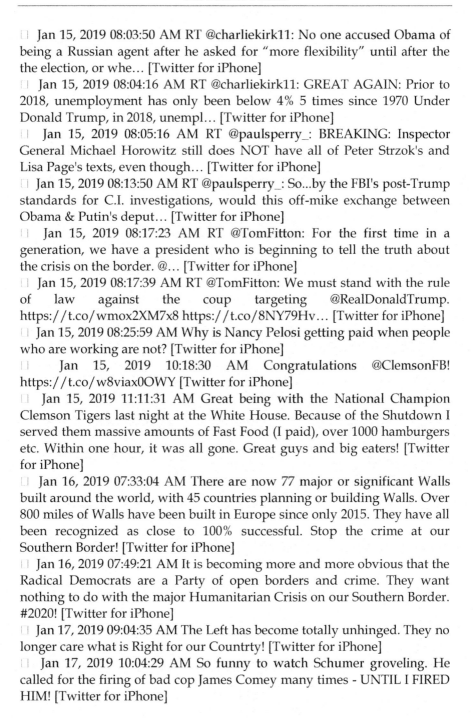

Jan 15, 2019 08:03:50 AM RT @charliekirk11: No one accused Obama of being a Russian agent after he asked for "more flexibility" until after the the election, or whe... [Twitter for iPhone]

Jan 15, 2019 08:04:16 AM RT @charliekirk11: GREAT AGAIN: Prior to 2018, unemployment has only been below 4% 5 times since 1970 Under Donald Trump, in 2018, unempl... [Twitter for iPhone]

Jan 15, 2019 08:05:16 AM RT @paulsperry_: BREAKING: Inspector General Michael Horowitz still does NOT have all of Peter Strzok's and Lisa Page's texts, even though... [Twitter for iPhone]

Jan 15, 2019 08:13:50 AM RT @paulsperry_: So...by the FBI's post-Trump standards for C.I. investigations, would this off-mike exchange between Obama & Putin's deput... [Twitter for iPhone]

Jan 15, 2019 08:17:23 AM RT @TomFitton: For the first time in a generation, we have a president who is beginning to tell the truth about the crisis on the border. @... [Twitter for iPhone]

Jan 15, 2019 08:17:39 AM RT @TomFitton: We must stand with the rule of law against the coup targeting @RealDonaldTrump. https://t.co/wmox2XM7x8 https://t.co/8NY79Hv... [Twitter for iPhone]

Jan 15, 2019 08:25:59 AM Why is Nancy Pelosi getting paid when people who are working are not? [Twitter for iPhone]

Jan 15, 2019 10:18:30 AM Congratulations @ClemsonFB! https://t.co/w8viax0OWY [Twitter for iPhone]

Jan 15, 2019 11:11:31 AM Great being with the National Champion Clemson Tigers last night at the White House. Because of the Shutdown I served them massive amounts of Fast Food (I paid), over 1000 hamburgers etc. Within one hour, it was all gone. Great guys and big eaters! [Twitter for iPhone]

Jan 16, 2019 07:33:04 AM There are now 77 major or significant Walls built around the world, with 45 countries planning or building Walls. Over 800 miles of Walls have been built in Europe since only 2015. They have all been recognized as close to 100% successful. Stop the crime at our Southern Border! [Twitter for iPhone]

Jan 16, 2019 07:49:21 AM It is becoming more and more obvious that the Radical Democrats are a Party of open borders and crime. They want nothing to do with the major Humanitarian Crisis on our Southern Border. #2020! [Twitter for iPhone]

Jan 17, 2019 09:04:35 AM The Left has become totally unhinged. They no longer care what is Right for our Countrty! [Twitter for iPhone]

Jan 17, 2019 10:04:29 AM So funny to watch Schumer groveling. He called for the firing of bad cop James Comey many times - UNTIL I FIRED HIM! [Twitter for iPhone]

Jan 17, 2019 10:29:19 AM RT @Lrihendry: @realDonaldTrump They are eaten alive by hate for our President & his voters! They care more about illegal immigrants than… [Twitter for iPhone]

Jan 17, 2019 08:18:04 PM RT @realDonaldTrump: ….I am doing exactly what I pledged to do, and what I was elected to do by the citizens of our great Country. Just a… [Twitter for iPhone]

Jan 17, 2019 08:18:07 PM RT @realDonaldTrump: For decades, politicians promised to secure the border, fix our trade deals, bring back our factories, get tough on Ch… [Twitter for iPhone]

Jan 17, 2019 08:36:01 PM Thank you to Amy Kremer, Women for Trump Co-Founder, for doing such a great interview with Martha MacCallum…and by the way, women have the lowest unemployment numbers in many decades - at the highest pay ever. Proud of that! [Twitter for iPhone]

Jan 17, 2019 09:42:41 PM "In 2018 alone, 20,000 illegal aliens with criminal records were apprehended trying to cross the Border, and there was a 122% increase in fentanyl being smuggled between ports of entry. Last month alone, more than 20,000 minors were smuggled into the U.S." @seanhannity [Twitter for iPhone]

Jan 17, 2019 10:03:24 PM Gregg Jarrett: "Mueller's prosecutors knew the "Dossier" was the product of bias and deception." It was a Fake, just like so much news coverage in our Country. Nothing but a Witch Hunt, from beginning to end! [Twitter for iPhone]

Jan 18, 2019 08:22:53 AM Border rancher: "We've found prayer rugs out here. It's unreal." Washington Examiner People coming across the Southern Border from many countries, some of which would be a big surprise. [Twitter for iPhone]

Jan 18, 2019 09:00:17 AM Why would Nancy Pelosi leave the Country with other Democrats on a seven day excursion when 800,000 great people are not getting paid. Also, could somebody please explain to Nancy & her "big donors" in wine country that people working on farms (grapes) will have easy access in! [Twitter for iPhone]

Jan 18, 2019 09:08:24 AM "It's the Democrats keeping everything closed." @JimInhofe So true! [Twitter for iPhone]

Jan 18, 2019 09:13:56 AM Another big Caravan heading our way. Very hard to stop without a Wall! [Twitter for iPhone]

Jan 18, 2019 10:02:41 AM Kevin Corke, @FoxNews "Don't forget, Michael Cohen has already been convicted of perjury and fraud, and as recently as this week, the Wall Street Journal has suggested that he may have stolen tens of thousands of dollars…." Lying to reduce his jail time! Watch father-in-law! [Twitter for iPhone]

Jan 18, 2019 10:58:37 AM Never seen the Republican Party so unified. No "Cave" on the issue of Border and National Security. A beautiful thing to see, especially when you hear the new rhetoric spewing from the mouths of the Democrats who talk Open Border, High Taxes and Crime. Stop Criminals & Drugs now! [Twitter for iPhone]

Jan 18, 2019 10:59:35 AM MAKE AMERICA GREAT AGAIN! [Twitter for iPhone]

Jan 18, 2019 11:00:07 AM AMERICA FIRST! [Twitter for iPhone]

Jan 18, 2019 11:58:04 AM https://t.co/6xciJ0ubp0 [Twitter for iPhone]

Jan 18, 2019 05:51:00 PM I will be making a major announcement concerning the Humanitarian Crisis on our Southern Border, and the Shutdown, tomorrow afternoon at 3 P.M., live from the @WhiteHouse. [Twitter for iPhone]

Jan 18, 2019 08:06:38 PM RT @SchnurreZueri: @sethweathers @BuzzFeedNews Sadly so many will never get the memo that it was fake! [Twitter for iPhone]

Jan 18, 2019 08:12:08 PM Just a son who loves his Dad. Nice! https://t.co/ZI4012Ld7S [Twitter for iPhone]

Jan 18, 2019 08:14:30 PM RT @johncardillo: I told you all that the BuzzFeed story was nonsense. https://t.co/gbTXPjpVtk [Twitter for iPhone]

Jan 18, 2019 08:16:18 PM RT @dbongino: We called it. FAKE NEWS! "More Buzzfeed B.S." https://t.co/aOIPJJu0vH [Twitter for iPhone]

Jan 18, 2019 08:42:51 PM RT @SebGorka: "We will b protected by grt men & women of r military & law enforcmt & most importantly, we will b protected by God" https://... [Twitter for iPhone]

Jan 18, 2019 08:44:59 PM RT @dbongino: When are we going to start investigating the REAL collusion scandal? The collusion between the Clinton & Obama teams and fore... [Twitter for iPhone]

Jan 18, 2019 08:46:08 PM RT @dbongino: Latino Job Approval of Trump SURGES in Midst of Govt Shutdown Over Border Wall Funding https://t.co/HAqstQDGw5 [Twitter for iPhone]

Jan 18, 2019 08:50:03 PM RT @parscale: This is just one of many fake news stories over the last several years. Sad so many journalists have lost their integrity. I... [Twitter for iPhone]

Jan 18, 2019 08:52:47 PM RT @GOPChairwoman: The entire premise of this story, which received wall-to-wall coverage, was based on "evidence" the reporters admitted t... [Twitter for iPhone]

Jan 18, 2019 09:14:11 PM RT @LindaSuhler: Dear God, Thank you for answering our prayers. A grateful Nation #GodBlessAmericaus #PresidentTrump #ElectionDay https://... [Twitter for iPhone]

Jan 18, 2019 09:14:44 PM https://t.co/wjqVvTqeky [Twitter for iPhone]

Jan 18, 2019 09:18:14 PM RT @RyanAFournier: The reporters never saw the evidence. They went off of a source who said it was "credible". This isn't journalism. Con... [Twitter for iPhone]

Jan 18, 2019 09:18:18 PM RT @ChatByCC: The Buzzfeed bombshell bombed. It blew up in their face and the rest of the fake news are casualties too. [Twitter for iPhone]

Jan 18, 2019 09:23:46 PM RT @CarmineZozzora: By the time their fake news campaigns are fully exposed they've already moved on to their next fake news campaign. A g... [Twitter for iPhone]

Jan 18, 2019 10:02:50 PM Remember it was Buzzfeed that released the totally discredited "Dossier," paid for by Crooked Hillary Clinton and the Democrats (as opposition research), on which the entire Russian probe is based! A very sad day for journalism, but a great day for our Country! [Twitter for iPhone]

Jan 18, 2019 10:22:29 PM RT @GeraldoRivera: At what point in fairness-after 2 years do Americans of good will say enough already? If the #SpecialCounsel had collusi... [Twitter for iPhone]

Jan 18, 2019 10:22:44 PM RT @GeraldoRivera: This is just the most egregious example of the rampant unfairness that has tainted this partisan witch-hunt from the beg... [Twitter for iPhone]

Jan 18, 2019 10:24:49 PM Fake News is truly the ENEMY OF THE PEOPLE! [Twitter for iPhone]

Jan 19, 2019 06:29:21 AM Will be leaving for Dover to be with the families of 4 very special people who lost their lives in service to our Country! [Twitter for iPhone]

Jan 19, 2019 07:11:38 AM .@newtgingrich just stated that there has been no president since Abraham Lincoln who has been treated worse or more unfairly by the media than your favorite President, me! At the same time there has been no president who has accomplished more in his first two years in office! [Twitter for iPhone]

Jan 19, 2019 07:51:30 AM The Economy is one of the best in our history, with unemployment at a 50 year low, and the Stock Market ready to again break a record (set by us many times) - & all you heard yesterday, based on a phony story, was Impeachment. You want to see a Stock Market Crash, Impeach Trump! [Twitter for iPhone]

Jan 19, 2019 08:50:09 AM Many people are saying that the Mainstream Media will have a very hard time restoring credibility because of the way they have treated me over the past 3 years (including the election lead-up), as highlighted by the disgraceful Buzzfeed story & the even more disgraceful coverage! [Twitter for iPhone]

Jan 19, 2019 09:09:37 AM Mexico is doing NOTHING to stop the Caravan which is now fully formed and heading to the United States. We stopped the last two - many are still in Mexico but can't get through our Wall, but it takes a lot of Border Agents if there is no Wall. Not easy! [Twitter for iPhone]

Jan 19, 2019 02:08:41 PM I will be live from the White House at 4:00 P.M. [Twitter for iPhone]

Jan 19, 2019 04:24:23 PM https://t.co/bJ81QkOObW [Twitter for iPhone]

Jan 20, 2019 07:40:04 AM Always heard that as President, "it's all about the economy!" Well, we have one of the best economies in the history of our Country. Big GDP, lowest unemployment, companies coming back to the U.S. in BIG numbers, great new trade deals happening, & more. But LITTLE media mention! [Twitter for iPhone]

Jan 20, 2019 07:59:35 AM Be careful and try staying in your house. Large parts of the Country are suffering from tremendous amounts of snow and near record setting cold. Amazing how big this system is. Wouldn't be bad to have a little of that good old fashioned Global Warming right now! [Twitter for iPhone]

Jan 20, 2019 08:11:51 AM Nancy Pelosi and some of the Democrats turned down my offer yesterday before I even got up to speak. They don't see crime & drugs, they only see 2020 - which they are not going to win. Best economy! They should do the right thing for the Country & allow people to go back to work. [Twitter for iPhone]

Jan 20, 2019 08:23:28 AM No, Amnesty is not a part of my offer. It is a 3 year extension of DACA. Amnesty will be used only on a much bigger deal, whether on immigration or something else. Likewise there will be no big push to remove the 11,000,000 plus people who are here illegally-but be careful Nancy! [Twitter for iPhone]

Jan 20, 2019 08:35:46 AM Nancy Pelosi has behaved so irrationally & has gone so far to the left that she has now officially become a Radical Democrat. She is so petrified of the "lefties" in her party that she has lost control...And by the way, clean up the streets in San Francisco, they are disgusting! [Twitter for iPhone]

Jan 20, 2019 08:51:26 AM Nancy, I am still thinking about the State of the Union speech, there are so many options - including doing it as per your written offer (made during the Shutdown, security is no problem), and my written acceptance. While a contract is a contract, I'll get back to you soon! [Twitter for iPhone]

Jan 20, 2019 09:03:26 AM Wow, just heard that my poll numbers with Hispanics has gone up 19%, to 50%. That is because they know the Border issue better than anyone, and they want Security, which can only be gotten with a Wall. [Twitter for iPhone]

Jan 20, 2019 09:20:57 AM Don't forget, we are building and renovating big sections of Wall right now. Moving quickly, and will cost far less than previous politicians thought possible. Building, after all, is what I do best, even when money is not readily available! [Twitter for iPhone]

Jan 20, 2019 09:33:25 AM Thank you David! https://t.co/zsmNfTjEDR [Twitter for iPhone]

Jan 20, 2019 01:16:22 PM The Media is not giving us credit for the tremendous progress we have made with North Korea. Think of where we were at the end of the Obama Administration compared to now. Great meeting this week with top Reps. Looking forward to meeting with Chairman Kim at end of February! [Twitter for iPhone]

Jan 20, 2019 01:16:46 PM https://t.co/yQkCrpooIT [Twitter for iPhone]

Jan 20, 2019 03:19:42 PM RT @charliekirk11: Breaking: A new NPR/PBS NewsHour/Marist poll shows Hispanic-Latino approval of President Donald Trump's job performance… [Twitter for iPhone]

Jan 20, 2019 03:20:19 PM RT @GOPChairwoman: Spot on. https://t.co/DnD5JlkdFb [Twitter for iPhone]

Jan 20, 2019 03:21:45 PM RT @GOP: "I commend the President for his leadership in proposing this bold solution to reopen the government, secure the border, and take… [Twitter for iPhone]

Jan 20, 2019 03:22:00 PM RT @GOPLeader: President Trump has put forward a serious and reasonable offer to reform parts of our broken immigration system and reopen g… [Twitter for iPhone]

Jan 20, 2019 03:22:33 PM RT @marklevinshow: I strongly support President Trump's immigration proposal today. Pelosi & Schumer rejected it even before the president… [Twitter for iPhone]

Jan 20, 2019 03:31:08 PM RT @sendavidperdue: President Trump again spoke directly to the American people about the national security crisis at our southern border.… [Twitter for iPhone]

Jan 20, 2019 03:31:25 PM RT @SenatorWicker: I support President @realDonaldTrump's plan. I will absolutely vote for this proposal when @senatemajldr brings up the b… [Twitter for iPhone]

Jan 20, 2019 03:31:36 PM RT @LindseyGrahamSC: A fantastic proposal Mr. President! Let's get it done! https://t.co/m8bzYGRLTw [Twitter for iPhone]

Jan 20, 2019 03:31:55 PM RT @VP: Today @POTUS proposed a common sense plan to secure our border, reopen our government, and KEEP AMERICANS SAFE. Now it's time for C… [Twitter for iPhone]

Jan 20, 2019 03:32:11 PM RT @senrobportman: .@POTUS has laid out a constructive new proposal that contains the basis for a bipartisan agreement. It includes many of… [Twitter for iPhone]

Jan 20, 2019 06:42:02 PM RT @SenThomTillis: My statement on the President's proposal to end the partial government #shutdown through a compromise on border security... [Twitter for iPhone]

Jan 20, 2019 06:42:27 PM RT @marcorubio: @POTUS offers to support 2 bills sponsored by Dems (TPS & DACA extensions)in exchange for Border Security (something Democr... [Twitter for iPhone]

Jan 20, 2019 06:42:41 PM RT @SenJohnThune: My statement on @POTUS's proposal to end the shutdown: https://t.co/VCO1vwzaC3 [Twitter for iPhone]

Jan 20, 2019 06:42:53 PM RT @RepMarkMeadows: This is the latest and most significant step yet of POTUS showing his willingness to negotiate and compromise with Demo... [Twitter for iPhone]

Jan 20, 2019 07:33:14 PM RT @JimInhofe: It is true and I'm glad to stand with you on this @realDonaldTrump. The Democrats need to come to the table so we can secure... [Twitter for iPhone]

Jan 20, 2019 07:33:45 PM RT @SenatorLankford: The President offered a reasonable compromise today to reopen the remainder of the government, and I look forward to c... [Twitter for iPhone]

Jan 20, 2019 07:35:02 PM RT @JerryMoran: This proposal, which incorporates provisions similar to legislation I introduced earlier this month with @SenRobPortman, in... [Twitter for iPhone]

Jan 20, 2019 07:35:32 PM RT @SenJohnHoeven: The president outlined a compromise proposal to strengthen border security & end the partial government shutdown. Read m... [Twitter for iPhone]

Jan 20, 2019 07:37:50 PM Will do a fantastic job! https://t.co/YkcenJhzsK [Twitter for iPhone]

Jan 20, 2019 07:39:09 PM RT @BudgetGOP: TODAY - @SenatorEnzi Welcomed new @BudgetGOP members @SenatorBraun, @SenRickScott and @SenKevinCramer https://t.co/yL31HsHXm... [Twitter for iPhone]

Jan 20, 2019 07:40:00 PM RT @GOPChairwoman: So many accomplishments from @realDonaldTrump and his administration over the past two years! https://t.co/GL1QplJhoI [Twitter for iPhone]

Jan 20, 2019 07:48:09 PM Thanks James! https://t.co/iTdCEEiiRv [Twitter for iPhone]

Jan 20, 2019 07:50:08 PM A truly great First Lady who doesn't get the credit she deserves! https://t.co/Wc9bYtoLKq [Twitter for iPhone]

Jan 20, 2019 07:51:44 PM RT @VP: Honored to serve as @POTUS Trump's Vice President these past two years, working to deliver historic results for the American people... [Twitter for iPhone]

Jan 20, 2019 07:51:57 PM RT @WhiteHouse: The historic results of President Donald J. Trump's first two years in office: https://t.co/xznAzXbrq3 [Twitter for iPhone]

Jan 20, 2019 08:25:06 PM To all of the great people who are working so hard for your Country and not getting paid I say, THANK YOU - YOU ARE GREAT PATRIOTS! We must now work together, after decades of abuse, to finally fix the Humanitarian, Criminal & Drug Crisis at our Border. WE WILL WIN BIG! [Twitter for iPhone]

Jan 20, 2019 10:43:06 PM Congratulations to Bob Kraft, Bill Belichick, Tom Brady and the entire New England Patriots team on a great game and season. Will be a fantastic Super Bowl! [Twitter for iPhone]

Jan 20, 2019 10:54:27 PM RT @DonaldJTrumpJr: Maybe the left will one day stop trying desperately to destroy my family and especially @realDonaldTrump. Till then the... [Twitter for iPhone]

Jan 20, 2019 11:08:13 PM Curt Schilling deserves to be in the Baseball Hall of Fame. Great record, especially when under pressure and when it mattered most. Do what everyone in Baseball knows is right! @marklevinshow [Twitter for iPhone]

Jan 21, 2019 12:03:01 AM "No President in modern times has kept more promises than Donald Trump!" Thank you Bill Bennett @SteveHiltonx [Twitter for iPhone]

Jan 21, 2019 10:22:36 AM Last year was the best year for American Manufacturing job growth since 1997, or 21 years. The previous administration said manufacturing will not come back to the U.S., "you would need a magic wand." I guess I found the MAGIC WAND - and it is only getting better! [Twitter for iPhone]

Jan 21, 2019 10:39:09 AM Today we celebrate Dr. Martin Luther King, Jr. for standing up for the self-evident truth Americans hold so dear, that no matter what the color of our skin or the place of our birth, we are all created equal by God. #MLKDay https://t.co/pEaVpCB8M4 [Twitter for iPhone]

Jan 21, 2019 10:40:50 AM Democrats campaigned on working within Washington and "getting things done!" How is that working out? #2020TAKEBACKTHEHOUSE [Twitter for iPhone]

Jan 21, 2019 10:41:23 AM RT @realDonaldTrump: To all of the great people who are working so hard for your Country and not getting paid I say, THANK YOU - YOU ARE GR... [Twitter for iPhone]

Jan 21, 2019 12:46:05 PM Today, it was my great honor to visit the Martin Luther King Jr. Memorial with @VP Mike Pence, in honor of #MLKDay https://t.co/YsDEA3kygd [Twitter for iPhone]

Jan 21, 2019 04:57:59 PM China posts slowest economic numbers since 1990 due to U.S. trade tensions and new policies. Makes so much sense for China to finally do a Real Deal, and stop playing around! [Twitter for iPhone]

Jan 21, 2019 05:08:55 PM If Nancy Pelosi thinks that Walls are "immoral," why isn't she requesting that we take down all of the existing Walls between the U.S. and Mexico, even the new ones just built in San Diego at their very strong urging. Let millions of unchecked "strangers" just flow into the U.S. [Twitter for iPhone]

Jan 21, 2019 06:37:28 PM Four people in Nevada viciously robbed and killed by an illegal immigrant who should not have been in our Country. 26 people killed on the Border in a drug and gang related fight. Two large Caravans from Honduras broke into Mexico and are headed our way. We need a powerful Wall! [Twitter for iPhone]

Jan 21, 2019 06:45:02 PM Democrats are kidding themselves (they don't really believe it!) if they say you can stop Crime, Drugs, Human Trafficking and Caravans without a Wall or Steel Barrier. Stop playing games and give America the Security it deserves. A Humanitarian Crisis! [Twitter for iPhone]

Jan 21, 2019 09:46:23 PM Looking like Nick Sandman & Covington Catholic students were treated unfairly with early judgements proving out to be false - smeared by media. Not good, but making big comeback! "New footage shows that media was wrong about teen's encounter with Native American" @TuckerCarlson [Twitter for iPhone]

Jan 21, 2019 11:43:14 PM RT @KayaJones: I want to show other celebrities who voted for @realDonaldTrump it's ok to come forward. Better yet let's show the world how… [Twitter for iPhone]

Jan 22, 2019 07:32:19 AM Nick Sandmann and the students of Covington have become symbols of Fake News and how evil it can be. They have captivated the attention of the world, and I know they will use it for the good - maybe even to bring people together. It started off unpleasant, but can end in a dream! [Twitter for iPhone]

Jan 22, 2019 07:35:46 AM "The Democrats are playing politics with Border Security." @foxandfriends [Twitter for iPhone]

Jan 22, 2019 07:48:22 AM Without a Wall our Country can never have Border or National Security. With a powerful Wall or Steel Barrier, Crime Rates (and Drugs) will go substantially down all over the U.S. The Dems know this but want to play political games. Must finally be done correctly. No Cave! [Twitter for iPhone]

Jan 22, 2019 08:15:09 AM FBI top lawyer confirms "unusual steps." They relied on the Clinton Campaign's Fake & Unverified "Dossier," which is illegal. "That has corrupted them. That has enabled them to gather evidence by UNCONSTITUTIONAL MEANS, and that's what they did to the President." Judge Napolitano [Twitter for iPhone]

Jan 22, 2019 08:25:03 AM Marist/NPR/PBS Poll shows President Trump's approval rating among Latinos going to 50%, an increase in one year of 19%. Thank you, working hard! [Twitter for iPhone]

Jan 22, 2019 09:48:46 AM Never seen @senatemajldr and Republicans so united on an issue as they are on the Humanitarian Crisis & Security on our Southern Border. If we create a Wall or Barrier which prevents Criminals and Drugs from flowing into our Country, Crime will go down by record numbers! [Twitter for iPhone]

Jan 22, 2019 10:00:04 AM Last time I went to Davos, the Fake News said I should not go there. This year, because of the Shutdown, I decided not to go, and the Fake News said I should be there. The fact is that the people understand the media better than the media understands them! [Twitter for iPhone]

Jan 22, 2019 10:01:11 AM The United States has a great economic story to tell. Number one in the World, by far! [Twitter for iPhone]

Jan 22, 2019 10:28:57 AM The reason Sarah Sanders does not go to the "podium" much anymore is that the press covers her so rudely & inaccurately, in particular certain members of the press. I told her not to bother, the word gets out anyway! Most will never cover us fairly & hence, the term, Fake News! [Twitter for iPhone]

Jan 22, 2019 10:53:58 AM Former FBI top lawyer James Baker just admitted involvement in FISA Warrant and further admitted there were IRREGULARITIES in the way the Russia probe was handled. They relied heavily on the unverified Trump "Dossier" paid for by the DNC & Clinton Campaign, & funded through a... [Twitter for iPhone]

Jan 22, 2019 11:06:31 AM ...big Crooked Hillary law firm, represented by her lawyer Michael Sussmann (do you believe this?) who worked Baker hard & gave him Oppo Research for "a Russia probe." This meeting, now exposed, is the subject of Senate inquiries and much more. An Unconstitutional Hoax. @FoxNews [Twitter for iPhone]

Jan 22, 2019 07:19:47 PM Congratulations to Mariano Rivera on unanimously being elected to the National Baseball Hall of Fame! Not only a great player but a great person. I am thankful for Mariano's support of the Opioid Drug Abuse Commission and @FitnessGov. #EnterSandman #HOF2019💯 https://t.co/reU1gKWHSQ [Twitter for iPhone]

Jan 22, 2019 09:00:56 PM Deroy Murdock, National Review: "We are now exporting oil, which is the first time in my lifetime - we are right now the largest producer of oil and gas. This is not good if you're Vladimir Putin where your chief export is oil. W.H. Agent - Not good for Kremlin." @TuckerCarlson [Twitter for iPhone]

Jan 23, 2019 07:48:55 AM Great unity in the Republican Party. Want to, once and for all, put an end to stoppable crime and drugs! Border Security and Wall. No doubt! [Twitter for iPhone]

Jan 23, 2019 07:57:29 AM BUILD A WALL & CRIME WILL FALL! This is the new theme, for two years until the Wall is finished (under construction now), of the Republican Party. Use it and pray! [Twitter for iPhone]

Jan 23, 2019 07:59:50 AM BUILD A WALL & CRIME WILL FALL! [Twitter for iPhone]

Jan 23, 2019 01:47:53 PM The citizens of Venezuela have suffered for too long at the hands of the illegitimate Maduro regime. Today, I have officially recognized the President of the Venezuelan National Assembly, Juan Guaido, as the Interim President of Venezuela. https://t.co/WItWPiG9jK [Twitter for iPhone]

Jan 23, 2019 02:00:06 PM Even Trump Haters like (MS)NBC acknowledge you "BUILD A WALL & CRIME WILL FALL!" https://t.co/bKIgmHUW5P [Twitter for iPhone]

Jan 23, 2019 02:09:40 PM "The Historic Results of President Donald J. Trump's First Two Years in Office" https://t.co/AFnWWiLlCa [Twitter for iPhone]

Jan 23, 2019 11:12:07 PM As the Shutdown was going on, Nancy Pelosi asked me to give the State of the Union Address. I agreed. She then changed her mind because of the Shutdown, suggesting a later date. This is her prerogative - I will do the Address when the Shutdown is over. I am not looking for an.... [Twitter for iPhone]

Jan 23, 2019 11:18:30 PM ....alternative venue for the SOTU Address because there is no venue that can compete with the history, tradition and importance of the House Chamber. I look forward to giving a "great" State of the Union Address in the near future! [Twitter for iPhone]

Jan 24, 2019 06:35:48 AM A great new book just out, "Game of Thorns," by Doug Wead, Presidential Historian and best selling author. The book covers the campaign of 2016, and what could be more exciting than that? [Twitter for iPhone]

Jan 24, 2019 06:51:52 AM "This is everything FDR dreamed about, the New Deal to put America back to work. Think of LBJ, he gave people food stamps & welfare. Donald Trump's giving them a job. He's got a lot of good things to talk about. News stories do not accurately cover him, should correct." @DougWead [Twitter for iPhone]

Jan 24, 2019 06:56:31 AM The economy is doing great. More people working in U.S.A. today than at any time in our HISTORY. Media barely covers! @foxandfriends [Twitter for iPhone]

Jan 24, 2019 07:48:32 AM So interesting that bad lawyer Michael Cohen, who sadly will not be testifying before Congress, is using the lawyer of Crooked Hillary Clinton to represent him - Gee, how did that happen? Remember July 4th weekend when Crooked went before FBI & wasn't sworn in, no tape, nothing? [Twitter for iPhone]

Jan 24, 2019 08:21:59 AM The Fake News Media loves saying "so little happened at my first summit with Kim Jong Un." Wrong! After 40 years of doing nothing with North Korea but being taken to the cleaners, & with a major war ready to start, in a short 15 months, relationships built, hostages & remains.... [Twitter for iPhone]

Jan 24, 2019 08:34:26 AM ...back home where they belong, no more Rockets or M's being fired over Japan or anywhere else and, most importantly, no Nuclear Testing. This is more than has ever been accomplished with North Korea, and the Fake News knows it. I expect another good meeting soon, much potential! [Twitter for iPhone]

Jan 24, 2019 08:37:59 AM Without a Wall there cannot be safety and security at the Border or for the U.S.A. BUILD THE WALL AND CRIME WILL FALL! [Twitter for iPhone]

Jan 24, 2019 11:16:03 AM Nancy just said she "just doesn't understand why?" Very simply, without a Wall it all doesn't work. Our Country has a chance to greatly reduce Crime, Human Trafficking, Gangs and Drugs. Should have been done for decades. We will not Cave! [Twitter for iPhone]

Jan 24, 2019 10:09:39 PM Great earnings coming out of Stock Market. Too bad Media doesn't devote much time to this! [Twitter for iPhone]

Jan 24, 2019 10:28:25 PM A third rate conman who interviewed me many years ago for just a short period of time has been playing his biggest con of all on Fake News CNN. Michael D'Antonio, a broken down hack who knows nothing about me, goes on night after night telling made up Trump stories. Disgraceful! [Twitter for iPhone]

Jan 25, 2019 11:16:09 AM Greatest Witch Hunt in the History of our Country! NO COLLUSION! Border Coyotes, Drug Dealers and Human Traffickers are treated better. Who alerted CNN to be there? [Twitter for iPhone]

Jan 25, 2019 02:39:28 PM https://t.co/RUFlgMxOUq [Twitter for iPhone]

Jan 25, 2019 07:33:50 PM I wish people would read or listen to my words on the Border Wall. This was in no way a concession. It was taking care of millions of people who were getting badly hurt by the Shutdown with the understanding that in 21 days, if no deal is done, it's off to the races! [Twitter for iPhone]

Jan 26, 2019 08:42:28 AM If Roger Stone was indicted for lying to Congress, what about the lying done by Comey, Brennan, Clapper, Lisa Page & lover, Baker and soooo many others? What about Hillary to FBI and her 33,000 deleted Emails? What about Lisa & Peter's deleted texts & Wiener's laptop? Much more! [Twitter for iPhone]

Jan 26, 2019 08:52:30 AM "I like the fact that the President is making the case (Border Security & Crime) to the American people. Now we know where Nancy Pelosi, Chuck Schumer & the Democrats stand, which is no Border Security. Will be big 2020 issue." Matt Schlapp, Chair, ACU. Bigger than anyone knows! [Twitter for iPhone]

Jan 26, 2019 09:01:48 AM 21 days goes very quickly. Negotiations with Democrats will start immediately. Will not be easy to make a deal, both parties very dug in. The case for National Security has been greatly enhanced by what has been happening at the Border & through dialogue. We will build the Wall! [Twitter for iPhone]

Jan 26, 2019 09:06:39 AM We have turned away, at great expense, two major Caravans, but a big one has now formed and is coming. At least 8000 people! If we had a powerful Wall, they wouldn't even try to make the long and dangerous journey. Build the Wall and Crime will Fall! [Twitter for iPhone]

Jan 26, 2019 09:23:29 AM Thank you to the Republican National Committee, (the RNC), who voted UNANIMOUSLY yesterday to support me in the upcoming 2020 Election. Considering that we have done more than any Administration in the first two years, this should be easy. More great things now in the works! [Twitter for iPhone]

Jan 26, 2019 09:32:46 AM "We absolutely need a physical barrier or Wall, whatever you want to call it. The President yesterday laid all that out. We need to do it all, including the Wall. I provided the same information to the previous administration, & it was ignored." Mark Morgan, Border Chief for "O"! [Twitter for iPhone]

Jan 26, 2019 11:42:32 AM BUILD A WALL & CRIME WILL FALL! https://t.co/a0G7GWi74k [Twitter for iPhone]

Jan 26, 2019 03:52:38 PM Only fools, or people with a political agenda, don't want a Wall or Steel Barrier to protect our Country from Crime, Drugs and Human Trafficking. It will happen - it always does! [Twitter for iPhone]

Jan 26, 2019 04:37:07 PM "Ax falls quickly at BuzzFeed and Huffpost!" Headline, New York Post. Fake News and bad journalism have caused a big downturn. Sadly, many others will follow. The people want the Truth! [Twitter for iPhone]

Jan 26, 2019 08:39:07 PM CBS reports that in the Roger Stone indictment, data was "released during the 2016 Election to damage Hillary Clinton." Oh really! What about the Fake and Unverified "Dossier," a total phony conjob, that was paid for by Crooked Hillary to damage me and the Trump Campaign? What... [Twitter for iPhone]

⌨ Jan 26, 2019 08:49:53 PM ....about all of the one sided Fake Media coverage (collusion with Crooked H?) that I had to endure during my very successful presidential campaign. What about the now revealed bias by Facebook and many others. Roger Stone didn't even work for me anywhere near the Election! [Twitter for iPhone]

⌨ Jan 26, 2019 08:51:57 PM WITCH HUNT! [Twitter for iPhone]

⌨ Jan 27, 2019 08:22:19 AM 58,000 non-citizens voted in Texas, with 95,000 non-citizens registered to vote. These numbers are just the tip of the iceberg. All over the country, especially in California, voter fraud is rampant. Must be stopped. Strong voter ID! @foxandfriends [Twitter for iPhone]

⌨ Jan 27, 2019 08:44:39 AM We are not even into February and the cost of illegal immigration so far this year is $18,959,495,168. Cost Friday was $603,331,392. There are at least 25,772,342 illegal aliens, not the 11,000,000 that have been reported for years, in our Country. So ridiculous! DHS [Twitter for iPhone]

⌨ Jan 27, 2019 10:11:55 AM Jens Stoltenberg, NATO Secretary General, just stated that because of me NATO has been able to raise far more money than ever before from its members after many years of decline. It's called burden sharing. Also, more united. Dems & Fake News like to portray the opposite! [Twitter for iPhone]

⌨ Jan 27, 2019 10:20:27 AM RT @ChatByCC: Strong people stand up for themselves—but stronger people stand up for others. Thank you President @realDonaldTrump for stan… [Twitter for iPhone]

⌨ Jan 27, 2019 10:27:29 AM Thank you to Brit. This is a very big deal in Europe. Fake News is the Enemy of the People! https://t.co/WX0o8gaiMC [Twitter for iPhone]

⌨ Jan 27, 2019 10:28:22 AM RT @KenPaxtonTX: VOTER FRAUD ALERT: The @TXsecofstate discovered approx 95,000 individuals identified by DPS as non-U.S. citizens have a ma… [Twitter for iPhone]

⌨ Jan 27, 2019 10:30:50 AM RT @GOP: "300 people are dying from heroin overdoses a week in this country, 90% of it is coming over the southern border… We've got to sto… [Twitter for iPhone]

⌨ Jan 27, 2019 01:04:38 PM #HolocaustMemorialDay https://t.co/zBQjfUOdtj https://t.co/hgTBGoECUU [Twitter for iPhone]

⌨ Jan 27, 2019 01:22:55 PM BUILD A WALL & CRIME WILL FALL! https://t.co/yDdCG5DCxn [Twitter for iPhone]

⌨ Jan 27, 2019 07:58:41 PM Never thought I'd say this but I think @johnrobertsFox and @JillianTurner @FoxNews have even less understanding of the Wall negotiations than the folks at FAKE NEWS CNN & NBC! Look to final results! Don't know how my poll numbers are so good, especially up 19% with Hispanics? [Twitter for iPhone]

Jan 27, 2019 08:08:09 PM Never thought I'd say this but I think @johnrobertsFox and @GillianHTurner @FoxNews have even less understanding of the Wall negotiations than the folks at FAKE NEWS CNN & NBC! Look to final results! Don't know how my poll numbers are so good, especially up 19% with Hispanics? [Twitter for iPhone]

Jan 27, 2019 08:09:49 PM After all that I have done for the Military, our great Veterans, Judges (99), Justices (2), Tax & Regulation Cuts, the Economy, Energy, Trade & MUCH MORE, does anybody really think I won't build the WALL? Done more in first two years than any President! MAKE AMERICA GREAT AGAIN! [Twitter for iPhone]

Jan 28, 2019 08:16:32 AM Tariffs on the "dumping" of Steel in the United States have totally revived our Steel Industry. New and expanded plants are happening all over the U.S. We have not only saved this important industry, but created many jobs. Also, billions paid to our treasury. A BIG WIN FOR U.S. [Twitter for iPhone]

Jan 28, 2019 08:21:15 AM Numerous states introducing Bible Literacy classes, giving students the option of studying the Bible. Starting to make a turn back? Great! [Twitter for iPhone]

Jan 28, 2019 08:41:52 AM Howard Schultz doesn't have the "guts" to run for President! Watched him on @60Minutes last night and I agree with him that he is not the "smartest person." Besides, America already has that! I only hope that Starbucks is still paying me their rent in Trump Tower! [Twitter for iPhone]

Jan 28, 2019 08:50:11 AM "In the Media's effort to destroy the President, they are actually destroying themselves. Given all of the tremendous headwinds this President has faced, it's amazing he has accomplished so much." DEROY MURDOCK @foxandfriends I agree! [Twitter for iPhone]

Jan 28, 2019 09:28:49 PM In the beautiful Midwest, windchill temperatures are reaching minus 60 degrees, the coldest ever recorded. In coming days, expected to get even colder. People can't last outside even for minutes. What the hell is going on with Global Waming? Please come back fast, we need you! [Twitter for iPhone]

Jan 28, 2019 09:46:02 PM How does Da Nang Dick (Blumenthal) serve on the Senate Judiciary Committee when he defrauded the American people about his so called War Hero status in Vietnam, only to later admit, with tears pouring down his face, that he was never in Vietnam. An embarrassment to our Country! [Twitter for iPhone]

Jan 29, 2019 08:45:55 AM A low level staffer that I hardly knew named Cliff Sims wrote yet another boring book based on made up stories and fiction. He pretended to be an insider when in fact he was nothing more than a gofer. He signed a non-disclosure agreement. He is a mess! [Twitter for iPhone]

Jan 29, 2019 11:00:56 PM "Our economy, right now, is the Gold Standard throughout the World." @IngrahamAngle So true, and not even close! [Twitter for iPhone]

Jan 30, 2019 06:02:54 AM Maduro willing to negotiate with opposition in Venezuela following U.S. sanctions and the cutting off of oil revenues. Guaido is being targeted by Venezuelan Supreme Court. Massive protest expected today. Americans should not travel to Venezuela until further notice. [Twitter for iPhone]

Jan 30, 2019 06:25:02 AM When I became President, ISIS was out of control in Syria & running rampant. Since then tremendous progress made, especially over last 5 weeks. Caliphate will soon be destroyed, unthinkable two years ago. Negotiating are proceeding well in Afghanistan after 18 years of fighting.. [Twitter for iPhone]

Jan 30, 2019 06:34:31 AM ....Fighting continues but the people of Afghanistan want peace in this never ending war. We will soon see if talks will be successful? North Korea relationship is best it has ever been with U.S. No testing, getting remains, hostages returned. Decent chance of Denuclearization... [Twitter for iPhone]

Jan 30, 2019 06:40:11 AM ...Time will tell what will happen with North Korea, but at the end of the previous administration, relationship was horrendous and very bad things were about to happen. Now a whole different story. I look forward to seeing Kim Jong Un shortly. Progress being made-big difference! [Twitter for iPhone]

Jan 30, 2019 06:49:26 AM If the committee of Republicans and Democrats now meeting on Border Security is not discussing or contemplating a Wall or Physical Barrier, they are Wasting their time! [Twitter for iPhone]

Jan 30, 2019 06:54:21 AM "Three separate caravans marching to our Border. The numbers are tremendous." @foxandfriends [Twitter for iPhone]

Jan 30, 2019 08:50:55 AM The Intelligence people seem to be extremely passive and naive when it comes to the dangers of Iran. They are wrong! When I became President Iran was making trouble all over the Middle East, and beyond. Since ending the terrible Iran Nuclear Deal, they are MUCH different, but.... [Twitter for iPhone]

Jan 30, 2019 08:56:00 AM ....a source of potential danger and conflict. They are testing Rockets (last week) and more, and are coming very close to the edge. There economy is now crashing, which is the only thing holding them back. Be careful of Iran. Perhaps Intelligence should go back to school! [Twitter for iPhone]

Jan 30, 2019 04:54:12 PM Dow just broke 25,000. Tremendous news! [Twitter for iPhone]

Jan 30, 2019 04:58:38 PM ....Large protests all across Venezuela today against Maduro. The fight for freedom has begun! [Twitter for iPhone]

Jan 30, 2019 04:58:38 PM Spoke today with Venezuelan Interim President Juan Guaido to congratulate him on his historic assumption of the presidency and reinforced strong United States support for Venezuela's fight to regain its democracy.... [Twitter for iPhone]

Jan 31, 2019 07:04:57 AM So great to watch & listen to all these people who write books & talk about my presidential campaign and so many others things related to winning, and how I should be doing "IT." As I take it all in, I then sit back, look around, & say "gee, I'm in the White House, & they're not! [Twitter for iPhone]

Jan 31, 2019 07:13:17 AM Large sections of WALL have already been built with much more either under construction or ready to go. Renovation of existing WALLS is also a very big part of the plan to finally, after many decades, properly Secure Our Border. The Wall is getting done one way or the other! [Twitter for iPhone]

Jan 31, 2019 07:16:49 AM Lets just call them WALLS from now on and stop playing political games! A WALL is a WALL! [Twitter for iPhone]

Jan 31, 2019 07:25:58 AM Very sadly, Murder cases in Mexico in 2018 rose 33% from 2017, to 33,341. This is a big contributor to the Humanitarian Crises taking place on our Southern Border and then spreading throughout our Country. Worse even than Afghanistan. Much caused by DRUGS. Wall is being built! [Twitter for iPhone]

Jan 31, 2019 07:32:16 AM With Murders up 33% in Mexico, a record, why wouldn't any sane person want to build a Wall! Construction has started and will not stop until it is finished. @LouDobbs @foxandfriends [Twitter for iPhone]

Jan 31, 2019 07:41:56 AM China's top trade negotiators are in the U.S. meeting with our representatives. Meetings are going well with good intent and spirit on both sides. China does not want an increase in Tariffs and feels they will do much better if they make a deal. They are correct. I will be...... [Twitter for iPhone]

Jan 31, 2019 07:48:13 AM ....meeting with their top leaders and representatives today in the Oval Office. No final deal will be made until my friend President Xi, and I, meet in the near future to discuss and agree on some of the long standing and more difficult points. Very comprehensive transaction.... [Twitter for iPhone]

Jan 31, 2019 07:56:36 AM ....China's representatives and I are trying to do a complete deal, leaving NOTHING unresolved on the table. All of the many problems are being discussed and will be hopefully resolved. Tariffs on China increase to 25% on March 1st, so all working hard to complete by that date! [Twitter for iPhone]

Jan 31, 2019 08:21:01 AM Republicans on the Homeland Security Committee are wasting their time. Democrats, despite all of the evidence, proof and Caravans coming, are not going to give money to build the DESPERATELY needed WALL. I've got you covered. Wall is already being built, I don't expect much help! [Twitter for iPhone]

Jan 31, 2019 08:36:29 AM Democrats are becoming the Party of late term abortion, high taxes, Open Borders and Crime! [Twitter for iPhone]

Jan 31, 2019 09:52:17 AM More troops being sent to the Southern Border to stop the attempted Invasion of Illegals, through large Caravans, into our Country. We have stopped the previous Caravans, and we will stop these also. With a Wall it would be soooo much easier and less expensive. Being Built! [Twitter for iPhone]

Jan 31, 2019 09:56:15 AM Looking for China to open their Markets not only to Financial Services, which they are now doing, but also to our Manufacturing, Farmers and other U.S. businesses and industries. Without this a deal would be unacceptable! [Twitter for iPhone]

Jan 31, 2019 10:08:03 AM Schumer and the Democrats are big fans of being weak and passive with Iran. They have no clue as to the danger they would be inflicting on our Country. Iran is in financial chaos now because of the sanctions and Iran Deal termination. Dems put us in a bad place - but now good! [Twitter for iPhone]

Jan 31, 2019 12:43:21 PM Very sadly, Murder cases in Mexico in 2018 rose 33% from 2017, to 33,341. This is a big contributor to the Humanitarian Crisis taking place on our Southern Border and then spreading throughout our Country. Worse even than Afghanistan. Much caused by DRUGS. Wall is being built! [Twitter for iPhone]

Jan 31, 2019 02:19:19 PM https://t.co/6wK5He4pk5 [Twitter for iPhone]

Jan 31, 2019 04:40:01 PM Just concluded a great meeting with my Intel team in the Oval Office who told me that what they said on Tuesday at the Senate Hearing was mischaracterized by the media - and we are very much in agreement on Iran, ISIS, North Korea, etc. Their testimony was distorted press.... https://t.co/Zl5aqBmpjF [Twitter for iPhone]

Jan 31, 2019 04:40:02 PM ....I would suggest you read the COMPLETE testimony from Tuesday. A false narrative is so bad for our Country. I value our intelligence community. Happily, we had a very good meeting, and we are all on the same page! [Twitter for iPhone]

Jan 31, 2019 07:14:37 PM Our great U.S. Border Patrol Agents made the biggest Fentanyl bust in our Country's history. Thanks, as always, for a job well done! [Twitter for iPhone]

Jan 31, 2019 10:03:56 PM Just out: The big deal, very mysterious Don jr telephone calls, after the innocent Trump Tower meeting, that the media & Dems said were made to his father (me), were just conclusively found NOT to be made to me. They were made to friends & business associates of Don. Really sad! [Twitter for iPhone]

Jan 31, 2019 10:16:58 PM Nellie Ohr, the wife of DOJ official Bruce Ohr, was long ago investigating for pay (GPS Fusion) members of my family, feeding it to her husband who was then giving it to the FBI, even though it was created by ousted & discredited Christopher Steele. Illegal! WITCH HUNT [Twitter for iPhone]

Jan 31, 2019 11:26:43 PM This Witch Hunt must end! https://t.co/3og7H4uUw2 [Twitter for iPhone]

Feb 1, 2019 08:23:07 AM I inherited a total mess in Syria and Afghanistan, the "Endless Wars" of unlimited spending and death. During my campaign I said, very strongly, that these wars must finally end. We spend $50 Billion a year in Afghanistan and have hit them so hard that we are now talking peace... [Twitter for iPhone]

Feb 1, 2019 08:35:16 AM ....after 18 long years. Syria was loaded with ISIS until I came along. We will soon have destroyed 100% of the Caliphate, but will be watching them closely. It is now time to start coming home and, after many years, spending our money wisely. Certain people must get smart! [Twitter for iPhone]

Feb 1, 2019 09:16:32 AM Best January for the DOW in over 30 years. We have, by far, the strongest economy in the world! [Twitter for iPhone]

Feb 1, 2019 10:48:06 AM JOBS, JOBS, JOBS! https://t.co/29dViqkEV7 [Twitter for iPhone]

Feb 1, 2019 01:44:08 PM Great news on Foxconn in Wisconsin after my conversation with Terry Gou! https://t.co/2wtuCdl7TX [Twitter for iPhone]

Feb 1, 2019 02:19:52 PM RT @WhiteHouse: "We added 304,000 jobs, which was a shocker to a lot of people. It wasn't a shocker to me." https://t.co/hHzogMtXG5 [Twitter for iPhone]

Feb 1, 2019 02:25:21 PM Thank you to Senator Rob Portman and Senator Cory Gardner for the early and warm endorsement. We will ALL WIN in 2020 together! [Twitter for iPhone]

Feb 1, 2019 03:07:50 PM National African American History Month is an occasion to rediscover the enduring stories of African Americans and the gifts of freedom, purpose, and opportunity they have bestowed on future generations...https://t.co/n9kf58NruZ [Twitter for iPhone]

Feb 2, 2019 01:10:12 PM Great morning at Trump National Golf Club in Jupiter, Florida with @JackNicklaus and @TigerWoods! https://t.co/mdPN4yvS8e [Twitter for iPhone]

Feb 2, 2019 07:39:31 PM Democrat Governor Ralph Northam of Virginia just stated, "I believe that I am not either of the people in that photo." This was 24 hours after apologizing for appearing in the picture and after making the most horrible statement on "super" late term abortion. Unforgivable! [Twitter for iPhone]

Feb 2, 2019 08:01:12 PM Ed Gillespie, who ran for Governor of the Great State of Virginia against Ralph Northam, must now be thinking Malpractice and Dereliction of Duty with regard to his Opposition Research Staff. If they find that terrible picture before the election, he wins by 20 points! [Twitter for iPhone]

Feb 2, 2019 11:37:02 PM I will be interviewed Sunday morning on @FaceTheNation and prior to the Super Bowl on @CBS at 3:30 P.M. Enjoy! [Twitter for iPhone]

Feb 3, 2019 04:14:39 PM Everyone is asking how Tiger played yesterday. The answer is Great! He was long, straight & putted fantastically well. He shot a 64. Tiger is back & will be winning Majors again! Not surprisingly, Jack also played really well. His putting is amazing! Jack & Tiger like each other. [Twitter for iPhone]

Feb 3, 2019 04:59:03 PM With Caravans marching through Mexico and toward our Country, Republicans must be prepared to do whatever is necessary for STRONG Border Security. Dems do nothing. If there is no Wall, there is no Security. Human Trafficking, Drugs and Criminals of all dimensionns - KEEP OUT! [Twitter for iPhone]

Feb 3, 2019 05:03:11 PM With Caravans marching through Mexico and toward our Country, Republicans must be prepared to do whatever is necessary for STRONG Border Security. Dems do nothing. If there is no Wall, there is no Security. Human Trafficking, Drugs and Criminals of all dimensions - KEEP OUT! [Twitter for iPhone]

Feb 4, 2019 03:13:35 PM I am pleased to announce that David Bernhardt, Acting Secretary of the Interior, will be nominated as Secretary of the Interior. David has done a fantastic job from the day he arrived, and we look forward to having his nomination officially confirmed! [Twitter for iPhone]

Feb 5, 2019 09:10:03 AM Tremendous numbers of people are coming up through Mexico in the hopes of flooding our Southern Border. We have sent additional military. We will build a Human Wall if necessary. If we had a real Wall, this would be a non-event! [Twitter for iPhone]

Feb 5, 2019 10:29:52 AM I see Schumer is already criticizing my State of the Union speech, even though he hasn't seen it yet. He's just upset that he didn't win the Senate, after spending a fortune, like he thought he would. Too bad we weren't given more credit for the Senate win by the media! [Twitter for iPhone]

⊔ Feb 5, 2019 12:08:34 PM Melania and I send our greetings to those celebrating the Lunar New Year. Today, people across the United States and around the world mark the beginning of the Lunar New Year with spectacular fireworks displays, joyful festivals, and family gatherings...https://t.co/yM6qZng5m0 [Twitter for iPhone]

⊔ Feb 5, 2019 04:41:35 PM Looking forward to tonight! #SOTU https://t.co/lGKkZeaxUZ [Twitter for iPhone]

⊔ Feb 5, 2019 10:40:40 PM #SOTU https://t.co/kL6SoClx4K [Twitter for iPhone]

⊔ Feb 5, 2019 10:54:08 PM RT @realDonaldTrump: #SOTU https://t.co/kL6SoClx4K [Twitter for iPhone]

⊔ Feb 6, 2019 12:34:05 PM RT @realDonaldTrump: #SOTU https://t.co/kL6SoClx4K [Twitter for iPhone]

⊔ Feb 6, 2019 05:14:10 PM https://t.co/tUDYZrc6w0 [Twitter for iPhone]

⊔ Feb 7, 2019 06:13:34 AM So now Congressman Adam Schiff announces, after having found zero Russian Collusion, that he is going to be looking at every aspect of my life, both financial and personal, even though there is no reason to be doing so. Never happened before! Unlimited Presidential Harassment.... [Twitter for iPhone]

⊔ Feb 7, 2019 06:26:48 AM ....The Dems and their committees are going "nuts." The Republicans never did this to President Obama, there would be no time left to run government. I hear other committee heads will do the same thing. Even stealing people who work at White House! A continuation of Witch Hunt! [Twitter for iPhone]

⊔ Feb 7, 2019 07:35:05 AM Democrats at the top are killing the Great State of Virginia. If the three failing pols were Republicans, far stronger action would be taken. Virginia will come back HOME Republican) in 2020! [Twitter for iPhone]

⊔ Feb 7, 2019 07:37:55 AM PRESIDENTIAL HARASSMENT! It should never be allowed to happen again! [Twitter for iPhone]

⊔ Feb 7, 2019 10:20:15 AM 2019 National Prayer Breakfast https://t.co/cKvv3ygOOt [Twitter for iPhone]

⊔ Feb 7, 2019 06:43:37 PM Today, it was my great honor to sign a Presidential Memorandum launching the Women's Global Development and Prosperity Initiative. #WGDP Read more: https://t.co/qr3jevdayp https://t.co/HyIPPm4Q7b [Twitter for iPhone]

⊔ Feb 7, 2019 07:01:43 PM Each year, America pauses to remember its fallen astronaut heroes and the great accomplishments for which they strived. @FLOTUS Melania and I mourn their passing and take to heart the lessons of their lives and the greater human potential to which they continue to inspire. https://t.co/P9d1bpapsd [Twitter for iPhone]

⊔ Feb 7, 2019 07:02:51 PM So nice how well my State of the Union speech was received. Thank you to all! [Twitter for iPhone]

Feb 7, 2019 09:05:56 PM Highly respected Senator Richard Burr, Chairman of Senate Intelligence, said today that, after an almost two year investigation, he saw no evidence of Russia collusion. "We don't have anything that would suggest there was collusion by the Trump campaign and Russia." Thank you! [Twitter for iPhone]

Feb 8, 2019 07:23:29 AM Not only did Senator Burr's Committee find No Collusion by the Trump Campaign and Russia, it's important because they interviewed 200 witnesses and 300,000 pages of documents, & the Committee has direct access to intelligence information that's Classified. @GreggJarrett [Twitter for iPhone]

Feb 8, 2019 08:41:16 AM Now we find out that Adam Schiff was spending time together in Aspen with Glenn Simpson of GPS Fusion, who wrote the fake and discredited Dossier, even though Simpson was testifying before Schiff. John Solomon of @thehill [Twitter for iPhone]

Feb 8, 2019 08:48:08 AM The mainstream media has refused to cover the fact that the head of the VERY important Senate Intelligence Committee, after two years of intensive study and access to Intelligence that only they could get, just stated that they have found NO COLLUSION between "Trump" & Russia.... [Twitter for iPhone]

Feb 8, 2019 08:59:10 AM ...It is all a GIANT AND ILLEGAL HOAX, developed long before the election itself, but used as an excuse by the Democrats as to why Crooked Hillary Clinton lost the Election! Someday the Fake News Media will turn honest & report that Donald J. Trump was actually a GREAT Candidate! [Twitter for iPhone]

Feb 8, 2019 03:10:15 PM Working hard, thank you! https://t.co/tnuHnw8kll [Twitter for iPhone]

Feb 8, 2019 03:13:06 PM Deepest sympathies to Congresswoman Debbie Dingell and the entire family of John Dingell. Longest serving Congressman in Country's history which, if people understand politics, means he was very smart. A great reputation and highly respected man. [Twitter for iPhone]

Feb 8, 2019 03:15:20 PM I was a big fan of Frank Robinson, both as a great player and man. He was the first African American manager in baseball and was highly respected at everything he did. He will he missed! [Twitter for iPhone]

Feb 8, 2019 07:33:45 PM My representatives have just left North Korea after a very productive meeting and an agreed upon time and date for the second Summit with Kim Jong Un. It will take place in Hanoi, Vietnam, on February 27 & 28. I look forward to seeing Chairman Kim & advancing the cause of peace! [Twitter for iPhone]

Feb 8, 2019 07:50:38 PM North Korea, under the leadership of Kim Jong Un, will become a great Economic Powerhouse. He may surprise some but he won't surprise me, because I have gotten to know him & fully understand how capable he is. North Korea will become a different kind of Rocket - an Economic one! [Twitter for iPhone]

Feb 9, 2019 08:56:24 AM It was great meeting some of our outstanding young military personnel who were wounded in both Syria and Afghanistan. Their wounds are deep but their spirit is sooo high. They will recoverer & be back very soon. America loves them. Walter Reed Hospital is AMAZING - Thank you all! [Twitter for iPhone]

Feb 9, 2019 09:30:36 AM The Democrats in Congress yesterday were vicious and totally showed their cards for everyone to see. When the Republicans had the Majority they never acted with such hatred and scorn! The Dems are trying to win an election in 2020 that they know they cannot legitimately win! [Twitter for iPhone]

Feb 9, 2019 09:36:06 AM We have a great economy DESPITE the Obama Administration and all of its job killing Regulations and Roadblocks. If that thinking prevailed in the 2016 Election, the U.S. would be in a Depression right now! We were heading down, and don't let the Democrats sound bites fool you! [Twitter for iPhone]

Feb 9, 2019 09:51:59 AM RT @seanhannity: TRUMP: "Not only did Senator Burr's Committee find No Collusion by the Trump Campaign and Russia, it's important because t… [Twitter for iPhone]

Feb 9, 2019 09:57:08 AM RT @seanhannity: https://t.co/rhKgdlJt8X [Twitter for iPhone]

Feb 9, 2019 09:57:57 AM RT @seanhannity: Adam Schiff, Glenn Simpson and their Forrest Gump-like encounter in Aspen https://t.co/j2lqrxflGH [Twitter for iPhone]

Feb 9, 2019 04:23:44 PM RT @Jim_Jordan: .@AdamSchiff: -Meets with Glenn Simpson, who hired Nellie Ohr and Chris Steele and paid for the Dossier -Doesn't disclose… [Twitter for iPhone]

Feb 9, 2019 04:28:12 PM RT @TomFitton: Inside @JudicialWatch: @RealDonaldTrump is first president in a generation to talk honestly about the border crisis. https:… [Twitter for iPhone]

Feb 9, 2019 04:34:15 PM RT @JudicialWatch: JW released State Dept docs showing the Clinton-linked Podesta Group run by Tony Podesta (the brother of John Podesta wh… [Twitter for iPhone]

Feb 9, 2019 04:39:09 PM RT @dbongino: The corrupt spying operation against Donald Trump's team is the biggest scandal in political history. Read my new book for th… [Twitter for iPhone]

Feb 9, 2019 04:44:42 PM RT @IngrahamAngle: The #IngrahamAngle goes to El Paso Monday, where I'll be interviewing @realDonaldTrump. Tune in! 10p ET @FoxNews [Twitter for iPhone]

⬜ Feb 9, 2019 05:02:33 PM The Democrats just don't seem to want Border Security. They are fighting Border Agents recommendations. If you believe news reports, they are not offering much for the Wall. They look to be making this a campaign issue. The Wall will get built one way or the other! [Twitter for iPhone]

⬜ Feb 9, 2019 05:54:05 PM Today Elizabeth Warren, sometimes referred to by me as Pocahontas, joined the race for President. Will she run as our first Native American presidential candidate, or has she decided that after 32 years, this is not playing so well anymore? See you on the campaign TRAIL, Liz! [Twitter for iPhone]

⬜ Feb 9, 2019 06:21:25 PM I think it is very important for the Democrats to press forward with their Green New Deal. It would be great for the so-called "Carbon Footprint" to permanently eliminate all Planes, Cars, Cows, Oil, Gas & the Military - even if no other country would do the same. Brilliant! [Twitter for iPhone]

⬜ Feb 10, 2019 07:41:34 AM Senator Richard Burr, The Chairman of the Senate Intelligence Committee, just announced that after almost two years, more than two hundred interviews, and thousands of documents, they have found NO COLLUSION BETWEEN TRUMP AND RUSSIA! Is anybody really surprised by this? [Twitter for iPhone]

⬜ Feb 10, 2019 09:53:58 AM African Americans are very angry at the double standard on full display in Virginia! [Twitter for iPhone]

⬜ Feb 10, 2019 10:24:57 AM Gallup Poll: "Open Borders will potentially attract 42 million Latin Americans." This would be a disaster for the U.S. We need the Wall now! [Twitter for iPhone]

⬜ Feb 10, 2019 11:17:21 AM I don't think the Dems on the Border Committee are being allowed by their leaders to make a deal. They are offering very little money for the desperately needed Border Wall & now, out of the blue, want a cap on convicted violent felons to be held in detention! [Twitter for iPhone]

⬜ Feb 10, 2019 11:24:40 AM It was a very bad week for the Democrats, with the GREAT economic numbers, The Virginia disaster and the State of the Union address. Now, with the terrible offers being made by them to the Border Committee, I actually believe they want a Shutdown. They want a new subject! [Twitter for iPhone]

⬜ Feb 10, 2019 01:27:03 PM The media was able to get my work schedule, something very easy to do, but it should have been reported as a positive, not negative. When the term Executive Time is used, I am generally working, not relaxing. In fact, I probably work more hours than almost any past President..... [Twitter for iPhone]

Feb 10, 2019 01:39:29 PM ....The fact is, when I took over as President, our Country was a mess. Depleted Military, Endless Wars, a potential War with North Korea, V.A., High Taxes & too many Regulations, Border, Immigration & HealthCare problems, & much more. I had no choice but to work very long hours! [Twitter for iPhone]

Feb 10, 2019 04:46:19 PM "President is on sound legal ground to declare a National Emergency. There have been 58 National Emergencies declared since the law was enacted in 1976, and 31 right now that are currently active, so this is hardly unprecedented." Congressman @tommcclintock [Twitter for iPhone]

Feb 10, 2019 04:54:00 PM The Border Committee Democrats are behaving, all of a sudden, irrationally. Not only are they unwilling to give dollars for the obviously needed Wall (they overrode recommendations of Border Patrol experts), but they don't even want to take muderers into custody! What's going on? [Twitter for iPhone]

Feb 10, 2019 05:04:48 PM Well, it happened again. Amy Klobuchar announced that she is running for President, talking proudly of fighting global warming while standing in a virtual blizzard of snow, ice and freezing temperatures. Bad timing. By the end of her speech she looked like a Snowman(woman)! [Twitter for iPhone]

Feb 10, 2019 05:10:06 PM RT @club4growth: Agreed! Senate needs to confirm @realDonaldTrump Admin appointees. #SOTU [Twitter for iPhone]

Feb 10, 2019 05:16:43 PM RT @club4growth: WE AGREE! The time is now! ☞ "The time has come to pass school choice for America's children." - @realDonaldTrump #SOTU [Twitter for iPhone]

Feb 10, 2019 05:28:30 PM The U.S. will soon control 100% of ISIS territory in Syria. @CNN (do you believe this?). [Twitter for iPhone]

Feb 10, 2019 05:38:12 PM RT @realDonaldTrump: Working hard, thank you! https://t.co/tnuHnw8kll [Twitter for iPhone]

Feb 11, 2019 07:41:49 AM "Fact checkers have become Fake News." @JesseBWatters So True! [Twitter for iPhone]

Feb 11, 2019 07:43:45 AM No president ever worked harder than me (cleaning up the mess I inherited)! [Twitter for iPhone]

Feb 11, 2019 08:18:57 AM The Democrats do not want us to detain, or send back, criminal aliens! This is a brand new demand. Crazy! [Twitter for iPhone]

Feb 11, 2019 09:19:08 AM The Democrats are so self righteous and ANGRY! Loosen up and have some fun. The Country is doing well! [Twitter for iPhone]

Feb 11, 2019 11:03:01 AM Will be heading to El Paso very soon. Big speech on Border Security and much else tonight. Tremendous crowd! See you later! [Twitter for iPhone]

Feb 11, 2019 02:33:18 PM https://t.co/LpR2JkYLcW [Twitter for iPhone]

Feb 11, 2019 02:58:03 PM 40 years of corruption. 40 years of repression. 40 years of terror. The regime in Iran has produced only #40YearsofFailure. The long-suffering Iranian people deserve a much brighter future. https://t.co/bA8YGsw9LA [Twitter for iPhone]

Feb 11, 2019 02:58:05 PM ۴۰ رژیم .تـ رور سال ۴۰ . سرکوب سال ۴۰ .فـ ساد سال رنـجـنـد در مدتـهـاست کـه ایـران مردم .اـست شده شـکـست_سال_چهل# موجب فـ قط ایـران تـه شایـ نده آیـ ری روشن تـ هسـ تـنـد https://t.co/nKMQCHQFCZ [Twitter for iPhone]

Feb 11, 2019 05:03:25 PM Coal is an important part of our electricity generation mix and @TVAnews should give serious consideration to all factors before voting to close viable power plants, like Paradise #3 in Kentucky! [Twitter for iPhone]

Feb 11, 2019 10:47:54 PM RT @DonaldJTrumpJr: Beto trying to counter-program @realdonaldtrump in his hometown and only drawing a few hundred people to Trump's 35,000... [Twitter for iPhone]

Feb 11, 2019 10:52:33 PM We are fighting for all Americans, from all backgrounds, of every age, race, religion, birthplace, color & creed. Our agenda is NOT a partisan agenda – it is the mainstream, common sense agenda of the American People. Thank you El Paso, Texas - I love you! https://t.co/4Lz4PUwKzV [Twitter for iPhone]

Feb 11, 2019 11:43:55 PM RT @DanScavino: 📹Happening Now: @realDonaldTrump overflow crowd in El Paso, Texas.... https://t.co/kqyDC66qRA [Twitter for iPhone]

Feb 11, 2019 11:45:41 PM RT @IngrahamAngle: It was 45 degrees outside and this was the overflow crowd. #ElPaso @realDonaldTrump https://t.co/FipvNxp8di [Twitter for iPhone]

Feb 12, 2019 11:35:52 AM Beautiful evening in El Paso, Texas last night. God Bless the USA! https://t.co/trqA75KxLN [Twitter for iPhone]

Feb 12, 2019 06:47:23 PM Was just presented the concept and parameters of the Border Security Deal by hard working Senator Richard Shelby. Looking over all aspects knowing that this will be hooked up with lots of money from other sources.... [Twitter for iPhone]

Feb 12, 2019 06:47:24 PM ....Will be getting almost $23 BILLION for Border Security. Regardless of Wall money, it is being built as we speak! [Twitter for iPhone]

Feb 12, 2019 06:52:28 PM Thank you to @MSNBC! https://t.co/VdRnirACAz [Twitter for iPhone]

Feb 12, 2019 09:47:16 PM RT @planetepics: They are soooo beautiful and magnificent! ❤☐❤☐❤☐❤☐ https://t.co/ISn5jo8CcD https://t.co/JcMpQUzIml [Twitter for iPhone]

Feb 12, 2019 09:53:27 PM RT @WhiteHouse: Americans pay 180 percent of what Europeans, Canadians, and Japanese pay for the exact same drugs! Our seniors aren't goin… [Twitter for iPhone]

Feb 12, 2019 09:54:10 PM RT @WhiteHouse: President Trump's commitment to improving the quality of life for all Americans has led to the largest single decline in dr… [Twitter for iPhone]

Feb 12, 2019 10:23:41 PM I want to thank all Republicans for the work you have done in dealing with the Radical Left on Border Security. Not an easy task, but the Wall is being built and will be a great achievement and contributor toward life and safety within our Country! [Twitter for iPhone]

Feb 12, 2019 10:25:44 PM RT @dbongino: I don't feel an ounce of empathy for all of the imbeciles who bought into the Russian collusion hoax now that it's been entir… [Twitter for iPhone]

Feb 13, 2019 05:58:03 AM The Senate Intelligence Committee: THERE IS NO EVIDENCE OF COLLUSION BETWEEN THE TRUMP CAMPAIGN AND RUSSIA! [Twitter for iPhone]

Feb 13, 2019 10:01:31 AM The Gallup Poll just announced that 69% of our great citizens expect their finances to improve next year, a 16 year high. Nice! [Twitter for iPhone]

Feb 13, 2019 03:51:14 PM Today, it was my great honor to address the @MjrCitiesChiefs Association and @MCSheriffs Conference in Washington, D.C. We will never forget your service, and we will never, ever let you down! We love you, and we thank God for you each and every day. https://t.co/9tuNcVcBqe [Twitter for iPhone]

Feb 13, 2019 05:52:11 PM RT @WhiteHouse: "Every American in every community and from every walk of life has a right to live in security and to live in peace. That i… [Twitter for iPhone]

Feb 13, 2019 07:24:33 PM https://t.co/ruL7Ctpdak [Twitter for iPhone]

Feb 13, 2019 07:41:14 PM https://t.co/BS162NF8HC [Twitter for iPhone]

Feb 13, 2019 07:55:37 PM RT @SenTedCruz: Report: Texas crude oil production breaks 1970s record https://t.co/RHpaMLX7G2 via @houstonchron [Twitter for iPhone]

Feb 13, 2019 08:29:43 PM California has been forced to cancel the massive bullet train project after having spent and wasted many billions of dollars. They owe the Federal Government three and a half billion dollars. We want that money back now. Whole project is a "green" disaster! [Twitter for iPhone]

Feb 14, 2019 09:39:50 AM Disgraced FBI Acting Director Andrew McCabe pretends to be a "poor little Angel" when in fact he was a big part of the Crooked Hillary Scandal & the Russia Hoax - a puppet for Leakin' James Comey. I.G. report on McCabe was devastating. Part of "insurance policy" in case I won.... [Twitter for iPhone]

Feb 14, 2019 09:55:09 AM ....Many of the top FBI brass were fired, forced to leave, or left. McCabe's wife received BIG DOLLARS from Clinton people for her campaign - he gave Hillary a pass. McCabe is a disgrace to the FBI and a disgrace to our Country. MAKE AMERICA GREAT AGAIN! [Twitter for iPhone]

Feb 14, 2019 12:21:51 PM funding bill [Twitter Web Client]

Feb 14, 2019 12:27:30 PM Reviewing the funding bill with my team at the @WhiteHouse! [Twitter for iPhone]

Feb 14, 2019 12:30:39 PM One year ago today, a horrific act of violence took the lives of 14 students and 3 educators in Parkland, Florida. On this somber anniversary, we honor their memory and recommit to ensuring the safety of all Americans, especially our Nation's children... https://t.co/MDnSX1BFeW https://t.co/EVAeSwA8oV [Twitter for iPhone]

Feb 14, 2019 09:58:26 PM "After The Flight 93 Election, The Vote That Saved America - And What We Still Have To Lose," by very talented Michael Anton, is a terrific read. Check it out! [Twitter for iPhone]

Feb 14, 2019 09:59:12 PM RT @WhiteHouse: .@PressSec: President Trump will sign the government funding bill, and as he has stated before, he will also take other exe… [Twitter for iPhone]

Feb 14, 2019 10:16:23 PM "Trying to use the 25th Amendment to try and circumvent the Election is a despicable act of unconstitutional power grabbing...which happens in third world countries. You have to obey the law. This is an attack on our system & Constitution." Alan Dershowitz. @TuckerCarlson [Twitter for iPhone]

Feb 15, 2019 10:37:40 AM RT @WhiteHouse: President Trump Speaks on the National Security & Humanitarian Crisis on Our Southern Border https://t.co/FqdfFORbv5 [Twitter for iPhone]

Feb 15, 2019 02:04:20 PM https://t.co/BliAo5YDqb [Twitter Media Studio]

Feb 15, 2019 06:11:15 PM Great job by law enforcement in Aurora, Illinois. Heartfelt condolences to all of the victims and their families. America is with you! [Twitter for iPhone]

Feb 16, 2019 11:43:32 AM https://t.co/f6Jd2FzayZ [Twitter for iPhone]

Feb 16, 2019 02:40:18 PM https://t.co/nJORBjwint [Twitter for iPhone]

Feb 16, 2019 07:10:04 PM BUILDING THE WALL! [Twitter for iPhone]

Feb 16, 2019 07:17:44 PM Trade negotiators have just returned from China where the meetings on Trade were very productive. Now at meetings with me at Mar-a-Lago giving the details. In the meantime, Billions of Dollars are being paid to the United States by China in the form of Trade Tariffs! [Twitter for iPhone]

Feb 16, 2019 07:17:54 PM RT @realDonaldTrump: https://t.co/nJORBjwint [Twitter for iPhone]

Feb 16, 2019 10:51:24 PM The United States is asking Britain, France, Germany and other European allies to take back over 800 ISIS fighters that we captured in Syria and put them on trial. The Caliphate is ready to fall. The alternative is not a good one in that we will be forced to release them........ [Twitter for iPhone]

Feb 16, 2019 11:01:37 PM ....The U.S. does not want to watch as these ISIS fighters permeate Europe, which is where they are expected to go. We do so much, and spend so much - Time for others to step up and do the job that they are so capable of doing. We are pulling back after 100% Caliphate victory! [Twitter for iPhone]

Feb 16, 2019 11:06:20 PM RT @real_defender: @realDonaldTrump Protecting America and putting Americans first. Thank you Mr. President! [Twitter for iPhone]

Feb 16, 2019 11:52:57 PM RT @TomFitton: BIG: Strzok/Page Docs Show More Collusion to Protect Hillary Clinton; Voter Fraud Crisis--Thousands of Aliens Illegally Voti... [Twitter for iPhone]

Feb 16, 2019 11:56:12 PM RT @TomFitton: Mueller Will Harass @RealDonaldTrump for Entire Term https://t.co/eoQVP6MsmF via @JudicialWatch [Twitter for iPhone]

Feb 16, 2019 11:56:32 PM RT @TomFitton: .@NYTIMES complains @realDonaldTrump crackdown on asylum scamming is working. https://t.co/K8j94ITalL [Twitter for iPhone]

Feb 17, 2019 07:00:26 AM Important meetings and calls on China Trade Deal, and more, today with my staff. Big progress being made on soooo many different fronts! Our Country has such fantastic potential for future growth and greatness on an even higher level! [Twitter for iPhone]

Feb 17, 2019 07:24:40 AM Democrats in the Senate are still slow walking hundreds of highly qualified people wanting to come into government. Never been such an abuse in our country's history. Mitch should not let Senate go home until all are approved. We need our Ambassadors and all others NOW! [Twitter for iPhone]

Feb 17, 2019 07:41:31 AM 52% Approval Rating, 93% in Republican Party (a record)! Pretty amazing considering that 93% (also) of my press is REALLY BAD. The "people" are SMART! [Twitter for iPhone]

⬜ Feb 17, 2019 07:52:38 AM Nothing funny about tired Saturday Night Live on Fake News NBC! Question is, how do the Networks get away with these total Republican hit jobs without retribution? Likewise for many other shows? Very unfair and should be looked into. This is the real Collusion! [Twitter for iPhone]

⬜ Feb 17, 2019 07:56:09 AM THE RIGGED AND CORRUPT MEDIA IS THE ENEMY OF THE PEOPLE! [Twitter for iPhone]

⬜ Feb 17, 2019 01:28:57 PM https://t.co/y61loNunTJ [Twitter for iPhone]

⬜ Feb 17, 2019 01:29:40 PM https://t.co/r8N9m5vQlF [Twitter for iPhone]

⬜ Feb 17, 2019 04:32:33 PM "These guys, the investigators, ought to be in jail. What they have done, working with the Obama intelligence agencies, is simply unprecedented. This is one of the greatest political hoaxes ever perpetrated on the people of this Country, and Mueller is a coverup." Rush Limbaugh [Twitter for iPhone]

⬜ Feb 17, 2019 06:45:13 PM The Mueller investigation is totally conflicted, illegal and rigged! Should never have been allowed to begin, except for the Collusion and many crimes committed by the Democrats. Witch Hunt! [Twitter for iPhone]

⬜ Feb 17, 2019 06:49:28 PM RT @realDonaldTrump: Disgraced FBI Acting Director Andrew McCabe pretends to be a "poor little Angel" when in fact he was a big part of the… [Twitter for iPhone]

⬜ Feb 17, 2019 06:49:31 PM RT @realDonaldTrump: ....Many of the top FBI brass were fired, forced to leave, or left. McCabe's wife received BIG DOLLARS from Clinton pe… [Twitter for iPhone]

⬜ Feb 17, 2019 11:21:07 PM William Barr is arriving at a Justice Department that desperately needs an infusion of credibility, writes @KimStrassel https://t.co/naY9XOxb12 via @WSJ [Twitter for iPhone]

⬜ Feb 17, 2019 11:28:34 PM RT @KimStrassel: Death of a California Dream https://t.co/sBnSecSriX via @WSJOpinion [Twitter for iPhone]

⬜ Feb 18, 2019 06:56:34 AM "After two years and interviewing more than two hundred witnesses, the Senate Intelligence Committee has NOT discovered any direct evidence of a conspiracy between the Trump Campaign and Russia." Ken Dilanian @NBCNews [Twitter for iPhone]

⬜ Feb 18, 2019 07:15:27 AM Wow, so many lies by now disgraced acting FBI Director Andrew McCabe. He was fired for lying, and now his story gets even more deranged. He and Rod Rosenstein, who was hired by Jeff Sessions (another beauty), look like they were planning a very illegal act, and got caught..... [Twitter for iPhone]

⬜ Feb 18, 2019 07:29:07 AM ....There is a lot of explaining to do to the millions of people who had just elected a president who they really like and who has done a great job for them with the Military, Vets, Economy and so much more. This was the illegal and treasonous "insurance policy" in full action! [Twitter for iPhone]

Feb 18, 2019 08:02:53 AM Great analysis by @foxandfriends! [Twitter for iPhone]

Feb 18, 2019 08:29:25 AM "This was an illegal coup attempt on the President of the United States." Dan Bongino on @foxandfriends True! [Twitter for iPhone]

Feb 18, 2019 03:22:58 PM Hope you are enjoying your President's Day, our Country is making unprecedented progress! [Twitter for iPhone]

Feb 18, 2019 03:34:14 PM RT @FLOTUS: A beautiful ceremony at @Nicklaus4kids hospital today to celebrate their new changes! I hope the garden nurtures & heals all th… [Twitter for iPhone]

Feb 18, 2019 05:26:51 PM We are here to proclaim that a new day is coming in Latin America. In Venezuela and across the Western Hemisphere, Socialism is DYING - and liberty, prosperity, and democracy are being REBORN...https://t.co/hPL5W48Pmg [Twitter for iPhone]

Feb 18, 2019 05:30:07 PM The people of Venezuela are standing for FREEDOM and DEMOCRACY – and the United States of America is standing right by their side! [Twitter for iPhone]

Feb 18, 2019 05:32:53 PM I ask every member of the Maduro regime: End this nightmare of poverty, hunger and death. LET YOUR PEOPLE GO. Set your country free! Now is the time for all Venezuelan Patriots to act together, as one united people. Nothing could be better for the future of Venezuela! [Twitter for iPhone]

Feb 18, 2019 08:17:17 PM Today more than 50 countries around the world now recognize the rightful government of Venezuela. The Venezuelan people have spoken and the world has heard their voice. They are turning the page on Socialism and Dictatorship; and there will be NO GOING BACK! https://t.co/C3DL5RFfiE [Twitter for iPhone]

Feb 18, 2019 09:53:59 PM "The biggest abuse of power and corruption scandal in our history, and it's much worse than we thought. Andrew McCabe (FBI) admitted to plotting a coup (government overthrow) when he was serving in the FBI, before he was fired for lying & leaking." @seanhannity @FoxNews Treason! [Twitter for iPhone]

Feb 18, 2019 10:00:50 PM Amazing! https://t.co/uUNCL1hPAk [Twitter for iPhone]

Feb 18, 2019 10:13:48 PM Thank you JT! https://t.co/L1HDeXWazc [Twitter for iPhone]

Feb 18, 2019 10:21:32 PM Thank you Andrew - We all miss beautiful Meadow! https://t.co/a5PLSwpJyx [Twitter for iPhone]

Feb 18, 2019 10:23:47 PM RT @real_defender: @realDonaldTrump Our country is making unprecedented progress thanks to the fact that we finally have a president who is… [Twitter for iPhone]

Feb 18, 2019 10:26:47 PM Remember this, Andrew McCabe didn't go to the bathroom without the approval of Leakin' James Comey! [Twitter for iPhone]

Feb 19, 2019 07:21:07 AM "....(The Witch Hunt) in time likely will become recognized as the greatest scandal in American political history, marking the first occasion in which the U.S. government bureaucrats sought to overturn an election (presidential)!" Victor Davis Hanson And got caught! @FoxNews [Twitter for iPhone]

Feb 19, 2019 07:30:03 AM Had the opposition party (no, not the Media) won the election, the Stock Market would be down at least 10,000 points by now. We are heading up, up, up! [Twitter for iPhone]

Feb 19, 2019 07:44:43 AM As I predicted, 16 cities, led mostly by Open Border Democrats and the Radical Left, have filed a lawsuit in, of course, the 9th Circuit! California, the state that has wasted billions of dollars on their out of control Fast Train, with no hope of completion, seems in charge! [Twitter for iPhone]

Feb 19, 2019 07:48:07 AM The failed Fast Train project in California, were the cost overruns are becoming world record setting, is hundreds of times more expensive than the desperately needed Wall! [Twitter for iPhone]

Feb 19, 2019 08:52:18 AM As I predicted, 16 states, led mostly by Open Border Democrats and the Radical Left, have filed a lawsuit in, of course, the 9th Circuit! California, the state that has wasted billions of dollars on their out of control Fast Train, with no hope of completion, seems in charge! [Twitter for iPhone]

Feb 19, 2019 08:53:35 AM The failed Fast Train project in California, where the cost overruns are becoming world record setting, is hundreds of times more expensive than the desperately needed Wall! [Twitter for iPhone]

Feb 19, 2019 10:22:23 AM The Washington Post is a Fact Checker only for the Democrats. For the Republicans, and for your all time favorite President, it is a Fake Fact Checker! [Twitter for iPhone]

Feb 19, 2019 11:05:01 AM I never said anything bad about Andrew McCabe's wife other than she (they) should not have taken large amounts of campaign money from a Crooked Hillary source when Clinton was under investigation by the FBI. I never called his wife a loser to him (another McCabe made up lie)! [Twitter for iPhone]

Feb 19, 2019 11:50:51 AM https://t.co/xRbxknI4Nf [Twitter for iPhone]

Feb 19, 2019 11:54:56 PM RT @GeraldoRivera: This is crazy scary. A cabal of unelected bureaucrats-angered & upset that @realDonaldTrump fired their boss-whispered a... [Twitter for iPhone]

Feb 20, 2019 07:03:18 AM "Andrew McCabe gave absolutely no evidence of any threat to substantiate his ABSURD claim." @LouDobbs [Twitter for iPhone]

Feb 20, 2019 07:07:14 AM Crazy Bernie has just entered the race. I wish him well! [Twitter for iPhone]

Feb 20, 2019 07:20:29 AM The Press has never been more dishonest than it is today. Stories are written that have absolutely no basis in fact. The writers don't even call asking for verification. They are totally out of control. Sadly, I kept many of them in business. In six years, they all go BUST! [Twitter for iPhone]

Feb 20, 2019 07:44:20 AM "The Washington Post ignored basic journalistic standards because it wanted to advance its well-known and easily documented biased agenda against President Donald J. Trump." Covington student suing WAPO. Go get them Nick. Fake News! [Twitter for iPhone]

Feb 20, 2019 07:54:33 AM "If thinking that James Comey is not a good FBI Director is tantamount to being an agent of Russia, than just list all the people that are agents of Russia - Chuck Schumer, Nancy Pelosi, Rod Rosenstein who wrote the memo to get rid of Comey, the Inspector General...." Trey Gowdy [Twitter for iPhone]

Feb 20, 2019 08:49:13 AM The New York Times reporting is false. They are a true ENEMY OF THE PEOPLE! [Twitter for iPhone]

Feb 20, 2019 09:13:25 AM California now wants to scale back their already failed "fast train" project by substantially shortening the distance so that it no longer goes from L.A. to San Francisco. A different deal and record cost overruns. Send the Federal Government back the Billions of Dollars WASTED! [Twitter for iPhone]

Feb 20, 2019 01:56:02 PM We have just built this powerful Wall in New Mexico. Completed on January 30, 2019 – 47 days ahead of schedule! Many miles more now under construction! #FinishTheWall https://t.co/TYkj3KRdOC [Twitter for iPhone]

Feb 20, 2019 04:05:41 PM I have instructed Secretary of State Mike Pompeo, and he fully agrees, not to allow Hoda Muthana back into the Country! [Twitter for iPhone]

Feb 21, 2019 08:55:02 AM I want 5G, and even 6G, technology in the United States as soon as possible. It is far more powerful, faster, and smarter than the current standard. American companies must step up their efforts, or get left behind. There is no reason that we should be lagging behind on......... [Twitter for iPhone]

Feb 21, 2019 08:59:39 AM ....something that is so obviously the future. I want the United States to win through competition, not by blocking out currently more advanced technologies. We must always be the leader in everything we do, especially when it comes to the very exciting world of technology! [Twitter for iPhone]

Feb 21, 2019 09:17:45 AM THE WALL IS UNDER CONSTRUCTION RIGHT NOW! https://t.co/exUJCiITsz [Twitter for iPhone]

Feb 21, 2019 11:09:57 AM .@JussieSmollett - what about MAGA and the tens of millions of people you insulted with your racist and dangerous comments!? #MAGA [Twitter for iPhone]

Feb 21, 2019 03:10:38 PM Senator John Cornyn has done an outstanding job for the people of Texas. He is strong on Crime, the Border, the Second Amendment and loves our Military and Vets. John has my complete and total endorsement. MAKE AMERICA GREAT AGAIN! [Twitter for iPhone]

Feb 21, 2019 07:27:07 PM We are here to honor the extraordinary contributions of African-Americans to every aspect of American Life, History and Culture. From the earliest days of this Nation, African-American Leaders, Pioneers, & Visionaries have uplifted & inspired our Country...https://t.co/VuFLkfd12j [Twitter for iPhone]

Feb 21, 2019 09:30:30 PM RT @FLOTUS: Wonderful evening at @WhiteHouse celebrating #AfricanAmericanHistoryMonth! https://t.co/ZBJop8kxTY [Twitter for iPhone]

Feb 22, 2019 09:11:44 AM Highly respected Senator Richard Burr, head of Senate Intelligence, said, after interviewing over 200 witnesses and studying over 2 million pages of documents, "WE HAVE FOUND NO COLLUSION BETWEEN THE TRUMP CAMPAIGN AND RUSSIA." The Witch Hunt, so bad for our Country, must end! [Twitter for iPhone]

Feb 22, 2019 09:55:25 AM Fake News is so bad for our Country! https://t.co/ZwA8E0URer [Twitter for iPhone]

Feb 22, 2019 11:01:59 AM A must read by @KimStrassel! https://t.co/Gfyrfpy55b [Twitter for iPhone]

Feb 22, 2019 05:51:34 PM RT @SecretarySonny: BREAKING: In Oval Office meeting today, the Chinese committed to buy an additional 10 million metric tons of U.S. soybe... [Twitter for iPhone]

Feb 22, 2019 06:02:53 PM ....Kelly has done an outstanding job representing our Nation and I have no doubt that, under her leadership, our Country will be represented at the highest level. Congratulations to Kelly and her entire family! [Twitter for iPhone]

Feb 22, 2019 06:02:53 PM I am pleased to announce that Kelly Knight Craft, our current Ambassador to Canada, is being nominated to be United States Ambassador to the United Nations.... [Twitter for iPhone]

Feb 23, 2019 11:12:07 AM Great new book: "The Case For Trump" by Victor Davis Hanson, Hoover Senior Fellow. [Twitter for iPhone]

Feb 23, 2019 12:30:21 PM God Bless the people of Venezuela! [Twitter for iPhone]

Feb 23, 2019 12:52:46 PM There is far more ENERGY on the Right than there is on the Left. That's why we just won the Senate and why we will win big in 2020. The Fake News just doesn't want to report the facts. Border Security is a big factor. The under construction Wall will stop Gangs, Drugs and Crime! [Twitter for iPhone]

Feb 23, 2019 02:55:27 PM RT @USMC: 74 years ago today, Marines on Iwo Jima raised the flag atop Mount Suribachi. Semper Fidelis. https://t.co/UsQ2z344Xp [Twitter for iPhone]

Feb 23, 2019 03:00:36 PM The people of Venezuela stand at the threshold of history, ready to reclaim their country – and their future.... https://t.co/ajxd1EN64c [Twitter for iPhone]

Feb 23, 2019 07:01:00 PM "There's not one shred of evidence that this president's done anything Constitutionally (or anything else) wrong." Graham Ledger. Thank you Graham, so true! [Twitter for iPhone]

Feb 23, 2019 10:33:16 PM RT @GOPChairwoman: Thank you @RonaldWeiser for serving the @MIGOP well and congratulations to my friend and new @MIGOPChair Laura Cox! I... [Twitter for iPhone]

Feb 23, 2019 10:35:24 PM So great being with you both in the Oval Office! https://t.co/9VoIV3NahE [Twitter for iPhone]

Feb 23, 2019 10:37:35 PM RT @LouDobbs: #AmericaFirst – @CLewandowski_ :The media doesn't want to give @realDonaldTrump the credit for once again exerting American do... [Twitter for iPhone]

Feb 23, 2019 10:40:15 PM RT @GOPChairwoman: Drug trafficking at our southern border has exploded. CBP seized nearly 5X as much methamphetamine in 2018 than it did... [Twitter for iPhone]

Feb 23, 2019 10:40:28 PM RT @PressSec: President @realDonaldTrump delivers more great news for our farmers. https://t.co/ACq0ujTFTS [Twitter for iPhone]

Feb 23, 2019 10:49:32 PM RT @TomFitton: MASSIVE @JudicialWatch Update: Lawsuit to Expose Coup Against @RealDonaldTrump, Another FBI Cover-up of potential Clinton e... [Twitter for iPhone]

Feb 23, 2019 10:56:41 PM RT @CortesSteve: Was wonderful to meet so many inspiring young patriots last night when I spoke to the @TPUSA Latino conference! @char... [Twitter for iPhone]

Feb 23, 2019 11:02:02 PM RT @seanhannity: **REPORT: "China is proposing that it could buy an additional $30 billion a year of U.S. agricultural products including s... [Twitter for iPhone]

Feb 24, 2019 07:43:52 AM HOLD THE DATE! We will be having one of the biggest gatherings in the history of Washington, D.C., on July 4th. It will be called "A Salute To America" and will be held at the Lincoln Memorial. Major fireworks display, entertainment and an address by your favorite President, me! [Twitter for iPhone]

Feb 24, 2019 07:58:20 AM Very productive talks yesterday with China on Trade. Will continue today! I will be leaving for Hanoi, Vietnam, early tomorrow for a Summit with Kim Jong Un of North Korea, where we both expect a continuation of the progress made at first Summit in Singapore. Denuclearization? [Twitter for iPhone]

Feb 24, 2019 08:05:49 AM President Xi of China has been very helpful in his support of my meeting with Kim Jong Un. The last thing China wants are large scale nuclear weapons right next door. Sanctions placed on the border by China and Russia have been very helpful. Great relationship with Chairman Kim! [Twitter for iPhone]

Feb 24, 2019 08:19:19 AM Chairman Kim realizes, perhaps better than anyone else, that without nuclear weapons, his country could fast become one of the great economic powers anywhere in the World. Because of its location and people (and him), it has more potential for rapid growth than any other nation! [Twitter for iPhone]

Feb 24, 2019 09:56:08 AM Poll: Suburban women are coming back into the Republican Party in droves "because of the Wall and Border Security. 70% support Border Security and the Wall." Not believing the Walls are immoral line. Beverly Hallberg, Independent Women's Forum @KatiePavlich A great USA issue! [Twitter for iPhone]

Feb 24, 2019 10:02:16 AM 93% Approval Rating in the Republican Party. 52% Approval Rating overall! Not bad considering I get the most unfair (BAD) press in the history of presidential politics! And don't forget the Witch Hunt! [Twitter for iPhone]

Feb 24, 2019 11:51:33 AM The only Collusion with the Russians was with Crooked Hillary Clinton and the Democratic National Committee...And, where's the Server that the DNC refused to give to the FBI? Where are the new Texts between Agent Lisa Page and her Agent lover, Peter S? We want them now! [Twitter for iPhone]

Feb 24, 2019 12:27:12 PM So funny to watch people who have failed for years, they got NOTHING, telling me how to negotiate with North Korea. But thanks anyway! [Twitter for iPhone]

Feb 24, 2019 05:39:17 PM I am pleased to report that the U.S. has made substantial progress in our trade talks with China on important structural issues including intellectual property protection, technology transfer, agriculture, services, currency, and many other issues. As a result of these very...... [Twitter for iPhone]

Feb 24, 2019 05:50:14 PM ....productive talks, I will be delaying the U.S. increase in tariffs now scheduled for March 1. Assuming both sides make additional progress, we will be planning a Summit for President Xi and myself, at Mar-a-Lago, to conclude an agreement. A very good weekend for U.S. & China! [Twitter for iPhone]

Feb 25, 2019 06:32:45 AM We have a State of Emergency at our Southern Border. Border Patrol, our Military and local Law Enforcement are doing a great job, but without the Wall, which is now under major construction, you cannot have Border Security. Drugs, Gangs and Human Trafficking must be stopped! [Twitter for iPhone]

Feb 25, 2019 06:36:32 AM RT @realDonaldTrump: Highly respected Senator Richard Burr, head of Senate Intelligence, said, after interviewing over 200 witnesses and st... [Twitter for iPhone]

Feb 25, 2019 06:50:18 AM Be nice if Spike Lee could read his notes, or better yet not have to use notes at all, when doing his racist hit on your President, who has done more for African Americans (Criminal Justice Reform, Lowest Unemployment numbers in History, Tax Cuts,etc.) than almost any other Pres! [Twitter for iPhone]

Feb 25, 2019 06:58:41 AM Oil prices getting too high. OPEC, please relax and take it easy. World cannot take a price hike - fragile! [Twitter for iPhone]

Feb 25, 2019 06:59:52 AM RT @IvankaTrump: This Admin is committed to ensuring more Americans have the skills needed to secure better jobs in our strong economy. I... [Twitter for iPhone]

Feb 25, 2019 07:30:55 AM RT @realDonaldTrump: So funny to watch people who have failed for years, they got NOTHING, telling me how to negotiate with North Korea. Bu... [Twitter for iPhone]

Feb 25, 2019 07:40:20 AM Meeting for breakfast with our Nation's Governors - then off to Vietnam for a very important Summit with Kim Jong Un. With complete Denuclearization, North Korea will rapidly become an Economic Powerhouse. Without it, just more of the same. Chairman Kim will make a wise decision! [Twitter for iPhone]

Feb 25, 2019 07:53:02 AM Former Senator Harry Reid (he got thrown out) is working hard to put a good spin on his failed career. He led through lies and deception, only to be replaced by another beauty, Cryin' Chuck Schumer. Some things just never change! [Twitter for iPhone]

Feb 25, 2019 07:58:41 AM I hope our great Republican Senators don't get led down the path of weak and ineffective Border Security. Without strong Borders, we don't have a Country - and the voters are on board with us. Be strong and smart, don't fall into the Democrats "trap" of Open Borders and Crime! [Twitter for iPhone]

Feb 25, 2019 10:01:23 AM "Why on earth would any Republican vote not to put up a Wall or against Border Security. Please explain that to me?" @Varneyco [Twitter for iPhone]

Feb 25, 2019 10:12:02 AM Since my election as President the Dow Jones is up 43% and the NASDAQ Composite almost 50%. Great news for your 401(k)s as they continue to grow. We are bringing back America faster than anyone thought possible! [Twitter for iPhone]

Feb 25, 2019 01:50:20 PM Congratulations to @DJohnsonPGA on his 20th PGA Tour WIN. Not only is Dustin a truly great golfer, he is a wonderful guy. Big year ahead for Dustin! [Twitter for iPhone]

Feb 25, 2019 02:08:55 PM It is my honor today to announce that Danny Burch, a United States citizen who has been held hostage in Yemen for 18 months, has been recovered and reunited with his wife and children. I appreciate the support of the United Arab Emirates in bringing Danny home... [Twitter for iPhone]

Feb 25, 2019 02:08:56 PM ...Danny's recovery reflects the best of what the United States & its partners can accomplish. We work every day to bring Americans home. We maintain constant and intensive diplomatic, intelligence, and law enforcement cooperation within the United States Government and with... [Twitter for iPhone]

Feb 25, 2019 02:08:57 PM ...our foreign partners. Recovering American hostages is a priority of my Admin, and with Danny's release, we have now secured freedom for 20 American captives since my election victory. We will not rest as we continue our work to bring the remaining American hostages back home! [Twitter for iPhone]

Feb 25, 2019 03:12:25 PM China Trade Deal (and more) in advanced stages. Relationship between our two Countries is very strong. I have therefore agreed to delay U.S. tariff hikes. Let's see what happens? [Twitter for iPhone]

Feb 25, 2019 03:17:02 PM Heading over to Vietnam for my meeting with Kim Jong Un. Looking forward to a very productive Summit! [Twitter for iPhone]

Feb 25, 2019 07:04:49 PM If a deal is made with China, our great American Farmers will be treated better than they have ever been treated before! [Twitter for iPhone]

Feb 25, 2019 08:50:36 PM Senate Democrats just voted against legislation to prevent the killing of newborn infant children. The Democrat position on abortion is now so extreme that they don't mind executing babies AFTER birth.... [Twitter for iPhone]

Feb 25, 2019 08:50:37 PM ....This will be remembered as one of the most shocking votes in the history of Congress. If there is one thing we should all agree on, it's protecting the lives of innocent babies. [Twitter for iPhone]

Feb 26, 2019 10:08:14 AM Just arrived in Vietnam. Thank you to all of the people for the great reception in Hanoi. Tremendous crowds, and so much love! [Twitter for iPhone]

Feb 26, 2019 09:31:21 PM Vietnam is thriving like few places on earth. North Korea would be the same, and very quickly, if it would denuclearize. The potential is AWESOME, a great opportunity, like almost none other in history, for my friend Kim Jong Un. We will know fairly soon - Very Interesting! [Twitter for iPhone]

Feb 26, 2019 09:36:29 PM The Democrats should stop talking about what I should do with North Korea and ask themselves instead why they didn't do "it" during eight years of the Obama Administration? [Twitter for iPhone]

Feb 27, 2019 02:51:36 AM RT @realDonaldTrump: ....This will be remembered as one of the most shocking votes in the history of Congress. If there is one thing we sho... [Twitter for iPhone]

Feb 27, 2019 02:51:38 AM RT @realDonaldTrump: Senate Democrats just voted against legislation to prevent the killing of newborn infant children. The Democrat positi... [Twitter for iPhone]

Feb 27, 2019 02:52:35 AM RT @IvankaTrump: No I did not. I support a minimum wage. I do not however believe in a minimum guarantee for people "unwilling to work" whi... [Twitter for iPhone]

Feb 27, 2019 02:58:32 AM I have now spent more time in Vietnam than Da Nang Dick Blumenthal, the third rate Senator from Connecticut (how is Connecticut doing?). His war stories of his heroism in Vietnam were a total fraud - he was never even there. We talked about it today with Vietnamese leaders! [Twitter for iPhone]

Feb 27, 2019 04:08:03 AM Michael Cohen was one of many lawyers who represented me (unfortunately). He had other clients also. He was just disbarred by the State Supreme Court for lying & fraud. He did bad things unrelated to Trump. He is lying in order to reduce his prison time. Using Crooked's lawyer! [Twitter for iPhone]

Feb 27, 2019 04:20:25 AM Fiat Chrysler will be adding more than 6,500 JOBS in Michigan (Detroit area), doubling its hourly workforce as part of a 4.5 Billion Dollar investment. Thank you Fiat Chrysler. They are all coming back to the USA, it's where the action is! [Twitter for iPhone]

Feb 27, 2019 04:45:59 AM All false reporting (guessing) on my intentions with respect to North Korea. Kim Jong Un and I will try very hard to work something out on Denuclearization & then making North Korea an Economic Powerhouse. I believe that China, Russia, Japan & South Korea will be very helpful! [Twitter for iPhone]

Feb 27, 2019 10:24:14 AM RT @WhiteHouse: https://t.co/t6egb4Neir [Twitter for iPhone]

Feb 27, 2019 10:24:16 AM RT @WhiteHouse: https://t.co/Wo4C4hsP43 [Twitter for iPhone]

Feb 27, 2019 10:36:56 AM Great meetings and dinner tonight in Vietnam with Kim Jong Un of North Korea. Very good dialogue. Resuming tomorrow! [Twitter for iPhone]

Feb 27, 2019 10:38:24 AM Great meeting and dinner with Kim Jong Un in Hanoi, Vietnam tonight. Looking forward to continuing our discussions tomorrow! #HanoiSummit https://t.co/J3x6lUGzjS [Twitter for iPhone]

Feb 27, 2019 11:25:33 AM RT @realDonaldTrump: Michael Cohen was one of many lawyers who represented me (unfortunately). He had other clients also. He was just disba... [Twitter for iPhone]

Feb 28, 2019 05:10:02 AM RT @StateDept: President @realDonaldTrump and @SecPompeo participate in a Press Conference in Hanoi, Vietnam, on February 28, 2019. https:/... [Twitter for iPhone]

Feb 28, 2019 05:25:18 AM THANK YOU to our generous hosts in Hanoi this week: President Trong, Prime Minister Phuc, and the wonderful people of Vietnam! https://t.co/AMqF0dfRhP [Twitter for iPhone]

Feb 28, 2019 08:12:26 PM Everyone MUST watch the opening to @TuckerCarlson - A Classic! @foxnews [Twitter for iPhone]

Feb 28, 2019 08:15:17 PM I will be interviewed by @seanhannity at 9:00 P.M. on @FoxNews. Enjoy! [Twitter for iPhone]

Feb 28, 2019 10:59:59 PM https://t.co/hUK9dSBM3M [Twitter for iPhone]

Feb 28, 2019 11:00:29 PM https://t.co/ywNk8EhOh0 [Twitter for iPhone]

Feb 28, 2019 11:35:26 PM Today in Alaska, it was my great honor to visit with our brave men and women of the United States Military at Joint Base Elmendorf-Richardson. We are forever grateful for their service and sacrifice. THANK YOU! https://t.co/4REVxKUsHT [Twitter for iPhone]

Mar 1, 2019 07:49:22 AM Great to be back from Vietnam, an amazing place. We had very substantive negotiations with Kim Jong Un - we know what they want and they know what we must have. Relationship very good, let's see what happens! [Twitter for iPhone]

Mar 1, 2019 08:00:17 AM Wow, just revealed that Michael Cohen wrote a "love letter to Trump" manuscript for a new book that he was pushing. Written and submitted long after Charlottesville and Helsinki, his phony reasons for going rogue. Book is exact opposite of his fake testimony, which now is a lie! [Twitter for iPhone]

Mar 1, 2019 08:08:02 AM Congress must demand the transcript of Michael Cohen's new book, given to publishers a short time ago. Your heads will spin when you see the lies, misrepresentations and contradictions against his Thursday testimony. Like a different person! He is totally discredited! [Twitter for iPhone]

Mar 1, 2019 08:19:44 AM Oh' I see! Now that the 2 year Russian Collusion case has fallen apart, there was no Collusion except bye Crooked Hillary and the Democrats, they say, "gee, I have an idea, let's look at Trump's finances and every deal he has ever done. Let's follow discredited Michael Cohen..... [Twitter for iPhone]

Mar 1, 2019 08:26:56 AM ...and the fraudulent and dishonest statements he made on Wednesday. No way, it's time to stop this corrupt and illegally brought Witch Hunt. Time to start looking at the other side where real crimes were committed. Republicans have been abused long enough. Must end now! [Twitter for iPhone]

Mar 1, 2019 08:37:09 AM Michael Cohen's book manuscript shows that he committed perjury on a scale not seen before. He must have forgotten about his book when he testified. What does Hillary Clinton's lawyer, Lanny Davis, say about this one. Is he being paid by Crooked Hillary. Using her lawyer? [Twitter for iPhone]

Mar 1, 2019 04:03:13 PM I never like being misinterpreted, but especially when it comes to Otto Warmbier and his great family. Remember, I got Otto out along with three others. The previous Administration did nothing, and he was taken on their watch. Of course I hold North Korea responsible.... [Twitter for iPhone]

Mar 1, 2019 04:03:14 PM ....for Otto's mistreatment and death. Most important, Otto Warmbier will not have died in vain. Otto and his family have become a tremendous symbol of strong passion and strength, which will last for many years into the future. I love Otto and think of him often! [Twitter for iPhone]

Mar 1, 2019 06:08:11 PM ....and I did not increase their second traunch of Tariffs to 25% on March 1st. This is very important for our great farmers - and me! [Twitter for iPhone]

Mar 1, 2019 06:08:11 PM I have asked China to immediately remove all Tariffs on our agricultural products (including beef, pork, etc.) based on the fact that we are moving along nicely with Trade discussions.... [Twitter for iPhone]

Mar 2, 2019 08:31:45 AM Very proud of perhaps the greatest golf course anywhere in the world. Also, furthers U.K. relationship! https://t.co/3xTzzJH6Iq [Twitter for iPhone]

Mar 2, 2019 08:40:37 AM Will be speaking at CPAC at 11:30 this morning. Record crowd, live broadcast. Enjoy! [Twitter for iPhone]

Mar 2, 2019 09:22:51 AM RT @TeamTrump: Get your OFFICIAL campaign merchandise @ https://t.co/avCW7TGIn1 or, if you're at @CPAC, check out our Official booth!" #Tea... [Twitter for iPhone]

Mar 2, 2019 09:23:21 AM RT @dcexaminer: Pence says President Trump has "no higher priority than the safety of the American people." #CPAC2019 https://t.co/fmBGjTBC... [Twitter for iPhone]

Mar 2, 2019 09:48:47 AM RT @realDonaldTrump: Since my election as President the Dow Jones is up 43% and the NASDAQ Composite almost 50%. Great news for your 401(k)... [Twitter for iPhone]

Mar 2, 2019 09:50:52 AM RT @realDonaldTrump: I hope our great Republican Senators don't get led down the path of weak and ineffective Border Security. Without stro... [Twitter for iPhone]

Mar 2, 2019 09:51:53 AM RT @realDonaldTrump: 93% Approval Rating in the Republican Party. 52% Approval Rating overall! Not bad considering I get the most unfair (B... [Twitter for iPhone]

Mar 2, 2019 10:44:33 AM @TeamCavuto It was a 3 day train ride to Vietnam, not 3 hours! [Twitter for iPhone]

Mar 2, 2019 11:21:42 AM Thank you @marklevinshow! https://t.co/dwQR11genG [Twitter for iPhone]

Mar 2, 2019 07:27:40 PM Virtually everything failed lawyer Michael Cohen said in his sworn testimony last week is totally contradicted in his just released manuscript for a book about me. It's a total new love letter to "Trump" and the pols must now use it rather than his lies for sentence reduction! [Twitter for iPhone]

Mar 2, 2019 07:34:51 PM The brand new manuscript for a new book by failed lawyer Michael Cohen shows his testimony was a total lie! Pundits should only use it. [Twitter for iPhone]

Mar 2, 2019 07:48:00 PM We've got NASA "rocking" again. Great activity and success. Congrats to SPACEX and all! [Twitter for iPhone]

Mar 2, 2019 08:39:36 PM https://t.co/PTLqvZNwqY [Twitter for iPhone]

Mar 3, 2019 10:44:10 AM ...said was a total lie, but Fake Media won't show it. I am an innocent man being persecuted by some very bad, conflicted & corrupt people in a Witch Hunt that is illegal & should never have been allowed to start - And only because I won the Election! Despite this, great success! [Twitter for iPhone]

Mar 3, 2019 11:02:13 AM After more than two years of Presidential Harassment, the only things that have been proven is that Democrats and other broke the law. The hostile Cohen testimony, given by a liar to reduce his prison time, proved no Collusion! His just written book manuscript showed what he..... [Twitter for iPhone]

Mar 3, 2019 02:23:01 PM "Look how they're acting now and how we act when we're in the majority. What the Democrats are doing is an abuse of power. They couldn't find anything...they took a Fake Dossier & couldn't find any Collusion. Now they have a fake witness in Cohen." Congressman Mark Green, (R-TN). [Twitter for iPhone]

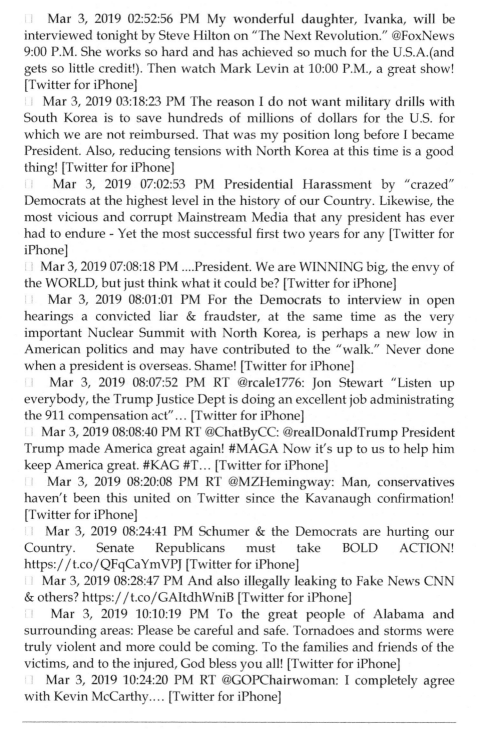

☐ Mar 3, 2019 02:52:56 PM My wonderful daughter, Ivanka, will be interviewed tonight by Steve Hilton on "The Next Revolution." @FoxNews 9:00 P.M. She works so hard and has achieved so much for the U.S.A.(and gets so little credit!). Then watch Mark Levin at 10:00 P.M., a great show! [Twitter for iPhone]

☐ Mar 3, 2019 03:18:23 PM The reason I do not want military drills with South Korea is to save hundreds of millions of dollars for the U.S. for which we are not reimbursed. That was my position long before I became President. Also, reducing tensions with North Korea at this time is a good thing! [Twitter for iPhone]

☐ Mar 3, 2019 07:02:53 PM Presidential Harassment by "crazed" Democrats at the highest level in the history of our Country. Likewise, the most vicious and corrupt Mainstream Media that any president has ever had to endure - Yet the most successful first two years for any [Twitter for iPhone]

☐ Mar 3, 2019 07:08:18 PM ....President. We are WINNING big, the envy of the WORLD, but just think what it could be? [Twitter for iPhone]

☐ Mar 3, 2019 08:01:01 PM For the Democrats to interview in open hearings a convicted liar & fraudster, at the same time as the very important Nuclear Summit with North Korea, is perhaps a new low in American politics and may have contributed to the "walk." Never done when a president is overseas. Shame! [Twitter for iPhone]

☐ Mar 3, 2019 08:07:52 PM RT @rcale1776: Jon Stewart "Listen up everybody, the Trump Justice Dept is doing an excellent job administrating the 911 compensation act"... [Twitter for iPhone]

☐ Mar 3, 2019 08:08:40 PM RT @ChatByCC: @realDonaldTrump President Trump made America great again! #MAGA Now it's up to us to help him keep America great. #KAG #T... [Twitter for iPhone]

☐ Mar 3, 2019 08:20:08 PM RT @MZHemingway: Man, conservatives haven't been this united on Twitter since the Kavanaugh confirmation! [Twitter for iPhone]

☐ Mar 3, 2019 08:24:41 PM Schumer & the Democrats are hurting our Country. Senate Republicans must take BOLD ACTION! https://t.co/QFqCaYmVPJ [Twitter for iPhone]

☐ Mar 3, 2019 08:28:47 PM And also illegally leaking to Fake News CNN & others? https://t.co/GAItdhWniB [Twitter for iPhone]

☐ Mar 3, 2019 10:10:19 PM To the great people of Alabama and surrounding areas: Please be careful and safe. Tornadoes and storms were truly violent and more could be coming. To the families and friends of the victims, and to the injured, God bless you all! [Twitter for iPhone]

☐ Mar 3, 2019 10:24:20 PM RT @GOPChairwoman: I completely agree with Kevin McCarthy.... [Twitter for iPhone]

⊔ Mar 4, 2019 09:52:14 AM FEMA has been told directly by me to give the A Plus treatment to the Great State of Alabama and the wonderful people who have been so devastated by the Tornadoes. @GovIvey, one of the best in our Country, has been so informed. She is working closely with FEMA (and me!). [Twitter for iPhone]

⊔ Mar 4, 2019 11:17:28 AM FEMA has been told directly by me to give the A Plus treatment to the Great State of Alabama and the wonderful people who have been so devastated by the Tornadoes. @GovernorKayIvey, one of the best in our Country, has been so informed. She is working closely with FEMA (and me!). [Twitter for iPhone]

⊔ Mar 4, 2019 02:53:49 PM The military drills, or war games as I call them, were never even discussed in my mtg w/ Kim Jong Un of NK — FAKE NEWS! I made that decision long ago because it costs the U.S. far too much money to have those "games", especially since we are not reimbursed for the tremendous cost! [Twitter for iPhone]

⊔ Mar 4, 2019 03:06:34 PM "Now that the Dems are going to try & switch from Collusion to some other reason, it makes them continue to look like sore losers who didn't accept the WILL OF THE PEOPLE in the last election - they will do anything to get rid of the President." @AriFleischer It will never work! [Twitter for iPhone]

⊔ Mar 4, 2019 03:17:23 PM "There is no Collusion. All of these investigations are in search of a crime. Democrats have no evidence to impeach President Trump. Ridiculous!" @DevinNunes @FoxNews [Twitter for iPhone]

⊔ Mar 4, 2019 03:53:21 PM RT @WhiteHouse: President Trump's message to those affected by the tornadoes in the Gulf states: "We grieve by your side and we pledge our… [Twitter for iPhone]

⊔ Mar 4, 2019 08:59:32 PM Presidential Harassment! https://t.co/2Cz5ckERcs [Twitter for iPhone]

⊔ Mar 4, 2019 09:04:29 PM "The American Media has changed forever. News organizations that seemed like a big deal are now extinct. Those that remain have now degraded themselves beyond recognition, like the New Yorker - or they've been purchased by Jeff Bezos to conduct unregistered lobbying for......... [Twitter for iPhone]

⊔ Mar 4, 2019 09:10:34 PM .... Amazon, like the Washington Post. It's hard to remember that not so long ago America had prestige media outlets, but not anymore." @TuckerCarlson The Fake News Media is the true Enemy of the People! [Twitter for iPhone]

⊔ Mar 4, 2019 09:24:38 PM RT @JudicialWatch: Right now, our borders are being used as gateways for drug cartels & violent criminals – each day adding to the millions… [Twitter for iPhone]

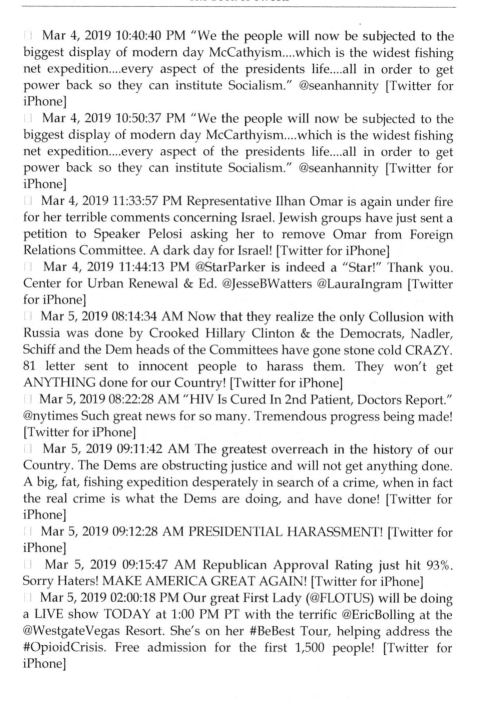

Mar 4, 2019 10:40:40 PM "We the people will now be subjected to the biggest display of modern day McCathyism....which is the widest fishing net expedition....every aspect of the presidents life....all in order to get power back so they can institute Socialism." @seanhannity [Twitter for iPhone]

Mar 4, 2019 10:50:37 PM "We the people will now be subjected to the biggest display of modern day McCarthyism....which is the widest fishing net expedition....every aspect of the presidents life....all in order to get power back so they can institute Socialism." @seanhannity [Twitter for iPhone]

Mar 4, 2019 11:33:57 PM Representative Ilhan Omar is again under fire for her terrible comments concerning Israel. Jewish groups have just sent a petition to Speaker Pelosi asking her to remove Omar from Foreign Relations Committee. A dark day for Israel! [Twitter for iPhone]

Mar 4, 2019 11:44:13 PM @StarParker is indeed a "Star!" Thank you. Center for Urban Renewal & Ed. @JesseBWatters @LauraIngram [Twitter for iPhone]

Mar 5, 2019 08:14:34 AM Now that they realize the only Collusion with Russia was done by Crooked Hillary Clinton & the Democrats, Nadler, Schiff and the Dem heads of the Committees have gone stone cold CRAZY. 81 letter sent to innocent people to harass them. They won't get ANYTHING done for our Country! [Twitter for iPhone]

Mar 5, 2019 08:22:28 AM "HIV Is Cured In 2nd Patient, Doctors Report." @nytimes Such great news for so many. Tremendous progress being made! [Twitter for iPhone]

Mar 5, 2019 09:11:42 AM The greatest overreach in the history of our Country. The Dems are obstructing justice and will not get anything done. A big, fat, fishing expedition desperately in search of a crime, when in fact the real crime is what the Dems are doing, and have done! [Twitter for iPhone]

Mar 5, 2019 09:12:28 AM PRESIDENTIAL HARASSMENT! [Twitter for iPhone]

Mar 5, 2019 09:15:47 AM Republican Approval Rating just hit 93%. Sorry Haters! MAKE AMERICA GREAT AGAIN! [Twitter for iPhone]

Mar 5, 2019 02:00:18 PM Our great First Lady (@FLOTUS) will be doing a LIVE show TODAY at 1:00 PM PT with the terrific @EricBolling at the @WestgateVegas Resort. She's on her #BeBest Tour, helping address the #OpioidCrisis. Free admission for the first 1,500 people! [Twitter for iPhone]

Mar 5, 2019 02:49:38 PM Just a few moments ago, I signed an EO addressing one of our nation's most heartbreaking tragedies: VETERANS SUICIDE. To every Veteran—I want you to know that you have an entire nation of more than 300 million people behind you. You will NEVER be forgotten.https://t.co/DKxiV5Ku3B [Twitter for iPhone]

Mar 5, 2019 03:54:27 PM ....Scott has helped us to lower drug prices, get a record number of generic drugs approved and onto the market, and so many other things. He and his talents will be greatly missed! [Twitter for iPhone]

Mar 5, 2019 03:54:27 PM Scott Gottlieb, who has done an absolutely terrific job as Commissioner of the FDA, plans to leave government service sometime next month.... [Twitter for iPhone]

Mar 5, 2019 05:18:31 PM "(Crooked) Hillary Clinton confirms she will not run in 2020, rules out a third bid for White House." Aw-shucks, does that mean I won't get to run against her again? She will be sorely missed! [Twitter for iPhone]

Mar 5, 2019 11:15:41 PM RT @PressSec: Statement on Chairman Nadler's fishing expedition. https://t.co/tBsVzrtGYg [Twitter for iPhone]

Mar 5, 2019 11:16:05 PM RT @GOPChairwoman: While @realDonaldTrump was successful in the private sector, career politicians enrich themselves by spending decades in… [Twitter for iPhone]

Mar 5, 2019 11:17:33 PM Presidential Harassment! https://t.co/AHz6kLliaC [Twitter for iPhone]

Mar 5, 2019 11:17:54 PM RT @Uncle_Jimbo: .@JerryNadler admits on #CNN they have no proof of Obstruction by @realDonaldTrump it's just his "personal opinion" Meet… [Twitter for iPhone]

Mar 5, 2019 11:27:18 PM Hans Von Spakovsky, "I haven't seen any evidence of actual violations of the law, which is usually a basis before you start an investigation. Adam Schiff seems to be copying Joseph McCarthy in wanting to open up investigations when they don't have any evidence of wrongdoing." [Twitter for iPhone]

Mar 5, 2019 11:43:07 PM RT @IngrahamAngle: Tune in tonight for blockbuster analysis of the Dems' colossally stupid decision to overreach with overbroad subpoenas..... [Twitter for iPhone]

Mar 5, 2019 11:45:07 PM RT @DonaldJTrumpJr: Weird that all of a sudden the Fake Dossier author (paid for by Hillary and the DNC etc) no longe wants to show up and… [Twitter for iPhone]

Mar 5, 2019 11:53:11 PM Weirdo Tom Steyer doesn't have the "guts" or money to run for President. He's all talk! https://t.co/klmVsCmeNE [Twitter for iPhone]

Mar 5, 2019 11:54:20 PM RT @DonaldJTrumpJr: Jim Jordan: No evidence of Trump colluding with Russia, but 'all kinds' showing Clinton campaign did https://t.co/XR2hU… [Twitter for iPhone]

Mar 6, 2019 12:54:06 PM Senate Republicans are not voting on constitutionality or precedent, they are voting on desperately needed Border Security & the Wall. Our Country is being invaded with Drugs, Human Traffickers, & Criminals of all shapes and sizes. That's what this vote is all about. STAY UNITED! [Twitter for iPhone]

Mar 6, 2019 02:50:45 PM It is shameful that House Democrats won't take a stronger stand against Anti-Semitism in their conference. Anti-Semitism has fueled atrocities throughout history and it's inconceivable they will not act to condemn it! [Twitter for iPhone]

Mar 6, 2019 05:04:13 PM American Workforce Policy Advisory Board Meeting at the @WhiteHouse! https://t.co/izb2tTrINB [Twitter for iPhone]

Mar 6, 2019 06:56:45 PM Congressman Chris Stewart: "No one is accusing the President of a crime and yet they (the Democrats) are issuing hundreds of subpoenas. This is unprecedented." They are desperately trying to find anything they can, even a punctuation mistake in a document! [Twitter for iPhone]

Mar 6, 2019 07:02:15 PM Wall Street Journal: "More migrant families crossing into the U.S. illegally have been arrested in the first five months of the federal fiscal year than in any prior full year." We are doing a great job at the border, but this is a National Emergency! [Twitter for iPhone]

Mar 6, 2019 07:05:33 PM Democrats just blocked @FoxNews from holding a debate. Good, then I think I'll do the same thing with the Fake News Networks and the Radical Left Democrats in the General Election debates! [Twitter for iPhone]

Mar 7, 2019 09:24:45 AM It was not a campaign contribution, and there were no violations of the campaign finance laws by me. Fake News! [Twitter for iPhone]

Mar 7, 2019 09:38:54 AM We are on track to APPREHEND more than one million people coming across the Southern Border this year. Great job by Border Patrol (and others) who are working in a Broken System. Can be fixed by Congress so easily and quickly if only the Democrats would get on board! [Twitter for iPhone]

Mar 7, 2019 05:39:11 PM Breaking News @MSNBC: "Cohen's lawyer contradicts Cohen's testimony about never seeking a Presidential Pardon." [Twitter for iPhone]

Mar 8, 2019 07:24:07 AM The Wall is being built and is well under construction. Big impact will be made. Many additional contracts are close to being signed. Far ahead of schedule despite all of the Democrat Obstruction and Fake News! [Twitter for iPhone]

Mar 8, 2019 07:26:00 AM Thank you @foxandfriends. Great show! [Twitter for iPhone]

⬜ Mar 8, 2019 07:32:44 AM I cannot believe the level of dishonesty in the media. It is totally out of control, but we are winning! [Twitter for iPhone]

⬜ Mar 8, 2019 07:34:24 AM PRESIDENTIAL HARASSMENT! [Twitter for iPhone]

⬜ Mar 8, 2019 08:30:46 AM Both the Judge and the lawyer in the Paul Manafort case stated loudly and for the world to hear that there was NO COLLUSION with Russia. But the Witch Hunt Hoax continues as you now add these statements to House & Senate Intelligence & Senator Burr. So bad for our Country! [Twitter for iPhone]

⬜ Mar 8, 2019 08:43:28 AM "This is as good a time as I can remember to be an American Worker. We have the strongest economy in the world." Stuart Varney @foxandfriends So true! [Twitter for iPhone]

⬜ Mar 8, 2019 08:54:57 AM We are apprehending record numbers of illegal immigrants - but we need the Wall to help our great Border Patrol Agents! [Twitter for iPhone]

⬜ Mar 8, 2019 08:58:29 AM Women's unemployment rate is down to 3.6% - was 7.9% in January, 2011. Things are looking good! [Twitter for iPhone]

⬜ Mar 8, 2019 09:13:54 AM On International Women's Day, we honor women worldwide for their vital role in shaping and strengthening our communities, families, governments, and businesses...https://t.co/VVnkuBPmhA [Twitter for iPhone]

⬜ Mar 8, 2019 09:59:22 AM Heading now to the Great State of Alabama! [Twitter for iPhone]

⬜ Mar 8, 2019 11:04:20 AM Bad lawyer and fraudster Michael Cohen said under sworn testimony that he never asked for a Pardon. His lawyers totally contradicted him. He lied! Additionally, he directly asked me for a pardon. I said NO. He lied again! He also badly wanted to work at the White House. He lied! [Twitter for iPhone]

⬜ Mar 8, 2019 01:47:33 PM ....as Secretary of the Air Force, and I know she will be equally great in the very important world of higher education. A strong thank you to Heather for her service. [Twitter for iPhone]

⬜ Mar 8, 2019 01:47:33 PM Congratulations to Heather Wilson, who is the sole finalist to become the next President of University of Texas at El Paso effective September 1, 2019. Heather has done an absolutely fantastic job... [Twitter for iPhone]

⬜ Mar 8, 2019 03:27:33 PM RT @IvankaTrump: We have reached 6,577,623 pledged new career opportunities, apprenticeships, continuing education and on-the-job training… [Twitter for iPhone]

⬜ Mar 8, 2019 03:30:48 PM RT @paulsperry_: Now that even some MSM acknowledging there never was a "collusion" scandal, when will MSM start investigating the real sca… [Twitter for iPhone]

Mar 8, 2019 03:31:15 PM RT @paulsperry_: Glenn Simpson & Christopher Steele r 2 of biggest villains in Russia collusion hoax, yet neither has faced serious scrutin... [Twitter for iPhone]

Mar 8, 2019 03:36:50 PM RT @paulsperry_: Despite running informants/stings on Trump camp, electronically spying for yr,unmasking NSA intercepts, rummaging thru Tru... [Twitter for iPhone]

Mar 8, 2019 03:36:53 PM RT @paulsperry_: BREAKING: Democratic Rep. Jerry "Joe McCarthy" Nadler, who just yesterday declared that Trump obstructed justice, just now... [Twitter for iPhone]

Mar 8, 2019 03:38:16 PM RT @paulsperry_: Cohen claimed his shady father-in-law's "in the clothing business" when in fact he's loan shark in same taxicab medallion... [Twitter for iPhone]

Mar 8, 2019 03:45:41 PM Aluminum prices are down 12% since I instituted Tariffs on Aluminum Dumping - and the U.S. will be taking in Billions, plus jobs. Nice! [Twitter for iPhone]

Mar 8, 2019 03:50:22 PM Sessions didn't have a clue! https://t.co/XlLpnINOBv [Twitter for iPhone]

Mar 8, 2019 03:52:06 PM RT @TomFitton: NEW: Cohen Testimony is Abuse of @RealDonaldTrump: Deep State Abuse and Leaks Targets Trump Family/WH On Security Clearances... [Twitter for iPhone]

Mar 8, 2019 03:52:15 PM RT @TomFitton: .@JudicialWatch exposed that Clinton operation and FBI paying Steele at the same time here: https://t.co/fICH35a59c https:/... [Twitter for iPhone]

Mar 8, 2019 04:23:18 PM RT @LouDobbs: #AmericaFirst – @marc_lotter: Democrats couldn't condemn anti-semitism. That's because the radical, left-wing socialists have... [Twitter for iPhone]

Mar 8, 2019 04:23:49 PM RT @LouDobbs: Radical Dimms embarrass themselves: Debate over anti-Semitism charges exposes divide in Democratic Party. https://t.co/xm4SD... [Twitter for iPhone]

Mar 8, 2019 04:26:51 PM RT @cvpayne: Jobs Report: Most Important Highlight Non-Supervisory Wages continue to surge and outpace overall wage increases This is amaz... [Twitter for iPhone]

Mar 8, 2019 04:28:49 PM RT @marklevinshow: Ron DeSantis, America's governor https://t.co/WmJ9yC922a [Twitter for iPhone]

Mar 8, 2019 04:30:25 PM RT @marklevinshow: Victor Davis Hanson is on next. His new book, the Case for Trump, is out now! https://t.co/u8JLoroBca [Twitter for iPhone]

Mar 8, 2019 05:46:23 PM RT @IvankaTrump: Happy International Women's Day! #IWD2019 #WGDP @USAID @WhiteHouse https://t.co/DOX6vGeCZd [Twitter for iPhone]

Mar 8, 2019 05:46:33 PM RT @FLOTUS: Happy #InternationalWomensDay2019 https://t.co/MtecsanuEo [Twitter for iPhone]

Mar 8, 2019 05:57:07 PM RT @IvankaTrump: Thank you for your exemplary service to our nation Secretary Wilson! https://t.co/sYGLGmOT4X [Twitter for iPhone]

Mar 8, 2019 06:00:56 PM Unimaginable loss - Such great people! https://t.co/AV9oi8XuaE [Twitter for iPhone]

Mar 8, 2019 06:02:29 PM RT @MSNBC: President Trump and First Lady Melania Trump view memorial crosses for the 23 people killed in the Alabama tornadoes. https://t.... [Twitter for iPhone]

Mar 8, 2019 06:18:27 PM .@RepMikeTurner "The only time that Michael Cohen told the truth is when he pled that he is guilty." Also when he said no collusion and I did not tell him to lie!" [Twitter for iPhone]

Mar 8, 2019 08:18:38 PM https://t.co/QUuEBfFo44 [Twitter for iPhone]

Mar 9, 2019 09:07:12 AM Border Patrol and Law Enforcement has apprehended (captured) large numbers of illegal immigrants at the Border. They won't be coming into the U.S. The Wall is being built and will greatly help us in the future, and now! [Twitter for iPhone]

Mar 9, 2019 03:35:24 PM RT @RepDanCrenshaw: Today I offered a motion to recommit #HR1 reaffirming that only US citizens should have the right to vote. Dems rejec... [Twitter for iPhone]

Mar 9, 2019 03:37:14 PM RT @dbongino: Is there anything that the Democrats stand for that aligns with American values anymore? Now that they've gone all-in on anti... [Twitter for iPhone]

Mar 9, 2019 03:37:14 PM RT @RepMarkMeadows: Before Michael Cohen's testimony last week, he and Adam Schiff met for TEN hours. But last Sunday, Schiff told CBS his... [Twitter for iPhone]

Mar 9, 2019 04:50:23 PM I hope the grandstanding Governor of California is able to spend his very highly taxed citizens money on asylum holds more efficiently than money has been spent on the so-called Fast Train, which is $Billions over budget & in total disarray. Time to reduce taxes in California! [Twitter for iPhone]

Mar 9, 2019 05:04:22 PM Wacky Nut Job @AnnCoulter, who still hasn't figured out that, despite all odds and an entire Democrat Party of Far Left Radicals against me (not to mention certain Republicans who are sadly unwilling to fight), I am winning on the Border. Major sections of Wall are being built... [Twitter for iPhone]

Mar 9, 2019 05:13:55 PM ....and renovated, with MUCH MORE to follow shortly. Tens of thousands of illegals are being apprehended (captured) at the Border and NOT allowed into our Country. With another President, millions would be pouring in. I am stopping an invasion as the Wall gets built. #MAGA [Twitter for iPhone]

Mar 9, 2019 05:19:10 PM The Witch Hunt continues! https://t.co/9W1iUgE0d6 [Twitter for iPhone]

Mar 9, 2019 05:20:01 PM RT @TimRunsHisMouth: Democrats so far in 2019: ✓Won't condemn anti-semitism in the House of Reps. ✓Do nothing against a racist Governor w... [Twitter for iPhone]

Mar 9, 2019 05:50:47 PM This is just the beginning! https://t.co/PYwFGVGUxX [Twitter for iPhone]

Mar 9, 2019 11:19:53 PM Will soon be 145 Judges! https://t.co/LoTbT4RFJj [Twitter for iPhone]

Mar 9, 2019 11:20:36 PM RT @GOPChairwoman: Since the mainstream media doesn't cover the booming @realDonaldTrump economy enough: - Wage growth just hit 3.4% – the... [Twitter for iPhone]

Mar 9, 2019 11:21:34 PM RT @WhiteHouse: Economic security is national security. That's the principle at work as President @realDonaldTrump helps our veterans tra... [Twitter for iPhone]

Mar 9, 2019 11:23:35 PM RT @TomFitton: .@JudicialWatch uncovers major Ohr-Steele-Fusion GPS collusion docs PLUS did Schiff conspire with Cohen to smear @RealDonald... [Twitter for iPhone]

Mar 9, 2019 11:32:18 PM "Donald Trump's Approval Rating is at or near his highest level ever. The media is not being honest about what is happening in this Country." Jesse Watters [Twitter for iPhone]

Mar 9, 2019 11:33:09 PM RT @mike_pence: Great to be in Kentucky! I'm proud to stand with @MattBevin who is working tirelessly for the great people of the Bluegrass... [Twitter for iPhone]

Mar 10, 2019 12:00:28 AM RT @WhiteHouse: "Public optimism in their personal economy has hit a 16-year high under President Trump." "The job market doesn't get much... [Twitter for iPhone]

Mar 10, 2019 07:02:20 AM Despite the most hostile and corrupt media in the history of American politics, the Trump Administration has accomplished more in its first two years than any other Administration. Judges, biggest Tax & Regulation Cuts, V.A. Choice, Best Economy, Lowest Unemployment & much more! [Twitter for iPhone]

Mar 10, 2019 07:05:46 AM More people are working today in the United States, 158,000,000, than at any time in our Country's history. That is a Big Deal! [Twitter for iPhone]

Mar 10, 2019 05:46:43 PM RT @paulsperry_: If Schiff wasn't coaching Cohen on how to go after Trump before his testimony and was just going over procedural issues, w... [Twitter for iPhone]

Mar 10, 2019 06:42:31 PM "There's not one shred of evidence that President Trump has done anything wrong." @GrahamLedger One America News. So true, a total Witch Hunt - All started illegally by Crooked Hillary Clinton, the DNC and others! [Twitter for iPhone]

⬜ Mar 10, 2019 07:12:36 PM RT @TomFitton: .@RepAdamSchiff has another ethics scandal as a result of his and his staff colluding with Cohen on his testimony, which was… [Twitter for iPhone]

⬜ Mar 10, 2019 07:13:59 PM RT @TomFitton: Top House Dem says Cohen likely to face DOJ perjury probe https://t.co/Xo1o4E6f5x #FoxNews [Twitter for iPhone]

⬜ Mar 10, 2019 07:14:15 PM RT @TomFitton: The real collusion scandal… why haven't Hillary Clinton and her lawyers been questioned about their collusion with Fusion… [Twitter for iPhone]

⬜ Mar 10, 2019 08:44:21 PM RT @paulsperry_: BREAKING: Even Mueller's case against Russia itself, for interfering in the 2016 election, is breaking down [Twitter for iPhone]

⬜ Mar 10, 2019 08:44:25 PM RT @paulsperry_: BREAKING: US Border Patrol says that after physical barriers were erected in San Diego and El Paso sectors, as well as Yum… [Twitter for iPhone]

⬜ Mar 10, 2019 08:51:43 PM RT @senatemajldr: H.R.1 is a blatant power grab to give Washington bureaucrats control over what American citizens can say about politics,… [Twitter for iPhone]

⬜ Mar 10, 2019 08:52:24 PM RT @LindseyGrahamSC: Executive Business meeting this morning on judicial nominees in the @senjudiciary committee. WATCH: https://t.co/AAzW… [Twitter for iPhone]

⬜ Mar 10, 2019 08:53:01 PM RT @USAmbIsrael: With @LindseyGrahamSC today touring a Gaza terror tunnel. Cost of tunnel = cost of 2 new schools = cost of 30 new homes. #… [Twitter for iPhone]

⬜ Mar 10, 2019 08:54:00 PM RT @TomFitton: BIG:@JudicialWatch Uncovers DOJ Docs Showing Numerous Bruce Ohr Communications with Clinton/DNC's Fusion GPS, Christopher St… [Twitter for iPhone]

⬜ Mar 10, 2019 08:58:07 PM RT @ChuckRossDC: NEW: Dark money group gave $2 Million DEMOCRACY INTEGRITY PROJECT, the org that hired Fusion GPS and Chris Steele to bolst… [Twitter for iPhone]

⬜ Mar 11, 2019 09:12:50 AM At a recent round table meeting of business executives, & long after formally introducing Tim Cook of Apple, I quickly referred to Tim + Apple as Tim/Apple as an easy way to save time & words. The Fake News was disparagingly all over this, & it became yet another bad Trump story! [Twitter for iPhone]

⬜ Mar 11, 2019 09:17:01 AM Making Daylight Saving Time permanent is O.K. with me! [Twitter for iPhone]

⬜ Mar 11, 2019 09:18:59 AM RT @GOPChairwoman: .@realDonaldTrump made history by including a national paid family leave proposal in a presidential budget. This invest… [Twitter for iPhone]

⬜ Mar 11, 2019 09:42:28 AM RT @RepAndyBiggsAZ: Kate Steinle. Sarah Root. Grant Ronnebeck. We willl no longer be bystanders to these crimes committed by illegal alien… [Twitter for iPhone]

Mar 11, 2019 10:27:50 AM Republican Senators have a very easy vote this week. It is about Border Security and the Wall (stopping Crime, Drugs etc.), not Constitutionality and Precedent. It is an 80% positive issue. The Dems are 100% United, as usual, on a 20% issue, Open Borders and Crime. Get tough R's! [Twitter for iPhone]

Mar 12, 2019 07:12:01 AM "Jewish people are leaving the Democratic Party. We saw a lot of anti Israel policies start under the Obama Administration, and it got worsts & worse. There is anti-Semitism in the Democratic Party. They don't care about Israel or the Jewish people." Elizabeth Pipko, Jexodus. [Twitter for iPhone]

Mar 12, 2019 07:29:48 AM Patrick Moore, co-founder of Greenpeace: "The whole climate crisis is not only Fake News, it's Fake Science. There is no climate crisis, there's weather and climate all around the world, and in fact carbon dioxide is the main building block of all life." @foxandfriends Wow! [Twitter for iPhone]

Mar 12, 2019 09:00:20 AM Airplanes are becoming far too complex to fly. Pilots are no longer needed, but rather computer scientists from MIT. I see it all the time in many products. Always seeking to go one unnecessary step further, when often old and simpler is far better. Split second decisions are.... [Twitter for iPhone]

Mar 12, 2019 09:12:27 AM ....needed, and the complexity creates danger. All of this for great cost yet very little gain. I don't know about you, but I don't want Albert Einstein to be my pilot. I want great flying professionals that are allowed to easily and quickly take control of a plane! [Twitter for iPhone]

Mar 12, 2019 11:27:42 AM RT @FLOTUS: While you may never personally become addicted, the chances of knowing someone who struggles with it are high. If you, or someo… [Twitter for iPhone]

Mar 12, 2019 05:17:13 PM New York State and its Governor, Andrew Cuomo, are now proud members of the group of PRESIDENTIAL HARASSERS. No wonder people are fleeing the State in record numbers. The Witch Hunt continues! [Twitter for iPhone]

Mar 12, 2019 10:28:12 PM RT @WhiteHouse: More good news today: "Real wages for American families are soaring," says @WhiteHouseCEA. And along with those rising wage… [Twitter for iPhone]

Mar 12, 2019 10:29:46 PM RT @WhiteHouse: Today, President @realDonaldTrump signed the John D. Dingell, Jr. Conservation, Management, and Recreation Act, which prote… [Twitter for iPhone]

Mar 12, 2019 10:30:19 PM RT @dcexaminer: For the first time in his presidency, @realDonaldTrump flipped an appeals court to now have a majority of Republican-appoin… [Twitter for iPhone]

⬜ Mar 12, 2019 10:34:25 PM RT @VP: Thank you @CUNA for hosting me today! As I told their members: we're asking every member of the US Senate: A vote against the Presi... [Twitter for iPhone]

⬜ Mar 12, 2019 10:34:48 PM RT @WhiteHouseCEA: Real average hourly earnings rose 1.9% during the past 12 months, well exceeding the 0.4% pace during the year-earlier p... [Twitter for iPhone]

⬜ Mar 12, 2019 10:37:29 PM RT @IvankaTrump: America's economy is stronger than ever & women in the workforce are thriving: - Female unemployment reached its LOW... [Twitter for iPhone]

⬜ Mar 12, 2019 10:37:43 PM RT @IvankaTrump: - Labor force participation of prime-age females reached 76% in January, matching the highest rate since '03 - Wages are... [Twitter for iPhone]

⬜ Mar 12, 2019 10:40:58 PM RT @WhiteHouse: All across America, hardworking taxpayers balance their household budgets, find ways to do more with less, and still manage... [Twitter for iPhone]

⬜ Mar 12, 2019 10:57:15 PM All part of the Witch Hunt! https://t.co/5HCCNFZXFN [Twitter for iPhone]

⬜ Mar 12, 2019 11:00:58 PM RT @Jim_Jordan: Why did @AdamSchiff fail to disclose that he met with Glenn Simpson (whose Dossier oppo research was funded by the Clinton... [Twitter for iPhone]

⬜ Mar 12, 2019 11:03:57 PM RT @DonaldJTrumpJr: Well done @SteveDaines! As we spoke about on the campaign trail and in hunting camp #publiclands is a big issue for us... [Twitter for iPhone]

⬜ Mar 12, 2019 11:04:29 PM RT @Jim_Jordan: Why did @AdamSchiff say that his talks with Michael Cohen were limited to inviting him and allaying any concerns about thre... [Twitter for iPhone]

⬜ Mar 12, 2019 11:05:16 PM RT @Jim_Jordan: Why did @AdamSchiff try to block Congress from learning that the Clinton campaign paid for the Dossier? [Twitter for iPhone]

⬜ Mar 12, 2019 11:07:08 PM RT @LindaSuhler: Dear God, Thank you for answering our prayers. A grateful Nation #GodBlessAmericaus #PresidentTrump #ElectionDay https://... [Twitter for iPhone]

⬜ Mar 12, 2019 11:10:51 PM RT @GOP: The NY Attorney General called President Trump an "illegitimate president." She has proven to have a vendetta against @realDonaldT... [Twitter for iPhone]

⬜ Mar 12, 2019 11:17:52 PM All part of the Witch Hunt Hoax. Started by little Eric Schneiderman & Coumo. So many leaving New York! https://t.co/5HCCNFZXFN [Twitter for iPhone]

⬜ Mar 12, 2019 11:27:04 PM All part of the Witch Hunt Hoax. Started by little Eric Schneiderman & Cuomo. So many leaving New York! https://t.co/5HCCNFZXFN [Twitter for iPhone]

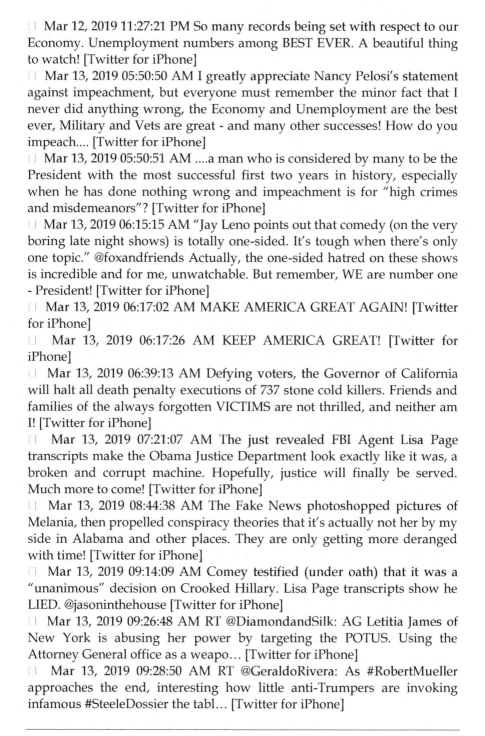

☐ Mar 12, 2019 11:27:21 PM So many records being set with respect to our Economy. Unemployment numbers among BEST EVER. A beautiful thing to watch! [Twitter for iPhone]

☐ Mar 13, 2019 05:50:50 AM I greatly appreciate Nancy Pelosi's statement against impeachment, but everyone must remember the minor fact that I never did anything wrong, the Economy and Unemployment are the best ever, Military and Vets are great - and many other successes! How do you impeach.... [Twitter for iPhone]

☐ Mar 13, 2019 05:50:51 AM ....a man who is considered by many to be the President with the most successful first two years in history, especially when he has done nothing wrong and impeachment is for "high crimes and misdemeanors"? [Twitter for iPhone]

☐ Mar 13, 2019 06:15:15 AM "Jay Leno points out that comedy (on the very boring late night shows) is totally one-sided. It's tough when there's only one topic." @foxandfriends Actually, the one-sided hatred on these shows is incredible and for me, unwatchable. But remember, WE are number one - President! [Twitter for iPhone]

☐ Mar 13, 2019 06:17:02 AM MAKE AMERICA GREAT AGAIN! [Twitter for iPhone]

☐ Mar 13, 2019 06:17:26 AM KEEP AMERICA GREAT! [Twitter for iPhone]

☐ Mar 13, 2019 06:39:13 AM Defying voters, the Governor of California will halt all death penalty executions of 737 stone cold killers. Friends and families of the always forgotten VICTIMS are not thrilled, and neither am I! [Twitter for iPhone]

☐ Mar 13, 2019 07:21:07 AM The just revealed FBI Agent Lisa Page transcripts make the Obama Justice Department look exactly like it was, a broken and corrupt machine. Hopefully, justice will finally be served. Much more to come! [Twitter for iPhone]

☐ Mar 13, 2019 08:44:38 AM The Fake News photoshopped pictures of Melania, then propelled conspiracy theories that it's actually not her by my side in Alabama and other places. They are only getting more deranged with time! [Twitter for iPhone]

☐ Mar 13, 2019 09:14:09 AM Comey testified (under oath) that it was a "unanimous" decision on Crooked Hillary. Lisa Page transcripts show he LIED. @jasoninthehouse [Twitter for iPhone]

☐ Mar 13, 2019 09:26:48 AM RT @DiamondandSilk: AG Letitia James of New York is abusing her power by targeting the POTUS. Using the Attorney General office as a weapo… [Twitter for iPhone]

☐ Mar 13, 2019 09:28:50 AM RT @GeraldoRivera: As #RobertMueller approaches the end, interesting how little anti-Trumpers are invoking infamous #SteeleDossier the tabl… [Twitter for iPhone]

Mar 13, 2019 09:28:54 AM RT @GeraldoRivera: @SpeakerPelosi statements vs #Impeachment are refreshing & conciliatory. Her conclusion that attempting to remove @realD... [Twitter for iPhone]

Mar 13, 2019 11:43:14 AM Democrats will have a unanimous vote on a 20% issue in opposing Republican Senators tomorrow. The Dems are for Open Borders and Crime! [Twitter for iPhone]

Mar 13, 2019 11:48:29 AM Republican Senators are overthinking tomorrow's vote on National Emergency. It is very simply Border Security/No Crime - Should not be thought of any other way. We have a MAJOR NATIONAL EMERGENCY at our Border and the People of our Country know it very well! [Twitter for iPhone]

Mar 13, 2019 01:54:10 PM https://t.co/2qWkPuFDL6 [Twitter Media Studio]

Mar 13, 2019 05:35:47 PM "Double Standard - Former FBI lawyer (Lisa Page) admits being told to go easy on Clinton." Very unfair! @FoxNews [Twitter for iPhone]

Mar 13, 2019 05:47:30 PM "The Lisa Page (FBI) transcript also confirms earlier reporting that Page testified Russian Collusion was still unproven when Special Counsel Robert Mueller was appointed." Catherine Herridge, @FoxNews In other words they appointed someone when there was (and is) no crime. Bad! [Twitter for iPhone]

Mar 13, 2019 05:52:42 PM I agree with Rand Paul. This is a total disgrace and should NEVER happen to another President! https://t.co/czcUbee9x7 [Twitter for iPhone]

Mar 13, 2019 08:12:29 PM RT @WhiteHouse: January 16, 2019: 247 illegal migrants rush the border in New Mexico. This is a national emergency. https://t.co/I6tLEQkbnX [Twitter for iPhone]

Mar 14, 2019 05:28:37 AM "Democrats are frantic to throw something else at the President. That's why you saw those 81 subpoenas. It's ridiculous. Just because your still upset over an election that happened 2 1/2 years ago, you should not be allowed to ruin people's lives like this." Lara Trump, @FoxNews [Twitter for iPhone]

Mar 14, 2019 05:44:56 AM A big National Emergency vote today by The United States Senate on Border Security & the Wall (which is already under major construction). I am prepared to veto, if necessary. The Southern Border is a National Security and Humanitarian Nightmare, but it can be easily fixed! [Twitter for iPhone]

Mar 14, 2019 06:22:13 AM My Administration looks forward to negotiating a large scale Trade Deal with the United Kingdom. The potential is unlimited! [Twitter for iPhone]

Mar 14, 2019 06:54:24 AM The Democrats are "Border Deniers." They refuse to see or acknowledge the Death, Crime, Drugs and Human Trafficking at our Southern Border! [Twitter for iPhone]

Mar 14, 2019 07:25:25 AM The three very weak and untalented late night "hosts" are "fighting over table scraps. Carson did a great job, it wasn't political. I don't know what they're going to do in 2024 when he's no longer President? Will be wacky in the unemployment line." Michael Loftus @foxandfriends [Twitter for iPhone]

Mar 14, 2019 07:40:51 AM Happy National Ag Day! https://t.co/hNkOh0TqvW [Twitter for iPhone]

Mar 14, 2019 09:13:13 AM Prominent legal scholars agree that our actions to address the National Emergency at the Southern Border and to protect the American people are both CONSTITUTIONAL and EXPRESSLY authorized by Congress.... [Twitter for iPhone]

Mar 14, 2019 09:13:14 AM ....If, at a later date, Congress wants to update the law, I will support those efforts, but today's issue is BORDER SECURITY and Crime!!! Don't vote with Pelosi! [Twitter for iPhone]

Mar 14, 2019 09:46:44 AM A vote for today's resolution by Republican Senators is a vote for Nancy Pelosi, Crime, and the Open Border Democrats! [Twitter for iPhone]

Mar 14, 2019 11:18:40 AM Congratulations @Toyota! BIG NEWS for U.S. Auto Workers! The USMCA is already fixing the broken NAFTA deal. https://t.co/f9iHprPk5B [Twitter for iPhone]

Mar 14, 2019 02:16:31 PM VETO! [Twitter for iPhone]

Mar 14, 2019 02:43:08 PM I look forward to VETOING the just passed Democrat inspired Resolution which would OPEN BORDERS while increasing Crime, Drugs, and Trafficking in our Country. I thank all of the Strong Republicans who voted to support Border Security and our desperately needed WALL! [Twitter for iPhone]

Mar 14, 2019 09:31:13 PM https://t.co/884dpZi52P [Twitter for iPhone]

Mar 14, 2019 10:05:36 PM Breitbart News Network https://t.co/HdGfwuASWC via @BreitbartNews [Twitter for iPhone]

Mar 15, 2019 06:41:18 AM My warmest sympathy and best wishes goes out to the people of New Zealand after the horrible massacre in the Mosques. 49 innocent people have so senselessly died, with so many more seriously injured. The U.S. stands by New Zealand for anything we can do. God bless all! [Twitter for iPhone]

Mar 15, 2019 07:03:10 AM The 'Jexodus' movement encourages Jewish people to leave the Democrat Party. Total disrespect! Republicans are waiting with open arms. Remember Jerusalem (U.S. Embassy) and the horrible Iran Nuclear Deal! @OANN @foxandfriends [Twitter for iPhone]

Mar 15, 2019 07:15:33 AM "New evidence that the Obama era team of the FBI, DOJ & CIA were working together to Spy on (and take out) President Trump, all the way back in 2015." A transcript of Peter Strzok's testimony is devastating. Hopefully the Mueller Report will be covering this. @OANN @foxandfriends [Twitter for iPhone]

Mar 15, 2019 08:47:58 AM So, if there was knowingly & acknowledged to be "zero" crime when the Special Counsel was appointed, and if the appointment was made based on the Fake Dossier (paid for by Crooked Hillary) and now disgraced Andrew McCabe (he & all stated no crime), then the Special Counsel....... [Twitter for iPhone]

Mar 15, 2019 08:55:16 AM ....should never have been appointed and there should be no Mueller Report. This was an illegal & conflicted investigation in search of a crime. Russian Collusion was nothing more than an excuse by the Democrats for losing an Election that they thought they were going to win..... [Twitter for iPhone]

Mar 15, 2019 08:56:26 AM .....THIS SHOULD NEVER HAPPEN TO A PRESIDENT AGAIN! [Twitter for iPhone]

Mar 15, 2019 12:42:42 PM I'd like to thank all of the Great Republican Senators who bravely voted for Strong Border Security and the WALL. This will help stop Crime, Human Trafficking, and Drugs entering our Country. Watch, when you get back to your State, they will LOVE you more than ever before! [Twitter for iPhone]

Mar 15, 2019 02:14:10 PM ....that we stand in solidarity with New Zealand – and that any assistance the U.S.A. can give, we stand by ready to help. We love you New Zealand! [Twitter for iPhone]

Mar 15, 2019 02:14:10 PM Just spoke with Jacinda Ardern, the Prime Minister of New Zealand, regarding the horrific events that have taken place over the past 24 hours. I informed the Prime Minister.... [Twitter for iPhone]

Mar 15, 2019 03:46:03 PM https://t.co/tEgQFkcMs1 [Twitter for iPhone]

Mar 15, 2019 04:16:15 PM Just spoke w/ @GovRicketts. The people of Nebraska & across the Midwest, especially the Farmers & Ranchers, are feeling the impacts from severe weather. The first responders & emergency response teams have done a great job dealing w/ record flooding, high winds, & road closures. [Twitter for iPhone]

Mar 16, 2019 10:50:36 AM https://t.co/B6NgsZuJdy [Twitter for iPhone]

Mar 16, 2019 10:56:22 AM https://t.co/lopau8H33l [Twitter for iPhone]

Mar 16, 2019 11:06:21 AM On the recent non-binding vote (420-0) in Congress about releasing the Mueller Report, I told leadership to let all Republicans vote for transparency. Makes us all look good and doesn't matter. Play along with the game! [Twitter for iPhone]

Mar 16, 2019 11:10:39 AM https://t.co/oCPqP4v1fH [Twitter for iPhone]

Mar 16, 2019 11:16:46 AM Veto Message to the House of Representatives for H.J. Res. 46: https://t.co/9Z5JHAUv6N https://t.co/1A4RSYTZo0 [Twitter for iPhone]

Mar 16, 2019 12:24:46 PM https://t.co/WQThgHWcg4 [Twitter for iPhone]

Mar 16, 2019 12:38:50 PM Mark Morgan, Former Border Patrol Chief with great experience in Law Enforcement, really understands the subjects of Immigration and the Border. Thank you Mark! @foxandfriends [Twitter for iPhone]

Mar 16, 2019 01:37:39 PM RT @WhiteHouse: Attorney General Bill Barr: "The crisis that we're dealing with today is right on our door step and it presents a real clea... [Twitter for iPhone]

Mar 16, 2019 02:09:36 PM RT @WhiteHouse: Sheriff Louderback: "The sheriffs and men and women of law enforcement in this room and across this nation owe you a debt o... [Twitter for iPhone]

Mar 16, 2019 02:09:39 PM RT @WhiteHouse: Sheriff Hodgson: "Mr. President, you have stood up and you've taken the action. And the American people are behind you and... [Twitter for iPhone]

Mar 16, 2019 02:32:23 PM This is a National Emergency... https://t.co/AAKBuNW2ro [Twitter for iPhone]

Mar 16, 2019 03:46:36 PM Spreading the fake and totally discredited Dossier "is unfortunately a very dark stain against John McCain." Ken Starr, Former Independent Counsel. He had far worse "stains" than this, including thumbs down on repeal and replace after years of campaigning to repeal and replace! [Twitter for iPhone]

Mar 16, 2019 04:01:21 PM Because the economy is so good, General Motors must get their Lordstown, Ohio, plant open, maybe in a different form or with a new owner, FAST! Toyota is investing 13.5 $Billion in U.S., others likewise. G.M. MUST ACT QUICKLY. Time is of the essence! [Twitter for iPhone]

Mar 16, 2019 04:07:46 PM Google is helping China and their military, but not the U.S. Terrible! The good news is that they helped Crooked Hillary Clinton, and not Trump....and how did that turn out? [Twitter for iPhone]

Mar 16, 2019 04:22:25 PM How is the Paris Environmental Accord working out for France? After 18 weeks of rioting by the Yellow Vest Protesters, I guess not so well! In the meantime, the United States has gone to the top of all lists on the Environment. [Twitter for iPhone]

Mar 16, 2019 04:34:04 PM RT @realDonaldTrump: "New evidence that the Obama era team of the FBI, DOJ & CIA were working together to Spy on (and take out) President T... [Twitter for iPhone]

Mar 16, 2019 04:34:15 PM RT @realDonaldTrump: So, if there was knowingly & acknowledged to be "zero" crime when the Special Counsel was appointed, and if the appoin... [Twitter for iPhone]

Mar 16, 2019 04:34:18 PM RT @realDonaldTrump: ....should never have been appointed and there should be no Mueller Report. This was an illegal & conflicted investiga... [Twitter for iPhone]

Mar 16, 2019 04:34:21 PM RT @realDonaldTrump: .....THIS SHOULD NEVER HAPPEN TO A PRESIDENT AGAIN! [Twitter for iPhone]

Mar 16, 2019 04:34:52 PM RT @realDonaldTrump: I'd like to thank all of the Great Republican Senators who bravely voted for Strong Border Security and the WALL. This... [Twitter for iPhone]

Mar 17, 2019 06:59:15 AM It's truly incredible that shows like Saturday Night Live, not funny/no talent, can spend all of their time knocking the same person (me), over & over, without so much of a mention of "the other side." Like an advertisement without consequences. Same with Late Night Shows...... [Twitter for iPhone]

Mar 17, 2019 07:13:58 AM ....Should Federal Election Commission and/or FCC look into this? There must be Collusion with the Democrats and, of course, Russia! Such one sided media coverage, most of it Fake News. Hard to believe I won and am winning. Approval Rating 52%, 93% with Republicans. Sorry! #MAGA [Twitter for iPhone]

Mar 17, 2019 07:23:30 AM Report: Christopher Steele backed up his Democrat & Crooked Hillary paid for Fake & Unverified Dossier with information he got from "send in watchers" of low ratings CNN. This is the info that got us the Witch Hunt! [Twitter for iPhone]

Mar 17, 2019 07:36:08 AM So it was indeed (just proven in court papers) "last in his class" (Annapolis) John McCain that sent the Fake Dossier to the FBI and Media hoping to have it printed BEFORE the Election. He & the Dems, working together, failed (as usual). Even the Fake News refused this garbage! [Twitter for iPhone]

Mar 17, 2019 07:41:15 AM So it was indeed (just proven in court papers) "last in his class" (Annapolis) John McCain that sent the Fake Dossier to the FBI and Media hoping to have it printed BEFORE the Election. He & the Dems, working together, failed (as usual). Even the Fake News refused this garbage! [Twitter for iPhone]

Mar 17, 2019 07:50:00 AM Happy St. Patrick's Day! ☘ https://t.co/WmuNzJSRr8 [Twitter for iPhone]

Mar 17, 2019 08:18:29 AM Bring back @JudgeJeanine Pirro. The Radical Left Democrats, working closely with their beloved partner, the Fake News Media, is using every trick in the book to SILENCE a majority of our Country. They have all out campaigns against @FoxNews hosts who are doing too well. Fox ..... [Twitter for iPhone]

☐ Mar 17, 2019 08:33:03 AM ....must stay strong and fight back with vigor. Stop working soooo hard on being politically correct, which will only bring you down, and continue to fight for our Country. The losers all want what you have, don't give it to them. Be strong & prosper, be weak & die! Stay true.... [Twitter for iPhone]

☐ Mar 17, 2019 08:43:17 AM https://t.co/gj32A6PowS [Twitter for iPhone]

☐ Mar 17, 2019 08:44:25 AM ....to the people that got you there. Keep fighting for Tucker, and fight hard for @JudgeJeanine. Your competitors are jealous - they all want what you've got - NUMBER ONE. Don't hand it to them on a silver platter. They can't beat you, you can only beat yourselves! [Twitter for iPhone]

☐ Mar 17, 2019 08:53:37 AM https://t.co/yvJpMzy3R4 [Twitter for iPhone]

☐ Mar 17, 2019 12:38:40 PM Democrat UAW Local 1112 President David Green ought to get his act together and produce. G.M. let our Country down, but other much better car companies are coming into the U.S. in droves. I want action on Lordstown fast. Stop complaining and get the job done! 3.8% Unemployment! [Twitter for iPhone]

☐ Mar 17, 2019 01:18:45 PM Were @FoxNews weekend anchors, @ArthelNeville and @LelandVittert, trained by CNN prior to their ratings collapse? In any event, that's where they should be working, along with their lowest rated anchor, Shepard Smith! [Twitter for iPhone]

☐ Mar 17, 2019 03:58:32 PM Those Republican Senators who voted in favor of Strong Border Security (and the Wall) are being uniformly praised as they return to their States. They know there is a National Emergency at the Southern Border, and they had the courage to ACT. Great job! [Twitter for iPhone]

☐ Mar 17, 2019 04:22:40 PM RT @Lrihendry: Meghan MCCain took a swipe at Trump suggesting "no one will ever love you like they loved my father" WRONG Meghan! Million... [Twitter for iPhone]

☐ Mar 17, 2019 04:25:35 PM RT @superyayadize: NPR Accidentally Admits Border Fences Are Effective - Over past several decades, migrants have turned to more rugged par... [Twitter for iPhone]

☐ Mar 17, 2019 04:31:06 PM RT @ChuckCallesto: President Trump Defends Judge Jeanine After Fox Censors Her Show https://t.co/NodG0t0w2I [Twitter for iPhone]

☐ Mar 17, 2019 04:31:42 PM RT @ChuckCallesto: Christopher Steele Admits Using Posts By 'Random Individuals' From CNN To Back Up Trump Dossier https://t.co/ejhRHBjoBV [Twitter for iPhone]

☐ Mar 17, 2019 04:34:13 PM RT @ChuckCallesto: BREAKING: ==> Minnesota Democrats make move to REMOVE Ilhan Omar from Congress... https://t.co/77LYHMQ96K [Twitter for iPhone]

Mar 17, 2019 04:34:16 PM RT @ChuckCallesto: REVEALED: Foreign Government Official Offered Hillary Campaign Dirt On Trump [Details] https://t.co/t9EMftRAIG [Twitter for iPhone]

Mar 17, 2019 04:36:00 PM RT @vmbb12: We have to fight back. They have not let up on President Trump, nor his supporters since they lost. They are losers, we are win… [Twitter for iPhone]

Mar 17, 2019 04:36:33 PM RT @LonewolfnDuke: @Lrihendry https://t.co/eVXFEQCkat [Twitter for iPhone]

Mar 17, 2019 04:36:53 PM RT @parscale: David Urban: Trump's PA popularity no accident | https://t.co/mMJ65vRLhc https://t.co/0XfqEBl4p6 [Twitter for iPhone]

Mar 17, 2019 04:38:26 PM RT @WhiteHouse: Happy St. Patrick's Day! ☘ https://t.co/GEGdysOWFB [Twitter for iPhone]

Mar 17, 2019 04:44:17 PM RT @SaraCarterDC: POWELL: Andrew Weissmann -- The Kingpin Of Prosecutorial Misconduct -- Leaves Mueller's Squad | The Daily Caller https://t…. [Twitter for iPhone]

Mar 17, 2019 04:44:57 PM RT @LindaSuhler: @realDonaldTrump @FoxNews @ArthelNeville @LelandVittert Absolutely true, President Trump. When those three show up, I turn… [Twitter for iPhone]

Mar 17, 2019 04:45:18 PM RT @JackPosobiec: "Teen stabbed about 100 times and set on fire in MS-13 murder, police say" https://t.co/Xrj1j9h7qe [Twitter for iPhone]

Mar 17, 2019 04:51:27 PM RT @JackPosobiec: Why did CNN cut her off after she destroyed their Islamophobia hoax? https://t.co/zYepQbVqn8 [Twitter for iPhone]

Mar 17, 2019 04:55:11 PM RT @williamcraddick: Russiagate was designed in part to help the UK counter Russian influence by baiting the United States into taking a ha… [Twitter for iPhone]

Mar 17, 2019 05:27:27 PM Just spoke to Mary Barra, CEO of General Motors about the Lordstown Ohio plant. I am not happy that it is closed when everything else in our Country is BOOMING. I asked her to sell it or do something quickly. She blamed the UAW Union -- I don't care, I just want it open! [Twitter for iPhone]

Mar 17, 2019 06:16:38 PM What the Democrats have done in trying to steal a Presidential Election, first at the "ballot box" and then, after that failed, with the "Insurance Policy," is the biggest Scandal in the history of our Country! [Twitter for iPhone]

Mar 17, 2019 09:04:11 PM MAKE AMERICA GREAT AGAIN! [Twitter for iPhone]

Mar 18, 2019 06:37:55 AM General Motors and the UAW are going to start "talks" in September/October. Why wait, start them now! I want jobs to stay in the U.S.A. and want Lordstown (Ohio), in one of the best economies in our history, opened or sold to a company who will open it up fast! Car companies..... [Twitter for iPhone]

Mar 18, 2019 06:45:19 AM ....are all coming back to the U.S. So is everyone else. We now have the best Economy in the World, the envy of all. Get that big, beautiful plant in Ohio open now. Close a plant in China or Mexico, where you invested so heavily pre-Trump, but not in the U.S.A. Bring jobs home! [Twitter for iPhone]

Mar 18, 2019 06:55:21 AM 93% Approval Rating in the Republican Party. Thank you! [Twitter for iPhone]

Mar 18, 2019 08:14:14 AM Joe Biden got tongue tied over the weekend when he was unable to properly deliver a very simple line about his decision to run for President. Get used to it, another low I.Q. individual! [Twitter for iPhone]

Mar 18, 2019 08:38:30 AM The Fake News Media is working overtime to blame me for the horrible attack in New Zealand. They will have to work very hard to prove that one. So Ridiculous! [Twitter for iPhone]

Mar 18, 2019 10:07:40 AM Wow! A Suffolk/USA Today Poll, just out, states, "50% of Americans AGREE that Robert Mueller's investigation is a Witch Hunt." @MSNBC Very few think it is legit! We will soon find out? [Twitter for iPhone]

Mar 18, 2019 11:00:58 AM GDP growth during the four quarters of 2018 was the fastest since 2005. This Administration is the first on record to have experienced economic growth that meets or exceeds its own forecasts in each of its first two years in office. GROWTH is beating MARKET EXPECTATIONS! [Twitter for iPhone]

Mar 18, 2019 11:12:03 AM https://t.co/sb4UfYkFWI [Twitter Media Studio]

Mar 18, 2019 03:52:32 PM My team is staying in close contact with Governor Kim Reynolds (@IAGovernor) of Iowa and the local officials managing these floods. We support you and thank all of the first responders working long hours to help the great people of Iowa! https://t.co/mZ4grxQ1Sa [Twitter for iPhone]

Mar 18, 2019 03:57:23 PM Our prayers are with the great people of South Dakota. We are staying in close contact with @GovKristiNoem and all the State and Local leaders during and after these devastating floods. Everyone be safe! https://t.co/9CNcPJZ3qi [Twitter for iPhone]

Mar 18, 2019 04:35:35 PM https://t.co/precsXDarx [Twitter Media Studio]

☐ Mar 18, 2019 05:29:29 PM While the press doesn't like writing about it, nor do I need them to, I donate my yearly Presidential salary of $400,000.00 to different agencies throughout the year, this to Homeland Security. If I didn't do it there would be hell to pay from the FAKE NEWS MEDIA! https://t.co/xqIGUOwh4x [Twitter for iPhone]

☐ Mar 18, 2019 08:32:29 PM Rep. Devin Nunes Files $250M Defamation Lawsuit Against Twitter, Two Anonymous Twitter Accounts https://t.co/fT9ZXdWg7z via @thedailybeast [Twitter for iPhone]

☐ Mar 18, 2019 08:38:48 PM https://t.co/QxJBMTAZqG [Twitter Media Studio]

☐ Mar 18, 2019 10:48:54 PM https://t.co/h2bZ1p3UlY [Twitter Media Studio]

☐ Mar 19, 2019 07:24:21 AM The Fake News Media has NEVER been more Dishonest or Corrupt than it is right now. There has never been a time like this in American History. Very exciting but also, very sad! Fake News is the absolute Enemy of the People and our Country itself! [Twitter for iPhone]

☐ Mar 19, 2019 07:34:40 AM A total loser! https://t.co/vm3Vv2f9jf [Twitter for iPhone]

☐ Mar 19, 2019 08:31:02 AM "You can't dispel this mood of positive energy." @Varneyco The Economy is Great! [Twitter for iPhone]

☐ Mar 19, 2019 08:57:04 AM Facebook, Google and Twitter, not to mention the Corrupt Media, are sooo on the side of the Radical Left Democrats. But fear not, we will win anyway, just like we did before! #MAGA [Twitter for iPhone]

☐ Mar 19, 2019 10:32:51 AM I will be looking into this! #StopTheBias https://t.co/ZTWQolvmdM [Twitter for iPhone]

☐ Mar 19, 2019 11:04:09 AM https://t.co/95I4towyEP [Twitter Media Studio]

☐ Mar 19, 2019 04:28:55 PM Amazingly, CNN just released a poll at 71%, saying that the economy is in the best shape since 2001, 18 years! WOW, is CNN becoming a believer? [Twitter for iPhone]

☐ Mar 19, 2019 06:23:33 PM Thank you @JesseBWatters, could not have said it any better myself! https://t.co/HirL10zwZl [Twitter for iPhone]

☐ Mar 19, 2019 07:33:50 PM RT @DonaldJTrumpJr: My latest OP-Ed on Tech Censorship - check it out and RT. Conservatives face a tough fight as Big Tech's censorship e… [Twitter for iPhone]

☐ Mar 19, 2019 09:05:48 PM Campaigning for the Popular Vote is much easier & different than campaigning for the Electoral College. It's like training for the 100 yard dash vs. a marathon. The brilliance of the Electoral College is that you must go to many States to win. With the Popular Vote, you go to.... [Twitter for iPhone]

Mar 19, 2019 09:17:39 PM ....just the large States - the Cities would end up running the Country. Smaller States & the entire Midwest would end up losing all power - & we can't let that happen. I used to like the idea of the Popular Vote, but now realize the Electoral College is far better for the U.S.A. [Twitter for iPhone]

Mar 19, 2019 10:53:03 PM Not a good situation! https://t.co/uaMcSrX4yM [Twitter for iPhone]

Mar 19, 2019 11:04:40 PM The Democrats are getting very "strange." They now want to change the voting age to 16, abolish the Electoral College, and Increase significantly the number of Supreme Court Justices. Actually, you've got to win it at the Ballot Box! [Twitter for iPhone]

Mar 20, 2019 06:51:40 AM George Conway, often referred to as Mr. Kellyanne Conway by those who know him, is VERY jealous of his wife's success & angry that I, with her help, didn't give him the job he so desperately wanted. I barely know him but just take a look, a stone cold LOSER & husband from hell! [Twitter for iPhone]

Mar 20, 2019 03:23:04 PM I am thrilled to be here in Ohio with the hardworking men and women of the Lima Army Tank Plant! We are here today to celebrate a resounding victory for all of you, for Northwest Ohio, for our GREAT MILITARY, and for our entire Country...https://t.co/ZWbjX0Be9m [Twitter for iPhone]

Mar 20, 2019 03:51:41 PM Great news from @Ford! They are investing nearly $1 BILLION in Flat Rock, Michigan for auto production on top of a $1 BILLION investment last month in a facility outside of Chicago. Companies are pouring back into the United States - they want to be where the action is! [Twitter for iPhone]

Mar 20, 2019 03:57:57 PM Really beautiful to see! https://t.co/DKq2TIeiSs [Twitter for iPhone]

Mar 20, 2019 04:25:57 PM ISIS Caliphate two years ago in red vs. ISIS Caliphate TODAY. (Was even worse in November 2016 before I took office). https://t.co/MUgfex4rCj [Twitter for iPhone]

Mar 20, 2019 06:37:42 PM https://t.co/ssJNhlTMzy [Twitter for iPhone]

Mar 20, 2019 07:07:50 PM Leaving the GREAT STATE of OHIO for the @WhiteHouse. A really great day! [Twitter for iPhone]

Mar 20, 2019 09:00:05 PM https://t.co/UhTjBuWY2h [Twitter for iPhone]

Mar 20, 2019 09:04:05 PM "The reason we have the Special Counsel investigation is that James Comey (a dirty cop) leaked his memos to a friend, who leaked them to the press, on purpose." @KennedyNation Totally illegal! [Twitter for iPhone]

Mar 20, 2019 09:40:55 PM "John Solomon: As Russia Collusion fades, Ukrainian plot to help Clinton emerges." @seanhannity @FoxNews [Twitter for iPhone]

Mar 21, 2019 11:50:46 AM After 52 years it is time for the United States to fully recognize Israel's Sovereignty over the Golan Heights, which is of critical strategic and security importance to the State of Israel and Regional Stability! [Twitter for iPhone]

Mar 21, 2019 03:12:40 PM We are here today to take historic action to defend American Students and American Values. In a few moments, I will be signing an Executive Order to protect FREE SPEECH on College Campuses. https://t.co/gFFnSl1bEF [Twitter for iPhone]

Mar 21, 2019 04:12:05 PM Today we celebrate the lives and achievements of Americans with Down Syndrome. @VP and I will always stand with these wonderful families, and together we will always stand for LIFE! #WorldDownSyndromeDay https://t.co/u7vrG7JnCP [Twitter for iPhone]

Mar 21, 2019 09:22:31 PM RT @WhiteHouse: Today, there are plenty of reasons for that trust. Manufacturing jobs are roaring back. Blue-collar workers are set to make… [Twitter for iPhone]

Mar 21, 2019 09:38:30 PM RT @WhiteHouse: President @realDonaldTrump's historic investments in our defense industrial base keep two of his biggest promises to voters… [Twitter for iPhone]

Mar 21, 2019 09:39:21 PM RT @DonaldJTrumpJr: Super excited today that @realdonaldTrump is signing an executive order today to protect free speech rights for ALL stu… [Twitter for iPhone]

Mar 21, 2019 09:39:49 PM RT @GOPChairwoman: You can't deny our economy is roaring: *fastest GDP growth in 13 years *1M more job openings than people looking for… [Twitter for iPhone]

Mar 22, 2019 05:49:07 AM RT @WhiteHouse: The American dream is back because President Trump understands what many experts don't: that restoring American greatness i… [Twitter for iPhone]

Mar 22, 2019 05:52:12 AM 3.1 GDP FOR THE YEAR, BEST NUMBER IN 14 YEARS! [Twitter for iPhone]

Mar 22, 2019 07:48:06 AM https://t.co/qjoe0rc3rQ [Twitter Media Studio]

Mar 22, 2019 07:57:45 AM "Our own Benjamin Hall is doing fantastic reporting on ISIS right on the from line (True). ISIS was willing to die but now, because of big pressure, save for a few people in caves, most have surrendered. A testament to our President." Thank you Pete Hegseth @foxandfriends [Twitter for iPhone]

Mar 22, 2019 08:13:18 AM https://t.co/du665IcD5H [Twitter for iPhone]

Mar 22, 2019 08:33:39 AM https://t.co/wbQiy4uGYM [Twitter for iPhone]

Mar 22, 2019 11:15:04 AM ISIS uses the internet better than almost anyone, but for all of those susceptible to ISIS propaganda, they are now being beaten badly at every level.... [Twitter for iPhone]

Mar 22, 2019 11:15:05 AM ....There is nothing to admire about them, they will always try to show a glimmer of vicious hope, but they are losers and barely breathing. Think about that before you destroy your lives and the lives of your family! [Twitter for iPhone]

Mar 22, 2019 11:47:33 AM It is my pleasure to announce that @StephenMoore, a very respected Economist, will be nominated to serve on the Fed Board. I have known Steve for a long time – and have no doubt he will be an outstanding choice! [Twitter for iPhone]

Mar 22, 2019 12:22:59 PM It was announced today by the U.S. Treasury that additional large scale Sanctions would be added to those already existing Sanctions on North Korea. I have today ordered the withdrawal of those additional Sanctions! [Twitter for iPhone]

Mar 22, 2019 03:15:46 PM Today in Florida, @FLOTUS and I were honored to welcome and meet with leaders from the Bahamas, Dominican Republic, Haiti, Jamaica, and Saint Lucia! https://t.co/tElFdkIYfC [Twitter for iPhone]

Mar 24, 2019 07:01:44 AM Good Morning, Have A Great Day! [Twitter for iPhone]

Mar 24, 2019 07:02:59 AM MAKE AMERICA GREAT AGAIN! [Twitter for iPhone]

Mar 24, 2019 03:42:19 PM No Collusion, No Obstruction, Complete and Total EXONERATION. KEEP AMERICA GREAT! [Twitter for iPhone]

Mar 25, 2019 05:10:14 AM "No matter your ideologies or your loyalties, this is a good day for America. No American conspired to cooperate with Russia in its efforts to interfere with the 2016 election, according to Robert Mueller, and that is good." @BretBaier @FoxNews [Twitter for iPhone]

Mar 25, 2019 05:20:12 AM "The Special Counsel did not find that the Trump Campaign, or anyone associated with it, conspired or coordinated with the Russian Government in these efforts, despite multiple offers from Russian-affiliated individuals to assist the Trump Campaign." [Twitter for iPhone]

Mar 25, 2019 05:25:23 AM "Breaking News: Mueller Report Finds No Trump-Russia Conspiracy." @MSNBC [Twitter for iPhone]

Mar 25, 2019 05:26:28 AM RT @realDonaldTrump: MAKE AMERICA GREAT AGAIN! [Twitter for iPhone]

Mar 25, 2019 05:26:33 AM RT @realDonaldTrump: No Collusion, No Obstruction, Complete and Total EXONERATION. KEEP AMERICA GREAT! [Twitter for iPhone]

Mar 25, 2019 05:26:39 AM RT @realDonaldTrump: Good Morning, Have A Great Day! [Twitter for iPhone]

⎵ Mar 25, 2019 10:22:40 AM https://t.co/DAT0cT72WX [Twitter Media Studio]

⎵ Mar 25, 2019 12:26:24 PM https://t.co/G4RNXzoWqc [Twitter for iPhone]

⎵ Mar 25, 2019 01:10:19 PM Today, it was my great honor to welcome Prime Minister @Netanyahu of Israel back to the @WhiteHouse where I signed a Presidential Proclamation recognizing Israel's sovereignty over the Golan Heights. Read more: https://t.co/yAAyR2Hxe4 https://t.co/gWp6nwRwsY [Twitter for iPhone]

⎵ Mar 25, 2019 08:54:43 PM WSJ: Obama Admin Must Account for 'Abuse of Surveillance Powers' https://t.co/mIE0vOFZae via @BreitbartNews [Twitter for iPhone]

⎵ Mar 25, 2019 09:05:36 PM RT @bmcnally14: The #Caps won a Stanley Cup so they get to spend the next hour here touring and meeting the President in a private event. h… [Twitter for iPhone]

⎵ Mar 25, 2019 09:06:51 PM RT @keeperofthecup: Hanging out in the Roosevelt Room, waiting to head into the oval office. #stanleycup @NHL @WhiteHouse @HockeyHallFame… [Twitter for iPhone]

⎵ Mar 25, 2019 09:08:59 PM A team of great champions! https://t.co/Pm5p9L6TaX [Twitter for iPhone]

⎵ Mar 25, 2019 09:09:25 PM RT @ScottABC7: The Stanley Cup and the Caps with President Trump in the Oval Office. What a picture! https://t.co/lKwBz3F1YL [Twitter for iPhone]

⎵ Mar 25, 2019 10:24:10 PM RT @ZacharyIvanPor1: @realDonaldTrump Thank you Mr. Presidentus for all of your sacrifice, your hard work, and your thoughtful leadership.… [Twitter for iPhone]

⎵ Mar 25, 2019 10:32:10 PM RT @DonaldJTrumpJr: Christmas came early this week. https://t.co/ypqkZgRkeR [Twitter for iPhone]

⎵ Mar 25, 2019 10:48:05 PM RT @TomFitton: Tom Fitton on @RealDonaldTrump Russia Mueller Probe: 'They've KNOWN There Was NO Collusion" And, by the way, @DevinNunes is… [Twitter for iPhone]

⎵ Mar 26, 2019 05:54:55 AM The Mainstream Media is under fire and being scorned all over the World as being corrupt and FAKE. For two years they pushed the Russian Collusion Delusion when they always knew there was No Collusion. They truly are the Enemy of the People and the Real Opposition Party! [Twitter for iPhone]

⎵ Mar 26, 2019 06:12:01 AM RT @TomFitton: Let's be clear, neither Mueller, Obama FBI, DOJ, CIA, Deep State, etc ever had good faith basis to pursue @realDonaldTrump o… [Twitter for iPhone]

Mar 26, 2019 09:42:40 AM "What we're seeing on Capital Hill right now is that the Democrats are walking back any charges of Collusion against the President." @ByronYork @BillHemmer Should never have been started, a disgrace! [Twitter for iPhone]

Mar 26, 2019 09:49:07 AM "What we're seeing on Capitol Hill right now is that the Democrats are walking back any charges of Collusion against the President." @ByronYork @BillHemmer Should never have been started, a disgrace! [Twitter for iPhone]

Mar 26, 2019 11:58:18 AM The Republican Party will become "The Party of Healthcare!" [Twitter for iPhone]

Mar 26, 2019 03:36:53 PM "A Catastrophic Media Failure" https://t.co/dkHo5kHwwf [Twitter for iPhone]

Mar 26, 2019 04:31:16 PM Thank you to the House Republicans for sticking together and the BIG WIN today on the Border. Today's vote simply reaffirms Congressional Democrats are the party of Open Borders, Drugs and Crime! [Twitter for iPhone]

Mar 26, 2019 06:15:06 PM "Proclamation on Recognizing the Golan Heights as Part of the State of Israel" https://t.co/yAAyR2Hxe4 https://t.co/VccUpjMJqZ [Twitter for iPhone]

Mar 26, 2019 07:39:17 PM "I think this is probably the most consequential media screwup of the last 25 to 50 years. It is difficult to comprehend or overstate the damage that the media did to the Country, to their own reputation or to the Constitution. An absolute catastrophe" Sean Davis @TuckerCarlson [Twitter for iPhone]

Mar 26, 2019 08:09:27 PM https://t.co/P46CNUBicX [Twitter for iPhone]

Mar 26, 2019 08:10:51 PM https://t.co/Ing9BhBQGi [Twitter for iPhone]

Mar 26, 2019 08:27:21 PM The Fake News Media has lost tremendous credibility with its corrupt coverage of the illegal Democrat Witch Hunt of your all time favorite duly elected President, me! T.V. ratings of CNN & MSNBC tanked last night after seeing the Mueller Report statement. @FoxNews up BIG! [Twitter for iPhone]

Mar 27, 2019 01:47:09 PM .@GreggJarrett: "Trump-Russia 'collusion' was always a hoax -- and dirtiest political trick in modern US history" https://t.co/H59Q1UL64g [Twitter for iPhone]

Mar 27, 2019 02:00:12 PM https://t.co/kTXRgcuk5x [Twitter for iPhone]

Mar 27, 2019 02:38:55 PM ....Also discussed political fairness and various things that @Google can do for our Country. Meeting ended very well! [Twitter for iPhone]

Mar 27, 2019 02:38:55 PM Just met with @SundarPichai, President of @Google, who is obviously doing quite well. He stated strongly that he is totally committed to the U.S. Military, not the Chinese Military.... [Twitter for iPhone]

⊔ Mar 27, 2019 03:48:47 PM We are here today to award America's highest military honor to a fallen hero who made the supreme sacrifice for our nation -- Staff Sergeant Travis Atkins...https://t.co/q3J8BhRnhA [Twitter for iPhone]

⊔ Mar 27, 2019 04:30:32 PM RT @seanhannity: #HANNITY EXCLUSIVE TONIGHT: One-on-one with @realdonaldtrump — the President's first interview since Mueller found no coll… [Twitter for iPhone]

⊔ Mar 27, 2019 06:17:42 PM https://t.co/lGxIGgf43F [Twitter for iPhone]

⊔ Mar 27, 2019 09:40:30 PM https://t.co/Tjz6ZjVV79 [Twitter for iPhone]

⊔ Mar 28, 2019 05:05:06 AM Will be heading to Grand Rapids, Michigan, tonight for a Big Rally. Will be talking about the many exciting things that are happening to our Country, but also the car companies, & others, that are pouring back into Michigan, Ohio, Pennsylvania, North & South Carolina & all over! [Twitter for iPhone]

⊔ Mar 28, 2019 05:13:14 AM The Fake News Media is going Crazy! They are suffering a major "breakdown," have ZERO credibility or respect, & must be thinking about going legit. I have learned to live with Fake News, which has never been more corrupt than it is right now. Someday, I will tell you the secret! [Twitter for iPhone]

⊔ Mar 28, 2019 05:24:04 AM Mexico is doing NOTHING to help stop the flow of illegal immigrants to our Country. They are all talk and no action. Likewise, Honduras, Guatemala and El Salvador have taken our money for years, and do Nothing. The Dems don't care, such BAD laws. May close the Southern Border! [Twitter for iPhone]

⊔ Mar 28, 2019 05:34:34 AM FBI & DOJ to review the outrageous Jussie Smollett case in Chicago. It is an embarrassment to our Nation! [Twitter for iPhone]

⊔ Mar 28, 2019 05:43:13 AM Congressman Adam Schiff, who spent two years knowingly and unlawfully lying and leaking, should be forced to resign from Congress! [Twitter for iPhone]

⊔ Mar 28, 2019 06:04:04 AM Wow, ratings for "Morning Joe," which were really bad in the first place, just "tanked" with the release of the Mueller Report. Likewise, other shows on MSNBC and CNN have gone down by as much as 50%. Just shows, Fake News never wins! [Twitter for iPhone]

⊔ Mar 28, 2019 07:30:04 AM Very important that OPEC increase the flow of Oil. World Markets are fragile, price of Oil getting too high. Thank you! [Twitter for iPhone]

⊔ Mar 28, 2019 10:11:47 AM https://t.co/b1bp3CGqwC [Twitter Media Studio]

⊔ Mar 28, 2019 11:11:27 AM https://t.co/3AFCELjprL [Twitter Media Studio]

Mar 28, 2019 02:41:11 PM The Republican Party will become the Party of Great HealthCare! ObamaCare is a disaster, far too expensive and deductibility ridiculously high - virtually unusable! Moving forward in Courts and Legislatively! [Twitter for iPhone]

Mar 28, 2019 02:51:49 PM We have a National Emergency at our Southern Border. The Dems refuse to do what they know is necessary - amend our immigration laws. Would immediately solve the problem! Mexico, with the strongest immigration laws in the World, refuses to help with illegal immigration & drugs! [Twitter for iPhone]

Mar 28, 2019 04:06:28 PM On my way to Grand Rapids, Michigan right now. See you all very soon! #MAGA https://t.co/JjGAijXlRT [Twitter for iPhone]

Mar 28, 2019 08:16:18 PM Beautiful #MAGARally tonight in Grand Rapids, Michigan - thank you, I love you! MAKE AMERICA GREAT AGAIN!! https://t.co/3xlMOaaTR5 [Twitter for iPhone]

Mar 28, 2019 09:30:19 PM Massive overflow crowds in Grand Rapids, Michigan tonight. Thank you for joining us tonight! #MAGA https://t.co/KQ5hTZAXsk [Twitter for iPhone]

Mar 28, 2019 09:41:35 PM MAKE AMERICA GREAT AGAIN! https://t.co/Y6UPREMY7u https://t.co/6r7wdYDf66 [Twitter for iPhone]

Mar 28, 2019 10:23:35 PM Working hard, thank you! #MAGA https://t.co/00hoL0to0u [Twitter for iPhone]

Mar 29, 2019 07:48:51 AM On this Vietnam War Veterans Day, we celebrate the brave Vietnam Veterans and all of America's Veterans. Thank you for your service to our great Nation! [Twitter for iPhone]

Mar 29, 2019 10:09:07 AM This has been an incredible couple of weeks for AMERICA! https://t.co/bqdB7DFx8P [Twitter for iPhone]

Mar 29, 2019 10:23:50 AM The DEMOCRATS have given us the weakest immigration laws anywhere in the World. Mexico has the strongest, & they make more than $100 Billion a year on the U.S. Therefore, CONGRESS MUST CHANGE OUR WEAK IMMIGRATION LAWS NOW, & Mexico must stop illegals from entering the U.S.... [Twitter for iPhone]

Mar 29, 2019 10:37:09 AM ....through their country and our Southern Border. Mexico has for many years made a fortune off of the U.S., far greater than Border Costs. If Mexico doesn't immediately stop ALL illegal immigration coming into the United States throug our Southern Border, I will be CLOSING..... [Twitter for iPhone]

Mar 29, 2019 10:43:46 AM ....the Border, or large sections of the Border, next week. This would be so easy for Mexico to do, but they just take our money and "talk." Besides, we lose so much money with them, especially when you add in drug trafficking etc.), that the Border closing would be a good thing! [Twitter for iPhone]

Mar 29, 2019 04:41:20 PM Had the Fed not mistakenly raised interest rates, especially since there is very little inflation, and had they not done the ridiculously timed quantitative tightening, the 3.0% GDP, & Stock Market, would have both been much higher & World Markets would be in a better place! [Twitter for iPhone]

Mar 29, 2019 05:31:49 PM Robert Mueller was a Hero to the Radical Left Democrats, until he ruled that there was No Collusion with Russia (so ridiculous to even say!). After more than two years since the "insurance policy" statement was made by a dirty cop, I got the answers I wanted, the Truth..... [Twitter for iPhone]

Mar 29, 2019 06:15:44 PM ...The problem is, no matter what the Radical Left Democrats get, no matter what we give them, it will never be enough. Just watch, they will Harass & Complain & Resist (the theme of their movement). So maybe we should just take our victory and say NO, we've got a Country to run! [Twitter for iPhone]

Mar 29, 2019 06:25:17 PM So funny that The New York Times & The Washington Post got a Pulitzer Prize for their coverage (100% NEGATIVE and FAKE!) of Collusion with Russia - And there was No Collusion! So, they were either duped or corrupt? In any event, their prizes should be taken away by the Committee! [Twitter for iPhone]

Mar 29, 2019 10:26:56 PM A huge thanks to @HeatherNauert for serving America at the @StateDept. Great work! I'm proud to have you join the Fulbright board! https://t.co/oq0ZaA3MID [Twitter for iPhone]

Mar 30, 2019 07:14:56 AM In honor of his past service to our Country, Navy Seal #EddieGallagher will soon be moved to less restrictive confinement while he awaits his day in court. Process should move quickly! @foxandfriends @RepRalphNorman [Twitter for iPhone]

Mar 30, 2019 03:31:22 PM It would be so easy to fix our weak and very stupid Democrat inspired immigration laws. In less than one hour, and then a vote, the problem would be solved. But the Dems don't care about the crime, they don't want any victory for Trump and the Republicans, even if good for USA! [Twitter for iPhone]

Mar 30, 2019 03:36:30 PM Mexico must use its very strong immigration laws to stop the many thousands of people trying to get into the USA. Our detention areas are maxed out & we will take no more illegals. Next step is to close the Border! This will also help us with stopping the Drug flow from Mexico! [Twitter for iPhone]

Mar 30, 2019 05:24:34 PM "The Trump Administration has succeeded in dramatically raising the costs to Iran for its sinister behavior, at no cost to the U.S. or our allies. That's the definition of a foreign-policy achievement." Bret Stephens, @nytimes We are getting stronger all over the world, watch! [Twitter for iPhone]

Mar 31, 2019 02:21:24 PM Everybody is asking how the phony and fraudulent investigation of the No Collusion, No Obstruction Trump Campaign began. We need to know for future generations to understand. This Hoax should never be allowed to happen to another President or Administration again! [Twitter for iPhone]

Mar 31, 2019 02:39:13 PM "Outrageous, it's the Adam Schiff problem. People abusing the access to classified data to then go out in public and make allegations that didn't prove to be true. You look at a decision to essentially investigate a political rival. Who made it?" James Freeman, @WSJ [Twitter for iPhone]

Mar 31, 2019 06:41:52 PM The Democrats are allowing a ridiculous asylum system and major loopholes to remain as a mainstay of our immigration system. Mexico is likewise doing NOTHING, a very bad combination for our Country. Homeland Security is being sooo very nice, but not for long! [Twitter for iPhone]

Apr 1, 2019 07:07:45 AM Now that the long awaited Mueller Report conclusions have been released, most Democrats and others have gone back to the pre-Witch Hunt phase of their lives before Collusion Delusion took over. Others are pretending that their former hero, Bob Mueller, no longer exists! [Twitter for iPhone]

Apr 1, 2019 07:13:29 AM Democrats, working with Republicans in Congress, can fix the Asylum and other loopholes quickly. We have a major National Emergency at our Border. GET IT DONE NOW! [Twitter for iPhone]

Apr 1, 2019 07:14:45 AM RT @realDonaldTrump: Everybody is asking how the phony and fraudulent investigation of the No Collusion, No Obstruction Trump Campaign bega... [Twitter for iPhone]

Apr 1, 2019 07:15:19 AM RT @realDonaldTrump: Mexico must use its very strong immigration laws to stop the many thousands of people trying to get into the USA. Our... [Twitter for iPhone]

Apr 1, 2019 08:03:28 AM Can you believe that the Radical Left Democrats want to do our new and very important Census Report without the all important Citizenship Question. Report would be meaningless and a waste of the $Billions (ridiculous) that it costs to put together! [Twitter for iPhone]

Apr 1, 2019 08:41:23 AM The cost of ObamaCare is far too high for our great citizens. The deductibles, in many cases way over $7000, make it almost worthless or unusable. Good things are going to happen! @SenRickScott @senatemajldr @SenJohnBarrasso @SenBillCassidy [Twitter for iPhone]

Apr 1, 2019 09:43:14 AM No matter what information is given to the crazed Democrats from the No Collusion Mueller Report, it will never be good enough. Behind closed doors the Dems are laughing! [Twitter for iPhone]

Apr 1, 2019 11:47:16 AM Democrats should stop fighting Sen. David Perdue's disaster relief bill. They are blocking funding and relief for our great farmers and rural America! [Twitter for iPhone]

Apr 1, 2019 09:13:25 PM Everybody agrees that ObamaCare doesn't work. Premiums & deductibles are far too high - Really bad HealthCare! Even the Dems want to replace it, but with Medicare for all, which would cause 180 million Americans to lose their beloved private health insurance. The Republicans..... [Twitter for iPhone]

Apr 1, 2019 09:23:55 PM ....are developing a really great HealthCare Plan with far lower premiums (cost) & deductibles than ObamaCare. In other words it will be far less expensive & much more usable than ObamaCare. Vote will be taken right after the Election when Republicans hold the Senate & win...... [Twitter for iPhone]

Apr 1, 2019 09:37:44 PM ....back the House. It will be truly great HealthCare that will work for America. Also, Republicans will always support Pre-Existing Conditions. The Republican Party will be known as the Party of Great HealtCare. Meantime, the USA is doing better than ever & is respected again! [Twitter for iPhone]

Apr 1, 2019 09:50:20 PM The Democrats today killed a Bill that would have provided great relief to Farmers and yet more money to Puerto Rico despite the fact that Puerto Rico has already been scheduled to receive more hurricane relief funding than any "place" in history. The people of Puerto Rico..... [Twitter for iPhone]

Apr 1, 2019 10:11:44 PM ....are GREAT, but the politicians are incompetent or corrupt. Puerto Rico got far more money than Texas & Florida combined, yet their government can't do anything right, the place is a mess - nothing works. FEMA & the Military worked emergency miracles, but politicians like..... [Twitter for iPhone]

Apr 1, 2019 10:38:29 PM ....the crazed and incompetent Mayor of San Juan have done such a poor job of bringing the Island back to health. 91 Billion Dollars to Puerto Rico, and now the Dems want to give them more, taking dollars away from our Farmers and so many others. Disgraceful! [Twitter for iPhone]

Apr 2, 2019 06:33:17 AM Puerto Rico got 91 Billion Dollars for the hurricane, more money than has ever been gotten for a hurricane before, & all their local politicians do is complain & ask for more money. The pols are grossly incompetent, spend the money foolishly or corruptly, & only take from USA.... [Twitter for iPhone]

Apr 2, 2019 06:45:26 AM ....The best thing that ever happened to Puerto Rico is President Donald J. Trump. So many wonderful people, but with such bad Island leadership and with so much money wasted. Cannot continue to hurt our Farmers and States with these massive payments, and so little appreciation! [Twitter for iPhone]

Apr 2, 2019 06:58:10 AM In 1998, Rep.Jerry Nadler strongly opposed the release of the Starr Report on Bill Clinton. No information whatsoever would or could be legally released. But with the NO COLLUSION Mueller Report, which the Dems hate, he wants it all. NOTHING WILL EVER SATISFY THEM! @foxandfriends [Twitter for iPhone]

Apr 2, 2019 07:02:02 AM World Autism Awareness Day 2019: Significance, history and theme via @htTweets https://t.co/kRLZoYEIJS [Twitter for iPhone]

Apr 2, 2019 07:46:29 AM Robert Mueller was a God-like figure to the Democrats, until he ruled No Collusion in the long awaited $30,000,000 Mueller Report. Now the Dems don't even acknowledge his name, have become totally unhinged, and would like to go through the whole process again. It won't happen! [Twitter for iPhone]

Apr 2, 2019 07:54:11 AM There is no amount of testimony or document production that can satisfy Jerry Nadler or Shifty Adam Schiff. It is now time to focus exclusively on properly running our great Country! [Twitter for iPhone]

Apr 2, 2019 09:41:50 AM After many years (decades), Mexico is apprehending large numbers of people at their Southern Border, mostly from Guatemala, Honduras and El Salvador. They have ALL been taking U.S. money for years, and doing ABSOLUTELY NOTHING for us, just like the Democrats in Congress! [Twitter for iPhone]

Apr 2, 2019 09:51:17 AM https://t.co/jVlodsTNNH [Twitter Media Studio]

Apr 2, 2019 09:52:09 AM "I haven't seen any Democrats down here at the Border working with us or asking to speak to any of us. They have an open invitation. We are getting overrun, our facilities are overcapacity. We are at an emergency crisis." Art Del Cueto, National Border Patrol Council. [Twitter for iPhone]

Apr 2, 2019 02:42:48 PM Today, we celebrate the tremendous accomplishments of Americans with ASD and reaffirm our commitment to work together to ensure that every member of our society is afforded equal opportunities to reach their full potential. #WorldAutismAwarenessDay https://t.co/JQbJ2TGA3P [Twitter for iPhone]

Apr 2, 2019 02:59:57 PM Today, it was my great honor to welcome @NATO Secretary General @JensStoltenberg to the @WhiteHouse! https://t.co/4drPHXZBWH [Twitter for iPhone]

Apr 3, 2019 08:26:53 AM I was never planning a vote prior to the 2020 Election on the wonderful HealthCare package that some very talented people are now developing for me & the Republican Party. It will be on full display during the Election as a much better & less expensive alternative to ObamaCare... [Twitter for iPhone]

Apr 3, 2019 08:37:14 AM ...This will be a great campaign issue. I never asked Mitch McConnell for a vote before the Election as has been incorrectly reported (as usual) in the @nytimes, but only after the Election when we take back the House etc. Republicans will always support pre-existing conditions! [Twitter for iPhone]

Apr 3, 2019 08:45:03 AM Congress must get together and immediately eliminate the loopholes at the Border! If no action, Border, or large sections of Border, will close. This is a National Emergency! [Twitter for iPhone]

Apr 3, 2019 12:09:19 PM The First Step Act proves that our Country can achieve amazing breakthroughs when we put politics aside, and put the interests of ALL Americans FIRST. https://t.co/dTKubkIBQn https://t.co/kILIFjXglO [Twitter for iPhone]

Apr 4, 2019 06:49:18 AM THE REPUBLICAN PARTY IS THE PARTY OF THE AMERICAN DREAM! [Twitter for iPhone]

Apr 4, 2019 07:01:15 AM Despite the unnecessary and destructive actions taken by the Fed, the Economy is looking very strong, the China and USMCA deals are moving along nicely, there is little or no Inflation, and USA optimism is very high! [Twitter for iPhone]

Apr 4, 2019 07:22:54 AM According to polling, few people seem to care about the Russian Collusion Hoax, but some Democrats are fighting hard to keep the Witch Hunt alive. They should focus on legislation or, even better, an investigation of how the ridiculous Collusion Delusion got started - so illegal! [Twitter for iPhone]

Apr 4, 2019 07:46:27 AM There is nothing we can ever give to the Democrats that will make them happy. This is the highest level of Presidential Harassment in the history of our Country! [Twitter for iPhone]

Apr 4, 2019 10:04:27 AM The New York Times had no legitimate sources, which would be totally illegal, concerning the Mueller Report. In fact, they probably had no sources at all! They are a Fake News paper who have already been forced to apologize for their incorrect and very bad reporting on me! [Twitter for iPhone]

Apr 4, 2019 12:53:08 PM WELCOME BACK JOE! https://t.co/b2NbBSX3sx [Twitter for iPhone]

Apr 4, 2019 05:55:46 PM Thank you @Trish_Regan! https://t.co/6CyCpHnR6x [Twitter for iPhone]

Apr 4, 2019 06:42:51 PM "Democrats need to help fix the border crisis or get out of Trump's way" https://t.co/IlQ8rbjlfg [Twitter for iPhone]

Apr 4, 2019 06:45:13 PM "Conservative support for Trump wall soars to 99 percent" https://t.co/Tblpox8Nsg [Twitter for iPhone]

Apr 4, 2019 06:47:02 PM .@ByronYork: "How bad does border have to be for Democrats to admit it's an emergency?" https://t.co/6LOPQQEKtP [Twitter for iPhone]

Apr 4, 2019 07:19:56 PM I am pleased to announce that Jovita Carranza will be nominated as the new @SBAgov Administrator. She will be replacing Linda McMahon, who has done an outstanding job. Jovita was a great Treasurer of the United States – and I look forward to her joining my Cabinet! [Twitter for iPhone]

Apr 5, 2019 06:58:46 AM "Trolling the Mueller Report. Democrats Lost On Collusion. Now They're Inventing A Coverup." @WSJopinion James Freeman @LouDobbs [Twitter for iPhone]

Apr 5, 2019 08:04:12 AM The Crazed and Dishonest Washington Post again purposely got it wrong. Mexico, for the first time in decades, is meaningfully apprehending illegals at THEIR Southern Border, before the long march up to the U.S. This is great and the way it should be. The big flow will stop....... [Twitter for iPhone]

Apr 5, 2019 08:11:36 AM ....However, if for any reason Mexico stops apprehending and bringing the illegals back to where they came from, the U.S. will be forced to Tariff at 25% all cars made in Mexico and shipped over the Border to us. If that doesn't work, which it will, I will close the Border....... [Twitter for iPhone]

Apr 5, 2019 08:19:46 AM ....This will supersede USMCA. Likewise I am looking at an economic penalty for the 500 Billion Dollars in illegal DRUGS that are shipped and smuggled through Mexico and across our Southern Border. Over 100,00 Americans die each year, sooo many families destroyed! [Twitter for iPhone]

Apr 5, 2019 08:22:13 AM Heading to the Southern Border to show a section of the new Wall being built! Leaving now! [Twitter for iPhone]

Apr 5, 2019 11:03:47 AM JOBS! JOBS! JOBS! https://t.co/3tukVpJpzN [Twitter for iPhone]

Apr 5, 2019 11:43:48 AM Congratulations to Brian Hagedorn on his big surprise win over a well funded Liberal Democrat in the Great State of Wisconsin for a very important Supreme Court seat. Republicans are producing big for Wisconsin! [Twitter for iPhone]

Apr 5, 2019 11:44:58 AM I've employed thousands of Electrical Workers. They will be voting for me! [Twitter for iPhone]

Apr 5, 2019 11:58:29 AM "America Created 196,000 Jobs in March, Beating Expectations for 170,000" https://t.co/TQ2LecXgfi [Twitter for iPhone]

Apr 5, 2019 12:41:29 PM The press is doing everything within their power to fight the magnificence of the phrase, MAKE AMERICA GREAT AGAIN! They can't stand the fact that this Administration has done more than virtually any other Administration in its first 2yrs. They are truly the ENEMY OF THE PEOPLE! [Twitter for iPhone]

Apr 5, 2019 12:48:18 PM Will soon be landing in Calexico, California to look at a portion of the new WALL being built on our Southern Border. Within two years we will have close to 400 miles built or under construction & keeping our Country SAFE – not easy when the Dems are always fighting to stop you! [Twitter for iPhone]

Apr 5, 2019 02:10:20 PM Just arrived in Calexico, California! https://t.co/lTChNxsHj6 [Twitter for iPhone]

Apr 5, 2019 03:33:09 PM Join me in California for a Roundtable on Immigration and Border Security! https://t.co/hLV86lWTtA [Twitter for iPhone]

Apr 5, 2019 05:16:20 PM Just checked out the new Wall on the Border - GREAT! Leaving now for L.A. [Twitter for iPhone]

Apr 5, 2019 06:05:14 PM RT @WhiteHouse: Americans will write our own economic destiny. Never believe the pessimists: Pro-growth, pro-worker policies work. America… [Twitter for iPhone]

Apr 5, 2019 06:06:42 PM Congratulations David, a very big deal! https://t.co/ymtI2ueAgA [Twitter for iPhone]

Apr 5, 2019 06:08:20 PM RT @Scavino45: 🎥 Happening Now: President @realDonaldTrump at the Southern Border with the great men and women who protect our country 24/7… [Twitter for iPhone]

Apr 5, 2019 06:09:51 PM RT @VP: The struggle in Venezuela is between dictatorship and democracy, and freedom has the momentum. Nicolas Maduro is a dictator with no… [Twitter for iPhone]

Apr 5, 2019 06:10:09 PM RT @WhiteHouse: Thank you to all of the brave men and women of CBP who protect our country each and every day. https://t.co/jpW7B5NK6p [Twitter for iPhone]

Apr 5, 2019 08:25:17 PM THANK YOU @DHSgov, @CBP, and @ICEgov! https://t.co/BzNwKoUJlg [Twitter for iPhone]

Apr 6, 2019 08:24:51 AM "The lowest average jobs number for any President since 1951, 4.1%. Economy doing great. If the Democrats win, it is all over." @Varneyco @foxandfriends I agree! [Twitter for iPhone]

Apr 6, 2019 08:41:23 AM "Collusion was a Hoax from day one." @dbongino @foxandfriends [Twitter for iPhone]

Apr 6, 2019 08:45:12 AM RT @JesseBWatters: TOMORROW: It's a star-studded FOX episode of @WattersWorld with @seanhannity , @LouDobbs , and @marklevinshow ! What wil… [Twitter for iPhone]

Apr 6, 2019 08:47:26 AM RT @WhiteHouse: "There is indeed an emergency on our southern border. It's been loud and clear." https://t.co/TJMJ5bhdDO [Twitter for iPhone]

Apr 6, 2019 08:51:06 AM RT @marc_lotter: Let me answer that question for you @MSNBC - NO!!! https://t.co/0QYxwKjGJ1 [Twitter for iPhone]

Apr 6, 2019 08:55:40 AM RT @WhiteHouse: Simply put: Walls work, and walls save lives. https://t.co/OyLatl4oyN [Twitter for iPhone]

Apr 6, 2019 08:57:36 AM Thank you to two great people! https://t.co/9VoIV44L9c [Twitter for iPhone]

Apr 6, 2019 09:22:26 AM I have not read the Mueller Report yet, even though I have every right to do so. Only know the conclusions, and on the big one, No Collusion. Likewise, recommendations made to our great A.G. who found No Obstruction. 13 Angry Trump hating Dems (later brought to 18) given two..... [Twitter for iPhone]

Apr 6, 2019 09:31:09 AM .....years and $30 million, and they found No Collusion, No Obstruction. But the Democrats, no matter what we give them, will NEVER be satisfied. A total waste of time. As @FrankLuntz has just stated, "Enough, America has had enough. What have you accomplished. Public is fed up." [Twitter for iPhone]

Apr 6, 2019 10:24:23 AM RT @ABC: NEW: Pres. Trump says he will hold a rally at an undetermined location rather than attend the White House Correspondents' Dinner,... [Twitter for iPhone]

Apr 6, 2019 10:49:40 AM So, let's get this straight! There was No Collusion and in fact the Phony Dossier was a Con Job that was paid for by Crooked Hillary and the DNC. So the 13 Angry Democrats were investigating an event that never happened and that was in fact a made up Fraud. I just fought back.... [Twitter for iPhone]

Apr 6, 2019 10:51:03 AM Will be speaking today at the Republican Jewish Coalition (@RJC) meeting in Las Vegas, Nevada. See everyone soon! https://t.co/RvNBLMC2nI [Twitter for iPhone]

Apr 6, 2019 10:52:54 AM So, let's get this straight! There was No Collusion and in fact the Phony Dossier was a Con Job that was paid for by Crooked Hillary and the DNC. So the 13 Angry Democrats were investigating an event that never happened and that was in fact a made up Fraud. I just fought back.... [Twitter for iPhone]

Apr 6, 2019 10:57:08 AM .... against something I knew never existed, Collusion with Russia (so ridiculous!) - No Obstruction. This Russia Hoax must never happen to another President, and Law Enforcement must find out, HOW DID IT START? [Twitter for iPhone]

Apr 6, 2019 03:03:52 PM To every member of the @RJC, thank you for your incredible support and your outstanding commitment to our Country, to our safety, and to electing MORE REPUBLICANS. Over the next 19 months, I know that the @RJC will help lead our party to another HISTORIC VICTORY! #TrumpAtRJC https://t.co/P1brsp3PxF [Twitter for iPhone]

Apr 6, 2019 03:19:23 PM Why should I be defending a fraudulent Russian Witch Hunt. It's about time the perpetrators of this fraud on me and the American People start defending their dishonest and treasonous acts. How and why did this terrible event begin? Never Forget! [Twitter for iPhone]

Apr 6, 2019 03:48:40 PM "Give Up, Trump-Haters" https://t.co/4wg4BUk9gP https://t.co/0Bt2jyorMn [Twitter for iPhone]

Apr 6, 2019 06:33:02 PM We have redeployed 750 agents at the Southern Border's specific Ports of Entry in order to help with the large scale surge of illegal migrants trying to make their way into the United States. This will cause traffic & commercial delays until such time as Mexico is able to use.... [Twitter for iPhone]

Apr 6, 2019 06:36:06 PM ....it's powerful common sense Immigration Laws to stop illegals from coming through Mexico into the U.S., and removing them back to their country of origin. Until Mexico cleans up this ridiculous & massive migration, we will be focusing on Border Security, not Ports of Entry.... [Twitter for iPhone]

Apr 6, 2019 06:36:56 PM ....In the meantime, the Democrats in Congress must help the Republicans (we need their votes) to end the horrible, costly and foolish loopholes in our Immigration Laws. Once that happens, all will be smooth. We can NEVER allow Open Borders! [Twitter for iPhone]

Apr 7, 2019 08:50:02 AM Looks like Bob Mueller's team of 13 Trump Haters & Angry Democrats are illegally leaking information to the press while the Fake News Media make up their own stories with or without sources - sources no longer matter to our corrupt & dishonest Mainstream Media, they are a Joke! [Twitter for iPhone]

Apr 7, 2019 02:50:54 PM Pleased to report that the American tourist and tour guide that were abducted in Uganda have been released. God bless them and their families! [Twitter for iPhone]

Apr 7, 2019 02:53:56 PM RT @mike_pence: The last 2 years, under @RealDonaldTrump, have been 2 years of action – it's been 2 years of results – & it's been 2 years… [Twitter for iPhone]

Apr 7, 2019 02:54:53 PM RT @mike_pence: .@RealDonaldTrump is doing his job to SECURE OUR BORDER! @CBP is doing their job. It's time for Congress to do its job and… [Twitter for iPhone]

Apr 7, 2019 05:02:03 PM Secretary of Homeland Security Kirstjen Nielsen will be leaving her position, and I would like to thank her for her service.... [Twitter for iPhone]

Apr 7, 2019 05:02:04 PM ....I am pleased to announce that Kevin McAleenan, the current U.S. Customs and Border Protection Commissioner, will become Acting Secretary for @DHSgov. I have confidence that Kevin will do a great job! [Twitter for iPhone]

Apr 7, 2019 07:45:32 PM More apprehensions (captures) at the Southern Border than in many years. Border Patrol amazing! Country is FULL! System has been broken for many years. Democrats in Congress must agree to fix loopholes - No Open Borders (Crimes & Drugs). Will Close Southern Border If necessary... [Twitter for iPhone]

Apr 7, 2019 08:03:25 PM ....Mexico must apprehend all illegals and not let them make the long march up to the United States, or we will have no other choice than to Close the Border and/or institute Tariffs. Our Country is FULL! [Twitter for iPhone]

Apr 8, 2019 06:39:34 AM "The reason the whole process seems so politicized is that Democrats made up this complete lie about Collusion ....and none of it happened." Charles Hurt. The Russian Hoax never happened, it was a fraud on the American people! [Twitter for iPhone]

Apr 8, 2019 06:44:16 AM "Jerry Nadler is not entitled to this information. He is doing this to get it to the Democrat 2020 nominee." @KatiePavlich [Twitter for iPhone]

Apr 8, 2019 07:06:29 AM RT @Jim_Jordan: Dem talk: -Abolish ICE - Borderless hemisphere -Walls are immoral -Illegals should vote -Raise taxes @POTUS action: -Regs r... [Twitter for iPhone]

Apr 8, 2019 07:09:19 AM RT @Jim_Jordan: Dems want President's tax returns for purely political purposes! Frightening, but shouldn't surprise us — same folks used th... [Twitter for iPhone]

Apr 8, 2019 07:09:45 AM RT @cspan: Rep. @Jim_Jordan on President Trump's tax returns: "There's no law that says they have to be public." Watch full #Newsmakers in... [Twitter for iPhone]

Apr 8, 2019 07:22:03 AM Uganda must find the kidnappers of the American Tourist and guide before people will feel safe in going there. Bring them to justice openly and quickly! [Twitter for iPhone]

Apr 8, 2019 11:48:48 AM The Democrats will never be satisfied, no matter what they get, how much they get, or how many pages they get. It will never end, but that's the way life goes! [Twitter for iPhone]

Apr 8, 2019 06:57:29 PM Congratulations to the Baylor Lady Bears on their amazing win last night against Notre Dame to become the 2019 NCAA Women's Basketball National Champions! https://t.co/cogqxFgnRn [Twitter for iPhone]

Apr 8, 2019 10:10:33 PM A 9th Circuit Judge just ruled that Mexico is too dangerous for migrants. So unfair to the U.S. OUT OF CONTROL! https://t.co/XF8o3jMDle [Twitter for iPhone]

Apr 8, 2019 10:13:29 PM RT @TeamTrump: BIGGER paychecks under President @realDonaldTrump! 💰 https://t.co/GAezgi2RI5 [Twitter for iPhone]

Apr 8, 2019 11:43:57 PM Congratulations to Virginia - Great game! [Twitter for iPhone]

Apr 8, 2019 11:50:22 PM RT @WhiteHouse: The newly constructed 30-foot wall in Calexico, CA, replaces a barrier made of surplus corrugated steel landing mats from t... [Twitter for iPhone]

Apr 8, 2019 11:51:09 PM RT @GOPChairwoman: Our economy is on fire. Jobs are up, unemployment is at record lows, and wages are still rising. But Democrats would... [Twitter for iPhone]

Apr 9, 2019 06:34:39 AM The World Trade Organization finds that the European Union subsidies to Airbus has adversely impacted the United States, which will now put Tariffs on $11 Billion of EU products! The EU has taken advantage of the U.S. on trade for many years. It will soon stop! [Twitter for iPhone]

Apr 9, 2019 07:16:54 AM Congressman Jerry Nadler fought me for years on a very large development I built on the West Side of Manhattan. He wanted a Rail Yard built underneath the development or even better, to stop the job. He didn't get either & the development became VERY successful. Nevertheless,.... [Twitter for iPhone]

Apr 9, 2019 07:33:09 AM ....I got along very well with Jerry during the zoning and building process. Then I changed course (slightly), became President, and now I am dealing with Congressman Nadler again. Some things never end, but hopefully it will all go well for everyone. Only time will tell! [Twitter for iPhone]

Apr 9, 2019 07:44:17 AM The Mainstream Media has never been more inaccurate or corrupt than it is today. It only seems to get worse. So much Fake News! [Twitter for iPhone]

Apr 9, 2019 10:31:21 AM On National Former Prisoner of War Recognition Day, we honor the Americans captured and imprisoned by foreign powers while carrying out their duties to defend this great Nation...https://t.co/dEVfRo5uy7 [Twitter for iPhone]

Apr 9, 2019 10:36:17 AM "What's completely unacceptable is for Congesswoman Omar to target Jews, in this case Stephen Miller." Jeff Ballabon, B2 Strategic, CEO. @Varneyco [Twitter for iPhone]

Apr 9, 2019 10:38:27 AM https://t.co/OIpp7mL2uD [Twitter Media Studio]

Apr 9, 2019 11:09:58 AM "She (Congresswoman Omar) keeps on assaulting Jews..." Jeff Ballabon, B2 Strategic, CEO https://t.co/WMKN9RQm2n [Twitter Media Studio]

Apr 9, 2019 12:58:35 PM Today, it was my great honor to welcome President @AlsisiOfficial of the Arab Republic of Egypt to the @WhiteHouse! https://t.co/yBox7EhToT [Twitter for iPhone]

Apr 9, 2019 01:32:44 PM Check this out - TRUTH! https://t.co/2HNVeEpKDu [Twitter for iPhone]

Apr 9, 2019 02:15:26 PM THANK YOU, WORKING HARD! https://t.co/3OUESGRw43 [Twitter for iPhone]

Apr 9, 2019 03:43:35 PM MAKE AMERICA GREAT AGAIN! https://t.co/diXWQHuyGj [Twitter Media Studio]

Apr 9, 2019 08:01:51 PM "The underlying issue remains the same without a single American being indicted for Collusion with Russia, & that is a stunning end considering we were led to believe (Fake News) that something much more dramatic would happen. Why did people fall for this?" @TuckerCarlson Molly H [Twitter for iPhone]

Apr 9, 2019 08:22:19 PM The Democrats must end the loopholes on immigration. So easy to solve! [Twitter for iPhone]

Apr 9, 2019 09:00:46 PM RT @HeyTammyBruce: Trump Job Approval Jumps to 53% - Seven Points Higher Than Obama https://t.co/cv40yIrU2M [Twitter for iPhone]

Apr 9, 2019 09:05:47 PM RT @IWV: .@POTUS @realDonaldTrump has "delivered on his promises...He has a background in delivering economically. He's promised to do cert... [Twitter for iPhone]

Apr 9, 2019 09:22:07 PM Everybody is now acknowledging that, right from the time I announced my run for President, I was 100% correct on the Border. Remember the heat I took? Democrats should now get rid of the loopholes. The Border is being fixed. Mexico will not let people through! [Twitter for iPhone]

Apr 9, 2019 09:59:40 PM RT @JudicialWatch: BREAKING: JW announced today that it uncovered 422 pages of FBI documents showing evidence of "cover up" discussions rel... [Twitter for iPhone]

Apr 9, 2019 10:02:43 PM RT @JudicialWatch: Judicial Watch President @TomFitton discussed the Trump coup in his Weekly Update: It was all based on this fraudulent d... [Twitter for iPhone]

Apr 10, 2019 09:48:02 AM Trump flags being waived at the Bibi @Netanyahu VICTORY celebration last night! https://t.co/SX8RVAALYW [Twitter for iPhone]

Apr 10, 2019 02:17:19 PM Spoke to Bibi @Netanyahu to congratulate him on a great and hard-fought win. The United States is with him and the People of Israel all the way! https://t.co/OfFI6aKSOb [Twitter for iPhone]

⬜ Apr 10, 2019 02:45:55 PM So, it has now been determined, by 18 people that truly hate President Trump, that there was No Collusion with Russia. In fact, it was an illegal investigation that should never have been allowed to start. I fought back hard against this Phony & Treasonous Hoax! [Twitter for iPhone]

⬜ Apr 10, 2019 04:37:40 PM Join me in Crosby, Texas as I deliver remarks and sign Executive Orders on Energy and Infrastructure! https://t.co/oun56uzi53 [Twitter for iPhone]

⬜ Apr 10, 2019 04:41:06 PM THANK YOU Texas, I love you! https://t.co/24D4K9ILFd [Twitter for iPhone]

⬜ Apr 10, 2019 08:55:55 PM CONGRATULATIONS to @EricTrump and @LaraLeaTrump on the great news. So proud! [Twitter for iPhone]

⬜ Apr 10, 2019 09:20:39 PM RT @DHSgov: Today, @CBP Commissioner Kevin McAleenan was sworn-in to lead DHS as the Acting Secretary. The ceremony took place at the new D… [Twitter for iPhone]

⬜ Apr 10, 2019 09:33:10 PM I think what the Democrats are doing with the Border is TREASONOUS. Their Open Border mindset is putting our Country at risk. Will not let this happen! [Twitter for iPhone]

⬜ Apr 10, 2019 09:52:50 PM Too bad that the European Union is being so tough on the United Kingdom and Brexit. The E.U. is likewise a brutal trading partner with the United States, which will change. Sometimes in life you have to let people breathe before it all comes back to bite you! [Twitter for iPhone]

⬜ Apr 11, 2019 06:20:18 AM Great news! #MAGA https://t.co/haZ1HbVpNu [Twitter for iPhone]

⬜ Apr 11, 2019 10:20:19 AM "SPY GAMES: TIME FOR ANSWERS" https://t.co/tRw7fb7Tys [Twitter Media Studio]

⬜ Apr 11, 2019 10:35:36 AM "Biggest scandal of our time - the coup that failed!" @MariaBartiromo https://t.co/7JuifNK79T [Twitter Media Studio]

⬜ Apr 11, 2019 04:23:33 PM Beautiful afternoon in the Oval Office today with a few great American HEROES! https://t.co/HYEI83NVrm [Twitter Media Studio]

⬜ Apr 11, 2019 06:14:47 PM House Democrats want to negotiate a $2 TRILLION spending increase but can't even pass their own plan. We can't afford it anyway, and it's not happening! [Twitter for iPhone]

⬜ Apr 11, 2019 06:45:38 PM RT @ArthurSchwartz: Wow. @tedlieu got a well deserved ass kicking. Shame on you Ted. https://t.co/R6Yb95EzYX [Twitter for iPhone]

⬜ Apr 11, 2019 06:57:01 PM "And the Radical Dems reeling in disarray as the President continues to Win, Win and Win again! The Left is PRETENDING to be shocked by A.G. William Barr's testimony before Congress in which he said SPYING did occur on the Trump 2016 Campaign." @LouDobbs @FoxNews [Twitter for iPhone]

Apr 11, 2019 07:24:09 PM RT @DailyCaller: Rod Rosenstein Defends Attorney General's Handling Of Mueller Report https://t.co/qMmzaPYrK4 [Twitter for iPhone]

Apr 11, 2019 07:29:17 PM Great heroes! https://t.co/ltiNOcBBeo [Twitter for iPhone]

Apr 11, 2019 07:32:40 PM RT @DailyCaller: Every CNN Presidential Town Hall Finished Behind MSNBC And Fox News In Ratings https://t.co/muDZgLT4u7 [Twitter for iPhone]

Apr 11, 2019 07:44:16 PM RT @chuckwoolery: President Trump continues to tally up wins for our country as Americans just saw the best income gains in over 50 years.... [Twitter for iPhone]

Apr 11, 2019 07:46:56 PM JOBLESS CLAIMS AT 50 YEAR LOW! [Twitter for iPhone]

Apr 12, 2019 08:06:42 AM "I don't need to know any more. We're done, absolutely done, he (Mueller) tried the case. There's NO COLLUSION." @LindseyGrahamSC @foxandfriends No matter what we do or give to the Radical Left, it will never be enough! [Twitter for iPhone]

Apr 12, 2019 08:37:30 AM President Obama's top White House lawyer, Gregory B. Craig, was indicted yesterday on very serious charges. This is a really big story, but the Fake News New York Times didn't even put it on page one, rather page 16. @washingtonpost not much better, "tiny" page one. Corrupt News! [Twitter for iPhone]

Apr 12, 2019 08:46:27 AM "Democrats don't like the results of the Mueller Report, so now they're trying everything else." @RepDougCollins They should stop wasting time and money and get back to real legislating, especially on the Border! [Twitter for iPhone]

Apr 12, 2019 09:19:36 AM Even the Democrats now say that our Southern Border is a Crisis and a National Emergency. Hopefully, we will not be getting any more BAD (outrageous) court decisions! [Twitter for iPhone]

Apr 12, 2019 11:38:02 AM ....The Radical Left always seems to have an Open Borders, Open Arms policy – so this should make them very happy! [Twitter for iPhone]

Apr 12, 2019 11:38:02 AM Due to the fact that Democrats are unwilling to change our very dangerous immigration laws, we are indeed, as reported, giving strong considerations to placing Illegal Immigrants in Sanctuary Cities only.... [Twitter for iPhone]

Apr 12, 2019 04:35:31 PM WE WILL NEVER FORGET! https://t.co/VxrGFRFeJM [Twitter Media Studio]

Apr 12, 2019 05:38:45 PM RT @trish_regan: .@CLewandowski_ says he is POSITIVE orders to spy on the #Trump campaign during 2016 came from the HIGHEST levels – perhap... [Twitter for iPhone]

Apr 12, 2019 06:26:32 PM WSJ's Strassel: Barr 'Right' to Say 'Spying' Occurred on Trump Campaign | Breitbart https://t.co/YuC9IX01GF via @BreitbartNews [Twitter for iPhone]

Apr 12, 2019 09:30:47 PM If the Radical Left Democrats all of a sudden don't want the Illegal Migrants in their Sanctuary Cities (no more open arms), why should others be expected to take them into their communities? Go home and come into our Country legally and through a system of Merit! [Twitter for iPhone]

Apr 12, 2019 09:35:03 PM Thank you Jeh, so well stated! https://t.co/4QmP6XrUVA [Twitter for iPhone]

Apr 12, 2019 09:38:54 PM Finally great news at the Border! https://t.co/nofzYa2Qs7 [Twitter for iPhone]

Apr 12, 2019 09:42:07 PM Finally, great news at the Border! https://t.co/nofzYa2Qs7 [Twitter for iPhone]

Apr 12, 2019 09:45:25 PM RT @dbongino: With the exception of FISA warrants, the use of human intelligence assets, the use of national security letters, & the unprec... [Twitter for iPhone]

Apr 12, 2019 09:51:24 PM RT @politicalelle: How is this woman walking the halls of Congress. How. https://t.co/CrtK7j3wpZ [Twitter for iPhone]

Apr 12, 2019 09:59:36 PM A Fake Story by Politico. Made up sources. Thank you Mount Vernon! https://t.co/Pf60zBy6Sw [Twitter for iPhone]

Apr 12, 2019 10:33:05 PM Another Fake Story on @NBCNews that I offered Pardons to Homeland Securiy personnel in case they broke the law regarding illegal immigration and sanctuary cities. Of course this is not true. Mainstream Media is corrupt and getting worse, if that is possible, every day! [Twitter for iPhone]

Apr 12, 2019 10:51:00 PM In New York State, Democrats blocked a Bill expanding College Tuition for Gold Star families after approving aid for illegal immigrants. No wonder so many people are leaving N.Y. Very Sad! [Twitter for iPhone]

Apr 13, 2019 06:54:45 AM I agree with Kim Jong Un of North Korea that our personal relationship remains very good, perhaps the term excellent would be even more accurate, and that a third Summit would be good in that we fully understand where we each stand. North Korea has tremendous potential for....... [Twitter for iPhone]

Apr 13, 2019 07:04:18 AM ....extraordinary growth, economic success and riches under the leadership of Chairman Kim. I look forward to the day, which could be soon, when Nuclear Weapons and Sanctions can be removed, and then watching North Korea become one of the most successful nations of the World! [Twitter for iPhone]

Apr 13, 2019 07:21:05 AM Why should Radical Left Democrats in Congress have a right to retry and examine the $35,000,000 (two years in the making) No Collusion Mueller Report, when the crime committed was by Crooked Hillary, the DNC and Dirty Cops? Attorney General Barr will make the decision! [Twitter for iPhone]

Apr 13, 2019 11:01:11 AM RT @realDonaldTrump: WE WILL NEVER FORGET! https://t.co/VxrGFRFeJM [Twitter for iPhone]

Apr 13, 2019 05:37:52 PM Great playing by @TigerWoods (at the) @TheMasters. Tomorrow will be a big and exciting day for golf and for sports. Many fantastic players in the hunt. Ratings Gold - Good luck to all! [Twitter for iPhone]

Apr 13, 2019 06:30:41 PM The New York Times Sanctuary Cities/Immigration story today was knowingly wrong on almost every fact. They never call to check for truth. Their sources often don't even exist, a fraud. They will lie & cheat anyway possible to make me look bad. In 6 years they will be gone........ [Twitter for iPhone]

Apr 13, 2019 06:38:27 PM ....When I won the Election in 2016, the @nytimes had to beg their fleeing subscribers for forgiveness in that they covered the Election (and me) so badly. They didn't have a clue, it was pathetic. They even apologized to me. But now they are even worse, really corrupt reporting! [Twitter for iPhone]

Apr 13, 2019 06:51:55 PM I never offered Pardons to Homeland Security Officials, never ordered anyone to close our Southern Border (although I have the absolute right to do so, and may if Mexico does not apprehend the illegals coming to our Border), and am not "frustrated." It is all Fake & Corrupt News! [Twitter for iPhone]

Apr 13, 2019 07:01:02 PM ....So interesting to see the Mayor of Oakland and other Sanctuary Cities NOT WANT our currently "detained immigrants" after release due to the ridiculous court ordered 20 day rule. If they don't want to serve our Nation by taking care of them, why should other cities & towns? [Twitter for iPhone]

Apr 13, 2019 07:08:37 PM Democrats must change the Immigration Laws FAST. If not, Sanctuary Cities must immediately ACT to take care of the Illegal Immigrants - and this includes Gang Members, Drug Dealers, Human Traffickers, and Criminals of all shapes, sizes and kinds. CHANGE THE LAWS NOW! [Twitter for iPhone]

Apr 13, 2019 08:38:33 PM RT @WhiteHouse: No law that kicks 180 million Americans off their plans is acceptable. While Democrats abandon Obamacare for more socialism... [Twitter for iPhone]

Apr 13, 2019 08:47:25 PM Just out: The USA has the absolute legal right to have apprehended illegal immigrants transferred to Sanctuary Cities. We hereby demand that they be taken care of at the highest level, especially by the State of California, which is well known or its poor management & high taxes! [Twitter for iPhone]

Apr 14, 2019 09:04:00 AM If the Fed had done its job properly, which it has not, the Stock Market would have been up 5000 to 10,000 additional points, and GDP would have been well over 4% instead of 3%...with almost no inflation. Quantitative tightening was a killer, should have done the exact opposite! [Twitter for iPhone]

Apr 14, 2019 12:57:15 PM Great Masters going on right now. @TigerWoods is leading with 2 holes left to play. Very exciting, tune in! [Twitter for iPhone]

Apr 14, 2019 01:27:57 PM Watching final hole of @TheMasters. @TigerWoods is looking GREAT! [Twitter for iPhone]

Apr 14, 2019 01:36:00 PM Congratulations to @TigerWoods., a truly Great Champion! [Twitter for iPhone]

Apr 14, 2019 02:10:18 PM Love people who are great under pressure. What a fantastic life comeback for a really great guy! https://t.co/41MtJtYEjq [Twitter for iPhone]

Apr 14, 2019 07:28:09 PM Such a "puff piece" on Nancy Pelosi by @60minutes, yet her leadership has passed no meaningful Legislation. All they do is Investigate, as it turns out, crimes that they instigated & committed. The Mueller No Collusion decision wasn't even discussed-and she was a disaster at W.H. [Twitter for iPhone]

Apr 14, 2019 08:31:56 PM .@SteveHiltonx "This is President Trump trying to deliver on his promises while the bureaucratic machine fights his agenda. He needs populist allies. These changes are not chaos, but rather progress. All this is President Trump at his absolute best." Thank you Steve! [Twitter for iPhone]

Apr 14, 2019 08:42:58 PM Chinese Telecom Giant Huawei hires former Obama Cyber Security Official as a lobbyist. This is not good, or acceptable! @FoxNews @SteveHiltonx [Twitter for iPhone]

Apr 14, 2019 08:49:26 PM RT @WSJ: Opinion: Trump's adversaries have spent more than two years trying to dodge accountability, writes @kimstrassel https://t.co/NXW4k... [Twitter for iPhone]

Apr 14, 2019 08:50:15 PM RT @KimStrassel: Actually, they chose NOT to give give GOP House a lot of what GOP investigators wanted--easily more than 400 pages. It's a... [Twitter for iPhone]

Apr 15, 2019 05:29:27 AM What do I know about branding, maybe nothing (but I did become President!), but if I were Boeing, I would FIX the Boeing 737 MAX, add some additional great features, & REBRAND the plane with a new name. No product has suffered like this one. But again, what the hell do I know? [Twitter for iPhone]

Apr 15, 2019 06:15:28 AM Mueller, and the A.G. based on Mueller findings (and great intelligence), have already ruled No Collusion, No Obstruction. These were crimes committed by Crooked Hillary, the DNC, Dirty Cops and others! INVESTIGATE THE INVESTIGATORS! [Twitter for iPhone]

Apr 15, 2019 06:28:47 AM Congress should come back to D.C. now and FIX THE IMMIGRATION LAWS! [Twitter for iPhone]

Apr 15, 2019 08:30:46 AM Before Nancy, who has lost all control of Congress and is getting nothing done, decides to defend her leader, Rep. Omar, she should look at the anti-Semitic, anti-Israel and ungrateful U.S. HATE statements Omar has made. She is out of control, except for her control of Nancy! [Twitter for iPhone]

Apr 15, 2019 08:52:45 AM THEY SPIED ON MY CAMPAIGN (We will never forget)! [Twitter for iPhone]

Apr 15, 2019 09:15:58 AM The Radical Left Democrats will never be satisfied with anything we give them. They will always Resist and Obstruct! [Twitter for iPhone]

Apr 15, 2019 10:33:36 AM I finally agree with @Cher! https://t.co/i5acSgUrCk [Twitter for iPhone]

Apr 15, 2019 10:33:56 AM Mark Morgan, President Obama's Border Patrol Chief, gave the following message to me: "President Trump, stay the course." I agree, and believe it or not, we are making great progress with a system that has been broken for many years! [Twitter for iPhone]

Apr 15, 2019 11:05:21 AM Those Illegal Immigrants who can no longer be legally held (Congress must fix the laws and loopholes) will be, subject to Homeland Security, given to Sanctuary Cities and States! [Twitter for iPhone]

Apr 15, 2019 11:21:01 AM The Mueller Report, which was written by 18 Angry Democrats who also happen to be Trump Haters (and Clinton Supporters), should have focused on the people who SPIED on my 2016 Campaign, and others who fabricated the whole Russia Hoax. That is, never forget, the crime..... [Twitter for iPhone]

Apr 15, 2019 11:24:39 AM ....Since there was no Collusion, why was there an Investigation in the first place! Answer - Dirty Cops, Dems and Crooked Hillary! [Twitter for iPhone]

Apr 15, 2019 11:36:19 AM Heading to the Great State of Minnesota! [Twitter for iPhone]

⬜ Apr 15, 2019 12:35:41 PM Spoke to @TigerWoods to congratulate him on the great victory he had in yesterday's @TheMasters, & to inform him that because of his incredible Success & Comeback in Sports (Golf) and, more importantly, LIFE, I will be presenting him with the PRESIDENTIAL MEDAL OF FREEDOM! [Twitter for iPhone]

⬜ Apr 15, 2019 12:39:48 PM So horrible to watch the massive fire at Notre Dame Cathedral in Paris. Perhaps flying water tankers could be used to put it out. Must act quickly! [Twitter for iPhone]

⬜ Apr 15, 2019 04:57:02 PM The forgotten voters of the 2016 Election are now doing great. The Steel Industry is rebuilding and expanding at a pace that it hasn't seen in decades. Our Country has one of the best Economies in many years, perhaps ever. Unemployment numbers best in 51 years. Wow! [Twitter for iPhone]

⬜ Apr 15, 2019 04:58:34 PM God bless the people of France! [Twitter for iPhone]

⬜ Apr 16, 2019 08:02:23 AM A must read, Andy McCarthy's column today, "Dirty dealings of dirt devils who concocted Trump-Russia probe." The greatest Scam in political history. If the Mainstream Media were honest, which they are not, this story would be bigger and more important than Watergate. Someday! [Twitter for iPhone]

⬜ Apr 16, 2019 08:34:55 AM No Collusion - No Obstruction! [Twitter for iPhone]

⬜ Apr 16, 2019 09:11:46 AM So weird to watch Crazy Bernie on @FoxNews. Not surprisingly, @BretBaier and the "audience" was so smiley and nice. Very strange, and now we have @donnabrazile? [Twitter for iPhone]

⬜ Apr 16, 2019 01:01:11 PM I will be in Green Bay, Wisconsin on Saturday, April 27th at the Resch Center — 7:00pm (CDT). Big crowd expected! #MAGA https://t.co/BPYK8PF0O8 [Twitter for iPhone]

⬜ Apr 16, 2019 01:59:17 PM No Collusion - No Obstruction! https://t.co/cbFOEEyLtM [Twitter Media Studio]

⬜ Apr 16, 2019 05:39:26 PM Just signed a critical bill to formalize drought contingency plans for the Colorado River. Thanks to @SenMcSallyAZ for getting it done. Big deal for Arizona! [Twitter for iPhone]

⬜ Apr 16, 2019 07:57:41 PM Many Trump Fans & Signs were outside of the @FoxNews Studio last night in the now thriving (Thank you President Trump) Bethlehem, Pennsylvania, for the interview with Crazy Bernie Sanders. Big complaints about not being let in-stuffed with Bernie supporters. What's with @FoxNews? [Twitter for iPhone]

Apr 16, 2019 08:11:47 PM Bernie Sanders and wife should pay the Pre-Trump Taxes on their almost $600,000 in income. He is always complaining about these big TAX CUTS, except when it benefits him. They made a fortune off of Trump, but so did everyone else - and that's a good thing, not a bad thing! [Twitter for iPhone]

Apr 16, 2019 08:24:39 PM I believe it will be Crazy Bernie Sanders vs. Sleepy Joe Biden as the two finalists to run against maybe the best Economy in the history of our Country (and MANY other great things)! I look forward to facing whoever it may be. May God Rest Their Soul! [Twitter for iPhone]

Apr 16, 2019 08:45:26 PM RT @charliekirk11: It is miraculous that Trump not only beat the Bush dynasty, 16 Republicans, the FBI, the media, voter fraud cheaters, th... [Twitter for iPhone]

Apr 16, 2019 11:27:01 PM On Trumps ICC Win, Dems and Republicans See Eye to Eye | RealClearPolitics https://t.co/6S6mP6yH3A [Twitter for iPhone]

Apr 17, 2019 06:34:45 AM Wow! FBI made 11 payments to Fake Dossier's discredited author, Trump hater Christopher Steele. @OANN @JudicialWatch The Witch Hunt has been a total fraud on your President and the American people! It was brought to you by Dirty Cops, Crooked Hillary and the DNC. [Twitter for iPhone]

Apr 17, 2019 06:45:14 AM Democrats in Congress must return from their Vacations and change the Immigration Laws, or the Border, despite the great job being done by Border Patrol, will only get worse. Big sections of Wall now being built! [Twitter for iPhone]

Apr 17, 2019 11:14:52 AM ....in my conversation yesterday with President @EmmanuelMacron of France. I also wished both Pope Francis and President Macron a very Happy Easter! [Twitter for iPhone]

Apr 17, 2019 11:14:52 AM Just had a wonderful conversation with @Pontifex Francis offering condolences from the People of the United States for the horrible and destructive fire at Notre Dame Cathedral. I offered the help of our great experts on renovation and construction as I did.... [Twitter for iPhone]

Apr 17, 2019 01:52:33 PM RT @WhiteHouse: LIVE NOW: President Trump at the White House Opportunity Zones Conference https://t.co/whaCFJdEiK [Twitter for iPhone]

Apr 17, 2019 05:26:28 PM RT @Team_Mitch: Today, we're officially launching our re-election campaign. Check out our first video below and visit our new website here:... [Twitter for iPhone]

Apr 17, 2019 08:07:04 PM Nolte: Poll Shows Media Failed to Gaslight Public About Trump Campaign Spying https://t.co/06OZcBE08b via @BreitbartNews [Twitter for iPhone]

Apr 18, 2019 06:54:39 AM The Greatest Political Hoax of all time! Crimes were committed by Crooked, Dirty Cops and DNC/The Democrats. [Twitter for iPhone]

Apr 18, 2019 07:07:08 AM PRESIDENTIAL HARASSMENT! [Twitter for iPhone]

Apr 18, 2019 07:11:29 AM RT @JudicialWatch: BREAKING: JW announced today that it filed a FOIA lawsuit against the DOJ for records of communications and payments bet... [Twitter for iPhone]

Apr 18, 2019 07:11:50 AM RT @JudicialWatch: JW President @TomFitton discusses Clinton's memo: "She signed a memo saying 'due to recent targeting of personal email a... [Twitter for iPhone]

Apr 18, 2019 07:12:50 AM RT @JudicialWatch: JW President @TomFitton appeared on "Fox and Friends First" to discuss AG Bill Barr's testimony and Spygate: They know i... [Twitter for iPhone]

Apr 18, 2019 07:13:44 AM RT @JudicialWatch: JW announced that it uncovered 422 pages of FBI documents showing evidence of "cover up" discussions related to the Clin... [Twitter for iPhone]

Apr 18, 2019 07:15:00 AM RT @JudicialWatch: Judicial Watch announced it received 756 pages of newly uncovered emails that were among the materials former Secretary... [Twitter for iPhone]

Apr 18, 2019 07:15:19 AM RT @JudicialWatch: On "Hannity", @seanhannity discussed some key findings from Judicial Watch in regards to the Clinton cover-up: "We are f... [Twitter for iPhone]

Apr 18, 2019 07:16:50 AM RT @DanScavino: Nadler (2019) vs. Nadler (1998) https://t.co/IVg7RW3f0F [Twitter for iPhone]

Apr 18, 2019 07:31:03 AM Attorney General William Barr's Press Conference today at 9:30 AM ET. Watch on @FoxNews @OANN [Twitter for iPhone]

Apr 18, 2019 07:54:47 AM No Collusion - No Obstruction! https://t.co/diggF8V3hl [Twitter for iPhone]

Apr 18, 2019 08:57:33 AM https://t.co/222atp7wuB [Twitter for iPhone]

Apr 18, 2019 11:59:04 AM As I have been saying all along, NO COLLUSION - NO OBSTRUCTION! https://t.co/BnMB5mvHAM [Twitter for iPhone]
! [Twitter for iPhone]

Apr 19, 2019 04:14:33 PM RT @JudicialWatch: JWPrez @TomFitton Mueller Report Confirms Russia Hoax, NEW Deep State Lawsuit, John Kerry Colluding w/ Iran? https://t.... [Twitter for iPhone]

Apr 19, 2019 04:23:10 PM The Washington Post and New York Times are, in my opinion, two of the most dishonest media outlets around. Truly, the Enemy of the People! https://t.co/AG3vccsJvg [Twitter for iPhone]

Apr 19, 2019 04:30:39 PM RT @ScottFantasy: @jdawsey1 This is why nobody but the @DNC circle jerk takes this seriously anymore. That front page is a disgrace but in... [Twitter for iPhone]

Apr 19, 2019 04:41:10 PM Time for Democrats to accept reality https://t.co/3SyAnkSVlX [Twitter for iPhone]

Apr 19, 2019 04:42:51 PM RT @TeamCavuto: .@RepMarkMeadows It's a good day for America and it's a good day for the President https://t.co/z2mpJu2JWJ [Twitter for iPhone]

Apr 19, 2019 04:44:40 PM RT @RepMattGaetz: "You have guys that come through here that do this for a living...they bring groups across, they bring drugs across." Sher... [Twitter for iPhone]

Apr 19, 2019 05:45:23 PM RT @marklevinshow: More on the phony collusion scam https://t.co/pYwRe1ojNI [Twitter for iPhone]

Apr 19, 2019 05:46:13 PM RT @seanhannity: Mueller's Final Report 'Completely Vindicates' President Trump 👆 https://t.co/t97JxHWdji [Twitter for iPhone]

Apr 19, 2019 05:51:04 PM "TRUMP HAS BEEN TOTALLY VINDICATED" https://t.co/ZjmmVD1T4z [Twitter for iPhone]

Apr 19, 2019 06:10:40 PM Wishing a Happy Passover to all those celebrating in America, Israel, and around the world! https://t.co/h3wgLZ4mxS [Twitter for iPhone]

Apr 20, 2019 06:53:29 AM Despite the fact that the Mueller Report should not have been authorized in the first place & was written as nastily as possible by 13 (18) Angry Democrats who were true Trump Haters, including highly conflicted Bob Mueller himself, the end result is No Collusion, No Obstruction! [Twitter for iPhone]

Apr 20, 2019 07:02:38 AM The Fake News Media is doing everything possible to stir up and anger the pols and as many people as possible seldom mentioning the fact that the Mueller Report had as its principle conclusion the fact that there was NO COLLUSION WITH RUSSIA. The Russia Hoax is dead! [Twitter for iPhone]

Apr 20, 2019 07:07:54 AM United States weekly jobless claims just hit a 50 year low. The economy is doing GREAT! [Twitter for iPhone]

Apr 20, 2019 07:15:41 AM The end result of the greatest Witch Hunt in U.S. political history is No Collusion with Russia (and No Obstruction). Pretty Amazing! [Twitter for iPhone]

Apr 20, 2019 10:52:34 AM https://t.co/yoWCQLuxbD [Twitter for iPhone]

Apr 20, 2019 12:52:31 PM RT @IvankaTrump: Thank you for an incredible trip Ethiopia! USET https://t.co/lqE2XLQ25I [Twitter for iPhone]

⊔ Apr 20, 2019 12:52:41 PM RT @IvankaTrump: Wonderful and productive visit to Côte d'Ivoire! #WGDP! 📹: https://t.co/zzEsYYOyUp [Twitter for iPhone]

⊔ Apr 20, 2019 04:46:09 PM https://t.co/bCvpOGCD4t [Twitter for iPhone]

⊔ Apr 20, 2019 04:48:05 PM RT @DanScavino: I am with the President at the Southern White House, I have never seen him happier! [Twitter for iPhone]

⊔ Apr 20, 2019 04:55:17 PM RT @marklevinshow: My appearance on Fox & Friends this morning https://t.co/d8qrERYmeD [Twitter for iPhone]

⊔ Apr 20, 2019 05:09:33 PM If @MittRomney spent the same energy fighting Barack Obama as he does fighting Donald Trump, he could have won the race (maybe)! https://t.co/p5imhMJqS1 [Twitter for iPhone]

⊔ Apr 20, 2019 06:02:54 PM Check out @MarkLevinShow: Life, Liberty & Levin on @FoxNews now (7pm)! [Twitter for iPhone]

⊔ Apr 20, 2019 06:20:08 PM RT @MariaBartiromo: Happening now: @LindseyGrahamSC "we are working on a package to change the immigration laws & asylum laws. We will intr… [Twitter for iPhone]

⊔ Apr 20, 2019 06:20:25 PM RT @MariaBartiromo: Tomorrow #EXCLUSIVE @SundayFutures @FoxNews #BreakingNews 10am et @LindseyGrahamSC @RepDougCollins @RepCartwright @Rep… [Twitter for iPhone]

⊔ Apr 20, 2019 06:22:28 PM RT @LouDobbs: #DrainTheSwamp - @GreggJarrett: No one takes anything Schiff says seriously because he lost all credibility. For 2 years he c… [Twitter for iPhone]

⊔ Apr 20, 2019 06:34:04 PM Good night of television! 8:00 PM @WattersWorld 9:00 PM @JudgeJeanine with interview of @RudyGiuliani followed by Greg G. Honest commentary is always nice! [Twitter for iPhone]

⊔ Apr 20, 2019 06:35:46 PM RT @RepDougCollins: This is ridiculous. AG Barr gives Democrats unprecedented accommodations, and they refuse them hours after Chairman Nad… [Twitter for iPhone]

⊔ Apr 20, 2019 08:44:34 PM https://t.co/xiMQFztJlV [Twitter for iPhone]

⊔ Apr 20, 2019 08:53:02 PM Thank you @JesseBWatters and @DBongino! https://t.co/aGH4GBzhqh [Twitter for iPhone]

⊔ Apr 20, 2019 10:10:43 PM RT @seanhannity: Prior Reporting Confirmed That Some FBI Agents Were FED UP With Comey https://t.co/xKVZMVnOQI [Twitter for iPhone]

⊔ Apr 20, 2019 11:01:18 PM RT @ByronYork: Lotta stuff in the report. From @SecretsBedard: Kushner cleared of seeking Russian money to pay real estate debt. https://t…. [Twitter for iPhone]

Apr 21, 2019 05:48:20 AM Heartfelt condolences from the people of the United States to the people of Sri Lanka on the horrible terrorist attacks on churches and hotels that have killed at least 138 million people and badly injured 600 more. We stand ready to help! [Twitter for iPhone]

Apr 21, 2019 06:04:01 AM Happy Easter! I have never been happier or more content because your Country is doing so well, with an Economy that is the talk of the World and may be stronger than it has ever been before. Have a great day! [Twitter for iPhone]

Apr 21, 2019 06:20:25 AM 138 people have been killed in Sri Lanka, with more that 600 badly injured, in a terrorist attack on churches and hotels. The United States offers heartfelt condolences to the great people of Sri Lanka. We stand ready to help! [Twitter for iPhone]

Apr 21, 2019 06:40:29 AM Do you believe this? The New York Times Op-Ed: MEDIA AND DEMOCRATS OWE TRUMP AN APOLOGY. Well, they got that one right! [Twitter for iPhone]

Apr 21, 2019 07:37:43 AM The Trump Haters and Angry Democrats who wrote the Mueller Report were devastated by the No Collusion finding! Nothing but a total "hit job" which should never have been allowed to start in the first place! [Twitter for iPhone]

Apr 21, 2019 07:51:49 AM Despite No Collusion, No Obstruction, The Radical Left Democrats do not want to go on to Legislate for the good of the people, but only to Investigate and waste time. This is costing our Country greatly, and will cost the Dems big time in 2020! [Twitter for iPhone]

Apr 21, 2019 08:55:27 AM Jobless claims in the United States have reached their lowest (BEST) level in over 50 years! [Twitter for iPhone]

Apr 21, 2019 09:23:37 AM Can you believe that I had to go through the worst and most corrupt political Witch Hunt in the history of the United States (No Collusion) when it was the "other side" that illegally created the diversionary & criminal event and even spied on my campaign? Disgraceful! [Twitter for iPhone]

Apr 21, 2019 05:35:16 PM How do you impeach a Republican President for a crime that was committed by the Democrats? MAKE AMERICA GREAT AGAIN! [Twitter for iPhone]

Apr 22, 2019 07:52:46 AM So true - thanks @SteveHiltonx @NextRevFNC! https://t.co/2UK8RgzRQL [Twitter for iPhone]

Apr 22, 2019 08:37:10 AM Saudi Arabia and others in OPEC will more than make up the Oil Flow difference in our now Full Sanctions on Iranian Oil. Iran is being given VERY BAD advice by @JohnKerry and people who helped him lead the U.S. into the very bad Iran Nuclear Deal. Big violation of Logan Act? [Twitter for iPhone]

Apr 22, 2019 08:47:41 AM Only high crimes and misdemeanors can lead to impeachment. There were no crimes by me (No Collusion, No Obstruction), so you can't impeach. It was the Democrats that committed the crimes, not your Republican President! Tables are finally turning on the Witch Hunt! [Twitter for iPhone]

Apr 22, 2019 09:11:30 AM Thank you @MarkLevinShow! #MAGA https://t.co/kff84hFgKP [Twitter Media Studio]

Apr 22, 2019 09:18:24 AM Congratulations! https://t.co/1qWbGqCCyj [Twitter for iPhone]

Apr 22, 2019 11:16:38 AM My friend Herman Cain, a truly wonderful man, has asked me not to nominate him for a seat on the Federal Reserve Board. I will respect his wishes. Herman is a great American who truly loves our Country! [Twitter for iPhone]

Apr 22, 2019 11:58:22 AM RT @realDonaldTrump: How do you impeach a Republican President for a crime that was committed by the Democrats? MAKE AMERICA GREAT AGAIN! [Twitter for iPhone]

Apr 22, 2019 12:47:14 PM Spoke to President Maithripala Sirisena of Sri Lanka yesterday to inform him that the United States stands by him and his country in the fight against terrorism. Also expressed condolences on behalf of myself and the People of the United States. [Twitter for iPhone]

Apr 22, 2019 01:05:04 PM Spoke to Prime Minister Ranil Wickremesinghe of Sri Lanka this morning to inform him that the United States stands by him and his country in the fight against terrorism. Also expressed condolences on behalf of myself and the People of the United States! [Twitter for iPhone]

Apr 22, 2019 01:06:59 PM Spoke to the Prime Minister of Italy, Giuseppe Conte, mostly concerning Immigration, Taxes, Trade, and the Economy of both of our countries. Very good call! [Twitter for iPhone]

Apr 22, 2019 01:25:26 PM SOUTHERN BORDER CRISIS! @LouDobbs https://t.co/2w3Qt9p8ER [Twitter Media Studio]

Apr 22, 2019 01:59:19 PM "The Obama Administration did not do itself proud in this." @ByronYork https://t.co/6IDI1vEqFV [Twitter for iPhone]

Apr 22, 2019 02:04:11 PM "A very exculpatory section of the Mueller Report: NO CONSPIRACY, COORDINATION or COLLUSION with the Trump Campaign and the Russians. You can't be more clear than that!" @GreggJarrett https://t.co/bcFCtD0DRP [Twitter Media Studio]

Apr 22, 2019 02:31:49 PM Isn't it amazing that the people who were closest to me, by far, and knew the Campaign better than anyone, were never even called to testify before Mueller. The reason is that the 18 Angry Democrats knew they would all say 'NO COLLUSION' and only very good things! [Twitter for iPhone]

Apr 22, 2019 02:41:59 PM Today, @FLOTUS Melania and I are honored to host the 2019 @WhiteHouse Easter Egg Roll! https://t.co/dKxSefCl7H [Twitter for iPhone]

Apr 22, 2019 03:46:12 PM Just spoke to @LouDobbs. Will be doing a very interesting show tonight at 7:00 P.M. Eastern on @FoxBusiness! [Twitter for iPhone]

Apr 22, 2019 04:30:57 PM This should NEVER happen to another President AGAIN! https://t.co/9fnYIzjKQX [Twitter Media Studio]

Apr 22, 2019 04:35:18 PM PRESIDENTIAL HARASSMENT! https://t.co/G3f6QBNSMa [Twitter Media Studio]

Apr 22, 2019 06:28:13 PM RT @MariaBartiromo: Rep. Ratcliffe: Mueller report proves Donald Trump was telling the truth about collusion https://t.co/dD5kCNBwKl @Sund… [Twitter for iPhone]

Apr 22, 2019 06:30:26 PM RT @GOPChairwoman: Joe Biden has been losing presidential elections since the 1980s. 2020 will be no different. Biden will have to ans… [Twitter for iPhone]

Apr 22, 2019 06:31:56 PM RT @TomFitton: COUP Update: Mueller Report vindicates @RealDonaldTrump even as it tries to smear him PLUS new @JudicialWatch lawsuits on FB… [Twitter for iPhone]

Apr 22, 2019 06:32:50 PM RT @TomFitton: Mueller report full of gossip targeting @realDonaldTrump. https://t.co/lPEroontdg [Twitter for iPhone]

Apr 22, 2019 06:33:01 PM RT @TomFitton: President @realDonaldTrump Should File a Criminal Complaint with DOJ over Illicit Targeting - @JudicialWatch https://t.co/oR… [Twitter for iPhone]

Apr 22, 2019 06:33:41 PM RT @TomFitton: UNPRECEDENTED Spying Campaign on @RealDonaldTrump: DOJ/FBI/NSA/CIA/State -- "all hands on deck" in Obama administration's go… [Twitter for iPhone]

Apr 22, 2019 06:34:41 PM RT @drudgefeed: Woodward: Investigate FBICIA Handling of 'Garbage' Dossier... https://t.co/Py5AwZpRfy [Twitter for iPhone]

Apr 22, 2019 06:37:07 PM RT @TomFitton: COUP UPDATE: Who needs to be investigated on #Spygate and other abuses targeting @RealDonaldTrump? Partial list: Obama Bid… [Twitter for iPhone]

Apr 22, 2019 06:37:29 PM RT @TomFitton: COUP: @RealDonaldTrump was right -- Mueller witchhunt part of #Spygate abuse begun by Obama DOJ/FBI, working with Hillary Cl… [Twitter for iPhone]

Apr 22, 2019 06:38:14 PM RT @DevinNunes: Byron York: For some Dems, breaking up with dossier is hard to do 🎵@ByronYork🎵 https://t.co/aVdNgcGv4m [Twitter for iPhone]

Apr 22, 2019 06:38:27 PM RT @DevinNunes: Victor Davis Hanson: Mueller Probe Could Backfire on Those Who Fabricated Russia-Collusion Narrative - YouTube https://t.co… [Twitter for iPhone]

Apr 22, 2019 06:39:02 PM RT @DevinNunes: Carter Page: Mueller Report Shows He's Mr. Clean | National Review https://t.co/ArJwbs3izo [Twitter for iPhone]

Apr 22, 2019 06:43:02 PM RT @GOPoversight: Days since @RepCummings promised accountability for #MichaelCohen's lies: 54 https://t.co/no25hstV69 [Twitter for iPhone]

Apr 22, 2019 06:43:26 PM RT @Jim_Jordan: Dems holding a conference call today to discuss their next moves now that Mueller announced no collusion and no obstruction… [Twitter for iPhone]

Apr 22, 2019 06:43:44 PM RT @Jim_Jordan: "Rep. Jim Jordan on plans to investigate the origins of the Russia collusion investigation" https://t.co/4TraSR2jaM [Twitter for iPhone]

Apr 22, 2019 06:44:32 PM RT @RepMarkMeadows: Think about this: we had a President under a constant 2 year investigation for a fabricated collusion conspiracy, and y… [Twitter for iPhone]

Apr 22, 2019 06:44:56 PM RT @RepMarkMeadows: Absolutely devastating to see the news out of Sri Lanka this morning. These were Christians targeted simply for practic… [Twitter for iPhone]

Apr 22, 2019 06:45:33 PM RT @replouiegohmert: What I have accumulated here is absolutely shocking upon the realization that #Mueller's disreputable, twisted history… [Twitter for iPhone]

Apr 22, 2019 06:55:46 PM RT @WhiteHouse: The 2019 Easter Egg Roll is almost here! President @realDonaldTrump and @FLOTUS will welcome guests to the White House fo… [Twitter for iPhone]

Apr 22, 2019 06:55:55 PM RT @FLOTUS: Another wonderful Easter Egg roll! @POTUS and I enjoyed meeting everyone! Thank you to the many volunteers and vendors who wo… [Twitter for iPhone]

Apr 22, 2019 06:57:10 PM RT @GOP: "In the heartland, they want legislating, not investigating." -@kayleighmcenany https://t.co/g6GNhJQGFS [Twitter for iPhone]

Apr 22, 2019 06:58:28 PM RT @SenCapito: Last year, @SenatorTimScott and I toured #OpportunityZones in Huntington and saw the incredible potential in these designate… [Twitter for iPhone]

Apr 22, 2019 06:58:58 PM RT @SenKevinCramer: Created under the Tax Cuts and Jobs Act, Opportunity Zones help lift low income Americans out of poverty by encouraging… [Twitter for iPhone]

Apr 22, 2019 06:59:38 PM RT @MarshaBlackburn: Here's what #TaxReform has brought to our country: ✅3.2 million new jobs ✅A bigger paycheck for ~90% of taxpayers ✅Lo… [Twitter for iPhone]

Apr 22, 2019 10:05:21 PM RT @realDonaldTrump: Thank you @MarkLevinShow! #MAGA https://t.co/kff84hFgKP [Twitter for iPhone]

⊔ Apr 22, 2019 10:06:12 PM RT @realDonaldTrump: PRESIDENTIAL HARASSMENT! https://t.co/G3f6QBNSMa [Twitter for iPhone]

⊔ Apr 23, 2019 04:59:49 AM Paul Krugman, of the Fake News New York Times, has lost all credibility, as has the Times itself, with his false and highly inaccurate writings on me. He is obsessed with hatred, just as others are obsessed with how stupid he is. He said Market would crash, Only Record Highs! [Twitter for iPhone]

⊔ Apr 23, 2019 05:08:03 AM I wonder if the New York Times will apologize to me a second time, as they did after the 2016 Election. But this one will have to be a far bigger & better apology. On this one they will have to get down on their knees & beg for forgiveness-they are truly the Enemy of the People! [Twitter for iPhone]

⊔ Apr 23, 2019 05:14:24 AM I will be going to Green Bay, Wisconsin, for a really big Rally on Saturday Evening. Big crowd expected, much to talk about. MAKE AMERICA GREAT AGAIN! [Twitter for iPhone]

⊔ Apr 23, 2019 05:18:42 AM The Radical Left Democrats, together with their leaders in the Fake News Media, have gone totally insane! I guess that means that the Republican agenda is working. Stay tuned for more! [Twitter for iPhone]

⊔ Apr 23, 2019 05:27:06 AM In the "old days" if you were President and you had a good economy, you were basically immune from criticism. Remember, "It's the economy stupid." Today I have, as President, perhaps the greatest economy in history...and to the Mainstream Media, it means NOTHING. But it will! [Twitter for iPhone]

⊔ Apr 23, 2019 05:44:33 AM Sorry to say but @foxandfriends is by far the best of the morning political shows on television. It rightfully has BY FAR the highest ratings, not even close. Morning Psycho (Joe), who helped get me elected in 2016 by having me on (free) all the time, has nosedived, too Angry... [Twitter for iPhone]

⊔ Apr 23, 2019 05:54:34 AM ....Dumb and Sick. A really bad show with low ratings - and will only get worse. CNN has been a proven and long term ratings and beyond disaster. In fact, it rewarded Chris Cuomo with a now unsuccessful prime time slot, despite his massive failure in the morning. Only on CNN! [Twitter for iPhone]

⊔ Apr 23, 2019 06:04:37 AM "Harley Davidson has struggled with Tariffs with the EU, currently paying 31%. They've had to move production overseas to try and offset some of that Tariff that they've been hit with which will rise to 66% in June of 2021." @MariaBartiromo So unfair to U.S. We will Reciprocate! [Twitter for iPhone]

Apr 23, 2019 06:26:40 AM "The best thing ever to happen to Twitter is Donald Trump." @MariaBartiromo So true, but they don't treat me well as a Republican. Very discriminatory, hard for people to sign on. Constantly taking people off list. Big complaints from many people. Different names- over 100 M..... [Twitter for iPhone]

Apr 23, 2019 06:32:19 AM .....But should be much higher than that if Twitter wasn't playing their political games. No wonder Congress wants to get involved - and they should. Must be more, and fairer, companies to get out the WORD! [Twitter for iPhone]

Apr 23, 2019 06:46:34 AM The Wall is being rapidly built! The Economy is GREAT! Our Country is Respected again! [Twitter for iPhone]

Apr 23, 2019 06:47:36 AM KEEP AMERICA GREAT! [Twitter for iPhone]

Apr 23, 2019 10:47:42 AM Great interview by Jared. Nice to have extraordinarily smart people serving our Country! https://t.co/d6Tgrn4Tzn [Twitter for iPhone]

Apr 23, 2019 12:34:42 PM Great golf champion & friend, Ernie Els (@TheBig_Easy), has done a tremendous job in assisting those w/ Autism through his Els for Autism Fdn, focusing on Education, Research, Global Outreach, Recreation Services, Therapy Services, & Adult Services. #NationalAutismAwarenessMonth [Twitter for iPhone]

Apr 23, 2019 01:08:55 PM I will be in Green Bay, Wisconsin this Saturday, April 27th at the Resch Center -- 7:00pm (CDT). Big crowd expected! #MAGA https://t.co/BPYK8PF0O8 [Twitter for iPhone]

Apr 23, 2019 03:54:56 PM Great meeting this afternoon at the @WhiteHouse with @Jack from @Twitter. Lots of subjects discussed regarding their platform, and the world of social media in general. Look forward to keeping an open dialogue! https://t.co/QnZi579eFb [Twitter for iPhone]

Apr 23, 2019 05:43:34 PM You mean the Stock Market hit an all-time record high today and they're actually talking impeachment!? Will I ever be given credit for anything by the Fake News Media or Radical Liberal Dems? NO COLLUSION! [Twitter for iPhone]

Apr 23, 2019 07:46:04 PM Thanks Rush! @FoxNews https://t.co/x8XogwA8VX [Twitter Media Studio]

Apr 24, 2019 06:04:17 AM "Former CIA analyst Larry Johnson accuses United Kingdom Intelligence of helping Obama Administration Spy on the 2016 Trump Presidential Campaign." @OANN WOW! It is now just a question of time before the truth comes out, and when it does, it will be a beauty! [Twitter for iPhone]

Apr 24, 2019 06:18:08 AM The American people deserve to know who is in this Country. Yesterday, the Supreme Court took up the Census Citizenship question, a really big deal. MAKE AMERICA GREAT AGAIN! [Twitter for iPhone]

Apr 24, 2019 06:25:43 AM A very big Caravan of over 20,000 people started up through Mexico. It has been reduced in size by Mexico but is still coming. Mexico must apprehend the remainder or we will be forced to close that section of the Border & call up the Military. The Coyotes & Cartels have weapons! [Twitter for iPhone]

Apr 24, 2019 07:00:46 AM Mexico's Soldiers recently pulled guns on our National Guard Soldiers, probably as a diversionary tactic for drug smugglers on the Border. Better not happen again! We are now sending ARMED SOLDIERS to the Border. Mexico is not doing nearly enough in apprehending & returning! [Twitter for iPhone]

Apr 24, 2019 07:10:06 AM The Mueller Report, despite being written by Angry Democrats and Trump Haters, and with unlimited money behind it ($35,000,000), didn't lay a glove on me. I DID NOTHING WRONG. If the partisan Dems ever tried to Impeach, I would first head to the U.S. Supreme Court. Not only...... [Twitter for iPhone]

Apr 24, 2019 07:18:31 AM .....are there no "High Crimes and Misdemeanors," there are no Crimes by me at all. All of the Crimes were committed by Crooked Hillary, the Dems, the DNC and Dirty Cops - and we caught them in the act! We waited for Mueller and WON, so now the Dems look to Congress as last hope! [Twitter for iPhone]

Apr 24, 2019 08:34:41 AM Can anyone comprehend what a GREAT job Border Patrol and Law Enforcement is doing on our Southern Border. So far this year they have APPREHENDED 418,000 plus illegal immigrants, way up from last year. Mexico is doing very little for us. DEMS IN CONGRESS MUST ACT NOW! [Twitter for iPhone]

Apr 24, 2019 08:47:54 AM No Collusion, No Obstruction - there has NEVER been a President who has been more transparent. Millions of pages of documents were given to the Mueller Angry Dems, plus I allowed everyone to testify, including W.H. counsel. I didn't have to do this, but now they want more..... [Twitter for iPhone]

Apr 24, 2019 08:52:04 AM ....Congress has no time to legislate, they only want to continue the Witch Hunt, which I have already won. They should start looking at The Criminals who are already very well known to all. This was a Rigged System - WE WILL DRAIN THE SWAMP! [Twitter for iPhone]

Apr 24, 2019 09:09:35 AM I didn't call Bob Costa of the Washington Post, he called me (Returned his call)! Just more Fake News. [Twitter for iPhone]

Apr 24, 2019 11:48:54 AM Rep. Occasio-Cortez is correct, the VA is not broken, it is doing great. But that is only because of the Trump Administration. We got Veterans Choice & Accountability passed. "President Trump deserves a lot of credit." Dan Caldwell, Concerned Veterans of America [Twitter for iPhone]

Apr 24, 2019 11:54:54 AM Rep. Alexandria Ocasio-Cortez is correct, the VA is not broken, it is doing great. But that is only because of the Trump Administration. We got Veterans Choice & Accountability passed. "President Trump deserves a lot of credit." Dan Caldwell, Concerned Veterans of America [Twitter for iPhone]

Apr 24, 2019 01:36:46 PM Today, @FLOTUS Melania and I were honored to join thousands of leaders from across the Country for the 2019 Prescription Drug Abuse and Heroin Summit (@RxSummit) in Atlanta, Georgia! #RxSummit2019 https://t.co/LfkFisfN22 [Twitter for iPhone]

Apr 24, 2019 01:40:18 PM As ONE UNITED NATION, we will work, we will pray, and we will fight for the day when every family across our land can live in a DRUG FREE AMERICA! #RxSummit2019 https://t.co/FqpHhaafkD [Twitter for iPhone]

Apr 24, 2019 02:48:32 PM .@SenMikeLee of the great state of Utah has written a wonderful new book entitled, "Our Lost Declaration." Highly recommended! [Twitter for iPhone]

Apr 24, 2019 06:01:43 PM The Great State of Tennessee is so close to passing School Choice. All of our Nation's children, regardless of background, deserve a shot at achieving the American Dream! Time to get this done, so important! [Twitter for iPhone]

Apr 25, 2019 06:47:12 AM As has been incorrectly reported by the Fake News Media, I never told then White House Counsel Don McGahn to fire Robert Mueller, even though I had the legal right to do so. If I wanted to fire Mueller, I didn't need McGahn to do it, I could have done it myself. Nevertheless,.... [Twitter for iPhone]

Apr 25, 2019 06:57:24 AM ....Mueller was NOT fired and was respectfully allowed to finish his work on what I, and many others, say was an illegal investigation (there was no crime), headed by a Trump hater who was highly conflicted, and a group of 18 VERY ANGRY Democrats. DRAIN THE SWAMP! [Twitter for iPhone]

Apr 25, 2019 07:09:42 AM .....Despite the fact that the Mueller Report was "composed" by Trump Haters and Angry Democrats, who had unlimited funds and human resources, the end result was No Collusion, No Obstruction. Amazing! [Twitter for iPhone]

⬜ Apr 25, 2019 07:22:18 AM Welcome to the race Sleepy Joe. I only hope you have the intelligence, long in doubt, to wage a successful primary campaign. It will be nasty - you will be dealing with people who truly have some very sick & demented ideas. But if you make it, I will see you at the Starting Gate! [Twitter for iPhone]

⬜ Apr 25, 2019 08:27:59 AM RT @Jim_Jordan: Peter Strzok told us that he would "love to answer each and every one of [our] questions" once the Mueller investigation co... [Twitter for iPhone]

⬜ Apr 25, 2019 08:29:00 AM RT @GOPoversight: Democrats are obsessed with @realDonaldTrump. It's time to move on and solve problems for the American people. https://t.... [Twitter for iPhone]

⬜ Apr 25, 2019 08:30:14 AM RT @Jim_Jordan: It's time to figure out what the Comey Cabal did at the start of the fake "Russia collusion" investigation. Comey, Andy Mc... [Twitter for iPhone]

⬜ Apr 25, 2019 08:31:11 AM RT @RepMarkMeadows: Reminder: Democrats demanding an unredacted Mueller report (exposing even classified info) spent a year attacking mysel... [Twitter for iPhone]

⬜ Apr 25, 2019 08:31:38 AM RT @dcexaminer: "The collusion delusion fell flat." @RepMarkMeadows suggests Democrats are too blinded by hatred of @realDonaldTrump to l... [Twitter for iPhone]

⬜ Apr 25, 2019 08:32:26 AM RT @RepMarkMeadows: We knew they wouldn't give up. The collusion delusion fell flat, and now reports say House Democrats are preparing to... [Twitter for iPhone]

⬜ Apr 25, 2019 08:35:36 AM RT @RepMattGaetz: Volume 1 of the Mueller Report is based on evidence, while Volume 2 seems to rely heavily on the reporting of news outlet... [Twitter for iPhone]

⬜ Apr 25, 2019 08:35:56 AM RT @RepAndyBiggsAZ: I'm grateful for my colleagues who accompanied me to the border to view the crisis w/ their own eyes. It's one thing to... [Twitter for iPhone]

⬜ Apr 25, 2019 08:47:45 AM RT @GOP: Do you want to go back to a bad economy, failed foreign policy, and more broken promises? https://t.co/TibOT2Bi5l [Twitter for iPhone]

⬜ Apr 25, 2019 08:48:02 AM RT @GOPChairwoman: Joe Biden literally can't hide from the economic successes of @realDonaldTrump's administration. Biden chose Pennsylv... [Twitter for iPhone]

⬜ Apr 25, 2019 09:01:57 AM RT @GOPChairwoman: If Joe Biden wants to keep score: In 8 years, Biden & Obama had a net loss of 193,000 manufacturing jobs. In just over... [Twitter for iPhone]

⬜ Apr 25, 2019 09:03:37 AM RT @RepMattGaetz: "The man who killed my son never did a day in prison. Not one day." On January 22nd, 2015, Grant Ronnebeck was shot and... [Twitter for iPhone]

⬜ Apr 25, 2019 09:35:11 AM I will be interviewed by @seanhannity tonight at 9:00 PM on @FoxNews. Enjoy! [Twitter for iPhone]

Apr 25, 2019 11:32:44 AM Look forward to seeing everyone in Indianapolis, Indiana tomorrow! https://t.co/3soeEjsMA3 [Twitter for iPhone]

Apr 25, 2019 12:17:56 PM RT @WhiteHouse: President @realDonaldTrump and @FLOTUS traveled to Atlanta, Georgia, yesterday for the Rx Drug Abuse and Heroin Summit, con... [Twitter for iPhone]

Apr 25, 2019 01:09:25 PM Our Border Control Agents have done an incredible job under very adverse conditions. I am very proud to have increased their salaries because of the great job they do. Nobody deserves it more. THANK YOU and keep up the outstanding work! https://t.co/ljy3hZOgfL [Twitter for iPhone]

Apr 25, 2019 01:11:16 PM Thank you! #MAGAus https://t.co/EWjwRlmIve [Twitter for iPhone]

Apr 25, 2019 07:59:14 PM I will be interviewed on @seanhannity at 9:00 PM. In 5 minutes - Enjoy! [Twitter for iPhone]

Apr 26, 2019 06:12:21 AM No money was paid to North Korea for Otto Warmbier, not two Million Dollars, not anything else. This is not the Obama Administration that paid 1.8 Billion Dollars for four hostages, or gave five terroist hostages plus, who soon went back to battle, for traitor Sgt. Bergdahl! [Twitter for iPhone]

Apr 26, 2019 06:32:40 AM "President Donald J. Trump is the greatest hostage negotiator that I know of in the history of the United States. 20 hostages, many in impossible circumstances, have been released in last two years. No money was paid." Cheif Hostage Negotiator, USA! [Twitter for iPhone]

Apr 26, 2019 07:39:55 AM Weirdo Tom Steyer, who didn't have the "guts" or money to run for President, is still trying to remain relevant by putting himself on ads begging for impeachment. He doesn't mention the fact that mine is perhaps the most successful first 2 year presidency in history & NO C OR O! [Twitter for iPhone]

Apr 26, 2019 07:47:07 AM Heading to Indianapolis to speak at the big NRA Conference. Love being in Indiana. The @NRA is getting stronger & stronger and doing some really great and important work. Having their powerful support has been vital to #MAGA! [Twitter for iPhone]

Apr 26, 2019 09:25:28 AM Just out: Real GDP for First Quarter grew 3.2% at an annual rate. This is far above expectations or projections. Importantly, inflation VERY LOW. MAKE AMERICA GREAT AGAIN! [Twitter for iPhone]

Apr 26, 2019 12:34:33 PM Great NRA crowd and enthusiasm in Indiana. Thank you! Leaving now for meetings in the Oval Office. [Twitter for iPhone]

Apr 26, 2019 01:31:47 PM Spoke to Saudi Arabia and others about increasing oil flow. All are in agreement. The California tax on gasoline is causing big problems on pricing for that state. Speak to your Governor about reducing. Economic numbers, 3.2% GDP for what is often worst quarter, looking good! [Twitter for iPhone]

Apr 26, 2019 02:03:05 PM RT @WhiteHouse: "Under my Administration, we will never surrender American sovereignty to anyone. We will never allow foreign bureaucrats t... [Twitter for iPhone]

Apr 26, 2019 02:03:10 PM RT @WhiteHouse: "With God as our witness, we swear today that we will defend our rights, we will safeguard our freedoms, we will uphold our... [Twitter for iPhone]

Apr 26, 2019 02:13:29 PM "U.S. Economy Grows 3.2% in Q1, Smashing Expectations" https://t.co/HltPdlkOD0 [Twitter for iPhone]

Apr 26, 2019 05:57:34 PM THANK YOU @NRA! #NRAAM https://t.co/SWkpe1eFhT [Twitter for iPhone]

Apr 27, 2019 07:06:03 AM Congratulations to Nick Bosa on being picked number two in the NFL Draft. You will be a great player for years to come, maybe one of the best. Big Talent! San Francisco will embrace you but most importantly, always stay true to yourself. MAKE AMERICA GREAT AGAIN! [Twitter for iPhone]

Apr 27, 2019 11:23:37 AM RT @WhiteHouse: Today is National Drug Take Back Day! Find a collection site near you and join the fight against opioid abuse. https://t.co... [Twitter for iPhone]

Apr 27, 2019 11:30:13 AM RT @FLOTUS: #TakeBackDay is a reminder to dispose of your unused prescription drugs responsibly! Find your nearest collection center at htt... [Twitter for iPhone]

Apr 27, 2019 11:41:38 AM We must end the Opioid Crisis. Do your part today by participating in prescription drug #TakeBackDay at over 4,000 locations across the Country! https://t.co/09LeIplOsp https://t.co/5nVH5AT2Fw [Twitter for iPhone]

Apr 27, 2019 12:05:36 PM We must end the Opioid Crisis. Do your part today by participating in prescription drug #TakeBackDay at over 4,000 locations across the Country! https://t.co/xvwO9fcu42 https://t.co/y96Y9MBpaz [Twitter for iPhone]

Apr 27, 2019 04:41:05 PM Thoughts and prayers to all of those affected by the shooting at the Synagogue in Poway, California. God bless you all. Suspect apprehended. Law enforcement did outstanding job. Thank you! [Twitter for iPhone]

Apr 27, 2019 05:00:23 PM Leaving now for Green Bay, Wisconsin - BIG CROWD, will be there shortly! #MAGA [Twitter for iPhone]

⊔ Apr 27, 2019 05:14:25 PM Great day with Prime Minister @AbeShinzo of Japan. We played a quick round of golf by the beautiful Potomac River while talking Trade and many other subjects. He has now left for Japan and I am on my way to Wisconsin where a very large crowd of friends await! https://t.co/ZvyxJ8sIw2 [Twitter for iPhone]

⊔ Apr 27, 2019 05:47:01 PM Sincerest THANK YOU to our great Border Patrol Agent who stopped the shooter at the Synagogue in Poway, California. He may have been off duty but his talents for Law Enforcement weren't! [Twitter for iPhone]

⊔ Apr 27, 2019 06:46:06 PM Just arrived in Green Bay, Wisconsin for a #MAGA Rally. Big crowds - join me at 8:00 P.M. Eastern, live on @FoxNews! [Twitter for iPhone]

⊔ Apr 27, 2019 08:58:39 PM Beautiful #TrumpRally tonight in Green Bay, Wisconsin with a massive crowd. Thank you for joining me, I love you! #MAGAushttps://t.co/JRyhOXH7EE [Twitter for iPhone]

⊔ Apr 27, 2019 09:07:11 PM Thank you Green Bay, Wisconsin! MAKE AMERICA GREAT AGAIN!! https://t.co/chGLxGsPQh [Twitter for iPhone]

⊔ Apr 27, 2019 09:57:31 PM Thank you to brilliant and highly respected attorney Alan Dershowitz for destroying the very dumb legal argument of "Judge" Andrew Napolitano.... [Twitter for iPhone]

⊔ Apr 27, 2019 09:57:32 PM ....Ever since Andrew came to my office to ask that I appoint him to the U.S. Supreme Court, and I said NO, he has been very hostile! Also asked for pardon for his friend. A good "pal" of low ratings Shepard Smith. [Twitter for iPhone]

⊔ Apr 27, 2019 10:10:24 PM The Democratic National Committee, sometimes referred to as the DNC, is again working its magic in its quest to destroy Crazy Bernie Sanders.... [Twitter for iPhone]

⊔ Apr 27, 2019 10:10:25 PM ....for the more traditional, but not very bright, Sleepy Joe Biden. Here we go again Bernie, but this time please show a little more anger and indignation when you get screwed! [Twitter for iPhone]

⊔ Apr 27, 2019 11:12:16 PM RT @AbeShinzo: 昨日の首脳会談、4人だけの夕食会、そして本日のゴルフと、トランプ大統領と10時間以上を共に過ごすなかで、北朝鮮問題への対応、経済、G20大阪サミット、更には世界情勢に至るまで、様々な課題についてじっくりと話をすることができました。 https://... [Twitter for iPhone]

⊔ Apr 28, 2019 07:59:53 AM Will be interviewed by @MariaBartiromo on @FoxNews at 10:00 AM. Talking about the Southern Border and how the Dems MUST act fast to change our pathetic immigration laws. Will be tough, watch! [Twitter for iPhone]

Apr 29, 2019 05:49:10 AM I spoke at length yesterday to Rabbi Yisroel Goldstein, Chabad of Poway, where I extended my warmest condolences to him and all affected by the shooting in California. What a great guy. He had a least one finger blown off, and all he wanted to do is help others. Very special! [Twitter for iPhone]

Apr 29, 2019 07:18:25 AM The NRA is under siege by Cuomo and the New York State A.G., who are illegally using the State's legal apparatus to take down and destroy this very important organization, & others. It must get its act together quickly, stop the internal fighting, & get back to GREATNESS - FAST! [Twitter for iPhone]

Apr 29, 2019 08:23:32 AM ....People are fleeing New York State because of high taxes and yes, even oppression of sorts. They didn't even put up a fight against SALT - could have won. So much litigation. The NRA should leave and fight from the outside of this very difficult to deal with (unfair) State! [Twitter for iPhone]

Apr 29, 2019 09:32:39 AM I'll never get the support of Dues Crazy union leadership, those people who rip-off their membership with ridiculously high dues, medical and other expenses while being paid a fortune. But the members love Trump. They look at our record economy, tax & reg cuts, military etc. WIN! [Twitter for iPhone]

Apr 29, 2019 09:42:12 AM The Media (Fake News) is pushing Sleepy Joe hard. Funny, I'm only here because of Biden & Obama. They didn't do the job and now you have Trump, who is getting it done - big time! [Twitter for iPhone]

Apr 29, 2019 09:51:03 AM Sleepy Joe Biden is having his first rally in the Great State of Pennsylvania. He obviously doesn't know that Pennsylvania is having one of the best economic years in its history, with lowest unemployment EVER, a now thriving Steel Industry (that was dead) & great future!........ [Twitter for iPhone]

Apr 29, 2019 09:55:09 AM The Dues Sucking firefighters leadership will always support Democrats, even though the membership wants me. Some things never change! [Twitter for iPhone]

Apr 29, 2019 10:06:11 AM Bob Mueller was a great HERO to the Radical Left Democrats. Now that the Mueller Report is finished, with a finding of NO COLLUSION & NO OBSTRUCTION (based on a review of Report by our highly respected A.G.), the Dems are going around saying, "Bob who, sorry, don't know the man." [Twitter for iPhone]

Apr 29, 2019 10:20:34 AM The New York Times has apologized for the terrible Anti-Semitic Cartoon, but they haven't apologized to me for this or all of the Fake and Corrupt news they print on a daily basis. They have reached the lowest level of "journalism," and certainly a low point in @nytimes history! [Twitter for iPhone]

Apr 29, 2019 04:34:37 PM RT @BaylorWBB: Thank you to @realDonaldTrump and the @WhiteHouse staff for a great experience for the Lady Bears! #SicEm https://t.co/SR7no... [Twitter for iPhone]

Apr 29, 2019 06:13:49 PM Pittsburgh jobless rate hits lowest point since the early 1970s (maybe even better than that) and Sleepy Joe just had his first rally there. Fact is, every economic aspect of our Country is the best it has ever been! https://t.co/kWriC0DIuW [Twitter for iPhone]

Apr 29, 2019 08:17:20 PM The Coyotes and Drug Cartels are in total control of the Mexico side of the Southern Border. They have labs nearby where they make drugs to sell into the U.S. Mexico, one of the most dangerous country's in the world, must eradicate this problem now. Also, stop the MARCH to U.S. [Twitter for iPhone]

Apr 29, 2019 08:23:49 PM If the Democrats don't give us the votes to change our weak, ineffective and dangerous Immigration Laws, we must fight hard for these votes in the 2020 Election! [Twitter for iPhone]

Apr 30, 2019 11:31:49 AM We have 1,800 ISIS Prisoners taken hostage in our final battles to destroy 100% of the Caliphate in Syria. Decisions are now being made as to what to do with these dangerous prisoners.... [Twitter for iPhone]

Apr 30, 2019 11:31:50 AM ....European countries are not helping at all, even though this was very much done for their benefit. They are refusing to take back prisoners from their specific countries. Not good! [Twitter for iPhone]

Apr 30, 2019 12:56:57 PM China is adding great stimulus to its economy while at the same time keeping interest rates low. Our Federal Reserve has incessantly lifted interest rates, even though inflation is very low, and instituted a very big dose of quantitative tightening. We have the potential to go... [Twitter for iPhone]

Apr 30, 2019 01:05:02 PM ....up like a rocket if we did some lowering of rates, like one point, and some quantitative easing. Yes, we are doing very well at 3.2% GDP, but with our wonderfully low inflation, we could be setting major records &, at the same time, make our National Debt start to look small! [Twitter for iPhone]

Apr 30, 2019 01:23:28 PM I am monitoring the situation in Venezuela very closely. The United States stands with the People of Venezuela and their Freedom! [Twitter for iPhone]

Apr 30, 2019 03:20:10 PM CONGRATULATIONS to the 2018 @NASCAR Cup Series Champion, @JoeyLogano! https://t.co/uHGTUVyRIC [Twitter for iPhone]

Apr 30, 2019 04:09:13 PM ....embargo, together with highest-level sanctions, will be placed on the island of Cuba. Hopefully, all Cuban soldiers will promptly and peacefully return to their island! [Twitter for iPhone]

Apr 30, 2019 04:09:13 PM If Cuban Troops and Militia do not immediately CEASE military and other operations for the purpose of causing death and destruction to the Constitution of Venezuela, a full and complete.... [Twitter for iPhone]

Apr 30, 2019 06:21:16 PM Today, it was my great honor to welcome and host the 2018 @NASCAR Cup Series Champion, @JoeyLogano and @Team_Penske to the @WhiteHouse! https://t.co/ExCangG6Kc [Twitter for iPhone]

May 1, 2019 04:56:00 AM I've done more for Firefighters than this dues sucking union will ever do, and I get paid ZERO! https://t.co/Tw0qwTiUD6 [Twitter for iPhone]

May 1, 2019 04:56:14 AM RT @dpparadis123: @dbongino My neighbor is a fireman and he loves trump [Twitter for iPhone]

May 1, 2019 04:56:34 AM RT @icemanTom: @dbongino I'm a firefighter and I don't endorse Joe Biden My vote goes to President Donald Trump!!!! [Twitter for iPhone]

May 1, 2019 04:56:39 AM RT @ro18007212: @dbongino I have fire fighter friends and they support Trump. [Twitter for iPhone]

May 1, 2019 04:56:52 AM RT @OrzechEd: @dbongino Im a firefighter and im NOT voting for Joe. [Twitter for iPhone]

May 1, 2019 04:56:59 AM RT @TheKevinNash61: @dbongino None. We are all pissed about this. I have withdrawn my support for firePAC [Twitter for iPhone]

May 1, 2019 04:57:10 AM RT @mitchraider60: @dbongino How any firefighter in NY can support any Dem is disgusting after DiBlasio went to the G2 last year to rip our... [Twitter for iPhone]

May 1, 2019 04:57:18 AM RT @JimmyMac233: @dbongino Agreed Dan. NYC FD inions haven't made a peep but the known rank and file are Trump guys. [Twitter for iPhone]

May 1, 2019 04:57:34 AM RT @jcoreybates: @dbongino 🖖 This career firefighter will not be voting for any Democrat on the ticket. I will be voting for @POTUS again. [Twitter for iPhone]

May 1, 2019 04:57:49 AM RT @G4TTO21: @dbongino My father is a fireman and his entire firehouse loves Trump [Twitter for iPhone]

May 1, 2019 04:59:54 AM RT @TGrande7: @dbongino All firefighters I work with said No way !!!!!! Fake News [Twitter for iPhone]

May 1, 2019 05:00:07 AM RT @CwElliott2: @dbongino You are correct, 100%, Dan. A bunch of us have been talking, and this is just the DNC buying and paying for the... [Twitter for iPhone]

May 1, 2019 05:00:28 AM RT @JA_Loans: @dbongino Does he know 90% of the Firemen's retirement is dependent on the US Economy and invested in US Stock? Do not think... [Twitter for iPhone]

May 1, 2019 05:00:40 AM RT @wadar1969: @dbongino The union bureaucrats endorse him but the due paying members don't, and they wonder why unions are getting smaller... [Twitter for iPhone]

May 1, 2019 05:00:50 AM RT @QuaglianoJohn: @dbongino Roger that....firefighters will vote Trump! The union may not be representing its membership appropriately in... [Twitter for iPhone]

May 1, 2019 05:01:01 AM RT @mscrosswi: @dbongino Nowhere have I heard the firefighters were supporting Joe Biden. The leadership of the firefighters union, on the... [Twitter for iPhone]

May 1, 2019 05:01:19 AM RT @woofeous: @dbongino "Over Charging Union Dues Alert". Dan, how about Union leadership opening up books to own members since they have s... [Twitter for iPhone]

May 1, 2019 05:01:28 AM RT @joelle_palombo: @dbongino This fire family does NOT support Joe Biden for President. #TRUMP2020us [Twitter for iPhone]

May 1, 2019 05:01:46 AM RT @Korryb: @dbongino I certainly won't be voting for this guy! [Twitter for iPhone]

May 1, 2019 05:02:04 AM RT @Daniel4SCBoone: @dbongino I bet if someone did a fireman's poll, President Trump would win by a landslide. [Twitter for iPhone]

May 1, 2019 05:02:13 AM RT @JeffreyKStewart: @dbongino Just the union leadership supports Biden. Members support Trump. This applies to most unions. [Twitter for iPhone]

May 1, 2019 05:02:26 AM RT @bobahide: @dbongino Not I [Twitter for iPhone]

May 1, 2019 05:02:27 AM RT @wargs8: @dbongino Fact!! [Twitter for iPhone]

May 1, 2019 05:05:28 AM RT @JeffNeely11: @dbongino No, we don't support Crazy Joe!! And our members in our Local are up in arms! [Twitter for iPhone]

May 1, 2019 05:05:52 AM RT @cmd629: @dbongino Yea right, until they get in the voting booth! [Twitter for iPhone]

May 1, 2019 05:05:56 AM RT @Bones_zoom: @dbongino He has NO chance. [Twitter for iPhone]

May 1, 2019 05:06:04 AM RT @JoanWil57769727: @dbongino Well there could be a small group of Obama people, anyone in his right mind would not support Joe Biden [Twitter for iPhone]

May 1, 2019 05:06:10 AM RT @clintwelborn1: @dbongino Happy im not a member of IAFF anymore [Twitter for iPhone]

May 1, 2019 05:06:16 AM RT @HikeAmerica440: @dbongino None that I know of in my home town either [Twitter for iPhone]

May 1, 2019 05:06:29 AM RT @LisaLimaaa: @dbongino Shouldn't the fireman have a say? [Twitter for iPhone]

May 1, 2019 05:06:45 AM RT @Kimberl40855897: @dbongino The rank and file know who has their back and remember no one knows who you vote for ! [Twitter for iPhone]

May 1, 2019 05:06:59 AM RT @CurtisVincent5: @dbongino This firefighter won't be voting for creepy @JoeBiden [Twitter for iPhone]

May 1, 2019 05:07:12 AM RT @23Mcguire: @dbongino Not 🦮☐♂☐nor my brother [Twitter for iPhone]

May 1, 2019 05:07:28 AM RT @broncolee70: @dbongino @KurtSchlichter That's why I am not in the IFFA. Don't want my $$$ going to dems [Twitter for iPhone]

May 1, 2019 05:08:02 AM RT @Steverefresh: @dbongino They will take union dues from trump voters and give to creepy though [Twitter for iPhone]

May 1, 2019 05:08:11 AM RT @mw_canterbury: @dbongino This is why more lawsuits are going to presented by union members because of misrepresentation by the top eche... [Twitter for iPhone]

May 1, 2019 05:08:20 AM RT @BradyBbum1957: @dbongino When the union backs you but the people in the union don't [Twitter for iPhone]

May 1, 2019 05:08:33 AM RT @Scooter172: @dbongino The fire fighters union bosses are endorsing a failure. [Twitter for iPhone]

May 1, 2019 05:08:56 AM RT @GWKohn1: @dbongino None of the MEN I know are either. [Twitter for iPhone]

May 1, 2019 05:09:06 AM RT @VanhortonM: @dbongino Smoke and mirrors Biden. [Twitter for iPhone]

May 1, 2019 05:09:22 AM RT @chrisgogarty: @dbongino Add me to your list Dan. I am furious that the board would make such an announcement without even taking the me... [Twitter for iPhone]

May 1, 2019 05:09:28 AM RT @JCryptoseed: @dbongino Never Supporting a Fireman's Ball again... [Twitter for iPhone]

May 1, 2019 05:11:05 AM RT @firemanbrawls: @dbongino I know a couple in my department. Granted I am in Alabama but most of the firefighters I talk to are voting @r... [Twitter for iPhone]

May 1, 2019 05:11:14 AM RT @blinddog007: @dbongino I know the police officers Union is backing Donald Trump...I back the blue #bluelivesmatter [Twitter for iPhone]

May 1, 2019 05:11:39 AM RT @KRobbio: @dbongino He used there dues when they support trump [Twitter for iPhone]

May 1, 2019 05:12:36 AM RT @flamingoHeels: @dbongino Joe Biden is not even his party's candidate yet. Firemen 🚒 can't say they endorse him. He may not even be on b... [Twitter for iPhone]

⊔ May 1, 2019 05:13:15 AM RT @RealDanKida: @dbongino The Unions have become Corporations representing themselves, Our President represents the people. #MAGA @realDon... [Twitter for iPhone]

⊔ May 1, 2019 05:14:02 AM RT @glamourizes: @dbongino My husband a New York City firefighter for 15 years will be voting Trump 2020 all the way!! [Twitter for iPhone]

⊔ May 1, 2019 05:14:13 AM RT @harrypeterson_: @dbongino It doesn't matter who they endorse, the only person winning in 2020 is President Trump! [Twitter for iPhone]

⊔ May 1, 2019 05:14:35 AM RT @kshaferus: @dbongino This statement is like so many others—liberal lies. Why would the military or emergency workers support a candidat... [Twitter for iPhone]

⊔ May 1, 2019 05:15:57 AM RT @mr36561: @dbongino Stick in the eye by union...Trump has worked very hard for our first responders and union members...fighting very ha... [Twitter for iPhone]

⊔ May 1, 2019 05:16:15 AM RT @OmastaSkip: @dbongino As a retired FF I know that the majority of the rank and file are conservative or moderate and DO NOT support lib... [Twitter for iPhone]

⊔ May 1, 2019 05:16:28 AM RT @tedbartley: @dbongino As a retired Firefighter, I can only speak for my fellow retirees,and I can assure you NONE of us support him,OR... [Twitter for iPhone]

⊔ May 1, 2019 05:16:48 AM RT @TheDJDaniel01: @dbongino Why would any firefighter of service vote for him? @realDonaldTrump is the way to go. [Twitter for iPhone]

⊔ May 1, 2019 05:17:01 AM RT @gr84u2c: @dbongino @DebbieB1230 Lousy choice [Twitter for iPhone]

⊔ May 1, 2019 05:17:13 AM RT @BIGGeorgeAZ: @dbongino Nope not me either. I'm not voting for crazy Joe. My support is behind @realDonaldTrump in 2020! [Twitter for iPhone]

⊔ May 1, 2019 05:17:21 AM RT @proudtexanbrew: @dbongino I'm a retired volunteer firefighter and I'd be PISSED if my dues were going to this [Twitter for iPhone]

⊔ May 1, 2019 05:17:41 AM RT @Jrag19601: @dbongino The ONLY reason why Joe Biden is able to get into this race is he knows for a fact that the democrat media will ne... [Twitter for iPhone]

⊔ May 1, 2019 05:17:51 AM RT @TomLewi86961554: @dbongino Im a Firefighter and I'm a YUGE trump supporter! I got banned from the IAFF web. [Twitter for iPhone]

⊔ May 1, 2019 05:18:08 AM RT @ScottBepler: @dbongino 24 years plus firefighter here,& there's no chance Biden is my choice. #NoMoJoe Actually, no one on the left ha... [Twitter for iPhone]

⊔ May 1, 2019 05:18:13 AM RT @saulpavsr: @dbongino I cannot wait to vote for the greatest president ever [Twitter for iPhone]

May 1, 2019 05:36:14 AM "The Democrats can't come to grips with the fact that there was No Collusion, there was No Conspiracy, there was No Obstruction. What we should be focused on is what's been going on in our government, at the highest levels of the FBI...." Senator Josh Hawley [Twitter for iPhone]

May 1, 2019 05:50:34 AM I am overriding the Decommission Order of the magnificent aircraft carrier Harry S. Truman, built in 1998 (fairly new), and considered one of the largest and finest in the world. It will be updated at a fraction of the cost of a new one (which also are being built)! [Twitter for iPhone]

May 1, 2019 06:01:15 AM Gallup Poll: 56% of Americans rate their financial situation as excellent or good. This is the highest number since 2002, and up 10 points since 2016. [Twitter for iPhone]

May 1, 2019 06:11:42 AM "No President in history has endured such vicious personal attacks by political opponents. Still, the President's record is unparalleled." @LouDobbs [Twitter for iPhone]

May 1, 2019 07:06:10 AM Congress must change the Immigration Laws now, Dems won't act. Wall is being built - 400 miles by end of next year. Mexico must stop the march to Border! @foxandfriends [Twitter for iPhone]

May 1, 2019 07:28:53 AM Why didn't President Obama do something about Russia in September (before November Election) when told by the FBI? He did NOTHING, and had no intention of doing anything! [Twitter for iPhone]

May 1, 2019 08:03:41 AM NO COLLUSION, NO OBSTRUCTION. Besides, how can you have Obstruction when not only was there No Collusion (by Trump), but the bad actions were done by the "other" side? The greatest con-job in the history of American Politics! [Twitter for iPhone]

May 1, 2019 07:31:57 PM RT @aldresser: As a Phoenix firefighter and member of the IAFF I was surprised and pleased to learn that the only money that goes to feder... [Twitter for iPhone]

May 1, 2019 07:33:40 PM RT @michi83: Barr: Was my letter inaccurate? Mueller: No. Barr: Was the media coverage of my letter inaccurate? Mueller: Yes. [Twitter for iPhone]

May 1, 2019 07:49:36 PM RT @EricTrump: The Democratic Party has no message, accomplishments or leadership so all they do is harass my father & our family. Congress... [Twitter for iPhone]

May 1, 2019 07:50:37 PM RT @EricTrump: .@CNN you might want to rethink your narrative - clearly people don't like your message. Truly shocking to me that any of yo... [Twitter for iPhone]

May 1, 2019 07:53:23 PM RT @marklevinshow: Audience to CNN, adios https://t.co/JvQy4oTfNj [Twitter for iPhone]

May 1, 2019 07:57:17 PM RT @TomFitton: BREAKING: Obama knew -- FBI admits it found Clinton Emails in Obama WH! PLUS @JudicialWatch is already investigating the inv... [Twitter for iPhone]

May 1, 2019 07:57:48 PM RT @TomFitton: .@JudicialWatch FOIA disclosures help lead to criminal referral on Russiagate targeting of @realDonaldTrump. https://t.co/aS... [Twitter for iPhone]

May 1, 2019 07:58:56 PM RT @JudicialWatch: JW announced that it filed a FOIA lawsuit against the DOJ for records of communications and payments between the FBI & f... [Twitter for iPhone]

May 1, 2019 07:59:22 PM RT @JudicialWatch: Judicial Watch announced it received 756 pages of newly uncovered emails that were among the materials former Secretary... [Twitter for iPhone]

May 1, 2019 07:59:51 PM RT @JudicialWatch: JW President @TomFitton appeared on "Hannity" to discuss the Deep State coup effort against @realDonaldTrump : "The DNC... [Twitter for iPhone]

May 1, 2019 08:00:19 PM RT @JudicialWatch: .@TomFitton discusses that "Obama, Biden, Clinton, Susan Rice, the DNC, John Brennan, Comey, Clapper, Kerry, McCabe, Lor... [Twitter for iPhone]

May 1, 2019 08:01:44 PM RT @JudicialWatch: JW President @TomFitton: "Obama allowed his DOJ & FBI to spy on @realDonaldTrump. That's the scandal of our generation &... [Twitter for iPhone]

May 1, 2019 08:58:10 PM https://t.co/S34Q0NY6Ju [Twitter for iPhone]

May 1, 2019 09:53:39 PM I am continuing to monitor the situation in Venezuela very closely. The United States stands with the People of Venezuela and their Freedom! https://t.co/rtGfjQjc1u [Twitter for iPhone]

May 1, 2019 10:09:34 PM The Collusion Delusion is OVER! https://t.co/sRnHoDmzFJ [Twitter Media Studio]

May 1, 2019 10:14:36 PM "The Mueller Witch Hunt is completely OVER!" @SeanHannity https://t.co/bE13T2Kt48 [Twitter Media Studio]

May 2, 2019 06:21:17 AM RT @RichLowry: NR's editorial: "Not for the first time, or we expect, the last, Bill Barr's critics are demonstrating their lack of judgme... [Twitter for iPhone]

May 2, 2019 06:21:52 AM RT @kenvogel: NEW: The BIDENS are entangled in a Ukrainian corruption scandal: @JoeBiden pushed Ukraine to fire a prosecutor seen as corrup... [Twitter for iPhone]

May 2, 2019 06:26:25 AM RT @ByronYork: I understand the talk about Mueller not deciding on Trump obstruction. But he did decide, didn't he? If you're investigated... [Twitter for iPhone]

May 2, 2019 11:29:21 AM Steve Moore, a great pro-growth economist and a truly fine person, has decided to withdraw from the Fed process. Steve won the battle of ideas including Tax Cuts.... [Twitter for iPhone]

May 2, 2019 11:29:22 AM ....and deregulation which have produced non-inflationary prosperity for all Americans. I've asked Steve to work with me toward future economic growth in our Country. [Twitter for iPhone]

May 2, 2019 11:56:07 AM As we unite on this day of prayer, we renew our resolve to protect communities of faith – and ensure that ALL of our people can live, pray and worship IN PEACE. #NationalDayOfPrayer https://t.co/1a7zphaE6z [Twitter for iPhone]

May 2, 2019 03:55:09 PM On this day of prayer, we once again place our hopes in the hands of our Creator. We give thanks for this wondrous land of liberty, & we pray that THIS nation – OUR home – these United States – will forever be strengthened by the Goodness and the Grace & the eternal GLORY OF GOD! https://t.co/RtSI3j1GWH [Twitter for iPhone]

May 2, 2019 04:33:57 PM Congrats to @U_S_Steel for investing $1+ BILLION in America's most INNOVATIVE steel mill. 232 Tariffs make Pennsylvania and USA more prosperous/secure by bringing Steel and Aluminum industries BACK. Tariffs are working. Pittsburgh is again The Steel City. USA Economy is BOOMING! https://t.co/XPXjxli6uc [Twitter for iPhone]

May 2, 2019 07:11:07 PM Proclamation on Days of Remembrance of Victims of the Holocaust: https://t.co/l5nVFKI9fr https://t.co/vGPOelEesM [Twitter for iPhone]

May 2, 2019 08:01:02 PM Thank you, working hard! #MAGA https://t.co/jwsb75t0WW [Twitter for iPhone]

May 2, 2019 10:45:29 PM ...at every turn in attempts to gain access. But now Republicans and Democrats must come together for the good of the American people. No more costly & time consuming investigations. Lets do Immigration (Border), Infrastructure, much lower drug prices & much more - and do it now! [Twitter for iPhone]

May 2, 2019 10:45:29 PM OK, so after two years of hard work and each party trying their best to make the other party look as bad as possible, it's time to get back to business. The Mueller Report strongly stated that there was No Collusion with Russia (of course) and, in fact, they were rebuffed..... [Twitter for iPhone]

May 3, 2019 07:12:09 AM RT @WhiteHouse: Happy National Space Day! 🚀 America is the best in space, and President @realDonaldTrump is making sure no other country… [Twitter for iPhone]

May 3, 2019 07:12:25 AM RT @WhiteHouse: President @realDonaldTrump is fixing American trade to bring our steel and manufacturing jobs back HOME! https://t.co/PjD6… [Twitter for iPhone]

May 3, 2019 07:13:12 AM RT @MariaBartiromo: This will become an imp & bigger story going into #2020 @GOPLeader @realDonaldTrump @MorningsMaria @FoxBusiness… [Twitter for iPhone]

May 3, 2019 07:13:32 AM RT @MariaBartiromo: "I will declassify soon" - @POTUS @realDonaldTrump @FoxNews @FoxBusiness [Twitter for iPhone]

May 3, 2019 07:22:02 AM Finally, Mainstream Media is getting involved - too "hot" to avoid. Pulitzer Prize anyone? The New York Times, on front page (finally), "Details effort to spy on Trump Campaign." @foxandfriends This is bigger than WATERGATE, but the reverse! [Twitter for iPhone]

May 3, 2019 08:35:49 AM JOBS, JOBS, JOBS! "Jobs surge in April, unemployment rate falls to the lowest since 1969" https://t.co/4DGpumMISf [Twitter for iPhone]

May 3, 2019 10:18:50 AM "The U.S. Created 263,000 Jobs in April, Unemployment Fell to Lowest Level Since 1969" https://t.co/TtQy5yJDku [Twitter for iPhone]

May 3, 2019 11:22:14 AM We can all agree that AMERICA is now #1. We are the ENVY of the WORLD -- and the best is yet to come! https://t.co/Uc81DzHbu2 [Twitter for iPhone]

May 3, 2019 12:06:31 PM ....We discussed Trade, Venezuela, Ukraine, North Korea, Nuclear Arms Control and even the "Russian Hoax." Very productive talk! [Twitter for iPhone]

May 3, 2019 12:06:31 PM Had a long and very good conversation with President Putin of Russia. As I have always said, long before the Witch Hunt started, getting along with Russia, China, and everyone is a good thing, not a bad thing.... [Twitter for iPhone]

May 3, 2019 02:39:10 PM Fred Keller of the Great State of Pennsylvania has been an outstanding State Rep. Now he is running as the Republican Nominee for Congress, and has my Complete and Total Endorsement. Strong on Crime, Second Amendment, Military, Vets, and Healthcare. He will do a fantastic job! [Twitter for iPhone]

May 3, 2019 04:48:37 PM RT @WhiteHouse: President Trump welcomed Prime Minister Peter Pellegrini of the Slovak Republic for his first visit in the Oval Office toda… [Twitter for iPhone]

May 3, 2019 05:53:05 PM The International Association of Firefighters Union is rebelling on their very foolish leader. Perhaps they will vote him out of office. He doesn't get it! https://t.co/NmaasMxOLE https://t.co/7tMG5NtvwO [Twitter for iPhone]

May 3, 2019 05:55:02 PM I am continuing to monitor the censorship of AMERICAN CITIZENS on social media platforms. This is the United States of America — and we have what's known as FREEDOM OF SPEECH! We are monitoring and watching, closely!! [Twitter for iPhone]

May 3, 2019 06:23:13 PM The wonderful Diamond and Silk have been treated so horribly by Facebook. They work so hard and what has been done to them is very sad - and we're looking into. It's getting worse and worse for Conservatives on social media! [Twitter for iPhone]

May 3, 2019 06:25:35 PM So surprised to see Conservative thinkers like James Woods banned from Twitter, and Paul Watson banned from Facebook! https://t.co/eHX3Z5CMXb [Twitter for iPhone]

May 3, 2019 06:45:22 PM As the great people of IA, IL, & MO continue to confront the devastating flooding, know we are here for you and ready to help! My team remains in close contact with @IAGovernor, @GovParsonMO, @GovPritzker, and the local officials managing the impacts of the destructive flooding. [Twitter for iPhone]

May 3, 2019 08:52:31 PM "They wanted to know what Trump was up to with the Russians - which of course is nonsense. This whole thing was a complete setup." George Papadopoulos to @seanhannity [Twitter for iPhone]

May 3, 2019 11:02:51 PM RT @DevinNunes: Perhaps the best @ChuckGrassley clip of all time... https://t.co/aMzUz516Dn [Twitter for iPhone]

May 4, 2019 06:56:15 AM There is nothing easy about a USA Infrastructure Plan, especially when our great Country has spent an astounding 7 trillion dollars in the Middle East over the last 19 years, but I am looking hard at a bipartisan plan of 1 to 2 trillion dollars. Badly needed! [Twitter for iPhone]

May 4, 2019 07:00:37 AM So great to watch this! https://t.co/pYoiLjM0pz [Twitter for iPhone]

May 4, 2019 07:09:42 AM RT @EricTrump: Great being with the team at @TrumpGolfPhilly! Such an unbelievable course and property! This is truly one of #TomFazios gre... [Twitter for iPhone]

May 4, 2019 07:11:55 AM RT @PrisonPlanet: The support for me has been incredible. This could actually lead to some genuine change. Keep up the pressure. Don't let... [Twitter for iPhone]

May 4, 2019 07:14:05 AM RT @SharylAttkisson: When did we quit teaching/understanding that free speech means protecting the distasteful, lest we open the door for g... [Twitter for iPhone]

May 4, 2019 07:15:09 AM RT @SharylAttkisson: When did we decide, as Americans, that it's ok fo govt & 3d parties to censor/ curate our info? That we cannot be trus... [Twitter for iPhone]

May 4, 2019 07:15:28 AM RT @JeremyDBoreing: Those suggesting Facebook can ban anyone for any reason because they are a private company do not understand the platfo... [Twitter for iPhone]

May 4, 2019 07:17:01 AM RT @Lauren_Southern: Lmao at establishment conservatives who think they won't be labeled the new "dangerous" / "extremist" voices when thos… [Twitter for iPhone]

May 4, 2019 07:18:56 AM RT @iheartmindy: So James Woods was kicked off Twitter for quoting Ralph Waldo Emerson...but @TalbertSwan the racist fake man of God, that'… [Twitter for iPhone]

May 4, 2019 07:21:15 AM RT @PrisonPlanet: "Dangerous". My opinions? Or giving a handful of giant partisan corporations the power to decide who has free speech?… [Twitter for iPhone]

May 4, 2019 07:34:07 AM When will the Radical Left Wing Media apologize to me for knowingly getting the Russia Collusion Delusion story so wrong? The real story is about to happen! Why is @nytimes, @washingtonpost, @CNN, @MSNBC allowed to be on Twitter & Facebook. Much of what they do is FAKE NEWS! [Twitter for iPhone]

May 4, 2019 08:31:28 AM RT @realDonaldTrump: So great to watch this! https://t.co/pYoiLjM0pz [Twitter for iPhone]

May 4, 2019 08:42:21 AM Anything in this very interesting world is possible, but I believe that Kim Jong Un fully realizes the great economic potential of North Korea, & will do nothing to interfere or end it. He also knows that I am with him & does not want to break his promise to me. Deal will happen! [Twitter for iPhone]

May 4, 2019 08:49:27 AM Very good call yesterday with President Putin of Russia. Tremendous potential for a good/great relationship with Russia, despite what you read and see in the Fake News Media. Look how they have misled you on "Russia Collusion." The World can be a better and safer place. Nice! [Twitter for iPhone]

May 4, 2019 08:53:28 AM RT @WhiteHouse: We're killing it on the economy! 🔥 https://t.co/hme0eihP9c [Twitter for iPhone]

May 4, 2019 08:53:56 AM RT @charliekirk11: BOOM: Despite horrendous media treatment coverage Trump stands at 51% approval rating! They tried to defame him They… [Twitter for iPhone]

May 4, 2019 08:54:28 AM RT @TrumpStudents: @realDonaldTrump With President Trump leading us, America is a BETTER and SAFER placeus [Twitter for iPhone]

May 4, 2019 08:56:03 AM RT @anshulblp1996: @realDonaldTrump https://t.co/JE35yONsry [Twitter for iPhone]

May 4, 2019 12:00:12 PM RT @IvankaTrump: The last time the unemployment rate was this low we were about to land for the first time on the moon! Happy April #Jobs… [Twitter for iPhone]

May 4, 2019 12:53:42 PM Today, May 4th - is International Firefighters Day! We remember all of those who put their lives on the line to save others, and are grateful to those who continue to do so 24/7/365. We love our great firefighters, thank you! #ThankAFirefighter https://t.co/LBSfQRFZ7k [Twitter for iPhone]

May 4, 2019 01:31:06 PM How can it be possible that James Woods (and many others), a strong but responsible Conservative Voice, is banned from Twitter? Social Media & Fake News Media, together with their partner, the Democrat Party, have no idea the problems they are causing for themselves. VERY UNFAIR! [Twitter for iPhone]

May 4, 2019 08:44:39 PM Mike has been a fantastic Senator! https://t.co/WKSAfbeARz [Twitter for iPhone]

May 4, 2019 08:45:40 PM RT @DailyCaller: April Jobs Report: 263,000 Jobs Added, Unemployment At 3.6 Percent https://t.co/ham2RwREKA [Twitter for iPhone]

May 4, 2019 08:48:39 PM RT @DailyCaller: Trump Cuts Off States From Skimming Medicaid Payments For Big Labor https://t.co/nWI8A8tomB [Twitter for iPhone]

May 4, 2019 08:49:05 PM RT @DailyCaller: CNN's Tapper: Is Trump Not Getting Enough Credit For The Economy? https://t.co/zTWeMmZKF8 [Twitter for iPhone]

May 4, 2019 08:49:24 PM RT @DailyCaller: DOJ Asks Courts To Lighten Up On Qualcomm As It Battles China For 5G Supremacy https://t.co/6CEMpAwJZF [Twitter for iPhone]

May 4, 2019 10:32:28 PM RT @mike_pence: Congratulations to @derekbrownutah on becoming Chairman of the @UtahGOP! Utah's economy is on FIRE thanks to the leadership... [Twitter for iPhone]

May 5, 2019 08:16:11 AM The Kentuky Derby decision was not a good one. It was a rough and tumble race on a wet and sloppy track, actually, a beautiful thing to watch. Only in these days of political correctness could such an overturn occur. The best horse did NOT win the Kentucky Derby - not even close! [Twitter for iPhone]

May 5, 2019 08:19:37 AM RT @HH41848213: When you look at the continuous incorrect statements by Napolitano over the past 2 years, it is fair to ask FNC why they al... [Twitter for iPhone]

May 5, 2019 08:45:16 AM RT @JudicialWatch: .@realDonaldTrump retweeted our petition! Right now, our borders are being used as gateways for drug cartels & violent c... [Twitter for iPhone]

May 5, 2019 08:45:34 AM RT @JudicialWatch: Judicial Watch President @TomFitton breaks down a list of lawsuits that Judicial Watch has filed to get to the truth abo... [Twitter for iPhone]

May 5, 2019 08:47:08 AM RT @JudicialWatch: JW announced that a senior FBI official admitted, in writing and under oath, that the agency found Clinton email records... [Twitter for iPhone]

May 5, 2019 08:48:07 AM RT @JudicialWatch: Judicial Watch announced it received 756 pages of newly uncovered emails that were among the materials former Secretary... [Twitter for iPhone]

May 5, 2019 09:46:47 AM RT @VP: Joined the pastors of Mt Pleasant Baptist Church, St. Mary Baptist Church, & Greater Union Baptist Church at what remains of Mt Pl... [Twitter for iPhone]

May 5, 2019 09:46:50 AM RT @VP: Honored to be with these congregations. @POTUS & I are with you. Our prayers are with you. Your resilience, your faith, and your co... [Twitter for iPhone]

May 5, 2019 09:48:15 AM RT @ericbolling: Hispanic Unemployment hit a record low today! Here's a clip of a big Special "AMericA" airing today I chatted with a gro... [Twitter for iPhone]

May 5, 2019 09:55:18 AM I am pleased to inform all of those that believe in a strong, fair and sound Immigration Policy that Mark Morgan will be joining the Trump Administration as the head of our hard working men and women of ICE. Mark is a true believer and American Patriot. He will do a great job! [Twitter for iPhone]

May 5, 2019 10:59:36 AM The Kentucky Derby decision was not a good one. It was a rough & tumble race on a wet and sloppy track, actually, a beautiful thing to watch. Only in these days of political correctness could such an overturn occur. The best horse did NOT win the Kentucky Derby - not even close! [Twitter for iPhone]

May 5, 2019 11:08:46 AM ....of additional goods sent to us by China remain untaxed, but will be shortly, at a rate of 25%. The Tariffs paid to the USA have had little impact on product cost, mostly borne by China. The Trade Deal with China continues, but too slowly, as they attempt to renegotiate. No! [Twitter for iPhone]

May 5, 2019 11:08:46 AM For 10 months, China has been paying Tariffs to the USA of 25% on 50 Billion Dollars of High Tech, and 10% on 200 Billion Dollars of other goods. These payments are partially responsible for our great economic results. The 10% will go up to 25% on Friday. 325 Billions Dollars.... [Twitter for iPhone]

May 5, 2019 01:03:29 PM ....to testify. Are they looking for a redo because they hated seeing the strong NO COLLUSION conclusion? There was no crime, except on the other side (incredibly not covered in the Report), and NO OBSTRUCTION. Bob Mueller should not testify. No redos for the Dems! [Twitter for iPhone]

May 5, 2019 01:03:29 PM After spending more than $35,000,000 over a two year period, interviewing 500 people, using 18 Trump Hating Angry Democrats & 49 FBI Agents - all culminating in a more than 400 page Report showing NO COLLUSION - why would the Democrats in Congress now need Robert Mueller....... [Twitter for iPhone]

May 5, 2019 03:01:49 PM "The Report sounded an awful lot as being Comeyesque, in other words, I'm not going to charge this person (there wasn't even close to being a crime), but I'm going to criticize him on the way out the door. That's unfortunate because it's stepping outside of the role." Robert Ray [Twitter for iPhone]

May 5, 2019 03:03:58 PM "This is not Congressional Oversight, this is bullying." Jason Riley, The Wall Street Journal [Twitter for iPhone]

May 5, 2019 03:21:11 PM RT @GOPChairwoman: Comey's FBI sent undercover agents to spy on @realDonaldTrump's campaign. It's a stunning revelation of the lengths the... [Twitter for iPhone]

May 5, 2019 03:21:41 PM RT @MariaBartiromo: most important from @GeorgePapa19 interview @SundayFutures @FoxNews was the London Cntr for int'l law reached out to hi... [Twitter for iPhone]

May 5, 2019 03:22:10 PM RT @IngrahamAngle: Excellent decision by @realDonaldTrump! No other president has had the guts to take on the China challenge. #AmericaNow... [Twitter for iPhone]

May 5, 2019 03:24:39 PM RT @JerryFalwellJr: After the best week ever for @realDonaldTrump - no obstruction, no collusion, NYT admits @BarackObama did spy on his ca... [Twitter for iPhone]

May 5, 2019 03:46:39 PM RT @GOPChairwoman: Our economy: *263,000 jobs in April, beating expectations. *5.4M jobs created since @realDonaldTrump took office. *Un... [Twitter for iPhone]

May 5, 2019 04:26:47 PM ....The Witch Hunt is over but we will never forget. MAKE AMERICA GREAT AGAIN! [Twitter for iPhone]

May 5, 2019 04:26:47 PM Despite the tremendous success that I have had as President, including perhaps the greatest ECONOMY and most successful first two years of any President in history, they have stollen two years of my (our) Presidency (Collusion Delusion) that we will never be able to get back..... [Twitter for iPhone]

May 5, 2019 07:08:20 PM Pending the confirmation of Mark Morgan as our Nation's new ICE Director, Matt Albence will serve in the role of Acting Director. Matt is tough and dedicated and has my full support to deploy ICE to the maximum extent of the law! #MAGA [Twitter for iPhone]

May 5, 2019 07:13:59 PM ....To the Gazan people — these terrorist acts against Israel will bring you nothing but more misery. END the violence and work towards peace - it can happen! [Twitter for iPhone]

May 5, 2019 07:13:59 PM Once again, Israel faces a barrage of deadly rocket attacks by terrorist groups Hamas and Islamic Jihad. We support Israel 100% in its defense of its citizens.... [Twitter for iPhone]

May 5, 2019 10:05:35 PM .....The Witch Hunt is over but we will never forget. MAKE AMERICA GREAT AGAIN! [Twitter for iPhone]

May 5, 2019 10:05:35 PM Despite the tremendous success that I have had as President, including perhaps the greatest ECONOMY and most successful first two years of any President in history, they have stolen two years of my (our) Presidency (Collusion Delusion) that we will never be able to get back..... [Twitter for iPhone]

May 6, 2019 05:46:01 AM Also, there are "No High Crimes & Misdemeanors," No Collusion, No Conspiracy, No Obstruction. ALL THE CRIMES ARE ON THE OTHER SIDE, and that's what the Dems should be looking at, but they won't. Nevertheless, the tables are turning! [Twitter for iPhone]

May 6, 2019 05:46:01 AM "Democrat Texas Congressman Al Green says impeachment is the only thing that can prevent President Trump from re-election in 2020." @OANN In other words, Dems can't win the election fairly. You can't impeach a president for creating the best economy in our country's history..... [Twitter for iPhone]

May 6, 2019 06:08:41 AM The United States has been losing, for many years, 600 to 800 Billion Dollars a year on Trade. With China we lose 500 Billion Dollars. Sorry, we're not going to be doing that anymore! [Twitter for iPhone]

May 6, 2019 08:30:14 AM Scott Walker is 100% correct when he says that the Republicans must WAKE UP to the Democrats State by State power grab. They play very dirty, actually, like never before. Don't allow them to get away with what they are doing! [Twitter for iPhone]

May 6, 2019 08:48:41 AM ....Alabama, Iowa, Nebraska, Georgia, South Carolina, North Carolina and others unless much more money is given to Puerto Rico. The Dems don't want farmers to get any help. Puerto Rico should be very happy and the Dems should stop blocking much needed Disaster Relief! [Twitter for iPhone]

May 6, 2019 08:48:41 AM Puerto Rico has been given more money by Congress for Hurricane Disaster Relief, 91 Billion Dollars, than any State in the history of the U.S. As an example, Florida got $12 Billion & Texas $39 Billion for their monster hurricanes. Now the Democrats are saying NO Relief to...... [Twitter for iPhone]

May 6, 2019 08:51:49 AM Just spoke to Prime Minister Abe of Japan concerning North Korea and Trade. Very good conversation! [Twitter for iPhone]

May 6, 2019 12:21:54 PM Congratulations @ArmyWP_Football! https://t.co/jzc35XNLl3 [Twitter for iPhone]

May 6, 2019 03:00:35 PM Today, it was my true honor to present the Commander-in-Chief's Trophy—for the second year in a row, to the @ArmyWP_Football Black Knights. Congratulations once again on your historic victories, and keep on making us proud! https://t.co/nGOC4PQn6S [Twitter for iPhone]

May 7, 2019 09:49:02 AM Democrats in Congress must vote to close the terrible loopholes at the Southern Border. If not, harsh measures will have to be taken! [Twitter for iPhone]

May 7, 2019 11:37:24 AM RT @WhiteHouse: On the one year anniversary of @FLOTUS' initiative, Be Best, take a look back at some of the highlights! #BeBest https://t.... [Twitter for iPhone]

May 7, 2019 01:57:23 PM Congratulations @TigerWoods - you are truly one of a kind! https://t.co/B6YpeLZiIo [Twitter for iPhone]

May 7, 2019 08:04:22 PM 'Forgotten Man' Story: Under Trump, Red Counties Economically Thrive https://t.co/eboFUSJH1u via @BreitbartNews [Twitter for iPhone]

May 7, 2019 08:15:40 PM He wants to impeach because they can't win election. Sad! https://t.co/oFO6wMVhYt [Twitter for iPhone]

May 7, 2019 08:16:14 PM RT @GOPChairwoman: Ever wonder why the Democrats are so obsessed with Russia? They want to distract from how strong our economy is under... [Twitter for iPhone]

May 7, 2019 08:16:31 PM RT @TeamTrump: President @realDonaldTrump is hard at work for the American people! #ThanksPresidentTrump #MAGA https://t.co/ehPs7iEn1u [Twitter for iPhone]

May 7, 2019 08:17:08 PM RT @TeamTrump: BIG NEWS: Nearly HALF of @realdonaldtrump's 2020 campaign contributions this year have come from WOMEN donors. #WomenForTru... [Twitter for iPhone]

May 7, 2019 08:17:38 PM RT @GOPChairwoman: Hillary Clinton is STILL claiming the election was "stolen" from her. It wasn't. She had a failed message and complet... [Twitter for iPhone]

May 7, 2019 08:22:17 PM RT @TigerWoods: It's an incredible privilege to be awarded the Presidential Medal of Freedom. Considering the recipients, history, and what... [Twitter for iPhone]

May 7, 2019 08:51:39 PM I am pleased to inform you that THE BIG FIREWORKS, after many years of not having any, are coming back to beautiful Mount Rushmore in South Dakota. Great work @GovKristiNoem and @SecBernhardt! #MAGA [Twitter for iPhone]

May 7, 2019 09:21:33 PM RT @realDonaldTrump: ....Alabama, Iowa, Nebraska, Georgia, South Carolina, North Carolina and others unless much more money is given to Pue... [Twitter for iPhone]

May 7, 2019 09:21:37 PM RT @realDonaldTrump: Puerto Rico has been given more money by Congress for Hurricane Disaster Relief, 91 Billion Dollars, than any State in... [Twitter for iPhone]

May 7, 2019 09:29:25 PM RT @WhiteHouse: LIVE NOW: President Trump Presents the Presidential Medal of Freedom to Tiger Woods https://t.co/tqZdiXay5T [Twitter for iPhone]

May 8, 2019 05:08:47 AM McConnell Backs Trump: Mueller Report Is 'Case Closed' | Breitbart https://t.co/eOWQSJX7lO via @BreitbartNews [Twitter for iPhone]

May 8, 2019 05:17:21 AM "CASE CLOSED!" @SenateMajLDR https://t.co/TOIatsmu4U [Twitter for iPhone]

May 8, 2019 05:56:32 AM ....you would get it by building, or even buying. You always wanted to show losses for tax purposes....almost all real estate developers did - and often re-negotiate with banks, it was sport. Additionally, the very old information put out is a highly inaccurate Fake News hit job! [Twitter for iPhone]

May 8, 2019 05:56:32 AM Real estate developers in the 1980's & 1990's, more than 30 years ago, were entitled to massive write offs and depreciation which would, if one was actively building, show losses and tax losses in almost all cases. Much was non monetary. Sometimes considered "tax shelter," ...... [Twitter for iPhone]

May 8, 2019 07:10:40 AM RT @GOPLeader: I am grateful to the millions of teachers who put their heart (and countless hours!) into their work. Thank you for your pas... [Twitter for iPhone]

May 8, 2019 07:10:48 AM RT @TXRandy14: Today, I led my Republican colleagues in asking for the #BornAliveAct to be taken up. Dem Leadership again denied our reques... [Twitter for iPhone]

May 8, 2019 07:11:04 AM RT @GOPLeader: Democrats and Republicans should be working together to lower the cost of prescription drugs. What are Democrats doing in... [Twitter for iPhone]

May 8, 2019 07:48:15 AM The reason for the China pullback & attempted renegotiation of the Trade Deal is the sincere HOPE that they will be able to "negotiate" with Joe Biden or one of the very weak Democrats, and thereby continue to ripoff the United States (($500 Billion a year)) for years to come.... [Twitter for iPhone]

May 8, 2019 07:48:16 AM ....Guess what, that's not going to happen! China has just informed us that they (Vice-Premier) are now coming to the U.S. to make a deal. We'll see, but I am very happy with over $100 Billion a year in Tariffs filling U.S. coffers...great for U.S., not good for China! [Twitter for iPhone]

May 8, 2019 07:57:35 AM "The real "Obstruction of Justice" is what the Democrats are trying to do to this Attorney General." Congressman Jim Jordan (R-Ohio). @MariaBartiromo [Twitter for iPhone]

May 8, 2019 08:23:07 AM "Shouldn't 2015 and 2016 be revealed, how Intelligence Agencies, FBI, tried to sabotage a particular campaign - never been done before?" @SteveForbesCEO @MariaBartiromo [Twitter for iPhone]

May 8, 2019 08:42:36 AM Big Court win at our Southern Border! We are getting there - and Wall is being built! [Twitter for iPhone]

May 8, 2019 09:38:49 AM "Everyone wants to know who needs to be accountable, because it took up two years of our lives talking about this Russian involvement. It proved No Collusion, & people want to trace it back to see how this all happened?" @ainsleyearhardt @foxandfriends TREASONOUS HOAX! [Twitter for iPhone]

May 8, 2019 09:42:26 AM "This British Spy, Christopher Steele, tried so hard to get this (the Fake Dossier) out before the Election. Why?" @kilmeade @foxandfriends [Twitter for iPhone]

May 8, 2019 09:45:07 AM RT @realDonaldTrump: "CASE CLOSED!" @SenateMajLDR https://t.co/TOIatsmu4U [Twitter for iPhone]

May 8, 2019 09:45:20 AM RT @realDonaldTrump: ....you would get it by building, or even buying. You always wanted to show losses for tax purposes....almost all real... [Twitter for iPhone]

May 8, 2019 09:45:23 AM RT @realDonaldTrump: Real estate developers in the 1980's & 1990's, more than 30 years ago, were entitled to massive write offs and depreci... [Twitter for iPhone]

May 8, 2019 10:18:41 AM GREAT NEWS FOR OHIO! Just spoke to Mary Barra, CEO of General Motors, who informed me that, subject to a UAW agreement etc., GM will be selling their beautiful Lordstown Plant to Workhorse, where they plan to build Electric Trucks. GM will also be spending $700,000,000 in Ohio... [Twitter for iPhone]

May 8, 2019 10:18:42 AM ....in 3 separate locations, creating another 450 jobs. I have been working nicely with GM to get this done. Thank you to Mary B, your GREAT Governor, and Senator Rob Portman. With all the car companies coming back, and much more, THE USA IS BOOMING! [Twitter for iPhone]

May 8, 2019 10:48:06 AM Republicans shouldn't vote for H.R. 312, a special interest casino Bill, backed by Elizabeth (Pocahontas) Warren. It is unfair and doesn't treat Native Americans equally! [Twitter for iPhone]

May 8, 2019 12:42:44 PM Our Nation grieves at the unspeakable violence that took a precious young life and badly injured others in Colorado. God be with the families and thank you to the First Responders for bravely intervening. We are in close contact with Law Enforcement. [Twitter for iPhone]

May 8, 2019 12:54:40 PM Thank you @NewtGingrich & @FoxandFriends! https://t.co/GYJ7U2k7nn [Twitter Media Studio]

☐ May 8, 2019 02:30:31 PM Getting ready to leave for one of my favorite places, the Florida Panhandle, where we've given, and are giving, billions of $$$ for the devastation caused by Hurricane Michael. Even though the Dems are totally in our way (they don't want money to go there) we're getting it done! [Twitter for iPhone]

☐ May 8, 2019 03:58:40 PM "The reality is, with the Tariffs, the economy has grown more rapidly in the United States and much more slowly in China." Peter Morici, Former Chief Economist, USITC [Twitter for iPhone]

☐ May 8, 2019 04:01:36 PM Big announcement today: Drug companies have to come clean about their prices in TV ads. Historic transparency for American patients is here. If drug companies are ashamed of those prices—lower them! [Twitter for iPhone]

☐ May 8, 2019 06:13:58 PM Just landed in Panama City Beach, Florida for a rally beginning at 8:00 P.M. Eastern. Will be live on @FoxNews! #MAGA @tuckercarlson @seanhannity [Twitter for iPhone]

☐ May 8, 2019 06:32:51 PM Big crowds in Panama City Beach, Florida. See everyone in 30 minutes! @FoxNews @TuckerCarlson @SeanHannity https://t.co/57tngL1W2i [Twitter for iPhone]

☐ May 8, 2019 08:51:19 PM Beautiful evening in Panama City Beach, Florida. Thank you! #MAGA https://t.co/lNBM9sED2f [Twitter for iPhone]

☐ May 8, 2019 10:05:42 PM MAKE AMERICA GREAT AGAIN! https://t.co/gOXXHnHHG5 [Twitter for iPhone]

☐ May 8, 2019 10:18:10 PM After a great rally in Panama City Beach, Florida - I am returning to Washington, D.C. with @SenRickScott and Senator @MarcoRubio, discussing the terrible abuses by Maduro. America stands with the GREAT PEOPLE of Venezuela for however long it takes! https://t.co/KcBoNfEibv [Twitter for iPhone]

☐ May 9, 2019 05:34:32 PM Great news today: My Administration just secured a historic donation of HIV prevention drugs from Gilead to help expand access to PrEP for the uninsured and those at risk. Will help us achieve our goal of ending the HIV epidemic in America! https://t.co/wux5QasWgW [Twitter for iPhone]

☐ May 9, 2019 05:50:19 PM Today, it was my honor to welcome the 2018 World Series Champion Boston @RedSox to the @WhiteHouse! https://t.co/yHAClpttLM [Twitter for iPhone]

☐ May 9, 2019 06:11:00 PM House Republicans should not vote for the BAD DEMOCRAT Disaster Supplemental Bill which hurts our States, Farmers & Border Security. Up for vote tomorrow. We want to do much better than this. All sides keep working and send a good BILL for immediate signing! [Twitter for iPhone]

May 9, 2019 08:31:02 PM RT @VP: Great to be at R&J Johnson Farms in Glyndon, Minnesota today! Since the earliest days of our administration, @POTUS has promised t... [Twitter for iPhone]

May 9, 2019 08:35:10 PM RT @DanCrenshawTX: We reached a new low in deceitful politics today. The lies about protection for pre-existing conditions continue. Th... [Twitter for iPhone]

May 9, 2019 08:35:26 PM RT @HouseGOP: D's bill on the floor today has nothing to do w/ pre-existing conditions. But it will prevent states from reducing the pric... [Twitter for iPhone]

May 9, 2019 08:36:22 PM RT @seanhannity: HANNITY IS ON LIVE with The Great One @MarkLevinShow! We'll break down the Democrats' disregard for the rule of law and Hi... [Twitter for iPhone]

May 9, 2019 08:36:37 PM RT @GOPChairwoman: Why do Democrats keeping fixating on the same Russia collusion lies? Because they don't want to admit that: -our econom... [Twitter for iPhone]

May 9, 2019 08:37:01 PM RT @DonaldJTrumpJr: Awesome!!! 🖐 https://t.co/SOWlOLzRxs [Twitter for iPhone]

May 9, 2019 08:38:01 PM RT @WhiteHouse: President @realDonaldTrump hosted the 2018 World Series Champions, the Boston @RedSox, at the White House! https://t.co/68f... [Twitter for iPhone]

May 9, 2019 08:38:23 PM RT @TeamTrump: President Trump is committed to protecting patients and their families from surprise medical bills. Hospitals and insurance... [Twitter for iPhone]

May 9, 2019 10:00:20 PM James Comey is a disgrace to the FBI & will go down as the worst Director in its long and once proud history. He brought the FBI down, almost all Republicans & Democrats thought he should be FIRED, but the FBI will regain greatness because of the great men & women who work there! [Twitter for iPhone]

May 9, 2019 10:58:03 PM Republicans must stick together! https://t.co/APrvcjpqOp [Twitter for iPhone]

May 10, 2019 05:53:55 AM ....The process has begun to place additional Tariffs at 25% on the remaining 325 Billion Dollars. The U.S. only sells China approximately 100 Billion Dollars of goods & products, a very big imbalance. With the over 100 Billion Dollars in Tariffs that we take in, we will buy..... [Twitter for iPhone]

May 10, 2019 05:53:55 AM Talks with China continue in a very congenial manner - there is absolutely no need to rush - as Tariffs are NOW being paid to the United States by China of 25% on 250 Billion Dollars worth of goods & products. These massive payments go directly to the Treasury of the U.S....... [Twitter for iPhone]

May 10, 2019 05:53:56 AM ....If we bought 15 Billion Dollars of Agriculture from our Farmers, far more than China buys now, we would have more than 85 Billion Dollars left over for new Infrastructure, Healthcare, or anything else. China would greatly slow down, and we would automatically speed up! [Twitter for iPhone]

May 10, 2019 05:53:56 AM Tariffs will bring in FAR MORE wealth to our country than even a phenomenal deal of the traditional kind. Also, much easier & quicker to do. Our Farmers will do better, faster, and starving nations can now be helped. Waivers on some products will be granted, or go to new source! [Twitter for iPhone]

May 10, 2019 05:53:56 AM ....agricultural products from our Great Farmers, in larger amounts than China ever did, and ship it to poor & starving countries in the form of humanitarian assistance. In the meantime we will continue to negotiate with China in the hopes that they do not again try to redo deal! [Twitter for iPhone]

May 10, 2019 06:22:21 AM Tariffs will bring in FAR MORE wealth to our Country than even a phenomenal deal of the traditional kind. Also, much easier & quicker to do. Our Farmers will do better, faster, and starving nations can now be helped. Waivers on some products will be granted, or go to new source! [Twitter for iPhone]

May 10, 2019 06:22:22 AM ....If we bought 15 Billion Dollars of Agriculture from our Farmers, far more than China buys now, we would have more than 85 Billion Dollars left over for new Infrastructure, Healthcare, or anything else. China would greatly slow down, and we would automatically speed up! [Twitter for iPhone]

May 10, 2019 06:22:22 AM Tariffs will bring in FAR MORE wealth to our Country than even a phenomenal deal of the traditional kind. Also, much easier & quicker to do. Our Farmers will do better, faster, and starving nations can now be helped. Waivers on some products will be granted, or go to new source! [Twitter for iPhone]

May 10, 2019 06:22:22 AM ....agricultural products from our Great Farmers, in larger amounts than China ever did, and ship it to poor & starving countries in the form of humanitarian assistance. In the meantime we will continue to negotiate with China in the hopes that they do not again try to redo deal! [Twitter for iPhone]

May 10, 2019 06:22:22 AM ....The process has begun to place additional Tariffs at 25% on the remaining 325 Billion Dollars. The U.S. only sells China approximately 100 Billion Dollars of goods & products, a very big imbalance. With the over 100 Billion Dollars in Tariffs that we take in, we will buy..... [Twitter for iPhone]

May 10, 2019 06:24:39 AM We have lost 500 Billion Dollars a year, for many years, on Crazy Trade with China. NO MORE! [Twitter for iPhone]

May 10, 2019 06:27:35 AM V.P. Mike Pence will be interviewed on @foxandfriends at 7:30 A.M. Enjoy! [Twitter for iPhone]

May 10, 2019 06:43:56 AM Talks with China continue in a very congenial manner - there is absolutely no need to rush - as Tariffs are NOW being paid to the United States by China of 25% on 250 Billion Dollars worth of goods & products. These massive payments go directly to the Treasury of the U.S.... [Twitter for iPhone]

May 10, 2019 06:43:56 AM ....agricultural products from our Great Farmers, in larger amounts than China ever did, and ship it to poor & starving countries in the form of humanitarian assistance. In the meantime we will continue to negotiate with China in the hopes that they do not again try to redo deal! [Twitter for iPhone]

May 10, 2019 06:43:56 AM ....The process has begun to place additional Tariffs at 25% on the remaining 325 Billion Dollars. The U.S. only sells China approximately 100 Billion Dollars of goods & products, a very big imbalance. With the over 100 Billion Dollars in Tariffs that we take in, we will buy..... [Twitter for iPhone]

May 10, 2019 06:46:16 AM Tariffs will bring in FAR MORE wealth to our Country than even a phenomenal deal of the traditional kind. Also, much easier & quicker to do. Our Farmers will do better, faster, and starving nations can now be helped. Waivers on some products will be granted, or go to new source! [Twitter for iPhone]

May 10, 2019 06:48:26 AM Tariffs will make our Country MUCH STRONGER, not weaker. Just sit back and watch! In the meantime, China should not renegotiate deals with the U.S. at the last minute. This is not the Obama Administration, or the Administration of Sleepy Joe, who let China get away with "murder!" [Twitter for iPhone]

May 10, 2019 06:54:19 AM The average 401(k) balance has SOARED since the bottom of the market - 466%. Wow! [Twitter for iPhone]

May 10, 2019 07:02:11 AM Build your products in the United States and there are NO TARIFFS! [Twitter for iPhone]

May 10, 2019 07:07:24 AM ....If we bought 15 Billion Dollars of Agriculture from our Farmers, far more than China buys now, we would have more than 85 Billion Dollars left over for new Infrastructure, Healthcare, or anything else. China would greatly slow down, and we would automatically speed up! [Twitter for iPhone]

May 10, 2019 07:08:32 AM Build your products in the United States and there are NO TARIFFS! [Twitter for iPhone]

May 10, 2019 07:55:27 AM Your all time favorite President got tired of waiting for China to help out and start buying from our FARMERS, the greatest anywhere in the World! [Twitter for iPhone]

May 10, 2019 08:01:47 AM Great Consumer Price Index just out. Really good, very low inflation! We have a great chance to "really rock!" Good numbers all around. [Twitter for iPhone]

May 10, 2019 08:11:04 AM RT @realDonaldTrump: Republicans must stick together! https://t.co/APrvcjpqOp [Twitter for iPhone]

May 10, 2019 08:20:35 AM Looks to me like it's going to be SleepyCreepy Joe over Crazy Bernie. Everyone else is fading fast! [Twitter for iPhone]

May 10, 2019 08:39:11 AM "We have been engaged in an unfair relationship with China for a long time. They have reneged on the commitments they made to the WTO, particularly around intellectual property." Carly Fiorina @MariaBartiromo [Twitter for iPhone]

May 10, 2019 12:57:00 PM Great Republican vote today on Disaster Relief Bill. We will now work out a bipartisan solution that gets relief for our great States and Farmers. Thank you to all. Get me a Bill that I can quickly sign! [Twitter for iPhone]

May 10, 2019 02:14:04 PM ....into the future will continue. In the meantime, the United States has imposed Tariffs on China, which may or may not be removed depending on what happens with respect to future negotiations! [Twitter for iPhone]

May 10, 2019 02:14:04 PM Over the course of the past two days, the United States and China have held candid and constructive conversations on the status of the trade relationship between both countries. The relationship between President Xi and myself remains a very strong one, and conversations.... [Twitter for iPhone]

May 10, 2019 04:13:28 PM Military spouses share an admirable legacy of unwavering devotion to their loved ones in uniform and to the cause of freedom. On Military Spouse Day, we honor our Nation's military spouses and express our deep appreciation for all that they do! https://t.co/B3NrKc698y [Twitter for iPhone]

May 10, 2019 06:41:41 PM RT @realDonaldTrump: Tariffs will bring in FAR MORE wealth to our Country than even a phenomenal deal of the traditional kind. Also, much e… [Twitter for iPhone]

May 10, 2019 07:11:23 PM RT @realDonaldTrump: ....If we bought 15 Billion Dollars of Agriculture from our Farmers, far more than China buys now, we would have more… [Twitter for iPhone]

May 10, 2019 09:10:08 PM RT @GOPChairwoman: The @realDonaldTrump re-election campaign has reported more female donors than any other candidate – and it's not even c… [Twitter for iPhone]

May 10, 2019 09:11:48 PM RT @TomFitton: SPYGATE CRIMES: Nadler abuse targeting AG Barr and @RealDonaldTrump designed to distract from the fact that the DNC/Dem Part… [Twitter for iPhone]

[] May 11, 2019 06:46:07 AM RT @Politi_Chatter: @realDonaldTrump Today Twitter crossed the line & Suspended the Conservative run @WeSupport45 account without explanati... [Twitter for iPhone]

[] May 11, 2019 06:52:39 AM RT @SenThomTillis: Please watch and share this testimony from Carla Provost, @USBPChief, Chief of the US Border Patrol about the ongoing cr... [Twitter for iPhone]

[] May 11, 2019 06:54:03 AM RT @SenThomTillis: I agree with Leader McConnell: this case is closed. The Mueller Report cleared @DonaldJTrumpJr and he's already spent 27... [Twitter for iPhone]

[] May 11, 2019 06:57:17 AM RT @TomFitton: BREAKING: New emails show Obama WH orchestrated Clinton email coverup; Illegal spying on @realDonaldTrump biggest corruption... [Twitter for iPhone]

[] May 11, 2019 06:57:54 AM RT @hughhewitt: The Mueller probe has concluded, after vast effort, that there was no collusion. Senate Intel subpoena to @DonaldJTrumpJr s... [Twitter for iPhone]

[] May 11, 2019 06:58:42 AM RT @TomFitton: Coming up! https://t.co/bOwV0Gs262 [Twitter for iPhone]

[] May 11, 2019 06:59:05 AM RT @TomFitton: FBI Official: Barack Obama's White House Was A "Repository" For Hillary Clinton's Emails - @JudicialWatch https://t.co/8bONh... [Twitter for iPhone]

[] May 11, 2019 06:59:44 AM RT @TomFitton: Of course, there's a #NationalEmergency on the border. @RealDonaldTrump is absolutely right about the border crisis and shou... [Twitter for iPhone]

[] May 11, 2019 07:00:03 AM RT @TomFitton: A federal court granted @JudicialWatch discovery on Clinton emails because the court wanted answers about the cover-up. And... [Twitter for iPhone]

[] May 11, 2019 07:00:59 AM RT @RMConservative: Today's show: Congress Believes Everything is a Disaster and Emergency Except for the Border https://t.co/678oIdCKJx [Twitter for iPhone]

[] May 11, 2019 07:02:10 AM RT @TomFitton: List of Hillary's spies. Deep State DOJ redacted Bruce Ohr's list of "intermediaries" used by Obama-Clinton-DNC's Fusion GPS... [Twitter for iPhone]

[] May 11, 2019 07:02:21 AM RT @TomFitton: DNC Worked With Russian Intel to Overthrow President @RealDonaldTrump. THIS is why we have the abusive contempt attack on AG... [Twitter for iPhone]

[] May 11, 2019 07:03:17 AM RT @TomFitton: ICYMI: Mueller Report Was A Political Tool To Attack President @RealDonaldTrump https://t.co/cSuMc56cni via @JudicialWatch @... [Twitter for iPhone]

[] May 11, 2019 07:04:23 AM RT @DonaldJTrumpJr: Very proud to have a President do what what he said he was going to do. For decades now @realdonaldtrump has been signa... [Twitter for iPhone]

May 11, 2019 07:04:53 AM RT @RealSaavedra: BREAKING: The father of one of the STEM School Highlands Ranch shooters was a *criminal illegal alien from Mexico* who wa... [Twitter for iPhone]

May 11, 2019 07:05:54 AM RT @johncatsjr: Trump Economy vs Obama Economy Manufacturing jobs created: Trump: 470,000 Obama: -206,000 Under Obama, unemployment decli... [Twitter for iPhone]

May 11, 2019 07:06:27 AM RT @RudyGiuliani: The evidence is mounting that Comey deceived the FISA court concerning the Steele dossier. State did a quick verification... [Twitter for iPhone]

May 11, 2019 07:06:57 AM RT @GOPChairwoman: We've added 6 MILLION jobs since @realDonaldTrump's election, unemployment is at record lows & wages are on the rise. O... [Twitter for iPhone]

May 11, 2019 07:07:11 AM RT @LindseyGrahamSC: @realDonaldTrump When it comes to China, we must be willing to accept short term pain for long term gain. Stick to y... [Twitter for iPhone]

May 11, 2019 07:07:33 AM RT @LindseyGrahamSC: Will stand behind President @realDonaldTrump and his team as he insists on a great deal with China. It's our last... [Twitter for iPhone]

May 11, 2019 07:07:57 AM RT @robbystarbuck: Why is this not the #1 news on every major news outlet tonight? President Trump's Admin secured a historic donation of H... [Twitter for iPhone]

May 11, 2019 07:08:19 AM RT @TommyHicksGOP: For years, China has engaged in unfair trade practices. While the US-China relationship is important, @realDonaldTrump i... [Twitter for iPhone]

May 11, 2019 07:08:40 AM RT @kimguilfoyle: Nolte: Trump's Job Approval Booms to Highest Mark Since Inauguration https://t.co/QtySKQ9OrP via @BreitbartNews [Twitter for iPhone]

May 11, 2019 07:08:51 AM RT @realDonaldTrump: Build your products in the United States and there are NO TARIFFS! [Twitter for iPhone]

May 11, 2019 07:09:07 AM RT @Jim_Jordan: Bill Barr used two frightening terms when he testified in front of the Senate last month: - Unauthorized surveillance -Poli... [Twitter for iPhone]

May 11, 2019 07:09:39 AM RT @GovMikeHuckabee: If Sen Burr didn't get enough flesh out of @DonaldJTrumpJr in the 1st 29 hrs of hammering, then hold him back a grade... [Twitter for iPhone]

May 11, 2019 07:10:10 AM RT @DonaldJTrumpJr: Because his family is on their payroll... https://t.co/73nygpO6k2 [Twitter for iPhone]

May 11, 2019 07:10:25 AM RT @TomFitton: .@SenatorBurr harasses @DonaldJTrumpJr with another subpoena while excusing unprecedented corruption targeting @realDonaldTr... [Twitter for iPhone]

May 11, 2019 07:11:39 AM RT @thehill: Mike Huckabee: "Did senators forget that Trump Jr. answered the questions already?" via @TheHillOpinion https://t.co/sL00Z17A3... [Twitter for iPhone]

⊡ May 11, 2019 07:12:22 AM RT @hughhewitt: I don't know, have never met or spoken w/ @DonaldJTrumpJr, but his being subpoenaed by Senate Intel AFTER SC report finds n... [Twitter for iPhone]

⊡ May 11, 2019 07:13:47 AM RT @KimStrassel: This is a very important story. https://t.co/G4w2LDXEm8 [Twitter for iPhone]

⊡ May 11, 2019 07:14:14 AM RT @RealSaavedra: .@RudyGiuliani goes off on Republican @SenatorBurr for continuing to issue subpoenas after @senatemajldr Mitch McConnell... [Twitter for iPhone]

⊡ May 11, 2019 07:14:54 AM RT @LindseyGrahamSC: When it comes to China, they will never change their behavior until someone stands up to them. I'm proud of President... [Twitter for iPhone]

⊡ May 11, 2019 07:15:36 AM RT @RealSaavedra: Sean Hannity slams @SenatorBurr: "Are you a collusion truther? How many times do you want Donald Trump Jr. and other peop... [Twitter for iPhone]

⊡ May 11, 2019 07:16:00 AM RT @DevinNunes: FBI's Steele story falls apart: False intel and media contacts were flagged before FISA | ⊡@jsolomonReports⊡ https://t.co/... [Twitter for iPhone]

⊡ May 11, 2019 07:16:08 AM RT @GOP: "This is crazy... China not being a threat? [Biden is] so out of touch." -@kayleighmcenany https://t.co/wlpYxS7wTS [Twitter for iPhone]

⊡ May 11, 2019 07:17:17 AM RT @BreitbartNews: .@tedcruz joins the ranks of Republican lawmakers criticizing Sen. Richard Burr (R-NC) for keeping the Collusion Hoax al... [Twitter for iPhone]

⊡ May 11, 2019 07:17:36 AM RT @JeffLandry: It's very concerning a U.S. Senate Committee would subpoena @DonaldJTrumpJr after he already testified for hours before a S... [Twitter for iPhone]

⊡ May 11, 2019 07:17:49 AM RT @GOPChairwoman: While @realDonaldTrump is standing up to China's unfair trade practices, Joe Biden says they are not "competition for us... [Twitter for iPhone]

⊡ May 11, 2019 07:18:13 AM RT @dbongino: "I think it's all about trying to destroy Bill Barr because Democrats are nervous he's going to get to the bottom of everythi... [Twitter for iPhone]

⊡ May 11, 2019 07:19:09 AM RT @ThomTillis: Case closed! The Mueller Report has cleared @DonaldJTrumpJr and the dems are now making this all about politics. Let's mov... [Twitter for iPhone]

⊡ May 11, 2019 07:19:24 AM RT @RepPeteKing: Hard to justify Senate subpoena of @DonaldJTrumpJr. After two years of investigations by Mueller, Senate & House as well a... [Twitter for iPhone]

⊡ May 11, 2019 07:19:42 AM RT @GovMikeHuckabee: I sure wish Sen Richard Burr was as interested in Biden's cushy deals w/ Ukraine & China while VP than he is in the ha... [Twitter for iPhone]

May 11, 2019 07:20:24 AM RT @tedcruz: The Russia investigation is over. After 2 years of Dem & media hysteria, after millions of dollars, after 2800 subpoenas, the... [Twitter for iPhone]

May 11, 2019 07:20:39 AM RT @SergioGor: Speaking to reporters just now @RandPaul calls for an end to the Senate intel investigation. As we've heard from @senatemajl... [Twitter for iPhone]

May 11, 2019 07:20:58 AM RT @RepMarkMeadows: Serving a subpoena to Don Trump Jr.—a private citizen who voluntarily testified before 3 Congressional committees for 2... [Twitter for iPhone]

May 11, 2019 07:21:15 AM RT @Jim_Jordan: Senate Intel subpoenas @DonaldJTrumpJr. He's already testified for 25 hours. But they're bringing him back based on Micha... [Twitter for iPhone]

May 11, 2019 07:21:58 AM RT @jason_donner: Chuck Grassley: "I think about the time that he [Trump Jr.] spent hours w/our staff & testimony...everything post the Mue... [Twitter for iPhone]

May 11, 2019 07:22:16 AM RT @MZanona: .@GOPLeader Kevin McCarthy says GOP-led Senate Intelligence Committee was wrong to subpoena Donald Trump Jr. [Twitter for iPhone]

May 11, 2019 07:22:37 AM RT @BradleyByrne: Despite spending millions and countless hours on an investigation that found NOTHING, some want to keep this nonsense goi... [Twitter for iPhone]

May 11, 2019 07:23:28 AM RT @AriFleischer: Of all the radical ideas in the D primary, this may be the most radical. This is a magnet that will make more people ente... [Twitter for iPhone]

May 11, 2019 07:23:53 AM RT @GeraldoRivera: If you were @DonaldJTrumpJr & had already testified for 30+ hours about same damn singular meeting at #TrumpTower wouldn... [Twitter for iPhone]

May 11, 2019 07:25:08 AM RT @brithume: Are Democratic voters really fooled by this show? Jerry Nadler's strategy clearly aims at provoking a confrontation for polit... [Twitter for iPhone]

May 11, 2019 07:25:23 AM RT @KamVTV: The FBI should be ASHAMED! They used unverified OPPOSITION research to get a FISA warrant to SPY on an American citizen?! They... [Twitter for iPhone]

May 11, 2019 07:26:02 AM RT @nedryun: Reminder: this guy is still on Twitter. Laura Loomer is not. The solution is not to ban this anti-Semite. The goal is to have... [Twitter for iPhone]

May 11, 2019 07:26:21 AM RT @theamgreatness: More than 1,000 Conservatives Rally at Philly Planned Parenthood Where Unhinged Dem Bullied Pro-Lifers https://t.co/k5r... [Twitter for iPhone]

May 11, 2019 07:28:10 AM RT @nedryun: Exactly. https://t.co/Fj6UiFWekS [Twitter for iPhone]

May 11, 2019 07:29:45 AM RT @WhiteHouse: Sen. @HawleyMO: "Large quantities of drugs are smuggled across the border. Isn't that right?" Border Patrol Chief: "That i... [Twitter for iPhone]

May 11, 2019 07:30:11 AM RT @nedryun: Love how Comey and Baker trying to get out there ahead of FISA report. But sorry, boys. Barr doesn't give a rip about public o... [Twitter for iPhone]

May 11, 2019 07:32:45 AM RT @ByronYork: If she was part of Russia 2016 campaign operation, odd that Mueller wasn't interested... RT @texan_21c: @ByronYork She was a... [Twitter for iPhone]

May 11, 2019 08:55:14 AM Such an easy way to avoid Tariffs? Make or produce your goods and products in the good old USA. It's very simple! [Twitter for iPhone]

May 11, 2019 01:32:12 PM I won the 2016 Election partially based on no Tax Returns while I am under audit (which I still am), and the voters didn't care. Now the Radical Left Democrats want to again relitigate this matter. Make it a part of the 2020 Election! [Twitter for iPhone]

May 11, 2019 01:44:07 PM So now the Radical Left Dems don't talk about Collusion anymore, because the Mueller Report said there was No Collusion, they only want to talk about Obstruction, even though there was No Obstruction or No Crime - except for the crimes committed by the other side! [Twitter for iPhone]

May 11, 2019 05:18:30 PM I think that China felt they were being beaten so badly in the recent negotiation that they may as well wait around for the next election, 2020, to see if they could get lucky & have a Democrat win - in which case they would continue to rip-off the USA for $500 Billion a year.... [Twitter for iPhone]

May 11, 2019 05:18:31 PM ....The only problem is that they know I am going to win (best economy & employment numbers in U.S. history, & much more), and the deal will become far worse for them if it has to be negotiated in my second term. Would be wise for them to act now, but love collecting BIG TARIFFS! [Twitter for iPhone]

May 11, 2019 05:39:44 PM I was NOT going to fire Bob Mueller, and did not fire Bob Mueller. In fact, he was allowed to finish his Report with unprecedented help from the Trump Administration. Actually, lawyer Don McGahn had a much better chance of being fired than Mueller. Never a big fan! [Twitter for iPhone]

May 11, 2019 06:27:40 PM RT @GOPChairwoman: An Ohio manufacturing CEO explains that cracking down on China has meant stability and predictability for his business.... [Twitter for iPhone]

May 11, 2019 06:32:03 PM RT @TomFitton: Democratic leaders don't want to talk about the criminal conspiracy their party was involved in related to the illegal spyin... [Twitter for iPhone]

May 11, 2019 10:40:23 PM RT @realDonaldTrump: ....The only problem is that they know I am going to win (best economy & employment numbers in U.S. history, & much mo... [Twitter for iPhone]

May 11, 2019 10:40:29 PM RT @realDonaldTrump: I think that China felt they were being beaten so badly in the recent negotiation that they may as well wait around fo... [Twitter for iPhone]

May 11, 2019 10:41:09 PM RT @realDonaldTrump: Such an easy way to avoid Tariffs? Make or produce your goods and products in the good old USA. It's very simple! [Twitter for iPhone]

May 12, 2019 05:33:41 AM ....President who is willing to have the battle, and we have a great Attorney General who is willing to lead the battle, and they are going to get to the bottom of it." @EdRollins @LouDobbs [Twitter for iPhone]

May 12, 2019 05:33:41 AM "The Democrats have nothing. Just want to distract from this President. The FBI was not doing its job, the State Department was covering things up everyday for Hillary. At the end of the day they're fearful of what they did, and should be fearful. This is a tough..... [Twitter for iPhone]

May 12, 2019 05:34:06 AM RT @VP: Under the leadership of @Potus Trump our economy is roaring. Businesses large and small have created more than 5.8 million jobs, un... [Twitter for iPhone]

May 12, 2019 06:04:04 AM ....Hoax. My campaign was being seriously spied upon by intel agencies and the Democrats. This never happened before in American history, and it all turned out to be a total scam, a Witch Hunt, that yielded No Collusion, No Obstruction. This must never be allowed to happen again! [Twitter for iPhone]

May 12, 2019 06:04:04 AM Think of it. I became President of the United States in one of the most hard fought and consequential elections in the history of our great nation. From long before I ever took office, I was under a sick & unlawful investigation concerning what has become known as the Russian.... [Twitter for iPhone]

May 12, 2019 12:11:31 PM https://t.co/NIL3YNhxly [Twitter for iPhone]

May 12, 2019 12:12:48 PM Big attacks on Republicans and Conservatives by Social Media. Not good! [Twitter for iPhone]

May 12, 2019 12:29:12 PM RT @TheRightMelissa: @RealCandaceO Because if they acknowledge the reality that Trump is neither of those things, they would be essentially... [Twitter for iPhone]

May 12, 2019 12:30:44 PM RT @TheRightMelissa: @RealCandaceO Yap Candace! No one in their right mind believes the crazy looney toon things coming out of the left. T... [Twitter for iPhone]

May 12, 2019 12:39:56 PM RT @LisaMei62: .@KimStrassel discusses what she wrote about in her column today re: how very powerful people in DC are panicking because AG... [Twitter for iPhone]

May 12, 2019 12:48:10 PM RT @RichLowry: I know he won't do this, because obviously the political narrative is important to him and people around him, but Mueller sh... [Twitter for iPhone]

May 12, 2019 12:52:27 PM https://t.co/6Xc1NJnf1Z [Twitter for iPhone]

May 12, 2019 12:54:51 PM Really sad! https://t.co/OjzNjhJeHt [Twitter for iPhone]

May 12, 2019 01:00:16 PM RT @TomFitton: Schiff knew. Comey knew. Obama knew. Susan Rice knew. Biden knew. Brennan knew. Clapper knew. Peter Strzok kne... [Twitter for iPhone]

May 12, 2019 01:02:30 PM RT @WhiteHouse: President @realDonaldTrump put forward 4 principles to protect American patients from the financial devastation of surprise... [Twitter for iPhone]

May 12, 2019 01:02:57 PM RT @GOPChairwoman: Republicans and @realDonaldTrump are delivering for Americans: *6M new jobs *Unemployment at 3.6%, the lowest since... [Twitter for iPhone]

May 12, 2019 01:03:38 PM RT @GOPChairwoman: The @realDonaldTrump effect on the 2020 Senate Map: Chuck Schumer is 0-7 in recruiting Senate challengers! https://t.c... [Twitter for iPhone]

May 12, 2019 04:06:05 PM ....We will then spend (match or better) the money that China may no longer be spending with our Great Patriot Farmers (Agriculture), which is a small percentage of total Tariffs received, and distribute the food to starving people in nations around the world! GREAT! #MAGA [Twitter for iPhone]

May 12, 2019 04:06:05 PM We are right where we want to be with China. Remember, they broke the deal with us & tried to renegotiate. We will be taking in Tens of Billions of Dollars in Tariffs from China. Buyers of product can make it themselves in the USA (ideal), or buy it from non-Tariffed countries... [Twitter for iPhone]

May 12, 2019 04:35:41 PM ....employment numbers ever, low taxes & regulations, a rebuilt military & V.A., many great new judges, & so much more. But we have had a giant SCAM perpetrated upon our nation, a Witch Hunt, a Treasonous Hoax. That is the Constitutional Crisis & hopefully guilty people will pay! [Twitter for iPhone]

May 12, 2019 04:35:41 PM The Democrats new and pathetically untrue sound bite is that we are in a "Constitutional Crisis." They and their partner, the Fake News Media, are all told to say this as loud and as often as possible. They are a sad JOKE! We may have the strongest Economy in our history, best... [Twitter for iPhone]

⬜ May 12, 2019 06:03:16 PM Despite two years and millions of dollars spent, the Democrats are acting like crazed lunatics ever since the results of the Mueller Report were made public. But they knew there was NOTHING even before the Report was started. It is all a big Hoax, the biggest in American history! [Twitter for iPhone]

⬜ May 12, 2019 06:10:43 PM Ever since the Mueller Report showed No Collusion & No Obstruction, the Dems have been working overtime to damage me and the Republican Party by issuing over 80 demands for documents and testimonies, and with NO REASON. That's all they want to do - don't care about anything else! [Twitter for iPhone]

⬜ May 12, 2019 06:16:10 PM When the Mueller Report came out showing NO Collusion with Russia (of course), it was supposed to be over, back to work for the people. But the Dems have gone "nuts," and it has actually gotten worse! Hope the Republicans win back the House in 2020, or little will get done! [Twitter for iPhone]

⬜ May 12, 2019 06:19:39 PM The "Constitutional Crisis" is the Democrats refusing to work. Let them start by fixing the mess that their Immigration Laws have caused at the Southern Border. [Twitter for iPhone]

⬜ May 12, 2019 06:22:39 PM China is DREAMING that Sleepy Joe Biden, or any of the others, gets elected in 2020. They LOVE ripping off America! [Twitter for iPhone]

⬜ May 12, 2019 08:19:46 PM "Even Director James Clapper admits that the FBI actions against the Trump Presidential Campaign do in fact meet the definition of spying, perhaps FBI Director Christopher Wray will be the next to do so." @LouDobbs [Twitter for iPhone]

⬜ May 12, 2019 09:00:47 PM ....overthrow the President through an illegal coup." (Recommended by previous DOJ) @TomFitton @JudicialWatch [Twitter for iPhone]

⬜ May 12, 2019 09:00:47 PM ....and the Democrat National Committee-The Democrat Party apparatus-has been caught using donor Dollars to Collude with Russian Intelligence to attack a domestic political opponent (me). The FBI has no leadership. The Director is protecting the same gang.....that tried to.... [Twitter for iPhone]

⬜ May 12, 2019 09:00:47 PM "Just another abuse of power in a long series of abuses of power by the Democrats that began during the Obama Administration, continued through the Mueller FBI operation, & now the baton has been passed to Jerry Nadler to continue to abuse power to harass President Trump.. [Twitter for iPhone]

⬜ May 13, 2019 05:09:51 AM information! As long as President Trump is President, his opposition will use every tool, and misuse every tool available, to make his life miserable." @TomFitton @JudicialWatch @LouDobbs Sadly, this proves I am doing a great job - Also, Best Economy and Employment Numbers EVER! [Twitter for iPhone]

May 13, 2019 05:09:51 AM "It's the attack strategy of harass. This is not about the Attorney General, who is very sophisticated & knows it isn't about him, it's about trying to destroy President Trump through an assault on his AG for upholding the rule of law. He released a massive amount of...... [Twitter for iPhone]

May 13, 2019 05:40:25 AM ..There will be nobody left in China to do business with. Very bad for China, very good for USA! But China has taken so advantage of the U.S. for so many years, that they are way ahead (Our Presidents did not do the job). Therefore, China should not retaliate-will only get worse! [Twitter for iPhone]

May 13, 2019 05:40:25 AM ....completely avoided if you by from a non-Tariffed Country, or you buy the product inside the USA (the best idea). That's Zero Tariffs. Many Tariffed companies will be leaving China for Vietnam and other such countries in Asia. That's why China wants to make a deal so badly!... [Twitter for iPhone]

May 13, 2019 05:40:25 AM Their is no reason for the U.S. Consumer to pay the Tariffs, which take effect on China today. This has been proven recently when only 4 points were paid by the U.S., 21 points by China because China subsidizes product to such a large degree. Also, the Tariffs can be..... [Twitter for iPhone]

May 13, 2019 05:49:24 AM I say openly to President Xi & all of my many friends in China that China will be hurt very badly if you don't make a deal because companies will be forced to leave China for other countries. Too expensive to buy in China. You had a great deal, almost completed, & you backed out! [Twitter for iPhone]

May 13, 2019 05:52:30 AM Thank you @foxandfriends, great show this morning and congratulations on your number one (by far) rating. Well deserved! [Twitter for iPhone]

May 13, 2019 05:56:22 AM Also, congratulations to @OANN on the great job you are doing and the big ratings jump ("thank you President Trump")! [Twitter for iPhone]

May 13, 2019 06:02:18 AM The unexpectedly good first quarter 3.2% GDP was greatly helped by Tariffs from China. Some people just don't get it! [Twitter for iPhone]

May 13, 2019 06:29:13 AM Has anyone noticed that all the Boston @RedSox have done is WIN since coming to the White House! Others also have done very well. The White House visit is becoming the opposite of being on the cover of Sports Illustrated! By the way, the Boston players were GREAT guys! [Twitter for iPhone]

May 13, 2019 08:12:14 AM RT @GOPChairwoman: Joe Biden let China get away with cheating when he was Vice President, and he continues to naively dismiss China today.... [Twitter for iPhone]

May 13, 2019 08:13:53 AM RT @GOPChairwoman: Asian Americans are winning with @realDonaldTrump: 2.1% unemployment rate – the lowest in history! Asian taxpayers re… [Twitter for iPhone]

May 13, 2019 08:59:34 AM Bernie Sanders, "The Economy is doing well, and I'm sure I don't have to give Trump any credit - I'm sure he'll take all the credit that he wants." Wrong Bernie, the Economy is doing GREAT, and would have CRASHED if my opponent (and yours), Crooked Hillary Clinton, had ever won! [Twitter for iPhone]

May 13, 2019 09:09:18 AM Democrat Rep. Tlaib is being slammed for her horrible and highly insensitive statement on the Holocaust. She obviously has tremendous hatred of Israel and the Jewish people. Can you imagine what would happen if I ever said what she said, and says? [Twitter for iPhone]

May 13, 2019 10:55:22 AM ...completely avoided if you buy from a non-Tariffed Country, or you buy the product inside the USA (the best idea). That's Zero Tariffs. Many Tariffed companies will be leaving China for Vietnam and other such countries in Asia. That's why China wants to make a deal so badly!... [Twitter for iPhone]

May 13, 2019 10:55:22 AM There is no reason for the U.S. Consumer to pay the Tariffs, which take effect on China today. This has been proven recently when only 4 points were paid by the U.S., 21 points by China because China subsidizes product to such a large degree. Also, the Tariffs can be..... [Twitter for iPhone]

May 13, 2019 10:55:23 AM ..There will be nobody left in China to do business with. Very bad for China, very good for USA! But China has taken so advantage of the U.S. for so many years, that they are way ahead (Our Presidents did not do the job). Therefore, China should not retaliate-will only get worse! [Twitter for iPhone]

May 13, 2019 03:02:22 PM RT @WhiteHouse: This afternoon, President Trump welcomed Prime Minister Viktor Orban of Hungary to the Oval Office. https://t.co/OgdONwKRB6 [Twitter for iPhone]

May 13, 2019 04:32:11 PM My Administration will be fighting for $200 million for the Army Corps Everglades restoration work this year. Congress needs to help us complete the world's largest intergovernmental watershed restoration project ASAP! Good for Florida and good for the environment. [Twitter for iPhone]

May 13, 2019 04:34:50 PM Under my Administration, we are restoring @NASA to greatness and we are going back to the Moon, then Mars. I am updating my budget to include an additional $1.6 billion so that we can return to Space in a BIG WAY! [Twitter for iPhone]

May 13, 2019 04:38:29 PM We must protect our Great Lakes, keeping them clean and beautiful for future generations. That's why I am fighting for $300 million in my updated budget for the Great Lakes Restoration Initiative. [Twitter for iPhone]

May 13, 2019 04:41:51 PM Today, I officially updated my budget to include $18 million for our GREAT @SpecialOlympics, whose athletes inspire us and make our Nation so PROUD! [Twitter for iPhone]

May 13, 2019 04:53:28 PM Great to welcome Chairman Shin from Lotte Group to the WH. They just invested $3.1 BILLION into Louisiana-biggest investment in U.S. EVER from a South Korean company, & thousands more jobs for Americans. Great partners like ROK know the U.S. economy is running stronger than ever! https://t.co/WaJxDeTuxj [Twitter for iPhone]

May 13, 2019 05:31:22 PM Wishing former President Jimmy Carter a speedy recovery from his hip surgery earlier today. He was in such good spirits when we spoke last month - he will be fine! [Twitter for iPhone]

May 13, 2019 06:15:34 PM I met Marine Sgt. John Peck, a quadruple amputee who has received a double arm transplant, at Walter Reed in 2017. Today, it was my honor to welcome John (HERO) to the Oval, with his wonderful wife Jessica. He also wrote a book that I highly recommend, "Rebuilding Sergeant Peck." https://t.co/eiNnHcEU7x [Twitter for iPhone]

May 14, 2019 05:15:50 AM In one year Tariffs have rebuilt our Steel Industry - it is booming! We placed a 25% Tariff on "dumped" steel from China & other countries, and we now have a big and growing industry. We had to save Steel for our defense and auto industries, both of which are coming back strong! [Twitter for iPhone]

May 14, 2019 05:31:10 AM China buys MUCH less from us than we buy from them, by almost 500 Billion Dollars, so we are in a fantastic position. Make your product at home in the USA and there is no Tariff. You can also buy from a non-Tariffed country instead of China. Many companies are leaving China..... [Twitter for iPhone]

May 14, 2019 05:31:11 AM ....so that they will be more competitive for USA buyers. We are now a much bigger economy than China, and have substantially increased in size since the great 2016 Election. We are the "piggy bank" that everyone wants to raid and take advantage of. NO MORE! [Twitter for iPhone]

May 14, 2019 05:51:41 AM Billions of Dollars, and moving jobs back to the USA where they belong. Other countries are already negotiating with us because they don't want this to happen to them. They must be a part of USA action. This should have been done by our leaders many years ago. Enjoy! [Twitter for iPhone]

May 14, 2019 05:51:41 AM We can make a deal with China tomorrow, before their companies start leaving so as not to lose USA business, but the last time we were close they wanted to renegotiate the deal. No way! We are in a much better position now than any deal we could have made. Will be taking in..... [Twitter for iPhone]

May 14, 2019 06:16:58 AM ....of the tremendous ground we have lost to China on Trade since the ridiculous one sided formation of the WTO. It will all happen, and much faster than people think! [Twitter for iPhone]

May 14, 2019 06:16:58 AM When the time is right we will make a deal with China. My respect and friendship with President Xi is unlimited but, as I have told him many times before, this must be a great deal for the United States or it just doesn't make any sense. We have to be allowed to make up some..... [Twitter for iPhone]

May 14, 2019 06:29:35 AM ....This money will come from the massive Tariffs being paid to the United States for allowing China, and others, to do business with us. The Farmers have been "forgotten" for many years. Their time is now! [Twitter for iPhone]

May 14, 2019 06:29:35 AM Our great Patriot Farmers will be one of the biggest beneficiaries of what is happening now. Hopefully China will do us the honor of continuing to buy our great farm product, the best, but if not your Country will be making up the difference based on a very high China buy...... [Twitter for iPhone]

May 14, 2019 06:39:01 AM Our great Senator (and Star) from the State of Arkansas, @TomCottonAR, has just completed a wonderful book, "Sacred Duty," about Arlington National Cemetary and the men and women who serve with such love and devotion. On sale today, make it big! [Twitter for iPhone]

May 14, 2019 07:35:41 AM China will be pumping money into their system and probably reducing interest rates, as always, in order to make up for the business they are, and will be, losing. If the Federal Reserve ever did a "match," it would be game over, we win! In any event, China wants a deal! [Twitter for iPhone]

May 14, 2019 09:59:17 AM Our great Senator (and Star) from the State of Arkansas, @TomCottonAR, has just completed a wonderful book, "Sacred Duty," about Arlington National Cemetery and the men and women who serve with such love and devotion. On sale today, make it big! [Twitter for iPhone]

May 14, 2019 10:43:19 AM When Prime Minister @AbeShinzo of Japan visited with me in the @WhiteHouse two weeks ago, I told him that I would be going to the G20 in Osaka, Japan. I look forward to being with him and other World Leaders! [Twitter for iPhone]

May 14, 2019 11:27:22 AM Today marks the one-year anniversary of the opening of the United States Embassy in Jerusalem, Israel. Our beautiful embassy stands as a proud reminder of our strong relationship with Israel and of the importance of keeping a promise and standing for the truth. [Twitter for iPhone]

May 14, 2019 03:45:21 PM It is great to be here in Hackberry, Louisiana with the incredible men and women who are making America into the energy superpower of the world! https://t.co/l0DrjtHf62 [Twitter for iPhone]

May 14, 2019 04:14:12 PM With incredible grit, skill, and pride, the 7,000 workers here at Sempra Energy are helping lead the American Energy Revolution. They are not only making our nation WEALTHIER but they are making America SAFER by building a future of American Energy INDEPENDENCE! https://t.co/Hqn9wEIXo9 [Twitter for iPhone]

May 14, 2019 07:25:44 PM The golden era of American energy is now underway! https://t.co/gEmhoMlLoc [Twitter for iPhone]

May 14, 2019 10:48:11 PM RT @EricTrump: Spare me? First you have never created a job in your life. Second, our great city has gone to shit under your leadership. Cr... [Twitter for iPhone]

May 15, 2019 07:48:33 AM RT @EricTrump: Very proud of @realDonaldTrump - he is going an amazing job! Trump Average Approval Ratings Skyrocket To Highest Point In Y... [Twitter for iPhone]

May 15, 2019 07:53:28 AM Thank you Joe and remember, the BRAIN is much sharper also! https://t.co/h1fG1GRQ99 [Twitter for iPhone]

May 15, 2019 01:20:30 PM The courage & sacrifice of our heroes is the reason our flag stands tall, our hearts beat with pride, and our Country remains one people, one family, and one NATION UNDER GOD. Today, we thank you, we honor you, & we forever cherish the memory of our Fallen Men and Women in Blue! https://t.co/ARHYgDVi3M [Twitter for iPhone]

May 15, 2019 01:56:51 PM We stand firmly, strongly, and proudly with the incredible men and women of law enforcement. You do not hear it nearly enough, but Americans across this Country love you, support you, and respect you more than you could possibly know! #PeaceOfficersMemorialDay https://t.co/T0qB5zN7WG [Twitter for iPhone]

May 15, 2019 02:10:47 PM ....Different opinions are expressed and I make a decisive and final decision - it is a very simple process. All sides, views, and policies are covered. I'm sure that Iran will want to talk soon. [Twitter for iPhone]

May 15, 2019 02:10:47 PM The Fake News Washington Post, and even more Fake News New York Times, are writing stories that there is infighting with respect to my strong policy in the Middle East. There is no infighting whatsoever.... [Twitter for iPhone]

May 15, 2019 08:51:56 PM RT @Trump: Ahead of the @PGAChampionship this week, @B_Dechambeau and @DJohnsonPGA joined us at @TrumpFerryPoint in support of @Curetivity!... [Twitter for iPhone]

May 15, 2019 09:48:07 PM RT @WhiteHouse: Tonight, the White House was lit in blue in honor of Peace Officers Memorial Day. https://t.co/Tv9nAn5M2G [Twitter for iPhone]

May 16, 2019 07:33:40 AM The Dems are getting another beauty to join their group. Bill de Blasio of NYC, considered the worst mayor in the U.S., will supposedly be making an announcement for president today. He is a JOKE, but if you like high taxes & crime, he's your man. NYC HATES HIM! [Twitter for iPhone]

May 16, 2019 07:34:38 AM RT @realDonaldTrump: ....Different opinions are expressed and I make a decisive and final decision - it is a very simple process. All sides... [Twitter for iPhone]

May 16, 2019 07:34:45 AM RT @realDonaldTrump: The Fake News Washington Post, and even more Fake News New York Times, are writing stories that there is infighting wi... [Twitter for iPhone]

May 16, 2019 11:53:23 AM Congratulations to Dan Bishop on his big Republican Primary victory in the 9th Congressional District of North Carolina. Dan is strong on Crime, Loves our Military, Vets, 2A, and great Healthcare. He has my Complete and Total Endorsement! #MAGA [Twitter for iPhone]

May 16, 2019 02:13:58 PM We are here on this beautiful spring day to unveil our plan to create a fair, modern & LAWFUL system of immigration for the U.S. If adopted, our plan will transform America's immigration system into the pride of our Nation and the envy of the modern world. https://t.co/YqyTYgTByD [Twitter for iPhone]

May 16, 2019 04:29:04 PM RT @WhiteHouse: "Our plan includes a sweeping modernization of our dysfunctional legal immigration process . . . The system will finally be... [Twitter for iPhone]

May 16, 2019 04:29:29 PM RT @WhiteHouse: "America's last major overhaul of our legal admissions policy was 54 YEARS ago. Think of that. So a major update, and that'... [Twitter for iPhone]

May 16, 2019 05:11:37 PM .@BilldeBlasio is the worst Mayor in the history of New York City - he won't last long! https://t.co/NyYntsX573 [Twitter for iPhone]

May 17, 2019 05:36:38 AM The Democrats now realize that there is a National Emergency at the Border and that, if we work together, it can be immediately fixed. We need Democrat votes and all will be well! [Twitter for iPhone]

May 17, 2019 05:44:53 AM Border Patrol is apprehending record numbers of people at the Southern Border. The bad "hombres," of which there are many, are being detained & will be sent home. Those which we release under the ridiculous Catch & Telease loophole, are being registered and will be removed later! [Twitter for iPhone]

May 17, 2019 05:51:34 AM All people that are illegally coming into the United States now will be removed from our Country at a later date as we build up our removal forces and as the laws are changed. Please do not make yourselves too comfortable, you will be leaving soon! [Twitter for iPhone]

May 17, 2019 05:53:25 AM Will the Democrats give our Country a badly needed immigration win before the election? Good chance! [Twitter for iPhone]

May 17, 2019 05:58:43 AM "What happened is that Donald Trump won. Down goes Comey." @foxandfriends [Twitter for iPhone]

May 17, 2019 06:00:06 AM DRAIN THE SWAMP! [Twitter for iPhone]

May 17, 2019 06:01:01 AM MAKE AMERICA GREAT AGAIN! [Twitter for iPhone]

May 17, 2019 06:05:30 AM New Fox Poll: 58% of people say that the FBI broke the law in investigating Donald J. Trump. @foxandfriends [Twitter for iPhone]

May 17, 2019 06:11:45 AM My Campaign for President was conclusively spied on. Nothing like this has ever happened in American Politics. A really bad situation. TREASON means long jail sentences, and this was TREASON! [Twitter for iPhone]

May 17, 2019 07:16:40 AM Will Jerry Nadler ever look into the fact that Crooked Hillary deleted and acid washed 33,000 emails AFTER getting a most powerful demand notice for them from Congress? [Twitter for iPhone]

May 17, 2019 08:44:35 AM The Fake News Media is hurting our Country with its fraudulent and highly inaccurate coverage of Iran. It is scattershot, poorly sourced (made up), and DANGEROUS. At least Iran doesn't know what to think, which at this point may very well be a good thing! [Twitter for iPhone]

May 17, 2019 09:35:05 AM It now seems the General Flynn was under investigation long before was common knowledge. It would have been impossible for me to know this but, if that was the case, and with me being one of two people who would become president, why was I not told so that I could make a change? [Twitter for iPhone]

⊔ May 17, 2019 11:53:00 AM With all of the Fake and Made Up News out there, Iran can have no idea what is actually going on! [Twitter for iPhone]

⊔ May 17, 2019 02:41:59 PM Today, it was my great honor to address the the National Association of REALTORS! https://t.co/LQNExa57ne [Twitter for iPhone]

⊔ May 17, 2019 05:49:34 PM Consumer Sentiment in the month of May is the highest in 15 years. Very nice! @FoxNews [Twitter for iPhone]

⊔ May 18, 2019 10:55:17 AM Our courageous and vigilant Armed Forces safeguard the blessings of liberty for us and for future generations by selflessly answering the call of duty. Today, and every day, we acknowledge and celebrate all who proudly wear our Nation's uniforms! https://t.co/w4DNjyPqvw https://t.co/BPXkmobseQ [Twitter for iPhone]

⊔ May 18, 2019 03:59:13 PM Congratulations to Scott on a GREAT WIN! https://t.co/IKxDrQmHfV [Twitter for iPhone]

⊔ May 18, 2019 04:00:20 PM RT @callme_Chari: @newscomauHQ If he's anything like Trump congratulations to you all. You have a leader who loves your country and will pu... [Twitter for iPhone]

⊔ May 18, 2019 04:08:35 PM Word is out that book is GREAT! https://t.co/mTA1xcz9eQ [Twitter for iPhone]

⊔ May 18, 2019 04:12:31 PM Thank you Dan! https://t.co/TdvC2eVo4H [Twitter for iPhone]

⊔ May 18, 2019 04:14:50 PM RT @TomFitton: Comey has significant potential criminal liability for his Spygate targeting of @RealDonaldTrump. @JudicialWatch @FoxNews ht... [Twitter for iPhone]

⊔ May 18, 2019 04:15:17 PM RT @TomFitton: Sure enough, Weissmann had key role in hiring the "13 angry Democrats" for Mueller @realDonaldTrump harassment operation --... [Twitter for iPhone]

⊔ May 18, 2019 04:15:59 PM RT @TomFitton: Now THIS is obstruction: FBI notes: "Hillary cover up operation work ticket archive cleanup." FBI knew of cover-up related... [Twitter for iPhone]

⊔ May 18, 2019 04:16:18 PM RT @TomFitton: Never in American history has there been such a spy effort against a candidate (@RealDonaldTrump) and abuse of power targeti... [Twitter for iPhone]

⊔ May 18, 2019 04:23:43 PM RT @realDonaldTrump: All people that are illegally coming into the United States now will be removed from our Country at a later date as we... [Twitter for iPhone]

⊔ May 18, 2019 04:23:49 PM RT @realDonaldTrump: MAKE AMERICA GREAT AGAIN! [Twitter for iPhone]

⊔ May 18, 2019 04:23:59 PM RT @realDonaldTrump: My Campaign for President was conclusively spied on. Nothing like this has ever happened in American Politics. A reall... [Twitter for iPhone]

May 18, 2019 04:24:02 PM RT @realDonaldTrump: Will Jerry Nadler ever look into the fact that Crooked Hillary deleted and acid washed 33,000 emails AFTER getting a m… [Twitter for iPhone]

May 18, 2019 05:33:48 PM Courts & Dems in Congress, neither of which have a clue, are trying to FORCE migrants into our Country! OUR COUNTRY IS FULL, OUR DETENTION CENTERS, HOSPITALS & SCHOOLS ARE PACKED. Crazy! [Twitter for iPhone]

May 18, 2019 10:37:08 PM As most people know, and for those who would like to know, I am strongly Pro-Life, with the three exceptions - Rape, Incest and protecting the Life of the mother - the same position taken by Ronald Reagan. We have come very far in the last two years with 105 wonderful new..... [Twitter for iPhone]

May 18, 2019 10:37:09 PM ....for Life in 2020. If we are foolish and do not stay UNITED as one, all of our hard fought gains for Life can, and will, rapidly disappear! [Twitter for iPhone]

May 18, 2019 10:37:09 PM ....Federal Judges (many more to come), two great new Supreme Court Justices, the Mexico City Policy, and a whole new & positive attitude about the Right to Life. The Radical Left, with late term abortion (and worse), is imploding on this issue. We must stick together and Win.... [Twitter for iPhone]

May 19, 2019 07:49:32 AM ....was a depleted disaster, will soon be stronger than ever before, our Vets are finally being taken care of and now have Choice, our Courts will have 145 great new Judges, and 2 Supreme Court Justices, got rid of the disastrous Individual Mandate & will protect Pre-Existing.... [Twitter for iPhone]

May 19, 2019 07:49:32 AM For all of the Fake News Sunday Political Shows, whose bias & dishonesty is greater than ever seen in our Country before, please inform your viewers that our Economy is setting records, with more people employed today than at any time in U.S. history, our Military, which.... [Twitter for iPhone]

May 19, 2019 07:49:33 AM ....Conditions, drug prices down for first time in 51 years (& soon will drop much further), Right to Try, protecting your 2nd Amendment, big Tax & Reg Cuts, 3.2 GDP, Strong Foreign Policy, & much much more that nobody else would have been able to do. Our Country is doing GREAT! [Twitter for iPhone]

May 19, 2019 08:55:07 AM ....he would see that it was nevertheless strong on NO COLLUSION and, ultimately, NO OBSTRUCTION...Anyway, how do you Obstruct when there is no crime and, in fact, the crimes were committed by the other side? Justin is a loser who sadly plays right into our opponents hands! [Twitter for iPhone]

May 19, 2019 08:55:07 AM Never a fan of @justinamash, a total lightweight who opposes me and some of our great Republican ideas and policies just for the sake of getting his name out there through controversy. If he actually read the biased Mueller Report, "composed" by 18 Angry Dems who hated Trump,.... [Twitter for iPhone]

May 19, 2019 01:50:37 PM Watched some of the Fake News Political Shows this morning and continue to be amazed at how every question is asked in the most negative way. The Mainstream Media should be ashamed of itself - But the good news is that the USA is wise to your game of dishonesty and deception! [Twitter for iPhone]

May 19, 2019 02:38:34 PM I will be interviewed by Steve Hilton tonight at 8:00 P.M. on @FoxNews. Enjoy! [Twitter for iPhone]

May 19, 2019 02:48:45 PM With the wonderful College, University and other Graduations taking place all over the USA, there has never been a better time than now to graduate. Best jobs market ever, great housing and financing. Go out there, work hard, & have a GREAT life. You deserve it. Congratulations! [Twitter for iPhone]

May 19, 2019 02:54:34 PM Our Economy and Jobs Market is BOOMING, the best in the World and in our Country's history - and we have just started! [Twitter for iPhone]

May 19, 2019 03:15:23 PM False reporting yesterday. "There are no plans to send migrants to Northern or Coastal Border facilities, including Florida." @FoxNews Not by airplanes or any other way. Our Country is FULL, will not, and can not, take you in! [Twitter for iPhone]

May 19, 2019 03:25:34 PM If Iran wants to fight, that will be the official end of Iran. Never threaten the United States again! [Twitter for iPhone]

May 19, 2019 03:39:31 PM I will be interviewed by Steve Hilton tonight at 9:00 P.M. on @FoxNews. Enjoy! [Twitter for iPhone]

May 19, 2019 04:15:50 PM ....who got them there. Chris Wallace said, "I actually think, whether you like his opinions or not, that Mayor Pete has a lot of substance...fascinating biography." Gee, he never speaks well of me - I like Mike Wallace better...and Alfred E. Newman will never be President! [Twitter for iPhone]

May 19, 2019 04:15:50 PM Hard to believe that @FoxNews is wasting airtime on Mayor Pete, as Chris Wallace likes to call him. Fox is moving more and more to the losing (wrong) side in covering the Dems. They got dumped from the Democrats boring debates, and they just want in. They forgot the people..... [Twitter for iPhone]

May 19, 2019 05:33:29 PM RT @realDonaldTrump: I will be interviewed by Steve Hilton tonight at 9:00 P.M. on @FoxNews. Enjoy! [Twitter for iPhone]

May 19, 2019 09:16:24 PM A great win for Brooks. Congratulations to a great champion! https://t.co/74z0n2icuA [Twitter for iPhone]

May 19, 2019 09:29:27 PM Starting Monday, our great Farmers can begin doing business again with Mexico and Canada. They have both taken the tariff penalties off of your great agricultural product. Please be sure that you are treated fairly. Any complaints should immediately go to @SecretarySonny Perdue! [Twitter for iPhone]

May 19, 2019 09:32:36 PM The Mainstream Media hates to cover this! https://t.co/EMhAVWCjVf [Twitter for iPhone]

May 19, 2019 09:47:21 PM RT @LouDobbs: God Bless President Trump--- Iran's so called leaders must think they're dealing with Bush or Obama. #MAGA #AmericaFirst #Do... [Twitter for iPhone]

May 20, 2019 06:20:53 AM ....Now the new big story is that Trump made a lot of money and buys everything for cash, he doesn't need banks. But where did he get all of that cash? Could it be Russia? No, I built a great business and don't need banks, but if I did they would be there...and DeutscheBank...... [Twitter for iPhone]

May 20, 2019 06:20:53 AM The Mainstream Media has never been as corrupt and deranged as it is today. FAKE NEWS is actually the biggest story of all and is the true ENEMY OF THE PEOPLE! That's why they refuse to cover the REAL Russia Hoax. But the American people are wise to what is going on..... [Twitter for iPhone]

May 20, 2019 06:20:53 AM ....fashioned, but true. When you don't need or want money, you don't need or want banks. Banks have always been available to me, they want to make money. Fake Media only says this to disparage, and always uses unnamed sources (because their sources don't even exist)...... [Twitter for iPhone]

May 20, 2019 06:20:53 AM The Failing New York Times (it will pass away when I leave office in 6 years), and others of the Fake News Media, keep writing phony stories about how I didn't use many banks because they didn't want to do business with me. WRONG! It is because I didn't need money. Very old [Twitter for iPhone]

May 20, 2019 06:20:54 AM .....was very good and highly professional to deal with - and if for any reason I didn't like them, I would have gone elsewhere....there was always plenty of money around and banks to choose from. They would be very happy to take my money. Fake News! [Twitter for iPhone]

May 20, 2019 06:35:31 AM Two Tweets missing from last batch, probably a Twitter error. No time for a redo! Only the Dems get redos! [Twitter for iPhone]

May 20, 2019 07:07:33 AM "We have a booming economy, and working people are making gains that they haven't seen in decades." Stuart Varney @foxandfriends [Twitter for iPhone]

May 20, 2019 07:13:31 AM Why are the Democrats not looking into all of the crimes committed by Crooked Hillary and the phony Russia Investigation? They would get back their credibility. Jerry Nadler, Schiff, would have a whole new future open to them. Perhaps they could even run for President! [Twitter for iPhone]

May 20, 2019 09:08:04 AM Looks like Bernie Sanders is history. Sleepy Joe Biden is pulling ahead and think about it, I'm only here because of Sleepy Joe and the man who took him off the 1% trash heap, President O! China wants Sleepy Joe BADLY! [Twitter for iPhone]

May 20, 2019 12:28:03 PM On this Cuban Independence Day, we stand by the people of Cuba in their quest for freedom, democracy and prosperity. The Cuban regime must end its repression of Cubans & Venezuelans. The United States will not stand idly by as Cuba continues to subvert democracy in the Americas! [Twitter for iPhone]

May 20, 2019 12:30:35 PM ....Iran will call us if and when they are ever ready. In the meantime, their economy continues to collapse - very sad for the Iranian people! [Twitter for iPhone]

May 20, 2019 12:30:35 PM The Fake News put out a typically false statement, without any knowledge that the United States was trying to set up a negotiation with Iran. This is a false report.... [Twitter for iPhone]

May 20, 2019 12:40:23 PM See you tonight at 7:00 P.M. Eastern, Montoursville, Pennsylvania! #MAGA https://t.co/Ij2AjXfRZa [Twitter for iPhone]

May 20, 2019 01:07:30 PM Fred Keller of the Great State of Pennsylvania has been an outstanding State Representative. Now he is running as the Republican Nominee for Congress, and has my Complete and Total Endorsement. He will do a fantastic job - I look forward to seeing everyone tonight! #MAGA [Twitter for iPhone]

May 20, 2019 05:39:53 PM Landing shortly in Montoursville, Pennsylvania - see everyone shortly! https://t.co/R67IxP3QPL [Twitter for iPhone]

May 20, 2019 07:45:41 PM Beautiful evening for a MAKE AMERICA GREAT AGAIN rally tonight in Pennsylvania. Thank you, I love you! #MAGA https://t.co/6oqbA5Y5zU [Twitter for iPhone]

May 20, 2019 08:04:55 PM Massive crowds in Pennsylvania tonight. Thank you for joining me! https://t.co/v1e0d0AHHo [Twitter for iPhone]

May 20, 2019 09:02:28 PM Megan King, who is running for Superior Court Judge in the Pennsylvania election, has my Full and Total Endorsement. She is tough on crime and fully understands all aspects of the law. Vote for Megan tomorrow (Tuesday). [Twitter for iPhone]

May 20, 2019 09:06:31 PM Just returned to the beautiful @WhiteHouse after a great evening in Pennsylvania! https://t.co/wMeh9k9knv [Twitter for iPhone]

May 21, 2019 06:34:18 AM RT @realDonaldTrump: Megan King, who is running for Superior Court Judge in the Pennsylvania election, has my Full and Total Endorsement. S... [Twitter for iPhone]

May 21, 2019 06:34:29 AM RT @realDonaldTrump: Fred Keller of the Great State of Pennsylvania has been an outstanding State Representative. Now he is running as the... [Twitter for iPhone]

May 21, 2019 10:25:09 AM To the great people of Kentucky, please go out and vote for Matt Bevin today. Very important. He has done a fantastic job for you and America! #MAGA [Twitter for iPhone]

May 21, 2019 11:16:53 AM I am very disappointed that Mexico is doing virtually nothing to stop illegal immigrants from coming to our Southern Border where everyone knows that because of the Democrats, our Immigration Laws are totally flawed & broken... [Twitter for iPhone]

May 21, 2019 11:16:54 AM ...Mexico's attitude is that people from other countries, including Mexico, should have the right to flow into the U.S. & that U.S. taxpayers should be responsible for the tremendous costs associated w/this illegal migration. Mexico is wrong and I will soon be giving a response! [Twitter for iPhone]

May 21, 2019 11:38:40 AM Pennsylvania - Don't forget to get out and VOTE TODAY for Republican Fred Keller for Congress. Fred is Strong on Crime, Second Amendment, Military, Vets, and Healthcare. He has my Complete and Total Endorsement! [Twitter for iPhone]

May 21, 2019 03:52:46 PM I am pleased to announce my nomination of Barbara Barrett of Arizona, and former Chairman of the Aerospace Corporation, to be the next Secretary of the Air Force. She will be an outstanding Secretary! #FlyFightWin [Twitter for iPhone]

May 21, 2019 04:22:52 PM ....at a conclusion of NO COLLUSION and NO OBSTRUCTION! The Dems were unhappy with the outcome of the $40M Mueller Report, so now they want a do-over. [Twitter for iPhone]

May 21, 2019 04:22:52 PM So even though I didn't have to do it with Presidential Privilege, I allowed everyone to testify, including White House Counsel Don McGahn (for over 30 hours), to Robert Mueller and the 18 Angry Trump-Hating Democrats, and they arrived.... [Twitter for iPhone]

May 21, 2019 04:53:23 PM Johnny, we will miss you – you did a great job! https://t.co/eXaASLgeSh [Twitter for iPhone]

May 21, 2019 05:00:15 PM Wow, Mark Levin's new book opened at #1. It is great – keep it there for a long time! https://t.co/3F1xybks0R [Twitter for iPhone]

May 21, 2019 05:48:50 PM Shahira Knight has done a wonderful job as my Legislative Affairs Director at the White House. She was outstanding for us and for our Country - will be a tremendous success in the private sector! [Twitter for iPhone]

May 21, 2019 07:32:40 PM After spending 40 Million Dollars, reviewing 1.4 million pages of documents, & interviewing 500 people with the total support of the White House, the Mueller Report was a BIG DISAPPOINTMENT to the Democrats, so they want a DO OVER. It doesn't work that way-so bad for our Country! [Twitter for iPhone]

May 21, 2019 07:51:43 PM The Democrats are on a fishing expedition, wanting to interview the same people, and see the same things, as we just went through for two years with Robert Mueller and the 18 Angry Dems. Never happened to a president before. Never even happened to President Obama! [Twitter for iPhone]

May 21, 2019 08:02:38 PM John Brennan on the Mueller probe, "I don't know if I received bad information, but I THINK I SUSPECTED THAT THERE WAS MORE THAN THERE ACTUALLY WAS." Wow, he admits he was wrong! Congress should go back to work on drug prices etc. [Twitter for iPhone]

May 21, 2019 09:20:51 PM Great news for Republicans: Fred Keller has just won the hard fought for Pennsylvania Congressional contest in a LANDSLIDE, over 70% of the vote. Thanks to the thousands who showed up for the Rally last night. Congratulations to Fred and his wonderful family! [Twitter for iPhone]

May 21, 2019 09:29:40 PM Congratulations to Governor @MattBevin on winning the Republican Primary for Governor tonight in the Great State of KENTUCKY. Matt, you are doing a fantastic job! [Twitter for iPhone]

May 22, 2019 04:55:14 AM Everything the Democrats are asking me for is based on an illegally started investigation that failed for them, especially when the Mueller Report came back with a NO COLLUSION finding. Now they say Impeach President Trump, even though he did nothin wrong, while they "fish!" [Twitter for iPhone]

May 22, 2019 04:58:59 AM After two years of an expensive and comprehensive Witch Hunt, the Democrats don't like the result and they want a DO OVER. In other words, the Witch Hunt continues! [Twitter for iPhone]

May 22, 2019 05:02:55 AM The Democrats are getting ZERO work done in Congress. All they are focused on is trying to prove the Mueller Report wrong, the Witch Hunt! [Twitter for iPhone]

May 22, 2019 05:03:51 AM PRESIDENTIAL HARASSMENT! [Twitter for iPhone]

May 22, 2019 05:37:02 AM RT @J_TrumpIN: Twitter VICIOUS censorship still hitting MAGA movement HARD. JAMES WOODS SUSPENDED DAY 32! If you think this is TOTAL BS,... [Twitter for iPhone]

May 22, 2019 05:38:30 AM RT @RepMarkMeadows: A question every American should ask: what on earth was the point of a taxpayer funded special counsel if we're going t... [Twitter for iPhone]

May 22, 2019 05:39:55 AM RT @RepMarkMeadows: This week you'll see more efforts from Democrats to re-do the Mueller investigation—hoping this time they'll stumble on... [Twitter for iPhone]

May 22, 2019 05:40:02 AM RT @dcexaminer: .@RepMarkMeadows: Declassification of Russia investigation docs is "right around the corner." https://t.co/6CpqRdCD8V [Twitter for iPhone]

May 22, 2019 05:40:57 AM RT @ChuckGrassley: Another trade breakthru 2day w Japan lifting restrictions on US beef products. US beef into Japan has been 1 of the most... [Twitter for iPhone]

May 22, 2019 05:41:53 AM RT @ChuckGrassley: Thx to Pres Trump/Amb Lighthizer & Canada/Mexico for working to get to this pt Now it's time for Congress to do its job... [Twitter for iPhone]

May 22, 2019 05:43:26 AM RT @GOPoversight: #ICYMI: Watch @RepMarkMeadows's opening statement from today's Government Operations Subcommittee hearing. Mr. Meadows i... [Twitter for iPhone]

May 22, 2019 05:44:26 AM RT @LindseyGrahamSC: Very pleased to have confirmed another conservative judge to the Ninth Circuit. Daniel Collins will be an outstanding... [Twitter for iPhone]

May 22, 2019 05:44:58 AM RT @LindseyGrahamSC: The only way to protect Americans serving overseas is to have their back. I am proud President Trump is standing up... [Twitter for iPhone]

May 22, 2019 05:46:03 AM RT @DevinNunes: Mueller changed everything- □@ByronYork□ #muellerdossier https://t.co/BU8rGW35CM [Twitter for iPhone]

May 22, 2019 05:48:31 AM RT @DevinNunes: "Warrior for the western alliance" 🙂 - Why does he wait 2 months to bring USA this important information? https://t.co/tY0... [Twitter for iPhone]

May 22, 2019 05:50:06 AM RT @senatemajldr: Today, tens of thousands of peace officers gathered in our nation's capital to honor the service and sacrifice of their f... [Twitter for iPhone]

May 22, 2019 06:00:15 AM Without the ILLEGAL Witch Hunt, my poll numbers, especially because of our historically "great" economy, would be at 65%. Too bad! The greatest Hoax in American History. [Twitter for iPhone]

May 22, 2019 06:22:36 AM Also, tremendous work is being done on pure renovation - fixing existing Walls that are in bad condition and ineffective, and bringing them to a very high standard! [Twitter for iPhone]

May 22, 2019 06:22:36 AM Much of the Wall being built at the Southern Border is a complete demolition and rebuilding of old and worthless barriers with a brand new Wall and footings. Problem is, the Haters say that is not a new Wall, but rather a renovation. Wrong, and we must build where most needed.... [Twitter for iPhone]

May 22, 2019 08:50:42 AM Everybody, including me, thought that when the 40 Million Dollar Mueller Report was released with No Collusion and No Obstruction (of a crime caused by others), that was the end. But no, the Democrats want to keep it going in an effort to help them in 2020. Bad for the Country! [Twitter for iPhone]

May 22, 2019 08:54:27 AM "The Democrats are in danger of becoming irrelevant because of their decision to keep taking the country on wild goose chases. They ought to start governing. You know, for a change." Michael Goodwin @newyorkpost [Twitter for iPhone]

May 22, 2019 10:11:15 AM "He (Jerry Nadler) wants a show. He wants to use Mr. McGahn as a prop to spend three hours claiming that Mr. Trump tried to obstruct the Mueller investigation. YET MR. MUELLER WASN'T OBSTRUCTED IN ANY WAY, HIS COPIOUS REPORT WAS RELEASED FOR ALL TO SEE, & THERE WAS NO COLLUSION.. [Twitter for iPhone]

May 22, 2019 10:11:16 AM ..BETWEEN RUSSIA AND THE TRUMP CAMPAIGN. Mr. McGahn can be forgiven for declining the honor of appearing in Mr. Nadler's pseudo-impeachment drama." Wall Street Journal Editorial Board Today - May 21, 2019 [Twitter for iPhone]

May 22, 2019 10:15:40 AM As I have long been saying, and has now been proven out, this is a Witch Hunt against the Republican Party and myself, and it was the other side that caused the problem, not us! [Twitter for iPhone]

May 22, 2019 11:57:35 AM https://t.co/Oe8E5kk8OA [Twitter for iPhone]

May 22, 2019 12:01:21 PM So sad that Nancy Pelosi and Chuck Schumer will never be able to see or understand the great promise of our Country. They can continue the Witch Hunt which has already cost $40M and been a tremendous waste of time and energy for everyone in America, or get back to work.... [Twitter for iPhone]

May 22, 2019 12:01:22 PM ....In the meantime, my Administration is achieving things that have never been done before, including unleashing perhaps the Greatest Economy in our Country's history.... [Twitter for iPhone]

May 22, 2019 12:01:22 PM ....But they really want a do-over! You can't investigate and legislate simultaneously - it just doesn't work that way. You can't go down two tracks at the same time. Let Chuck, Nancy, Jerry, Adam and all of the rest finish playing their games.... [Twitter for iPhone]

May 22, 2019 12:02:23 PM ....Democrat leadership is tearing the United States apart, but I will continue to set records for the American People – and Nancy, thank you so much for your prayers, I know you truly mean it! [Twitter for iPhone]

May 22, 2019 03:46:35 PM I want to welcome you all to the @WhiteHouse as we award our very bravest law enforcement officers and firefighters our nation's highest public safety award – The Medal of Valor...https://t.co/68EeQk8ZHr [Twitter for iPhone]

May 22, 2019 09:28:36 PM In a letter to her House colleagues, Nancy Pelosi said: "President Trump had a temper tantrum for us all to see." This is not true. I was purposely very polite and calm, much as I was minutes later with the press in the Rose Garden. Can be easily proven. It is all such a lie! [Twitter for iPhone]

May 22, 2019 09:31:52 PM Zero is getting done with the Democrats in charge of the House. All they want to do is put the Mueller Report behind them and start all over again. No Do-Overs! [Twitter for iPhone]

May 22, 2019 09:54:59 PM Democrats don't want to fix the loopholes at the Border. They don't want to do anything. Open Borders and crime! [Twitter for iPhone]

May 22, 2019 10:59:15 PM RT @TomFitton: .@RealDonaldTrump faces a criminal conspiracy against him.... https://t.co/JbxAxW3Sha [Twitter for iPhone]

May 23, 2019 06:56:03 AM The Democrats are getting nothing done in Congress. All of their effort is about a Re-Do of the Mueller Report, which didn't turn out the way they wanted. It is not possible for them to investigate and legislate at the same time. Their heart is not into Infrastructure, lower..... [Twitter for iPhone]

May 23, 2019 06:56:04 AM ....drug prices, pre-existing conditions and our great Vets. All they are geared up to do, six committees, is squander time, day after day, trying to find anything which will be bad for me. A pure fishing expedition like this never happened before, & it should never happen again! [Twitter for iPhone]

May 23, 2019 06:58:57 AM The Democrats have become known as THE DO NOTHING PARTY! [Twitter for iPhone]

May 23, 2019 07:29:04 AM Rex Tillerson, a man who is "dumb as a rock" and totally ill prepared and ill equipped to be Secretary of State, made up a story (he got fired) that I was out-prepared by Vladimir Putin at a meeting in Hamburg, Germany. I don't think Putin would agree. Look how the U.S. is doing! [Twitter for iPhone]

May 23, 2019 09:13:39 AM I was extremely calm yesterday with my meeting with Pelosi and Schumer, knowing that they would say I was raging, which they always do, along with their partner, the Fake News Media. Well, so many stories about the meeting use the Rage narrative anyway - Fake & Corrupt Press! [Twitter for iPhone]

May 23, 2019 09:27:34 AM When the Democrats in Congress refinish, for the 5th time, their Fake work on their very disappointing Mueller Report finding, they will have the time to get the REAL work of the people done. Move quickly! [Twitter for iPhone]

May 23, 2019 12:05:25 PM Our hearts go out to the people of Missouri as they woke up to assess the damage from storms. You are strong and resilient, and we are here to assist. https://t.co/paeOVcUQWn [Twitter for iPhone]

May 23, 2019 12:07:28 PM .@NWS and @USACEHQ are monitoring the damaging storms and flooding in Oklahoma. Listen to the warnings of your local officials and stay safe. We are with you! [Twitter for iPhone]

May 23, 2019 12:13:14 PM Congratulations to Prime Minister @NarendraModi and his BJP party on their BIG election victory! Great things are in store for the US-India partnership with the return of PM Modi at the helm. I look forward to continuing our important work together! [Twitter for iPhone]

May 23, 2019 06:34:53 PM We will never forget our fallen HEROES. It was our great honor to be with you today! #FlagsIn https://t.co/Z6OvQUr8lT [Twitter for iPhone]

May 23, 2019 07:11:19 PM The U.S. Senate has just approved a 19 Billion Dollar Disaster Relief Bill, with my total approval. Great! [Twitter for iPhone]

May 23, 2019 07:16:44 PM @FoxNews Poll: A majority of Americans want the Democrats to stop investigating President Trump. The Mueller Report said very strongly NO COLLUSION, which led to NO OBSTRUCTION. The Dems can't get over 2016 or the conclusive Mueller findings. They are now the Do Nothing Party! [Twitter for iPhone]

May 23, 2019 07:19:32 PM ....Today's action will help ensure that all Americans learn the truth about the events that occurred, and the actions that were taken, during the last Presidential election and will restore confidence in our public institutions." @PressSec [Twitter for iPhone]

May 23, 2019 07:19:32 PM ....during the 2016 Presidential election. The Attorney General has also been delegated full and complete authority to declassify information pertaining to this investigation, in accordance with the long-established standards for handling classified information.... [Twitter for iPhone]

May 23, 2019 07:19:32 PM "Today, at the request and recommendation of the Attorney General of the United States, President Donald J. Trump directed the intelligence community to quickly and fully cooperate with the Attorney General's investigation into surveillance activities.... [Twitter for iPhone]

May 23, 2019 07:39:52 PM "Nancy Pelosi should not be out there doing the kinds of things she is doing. She will diminish herself and her membership. She cannot put a subject with a predicate in the same sentence. What's going on?" Ed Rollins @GreggJarrett @LouDobbs [Twitter for iPhone]

May 23, 2019 07:40:47 PM RT @AviBerkow: Congrats @IvankaTrump on receiving the Internet Association's 2019 Internet Freedom Award this evening. https://t.co/dE6Zh... [Twitter for iPhone]

May 23, 2019 08:09:33 PM "PELOSI STAMMERS THROUGH NEWS CONFERENCE" https://t.co/1OyCyqRTuk [Twitter for iPhone]

May 23, 2019 08:18:27 PM RT @DonaldJTrumpJr: A friendly reminder from @LizRNC that the Main Stream Media who suffer from Trump Detangment Syndrome made this clown a... [Twitter for iPhone]

May 23, 2019 08:19:25 PM 71% of Voters rate the Economy as Excellent or Good. The highest number in more than 18 years! @QuinnipiacPoll [Twitter for iPhone]

May 23, 2019 09:48:08 PM RT @TomFitton: FBI refuses to search text messages under FOIA. Director Wray needs to step up and stop this stonewalling that protects corr... [Twitter for iPhone]

May 23, 2019 09:49:03 PM RT @TomFitton: BIG: @realDonaldTrump authorizes AG Barr to declassify #Spygate docs from all agencies! Coming up! https://t.co/PzzU0kNQfL [Twitter for iPhone]

May 23, 2019 09:56:00 PM RT @TPUSA: SPEAKER ANNOUNCEMENT! Fox News Contributor @LisaMarieBooth Has Just Been Added To Our AMAZING Line-Up Of Speakers For #YWLS2019... [Twitter for iPhone]

May 23, 2019 10:00:00 PM RT @NikkiHaley: A great night. Thank you. ♥ https://t.co/EIKFo2UMLy [Twitter for iPhone]

May 23, 2019 10:02:29 PM RT @HeyTammyBruce: Very excited to join the @foxnation team! "Fox Nation Rolls Out Slate With Tyrus, Kat Timpf, Tammy Bruce, Lawrence Jones... [Twitter for iPhone]

May 23, 2019 10:19:46 PM Wow! CNN Ratings are WAY DOWN, record lows. People are getting tired of so many Fake Stories and Anti-Trump lies. Chris Cuomo was rewarded for lowest morning ratings with a prime time spot - which is failing badly and not helping the dumbest man on television, Don Lemon! [Twitter for iPhone]

May 23, 2019 10:29:22 PM When is Twitter going to allow the very popular Conservative Voices that it has so viciously shut down, back into the OPEN? IT IS TIME! [Twitter for iPhone]

May 23, 2019 10:49:49 PM "Intelligence Agencies were used against an American President." @DevinNunes @ShannonBream @FoxNews This should NEVER happen to a President again! Dems are furious at Robert Mueller for his findings - NO COLLUSION, NO OBSTRUCTION. Now they should go back to work and legislate! [Twitter for iPhone]

May 24, 2019 07:19:56 AM "If they try to Impeach President Trump, who has done nothing wrong (No Collusion), they will end up getting him re-elected" @LindseyGrahamSC Impeachment is for High Crimes and Misdemeanors. There were no High Crimes and Misdemeanors, except for those committed by the other side! [Twitter for iPhone]

May 24, 2019 07:34:47 AM I don't know why the Radical Left Democrats want Bob Mueller to testify when he just issued a 40 Million Dollar Report that states, loud & clear & for all to hear, No Collusion and No Obstruction (how do you Obstruct a NO crime?) Dems are just looking for trouble and a Do-Over! [Twitter for iPhone]

May 24, 2019 12:31:18 PM Congratulations to Tom Cotton - his book, "Sacred Duty: A Solider's Tour at Arlington National Cemetery" just hit the best sellers list. I was at @ArlingtonNatl yesterday & the people there were so grateful for Tom's inspiring portrait of "The Old Guard." Great job @TomCottonAR! [Twitter for iPhone]

May 24, 2019 01:00:27 PM Just spoke to Prime Minister @NarendraModi where I congratulated him on his big political victory. He is a great man and leader for the people of India - they are lucky to have him! [Twitter for iPhone]

May 24, 2019 01:16:37 PM I am on Air Force one with the First Lady heading to Japan and looking forward to honoring, on behalf of the United States, His Majesty, the Emperor of Japan. I will also be discussing Trade and Military with my friend, Prime Minister @AbeShinzo. [Twitter for iPhone]

May 24, 2019 02:01:48 PM Departed the @WhiteHouse and am now on Air Force One with the First Lady heading to Japan and looking forward to honoring, on behalf of the United States, His Majesty, the Emperor of Japan. I will also be discussing Trade and Military with my friend, Prime Minister @AbeShinzo. https://t.co/uwEjQNbEXE [Twitter for iPhone]

May 24, 2019 03:22:08 PM https://t.co/8GRaqVxR8S [Twitter for iPhone]

May 24, 2019 03:56:31 PM Mitch McConnell and our Republican Senators have been very solid and strong. We have accomplished a great deal together, in particular with our Courts, 107 Federal Judges.... [Twitter for iPhone]

May 24, 2019 03:56:32 PM ....(with many more to come) and 2 Supreme Court Justices - we are getting into record territory! Thank you all and have a great Memorial Day Weekend. [Twitter for iPhone]

May 24, 2019 04:41:43 PM .....The Dems want a second shot at Bob Mueller, are very unhappy with the No Collusion Report. They should not be allowed to play this game any longer - no second chances - must get back to work. So bad for our Country! [Twitter for iPhone]

May 24, 2019 07:38:25 PM In Alaska with our GREAT TROOPS, departing shortly for Japan! https://t.co/9a72TMftpN [Twitter for iPhone]

May 25, 2019 01:51:19 AM RT @Jim_Jordan: Democrats are engaged in presidential obstruction. They're so desperate to stop the President that they won't help the coun... [Twitter for iPhone]

May 25, 2019 01:51:37 AM RT @Jim_Jordan: We could work together on the big problems facing America. We could solve the border crisis, lower the cost of prescriptio... [Twitter for iPhone]

May 25, 2019 01:57:23 AM The real trade war began 30 years ago, and we lost. This is a bright new Age, the Age of Enlightenment. We don't lose anymore! https://t.co/5ECmBpsI6D [Twitter for iPhone]

May 25, 2019 02:00:22 AM RT @Jim_Jordan: "Rep. Jordan: When your focus is attacking Trump, you can't do what's best for America" https://t.co/prJJfetQel [Twitter for iPhone]

May 25, 2019 02:20:36 AM Democrat Senator Mark Warner is acting and talking like he is in total control of the Senate Intelligence Committee. Their is nothing bipartisan about him. He should not be allowed to take "command" of that Committee. Too important! Remember when he spoke to the Russian jokester? [Twitter for iPhone]

May 25, 2019 02:32:43 AM Can't believe that Rolling Thunder would be given a hard time with permits in Washington, D.C. They are great Patriots who I have gotten to know and see in action. They love our Country and love our Flag. If I can help, I will! [Twitter for iPhone]

May 25, 2019 02:48:39 AM Getting ready to land in Japan with First Lady Melania. We look forward to seeing everyone soon!usjp [Twitter for iPhone]

May 25, 2019 07:22:30 AM RT @WhiteHouse: After arriving in Tokyo, President @realDonaldTrump spoke with Japanese business leaders at the U. S. Ambassador to Japan's... [Twitter for iPhone]

May 25, 2019 02:35:19 PM Another activist Obama appointed judge has just ruled against us on a section of the Southern Wall that is already under construction. This is a ruling against Border Security and in favor of crime, drugs and human trafficking. We are asking for an expedited appeal! [Twitter for iPhone]

May 25, 2019 02:55:52 PM Thank you John, so nice! https://t.co/cfcXpzjYn7 [Twitter for iPhone]

May 25, 2019 03:03:26 PM RT @jonvoight: To my fellow Americans. Part 2. https://t.co/uhqpbzwHhS [Twitter for iPhone]

May 25, 2019 03:23:30 PM RT @GOPChairwoman: Democrats and the mainstream media loved to talk about transparency until they learned @realDonaldTrump was declassifyin… [Twitter for iPhone]

May 25, 2019 03:25:44 PM RT @JesseBWatters: TOMORROW: Senator @LindseyGrahamSC splashes into @WattersWorld to discuss his relationship with President @realDonaldTru… [Twitter for iPhone]

May 25, 2019 03:27:47 PM RT @TeamTrump: Dems plan a government TAKEOVER of healthcare. That means ELIMINATING private plans (like Blue Cross/Blue Shield)! @reald… [Twitter for iPhone]

May 25, 2019 03:43:42 PM In addition to great incompetence and corruption, The Smollett case in Chicago is also about a Hate Crime. Remember, "MAGA COUNTRY DID IT!" That turned out to be a total lie, had nothing to do with "MAGA COUNTRY." Serious stuff, and not even an apology to millions of people! [Twitter for iPhone]

May 25, 2019 03:45:45 PM RT @GOPChairwoman: The @realDonaldTrump administration's fight for better trade deals doesn't end with China. The president is working ha… [Twitter for iPhone]

May 25, 2019 05:29:56 PM North Korea fired off some small weapons, which disturbed some of my people, and others, but not me. I have confidence that Chairman Kim will keep his promise to me, & also smiled when he called Swampman Joe Bidan a low IQ individual, & worse. Perhaps that's sending me a signal? [Twitter for iPhone]

May 25, 2019 06:24:17 PM RT @USAmbJapan: .@POTUS kicks off historic state visit by discussing ways to deepen economic ties with business leaders. #POTUSinJapan #All… [Twitter for iPhone]

May 25, 2019 06:47:33 PM RT @AbeShinzo: President Trump and the First Lady are staying in Japan as the first State Guests of the new era "Reiwa"! TOKYO SKYTREE welc… [Twitter for iPhone]

May 25, 2019 07:33:54 PM Going to play golf right now with @AbeShinzo. Japan loves the game. Tremendous fans of @JackNicklaus, @TigerWoods, and @PhilMickelson — I said what about @GaryPlayer, they said we love Gary too! [Twitter for iPhone]

May 25, 2019 08:32:08 PM North Korea fired off some small weapons, which disturbed some of my people, and others, but not me. I have confidence that Chairman Kim will keep his promise to me, & also smiled when he called Swampman Joe Biden a low IQ individual, & worse. Perhaps that's sending me a signal? [Twitter for iPhone]

⎕ May 25, 2019 08:32:55 PM RT @USAmbJapan: Welcome back to Japan, Mr. President! @POTUS #POTUSinJapan #Alliance トランプ大統領、日本へようこそ！USJP https://t.co/kenxM9A7YF [Twitter for iPhone]

⎕ May 25, 2019 11:07:56 PM Great morning of golf with Prime Minister @AbeShinzo at Mobara Country Club in Chiba, Japan! https://t.co/EZeJ8znS51 [Twitter for iPhone]

⎕ May 25, 2019 11:14:52 PM RT @AbeShinzo: 令和初の国賓としてお迎えしたトランプ大統領と千葉でゴルフです。新しい令和の時代も日米同盟をさらに揺るぎないものとしていきたいと考えています。 https://t.co/8ol8790xWY [Twitter for iPhone]

⎕ May 25, 2019 11:37:52 PM Great fun and meeting with Prime Minister @AbeShinzo. Numerous Japanese officials told me that the Democrats would rather see the United States fail than see me or the Republican Party succeed - Death Wish! [Twitter for iPhone]

⎕ May 25, 2019 11:39:09 PM Great progress being made in our Trade Negotiations with Japan. Agriculture and beef heavily in play. Much will wait until after their July elections where I anticipate big numbers! [Twitter for iPhone]

⎕ May 26, 2019 06:48:05 AM Tonight in Tokyo, Japan at the Ryōgoku Kokugikan Stadium, it was my great honor to present the first-ever U.S. President's Cup to Sumo Grand Champion Asanoyama. Congratulations! A great time had by all, thank you @AbeShinzo!! https://t.co/nwwxJl6KXH [Twitter for iPhone]

⎕ May 26, 2019 07:26:12 AM Thank you @JPN_PMO @AbeShinzo! #POTUSinJapanUSJP https://t.co/fWToB1XotG [Twitter for iPhone]

⎕ May 26, 2019 07:40:07 AM "Why doesn't the press apologize to President Trump for the Russian Collusion Delusion?" @marklevinshow @JudgeJeanine How about the Dems also? [Twitter for iPhone]

⎕ May 26, 2019 07:53:07 AM The Great Patriots of Rolling Thunder WILL be coming back to Washington, D.C. next year, & hopefully for many years to come. It is where they want to be, & where they should be. Have a wonderful time today. Thank you to our great men & women of the Pentagon for working it out! [Twitter for iPhone]

⎕ May 26, 2019 03:48:18 PM Congratulations to the Great (and my friend) Roger Penske on winning his 18th (UNBELIEVABLE!) Indianapolis 500. I am in Japan, very early in the morning, but I got to watch Simon drive one of the greatest races in the history of the sport. I will see them both, & TEAM, at the WH! [Twitter for iPhone]

May 26, 2019 08:21:26 PM RT @usembassytokyo: トランプ大統領は安倍首相と共に皇居での歓迎式典に出席しました。@POTUS & @AbeShinzo at the Imperial Palace for the Welcome Ceremony. #POTUSinJapan USJP... [Twitter for iPhone]

May 26, 2019 10:27:31 PM Great evening last night, thank you! https://t.co/wPjj3yaaru [Twitter for iPhone]

May 26, 2019 10:27:50 PM RT @usembassytokyo: トランプ大統領とメラニア夫人は、天皇、皇后両陛下との会見に臨みました。@POTUS & @FLOTUS were received by Their Majesties the Emperor and Empress of Japan.... [Twitter for iPhone]

May 27, 2019 02:30:22 AM RT @WhiteHouse: President @realDonaldTrump and Prime Minister @AbeShinzo met for bilateral meetings and a working lunch at Akasaka Palace.... [Twitter for iPhone]

May 27, 2019 03:57:33 AM .@ianbremmer now admits that he MADE UP "a completely ludicrous quote," attributing it to me. This is what's going on in the age of Fake News. People think they can say anything and get away with it. Really, the libel laws should be changed to hold Fake News Media accountable! [Twitter for iPhone]

May 27, 2019 04:10:27 AM Impeach for what, having created perhaps the greatest Economy in our Country's history, rebuilding our Military, taking care of our Vets (Choice), Judges, Best Jobs Numbers Ever, and much more? Dems are Obstructionists! https://t.co/NrTIxU9ZnA [Twitter for iPhone]

May 27, 2019 04:13:59 AM The Dems are getting NOTHING done in Congress! They only want a Do-Over on Mueller! [Twitter for iPhone]

May 27, 2019 07:54:34 AM https://t.co/lZRn4j8SpD [Twitter for iPhone]

May 27, 2019 07:57:10 AM #MemorialDayUS https://t.co/FmwhvPvvQU [Twitter for iPhone]

May 27, 2019 08:35:26 AM RT @japantimes: U.S. President Donald Trump becomes first foreign leader to meet Japan's Emperor Naruhito. https://t.co/X9Hu4wH3Jz [Twitter for iPhone]

May 27, 2019 08:56:34 AM Liz Cheney: Statements by agents investigating Trump 'could well be treason' https://t.co/ViG9DSrsXY [Twitter for iPhone]

May 27, 2019 09:33:32 AM https://t.co/BmmWXDFMQP [Twitter for iPhone]

May 27, 2019 10:24:52 AM Hoping things will work out with Israel's coalition formation and Bibi and I can continue to make the alliance between America and Israel stronger than ever. A lot more to do! [Twitter for iPhone]

May 27, 2019 04:08:31 PM Anyone associated with the 1994 Crime Bill will not have a chance of being elected. In particular, African Americans will not be ble to vote for you. I, on the other hand, was responsible for Criminal Justice Reform, which had tremendous support, and helped fix the bad 1994 Bill! [Twitter for iPhone]

May 27, 2019 04:16:45 PM ....Super Predator was the term associated with the 1994 Crime Bill that Sleepy Joe Biden was so heavily involved in passing. That was a dark period in American History, but has Sleepy Joe apologized? No! [Twitter for iPhone]

May 27, 2019 05:35:35 PM Anyone associated with the 1994 Crime Bill will not have a chance of being elected. In particular, African Americans will not be able to vote for you. I, on the other hand, was responsible for Criminal Justice Reform, which had tremendous support, & helped fix the bad 1994 Bill! [Twitter for iPhone]

May 27, 2019 05:57:37 PM I will be making two stops this morning in Japan to visit with our Great Military, then a quick stop in Alaska and back to D.C. Meetings with Prime Minister Abe went very well, and getting to spend time with the new Emperor and Empress of Japan was a great honor! [Twitter for iPhone]

May 27, 2019 06:05:26 PM RT @MZHemingway: EXCITING NEWS: I've written a book on the Kavanaugh confirmation with the inimitable @JCNSeverino. A behind-the-scenes loo… [Twitter for iPhone]

May 27, 2019 07:36:35 PM Can't wait to see you all soon! https://t.co/KKAw4hqqx5 [Twitter for iPhone]

May 27, 2019 09:25:49 PM RT @USForcesJapan: LIVE remarks from @POTUS Donald J. Trump aboard #USSWasp in #Japan! https://t.co/BIliRI025v [Twitter for iPhone]

May 28, 2019 03:11:10 AM Spoke with @GovStitt of Oklahoma last night from Japan because of the devastating tornadoes. Told him that @FEMA and the federal government are fully behind him and the great people of Oklahoma. [Twitter for iPhone]

May 28, 2019 07:07:36 AM RT @kantei: 【SNS投稿】「本日、トランプ大統領と共に、海上自衛隊の護衛艦「かが」を訪問しました。日米両国の首脳が揃って、自衛隊、米軍を激励するのは、史上初めてのことです。」総理メッセージの続きは https://t.co/HLWIQcmaH7 https://t…. [Twitter for iPhone]

May 28, 2019 07:39:41 AM GOD BLESS THE USAus https://t.co/Y8HRT6wnWZ [Twitter for iPhone]

May 28, 2019 02:38:00 PM Storms overnight across Ohio and many other States were very dangerous and damaging. My team continues to update me with reports from emergency managers in the States affected. Listen to your local officials and be resilient. We are with you! [Twitter for iPhone]

May 28, 2019 02:40:20 PM .@GovMikeDeWine just updated me on the devastation from the many tornadoes that struck Ohio early this morning. My Administration fully supports the people of the great State of Ohio as they begin the cleanup and recovery. [Twitter for iPhone]

May 28, 2019 04:24:32 PM Just spoke to Governor @AsaHutchinson of the Great State of Arkansas to inform him that FEMA and the Federal Government will do whatever is necessary to help out with what has turned out to be Record Flooding. Asa and local officials are doing a great job! [Twitter for iPhone]

May 28, 2019 04:58:55 PM I was actually sticking up for Sleepy Joe Biden while on foreign soil. Kim Jong Un called him a "low IQ idiot," and many other things, whereas I related the quote of Chairman Kim as a much softer "low IQ individual." Who could possibly be upset with that? [Twitter for iPhone]

May 28, 2019 07:22:51 PM Back from Japan after a very successful trip. Big progress on MANY fronts. A great country with a wonderful leader in Prime Minister Abe! [Twitter for iPhone]

May 28, 2019 07:33:37 PM THANK YOU JAPAN!usjp https://t.co/ZvzEL8iQsi [Twitter for iPhone]

May 28, 2019 10:14:26 PM RT @realDonaldTrump: GOD BLESS THE USAus https://t.co/Y8HRT6wnWZ [Twitter for iPhone]

May 29, 2019 06:40:30 AM Republicans cannot allow themselves to again lose the Senate seat in the Great State of Alabama. This time it will be for Six Years, not just Two. I have NOTHING against Roy Moore, and unlike many other Republican leaders, wanted him to win. But he didn't, and probably won't..... [Twitter for iPhone]

May 29, 2019 06:40:31 AM ...If Alabama does not elect a Republican to the Senate in 2020, many of the incredible gains that we have made during my Presidency may be lost, including our Pro-Life victories. Roy Moore cannot win, and the consequences will be devastating....Judges and Supreme Court Justices! [Twitter for iPhone]

May 29, 2019 10:37:21 AM Nothing changes from the Mueller Report. There was insufficient evidence and therefore, in our Country, a person is innocent. The case is closed! Thank you. [Twitter for iPhone]

May 29, 2019 12:21:00 PM RT @kayleighmcenany: "Now it's time to turn to the origins of the Russia hoax and get to the bottom of why the Trump campaign was spied on... [Twitter for iPhone]

May 29, 2019 12:23:55 PM RT @PressSec: White House Statement on Mueller statement today: https://t.co/f5TXzf3Qpd [Twitter for iPhone]

May 29, 2019 07:32:06 PM How do you impeach a Republican President for a crime that was committed by the Democrats? WITCH-HUNT! [Twitter for iPhone]

May 29, 2019 07:46:39 PM Great show tonight @seanhannity, you really get it (9:00 P.M. @FoxNews), that's why you're Number One (by far)! Also, please tell Mark Levin congrats on having the Number One book! [Twitter for iPhone]

May 29, 2019 07:59:43 PM I was not informed about anything having to do with the Navy Ship USS John S. McCain during my recent visit to Japan. Nevertheless, @FLOTUS and I loved being with our great Military Men and Women - what a spectacular job they do! [Twitter for iPhone]

May 30, 2019 06:21:45 AM The Greatest Presidential Harassment in history. After spending $40,000,000 over two dark years, with unlimited access, people, resources and cooperation, highly conflicted Robert Mueller would have brought charges, if he had ANYTHING, but there were no charges to bring! [Twitter for iPhone]

May 30, 2019 06:38:15 AM ....say he fought back against this phony crime that didn't exist, this horrendous false acquisition, and he shouldn't fight back, he should just sit back and take it. Could this be Obstruction? No, Mueller didn't find Obstruction either. Presidential Harassment! [Twitter for iPhone]

May 30, 2019 06:38:15 AM Russia, Russia, Russia! That's all you heard at the beginning of this Witch Hunt Hoax...And now Russia has disappeared because I had nothing to do with Russia helping me to get elected. It was a crime that didn't exist. So now the Dems and their partner, the Fake News Media,...... [Twitter for iPhone]

May 30, 2019 06:57:47 AM ....say he fought back against this phony crime that didn't exist, this horrendous false accusation, and he shouldn't fight back, he should just sit back and take it. Could this be Obstruction? No, Mueller didn't find Obstruction either. Presidential Harassment! [Twitter for iPhone]

May 30, 2019 06:57:47 AM Russia, Russia, Russia! That's all you heard at the beginning of this Witch Hunt Hoax...And now Russia has disappeared because I had nothing to do with Russia helping me to get elected. It was a crime that didn't exist. So now the Dems and their partner, the Fake News Media,...... [Twitter for iPhone]

May 30, 2019 08:41:43 AM Congressman John Ratcliffe, "The Trump Campaign clearly did not conspire or collude." @FoxNews [Twitter for iPhone]

May 30, 2019 09:41:24 AM "Comey and Brennan are turning on each other." @kilmeade [Twitter for iPhone]

May 30, 2019 10:34:11 AM Robert Mueller came to the Oval Office (along with other potential candidates) seeking to be named the Director of the FBI. He had already been in that position for 12 years, I told him NO. The next day he was named Special Counsel - A total Conflict of Interest. NICE! [Twitter for iPhone]

May 30, 2019 11:27:19 AM Very sad to hear the news on the passing of my friend, Senator Thad Cochran. He was a real Senator with incredible values - even flew back to Senate from Mississippi for important Healthcare Vote when he was desperately ill. Thad never let our Country (or me) down! [Twitter for iPhone]

May 30, 2019 11:28:40 AM https://t.co/J80cxMYVDX [Twitter for iPhone]

May 30, 2019 11:30:01 AM Just arrived in Colorado. Getting ready to deliver the commencement speech at the Air Force Academy graduation. Very exciting - probably will be broadcast live on TV. They want good ratings! [Twitter for iPhone]

May 30, 2019 04:12:46 PM RT @WhiteHouse: Thank you to all of the brave men and women graduating from the United States Air Force Academy today! "You could have ch... [Twitter for iPhone]

May 30, 2019 04:12:49 PM RT @WhiteHouse: "You are ready to fly, fight, and win!" — President Donald J. Trump https://t.co/w6aWnp8K88 [Twitter for iPhone]

May 30, 2019 04:16:00 PM Yesterday, Border Patrol agents apprehended the largest group of illegal aliens ever: 1,036 people who illegally crossed the border in El Paso around 4am. Democrats need to stand by our incredible Border Patrol and finally fix the loopholes at our Border! https://t.co/6K1rIUzorM [Twitter for iPhone]

May 30, 2019 05:23:21 PM The Navy put out a disclaimer on the McCain story. Looks like the story was an exaggeration, or even Fake News - but why not, everything else is! [Twitter for iPhone]

May 30, 2019 06:30:19 PM On June 10th, the United States will impose a 5% Tariff on all goods coming into our Country from Mexico, until such time as illegal migrants coming through Mexico, and into our Country, STOP. The Tariff will gradually increase until the Illegal Immigration problem is remedied,.. [Twitter for iPhone]

May 30, 2019 06:30:20 PM ....at which time the Tariffs will be removed. Details from the White House to follow. [Twitter for iPhone]

May 30, 2019 08:52:12 PM I will be watching @AlanDersh on @IngrahamAngle at 10:00 P.M. He speaks the truth! [Twitter for iPhone]

May 30, 2019 08:52:40 PM RT @TheHillOpinion: Shame on Robert Mueller for exceeding his role Read the full story: https://t.co/lbU4at5q8E Via: @AlanDersh https://t... [Twitter for iPhone]

May 30, 2019 09:31:01 PM RT @realDonaldTrump: How do you impeach a Republican President for a crime that was committed by the Democrats? WITCH-HUNT! [Twitter for iPhone]

May 31, 2019 07:38:16 AM Sean Davis, The Federalist: "Mueller proved his entire operation was a political hit job. Still ZERO evidence of Trump-Russia Collusion, and no new evidence from Mueller." @TuckerCarlson @FoxNews [Twitter for iPhone]

May 31, 2019 07:51:10 AM Congratulations to the @AF_Academy Class of 2019! https://t.co/A4Rxd1BsVn [Twitter for iPhone]

May 31, 2019 08:14:26 AM Hard to believe that with the Crisis on the Border, the Dems won't do the quick and easy fix. Would solve the problem but they want Open Borders, which equals crime! [Twitter for iPhone]

May 31, 2019 08:30:29 AM Mexico has taken advantage of the United States for decades. Because of the Dems, our Immigration Laws are BAD. Mexico makes a FORTUNE from the U.S., have for decades, they can easily fix this problem. Time for them to finally do what must be done! [Twitter for iPhone]

May 31, 2019 09:27:51 AM In order not to pay Tariffs, if they start rising, companies will leave Mexico, which has taken 30% of our Auto Industry, and come back home to the USA. Mexico must take back their country from the drug lords and cartels. The Tariff is about stopping drugs as well as illegals! [Twitter for iPhone]

May 31, 2019 09:41:24 AM 90% of the Drugs coming into the United States come through Mexico & our Southern Border. 80,000 people died last year, 1,000,000 people ruined. This has gone on for many years & nothing has been done about it. We have a 100 Billion Dollar Trade Deficit with Mexico. It's time! [Twitter for iPhone]

May 31, 2019 01:08:33 PM Saddened to hear about the loss of John Pinto, a Navajo Code Talker in World War II, over the Memorial Day Weekend. The Code Talkers are true American HEROES and John never stopped serving his fellow citizens as a longtime New Mexico State Senator. John, Rest In Peace! [Twitter for iPhone]

May 31, 2019 01:11:25 PM .@SeanHannity is having a DEEP STATE SHOW tonight on Fox News at 9:00 PM (E), exposing the tremendous abuse of power that has been uncovered. Tremendous guests, a must see – Enjoy! [Twitter for iPhone]

May 31, 2019 02:12:32 PM ....on the basis of their sexual orientation. My Administration has launched a global campaign to decriminalize homosexuality and invite all nations to join us in this effort! [Twitter for iPhone]

May 31, 2019 02:12:32 PM As we celebrate LGBT Pride Month and recognize the outstanding contributions LGBT people have made to our great Nation, let us also stand in solidarity with the many LGBT people who live in dozens of countries worldwide that punish, imprison, or even execute individuals.... [Twitter for iPhone]

May 31, 2019 03:02:16 PM GREAT NEWS! #MAGA https://t.co/91Yk8B11bP [Twitter Media Studio]

May 31, 2019 03:35:41 PM I will be announcing my Second Term Presidential Run with First Lady Melania, Vice President Mike Pence, and Second Lady Karen Pence on June 18th in Orlando, Florida, at the 20,000 seat Amway Center. Join us for this Historic Rally! Tickets: https://t.co/1krDP2oQvG [Twitter for iPhone]

Jun 1, 2019 09:43:06 AM Spoke to Virginia Governor @RalphNortham last night, and the Mayor and Vice Mayor of Virginia Beach this morning, to offer condolences to that great community. The Federal Government is there, and will be, for whatever they may need. God bless the families and all! [Twitter for iPhone]

Jun 1, 2019 02:48:55 PM Emmet Flood, who came to the White House to help me with the Mueller Report, will be leaving service on June 14th. He has done an outstanding job – NO COLLUSION - NO OBSTRUCTION! Case Closed! Emmet is my friend, and I thank him for the GREAT JOB he has done. [Twitter for iPhone]

Jun 1, 2019 02:50:47 PM The United States stands ready to work with @NayibBukele to advance prosperity in El Salvador and the hemisphere. Congratulations President Bukele on your inauguration! [Twitter for iPhone]

Jun 1, 2019 03:37:03 PM Washington Post got it wrong, as usual. The U.S. is charging 25% against 250 Billion Dollars of goods shipped from China, not 200 BD. Also, China is paying a heavy cost in that they will subsidize goods to keep them coming, devalue their currency, yet companies are moving to..... [Twitter for iPhone]

Jun 1, 2019 03:37:04 PM ...travesty that is taking place in allowing millions of people to easily meander through their country and INVADE the U.S., not to mention the Drugs & Human Trafficking pouring in through Mexico. Are the Drug Lords, Cartels & Coyotes really running Mexico? We will soon find out! [Twitter for iPhone]

Jun 1, 2019 03:37:04 PM ....U.S. in order to avoid paying the 25% Tariff. Like Mexican companies will move back to the United States once the Tariff reaches the higher levels. They took many of our companies & jobs, the foolish Pols let it happen, and now they will come back unless Mexico stops the..... [Twitter for iPhone]

Jun 1, 2019 05:20:56 PM When you are the "Piggy Bank" Nation that foreign countries have been robbing and deceiving for years, the word TARIFF is a beautiful word indeed! Others must treat the United States fairly and with respect - We are no longer the "fools" of the past! [Twitter for iPhone]

Jun 1, 2019 06:14:18 PM Thank you so much, Franklin! https://t.co/LK7sHUGrZ7 [Twitter for iPhone]

Jun 1, 2019 06:14:27 PM RT @financialissues: .@Franklin_Graham will be joining me LIVE on Financial Issues to talk about the nationwide movement, Special Day of Pr… [Twitter for iPhone]

Jun 1, 2019 06:15:30 PM RT @Franklin_Graham: I also hope thousands of pastors across the nation will take a moment in their service this Sunday to pray for the Pre… [Twitter for iPhone]

Jun 1, 2019 06:15:44 PM RT @Franklin_Graham: Thank you to the thousands of people who have already let me know that you'll be praying this Sunday. If you'd like to… [Twitter for iPhone]

Jun 1, 2019 06:15:55 PM RT @Franklin_Graham: I want to remind everyone of the importance of praying for @POTUS @realDonaldTrump this Sun., June 2. We need to pray… [Twitter for iPhone]

Jun 1, 2019 06:16:09 PM RT @jackngraham: I'm joining my good friend @Franklin_Graham and hundreds of other faith leaders in asking our churches across America to p… [Twitter for iPhone]

Jun 1, 2019 06:18:33 PM RT @toddstarnes: Franklin Graham Calls for National Day of Prayer for President Trump - https://t.co/WS2nRB1oME https://t.co/Smu9eC9YAG [Twitter for iPhone]

Jun 1, 2019 06:19:53 PM RT @Franklin_Graham: Announcing Special Day of Prayer for the President - June 2 https://t.co/IxtApdsjOI [Twitter for iPhone]

Jun 1, 2019 06:23:49 PM We will all stick together and WIN! Thank you Franklin. https://t.co/IS7OfkmGKA [Twitter for iPhone]

Jun 1, 2019 06:25:54 PM RT @FaithandFreedom: We are encouraged to join together in prayer for Pres. @realDonaldTrump on June 2nd with faith leaders such as @Frankl… [Twitter for iPhone]

Jun 1, 2019 06:26:56 PM RT @JennaBrowder: "This is not a political endorsement. It's just simply praying for the president." - @Franklin_Graham tells me and @JohnJ… [Twitter for iPhone]

Jun 1, 2019 06:27:17 PM RT @JennaBrowder: #FaithNation everyday at 6pm eastern — join me and @JohnJessupCBN over on the new 24/7 CBN News Channel by downloading ou… [Twitter for iPhone]

Jun 1, 2019 06:31:48 PM RT @DavidBrodyCBN: .@jaketapper and @CNN are spreading a false story. This is a perfect example of how the liberal media takes something co… [Twitter for iPhone]

Jun 1, 2019 06:32:24 PM RT @peterbakernyt: Trump to award Medal of Freedom to Arthur Laffer, father of supply side economics that gained prominence in the Reagan y… [Twitter for iPhone]

Jun 1, 2019 06:32:56 PM RT @DavidBrodyCBN: Trump's approval rating hits highest point in two years https://t.co/TT09Ovd5r8 [Twitter for iPhone]

Jun 1, 2019 08:58:47 PM THE TRUTH! The Witch Hunt is dead. Thank you @marcthiessen. https://t.co/myKaSEnbs7 [Twitter for iPhone]

Jun 1, 2019 09:28:39 PM The Great Jerry West will be receiving our Nation's highest civilian honor, The Presidential Medal of Freedom, for his outstanding career, both on and off the court. Happy Birthday Jerry! @Sen_JoeManchin https://t.co/3kNEpteYfW [Twitter for iPhone]

Jun 2, 2019 05:55:30 AM RT @realDonaldTrump: I will be announcing my Second Term Presidential Run with First Lady Melania, Vice President Mike Pence, and Second La... [Twitter for iPhone]

Jun 2, 2019 06:09:50 AM The Democrats are doing nothing on the Border to address the Humanitarian and National Security Crisis! Could be fixed so easily if they would vote with Republicans to fix the loopholes. [Twitter for iPhone]

Jun 2, 2019 06:44:12 AM ....Coyotes and Illegal Immigrants, which they can do very easily, or our many companies and jobs that have been foolishly allowed to move South of the Border, will be brought back into the United States through taxation (Tariffs). America has had enough! [Twitter for iPhone]

Jun 2, 2019 06:44:12 AM People have been saying for years that we should talk to Mexico. The problem is that Mexico is an "abuser" of the United States, taking but never giving. It has been this way for decades. Either they stop the invasion of our Country by Drug Dealers, Cartels, Human Traffickers.... [Twitter for iPhone]

Jun 2, 2019 06:53:25 AM The Wall is under construction and moving along quickly, despite all of the Radical Liberal Democrat lawsuits. What are they thinking as our Country is invaded by so many people (illegals) and things (Drugs) that we do not want. Make America Great Again! [Twitter for iPhone]

Jun 2, 2019 07:30:10 AM NO COLLUSION, NO OBSTRUCTION, NO NOTHING! "What the Democrats are trying to do is the biggest sin in the impeachment business." David Rivkin, Constitutional Scholar. Meantime, the Dems are getting nothing done in Congress. They are frozen stiff. Get back to work, much to do! [Twitter for iPhone]

Jun 2, 2019 07:44:24 AM I never called Meghan Markle "nasty." Made up by the Fake News Media, and they got caught cold! Will @CNN, @nytimes and others apologize? Doubt it! [Twitter for iPhone]

Jun 2, 2019 07:45:31 AM RT @realDonaldTrump: GREAT NEWS! #MAGA https://t.co/91Yk8B11bP [Twitter for iPhone]

Jun 2, 2019 08:00:57 AM RT @realDonaldTrump: THE TRUTH! The Witch Hunt is dead. Thank you @marcthiessen. https://t.co/myKaSEnbs7 [Twitter for iPhone]

Jun 2, 2019 01:13:04 PM Peggy Noonan, the simplistic writer for Trump Haters all, is stuck in the past glory of Reagan and has no idea what is happening with the Radical Left Democrats, or how vicious and desperate they are. Mueller had to correct his ridiculous statement, Peggy never understood it! [Twitter for iPhone]

Jun 2, 2019 01:19:47 PM Mexico is sending a big delegation to talk about the Border. Problem is, they've been "talking" for 25 years. We want action, not talk. They could solve the Border Crisis in one day if they so desired. Otherwise, our companies and jobs are coming back to the USA! [Twitter for iPhone]

Jun 2, 2019 06:43:35 PM Democrats can't impeach a Republican President for crimes committed by Democrats. The facts are "pouring" in. The Greatest Witch Hunt in American History! Congress, go back to work and help us at the Border, with Drug Prices and on Infrastructure. [Twitter for iPhone]

Jun 2, 2019 06:49:30 PM Hearing word that Russia, Syria and, to a lesser extent, Iran, are bombing the hell out of Idlib Province in Syria, and indiscriminately killing many innocent civilians. The World is watching this butchery. What is the purpose, what will it get you? STOP! [Twitter for iPhone]

Jun 2, 2019 08:41:17 PM Kevin Hassett, who has done such a great job for me and the Administration, will be leaving shortly. His very talented replacement will be named as soon as I get back to the U.S. I want to thank Kevin for all he has done - he is a true friend! [Twitter for iPhone]

Jun 2, 2019 08:44:41 PM BIG NEWS! As I promised two weeks ago, the first shipment of LNG has just left the Cameron LNG Export Facility in Louisiana. Not only have thousands of JOBS been created in USA, we're shipping freedom and opportunity abroad! [Twitter for iPhone]

Jun 3, 2019 02:11:19 AM RT @SteveScalise: Thank you for your leadership on this, @realDonaldTrump! It was great to visit the Cameron LNG export facility with you l... [Twitter for iPhone]

Jun 3, 2019 02:51:18 AM .@SadiqKhan, who by all accounts has done a terrible job as Mayor of London, has been foolishly "nasty" to the visiting President of the United States, by far the most important ally of the United Kingdom. He is a stone cold loser who should focus on crime in London, not me...... [Twitter for iPhone]

Jun 3, 2019 02:51:19 AM ....Kahn reminds me very much of our very dumb and incompetent Mayor of NYC, de Blasio, who has also done a terrible job - only half his height. In any event, I look forward to being a great friend to the United Kingdom, and am looking very much forward to my visit. Landing now! [Twitter for iPhone]

Jun 3, 2019 03:54:30 AM Thank you! USGB https://t.co/hm6RXLeWpp [Twitter for iPhone]

Jun 3, 2019 05:07:11 AM China is subsidizing its product in order that it can continue to be sold in the USA. Many firms are leaving China for other countries, including the United States, in order to avoid paying the Tariffs. No visible increase in costs or inflation, but U.S. is taking Billions! [Twitter for iPhone]

Jun 3, 2019 05:37:28 AM Just arrived in the United Kingdom. The only problem is that @CNN is the primary source of news available from the U.S. After watching it for a short while, I turned it off. All negative & so much Fake News, very bad for U.S. Big ratings drop. Why doesn't owner @ATT do something? [Twitter for iPhone]

Jun 3, 2019 05:50:33 AM I believe that if people stoped using or subscribing to @ATT, they would be forced to make big changes at @CNN, which is dying in the ratings anyway. It is so unfair with such bad, Fake News! Why wouldn't they act. When the World watches @CNN, it gets a false picture of USA. Sad! [Twitter for iPhone]

Jun 3, 2019 11:42:35 AM RT @RoyalFamily: The President and Mrs Trump stand with The Queen, The Prince of Wales and The Duchess of Cornwall as the US and UK nationa... [Twitter for iPhone]

Jun 3, 2019 11:42:41 AM RT @RoyalFamily: The President and The Prince of Wales inspect a Guard of Honour formed by Nijmegen Company, Grenadier Guards. #USStateVisi... [Twitter for iPhone]

Jun 3, 2019 11:42:46 AM RT @RoyalFamily: The Queen, President Trump and the First Lady view a display of items from the Royal Collection illustrating the enduring... [Twitter for iPhone]

Jun 3, 2019 12:41:37 PM ....Fake News will be working hard to find them. Great love all around. Also, big Trade Deal is possible once U.K. gets rid of the shackles. Already starting to talk! [Twitter for iPhone]

Jun 3, 2019 12:41:37 PM London part of trip is going really well. The Queen and the entire Royal family have been fantastic. The relationship with the United Kingdom is very strong. Tremendous crowds of well wishers and people that love our Country. Haven't seen any protests yet, but I'm sure the.... [Twitter for iPhone]

Jun 3, 2019 12:44:55 PM Russia has informed us that they have removed most of their people from Venezuela. [Twitter for iPhone]

Jun 3, 2019 01:11:26 PM As a sign of good faith, Mexico should immediately stop the flow of people and drugs through their country and to our Southern Border. They can do it if they want! [Twitter for iPhone]

Jun 3, 2019 05:29:19 PM RT @RoyalFamily: The Prince of Wales, The Duchess of Cornwall @ClarenceHouse The Duke and Duchess of Cambridge @KensingtonRoyal, The Duke o... [Twitter for iPhone]

Jun 3, 2019 05:29:44 PM RT @WhiteHouse: President @realDonaldTrump and @FLOTUS are guests of Her Majesty Queen Elizabeth II for a State Banquet at Buckingham Palac... [Twitter for iPhone]

Jun 3, 2019 05:29:57 PM RT @WhiteHouse: "This evening, we thank God for the brave sons of the United Kingdom and the United States, who defeated the Nazis and the... [Twitter for iPhone]

Jun 3, 2019 05:29:59 PM RT @WhiteHouse: "On behalf of all Americans, I offer a toast to the eternal friendship of our people, the vitality of our nations, and to t... [Twitter for iPhone]

Jun 3, 2019 06:58:38 PM House just passed the 19.1 Billion Dollar Disaster Aid Bill. Great, now we will get it done in the Senate! Farmers, Puerto Rico and all will be very happy. [Twitter for iPhone]

Jun 4, 2019 03:17:46 AM #USStateVisitUSGB https://t.co/8eN2bvtLLU [Twitter for iPhone]

Jun 4, 2019 07:48:03 AM RT @TheDukeOfYork: GBUSOn Day 2 of the #USStateVisit, The Duke of York & Prime Minister @TheresaMay welcome President Donald Trump @POTUS t... [Twitter for iPhone]

Jun 4, 2019 08:52:02 AM https://t.co/tlGGQJahr1 [Twitter for iPhone]

Jun 4, 2019 09:50:13 AM Thank you @Theresa_May!USGB https://t.co/zFJj47UuHO [Twitter for iPhone]

Jun 4, 2019 01:09:31 PM Just had a big victory in Federal Court over the Democrats in the House on the desperately needed Border Wall. A big step in the right direction. Wall is under construction! [Twitter for iPhone]

Jun 4, 2019 05:07:17 PM RT @RoyalFamily: Tonight, The Prince of Wales and The Duchess of Cornwall attended a dinner in London hosted by @POTUS and @FLOTUS on the s... [Twitter for iPhone]

Jun 4, 2019 05:09:21 PM RT @USAmbUK: President @realdonaldtrump and @FLOTUS welcome The Prince of Wales and The Duchess of Cornwall as they arrive at Winfield Hous... [Twitter for iPhone]

Jun 4, 2019 07:04:58 PM Can you imagine Cryin' Chuck Schumer saying out loud, for all to hear, that I am bluffing with respect to putting Tariffs on Mexico. What a Creep. He would rather have our Country fail with drugs & Immigration than give Republicans a win. But he gave Mexico bad advice, no bluff! [Twitter for iPhone]

Jun 4, 2019 07:30:55 PM Washed up psycho @BetteMidler was forced to apologize for a statement she attributed to me that turned out to be totally fabricated by her in order to make "your great president" look really bad. She got caught, just like the Fake News Media gets caught. A sick scammer! [Twitter for iPhone]

Jun 5, 2019 12:41:54 AM #USStateVisitUSGB https://t.co/XKa0iJRQYO [Twitter for iPhone]

Jun 5, 2019 12:55:19 AM Plagiarism charge against Sleepy Joe Biden on his ridiculous Climate Change Plan is a big problem, but the Corrupt Media will save him. His other problem is that he is drawing flies, not people, to his Rallies. Nobody is showing up, I mean nobody. You can't win without people! [Twitter for iPhone]

Jun 5, 2019 01:01:19 AM I kept hearing that there would be "massive" rallies against me in the UK, but it was quite the opposite. The big crowds, which the Corrupt Media hates to show, were those that gathered in support of the USA and me. They were big & enthusiastic as opposed to the organized flops! [Twitter for iPhone]

Jun 5, 2019 01:46:23 AM RT @realDonaldTrump: Just had a big victory in Federal Court over the Democrats in the House on the desperately needed Border Wall. A big s… [Twitter for iPhone]

Jun 5, 2019 01:57:58 AM If the totally Corrupt Media was less corrupt, I would be up by 15 points in the polls based on our tremendous success with the economy, maybe Best Ever! If the Corrup Media was actually fair, I would be up by 25 points. Nevertheless, despite the Fake News, we're doing great! [Twitter for iPhone]

Jun 5, 2019 02:31:34 AM .@FLOTUS Melania and I send our deepest condolences to President Reuven Rivlin and the entire State of Israel upon the passing of Mrs. Nechama Rivlin. Mrs. Rivlin represented her beloved country with grace and stature. We will miss her along with all those who knew her. [Twitter for iPhone]

Jun 5, 2019 03:02:27 AM Could not have been treated more warmly in the United Kingdom by the Royal Family or the people. Our relationship has never been better, and I see a very big Trade Deal down the road. "This trip has been an incredible success for the President." @IngrahamAngle [Twitter for iPhone]

Jun 5, 2019 03:12:19 AM House Democrats, fresh off a Republican victory against them (in Federal Court) on the Wall, keep asking people to come and testify regarding the No Collusion Witch Hunt. They are very unhappy with the Mueller Report, especially with his corrective letter, & now want a Do Over! [Twitter for iPhone]

Jun 5, 2019 03:17:07 AM If the totally Corrupt Media was less corrupt, I would be up by 15 points in the polls based on our tremendous success with the economy, maybe Best Ever! If the Corrupt Media was actually fair, I would be up by 25 points. Nevertheless, despite the Fake News, we're doing great! [Twitter for iPhone]

Jun 5, 2019 03:20:14 AM "House Republicans support the President on Tariffs with Mexico all the way, & that makes any measure the President takes on the Border totally Veto proof. Why wouldn't you as Republicans support him when that will allow our President to make a better deal." Thank you @GOPLeader [Twitter for iPhone]

Jun 5, 2019 07:18:50 AM As we approach the 75th Anniversary of D-Day, we proudly commemorate those heroic and honorable patriots who gave their all for the cause of freedom during some of history's darkest hours. #DDay75 https://t.co/hjTkdM7VcN [Twitter for iPhone]

Jun 5, 2019 05:42:39 PM ....talks with Mexico will resume tomorrow with the understanding that, if no agreement is reached, Tariffs at the 5% level will begin on Monday, with monthly increases as per schedule. The higher the Tariffs go, the higher the number of companies that will move back to the USA! [Twitter for iPhone]

Jun 5, 2019 05:42:39 PM Immigration discussions at the White House with representatives of Mexico have ended for the day. Progress is being made, but not nearly enough! Border arrests for May are at 133,000 because of Mexico & the Democrats in Congress refusing to budge on immigration reform. Further... [Twitter for iPhone]

Jun 6, 2019 12:40:23 AM #DDay75thAnniversary #DDay75 https://t.co/BwfVEt7gTG [Twitter for iPhone]

Jun 6, 2019 12:55:49 AM "The President has received glowing reviews from the British Media. Here at home, not so much. MSNBC Ramps up hateful coverage and promotes conspiracy theories during Trump's trip to Europe." @seanhannity The good news is that @maddow is dying in the ratings, along with @CNN! [Twitter for iPhone]

Jun 6, 2019 12:57:16 AM A big and beautiful day today! [Twitter for iPhone]

Jun 6, 2019 02:38:28 AM Heading over to Normandy to celebrate some of the bravest that ever lived. We are eternally grateful! #DDay75thAnniversary #DDay75 https://t.co/rg15c32Gow [Twitter for iPhone]

Jun 6, 2019 06:50:25 AM #DDay75thAnniversary https://t.co/0fYfpvUghk [Twitter for iPhone]

Jun 6, 2019 11:36:32 AM So sorry to hear about the terrible accident involving our GREAT West Point Cadets. We mourn the loss of life and pray for the injured. God Bless them ALL! [Twitter for iPhone]

Jun 6, 2019 12:36:28 PM Today, we remember those who fell, and we honor all who fought, here in Normandy. They won back this ground for civilization. To more than 170 Veterans of the Second World War who join us today: You are among the very greatest Americans who will ever live! #DDay75thAnniversary https://t.co/n0uIVHlkRL [Twitter for iPhone]

Jun 6, 2019 12:55:38 PM To the men who sit behind me, and to the boys who rest in the field before me: your example will never grow old. Your legend will never tire, and your spirit - brave, unyielding, and true - will NEVER DIE! #DDay75thAnniversary https://t.co/5qwQjkvHdl [Twitter for iPhone]

Jun 6, 2019 01:06:50 PM Just signed Disaster Aid Bill to help Americans who have been hit by recent catastrophic storms. So important for our GREAT American farmers and ranchers. Help for GA, FL, IA, NE, NC, and CA. Puerto Rico should love President Trump. Without me, they would have been shut out! https://t.co/HXvYYdcNW5 [Twitter for iPhone]

Jun 6, 2019 02:04:14 PM #DDay75thAnniversary https://t.co/GIsoLML4NP [Twitter for iPhone]

Jun 6, 2019 02:32:42 PM RT @IngrahamAngle: For my full interview with @realDonaldTrump from Normandy, tune in tonight #IngrahamAngle @FoxNews 10pET https://t.c... [Twitter for iPhone]

Jun 7, 2019 01:49:32 AM John Solomon: Factual errors and major omissions in the Mueller Report show that it is totally biased against Trump. [Twitter for iPhone]

Jun 7, 2019 02:01:43 AM "Mueller's report was pure, political garbage!" @SeanHannity https://t.co/lRjtoPTiO8 [Twitter for iPhone]

Jun 7, 2019 02:43:36 AM #DDay75thAnniversary #DDay75 https://t.co/c8OTeHVScr [Twitter for iPhone]

Jun 7, 2019 06:02:16 AM https://t.co/INh7hQiQTN [Twitter for iPhone]

Jun 7, 2019 06:29:30 AM https://t.co/xrrzYhPu0i [Twitter for iPhone]

Jun 7, 2019 09:44:50 AM HAPPY BIRTHDAY to our great @VP Mike Pence! https://t.co/k2fmu5bR5R [Twitter for iPhone]

Jun 7, 2019 11:36:55 AM China is subsidizing its product in order that it can continue to be sold in the USA. Many firms are leaving China for other countries, including the United States, in order to avoid paying the Tariffs. No visible increase in costs or inflation, but U.S. is taking in Billions! [Twitter for iPhone]

Jun 7, 2019 11:44:10 AM Nervous Nancy Pelosi is a disgrace to herself and her family for having made such a disgusting statement, especially since I was with foreign leaders overseas. There is no evidence for such a thing to have been said. Nervous Nancy & Dems are getting Zero work done in Congress,... [Twitter for iPhone]

Jun 7, 2019 11:44:11 AM ....and have no intention of doing anything other going on a fishing expedition to see if they can find anything on me - both illegal & unprecedented in U.S. history. There was no Collusion - Investigate the Investigators! Go to work on Drug Price Reductions & Infrastructure! [Twitter for iPhone]

Jun 7, 2019 11:57:47 AM Nervous Nancy Pelosi is a disgrace to herself and her family for having made such a disgusting statement, especially since I was with foreign leaders overseas. There is no evidence for such a thing to have been said. Nervous Nancy & Dems are getting Zero work done in Congress.... [Twitter for iPhone]

Jun 7, 2019 11:57:48 AM ...and have no intention of doing anything other than going on a fishing expedition to see if they can find anything on me - both illegal & unprecedented in U.S. history. There was no Collusion - Investigate the Investigators! Go to work on Drug Price Reductions & Infrastructure! [Twitter for iPhone]

Jun 7, 2019 12:16:41 PM If we are able to make the deal with Mexico, & there is a good chance that we will, they will begin purchasing Farm & Agricultural products at very high levels, starting immediately. If we are unable to make the deal, Mexico will begin paying Tariffs at the 5% level on Monday! [Twitter for iPhone]

Jun 7, 2019 12:27:31 PM Democrats are incapable of doing a good and solid Immigration Bill! [Twitter for iPhone]

Jun 7, 2019 12:38:01 PM For all of the money we are spending, NASA should NOT be talking about going to the Moon - We did that 50 years ago. They should be focused on the much bigger things we are doing, including Mars (of which the Moon is a part), Defense and Science! [Twitter for iPhone]

Jun 7, 2019 12:43:38 PM Heading back to D.C. Many great things are happening for our Country! [Twitter for iPhone]

Jun 7, 2019 04:43:41 PM Dow Jones has best week of the year! [Twitter for iPhone]

Jun 7, 2019 07:25:20 PM ....stem the tide of Migration through Mexico, and to our Southern Border. This is being done to greatly reduce, or eliminate, Illegal Immigration coming from Mexico and into the United States. Details of the agreement will be released shortly be the State Department. Thank you! [Twitter for iPhone]

Jun 7, 2019 07:25:20 PM I am pleased to inform you that The United States of America has reached a signed agreement with Mexico. The Tariffs scheduled to be implemented by the U.S. on Monday, against Mexico, are hereby indefinitely suspended. Mexico, in turn, has agreed to take strong measures to...... [Twitter for iPhone]

Jun 7, 2019 07:31:07 PM ....stem the tide of Migration through Mexico, and to our Southern Border. This is being done to greatly reduce, or eliminate, Illegal Immigration coming from Mexico and into the United States. Details of the agreement will be released shortly by the State Department. Thank you! [Twitter for iPhone]

Jun 7, 2019 07:31:07 PM I am pleased to inform you that The United States of America has reached a signed agreement with Mexico. The Tariffs scheduled to be implemented by the U.S. on Monday, against Mexico, are hereby indefinitely suspended. Mexico, in turn, has agreed to take strong measures to.... [Twitter for iPhone]

Jun 8, 2019 05:47:38 AM While the reviews and reporting on our Border Immigration Agreement with Mexico have been very good, there has nevertheless been much false reporting (surprise!) by the Fake and Corrupt News Media, such as Comcast/NBC, CNN, @nytimes & @washingtonpost. These "Fakers" are Bad News! [Twitter for iPhone]

Jun 8, 2019 05:55:26 AM Brandon Judd, National Border Patrol Council: "That's going to be a huge deal because Mexico will be using their strong Immigration Laws - A game changer. People no longer will be released into the U.S." Also, 6000 Mexican Troops at their Southern Border. Currently there are few! [Twitter for iPhone]

Jun 8, 2019 06:02:17 AM Mexico will try very hard, and if they do that, this will be a very successful agreement for both the United States and Mexico! [Twitter for iPhone]

Jun 8, 2019 07:03:41 AM MEXICO HAS AGREED TO IMMEDIATELY BEGIN BUYING LARGE QUANTITIES OF AGRICULTURAL PRODUCT FROM OUR GREAT PATRIOT FARMERS! [Twitter for iPhone]

Jun 8, 2019 08:43:35 AM Nervous Nancy Pelosi & the Democrat House are getting nothing done. Perhaps they could lead the way with the USMCA, the spectacular & very popular new Trade Deal that replaces NAFTA, the worst Trade Deal in the history of the U.S.A. Great for our Farmers, Manufacturers & Unions! [Twitter for iPhone]

Jun 8, 2019 08:47:29 AM Everyone very excited about the new deal with Mexico! [Twitter for iPhone]

Jun 8, 2019 09:20:59 AM I would like to thank the President of Mexico, Andres Manuel Lopez Obrador, and his foreign minister, Marcelo Ebrard, together with all of the many representatives of both the United States and Mexico, for working so long and hard to get our agreement on immigration completed! [Twitter for iPhone]

Jun 8, 2019 06:25:11 PM Watched MSNBC this morning just to see what the opposition was saying about events of the past week. Such lies, almost everything they were saying was the opposite of the truth. Fake News! No wonder their ratings, along with CNN, are WAY DOWN. The hatred Comcast has is amazing! [Twitter for iPhone]

Jun 8, 2019 06:44:39 PM Just watched the Great @RickBarry44, Backetball Hall of Famer, on the @marklevinshow @FoxNews. A wonderful interview of a very smart and interesting guy by the man, Mark Levin, who has the number one bestselling book, Unfreedom of the Press. Two Winners! [Twitter for iPhone]

Jun 8, 2019 07:24:14 PM Just watched the Great @Rick24Barry, Basketball Hall of Famer, on the @marklevinshow @FoxNews. A wonderful interview of a very smart and interesting guy by the man, Mark Levin, who has the number one bestselling book, Unfreedom of the Press. Two Winners! [Twitter for iPhone]

Jun 8, 2019 10:54:08 PM ....other than to know he was, and is, a total Loser. When he makes statements about me, they are made up, he knows nothing! [Twitter for iPhone]

Jun 8, 2019 10:54:08 PM Little @DonnyDeutsch, whose show, like his previous shoebiz tries, is a disaster, has been saying that I had been a friend of his. This is false. He, & separately @ErinBurnett, used to BEG me to be on episodes of the Apprentice (both were bad), but that was it. Hardly knew him,.. [Twitter for iPhone]

Jun 8, 2019 11:08:26 PM I know it is not at all "Presidential" to hit back at the Corrupt Media, or people who work for the Corrupt Media, when they make false statements about me or the Trump Administration. Problem is, if you don't hit back, people believe the Fake News is true. So we'll hit back! [Twitter for iPhone]

Jun 8, 2019 11:09:51 PM RT @realDonaldTrump: MEXICO HAS AGREED TO IMMEDIATELY BEGIN BUYING LARGE QUANTITIES OF AGRICULTURAL PRODUCT FROM OUR GREAT PATRIOT FARMERS! [Twitter for iPhone]

Jun 8, 2019 11:10:44 PM RT @realDonaldTrump: ....stem the tide of Migration through Mexico, and to our Southern Border. This is being done to greatly reduce, or el... [Twitter for iPhone]

Jun 8, 2019 11:10:47 PM RT @realDonaldTrump: I am pleased to inform you that The United States of America has reached a signed agreement with Mexico. The Tariffs s... [Twitter for iPhone]

Jun 9, 2019 07:26:37 AM .....there is not, we can always go back to our previous, very profitable, position of Tariffs - But I don't believe that will be necessary. The Failing @nytimes, & ratings challenged @CNN, will do anything possible to see our Country fail! They are truly The Enemy of the People! [Twitter for iPhone]

Jun 9, 2019 07:26:37 AM .....not mentioned in yesterday press release, one in particular, were agreed upon. That will be announced at the appropriate time. There is now going to be great cooperation between Mexico & the USA, something that didn't exist for decades. However, if for some unknown reason... [Twitter for iPhone]

Jun 9, 2019 07:26:37 AM .....Mexico was not being cooperative on the Border in things we had, or didn't have, and now I have full confidence, especially after speaking to their President yesterday, that they will be very cooperative and want to get the job properly done. Importantly, some things..... [Twitter for iPhone]

Jun 9, 2019 07:26:37 AM Another false report in the Failing @nytimes. We have been trying to get some of these Border Actions for a long time, as have other administrations, but were not able to get them, or get them in full, until our signed agreement with Mexico. Additionally, and for many years,.... [Twitter for iPhone]

Jun 9, 2019 07:45:21 AM Twitter should let the banned Conservative Voices back onto their platform, without restriction. It's called Freedom of Speech, remember. You are making a Giant Mistake! [Twitter for iPhone]

Jun 9, 2019 08:26:08 AM If President Obama made the deals that I have made, both at the Border and for the Economy, the Corrupt Media would be hailing them as Incredible, & a National Holiday would be immediately declared. With me, despite our record setting Economy and all that I have done, no credit! [Twitter for iPhone]

Jun 9, 2019 08:36:36 AM RT @RepDougCollins: Our Border Patrol agents are superheroes dealing with the border crisis every day. They are doing their job, and it's t… [Twitter for iPhone]

Jun 9, 2019 05:50:57 PM ….No Obstruction. The Dems were devastated - after all this time and money spent ($40,000,000), the Mueller Report was a disaster for them. But they want a Redo, or Do Over. They are even bringing in @CNN sleazebag attorney John Dean. Sorry, no Do Overs - Go back to work! [Twitter for iPhone]

Jun 9, 2019 05:50:57 PM For two years all the Democrats talked about was the Mueller Report, because they knew that it was loaded up with 13 Angry Democrat Trump Haters, later increased to 18. But despite the bias, when the Report came out, the findings were No Collusion and facts that led to…….. [Twitter for iPhone]

Jun 9, 2019 05:57:11 PM The Failing @nytimes story on Mexico and Illegal Immigration through our Southern Border has now been proven shockingly false and untrue, bad reporting, and the paper is embarrassed by it. The only problem is that they knew it was Fake News before it went out. Corrupt Media! [Twitter for iPhone]

Jun 9, 2019 06:20:04 PM RT @SecAzar: Read more about the announcement here: https://t.co/fKZBchzJCh #HIV #EndHIVEpidemic [Twitter for iPhone]

Jun 9, 2019 06:20:06 PM RT @SecAzar: The majority of Americans who are at risk and who could protect themselves with PrEP are still not receiving the medication. T… [Twitter for iPhone]

Jun 9, 2019 06:20:10 PM RT @SecAzar: Under @POTUS's leadership, @HHSgov worked with Gilead to secure preventative medication for uninsured individuals at risk for… [Twitter for iPhone]

Jun 9, 2019 06:20:13 PM RT @SecAzar: The agreement will provide pre-exposure prophylaxis (PrEP) to treat individuals who are at risk for HIV and who are uninsured,… [Twitter for iPhone]

Jun 9, 2019 06:20:30 PM RT @SecAzar: I'm pleased to announce that as a result of discussions between the Trump Administration and Gilead Sciences, Inc., Gilead has… [Twitter for iPhone]

Jun 9, 2019 06:23:27 PM RT @TheRightMelissa: @realDonaldTrump For the few conservatives they have left on, twitter is engaged in shadow banning of conservative con... [Twitter for iPhone]

Jun 9, 2019 06:26:28 PM RT @RealCandaceO: Black America has been destroyed by liberal policies, a liberal media and a liberal stranglehold on culture. Democrats... [Twitter for iPhone]

Jun 9, 2019 06:29:33 PM RT @charliekirk11: It's amazing to see Democrats within a span of 2 days go from being against Trump's tariffs on Mexico to now being again... [Twitter for iPhone]

Jun 9, 2019 06:35:39 PM RT @mitchellvii: Trump wins historic landslide election. Democrats - "Russia did it." Trump sets economic records. Democrats - "Obama di... [Twitter for iPhone]

Jun 9, 2019 06:35:53 PM RT @mitchellvii: Next we get to watch the Democrat Civil War between the Socialists and the Establishment during the debates in a race to s... [Twitter for iPhone]

Jun 9, 2019 06:41:02 PM RT @BreitbartNews: .@senronjohnson: "I called the Mexican ambassador and said regardless of what you read in the press, understand if the p... [Twitter for iPhone]

Jun 9, 2019 06:51:44 PM RT @larryelder: The Trump-hating media/dems now face a YUGE dilemma--how NOT to give @realDonaldTrump credit. #MexicoCavesAfterTariffThrea... [Twitter for iPhone]

Jun 10, 2019 05:00:46 AM Now with our new deal, Mexico is doing more for the USA on Illegal Immigration than the Democrats. In fact, the Democrats are doing NOTHING, they want Open Borders, which means Illigal Immigration, Drugs and Crime. [Twitter for iPhone]

Jun 10, 2019 05:02:01 AM RT @realDonaldTrump: The Failing @nytimes story on Mexico and Illegal Immigration through our Southern Border has now been proven shockingl... [Twitter for iPhone]

Jun 10, 2019 05:02:33 AM RT @realDonaldTrump: ....No Obstruction. The Dems were devastated - after all this time and money spent ($40,000,000), the Mueller Report w... [Twitter for iPhone]

Jun 10, 2019 05:02:43 AM RT @realDonaldTrump: For two years all the Democrats talked about was the Mueller Report, because they knew that it was loaded up with 13 A... [Twitter for iPhone]

Jun 10, 2019 05:03:29 AM RT @realDonaldTrump: If President Obama made the deals that I have made, both at the Border and for the Economy, the Corrupt Media would be... [Twitter for iPhone]

Jun 10, 2019 05:04:30 AM RT @realDonaldTrump: Twitter should let the banned Conservative Voices back onto their platform, without restriction. It's called Freedom o... [Twitter for iPhone]

Jun 10, 2019 05:31:43 AM ....We do not anticipate a problem with the vote but, if for any reason the approval is not forthcoming, Tariffs will be reinstated! [Twitter for iPhone]

Jun 10, 2019 05:31:43 AM We have fully signed and documented another very important part of the Immigration and Security deal with Mexico, one that the U.S. has been asking about getting for many years. It will be revealed in the not too distant future and will need a vote by Mexico's Legislative body!.. [Twitter for iPhone]

Jun 10, 2019 06:09:08 AM When will the Failing New York Times admit that their front page story on the the new Mexico deal at the Border is a FRAUD and nothing more than a badly reported "hit job" on me, something that has been going on since the first day I announced for the presidency! Sick Journalism [Twitter for iPhone]

Jun 10, 2019 08:33:13 AM https://t.co/TwLPmiAB78 [Twitter for iPhone]

Jun 10, 2019 08:33:24 AM https://t.co/2O43Na2Nmr [Twitter for iPhone]

Jun 10, 2019 10:36:00 AM RT @VP: .@POTUS' strong stand got Mexico to do things they have never done before: 6,000 National Guard at their southern border, immigrati… [Twitter for iPhone]

Jun 10, 2019 10:43:11 AM Thank you @MarkLevinShow and John Eastman! https://t.co/PsoyEVynjT [Twitter Media Studio]

Jun 10, 2019 01:17:37 PM Can't believe they are bringing in John Dean, the disgraced Nixon White House Counsel who is a paid CNN contributor. No Collusion - No Obstruction! Democrats just want a do-over which they'll never get! [Twitter for iPhone]

Jun 10, 2019 01:52:10 PM I have been briefed on the helicopter crash in New York City. Phenomenal job by our GREAT First Responders who are currently on the scene. THANK YOU for all you do 24/7/365! The Trump Administration stands ready should you need anything at all. [Twitter for iPhone]

Jun 10, 2019 05:53:08 PM Congratulations to the 2019 Indianapolis 500 Winner @IMS, @SimonPagenaud and @Team_Penske! @IndyCar 🏆🏁 https://t.co/uxhfbhJ2p0 [Twitter for iPhone]

Jun 10, 2019 06:01:02 PM Despite the Phony Witch Hunt, we will continue to MAKE AMERICA GREAT AGAIN! Thank you!! https://t.co/MXuiolM745 [Twitter for iPhone]

Jun 10, 2019 09:21:55 PM https://t.co/V8TxJ3KVLZ [Twitter for iPhone]

Jun 10, 2019 09:23:54 PM https://t.co/RRcP8ZDy1e [Twitter for iPhone]

Jun 10, 2019 10:41:17 PM #AmericaFIRST #MAGAus https://t.co/Ae51wFELD0 [Twitter for iPhone]

Jun 11, 2019 06:14:32 AM New book just out, "The Real Deal, My Decade Fighting Battles and Winning Wars With Trump," is really wonderful. It is written by two people who are very smart & know me well, George Sorial & Damian Bates, as opposed to all the books where the author has no clue who I am. ENJOY! [Twitter for iPhone]

Jun 11, 2019 06:25:08 AM "Jerry Nadler's Trump Bashing Show Is A Bust." Headline, New York Post. @foxandfriends The Greatest Witch Hunt of all time continues. All crimes were by the other side, but the Committee refuses to even take a look. Deleting 33,000 Emails is the real Obstruction - and much more! [Twitter for iPhone]

Jun 11, 2019 06:49:37 AM "Mueller has spoken. He found No Collusion between the Trump Campaign and the Russians. The bottom line is what the Democrat House is doing is trying to destroy the Trump Presidency (which has been a tremendous success), and I can assure you that we're done with the Mueller...... [Twitter for iPhone]

Jun 11, 2019 06:49:38 AM ....investigation in the Senate. They can talk to John Dean until the cows come home, we're not doing anything in the Senate regarding the Mueller Report. We are going to harden our Infrastructure against 2020!" @LindseyGrahamSC [Twitter for iPhone]

Jun 11, 2019 06:51:43 AM PRESIDENTIAL HARASSMENT! [Twitter for iPhone]

Jun 11, 2019 06:54:41 AM Sad when you think about it, but Mexico right now is doing more for the United States at the Border than the Democrats in Congress! @foxandfriends [Twitter for iPhone]

Jun 11, 2019 06:57:19 AM RT @bopinion: European landmarks have a question they desperately need answering: How do you stop the tourists from coming? https://t.co/7R... [Twitter for iPhone]

Jun 11, 2019 07:08:30 AM This is because the Euro and other currencies are devalued against the dollar, putting the U.S. at a big disadvantage. The Fed Interest rate way to high, added to ridiculous quantitative tightening! They don't have a clue! https://t.co/0CpnUzJqB9 [Twitter for iPhone]

Jun 11, 2019 07:10:26 AM The United States has VERY LOW INFLATION, a beautiful thing! [Twitter for iPhone]

Jun 11, 2019 07:47:09 AM This is because the Euro and other currencies are devalued against the dollar, putting the U.S. at a big disadvantage. The Fed Interest rate way too high, added to ridiculous quantitative tightening! They don't have a clue! https://t.co/0CpnUzJqB9 [Twitter for iPhone]

Jun 11, 2019 07:50:43 AM Maria, Dagan, Steve, Stuart V - When you are the big "piggy bank" that other countries have been ripping off for years (to a level that is not to be believed), Tariffs are a great negotiating tool, a great revenue producers and, most importantly, a powerful way to get...... [Twitter for iPhone]

Jun 11, 2019 08:12:17 AM ...Companies to come to the U.S.A and to get companies that have left us for other lands to come back home. We stupidly lost 30% of our auto business to Mexico. If the Tariffs went on at the higher level, they would all come back, and pass. But very happy with the deal I made,... [Twitter for iPhone]

Jun 11, 2019 08:14:13 AM ....If Mexico produces (which I think they will). Biggest part of deal with Mexico has not yet been revealed! China is similar, except they devalue currency and subsidize companies to lessen effect of 25% Tariff. So far, little effect to consumer. Companies will relocate to U.S. [Twitter for iPhone]

Jun 11, 2019 08:55:01 AM Good day in the Stock Market. People have no idea the tremendous potential our Country has for GROWTH - and many other things! [Twitter for iPhone]

Jun 11, 2019 08:58:26 AM "Why did the Democrats run if they didn't want to do things?" @SenRickScott [Twitter for iPhone]

Jun 11, 2019 12:44:20 PM On my way to Iowa - just heard nearly 1,000 agriculture groups signed a letter urging Congress to approve the USMCA. Our Patriot Farmers & rural America have spoken! Now Congress must do its job & support these great men and women by passing the bipartisan USMCA Trade Agreement! [Twitter for iPhone]

Jun 11, 2019 04:45:32 PM Today, here in Iowa, we honor America's cherished farming heritage. We salute your commitment to American Energy Independence — and we celebrate the bright future we are forging together powered by clean, affordable AMERICAN ETHANOL! https://t.co/WhuPwrETYk [Twitter for iPhone]

Jun 11, 2019 05:20:30 PM "Trump administration gives final approval for year-round E15 use" https://t.co/WPrDiyfpIW [Twitter for iPhone]

Jun 11, 2019 08:21:39 PM Beautiful afternoon in Iowa. Thank you to all of our Nation's Farmers. May God bless you, and may God Bless America! https://t.co/VYA2bSzMWf [Twitter for iPhone]

Jun 11, 2019 11:28:40 PM "Someone should call Obama up. The Obama Administration spied on a rival presidential campaign using Federal Agencies. I mean, that seems like a headline to me?" @TuckerCarlson It will all start coming out, and the Witch Hunt will end. Presidential Harassment! [Twitter for iPhone]

Jun 12, 2019 07:04:23 AM Wow! Just got word that our June 18th, Tuesday, ANNOUNCEMENT in Orlando, Florida, already has 74,000 requests for a 20,000 seat Arena. With all of the big events that we have done, this tickets looks to be the "hottest" of them all. See you in Florida! [Twitter for iPhone]

Jun 12, 2019 07:19:49 AM The Fake News has never been more dishonest than it is today. Thank goodness we can fight back on Social Media. There new weapon of choice is Fake Polling, sometimes referred to as Suppression Polls (they suppress the numbers). Had it in 2016, but this is worse......... [Twitter for iPhone]

Jun 12, 2019 07:19:50 AM .....The Fake (Corrupt) News Media said they had a leak into polling done by my campaign which, by the way and despite the phony and never ending Witch Hunt, are the best numbers WE have ever had. They reported Fake numbers that they made up & don't even exist. WE WILL WIN AGAIN! [Twitter for iPhone]

Jun 12, 2019 07:20:10 AM RT @realDonaldTrump: Despite the Phony Witch Hunt, we will continue to MAKE AMERICA GREAT AGAIN! Thank you!! https://t.co/MXuiolM745 [Twitter for iPhone]

Jun 12, 2019 07:40:55 AM Wow! Just got word that our June 18th, Tuesday, ANNOUNCEMENT in Orlando, Florida, already has 74,000 requests for a 20,000 seat Arena. With all of the big events that we have done, this ticket looks to be the "hottest" of them all. See you in Florida! [Twitter for iPhone]

Jun 12, 2019 07:46:43 AM .....The Fake (Corrupt) News Media said they had a leak into polling done by my campaign which, by the way and despite the phony and never ending Witch Hunt, are the best numbers WE have ever had. They reported Fake numbers that they made up & don't even exist. WE WILL WIN AGAIN! [Twitter for iPhone]

Jun 12, 2019 07:46:43 AM The Fake News has never been more dishonest than it is today. Thank goodness we can fight back on Social Media. Their new weapon of choice is Fake Polling, sometimes referred to as Suppression Polls (they suppress the numbers). Had it in 2016, but this is worse..... [Twitter for iPhone]

Jun 12, 2019 07:34:26 PM It was a pleasure to host my friends President Andrzej Duda and Mrs. Agata Kornhauser-Duda of Poland at the @WhiteHouse today. U.S.-Poland ties are at an all-time high. Thank you for being such an exemplary Ally! https://t.co/tvhHIpsrFo [Twitter for iPhone]

Jun 12, 2019 09:23:17 PM RT @mike_pence: Great event this afternoon in Billings supporting @SteveDaines! Montana needs 4 more years of @realdonaldtrump in the White... [Twitter for iPhone]

Jun 12, 2019 09:23:49 PM RT @mike_pence: The American people will continue to be drawn to @realDonaldTrump's consistent, conservative leadership - and I couldn't be... [Twitter for iPhone]

Jun 12, 2019 09:27:30 PM Michael Whatley has been with us right from the beginning. A great Leader and @NCGOP Chairman! https://t.co/XQvnK9LD8R [Twitter for iPhone]

▢ Jun 12, 2019 09:32:10 PM RT @VP: President @realDonaldTrump made the opioid crisis a primary focus of his administration. Today, I am in Montana to further our supp... [Twitter for iPhone]

▢ Jun 12, 2019 09:32:57 PM Thank you! https://t.co/tagXwv2imY [Twitter for iPhone]

▢ Jun 12, 2019 09:33:10 PM RT @WhiteHouse: President @realDonaldTrump and @FLOTUS will welcome Polish President @andrzejduda and Mrs. Agata Kornhauser-Duda for their... [Twitter for iPhone]

▢ Jun 12, 2019 09:34:23 PM Our Farmers deserve this, they are GREAT! https://t.co/0dFkx0vUkl [Twitter for iPhone]

▢ Jun 12, 2019 09:37:37 PM Two Fantastic People! My friends from the very beginning. Thank you D&S. https://t.co/XmyedA1WZL [Twitter for iPhone]

▢ Jun 12, 2019 09:38:55 PM RT @WhiteHouse: Tonight's 1600 Daily looks at how President @realDonaldTrump is delivering on his promise to roll back the regulation that... [Twitter for iPhone]

▢ Jun 12, 2019 09:44:13 PM is = if (Spell)! Not like Chris. https://t.co/wBIGo2ffzB [Twitter for iPhone]

▢ Jun 12, 2019 09:45:16 PM Thank you very much! https://t.co/UOeTBUqfhE [Twitter for iPhone]

▢ Jun 12, 2019 10:07:58 PM "Biden would be America's Dream Candidate, because there would be no more Tariffs, no more demands that China stop stealing our IP, things would go back to the old days with America's manufacturers & workers getting shafted. He has Zero Credibility!" @IngrahamAngle So true! [Twitter for iPhone]

▢ Jun 12, 2019 10:32:36 PM "It's about peace and Properity, that's how Republican Presidents get elected, and this President has delivered on the Economy and he's delivered on keeping America Stronger and Safer. Our biggest enemy is not any one of these Democrats, it's the Media." John McLaughlin, pollster [Twitter for iPhone]

▢ Jun 12, 2019 10:50:45 PM "Biden would be China's Dream Candidate, because there would be no more Tariffs, no more demands that China stop stealing our IP, things would go back to the old days with America's manufacturers & workers getting shafted. He has Zero Credibility!" @IngrahamAngle So true! [Twitter for iPhone]

▢ Jun 12, 2019 10:52:12 PM "It's about peace and Prosperity, that's how Republican Presidents get elected, and this President has delivered on the Economy and he's delivered on keeping America Stronger & Safer. Our biggest enemy is not any one of these Democrats, it's the Media." John McLaughlin, pollster [Twitter for iPhone]

Jun 13, 2019 05:21:50 AM General Michael Flynn, the 33 year war hero who has served with distinction, has not retained a good lawyer, he has retained a GREAT LAWYER, Sidney Powell. Best Wishes and Good Luck to them both! [Twitter for iPhone]

Jun 13, 2019 05:51:13 AM Unrelated to Russia, Russia, Russia (although the Radical Left doesn't use the name Russia anymore since the issuance of the Mueller Report), House Committee now plays the seldom used "Contempt" card on our great A.G. & Sec. of Commerce - this time on the Census. Dems play a..... [Twitter for iPhone]

Jun 13, 2019 05:51:14 AM ....can to embarrass the Trump Administration (and Republicans), attack the Trump Administration. This is campaigning by the Dems." Attorney David Bruno. So true! In the meantime they are getting NO work done on Drug Pricing, Infrastructure & many other things. [Twitter for iPhone]

Jun 13, 2019 05:51:14 AM .....much tougher game than the Republicans did when they had the House Majority. Republicans will remember! "This has already been argued before the U.S. Supreme Court, but the House doesn't want to wait. This is a common thread between all of the Committees - do whatever you... [Twitter for iPhone]

Jun 13, 2019 06:03:24 AM "Congress cannot Impeach President Trump (did nothing wrong) because if they did they would be putting themselves above the law. The Constitution provides criteria for Impeachment - treason, bribery, high crimes & misdemeanors. Unless there is compelling evidence, Impeachment... [Twitter for iPhone]

Jun 13, 2019 06:03:25 AM ....is not Constitutionally Permissable." Alan Dershowitz, Constitutional Lawyer [Twitter for iPhone]

Jun 13, 2019 07:11:54 AM The Dems fight us at every turn - in the meantime they are accomplishing nothing for the people! They have gone absolutely "Loco," or Unhinged, as they like to say! [Twitter for iPhone]

Jun 13, 2019 07:59:56 AM I meet and talk to "foreign governments" every day. I just met with the Queen of England (U.K.), the Prince of Whales, the P.M. of the United Kingdom, the P.M. of Ireland, the President of France and the President of Poland. We talked about "Everything!" Should I immediately..... [Twitter for iPhone]

Jun 13, 2019 07:59:57 AM .....call the FBI about these calls and meetings? How ridiculous! I would never be trusted again. With that being said, my full answer is rarely played by the Fake News Media. They purposely leave out the part that matters. [Twitter for iPhone]

Jun 13, 2019 08:23:47 AM ....call the FBI about these calls and meetings? How ridiculous! I would never be trusted again. With that being said, my full answer is rarely played by the Fake News Media. They purposely leave out the part that matters. [Twitter for iPhone]

Jun 13, 2019 08:23:47 AM I meet and talk to "foreign governments" every day. I just met with the Queen of England (U.K.), the Prince of Wales, the P.M. of the United Kingdom, the P.M. of Ireland, the President of France and the President of Poland. We talked about "Everything!" Should I immediately.... [Twitter for iPhone]

Jun 13, 2019 08:37:47 AM When Senator @MarkWarnerVA spoke at length, and in great detail, about extremely negative information on me, with a talented entertainer purporting to be a Russian Operative, did he immediately call the FBI? NO, in fact he didn't even tell the Senate Intelligence Committee of.... [Twitter for iPhone]

Jun 13, 2019 08:37:48 AM ....which he is a member. When @RepAdamSchiff took calls from another person, also very successfully purporting to be a Russian Operative, did he call the FBI, or even think to call the FBI? NO! The fact is that the phony Witch Hunt is a giant scam where Democrats,... [Twitter for iPhone]

Jun 13, 2019 08:37:49 AM ....and other really bad people, SPIED ON MY CAMPAIGN! They even had an "insurance policy" just in case Crooked Hillary Clinton and the Democrats lost their race for the Presidency! This is the biggest & worst political scandal in the history of the United States of America. Sad! [Twitter for iPhone]

Jun 13, 2019 01:01:53 PM They've been wrong all along! https://t.co/z5tSV2JLEf [Twitter for iPhone]

Jun 13, 2019 01:13:40 PM While I very much appreciate P.M. Abe going to Iran to meet with Ayatollah Ali Khamenei, I personally feel that it is too soon to even think about making a deal. They are not ready, and neither are we! [Twitter for iPhone]

Jun 13, 2019 01:21:54 PM While I very much appreciate P.M. Abe going to Iran to meet with Ayatollah Ali Khamenei, I personally feel that it is too soon to even think about making a deal. They are not ready, and neither are we! [Twitter for iPhone]

Jun 13, 2019 02:01:24 PM "It is the assessment of the U.S. government that Iran is responsible for today's attacks in the Gulf of Oman...." @StateDept @SecPompeo https://t.co/sTIB0p1kCE [Twitter Media Studio]

Jun 13, 2019 03:10:26 PM ....She is a very special person with extraordinary talents, who has done an incredible job! I hope she decides to run for Governor of Arkansas - she would be fantastic. Sarah, thank you for a job well done! [Twitter for iPhone]

Jun 13, 2019 03:10:26 PM After 3 1/2 years, our wonderful Sarah Huckabee Sanders will be leaving the White House at the end of the month and going home to the Great State of Arkansas.... [Twitter for iPhone]

Jun 13, 2019 04:03:45 PM Today we announced vital new actions that we are taking to help former inmates find a job, live a crime-free life, and succeed beyond their dreams....https://t.co/BBQ8gpFunJ [Twitter for iPhone]

Jun 13, 2019 07:35:04 PM Thank you Jason Chaffetz! #MAGA https://t.co/sz6LiPXez6 [Twitter Media Studio]

Jun 14, 2019 05:51:04 AM Natalie Harp, fighting Stage 2 Cancer and doing really well, was a GREAT guest on @foxandfriends. Right To Try is producing some truly spectacular results. Proud of Natalie! [Twitter for iPhone]

Jun 14, 2019 05:55:27 AM I will be interviewed on @foxandfriends at 8:00 A.M. Enjoy! @FoxNews [Twitter for iPhone]

Jun 14, 2019 11:26:38 AM RT @WhiteHouse: https://t.co/c40BQpZFtW [Twitter for iPhone]

Jun 14, 2019 12:03:55 PM HAPPY BIRTHDAY to our GREAT @USArmy. America loves you! #ArmyBday https://t.co/MyypBVGMoW [Twitter for iPhone]

Jun 14, 2019 01:51:00 PM The Radical Left Dems are working hard, but THE PEOPLE are much smarter. Working hard, thank you! https://t.co/KDHH5jYbGV [Twitter for iPhone]

Jun 14, 2019 02:14:02 PM Announcing great, expanded HRAs—big win for small employers and workers. This is a fantastic plan! My Administration has worked very hard on creating more affordable health coverage. https://t.co/DQbUfGJc1I [Twitter for iPhone]

Jun 14, 2019 02:15:42 PM The dishonest media will NEVER keep us from accomplishing our objectives on behalf of our GREAT AMERICAN PEOPLE! #MAGA https://t.co/e36YM4QCEx [Twitter Media Studio]

Jun 14, 2019 04:06:27 PM Thank you Senator @MarshaBlackburn for fighting obstructionist Democrats led by Cryin' Chuck Schumer. Democrats continue to look for a do-over on the Mueller Report and will stop at nothing to distract the American people from the great accomplishments of this Administration! [Twitter for iPhone]

Jun 14, 2019 04:12:19 PM Thank you @senatemajldr Mitch McConnell for understanding the Democrats game of not playing it straight on the ridiclious Witch Hunt Hoax in the Senate. Cryin' Chuck will never stop. Did Senator @MarkWarner ever report speaking to a Russian!? [Twitter for iPhone]

Jun 14, 2019 04:28:59 PM Thank you @senatemajldr Mitch McConnell for understanding the Democrats game of not playing it straight on the ridiculous Witch Hunt Hoax in the Senate. Cryin' Chuck will never stop. Did Senator @MarkWarner ever report speaking to a Russian!? [Twitter for iPhone]

⊔ Jun 14, 2019 04:32:53 PM RT @RepMarkMeadows: This week President Trump was able to do something no one else could: get the left to care about foreign intel in our e… [Twitter for iPhone]

⊔ Jun 14, 2019 05:37:37 PM Just spoke to Marillyn Hewson, CEO of @LockheedMartin, about continuing operations for the @Sikorsky in Coatesville, Pennsylvania. She will be taking it under advisement and will be making a decision soon…. [Twitter for iPhone]

⊔ Jun 14, 2019 05:37:38 PM ….While Pennsylvania is BOOMING, I don't want there to be even a little glitch in Coatesville – every job counts. I want Lockhead to BOOM along with it! [Twitter for iPhone]

⊔ Jun 15, 2019 06:09:29 AM RT @TomFitton: Obama-Clinton-Russia: The REAL Collusion Scandal; Docs Show Obama State Dept. Launders Steele Dossier to Target @realDonald… [Twitter for iPhone]

⊔ Jun 15, 2019 06:09:36 AM RT @TomFitton: Coup Update: Bruce Ohr gets $28k bonus in middle of Russiagate spying on @RealDonaldTrump -- and then gets a raise AFTER he… [Twitter for iPhone]

⊔ Jun 15, 2019 06:10:22 AM RT @TomFitton: As Pelosi House slithers towards impeachment of @RealDonaldTrump, Mueller Report exposed as lying hit job on Trump. @Judici… [Twitter for iPhone]

⊔ Jun 15, 2019 06:10:49 AM RT @TomFitton: 4 FBI witness interview reports are "missing", along with the notes of a meeting between the FBI and the intelligence commun… [Twitter for iPhone]

⊔ Jun 15, 2019 06:12:16 AM RT @TomFitton: Tom Fitton: If There's Anything Watergate-Related, it's the Obama Admin's Actions Targeting @realDonaldTrump - @JudicialWatc… [Twitter for iPhone]

⊔ Jun 15, 2019 06:13:14 AM RT @hughhewitt: "It may be the single biggest political crime in the history of the United States" @realDonaldTrump says about #Spygate. "E… [Twitter for iPhone]

⊔ Jun 15, 2019 06:22:00 AM RT @marcorubio: Here is video of #IRGC navy returning to the scene of the crime to erase evidence by removing an unexploded Limpet mine fro… [Twitter for iPhone]

⊔ Jun 15, 2019 06:23:39 AM RT @marcorubio: Not just the intelligence shows Iran was behind gulf attacks,common sense does too. It is a fact that only the #IRGC Navy… [Twitter for iPhone]

⊔ Jun 15, 2019 06:24:40 AM RT @marcorubio: And yesterday's attack on a civilian airport in #SaudiArabia by the Houthis using cruise missiles supplied by #IRGC should… [Twitter for iPhone]

⊔ Jun 15, 2019 06:27:21 AM RT @marcorubio: This account is really off-base. MLB meeting with @potus wasn't about resurrecting the old deal,it was about a new & much m… [Twitter for iPhone]

⊔ Jun 15, 2019 06:29:25 AM RT @FLOTUS: This Administration remains committed to the fight against the opioid epidemic. Thank you to all who participated in this week'… [Twitter for iPhone]

Jun 15, 2019 06:29:39 AM RT @FLOTUS: Yesterday we honored the incredible friendship between the United States and Poland, and celebrated our proud Polish-American c... [Twitter for iPhone]

Jun 15, 2019 06:29:54 AM RT @FLOTUS: Great to welcome back President Duda & Mrs. Kornhauser-Duda of Poland at the @WhiteHouse today! https://t.co/A3UxqNUqzn [Twitter for iPhone]

Jun 15, 2019 06:30:09 AM RT @FLOTUS: We must never forget the lives lost and heroic actions made by so many on D-Day in Normandy, France. https://t.co/Uhl3VUPleq [Twitter for iPhone]

Jun 15, 2019 06:30:49 AM RT @WhiteHouse: Opioid addiction can happen to anyone—and we must work together to fight the stigma and save lives, says @Surgeon_General J... [Twitter for iPhone]

Jun 15, 2019 06:37:34 AM "The latest Polls find 51% of Americans approve of President Trump's Job Performance. Last month a Democrat Pollster said President Trump's approval rating has been the most steady of any President in history!" @OANN [Twitter for iPhone]

Jun 15, 2019 06:44:47 AM "With over a 50% Approval Rating at this point in his Presidency, analysts believe re-election in 2020 looks (very) promising!" @OANN Hey, we have accomplished more than any President in the first 2 1/2 years, WHY NOT? [Twitter for iPhone]

Jun 15, 2019 06:46:00 AM RT @CLewandowski_: Great to see a strong showing in NH for @realDonaldTrump on his Birthday. Happy Birthday @realDonaldTrump https://t.co/... [Twitter for iPhone]

Jun 15, 2019 06:47:12 AM RT @TeamTrump: Today, President @realDonaldTrump spoke on expanding health coverage options for American small businesses & workers. Presi... [Twitter for iPhone]

Jun 15, 2019 06:48:36 AM RT @WhiteHouse: NEXT UP: President @realDonaldTrump speaks on expanding health coverage options for small businesses & workers. https://t.c... [Twitter for iPhone]

Jun 15, 2019 06:49:05 AM RT @DanScavino: NEVER GETS OLD.... https://t.co/SJQE8zxoCm [Twitter for iPhone]

Jun 15, 2019 06:49:20 AM RT @DanScavino: https://t.co/85xnJ7mpp7 [Twitter for iPhone]

Jun 15, 2019 06:49:53 AM RT @DanScavino: As the worst Mayor in the history of New York City manages his bucket list in Iowa — he also remains steady at ZERO PERCENT... [Twitter for iPhone]

Jun 15, 2019 06:50:18 AM RT @DanScavino: .@realDonaldTrump stops by for an impromptu photo with local school kids in Ireland, who were hoping to catch a glimpse of... [Twitter for iPhone]

Jun 15, 2019 06:50:33 AM RT @DanScavino: President @realDonaldTrump stayed after his commencement speech at the @AF_Academy in Colorado Springs this past Thursday t... [Twitter for iPhone]

Jun 15, 2019 06:51:27 AM RT @DanScavino: Dems will keep their (embarrassing) games going on here in THE SWAMP until 2020 because they hate Trump & they think it hel... [Twitter for iPhone]

Jun 15, 2019 07:05:17 AM Despite the Greatest Presidential Harassment of all time by people that are very dishonest and want to destroy our Country, we are doing great in the Polls, even better than in 2016, and will be packed at the Tuesday Announcement Rally in Orlando, Florida. KEEP AMERICA GREAT! [Twitter for iPhone]

Jun 15, 2019 07:51:34 AM All in for Senator Steve Daines as he proposes an Amendment for a strong BAN on burning our American Flag. A no brainer! [Twitter for iPhone]

Jun 15, 2019 07:55:47 AM "President Trump to launch 2020 Campaign in Florida!" @foxandfriends Tuesday will be a Big Crowd and Big Day! [Twitter for iPhone]

Jun 15, 2019 08:44:20 AM The Trump Economy is setting records, and has a long way up to go....However, if anyone but me takes over in 2020 (I know the competition very well), there will be a Market Crash the likes of which has not been seen before! KEEP AMERICA GREAT [Twitter for iPhone]

Jun 15, 2019 01:44:37 PM RT @SteveScalise: For weeks Republicans have asked for an emergency funding bill to help fix the worsening border crisis. Immediate action... [Twitter for iPhone]

Jun 15, 2019 01:45:01 PM Thank you Steve & family! https://t.co/1lgfJjHRfH [Twitter for iPhone]

Jun 15, 2019 01:47:35 PM LONDON needs a new mayor ASAP. Khan is a disaster - will only get worse! https://t.co/n7qKI3BbD2 [Twitter for iPhone]

Jun 15, 2019 01:50:40 PM https://t.co/jlmmOCxk9H [Twitter for iPhone]

Jun 15, 2019 02:04:33 PM The Corrupt News Media is totally out of control - they have given up and don't even care anymore. Mainstream Media has ZERO CREDIBILITY - TOTAL LOSERS! [Twitter for iPhone]

Jun 15, 2019 06:07:00 PM RT @PressSec: I am blessed and forever grateful to @realDonaldTrump for the opportunity to serve and proud of everything he's accomplished.... [Twitter for iPhone]

Jun 15, 2019 06:17:09 PM He is a national disgrace who is destroying the City of London! https://t.co/l3qcUS17jh [Twitter for iPhone]

Jun 15, 2019 07:30:07 PM I enjoyed my interview with @GStephanopoulos on @abcnews. So funny to watch the Fake News Media try to dissect & distort every word in as negative a way as possible. It will be aired on Sunday night at 8:00 P.M., and is called, "President Trump: 30 Hours" (which is somewhat.... [Twitter for iPhone]

Jun 15, 2019 07:30:08 PM ....misleading in that I personally spent only a small fraction of that time doing interviews. I do have a few other things to do, you know!). Think I will do many more Network Interviews, as I did in 2016, in order to get the word out that no President has done what I have in... [Twitter for iPhone]

Jun 15, 2019 07:30:09 PM .....the first 2 1/2 years of his Presidency, including the fact that we have one of the best Economies in the history of our Country. It is called Earned Media. In any event, enjoy the show! [Twitter for iPhone]

Jun 15, 2019 07:51:19 PM I enjoyed my interview with @GStephanopoulos on @ABC. So funny to watch the Fake News Media try to dissect & distort every word in as negative a way as possible. It will be aired on Sunday night at 8:00 P.M., and is called, "President Trump: 30 Hours" (which is somewhat.... [Twitter for iPhone]

Jun 15, 2019 07:51:20 PM .....the first 2 1/2 years of his Presidency, including the fact that we have one of the best Economies in the history of our Country. It is called Earned Media. In any event, enjoy the show! [Twitter for iPhone]

Jun 15, 2019 07:51:20 PM ....misleading in that I personally spent only a small fraction of that time doing interviews. I do have a few other things to do, you know!). Think I will do many more Network Interviews, as I did in 2016, in order to get the word out that no President has done what I have in... [Twitter for iPhone]

Jun 15, 2019 08:15:23 PM Do you believe that the Failing New York Times just did a story stating that the United States is substantially increasing Cyber Attacks on Russia. This is a virtual act of Treason by a once great paper so desperate for a story, any story, even if bad for our Country..... [Twitter for iPhone]

Jun 15, 2019 08:15:24 PM .....ALSO, NOT TRUE! Anything goes with our Corrupt News Media today. They will do, or say, whatever it takes, with not even the slightest thought of consequence! These are true cowards and without doubt, THE ENEMY OF THE PEOPLE! [Twitter for iPhone]

Jun 15, 2019 11:51:04 PM Florida Governor Ron DeSantis just signed Bill banning Sanctuary Cities in State, & forcing all law enforcement agencies to cooperate with Federal Immigration authorities. Bill prohibits local Gov't from enacting Sanctuary policies that protect undocumented immigrants...@FoxNews [Twitter for iPhone]

Jun 15, 2019 11:51:05 PM ....More and more states want to do this but their governors and leaders don't have the courage to do so. The politics will soon mandate, however, because people from California, & all over the land, are demanding that Sanctuary Cities be GONE. No illegals, Drugs or Trafficking! [Twitter for iPhone]

Jun 16, 2019 06:03:13 AM Congratulations to great guy Pete Hegseth and wonderful Jenny Cunningham on their engagement. They will have a fantastic life together! @foxandfriends [Twitter for iPhone]

Jun 16, 2019 06:39:51 AM Yesterday was the Radical Left Democrats big Impeachment day. They worked so hard to make it something really big and special but had one problem - almost nobody showed up. "The Media admits low turnout for anti-Trump rallies." @FoxNews "All around the Country people are....... [Twitter for iPhone]

Jun 16, 2019 06:39:52 AM .....saying enough. Democrat voters want to hear the politicians talking about issues. This is a huge distraction and will only help Donald Trump get elected." @JedediahBila "Greatest President since Ronald Reagan" said a counter-protester. LehighValleyLive [Twitter for iPhone]

Jun 16, 2019 08:39:22 AM .....news is that at the end of 6 years, after America has been made GREAT again and I leave the beautiful White House (do you think the people would demand that I stay longer? KEEP AMERICA GREAT), both of these horrible papers will quickly go out of business & be forever gone! [Twitter for iPhone]

Jun 16, 2019 08:39:22 AM A poll should be done on which is the more dishonest and deceitful newspaper, the Failing New York Times or the Amazon (lobbyist) Washington Post! They are both a disgrace to our Country, the Enemy of the People, but I just can't seem to figure out which is worse? The good..... [Twitter for iPhone]

Jun 16, 2019 08:55:08 AM Happy Father's Day to all, including my worst and most vicious critics, of which there are fewer and fewer. This is a FANTASTIC time to be an American! KEEP AMERICA GREAT! [Twitter for iPhone]

Jun 16, 2019 11:58:13 AM https://t.co/9T50NuGW28 [Twitter for iPhone]

Jun 16, 2019 02:00:49 PM Thank you PM @Netanyahu and the State of Israel for this great honor!usi□ https://t.co/OUcf6s98UX [Twitter for iPhone]

Jun 16, 2019 03:36:10 PM When will the Fake News Media start asking Democrats if they are OK with the hiring of Christopher Steele, a foreign agent, paid for by Crooked Hillary and the DNC, to dig up "dirt" and write a phony Dossier against the Presidential Candidate of the opposing party......... [Twitter for iPhone]

Jun 16, 2019 03:36:12 PM ......If Republicans ever did that to the Democrats, there would be all hell to pay. It would be a scandal like no other! [Twitter for iPhone]

Jun 16, 2019 04:08:00 PM So nice! https://t.co/oraaFoPByj [Twitter for iPhone]

Jun 16, 2019 04:08:10 PM RT @DanScavino: "Millennial fighting rare bone cancer responds to @JoeBiden vow: Law supported by @realDonaldTrump helped save my life" htt... [Twitter for iPhone]

Jun 16, 2019 04:23:31 PM Almost 70% in new Poll say don't impeach. So ridiculous to even be talking about this subject when all of the crimes were committed by the other side. They can't win the election fairly! [Twitter for iPhone]

Jun 16, 2019 05:55:55 PM Rep. Alexandria Ocasio-Cortez. "I think we have a very real risk of losing the Presidency to Donald Trump." I agree, and that is the only reason they play the impeach card, which cannot be legally used! [Twitter for iPhone]

Jun 16, 2019 08:48:26 PM Congratulations to Gary Woodland in winning the United States Open Golf Championship. Fantastic playing, great heart - there will be more in Gary's future! [Twitter for iPhone]

Jun 16, 2019 08:51:16 PM RT @LindseyGrahamSC: Very glad to see Mexico working with President @realDonaldTrump to up their game and deal with immigration from Centra... [Twitter for iPhone]

Jun 16, 2019 08:59:07 PM RT @i24NEWS_EN: Earlier today, @netanyahu and @USAmbIsrael held a ceremony for the inauguration of 'Trump Heights' — a town in #Israel's Go... [Twitter for iPhone]

Jun 16, 2019 09:18:01 PM Thank you Mr. Prime Minister, a great honor! https://t.co/ozLz84g3i0 [Twitter for iPhone]

Jun 17, 2019 07:00:45 AM Big Rally tomorrow night in Orlando, Florida, looks to be setting records. We are building large movie screens outside to take care of everybody. Over 100,000 requests. Our Country is doing great, far beyond what the haters & losers thought possible - and it will only get better! [Twitter for iPhone]

Jun 17, 2019 07:07:00 AM Only Fake Polls show us behind the Motley Crew. We are looking really good, but it is far too early to be focused on that. Much work to do! MAKE AMERICA GREAT AGAIN! [Twitter for iPhone]

Jun 17, 2019 10:49:44 AM "Iran to defy Uranium Stockpile Limits" [Twitter for iPhone]

Jun 17, 2019 02:05:30 PM One size doesn't fit all - I support West Virginia Schools. Keep up the great work, @WVGovernor Big Jim Justice - I am with you! https://t.co/EomFLcBjlz [Twitter for iPhone]

Jun 17, 2019 06:49:43 PM .@FoxNews Polls are always bad for me. They were against Crooked Hillary also. Something weird going on at Fox. Our polls show us leading in all 17 Swing States. For the record, I didn't spend 30 hours with @abcnews, but rather a tiny fraction of that. More Fake News @BretBaier [Twitter for iPhone]

Jun 17, 2019 08:20:39 PM ....long before they get to our Southern Border. Guatemala is getting ready to sign a Safe-Third Agreement. The only ones who won't do anything are the Democrats in Congress. They must vote to get rid of the loopholes, and fix asylum! If so, Border Crisis will end quickly! [Twitter for iPhone]

Jun 17, 2019 08:20:39 PM Next week ICE will begin the process of removing the millions of illegal aliens who have illicitly found their way into the United States. They will be removed as fast as they come in. Mexico, using their strong immigration laws, is doing a very good job of stopping people....... [Twitter for iPhone]

Jun 17, 2019 08:39:40 PM Thousands of people are already lined up in Orlando, some two days before tomorrow nights big Rally. Large Screens and food trucks will be there for those that can't get into the 25,000 capacity arena. It will be a very exciting evening! Make America Great Again! [Twitter for iPhone]

Jun 17, 2019 09:13:41 PM The story in the @nytimes about the U.S. escalating attacks on Russia's power grid is Fake News, and the Failing New York Times knows it. They should immediately release their sources which, if they exist at all, which I doubt, are phony. Times must be held fully accountable! [Twitter for iPhone]

Jun 17, 2019 11:51:18 PM Wow! The State Department said it has identified 30 Security Incidents involving current or former employees and their handling of Crooked Hillary Clinton's Emails. @FoxNews This is really big. Never admitted before. Highly Classified Material. Will the Dems investigate this? [Twitter for iPhone]

Jun 18, 2019 12:10:06 AM Only a few people showed up for the so-called Impeachment rallies over the weekend. The numbers were anemic, no spirit, no hope. More importantly, No Collusion, No Obstruction! [Twitter for iPhone]

Jun 18, 2019 05:53:44 AM Mario Draghi just announced more stimulus could come, which immediately dropped the Euro against the Dollar, making it unfairly easier for them to compete against the USA. They have been getting away with this for years, along with China and others. [Twitter for iPhone]

Jun 18, 2019 06:21:34 AM European Markets rose on comments (unfair to U.S.) made today by Mario D! [Twitter for iPhone]

Jun 18, 2019 06:30:23 AM The Fake News doesn't report it, but Republican enthusiasm is at an all time high. Look what is going on in Orlando, Florida, right now! People have never seen anything like it (unless you play a guitar). Going to be wild - See you later! [Twitter for iPhone]

Jun 18, 2019 08:39:38 AM Had a very good telephone conversation with President Xi of China. We will be having an extended meeting next week at the G-20 in Japan. Our respective teams will begin talks prior to our meeting. [Twitter for iPhone]

Jun 18, 2019 09:09:23 AM "ECB officials see Rate Cut as primary tool for any new stimulus." @business [Twitter for iPhone]

Jun 18, 2019 09:22:52 AM German DAX way up due to stimulus remarks from Mario Draghi. Very unfair to the United States! [Twitter for iPhone]

Jun 18, 2019 11:59:12 AM ....I thank Pat for his outstanding service and will be naming Secretary of the Army, Mark Esper, to be the new Acting Secretary of Defense. I know Mark, and have no doubt he will do a fantastic job! [Twitter for iPhone]

Jun 18, 2019 11:59:12 AM Acting Secretary of Defense Patrick Shanahan, who has done a wonderful job, has decided not to go forward with his confirmation process so that he can devote more time to his family.... [Twitter for iPhone]

Jun 18, 2019 03:32:07 PM Departing for Orlando, Florida with @FLOTUS Melania! https://t.co/EB2ewYArUP [Twitter for iPhone]

Jun 18, 2019 06:54:28 PM Join me LIVE tonight in Orlando, Florida at 8:00 P.M. Eastern as we kickoff #Trump2020. Enjoy! [Twitter for iPhone]

Jun 18, 2019 08:48:36 PM THANK YOU ORLANDO, FLORIDA!https://t.co/Va9FhByJi0 [Twitter for iPhone]

Jun 18, 2019 08:52:19 PM Together, we are breaking the most sacred rule in Washington Politics: we are KEEPING our promises to the American People. Because my only special interest is YOU! #Trump2020 https://t.co/bYyK6sOrak [Twitter for iPhone]

Jun 18, 2019 08:58:51 PM On no issue are Democrats more extreme – and more depraved – than when it comes to Border Security. The Democrat Agenda of open borders is morally reprehensible. It is the great betrayal of the American Middle Class and our Country as a whole! #Trump2020 https://t.co/f9RJhpp50J [Twitter for iPhone]

Jun 18, 2019 09:04:07 PM In the ultimate act of moral cowardice, not one Democrat Candidate for president - not a single one - has stood up to defend the incredible men and women of ICE and Border Patrol. They don't have the character, the virtue, or the spine! #Trump2020 https://t.co/oULNnVtxmW [Twitter for iPhone]

Jun 18, 2019 09:13:11 PM Don't ever forget - this election is about YOU. It is about YOUR family, YOUR future, & the fate of YOUR COUNTRY. We begin our campaign with the best record, the best results, the best agenda, & the only positive VISION for our Country's future! #Trump2020 https://t.co/Vmu28hKQh6 [Twitter for iPhone]

Jun 19, 2019 07:54:55 AM THANK YOU! #Trump2020us https://t.co/recnmmYAFN [Twitter for iPhone]

Jun 19, 2019 09:18:11 AM The Dems are very unhappy with the Mueller Report, so after almost 3 years, they want a Redo, or Do Over. This is extreme Presidential Harassment. They gave Crooked Hillary's people complete Immunity, yet now they bring back Hope Hicks. Why aren't the Dems looking at the..... [Twitter for iPhone]

Jun 19, 2019 09:18:12 AM ....33,000 Emails that Hillary and her lawyer deleted and acid washed AFTER GETTING A SUBPOENA FROM CONGRESS? That is real Obstruction that the Dems want no part of because their hearings are RIGGED and a disgrace to our Country! [Twitter for iPhone]

Jun 19, 2019 09:20:04 AM DEMOCRAT CONGRESSIONAL HEARINGS ARE #RIGGED! [Twitter for iPhone]

Jun 19, 2019 10:09:18 AM If I didn't have the Phony Witch Hunt going on for 3 years, and if the Fake News Media and their partner in Crime, the Democrats, would have played it straight, I would be way up in the Polls right now - with our Economy, winning by 20 points. But I'm winning anyway! [Twitter for iPhone]

Jun 19, 2019 02:48:02 PM So sad that the Democrats are putting wonderful Hope Hicks through hell, for 3 years now, after total exoneration by Robert Mueller & the Mueller Report. They were unhappy with result so they want a Do Over. Very unfair & costly to her. Will it ever end? Why aren't they....... [Twitter for iPhone]

Jun 19, 2019 02:48:04 PM ....asking Hillary Clinton why she deleted and acid washed her Emails AFTER getting a subpoena from Congress? Anybody else would be in jail for that, yet the Dems refuse to even bring it up. Rigged House Committee [Twitter for iPhone]

Jun 19, 2019 03:29:24 PM I will be interviewed LIVE tonight by @seanhannity on @FoxNews 9 P.M. Enjoy! [Twitter for iPhone]

Jun 19, 2019 03:39:28 PM Just returning from Orlando and Doral (Miami), Florida, and heading to the Oval Office, where I will present the great Economist, Dr. Arthur Laffer, with the Presidential Medal of Freedom. [Twitter for iPhone]

Jun 19, 2019 06:01:59 PM Congratulations to President Lopez Obrador — Mexico voted to ratify the USMCA today by a huge margin. Time for Congress to do the same here! [Twitter for iPhone]

Jun 19, 2019 07:12:31 PM Since Election Day 2016, Stocks up almost 50%, Stocks gained 9.2 Trillion Dollars in value, and more than 5,000,000 new jobs added to the Economy. @LouDobbs If our opponent had won, there would have been a market crash, plain and simple! @TuckerCarlson @seanhannity @IngrahamAngle [Twitter for iPhone]

Jun 20, 2019 08:58:53 AM S&P opens at Record High! [Twitter for iPhone]

Jun 20, 2019 09:14:13 AM "The President has a really good story to tell. We have unemployment lower than we've seen in decades. We have people who stopped looking for work coming back into the labor force. We are in a record growth period." Michael Steel @MSNBC (do you believe?) [Twitter for iPhone]

Jun 20, 2019 09:15:04 AM Iran made a very big mistake! [Twitter for iPhone]

Jun 20, 2019 12:49:52 PM It was my great honor to host Canadian Prime Minister @JustinTrudeau at the @WhiteHouse today!usc https://t.co/orlejZ9FFs [Twitter for iPhone]

Jun 20, 2019 05:22:36 PM S&P closes at Record High! https://t.co/C5nOXIQ7EJ [Twitter for iPhone]

Jun 21, 2019 07:19:49 AM Just revealed that the Failing and Desperate New York Times was feeding false stories about me, & those associated with me, to the FBI. This shows the kind of unprecedented hatred I have been putting up with for years with this Crooked newspaper. Is what they have done legal?... [Twitter for iPhone]

Jun 21, 2019 07:19:50 AM ...."This Russia Collusion Hoax was perpetrated in part by people inside the government, and in part by a compliant (Fake News) media." Mollie Hemingway. @TuckerCarlson @foxandfriends The facts are starting to pour out. Stay tuned! [Twitter for iPhone]

Jun 21, 2019 08:03:14 AM President Obama made a desperate and terrible deal with Iran - Gave them 150 Billion Dollars plus I.8 Billion Dollars in CASH! Iran was in big trouble and he bailed them out. Gave them a free path to Nuclear Weapons, and SOON. Instead of saying thank you, Iran yelled..... [Twitter for iPhone]

Jun 21, 2019 08:03:16 AM ....Death to America. I terminated deal, which was not even ratified by Congress, and imposed strong sanctions. They are a much weakened nation today than at the beginning of my Presidency, when they were causing major problems throughout the Middle East. Now they are Bust!.... [Twitter for iPhone]

Jun 21, 2019 08:03:17 AM ....On Monday they shot down an unmanned drone flying in International Waters. We were cocked & loaded to retaliate last night on 3 different sights when I asked, how many will die. 150 people, sir, was the answer from a General. 10 minutes before the strike I stopped it, not.... [Twitter for iPhone]

Jun 21, 2019 08:03:18 AM ....proportionate to shooting down an unmanned drone. I am in no hurry, our Military is rebuilt, new, and ready to go, by far the best in the world. Sanctions are biting & more added last night. Iran can NEVER have Nuclear Weapons, not against the USA, and not against the WORLD! [Twitter for iPhone]

Jun 21, 2019 02:50:23 PM https://t.co/JDS4zUXXJG [Twitter for iPhone]

Jun 21, 2019 09:49:45 PM RT @GOP: Under @realDonaldTrump's leadership, Florida is THRIVING! Read more from Pam Bondi — former AG of Florida↓ https://t.co/pLNpaO4... [Twitter for iPhone]

Jun 21, 2019 09:51:59 PM RT @RepMarkMeadows: The irony of Washington Democrats all but ignoring the dire situation at the border: they're calling it a "manufactured... [Twitter for iPhone]

Jun 21, 2019 09:52:20 PM RT @Jim_Jordan: There is a crisis at our border. Time for Congress to wake up, secure the border, and #DoWhatWeSaid. https://t.co/GCCJ9sYDkR [Twitter for iPhone]

Jun 22, 2019 07:30:27 AM The people that Ice will apprehend have already been ordered to be deported. This means that they have run from the law and run from the courts. These are people that are supposed to go back to their home country. They broke the law by coming into the country, & now by staying. [Twitter for iPhone]

Jun 22, 2019 07:32:25 AM When people come into our Country illegally, they will be DEPORTED! [Twitter for iPhone]

Jun 22, 2019 08:53:27 AM Stock Market is on track to have the best June in over 50 years! Thank you Mr. President! @WallStreetJour [Twitter for iPhone]

Jun 22, 2019 09:13:16 AM Stock Market is on track to have the best June in over 50 years! Thank you Mr. President! @WSJ [Twitter for iPhone]

Jun 22, 2019 10:56:52 AM RT @EricTrump: Behind the scenes in #Orlando - what an amazing night! @DonaldJTrumpJr @IvankaTrump https://t.co/DRqicdEFFY [Twitter for iPhone]

Jun 22, 2019 10:58:15 AM Looking good. We MUST WIN to KEEP AMERICA GREAT! https://t.co/ADULIQ0tO1 [Twitter for iPhone]

Jun 22, 2019 10:58:37 AM RT @EricTrump: This isn't a campaign, this is a movement! Thank you Orlando - we love you! #Florida #KeepAmericaGreat ususus https://t.co/M... [Twitter for iPhone]

Jun 22, 2019 10:58:50 AM RT @EricTrump: The crowds and the spirit outside the Amway Center waiting for @realDonaldTrump is absolutely incredible! #Orlando #2020 #Ma... [Twitter for iPhone]

Jun 22, 2019 10:59:33 AM A great book! https://t.co/QwB46HVpmv [Twitter for iPhone]

Jun 22, 2019 11:47:20 AM Thank you Jessica! https://t.co/gxNRfFqZCm [Twitter for iPhone]

Jun 22, 2019 11:48:26 AM https://t.co/mUc2KZFZON [Twitter for iPhone]

Jun 22, 2019 11:55:49 AM I am at Camp David working on many things, including Iran! We have a great Economy, Tariffs have been very helpful both with respect to the huge Dollars coming IN, & on helping to make good Trade Deals. The Dow heading to BEST June in 80 years! Stock Market BEST June in 50 years! [Twitter for iPhone]

Jun 22, 2019 01:56:33 PM Iran cannot have Nuclear Weapons! Under the terrible Obama plan, they would have been on their way to Nuclear in a short number of years, and existing verification is not acceptable. We are putting major additional Sanctions on Iran on Monday. I look forward to the day that..... [Twitter for iPhone]

Jun 22, 2019 01:56:34 PM ....Sanctions come off Iran, and they become a productive and prosperous nation again - The sooner the better! [Twitter for iPhone]

Jun 22, 2019 01:56:35 PM At the request of Democrats, I have delayed the Illegal Immigration Removal Process (Deportation) for two weeks to see if the Democrats and Republicans can get together and work out a solution to the Asylum and Loophole problems at the Southern Border. If not, Deportations start! [Twitter for iPhone]

Jun 22, 2019 04:24:47 PM https://t.co/SSWnX8oQ65 [Twitter for iPhone]

Jun 22, 2019 05:58:10 PM I never called the strike against Iran "BACK," as people are incorrectly reporting, I just stopped it from going forward at this time! [Twitter for iPhone]

Jun 23, 2019 07:13:26 AM I want to give the Democrats every last chance to quickly negotiate simple changes to Asylum and Loopholes. This will fix the Southern Border, together with the help that Mexico is now giving us. Probably won't happen, but worth a try. Two weeks and big Deportation begins! [Twitter for iPhone]

Jun 23, 2019 08:20:39 AM Wonderful Church service at Camp David. Thank you! [Twitter for iPhone]

Jun 23, 2019 09:46:46 AM When our Country had no debt and built everything from Highways to the Military with CASH, we had a big system of Tariffs. Now we allow other countries to steal our wealth, treasure, and jobs - But no more! The USA is doing great, with unlimited upside into the future! [Twitter for iPhone]

Jun 23, 2019 07:41:13 PM https://t.co/gw9cXRTtaR [Twitter for iPhone]

Jun 23, 2019 07:50:08 PM https://t.co/GY34Y0OeAS [Twitter Media Studio]

Jun 24, 2019 06:03:06 AM RT @VP: Mexico has done more to secure our border in 10 days than Democrats in Congress have in 10 YEARS. The time to put Americans first i... [Twitter for iPhone]

⊔   Jun 24, 2019 06:06:10 AM RT @IvankaTrump: "The Trump administration served as a catalyst for perhaps the largest criminal justice public-private-partnership ever as… [Twitter for iPhone]

⊔   Jun 24, 2019 06:06:30 AM RT @HolcombForIN: Governor Holcomb is working hard alongside @IvankaTrump, Commerce @SecretaryRoss & America's top CEOs to scale Indiana's… [Twitter for iPhone]

⊔   Jun 24, 2019 06:07:36 AM RT @realDonaldTrump: https://t.co/GY34Y0OeAS [Twitter for iPhone]

⊔   Jun 24, 2019 06:13:16 AM RT @realDonaldTrump: https://t.co/gw9cXRTtaR [Twitter for iPhone]

⊔   Jun 24, 2019 06:13:24 AM RT @realDonaldTrump: https://t.co/SSWnX8oQ65 [Twitter for iPhone]

⊔ Jun 24, 2019 07:08:01 AM China gets 91% of its Oil from the Straight, Japan 62%, & many other countries likewise. So why are we protecting the shipping lanes for other countries (many years) for zero compensation. All of these countries should be protecting their own ships on what has always been.... [Twitter for iPhone]

⊔ Jun 24, 2019 07:08:02 AM ....a dangerous journey. We don't even need to be there in that the U.S. has just become (by far) the largest producer of Energy anywhere in the world! The U.S. request for Iran is very simple - No Nuclear Weapons and No Further Sponsoring of Terror! [Twitter for iPhone]

⊔ Jun 24, 2019 07:29:49 AM ....Think of what it could have been if the Fed had gotten it right. Thousands of points higher on the Dow, and GDP in the 4's or even 5's. Now they stick, like a stubborn child, when we need rates cuts, & easing, to make up for what other countries are doing against us. Blew it! [Twitter for iPhone]

⊔ Jun 24, 2019 07:29:49 AM Despite a Federal Reserve that doesn't know what it is doing - raised rates far to fast (very low inflation, other parts of world slowing, lowering & easing) & did large scale tightening, $50 Billion/month, we are on course to have one of the best Months of June in U.S. history.. [Twitter for iPhone]

⊔ Jun 24, 2019 07:53:34 AM ....Think of what it could have been if the Fed had gotten it right. Thousands of points higher on the Dow, and GDP in the 4's or even 5's. Now they stick, like a stubborn child, when we need rates cuts, & easing, to make up for what other countries are doing against us. Blew it! [Twitter for iPhone]

⊔ Jun 24, 2019 07:53:34 AM Despite a Federal Reserve that doesn't know what it is doing - raised rates far too fast (very low inflation, other parts of world slowing, lowering & easing) & did large scale tightening, $50 Billion/month, we are on course to have one of the best Months of June in US history... [Twitter for iPhone]

Jun 24, 2019 09:12:31 AM I am pleased to announce the launch of https://t.co/D1MY2aPC7f. This new platform will allow my campaign and other Republicans to compete with the Democrats money machine. This has been a priority of mine and I'm pleased to share that it is up and running! #KeepAmericaGreat [Twitter for iPhone]

Jun 25, 2019 06:58:45 AM RT @VP: Mexico is keeping its promise & now sending 15,000 troops to border to help with crisis. Meanwhile Dems won't fund beds for migrant... [Twitter for iPhone]

Jun 25, 2019 06:59:09 AM RT @mike_pence: Looking forward to being in Miami today to kick off the @TeamTrump Latino Coalition! Under @realDonaldTrump more Hispanic A... [Twitter for iPhone]

Jun 25, 2019 06:59:20 AM RT @SharylAttkisson: Who thinks the debates just won't be the same without Donna Brazile working on them behind the scenes? [Twitter for iPhone]

Jun 25, 2019 07:01:30 AM RT @SteveScalise: Thank you @IvankaTrump for joining me and our Republican Whip Team at the Capitol tonight to talk about the work you're d... [Twitter for iPhone]

Jun 25, 2019 07:11:59 AM Stock Market is heading for one of the best months (June) in the history of our Country. Thank you Mr. President! [Twitter for iPhone]

Jun 25, 2019 09:42:29 AM ....The wonderful Iranian people are suffering, and for no reason at all. Their leadership spends all of its money on Terror, and little on anything else. The U.S. has not forgotten Iran's use of IED's & EFP's (bombs), which killed 2000 Americans, and wounded many more... [Twitter for iPhone]

Jun 25, 2019 09:42:29 AM Iran leadership doesn't understand the words "nice" or "compassion," they never have. Sadly, the thing they do understand is Strength and Power, and the USA is by far the most powerful Military Force in the world, with 1.5 Trillion Dollars invested over the last two years alone.. [Twitter for iPhone]

Jun 25, 2019 09:42:30 AM ....Iran's very ignorant and insulting statement, put out today, only shows that they do not understand reality. Any attack by Iran on anything American will be met with great and overwhelming force. In some areas, overwhelming will mean obliteration. No more John Kerry & Obama! [Twitter for iPhone]

Jun 25, 2019 02:25:20 PM ....Martha is strong on Crime and Borders, the 2nd Amendment, and loves our Military and Vets. She has my Complete and Total Endorsement! [Twitter for iPhone]

Jun 25, 2019 02:25:20 PM A brave former fighter jet pilot and warrior, Senator Martha McSally of Arizona has done an outstanding job in D.C., and is fully supportive of our agenda – she is with us all the way.... [Twitter for iPhone]

Jun 25, 2019 03:27:19 PM Today, it was my great honor to present the Medal of Honor to Army Staff Sgt. David Bellavia (HERO) for his courageous actions as a squad leader in Fallujah. #MOH https://t.co/FkNCazkWWo [Twitter for iPhone]

Jun 25, 2019 04:38:42 PM Staff Sgt. David Bellavia - today, we honor your extraordinary courage, we salute your selfless service, and we thank you for carrying on the legacy of American Valor that has always made our blessed nation the strongest and mightiest in the world! https://t.co/pQ3dhhaSpE [Twitter for iPhone]

Jun 25, 2019 05:20:42 PM Senator Thom Tillis of North Carolina has really stepped up to the plate. Thom is tough on Crime, Strong on the Border and fights hard against Illegal Immigration. He loves our Military, our Vets and our great Second Amendment. I give Thom my Full and Total Endorsement! [Twitter for iPhone]

Jun 25, 2019 09:34:41 PM Presidential Harassment! [Twitter for iPhone]

Jun 26, 2019 05:22:31 AM RT @JudicialWatch: .@TomFitton: "CA settled with JW & is taking steps to remove 1.5M inactive voters from the rolls. It's important for ele… [Twitter for iPhone]

Jun 26, 2019 05:23:08 AM RT @JudicialWatch: Hillary Clinton is not above the law, yet she has a record of contempt for the rule of law. Our leaders are bound by the… [Twitter for iPhone]

Jun 26, 2019 05:23:32 AM RT @JudicialWatch: A Judicial Watch lawsuit forced the state of California to begin removing more than 1.5 million potentially invalid name… [Twitter for iPhone]

Jun 26, 2019 05:40:12 AM Wow, @FoxNews did great in the ratings. CNN is dead as a door nail (no credibility), and MSNBC is dying fast. @foxandfriends and @MariaBartiromo are doing great! https://t.co/0sFBVmjR7f [Twitter for iPhone]

Jun 26, 2019 05:41:00 AM RT @MariaBartiromo: Tomorrow exclusive join us as @POTUS @realDonaldTrump joins me #LIVE @MorningsMaria @FoxBusiness 8am et https:… [Twitter for iPhone]

Jun 26, 2019 05:41:22 AM RT @mike_pence: Latino Americans know that it was freedom, not socialism, that gave us the most prosperous and powerful nation in the histo… [Twitter for iPhone]

Jun 26, 2019 05:43:13 AM RT @realDonaldTrump: Staff Sgt. David Bellavia - today, we honor your extraordinary courage, we salute your selfless service, and we thank… [Twitter for iPhone]

Jun 26, 2019 05:44:29 AM RT @PressSec: .@StephGrisham45 will be an incredible asset to the President and the country. I'm sad to leave the WH, but so happy our team… [Twitter for iPhone]

Jun 26, 2019 05:44:43 AM RT @mike_pence: America needs 4 more years of prosperity, 4 more years of security, and 4 MORE YEARS of President @realDonaldTrump! #KeepAm... [Twitter for iPhone]

Jun 26, 2019 05:45:10 AM RT @EricTrump: I hope everyone reads and watches this video to see the corruption of big tech. @Google should be absolutely ashamed. Un... [Twitter for iPhone]

Jun 26, 2019 05:45:29 AM RT @IvankaTrump: Great keynoting the Senate's weekly policy lunch and discussing workforce development policy, Higher Ed Act reauthorizatio... [Twitter for iPhone]

Jun 26, 2019 05:46:22 AM RT @ericbolling: Great choice @realDonaldTrump choosing @StephGrisham45 as your @PressSec !! https://t.co/jpv8z421TQ [Twitter for iPhone]

Jun 26, 2019 05:47:07 AM RT @CLewandowski_: #BREAKING: Melania Trump's senior aide to replace Sarah Sanders–Stephanie Grisham will be press secretary AND communicat... [Twitter for iPhone]

Jun 26, 2019 05:47:32 AM RT @mike_pence: What Americans hear tomorrow night will only confirm that Mexico has done more in the last 10 DAYS to secure the southern b... [Twitter for iPhone]

Jun 26, 2019 05:47:59 AM RT @Jim_Jordan: Tomorrow's hearing on the "Hatch Act" is just the latest attempt to silence the Trump administration. @KellyannePolls is a... [Twitter for iPhone]

Jun 26, 2019 05:48:51 AM RT @dougducey: Proud to stand with 27 other governors in calling for Congress to ratify #USMCA. It updates our nation's trade agreements wi... [Twitter for iPhone]

Jun 26, 2019 05:50:05 AM RT @SecretaryAcosta: Headed to Texas today to discuss #apprenticeship expansion, #PledgetoAmericasWorkers, and the #USMCA. Texas has added... [Twitter for iPhone]

Jun 26, 2019 05:50:16 AM RT @realDonaldTrump: Stock Market is heading for one of the best months (June) in the history of our Country. Thank you Mr. President! [Twitter for iPhone]

Jun 26, 2019 05:51:27 AM RT @FLOTUS: Looking forward to collaborating with all of our #BeBest Ambassadors. Delighted to be working alongside so many people both ins... [Twitter for iPhone]

Jun 26, 2019 05:52:31 AM RT @ABC: Jared Kushner speaks at U.S. Mideast peace plan conference in Bahrain: "For a moment, imagine a new reality in the Middle East." h... [Twitter for iPhone]

Jun 26, 2019 06:01:04 AM Too bad the Dems in Congress won't do anything at all about Border Security. They want Open Borders, which means crime. But we are getting it done, including building the Wall! More people than ever before are coming because the USA Economy is so good, the best in history. [Twitter for iPhone]

Jun 26, 2019 06:05:24 AM I will be interviewed by @MariaBartiromo today at 8:15 A.M. on @FoxBusiness. Enjoy! [Twitter for iPhone]

Jun 26, 2019 06:13:58 AM Democrats want Open Borders, which equals violent crime, drugs and human trafficking. They also want very high taxes, like 90%. Republicans want what's good for America - the exact opposite! [Twitter for iPhone]

Jun 26, 2019 09:27:56 AM ....in our Country's history, and the poverty index is also best number EVER), leagues and teams love coming to the White House. I am a big fan of the American Team, and Women's Soccer, but Megan should WIN first before she TALKS! Finish the job! We haven't yet.... [Twitter for iPhone]

Jun 26, 2019 09:27:56 AM Women's soccer player, @meganrapino, just stated that she is "not going to the F...ing White House if we win." Other than the NBA, which now refuses to call owners, owners (please explain that I just got Criminal Justice Reform passed, Black unemployment is at the lowest level... [Twitter for iPhone]

Jun 26, 2019 09:27:58 AM ....invited Megan or the team, but I am now inviting the TEAM, win or lose. Megan should never disrespect our Country, the White House, or our Flag, especially since so much has been done for her & the team. Be proud of the Flag that you wear. The USA is doing GREAT! [Twitter for iPhone]

Jun 26, 2019 09:42:37 AM Women's soccer player, @mPinoe, just stated that she is "not going to the F...ing White House if we win." Other than the NBA, which now refuses to call owners, owners (please explain that I just got Criminal Justice Reform passed, Black unemployment is at the lowest level... [Twitter for iPhone]

Jun 26, 2019 09:42:38 AM ....invited Megan or the team, but I am now inviting the TEAM, win or lose. Megan should never disrespect our Country, the White House, or our Flag, especially since so much has been done for her & the team. Be proud of the Flag that you wear. The USA is doing GREAT! [Twitter for iPhone]

Jun 26, 2019 09:42:38 AM ....in our Country's history, and the poverty index is also best number EVER), leagues and teams love coming to the White House. I am a big fan of the American Team, and Women's Soccer, but Megan should WIN first before she TALKS! Finish the job! We haven't yet.... [Twitter for iPhone]

Jun 26, 2019 11:53:37 AM It was my great honor to speak at the Faith & Freedom Coalition Conference today in Washington, D.C. Thank you! #RTM2019 https://t.co/KknwcFhawb [Twitter for iPhone]

Jun 26, 2019 01:26:41 PM The Democrats should change the Loopholes and Asylum Laws so lives will be saved at our Southern Border. They said it was not a crisis at the Border, that it was all just "manufactured." Now they admit that I was right - But they must do something about it. Fix the Laws NOW! [Twitter for iPhone]

Jun 26, 2019 02:13:22 PM Just departed for the #G20 Summit in Osaka, Japan!usjp https://t.co/IdAYUOiWqf [Twitter for iPhone]

Jun 26, 2019 03:24:00 PM The Democrats would save many lives if they would change our broken and very DANGEROUS Immigration Laws. It can be done instantly! [Twitter for iPhone]

Jun 26, 2019 03:31:31 PM https://t.co/mudnBtvWO1 [Twitter for iPhone]

Jun 26, 2019 04:17:54 PM "I have been in office for many years, the Military is very important to me, and at no time in my professional life has the U.S. Military been as strong as it is right now." Thank you @LindseyGrahamSC [Twitter for iPhone]

Jun 26, 2019 04:46:45 PM According to Fake News (and low ratings) @CNN, "Democrats say hearings could change impeachment debate." That's because they have lost the impeachment debate (80% say NO), and they are hoping that yet another DO OVER, after 2 1/2 years and $40,000,000, will turn things around.... [Twitter for iPhone]

Jun 26, 2019 04:46:46 PM ....No Collusion, No Obstruction! Robert Mueller said he was done after his last 9 minute news conference, as later corrected. Now the Dems want to give it another try. Does it ever end? [Twitter for iPhone]

Jun 26, 2019 04:47:40 PM The Republican Senate just passed bipartisan humanitarian assistance for our Southern Border, 84-8! In addition to aid, Congress must close the catastrophic loopholes that are driving the Crisis. We must end incentives for Smuggling Children, Trafficking Women, and Selling Drugs. [Twitter for iPhone]

Jun 26, 2019 05:47:42 PM Why aren't the Democrats in the House calling Comey, Brennan, Clapper, Page and her FBI lover (whose invaluable phone records were illegally deleted), Crooked Hillary, Podesta, Ohr (and Nellie), the GPS Fusion characters, Christopher Steele, the DNC (& their missing server).... [Twitter for iPhone]

Jun 26, 2019 05:47:43 PM ....and all of the others who have leaked, lied and did so many other terrible things? How is it even possible that these people are not being brought forward? Because it is a Rigged Democrat Con Game, and the Fake and Corrupt Media loves every minute of it! [Twitter for iPhone]

Jun 26, 2019 06:14:52 PM For tonight's #DemDebate, be sure to follow @TeamTrump, @TrumpWarRoom, @Parscale, @KayleighMcEnany, @TimMurtaugh, and @Marc_Lotter for RAPID RESPONSE, FACT CHECKING, and the TRUTH! #MAGA #KAG Sorry, I'm on Air Force One, off to save the Free World! [Twitter for iPhone]

Jun 26, 2019 06:46:04 PM Ever since the passage of the Super Predator Crime Bill, pushed hard by @JoeBiden, together with Bill and Crooked Hillary Clinton, which inflicted great pain on many, but especially the African American Community, Democrats have tried and failed to pass Criminal Justice Reform... [Twitter for iPhone]

Jun 26, 2019 06:46:05 PM ....They came to me asking for help, and I got Criminal Justice Reform passed, with help from both Republicans and Democrats. Many said that nobody but President Trump could have done this. All previous administrations failed. Please ask why THEY failed to the candidates! [Twitter for iPhone]

Jun 26, 2019 06:52:03 PM .@ByronYork: "What now, for those who denied a 'crisis' at the border?" https://t.co/g0EO7Xs0yE [Twitter for iPhone]

Jun 26, 2019 07:02:08 PM These flyers depict Australia's policy on Illegal Immigration. Much can be learned! https://t.co/QgGU0gyjRS [Twitter for iPhone]

Jun 26, 2019 08:35:55 PM BORING! [Twitter for iPhone]

Jun 26, 2019 09:06:51 PM .@NBCNews and @MSNBC should be ashamed of themselves for having such a horrible technical breakdown in the middle of the debate. Truly unprofessional and only worthy of a FAKE NEWS Organization, which they are! [Twitter for iPhone]

Jun 26, 2019 09:33:50 PM Just stopped in Alaska and said hello to our GREAT troops! https://t.co/oLYn1mpaVm [Twitter for iPhone]

Jun 26, 2019 09:40:04 PM https://t.co/JDS4zVfyBe [Twitter for iPhone]

Jun 26, 2019 10:47:05 PM I look forward to speaking with Prime Minister Modi about the fact that India, for years having put very high Tariffs against the United States, just recently increased the Tariffs even further. This is unacceptable and the Tariffs must be withdrawn! [Twitter for iPhone]

Jun 27, 2019 04:36:39 AM Thank you @MSNBC, real professionals! @chucktodd @maddow https://t.co/7ZCkcUQ4yA [Twitter for iPhone]

Jun 27, 2019 08:28:46 AM Thank you! #G20Summit https://t.co/28Y5rPE3BE [Twitter for iPhone]

Jun 27, 2019 12:37:32 PM .....United States Supreme Court is given additional information from which it can make a final and decisive decision on this very critical matter. Can anyone really believe that as a great Country, we are not able the ask whether or not someone is a Citizen. Only in America! [Twitter for iPhone]

Jun 27, 2019 12:37:32 PM Seems totally ridiculous that our government, and indeed Country, cannot ask a basic question of Citizenship in a very expensive, detailed and important Census, in this case for 2020. I have asked the lawyers if they can delay the Census, no matter how long, until the..... [Twitter for iPhone]

Jun 27, 2019 05:22:39 PM Bipartisan Humanitarian Aid Bill for the Southern Border just passed. A great job done by all! Now we must work to get rid of the Loopholes and fix Asylum. Thank you also to Mexico for the work being done on helping with Illegal Immigration - a very big difference! [Twitter for iPhone]

Jun 27, 2019 07:46:37 PM Great to be back in Japan for the #G20OsakaSummit https://t.co/ZUwla1UMAQ [Twitter for iPhone]

Jun 27, 2019 08:37:04 PM All Democrats just raised their hands for giving millions of illegal aliens unlimited healthcare. How about taking care of American Citizens first!? That's the end of that race! [Twitter for iPhone]

Jun 28, 2019 04:12:18 AM The Stock Market went up massively from the day after I won the Election, all the way up to the day that I took office, because of the enthusiasm for the fact that I was going to be President. That big Stock Market increase must be credited to me. If Hillary won - a Big Crash! [Twitter for iPhone]

Jun 28, 2019 04:26:34 AM I am in Japan at the G-20, representing our Country well, but I heard it was not a good day for Sleepy Joe or Crazy Bernie. One is exhausted, the other is nuts - so what's the big deal? [Twitter for iPhone]

Jun 28, 2019 05:41:17 PM 54% in Poll! I would be at 75% (with our great economy, maybe the best ever) if not for the Phony Witch Hunt and the Fake News Media! [Twitter for iPhone]

Jun 28, 2019 05:51:41 PM After some very important meetings, including my meeting with President Xi of China, I will be leaving Japan for South Korea (with President Moon). While there, if Chairman Kim of North Korea sees this, I would meet him at the Border/DMZ just to shake his hand and say Hello(?)! [Twitter for iPhone]

Jun 29, 2019 05:11:32 AM Thank you #G20OsakaSummit https://t.co/9FCqSuR5Bp [Twitter for iPhone]

Jun 29, 2019 04:22:11 PM I had a great meeting with President Xi of China yesterday, far better than expected. I agreed not to increase the already existing Tariffs that we charge China while we continue to negotiate. China has agreed that, during the negotiation, they will begin purchasing large...... [Twitter for iPhone]

Jun 29, 2019 04:22:12 PM .....amounts of agricultural product from our great Farmers. At the request of our High Tech companies, and President Xi, I agreed to allow Chinese company Huawei to buy product from them which will not impact our National Security. Importantly, we have opened up negotiations... [Twitter for iPhone]

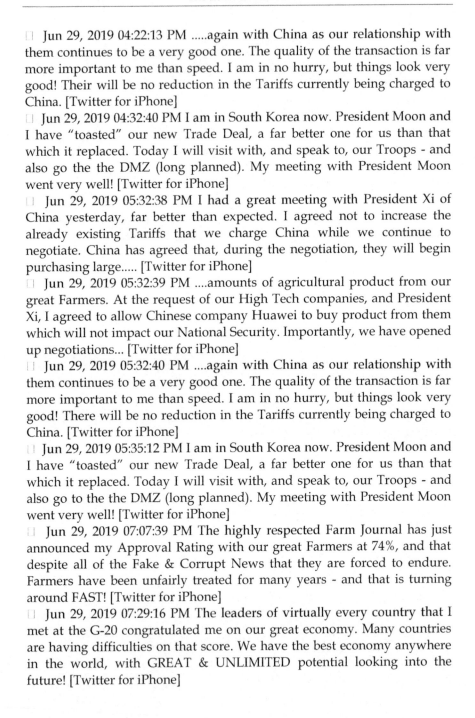

Jun 29, 2019 04:22:13 PM .....again with China as our relationship with them continues to be a very good one. The quality of the transaction is far more important to me than speed. I am in no hurry, but things look very good! Their will be no reduction in the Tariffs currently being charged to China. [Twitter for iPhone]

Jun 29, 2019 04:32:40 PM I am in South Korea now. President Moon and I have "toasted" our new Trade Deal, a far better one for us than that which it replaced. Today I will visit with, and speak to, our Troops - and also go the the DMZ (long planned). My meeting with President Moon went very well! [Twitter for iPhone]

Jun 29, 2019 05:32:38 PM I had a great meeting with President Xi of China yesterday, far better than expected. I agreed not to increase the already existing Tariffs that we charge China while we continue to negotiate. China has agreed that, during the negotiation, they will begin purchasing large..... [Twitter for iPhone]

Jun 29, 2019 05:32:39 PM ....amounts of agricultural product from our great Farmers. At the request of our High Tech companies, and President Xi, I agreed to allow Chinese company Huawei to buy product from them which will not impact our National Security. Importantly, we have opened up negotiations... [Twitter for iPhone]

Jun 29, 2019 05:32:40 PM ....again with China as our relationship with them continues to be a very good one. The quality of the transaction is far more important to me than speed. I am in no hurry, but things look very good! There will be no reduction in the Tariffs currently being charged to China. [Twitter for iPhone]

Jun 29, 2019 05:35:12 PM I am in South Korea now. President Moon and I have "toasted" our new Trade Deal, a far better one for us than that which it replaced. Today I will visit with, and speak to, our Troops - and also go to the the DMZ (long planned). My meeting with President Moon went very well! [Twitter for iPhone]

Jun 29, 2019 07:07:39 PM The highly respected Farm Journal has just announced my Approval Rating with our great Farmers at 74%, and that despite all of the Fake & Corrupt News that they are forced to endure. Farmers have been unfairly treated for many years - and that is turning around FAST! [Twitter for iPhone]

Jun 29, 2019 07:29:16 PM The leaders of virtually every country that I met at the G-20 congratulated me on our great economy. Many countries are having difficulties on that score. We have the best economy anywhere in the world, with GREAT & UNLIMITED potential looking into the future! [Twitter for iPhone]

Jun 30, 2019 05:21:00 AM RT @TheBlueHouseKR: @realDonaldTrump @moonriver365 @hellopolicy @mofa_kr @SecPompeo 오울렛 초소에서 브리핑을 받고 북측을 바라보며 대화하는 한.미 정상의 모습. 오울렛 초소는 한국전쟁... [Twitter for iPhone]

Jun 30, 2019 05:21:17 AM Leaving South Korea after a wonderful meeting with Chairman Kim Jong Un. Stood on the soil of North Korea, an important statement for all, and a great honor! [Twitter for iPhone]

Jun 30, 2019 07:47:37 PM https://t.co/ctb5YJL1Vb [Twitter for iPhone]

Jun 30, 2019 10:17:58 PM So many amazing things happened over the last three days. All, or at least most of those things, are great for the United States. Much was accomplished! [Twitter for iPhone]

Jun 30, 2019 10:27:29 PM "Stock had the Best First Half since 1997." @WallStreetJour Our Country is doing great - the talk of the world! [Twitter for iPhone]

Jun 30, 2019 10:32:07 PM "Stocks Cap Best First Half Since 1997" @WallStreetJour Our Country is doing great! [Twitter for iPhone]

Jun 30, 2019 10:50:10 PM "Stocks Cap Best First Half Since 1997" @WSJ Our Country is doing great! [Twitter for iPhone]

Jul 1, 2019 09:47:52 AM Congratulations to legislators in New Jersey for not passing taxes that would have driven large numbers of high end taxpayers out of the state. Many were planning to leave, & will now be staying. New York & others should start changing their thought process on taxes, fast! [Twitter for iPhone]

Jul 1, 2019 09:57:13 AM Thank you to President Moon of South Korea for hosting the American Delegation and me immediately following the very successful G-20 in Japan. While there, it was great to call on Chairman Kim of North Korea to have our very well covered meeting. Good things can happen for all! [Twitter for iPhone]

Jul 1, 2019 10:02:58 AM Congratulations to Prime Minister Abe of Japan for hosting such a fantastic and well run G-20. There wasn't a thing that was missing or a mistake that was made. PERFECT! The people of Japan must be very proud of their Prime Minister. [Twitter for iPhone]

Jul 1, 2019 10:42:09 AM https://t.co/k24a6VMTFu [Twitter for iPhone]

Jul 1, 2019 10:47:35 AM "In my opinion the President has done more good on the Korean issue in the last year and a half than President Obama did in eight years. If you look at the strides they made during the Obama years, which advocated strategic patience-they stuck their head in the sand. This is..... [Twitter for iPhone]

Jul 1, 2019 10:47:36 AM .....why President Trump has to deal with North Korea the way it is now. He had to figure out what to do with the Korea mess. I think this is why the President deserves a lot of credit." Harry Kazianis, Center for the National Interest. Thank you! [Twitter for iPhone]

Jul 1, 2019 11:10:44 AM ....more money than it had. Going on for years, originally brought by Crooked Hillary's Campaign Chair, A.G. Eric Schneiderman, until forced to resign for abuse against women. They never even looked at the disgusting Clinton Foundation. Now Cuomo's A.G. is harassing all of my.... [Twitter for iPhone]

Jul 1, 2019 11:10:44 AM It is very hard and expensive to live in New York. Governor Andrew Cuomo uses his Attorney General as a bludgeoning tool for his own purposes. They sue on everything, always in search of a crime. I even got sued on a Foundation which took Zero rent & expenses & gave away... [Twitter for iPhone]

Jul 1, 2019 11:10:45 AM ....New York businesses in search of anything at all they can find to make me look as bad as possible. So, on top of ridiculously high taxes, my children and companies are spending a fortune on lawyers. No wonder people and businesses are fleeing New York in record numbers! [Twitter for iPhone]

Jul 1, 2019 11:37:21 AM That's right, The Trump Foundation gave away 100% plus, with Zero rent or expenses charged, and has been being sued by Cuomo and New York State for years - another part of the political Witch Hunt. Just in case anyone is interested - Clinton Foundation never even looked at! [Twitter for iPhone]

Jul 1, 2019 05:15:29 PM I am excited to announce that @MercedesSchlapp will soon be joining our Campaign. She feels so strongly about our Country & its future. We are setting records in so many ways, & we will keep it going. Mercedes has done a fantastic job within the Administration & I am so thankful! [Twitter for iPhone]

Jul 1, 2019 05:16:51 PM It was great being with Chairman Kim Jong Un of North Korea this weekend. We had a great meeting, he looked really well and very healthy - I look forward to seeing him again soon.... [Twitter for iPhone]

Jul 1, 2019 05:17:52 PM ....In the meantime, our teams will be meeting to work on some solutions to very long term and persistent problems. No rush, but I am sure we will ultimately get there! [Twitter for iPhone]

Jul 1, 2019 05:18:55 PM I will be interviewed by @TuckerCarlson tonight at 8:00pm on @FoxNews! [Twitter for iPhone]

Jul 2, 2019 06:21:38 AM Mark Levin has written a big number one bestselling book called, conspicuously and accurately, "Unfreedom of the Press." It is a great book that tells it like it is, fake news and all. Keep this book number one! [Twitter for iPhone]

Jul 2, 2019 06:21:38 AM ...Texas will defend them & indemnify them against political harassment by New York State and Governor Cuomo. So many people are leaving New York for Texas and Florida that it is totally under siege. First New York taxes you too high, then they sue you, just to complete the job [Twitter for iPhone]

Jul 2, 2019 06:21:38 AM People are fleeing New York like never before. If they own a business, they are twice as likely to flee. And if they are a victim of harassment by the A.G. of the state, like what they are doing to our great NRA, which I think will move quickly to Texas, where they are loved..... [Twitter for iPhone]

Jul 2, 2019 06:38:22 AM As most people are aware, according to the Polls, I won EVERY debate, including the three with Crooked Hillary Clinton, despite the fact that in the first debate, they modulated the sound on me, and got caught. This crew looks somewhat easier than Crooked, but you never know? [Twitter for iPhone]

Jul 2, 2019 06:50:57 AM The Economy is the BEST IT HAS EVER BEEN! Even much of the Fake News is giving me credit for that! [Twitter for iPhone]

Jul 2, 2019 09:25:06 AM Big 4th of July in D.C. "Salute to America." The Pentagon & our great Military Leaders are thrilled to be doing this & showing to the American people, among other things, the strongest and most advanced Military anywhere in the World. Incredible Flyovers & biggest ever Fireworks! [Twitter for iPhone]

Jul 2, 2019 09:51:51 AM Robert Mueller is being asked to testify yet again. He said he could only stick to the Report, & that is what he would and must do. After so much testimony & total transparency, this Witch Hunt must now end. No more Do Overs. No Collusion, No Obstruction. The Great Hoax is dead! [Twitter for iPhone]

Jul 2, 2019 11:29:07 AM https://t.co/4FMs202NrW [Twitter for iPhone]

Jul 2, 2019 04:52:43 PM RT @IvankaTrump: Thank you Prime Minster Abe for inviting me to address heads of State on the economic + national security imperative of ec... [Twitter for iPhone]

Jul 2, 2019 05:05:56 PM Thanks to "Phantom Fireworks" and "Fireworks by Grucci" for their generosity in donating the biggest fireworks show Washington D.C. has ever seen. CEO's Bruce Zoldan and Phil Grucci are helping to make this the greatest 4th of July celebration in our Nations history! [Twitter for iPhone]

Jul 2, 2019 05:08:29 PM ....Prior to his current position, Christopher served as a professor and Chair of Economics at Notre Dame. [Twitter for iPhone]

Jul 2, 2019 05:08:29 PM I am pleased to announce that it is my intention to nominate Christopher Waller, Ph. D., Executive VP and Director of Research, Federal Reserve Bank of St. Louis, Missouri, to be on the board of the Federal Reserve.... [Twitter for iPhone]

Jul 2, 2019 05:10:44 PM I am pleased to announce that it is my intention to nominate Judy Shelton, Ph. D., U.S. Executive Dir, European Bank of Reconstruction & Development. Judy is a Founding Member of the board of directors of Empower America and has served on the board of directors of Hilton Hotels. [Twitter for iPhone]

Jul 2, 2019 05:36:48 PM ....Judy is a Founding Member of the board of directors of Empower America and has served on the board of directors of Hilton Hotels. [Twitter for iPhone]

Jul 2, 2019 05:36:48 PM I am pleased to announce that it is my intention to nominate Judy Shelton, Ph. D., U.S. Executive Dir, European Bank of Reconstruction & Development to be on the board of the Federal Reserve.... [Twitter for iPhone]

Jul 2, 2019 05:43:37 PM https://t.co/hWiNicShLY [Twitter for iPhone]

Jul 2, 2019 08:58:41 PM More great information from the @NatlParkService for Thursday's Fourth of July Celebration here in Washington, D.C. #SaluteToAmericaus https://t.co/AiZKkvBsh7 [Twitter for iPhone]

Jul 2, 2019 09:07:58 PM Thanks @RobertJeffress! https://t.co/wFZyCyh3W6 [Twitter for iPhone]

Jul 2, 2019 09:33:08 PM ....to do whatever is necessary to bring this most vital of questions, and this very important case, to a successful conclusion. USA! USA! USA! [Twitter for iPhone]

Jul 2, 2019 09:33:08 PM A very sad time for America when the Supreme Court of the United States won't allow a question of "Is this person a Citizen of the United States?" to be asked on the #2020 Census! Going on for a long time. I have asked the Department of Commerce and the Department of Justice.... [Twitter for iPhone]

Jul 2, 2019 11:06:20 PM Iran was violating the 150 Billion Dollar (plus 1.8 Billion Dollar in CASH) Nuclear Deal with the United States, and others who paid NOTHING, long before I became President - and they have now breached their stockpile limit. Not good! [Twitter for iPhone]

Jul 3, 2019 07:16:30 AM Our July 4th Salute to America at the Lincoln Memorial is looking to be really big. It will be the show of a lifetime! [Twitter for iPhone]

Jul 3, 2019 07:27:57 AM We have the greatest economy anywhere in the world. We have the greatest military anywhere in the world. Not bad! [Twitter for iPhone]

Jul 3, 2019 09:12:12 AM S&P 500 hits new record high. Up 19% for the year. Congratulations! [Twitter for iPhone]

Jul 3, 2019 09:21:52 AM China and Europe playing big currency manipulation game and pumping money into their system in order to compete with USA. We should MATCH, or continue being the dummies who sit back and politely watch as other countries continue to play their games - as they have for many years! [Twitter for iPhone]

Jul 3, 2019 09:30:33 AM The cost of our great Salute to America tomorrow will be very little compared to what it is worth. We own the planes, we have the pilots, the airport is right next door (Andrews), all we need is the fuel. We own the tanks and all. Fireworks are donated by two of the greats. Nice! [Twitter for iPhone]

Jul 3, 2019 09:47:57 AM Congratulations to Navy Seal Eddie Gallagher, his wonderful wife Andrea, and his entire family. You have been through much together. Glad I could help! [Twitter for iPhone]

Jul 3, 2019 10:06:40 AM The News Reports about the Department of Commerce dropping its quest to put the Citizenship Question on the Census is incorrect or, to state it differently, FAKE! We are absolutely moving forward, as we must, because of the importance of the answer to this question. [Twitter for iPhone]

Jul 3, 2019 02:31:49 PM .....came from, and in far safer conditions. No matter how good things actually look, even if perfect, the Democrat visitors will act shocked & aghast at how terrible things are. Just Pols. If they really want to fix them, change the Immigration Laws and Loopholes. So easy to do! [Twitter for iPhone]

Jul 3, 2019 02:31:49 PM Our Border Patrol people are not hospital workers, doctors or nurses. The Democrats bad Immigration Laws, which could be easily fixed, are the problem. Great job by Border Patrol, above and beyond. Many of these illegals aliens are living far better now than where they..... [Twitter for iPhone]

Jul 3, 2019 02:31:50 PM .....Now, if you really want to fix the Crisis at the Southern Border, both humanitarian and otherwise, tell migrants not to come into our country unless they are willing to do so legally, and hopefully through a system based on Merit. This way we have no problems at all! [Twitter for iPhone]

Jul 3, 2019 03:22:30 PM If Illegal Immigrants are unhappy with the conditions in the quickly built or refitted detentions centers, just tell them not to come. All problems solved! [Twitter for iPhone]

Jul 3, 2019 03:23:53 PM Mexico is doing a far better job than the Democrats on the Border. Thank you Mexico! [Twitter for iPhone]

Jul 3, 2019 03:33:24 PM Iran has just issued a New Warning. Rouhani says that they will Enrich Uranium to "any amount we want" if there is no new Nuclear Deal. Be careful with the threats, Iran. They can come back to bite you like nobody has been bitten before! [Twitter for iPhone]

Jul 3, 2019 10:44:03 PM Today's Stock Market is the highest in the history of our great Country! This is the 104th time since the Election of 2016 that we have reached a NEW HIGH. Congratulations USA! [Twitter for iPhone]

Jul 4, 2019 06:20:58 AM So important for our Country that the very simple and basic "Are you a Citizen of the United States?" question be allowed to be asked in the 2020 Census. Department of Commerce and the Department of Justice are working very hard on this, even on the 4th of July! [Twitter for iPhone]

Jul 4, 2019 06:23:30 AM HAPPY 4TH OF JULY! [Twitter for iPhone]

Jul 4, 2019 06:47:22 AM ....and advanced aircraft anywhere in the World. Perhaps even Aircraft One will do a low & loud sprint over the crowd. That will start at 6:00P.M., but be there early. Then, at 9:00 P.M., a great (to put it mildly) fireworks display. I will speak on behalf of our great Country! [Twitter for iPhone]

Jul 4, 2019 06:47:22 AM People are coming from far and wide to join us today and tonight for what is turning out to be one of the biggest celebrations in the history of our Country, SALUTE TO AMERICA, an all day event at the Lincoln Memorial, culminating with large scale flyovers of the most modern..... [Twitter for iPhone]

Jul 4, 2019 07:41:57 AM ....and advanced aircraft anywhere in the World. Perhaps even Air Force One will do a low & loud sprint over the crowd. That will start at 6:00P.M., but be there early. Then, at 9:00 P.M., a great (to put it mildly) fireworks display. I will speak on behalf of our great Country! [Twitter for iPhone]

Jul 4, 2019 07:41:57 AM People are coming from far and wide to join us today and tonight for what is turning out to be one of the biggest celebrations in the history of our Country, SALUTE TO AMERICA, an all day event at the Lincoln Memorial, culminating with large scale flyovers of the most modern..... [Twitter for iPhone]

Jul 4, 2019 07:42:23 AM RT @RealCandaceO: You cannot be a victim and a victor at the same time. You can either choose to win or accept your status as a loser.... [Twitter for iPhone]

Jul 4, 2019 07:45:51 AM RT @TheOfficerTatum: What I have seen from the last two nights isn't America. These candidates are disgraceful. All I saw was pandering.... [Twitter for iPhone]

Jul 4, 2019 08:05:17 AM Great news for the Republican Party as one of the dumbest & most disloyal men in Congress is "quitting" the Party. No Collusion, No Obstruction! Knew he couldn't get the nomination to run again in the Great State of Michigan. Already being challenged for his seat. A total loser! [Twitter for iPhone]

Jul 4, 2019 01:03:41 PM Looks like a lot of people already heading to SALUTE TO AMERICA at Lincoln Memorial. It will be well worth the trip and wait. See you there at 6:00 P.M. Amazing music and bands. Thank you ARMY! [Twitter for iPhone]

Jul 4, 2019 02:24:13 PM Been fully briefed on earthquake in Southern California. All seems to be very much under control! [Twitter for iPhone]

Jul 4, 2019 04:57:04 PM Weather looking good, clearing rapidly and temperatures going down fast. See you in 45 minutes, 6:30 to 7:00 P.M. at Lincoln Memorial! [Twitter for iPhone]

Jul 4, 2019 07:01:34 PM #SaluteToAmericaus#July4th https://t.co/CMxvvow5um [Twitter for iPhone]

Jul 4, 2019 07:28:07 PM A great crowd of tremendous Patriots this evening, all the way back to the Washington Monument! #SaluteToAmericaus https://t.co/nJghdfqIhX [Twitter for iPhone]

Jul 4, 2019 07:44:20 PM RT @AndrewHClark: Epic. #America #TrumpSpeech https://t.co/T3aQTIsucg [Twitter for iPhone]

Jul 4, 2019 07:50:59 PM RT @deronrossi: @realDonaldTrump The #SaluteToAmerica was awesome. Thanks to @FoxNews for covering it, the program and flyovers were great.... [Twitter for iPhone]

Jul 4, 2019 07:51:57 PM RT @JohnDePetroshow: Tonight is a perfect example where the critics of @realDonaldTrump criticize him and underestimate him. I have chills... [Twitter for iPhone]

Jul 4, 2019 07:53:33 PM RT @charliekirk11: Despite the left's best attempts at destroying a salute to America, the place is PACKED! God bless @realDonaldTrump and... [Twitter for iPhone]

Jul 4, 2019 07:54:14 PM RT @charliekirk11: RT if you are THANKFUL to have @realDonaldTrump as President this beautiful Independence Day! https://t.co/E0JljJOTgX [Twitter for iPhone]

Jul 4, 2019 07:55:00 PM RT @rnlynn1958: What a great celebration. I'm in tears and proud. Being a Navy Brat, I'm honestly overwhelmed with gratitude and pride. Th... [Twitter for iPhone]

Jul 4, 2019 07:56:03 PM RT @chuckwoolery: Rain? who cares. This is what it really looked like. https://t.co/CFxPjWeuNq [Twitter for iPhone]

Jul 4, 2019 07:56:54 PM RT @BreitbartNews: Communists BURN American flag near the White House on Independence Day. https://t.co/8lyfZ5EBwd [Twitter for iPhone]

Jul 4, 2019 07:59:15 PM RT @SenTedCruz: It is time to end the crisis at our border. And the only way we will end this crisis is for Congress to stop the political... [Twitter for iPhone]

Jul 4, 2019 08:04:02 PM RT @NBCNews: @NBCNewsNow Air Force One flies over the Lincoln Memorial Reflecting Pool at the start of President Trump's Fourth of July cel... [Twitter for iPhone]

Jul 4, 2019 08:31:51 PM RT @realDonaldTrump: #SaluteToAmericaυs#July4th https://t.co/CMxvvow5um [Twitter for iPhone]

Jul 4, 2019 08:31:55 PM RT @realDonaldTrump: A great crowd of tremendous Patriots this evening, all the way back to the Washington Monument! #SaluteToAmericaυs htt... [Twitter for iPhone]

Jul 4, 2019 08:54:41 PM RT @dcexaminer: "It'd be hard for the Democrats to say, 'well, we started an investigation we shouldn't have and continued it by breaking t... [Twitter for iPhone]

Jul 4, 2019 10:06:54 PM RT @dcexaminer: When Biden landed in Iowa this week, a new poll from A Focus on Rural America showed his support among Democrats in the sta... [Twitter for iPhone]

Jul 4, 2019 10:16:15 PM https://t.co/ldrobJIbrN [Twitter for iPhone]

Jul 4, 2019 10:42:21 PM RT @ByronYork: Attention Nike: The flag Colin Kaepernick told you was unacceptable on your shoes was displayed rather prominently at Barack... [Twitter for iPhone]

Jul 4, 2019 10:42:39 PM RT @KimStrassel: Trump's expansion of health reimbursement accounts is good news for workers. https://t.co/Qbj3qTNj5y via @WSJ [Twitter for iPhone]

Jul 4, 2019 10:44:27 PM RT @CBSNews: STUNNING: Fireworks filled the sky above the National Mall in Washington, D.C. on Independence Day. 🎆 https://t.co/76QfY3Q4oI... [Twitter for iPhone]

Jul 4, 2019 10:46:52 PM RT @ByronYork: Oh. That's different. From @AP: 'Harris says busing should be considered, not mandated.' https://t.co/uRRalGihR1 https://t.c... [Twitter for iPhone]

Jul 4, 2019 10:48:31 PM RT @Regnery: WATCH our first sneak peak of "Justice on Trial: The Kavanaugh Confirmation and the Future of the Supreme Court" by @MZHemingw... [Twitter for iPhone]

Jul 4, 2019 10:49:09 PM RT @MZHemingway: Good examples of corporate media failure here. "8 Times The Media Said There Was No Crisis At The Southern Border" https:/... [Twitter for iPhone]

Jul 4, 2019 10:50:32 PM Thank you Marc! https://t.co/JQBUPW2EHJ [Twitter for iPhone]

Jul 4, 2019 10:51:26 PM Thanks Ari! https://t.co/WOOzufbzOL [Twitter for iPhone]

Jul 4, 2019 10:52:49 PM Tammy is a great person! https://t.co/GRyl1OMsux [Twitter for iPhone]

Jul 4, 2019 10:53:38 PM RT @PressSec: Incredible to see all in attendance to hear our @POTUS speak & celebrate our great nation's Independence Day! υs https://t.co... [Twitter for iPhone]

Jul 4, 2019 10:55:38 PM RT @StewardshipAmer: Thank you, Mr. President. for a stupendous Independence Day tribute to our great nation, and to all who have donned ou... [Twitter for iPhone]

Jul 4, 2019 10:56:07 PM RT @StewardshipAmer: Spectacular ~ https://t.co/oh0Wca8YYJ [Twitter for iPhone]

Jul 4, 2019 10:56:23 PM RT @StewardshipAmer: Whenever you are in the Pensacola Florida area, go see the famous Blues; they will make you so proud ~ https://t.co/tB... [Twitter for iPhone]

Jul 4, 2019 10:56:48 PM RT @PastorDScott: Bruce Zoldon, Phil Grucci, Phantom Fireworks, and Fireworks by Grucci put on a TREMENDOUS display to cap off the Independ... [Twitter for iPhone]

Jul 4, 2019 10:59:47 PM RT @RandyRRQuaid: Wow! Rousing great speech, great air show, great bands! The great pilots, the great timing of the speech with the fly-ov... [Twitter for iPhone]

Jul 4, 2019 11:00:18 PM RT @JackPosobiec: Amazing Trump address and only @OANN covered the full day on cable! [Twitter for iPhone]

Jul 4, 2019 11:04:05 PM RT @GrahamLedger: https://t.co/BflJJEmkRp [Twitter for iPhone]

And the Cause of Freedom Marches On!

#AmericaFirst

And let us not be weary in well doing:
for in due season we shall reap, if we faint not.

~ Galatians 6:9

And I sought for a man among them,
that should build a wall,
and stand in the gap before me for the land,
that I should not destroy it.

~ Ezekiel 22:30

About the Editor

Judge Hal Moroz

Whether therefore ye eat, or drink, or whatsoever ye do, do all to the glory of God.

~ Psalm 37:23

The compiler and editor of this historical document is Judge Hal Moroz ...

Hal Moroz is an Attorney and Counselor at Law, who served as an Assistant District Attorney, a County Judge, and a city Chief Judge in the great State of Georgia. His practice in the law has ranged from prosecuting criminals on behalf of the State of Georgia to representing American military veterans in courts up to and including the Supreme Court of the United States.

Judge Moroz is also an accomplished soldier and statesman, as well as a retired U.S. Army officer, having served in the Airborne Infantry. Judge Moroz served on the faculty of Florida Coastal School of Law in Jacksonville,

Florida, and the State Bar of Georgia's Institute for Continuing Legal Education (ICLE) in the education of attorneys. He is a former candidate for the U.S. Congress, served as Special Counsel to the Georgia Republican Party's First Congressional District Committee in the 2000 primary and general elections, and was a Presidential Ballot Inspector-Observer during the 2000 Florida "Recount."

Hal Moroz is also a news and political commentator, sharing his insight of the law and politics on a variety of popular media programs. He was a supporter of Donald Trump from the start, and endorsed him in his campaign for President. Judge Moroz was repeatedly re-Tweeted and named in Tweets by @realDonaldTrump. He is also a prolific writer, having authored numerous legal articles, weekly legal newspaper columns, and books. Copies of his many books can be ordered at Amazon.com or any major online bookstore!

Hal Moroz can be reached through an internet search
or through his email at: hal@morozlaw.com or his website:
MorozLaw.com

Arise, shine; for thy light is come,
and the glory of the LORD is risen upon thee.

For, behold, the darkness shall cover the earth, and gross darkness the people: but the LORD shall arise upon thee, and his glory shall be seen upon thee.

~ Isaiah 60:1-2